# Lecture Notes in Artificial Intelligence     10965

## Subseries of Lecture Notes in Computer Science

### LNAI Series Editors

Randy Goebel
  *University of Alberta, Edmonton, Canada*
Yuzuru Tanaka
  *Hokkaido University, Sapporo, Japan*
Wolfgang Wahlster
  *DFKI and Saarland University, Saarbrücken, Germany*

### LNAI Founding Series Editor

Joerg Siekmann
  *DFKI and Saarland University, Saarbrücken, Germany*

More information about this series at http://www.springer.com/series/1244

Manuel Giuliani · Tareq Assaf
Maria Elena Giannaccini (Eds.)

# Towards Autonomous Robotic Systems

19th Annual Conference, TAROS 2018
Bristol, UK July 25–27, 2018
Proceedings

 Springer

*Editors*
Manuel Giuliani (iD)
University of the West of England
Bristol
UK

Maria Elena Giannaccini
University of Bristol
Bristol
UK

Tareq Assaf
University of Bath
Bath
UK

ISSN 0302-9743              ISSN 1611-3349   (electronic)
Lecture Notes in Artificial Intelligence
ISBN 978-3-319-96727-1        ISBN 978-3-319-96728-8   (eBook)
https://doi.org/10.1007/978-3-319-96728-8

Library of Congress Control Number: 2018948635

LNCS Sublibrary: SL7 – Artificial Intelligence

This Springer imprint is published by the registered company Springer Nature Switzerland AG
The registered company address is: Gewerbestrasse 11, 6330 Cham, Switzerland

# Preface

This volume contains the papers presented at TAROS 2018, the 19th Towards Autonomous Robotic Systems (TAROS) Conference, held at the Bristol Robotics Laboratory, Bristol, UK, during July 25–27, 2018 (http://www.brl.ac.uk/taros2018).

TAROS is the longest running UK-hosted international conference on robotics and autonomous systems (RAS), which is aimed at the presentation and discussion of the latest results and methods in autonomous robotics research and applications. The conference offers a friendly environment for robotics researchers and industry to take stock and plan future progress. It welcomes senior researchers and research students alike, and specifically provides opportunities for research students and young research scientists to present their work to the scientific community.

TAROS 2018 was held in the city centre of Bristol at M Shed, set on the harbour side in the heart of Bristol. The conference programme included an academic conference, industry exhibitions, robot demonstrations, a lab tour of the Bristol Robotics Laboratory, and a conference dinner. The programme highlights included:

- Keynote lectures by world-leading experts in robotics, including lectures by Professor Alan Winfield from the University of the West of England, Bristol, Professor Kerstin Dautenhahn from the University of Hertfordshire, and Silas Adekunle from Reach Robotics Limited.
- IET-sponsored evening lecture by Professor Brian Scassellati from Yale University.
- Oral presentations, covering topics of swarm and multi-robotic systems, human–robot interaction, robotic learning and imitation, robot navigation, planning and safety, soft and reconfigurable robots, service and industrial robots.
- Poster presentations, covering topics of humanoid and bio-inspired robots, mobile robots and vehicles, robot design and testing, detection and recognition, learning and adaptive behaviours, human–robot and robot–robot interaction.
- Presentations of the finalists of the Centre for Advanced Robotics at Queen Mary (ARQ) PhD thesis prize.
- Industrial and academic exhibition stands.

TAROS also offers several prizes for papers and posters. In 2018, the following papers were nominated by the Program Committee (PC):
Nominees for Best Paper Prize sponsored by the UK-RAS Network

- Jing Wu and Ze Ji, "Seeing the Unseen: Locating Objects from Reflections"
- Letizia Marchegiani and Paul Newman, "Learning to Listen to Your Ego-(motion): Metric Motion Estimation from Auditory Signals"
- Richard French, Alice Cryer, Gabriel Kapellmann, and Hector Marin-Reyes, "Evaluating the Radiation Tolerance of a Robotic Finger"

Nominees for Best Student Paper Prize in memory of Professor Ulrich Nehmzow

- James Wilson, Jonathan Timmis, and Andy Tyrrell, "A Hormone Arbitration System for Energy-Efficient Foraging In Robot Swarms"
- Cihan Uyanik, Sezgin Secil, Metin Ozkan, Helin Dutagaci, Kaya Turgut, Osman Parlaktuna, "SPGS: A New Method for Autonomous 3D Reconstruction of Unknown Objects by an Industrial Robot"
- Sergi Molina, Grzegorz Cielniak, Tomas Krajnik, and Tom Duckett, "Modelling and Predicting Rhythmic Flow Patterns in Dynamic Environments"

Nominees for Best Poster Prize sponsored by the UK-RAS Network

- Ke Wang, Aksat Shah, and Petar Kormushev, "SLIDER: A Novel Bipedal Walking Robot Without Knees"
- Barnali Das, Gordon Dobie, and Stephen Gareth Pierce, "State Estimation of Delays in Telepresence Robot Navigation Using Bayesian Approaches"

Nominees for IET Prize for Innovation in Robotics

- Tim Helps, Majid Taghavi, Sarah Manns, Ailie Turton, Jonathan Rossiter, "Easy Undressing with Soft Robotics"
- Khaled Elgeneidy, Pengcheng Liu, Simon Pearson, Niels Lohse, Gerhard Neumann, "Printable Soft Grippers with Integrated Bend Sensing for Handling of Crops"
- Alberto Caenazzo, Kaspar Althoefer, "Hypertonic Saline Solution for Signal Transmission and Steering in MRI-guided Intravascular Catheterisation"

The PC's Award Panel evaluated the presentations given by the shortlisted candidates during the conference and announced the winners at the award ceremony. The TAROS 2018 Organizing Committee would like to thank all the authors, reviewers, and the conference sponsors, including Maxon Motor UK Ltd., ROVCO Ltd, IET, and the UK-RAS Network.

May 2018                                                        Manuel Giuliani
                                                                     Tareq Assaf
                                                        Maria Elena Giannaccini

# Organization

## Program Chairs

| | |
|---|---|
| Manuel Giuliani | Bristol Robotics Laboratory, University of the West of England, UK |
| Tareq Assaf | Bristol Robotics Laboratory, University of the West of England, and University of Bath, UK |
| Maria Elena Giannaccini | Bristol Robotics Laboratory, University of Bristol, UK |

## Organizing Committee

| | |
|---|---|
| Appolinaire Etoundi | Bristol Robotics Laboratory, University of the West of England, UK |
| Alexander Fanourakis | Bristol Robotics Laboratory, University of the West of England, UK |
| Aghil Jafari | Bristol Robotics Laboratory, University of the West of England, UK |
| Marta Palau-Franco | Bristol Robotics Laboratory, University of the West of England, UK |
| Alex Smith | Bristol Robotics Laboratory, University of the West of England, UK |
| Alison Wilmot | Bristol Robotics Laboratory, University of the West of England, UK |

## Program Committee

| | |
|---|---|
| Komlan Jean Maxime Adjigble | University of Birmingham, UK |
| Lyuba Alboul | Sheffield Hallam University, UK |
| Farshad Arvin | University of Manchester, UK |
| Jacopo Banfi | Politecnico di Milano, Italy |
| Giacinto Barresi | Istituto Italiano di Tecnologia, Italy |
| Gytis Bernotas | University of the West of England, UK |
| Frank Broz | Heriot-Watt University, UK |
| Lola Canamero | University of Hertfordshire, UK |
| Andrew Conn | University of Bristol, UK |
| Luke Cramphorn | University of Bristol, UK |
| Giulio Dagnino | Imperial College London, UK |
| Steve Davis | University of Salford, UK |
| Geert De Cubber | Royal Military Academy, UK |
| Krishna Manaswi Digumarti | University of Bristol, UK |

| Sanja Dogramadzi | University of the West of England, UK |
| Kerstin Eder | University of Bristol, UK |
| Hatem Fakhruldeen | University of Bristol, UK |
| Fausto Ferreira | Centre for Maritime Research and Experimentation |
| Frank Foerster | University of Hertfordshire, UK |
| Mary Ellen Foster | University of Glasgow, UK |
| Swen Gaudl | Falmouth University, UK |
| Ioannis Georgilas | University of Bath, UK |
| Bruno Gil | Imperial College London, UK |
| Roderich Gross | The University of Sheffield, UK |
| Keir Groves | University of Manchester, UK |
| Dongbing Gu | University of Essex, UK |
| Heiko Hamann | University of Paderborn, Germany |
| Marc Hanheide | University of Lincoln, UK |
| Mark Hansen | University of the West of England, UK |
| Tim Helps | University of Bristol, UK |
| Andrew Hinitt | University of Bristol, UK |
| Patrick Holthaus | University of Hertfordshire, UK |
| Abdi Hadi Ibrahim | University of Djibouti, Djibouti |
| Roberto Iglesias Rodriguez | University of Santiago de Compostela, Spain |
| Aleksandar Jevtic | Institut de Robòtica i Informàtica Industrial, CSIC-UPC, Spain |
| Frederic Labrosse | Aberystwyth University, UK |
| Gabriella Lakatos | University of Hertfordshire, UK |
| Ben Mitchinson | University of Sheffield, UK |
| Lazaros Nalpantidis | Aalborg University, Denmark |
| Matthew Nancekievill | University of Manchester, UK |
| Martin Pearson | University of the West of England, UK |
| Ron Petrick | Heriot-Watt University, UK |
| Tony Pipe | University of the West of England, UK |
| Lenka Pitonakova | University of Bristol, UK |
| Efi Psomopoulou | University of the West of England, UK |
| Tom Rooney | University of the West of England, UK |
| Thomas Schmickl | Karl-Franzens University Graz, Austria |
| Mohammad Sobhani | University of the West of England, UK |
| Matthew Studley | University of the West of England, UK |
| Majid Taghavi | University of Bristol, UK |
| Lili Tao | University of the West of England, UK |
| Jonathan Timmis | University of York, UK |
| Antonia Tzemanaki | University of the West of England, UK |
| Hugo Vieira Neto | Federal University of Technology Parana, Brazil |
| Simon Watson | University of Manchester, UK |
| Andrew West | University of Manchester, UK |
| Craig West | University of the West of England, UK |
| James Whiting | University of the West of England, UK |
| Myra Wilson | Aberystwyth University, UK |

Ulf Witkowski                  South Westphalia University of Applied Sciences,
                                 Germany
Hartmut Witte                  Technische Universität Ilmenau, Germany
Luke Wood                      University of Hertfordshire, UK
Chaoqun Xiang                  University of Bristol, UK
Keren Yue                      University of Bristol, UK
Wenhao Zhang                   University of the West of England, UK
Anouk van Maris                University of the West of England, UK

# Contents

## HRI, Assistive and Medical Robotics

## Swarm Robotics

## Robotics Applications

# Object Manipulation and Locomotion

# Trajectory Optimization for High-Power Robots with Motor Temperature Constraints

Wei Xin Tan[1], Martim Brandão[1,2]([⊠]), Kenji Hashimoto[1,3],
and Atsuo Takanishi[1,3]

[1] Waseda University, Tokyo, Japan
[2] Oxford Robotics Institute, University of Oxford, Oxford, UK
`martim@robots.ox.ac.uk`
[3] Humanoid Robotics Institute, Waseda University, Tokyo, Japan

**Abstract.** Modeling heat transfer is an important problem in high-power electrical robots as the increase of motor temperature leads to both lower energy efficiency and the risk of motor damage. Power consumption itself is a strong restriction in these robots especially for battery-powered robots such as those used in disaster-response. In this paper, we propose to reduce power consumption and temperature for robots with high-power DC actuators without cooling systems only through motion planning. We first propose a parametric thermal model for brushless DC motors which accounts for the relationship between internal and external temperature and motor thermal resistances. Then, we introduce temperature variables and a thermal model constraint on a trajectory optimization problem which allows for power consumption minimization or the enforcing of temperature bounds during motion planning. We show that the approach leads to qualitatively different motion compared to typical cost function choices, as well as energy consumption gains of up to 40%.

**Keywords:** Trajectory optimization · Motion planning
Legged robots · Temperature · Thermal models

## 1 Introduction

High-power electrical robots have important applications in torque-demanding contexts from industry to disaster response. One crucial problem with such robots is to keep actuator temperatures within safe limits and electrical power or battery consumption to a minimum. For example, the 150[kg] high-power disaster-response legged robot WAREC-1 [1] was designed for high-torque tasks such as climbing vertical ladders and carrying heavy objects. Such tasks, however, will not only drain battery quickly but also generate high amounts of heat which puts some internal components at risk: in WAREC-1's case, encoders which have temperature limits from 70[°C] to 85[°C].

© Springer International Publishing AG, part of Springer Nature 2018
M. Giuliani et al. (Eds.): TAROS 2018, LNAI 10965, pp. 3–14, 2018.
https://doi.org/10.1007/978-3-319-96728-8_1

While the temperature problem can be tackled through the use of cooling, in this paper we claim that power consumption and temperature on such robots can also be reduced by careful motion design. We propose to integrate thermal models of the robot's actuators in motion planning using temperature variables and constraints on a trajectory optimization problem. The contributions of this paper are as follows

1. We propose a trajectory optimization formulation to motion planning in order to reduce robot actuator power consumption and temperature by using temperature variables and thermal model constraints,
2. We propose a thermal model for brushless DC actuators with justified modifications and integrate it into (1),
3. We evaluate our method in simulated and real experiments on the WAREC-1 robot. We show it is up to 40% more energy-efficient than typical optimization formulations.

## 2   Related Work

The problem of overheating in robotics is usually tackled by cooling systems using fluids [2]. The development of an actuator cooler is not always possible, however, due to either lack of expertise, funding, or permission to modify a robotic platform. Our complementary approach to the problem in this paper is to develop a thermal model of the actuator units which can be used to limit predicted temperature by changes in motion. This approach could also be used as a cost-effective alternative to designing a cooling system.

Work on the tree-climbing robot RiSE [3] also uses thermal models for constrained robot control. The system uses a 3-lump thermal model which is highly robust and valid within a large range of environmental temperatures. It requires two temperature sensors to measure internal and external temperature. Some actuators, however, have only one internal temperature sensor which severely limits the approach. In this paper, we assume the presence of only a single internal temperature sensor and use a model with extra parameters in an optimization problem to predict casing temperature.

Another paper which is similar to ours is [4]. It does time parameterization of pre-planned geometric robot paths using a time-optimization problem with a temperature constraint. In this paper we instead plan the (geometric) motion itself, for an underactuated legged-robot's joints with high degrees of freedom. Our problems are thus of considerably higher complexity, both in the number of variables and of constraints: including not only temperature but also kinematic, collision and stability limits. Finally, the thermal model in [4] considers heat transfer through conduction only, while ours considers both conduction and free convection.

Other related research includes temperature prediction for humanoid robots [5,6]. The robots used in that work (HRP-2, HRP-4R, STARO) cannot measure actuator winding temperature and the authors overcome this by assuming that the internal and external temperatures of the robot's actuators are the same.

This assumption could be problematic in high-power situations. For example, the temperature difference between the WAREC-1 robot's actuator windings and its casing is significantly large at high input power as seen in Fig. 4.

## 3   Methodology

### 3.1   Full-Body Trajectory Optimization with Motor Temperature Considerations

Based on [7], in this paper we formulate the motion planning problem as an optimization problem on a trajectory parameterized by $N$ waypoints (i.e. robot configurations at discrete instants of time). Here we further include temperature considerations in the following manner:

$$\underset{q^{(1)},...,q^{(N)},\dot{q}^{(1)},...,\dot{q}^{(N)},\tau^{(1)},...,\tau^{(N)},T^{(1)},...,T^{(N)},P_{\text{in}}^{(1)},...,P_{\text{in}}^{(N)}}{\text{minimize}} \sum_{i=1}^{N}\sum_{k=1}^{K} P_{\text{in},k}^{(i)} \tag{1a}$$

subject to

$$g_{\text{fwdkin}}(q^{(i)}) = s^{(i)} \quad \forall_{i\in 1,...,N} \tag{1b}$$

$$\dot{q}^{(i)} = \dot{q}(0) \tag{1c}$$

$$\dot{q}^{(i+1)} = (q^{(i+1)} - q^{(i)})/\Delta t \quad \forall_{i\in 1,...,N-1} \tag{1d}$$

$$\tau^{(i)} = g_{\text{torques}}(q^{(i)}) \quad \forall_{i\in 1,...,N} \tag{1e}$$

$$T^{(1)} = T(0) \tag{1f}$$

$$T^{(i+1)} = g_{\text{temp}}(T^{(i)}, P_{\text{in}}^{(i)}) \quad \forall_{i\in 1,...,N-1} \tag{1g}$$

$$P_{\text{in}}^{(i)} = g_{\text{power}}(T^{(i)}, \tau^{(i)}, \dot{q}^{(i)}) \quad \forall_{i\in 1,...,N} \tag{1h}$$

$$q_{\min} \le q^{(i)} \le q_{\max} \quad \forall_{i\in 1,...,N} \tag{1i}$$

$$\dot{q}_{\min} \le \dot{q}^{(i)} \le \dot{q}_{\max} \quad \forall_{i\in 1,...,N} \tag{1j}$$

$$h_{xy}(q^{(i)}) \in \mathcal{P}^{(i)} \quad \forall_{i\in 1,...,N} \tag{1k}$$

$$h_{\text{sd}}(q^{(i)}) \le 0 \quad \forall_{i\in 1,...,N}, \tag{1l}$$

where $q^{(i)} \in \mathbb{R}^D$ is the robot configuration at waypoint $i$, $D$ is the number of degrees-of-freedom, $\dot{q}^{(i)} \in \mathbb{R}^D$ are velocities, $\tau^{(i)} \in \mathbb{R}^K$ (static) joint torques, $P_{\text{in}}^{(i)} \in \mathbb{R}^K$ motor power, $T^{(i)} \in \mathbb{R}^{KL}$ motor temperatures. $K$ is the number of joints and $L$ the number of temperature values considered at each motor (e.g. if considering winding and case temperature then $L = 2$). The constant $\Delta t$ represents the time between two waypoints, $s^{(i)}$ represents the target link poses at waypoint $i$ and $\mathcal{P}^{(i)}$ the robot's support polygon at $i$. The objective of the problem is to minimize total power over all waypoints $i$ and joints $k$. Function $g_{\text{fwdkin}}$ implements forward kinematics, $g_{\text{temp}}$ temperature dynamics, $g_{\text{power}}$ the power consumption model, $h_{xy}$ the horizontal coordinates of the center-of-mass (COM) used for static stability, $h_{\text{sd}}$ a signed distance function for collision avoidance as in [8]. We define functions $g_{\text{temp}}$ and $g_{\text{power}}$ for brushless DC motors in Sects. 3.2 and 3.3, respectively.

## 3.2    Thermal Model for Brushless DC Motors

The thermal model constraints $g_{temp}$ in problem (1) are sufficiently general to account for different motor types. In this paper we derive $g_{temp}$ for brushless DC motors with no cooling, which we use in our experimental platform (Sect. 4). Brushless DC motors without cooling can be modeled using the lumped capacitance method [9] while considering heat transfer only through conduction and free convection. Based on [10], the model is generally of the form

$$m_w C_w \frac{dT_w}{dt} = P_{in} - \frac{T_w - T_c}{R_{wc}(T_w, T_c)}, \tag{2}$$

$$m_c C_c \frac{dT_c}{dt} = \frac{T_w - T_c}{R_{wc}(T_w, T_c)} - \frac{T_c - T_{env}}{R_{ca}(T_c)}, \tag{3}$$

where

- $m_w$, $m_c$ is the mass of the actuator windings and casing
- $C_w$, $C_c$ is the specific heat capacity of the windings and casing
- $T_w$, $T_c$, $T_{env}$ is the temperature of the windings, casing, and environment
- $P_{in}$, is the total input power being supplied to the actuator
- $R_{wc}$, is the thermal resistance between the windings and the casing, here modeled as a function of $T_w$ and $T_c$
- $R_{ca}$, is the thermal resistance between the casing and the ambient environment, here modeled as a function of $T_c$

Graphically, (2) and (3) can be represented by the diagram in Fig. 1, where the winding (red) and casing (blue) portions of the robot's actuator are each assumed to be made from one major material as seen in Fig. 1.

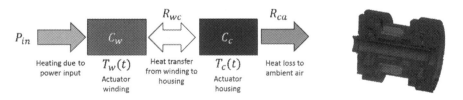

**Fig. 1.** Left: diagram of heat transfer for a DC actuator. Right: cross-section of WAREC-1's custom made actuator. (Color figure online)

Thermal resistances $R_{wc}(T_w, T_c)$, and $R_{ca}(T_c)$, can be obtained experimentally at steady state since

$$\frac{dT_w}{dt} \approx 0 \implies R_{wc}(T_w, T_c) = \frac{T_w - T_c}{P_{in}}, \tag{4}$$

$$\frac{dT_c}{dt} \approx 0 \implies R_{ca}(T_c) = \frac{T_c}{P_{in}}. \tag{5}$$

We discretize (2) and (3) using the Euler method to obtain $g_{\text{temp}}$:

$$T^{(i+1)} = g_{\text{temp}}(T^{(i)}, P_{\text{in}}^{(i)}) =$$

$$= \begin{bmatrix} T_{\text{w}}^{(i+1)} \\ T_{\text{c}}^{(i+1)} \end{bmatrix} = \begin{bmatrix} T_{\text{w}}^{(i)} + \frac{\Delta t}{C_{\text{w}}} * \left( P_{\text{in}}^{(i)} - \frac{T_{\text{w}}^{(i)} - T_{\text{c}}^{(i)}}{R_{\text{wc}}^{(i)}(T_{\text{w}}, T_{\text{c}})} \right) \\ T_{\text{c}}^{(i)} + \frac{\Delta t}{C_{\text{c}}} * \left( \frac{T_{\text{w}}^{(i)} - T_{\text{c}}^{(i)}}{R_{\text{wc}}^{(i)}(T_{\text{w}}, T_{\text{c}})} - \frac{T_{\text{c}}^{(i)}}{R_{\text{ca}}^{(i)}(T_{\text{c}})} \right) \end{bmatrix}. \quad (6)$$

The information at step $i+1$, can be determined from the information at the previous step, $i$, which means that the initial temperatures $T^{(1)}$ must be known. We assume this to be measured, or in case of a single sensor predicted by integration of the thermal model over time[1].

## 3.3  Power Consumption Model for Brushless DC Motors

Power needs to be predicted from motion during trajectory optimization, both for power minimization and temperature modeling (note that $g_{\text{temp}}$ depends on $P_{\text{in}}^{(i)}$). As such, an electrical model for a brushless DC actuator is required. Based on [11], the model used for brushed DC actuators is a good approximation for BLDC actuators at steady state. Assuming all input power is converted only into useful work and excess heat, the model is represented by

$$P_{\text{in}} = IV_o + I^2 R_a. \quad (7)$$

DC actuators have a linear relationship between input current $I$ and output torque $\tau$; between induced electromotive force $V_o$ and output angular velocity $\dot{q}$; and between winding resistance $R_a$ and winding temperature $T_{\text{w}}$. Therefore Eq. (7) can be rewritten as

$$P_{\text{in}} = |\tau \dot{q}| + \left( \frac{\tau}{K_\tau} \right)^2 R_{\text{ref}}(1 + \alpha(T_{\text{w}} - T_{\text{ref}})), \quad (8)$$

where $K_\tau$ is the actuator's torque constant, $R_{\text{ref}}$ is the actuator's terminal resistance at temperature $T_{\text{ref}}$ (usually found in the actuator's datasheet), and $\alpha$ is the temperature coefficient for the conductor used in the actuator's windings (typically copper).

One important issue to note is that at $P_{\text{in}} = 0$, (2) and (3) predict that the actuators experience cooling and will achieve temperatures below room temperature. This leads to erroneous results if used for motion planning. One way to overcome this particular problem is by adding a constant to (8), which we term $P_{\text{min}}$, which represents the minimum amount of power going into the actuator. This is justified from a real-world standpoint because even if an actuator is not moving, it will experience some small amount of current flowing through it the

---

[1] To avoid large accumulated error, another possible approximation would be to assume $T_{\text{c}}^{(1)} = T_{\text{w}}^{(1)}$.

moment it is connected to its power supply. This constant can be determined experimentally by determining the steady state temperatures of the actuator when it is only connected to its power supply and outputting no torque or angular velocity. As such, we use

$$P_{\text{in}} = P_{\text{min}} + |\tau\dot{q}| + \left(\frac{\tau}{K_\tau}\right)^2 R_{\text{ref}}(1 + \alpha(T_{\text{w}} - T_{\text{ref}})). \tag{9}$$

We discretize (9) using the Euler method to obtain the power constraint $g_{\text{power}}$ in (1):

$$P_{\text{in}}^{(i)} = g_{\text{power}}(T^{(i)}, \tau^{(i)}, \dot{q}^{(i)}) = P_{\text{min}} + |\tau^{(i)}\dot{q}^{(i)}| +$$
$$\left(\frac{\tau^{(i)}}{K_\tau}\right)^2 R_{\text{ref}}(1 + \alpha(T_{\text{w}}^{(i)} - T_{\text{ref}})). \tag{10}$$

## 4  Experimental Results

We empirically validated the proposed thermal models and trajectory optimization formulation by conducting motion planning experiments in both simulated and real environments. We used the legged-robot WAREC-1 (Fig. 5) in simulation and a single arm of the robot on real experiments. In what follows we will show the results of

- Determining the thermal resistances $R_{\text{wc}}(T_{\text{w}}, T_{\text{c}})$ and $R_{\text{ca}}(T_{\text{c}})$ of the robot's actuators through steady state experimentation (Sect. 4.1),
- Solving (1) on a biped walking and a reaching task, and comparing the results with other trajectory optimization formulations: IK-only and torque-minimization (Sect. 4.2).

### 4.1  Parameter Identification

Using [10] as a reference, we developed an experimental procedure utilizing an actuator testbed that was designed and assembled previously. The setup is shown in Fig. 2. The actuators contained an integrated platinum resistance temperature sensor made by Heraeus (model M222, 32208671). Since the actuators have a single internal temperature sensor, the external temperature of their casing was measured using an external 4-channel temperature data logger. Note that this external sensor does not exist on the real robot, and we used it only on the testbed for parameter identification.

To obtain the terminal resistance parameters we conducted experiments at different input power values and fitted parametric models to the collected points. We performed each experiment by setting up the electromagnetic powder brake such that the actuator's rotor was in a locked state during operation and used an oscilloscope to monitor the input power to the servo drive. Then, we monitored the internal and external temperatures of the actuator until they reached steady state, which took anywhere between 4–8 h to achieve.

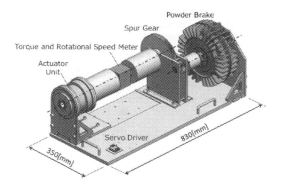

**Fig. 2.** Testbed setup and dimensions

Our robot platform contains large, medium and small-sized versions of the actuator as seen in Fig. 1. We conducted 10 experiments for the large-size and 8 for the small-size actuator. Due to time constraints, we used a linear interpolation of the two to determine the medium-sized actuator's thermal resistances. We then used MATLAB's curve fitting toolbox to fit parametric models to the data, as seen in Fig. 3. We used an exponential model for $R_{\mathrm{ca}}(T_c)$ based on [10] and Newton's law of cooling, and a linear model for $R_{\mathrm{wc}}(T_w, T_c)$ as that was sufficient for our operation range. The thermal resistances in (6) then become

$$R_{\mathrm{wc}}^{(i)}(T_w, T_c) = A_1 * (T_w^{(i)} - T_c^{(i)}) + A_2, \tag{11}$$

$$R_{\mathrm{ca}}^{(i)}(T_c) = B_1 + B_2 * e^{\left(-B_3 * T_c^{(i)}\right)}, \tag{12}$$

where parameters $A_1$, $A_2$, $B_1$, $B_2$, and $B_3$ are specific to each of the differently sized actuators being used by the robot.

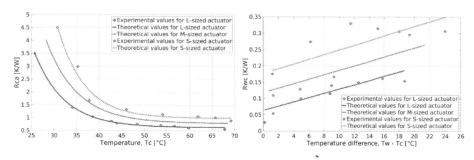

**Fig. 3.** Left: exponential curve for the different motor sizes. Right: linear curve for the different motor sizes. The M-sized actuator's $R_{\mathrm{ca}}$ values were obtained through linear interpolation between the curves for the L and S-sized actuators

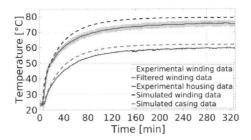

**Fig. 4.** Example of simulation results predicting temperature rise in Matlab

Figure 4 shows the results of a simulation obtained by numerical integration of the thermal models with the fitted resistance models. The figure shows a maximum error of around $2[°C]$ compared to the experimental values. Furthermore, the model can be considered safe as the temperatures predicted for large values of $P_{in}$ are above actual values (i.e. temperature constraints could safely be added to the optimization problem (1)).

## 4.2    Trajectory Optimization with Thermal Models

**Implementation Details.** We solve problem (1) with the Sequential Quadratic Programming method of [8]. At each iteration of the algorithm, the cost function and constraints are locally approximated by quadratic and linear functions, respectively. We compute these approximations symbolically wherever possible (i.e. all functions except static joint torques). We used MATLAB to symbolically obtain the partial derivatives of (6) and (10). Due to (10) being non-smooth, we replace the absolute function with the smooth approximation

$$|x| \approx \sqrt{x^2 + \epsilon} \quad \text{for some} \quad \epsilon > 0. \tag{13}$$

Note that $\sqrt{x^2 + \epsilon} \to |x|$ as $\epsilon \to 0$. We chose $\epsilon$ equal to $10^{-10}$.

**Biped Walking Experiment.** We first evaluated the capacity of our method to minimize power consumption on a biped walking task. We solved (1) on a sequence of 20 stances (20 waypoints) which lasted for a total duration of 10 min. We also compared the solution of (1) with that of

1. Inverse kinematics only: a similar optimization problem but with $q_i$ as the only variables, and without any cost function. We use exactly the same solver, parameters and nominal initialization
2. Minimum torques: same as (1) but with a sum-of-squared-torques cost function

The motion we obtained using the different methods actually varied enough that it is qualitatively visible. Figure 5 shows the motion obtained with our

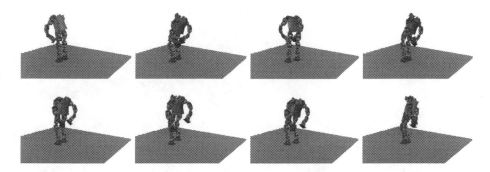

**Fig. 5.** Image sequence of the obtained full-body biped walking trajectories. Top: min squared-torques, Bottom: min power based on our thermal model.

approach and with torque-minimization. The postures obtained with our method are more consistent (arms always facing the same direction) and the trunk does not repeatedly lean back and forth.

Table 1 shows the predicted amount of total energy required by the robot's joints for the entire length of motion. Planning based on our temperature and power consumption model resulted in the most energy efficient motion. Energy for 10[min] of walking motion was reduced by more than 9% compared to a simple IK approach and 1% compared to torque minimization.

**Table 1.** Total predicted energy consumption on a simulation of biped walking

| Method | Predicted energy [kJ] |
|---|---|
| IK (no costs) | 165 |
| Min squared-torques | 151 |
| Min power w/temperature constr. (ours) | 149 |

**Real Robot Reaching Experiment.** We also evaluated our method on a second task which was to alternate between reaching for a certain location in space for 30[s] and resting the robot at a freely chosen location for another 30[s], repeatedly for 7[min]. This time we evaluated the method on a real robot which consists of a single arm of the legged WAREC-1 robot fixed to a base, as shown in Fig. 6. The same three methods were compared (IK-only, min torques, ours). The motion was then played open loop on the real system.

As can be seen from Table 2 and Fig. 7, real experiments show that our method reduced energy consumption by more than 7% when compared with the IK-only method and 40% with respect to torque minimization. It also kept motor temperature increases lower, as seen in Fig. 7. The reason for the low consumption of the IK-only method is related to the nominal posture of the

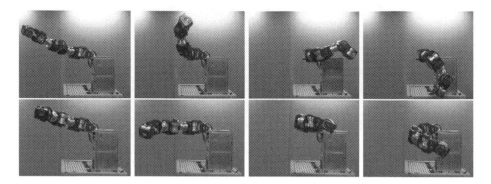

**Fig. 6.** Image sequence of a single arm experiment. Top: min squared-torques, Bottom: min power based on our thermal model.

robot, which is used for initializing the optimization, being coincidently close to the energetically optimal posture. Note that energetic performance of such an approach will be highly variable depending on the task and how "lucky" the initialization is.

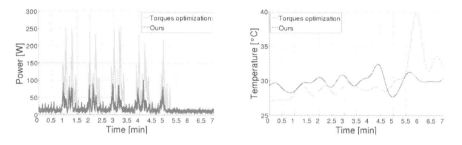

**Fig. 7.** Left: total power consumption on the real experiment. Right: winding temperature at the shoulder's roll joint.

Regarding the high energy consumption of torque minimization, an analysis of the experimental data revealed that the main contributing factor was the lack of friction modeling, leading to torque predictions up to 3 times larger than measured values. Although such modeling choice is common in optimization-based planners and controllers, our results show that this simplification can have drastic energetic effects. Note that the same torque computation is used in our method, and so improving the model should also improve the performance of our method.

**Table 2.** Total predicted and measured energy consumption on reaching experiments

| Method | Simulation [kJ] | Real experiment [kJ] |
|---|---|---|
| IK (no costs) | 34.7 | 10.4 |
| Min squared-torques | 29.4 | 16.0 |
| Min power w/temperature constr. (ours) | 29.2 | 9.7 |

## 5 Conclusion

In this paper, we introduced a parameterized thermal model for a robot's brush-less DC motors and applied it to an actuator with a single internal temperature sensor. We verified that the model was valid assuming only heat conduction within the actuator and free convection with the environmental where temperatures are between $23[°C]$ to $28[°]$. Using this model within motion planning, through trajectory optimization with temperature variables and constraints, resulted in energy efficiency gains between 1% and 9% in simulation, and up to 40% in the real robot when compared to simpler optimization-based planners. Importantly, the paper shows that squared-torque minimization, a common cost function in robotics, is a poor cost function for energy minimization as previously shown in the walking experiments of [12]. Trajectory optimization with a thermal model more accurately represents the capabilities of a robot's actuators and allows for the further flexibility of adding arbitrary constraints on temperature (e.g. enforcing temperature bounds).

Several interesting directions exist to further improve the proposed method. (1) Including time as a decision variable in the optimization problem, so that it becomes possible for the robot to stop (or slow down considerably) to allow its motors to cool down and keep their temperatures within safe bounds. (2) Modeling actuator friction to improve torque predictions, (3) Modeling the input current's trapezoidal waveform for BLDC motors [13], as well as the power from other sources such as the motor drivers and controlling PC [14], currently simplified as a constant $P_{min}$.

**Acknowledgment.** This work was supported by ImPACT TRC Program of Council for Science, Technology and Innovation (Cabinet Office, Government of Japan). Martim Brandão is supported by the EPSRC RAIN Hub, grant EP/R026084/1. Finally, we would like to thank N. Sakai for help with the open loop experiments and K. Kumagai for help with initially setting up the temperature experiments.

14    W. X. Tan et al.

# References

1. Hashimoto, K., et al.: WAREC-1 - a four-limbed robot having high locomotion ability with versatility in locomotion styles. In: IEEE International Symposium on Safety, Security and Rescue Robotics, pp. 172–178, October 2017
2. Urata, J., Nakanishi, Y., Okada, K., Inaba, M.: Design of high torque and high speed leg module for high power humanoid. In: 2010 IEEE/RSJ International Conference on Intelligent Robots and Systems, pp. 4497–4502, October 2010
3. Trujillo, S., Cutkosky, M.: Thermally constrained motor operation for a climbing robot. In: 2009 IEEE International Conference on Robotics and Automation, pp. 2362–2367, May 2009
4. Guilbert, M., Joly, L., Wieber, P.B.: Optimization of complex robot applications under real physical limitations. Int. J. Robot. Res. 27(5), 629–644 (2008)
5. Noda, S., Murooka, M., Nozawa, S., Kakiuchi, Y., Okada, K., Inaba, M.: Online maintaining behavior of high-load and unstable postures based on whole-body load balancing strategy with thermal prediction. In: 2014 IEEE International Conference on Automation Science and Engineering, pp. 1166–1171, August 2014
6. Kumagai, I., Noda, S., Nozawa, S., Kakiuchi, Y., Okada, K., Inaba, M.: Whole body joint load reduction control for high-load tasks of humanoid robot through adapting joint torque limitation based on online joint temperature estimation. In: IEEE-RAS International Conference on Humanoid Robots, pp. 463–468, November 2014
7. Brandao, M., Shiguematsu, Y.M., Hashimoto, K., Takanishi, A.: Material recognition CNNs and hierarchical planning for biped robot locomotion on slippery terrain. In: 16th IEEE-RAS International Conference on Humanoid Robots, pp. 81–88, November 2016
8. Schulman, J., et al.: Motion planning with sequential convex optimization and convex collision checking. Int. J. Robot. Res. 33(9), 1251–1270 (2014)
9. Bergman, T.L., Incropera, F.P.: Fundamentals of Heat and Mass Transfer. Wiley, Hoboken (2011)
10. Fussell, B.K.: Thermal effects on the torque-speed performance of a brushless DC motor. In: Proceedings of Electrical/Electronics Insulation Conference, pp. 403–411, October 1993
11. Sekalala, S.: Performance of a three-phase permanent magnet motor operating as a synchronous motor and a brushless dc motor. Master's thesis, Louisiana State University (2006)
12. Brandao, M., Hashimoto, K., Santos-Victor, J., Takanishi, A.: Optimizing energy consumption and preventing slips at the footstep planning level. In: 15th IEEE-RAS International Conference on Humanoid Robots, pp. 1–7, November 2015
13. Cham, C.L., Samad, Z.B.: Brushless dc motor electromagnetic torque estimation with single-phase current sensing. J. Electr. Eng. Technol. 9(3), 866–872 (2014)
14. Mei, Y., Lu, Y.H., Hu, Y.C., Lee, C.G.: A case study of mobile robot's energy consumption and conservation techniques. In: Proceedings of the 12th International Conference on Advanced Robotics, ICAR 2005, pp. 492–497. IEEE (2005)

# SPGS: A New Method for Autonomous 3D Reconstruction of Unknown Objects by an Industrial Robot

Cihan Uyanik[1], Sezgin Secil[2], Metin Ozkan[1(✉)], Helin Dutagaci[2],
Kaya Turgut[2], and Osman Parlaktuna[2]

[1] Department of Computer Engineering, Eskisehir Osmangazi University, Eskisehir, Turkey
{cuyanik,meozkan}@ogu.edu.tr
[2] Department of Electrical and Electronics Engineering, Eskisehir Osmangazi University,
Eskisehir, Turkey
{ssecil,oparlak}@ogu.edu.tr, helindutagaci@gmail.com,
kayaturgut@hotmail.com

**Abstract.** This paper presents the first findings of a new method called surface profile guided scan (SPGS) for 3D surface reconstruction of unknown small-scale objects. This method employs a laser profile sensor mounted on an industrial manipulator, a rotary stage, and a camera. The system requires no prior knowledge on the geometry of the object. The only information available is that the object is located on the rotary table, and is within the field of view of the camera and the working space of the industrial robot. First a number of surface profiles in the vertical direction around the object are generated from captured images. Then, a motion planning step is performed to position the laser sensor directed towards the profile normal. Finally, the 3D surface model is completed by hole detection and scanning process. The quality of surface models obtained from real objects with our system prove the effectiveness and the versatility of our 3D reconstruction method.

**Keywords:** Industrial robots · 3D reconstruction · Point clouds

## 1 Introduction

In this paper, we present a novel methodology to autonomously perform 3D surface modeling of objects via an industrial robot arm. 3D surface modeling of objects requires the acquisition of the complete geometric information from the surface of the object. The complete data acquisition process can be performed with different approaches, such as (i) moving the sensor around the object, (ii) moving the object around the sensor, or (iii) moving both. The motion of the object and/or the sensor can be realized either (a) manually, (b) using special mechanisms, or (c) robot arms. In all of these approaches, a major problem is to determine a configuration such that the sensor's field of view will contain the unscanned parts of the object. This problem is referred to as next-best-view planning (NBV) for autonomous 3D reconstruction systems.

© Springer International Publishing AG, part of Springer Nature 2018
M. Giuliani et al. (Eds.): TAROS 2018, LNAI 10965, pp. 15–27, 2018.
https://doi.org/10.1007/978-3-319-96728-8_2

Autonomous surface scanning methods may be implemented by either special mechanisms or robot manipulators. In [1], there is a fixed sensor projecting a laser ray for collecting surface data, and the object is placed on a moving band. In [2], an orthographic projector and a pair of planar mirrors are used to obtain the 3D shape of an object. In [3], the authors present a study for 3D measurement of large parts in a precise and convenient way for reverse engineering. This system consists of a CCD camera, a galvanometer and a laser projector. In [4], a stereo camera is used to identify candidate gaze positions perpendicular to a spherical surface surrounding the object. There are no details about how the final gaze positions are selected from the candidate points. As a test object, a simple object, such as a mask, was chosen. Some studies just focused on developing methods for the determination of NBV from the scanned surface model [5, 6], while in other studies robot manipulators are used to move the sensor to the NBV locations with motion planning [7–13].

In this study, we present an original method for autonomous 3D reconstruction of novel objects. We combine the strengths of an image-based sensor and a laser scanner to collect accurate data with high resolution while working with a wide field of view. The wide field of view is provided by the image sensor, and the information collected using the large view is used to guide the laser sensor to acquire highly accurate and dense distance information from the surface. The laser sensor needs to be located at a close distance to the surface of the object so that the surface remains within the sensing range. In this case, the rest of the object will remain unknown to the sensor, and the solution of the NBV problem becomes difficult. NBVs that are not computed sufficiently efficient can cause the sensor to hit the object or not to obtain enough data from the surface. The object profiles collected by the image sensor positioned at an adequate distance will provide guidance to move the laser sensor safely to a location with the next best view. The proposed Surface Profile Guided Scanning Method (SPGS) uses both modalities by exploiting their respective advantages.

The rest of the paper is organized as follows: In the next section, an overview of the autonomous modeling system is introduced. In Sect. 3, the proposed method is described. Experimental results are given in Sect. 4. Finally, the conclusion is given in Sect. 5.

## 2   System Overview

The proposed method is developed for a system comprised of four components: An industrial manipulator, a laser profile sensor, a camera, and a rotary stage. A picture of the experimental workspace including all of the system components can be seen in Fig. 1. A full implementation of the system is presented in [14].

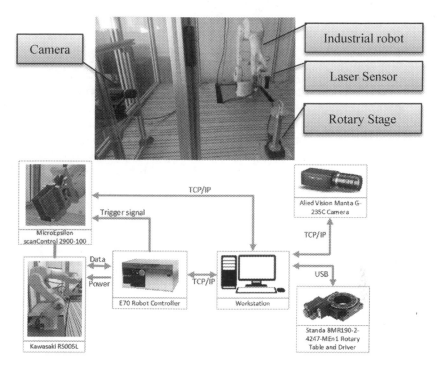

**Fig. 1.** The experimental workspace: (Top) A picture, (Bottom) A diagram.

*Laser Sensor:* A laser sensor is used to collect point clouds from the surface of objects with high accuracy and resolution. The high accuracy necessitates a narrow working range for the sensor. Thus, the laser sensor should be moved frequently to the next-best views in order to capture data from different regions of the object surface. In this study, a laser profile sensor is employed. However, an image sensor, that captures global views of the object, is used to help determine the next best views.

*Industrial Manipulator:* The laser sensor needs to be moved around the entire surface of the object for obtaining a complete point cloud. An industrial manipulator is used for this purpose. The laser sensor is mounted at the tip of the manipulator. The manipulator carries and rotates the laser sensor to the desired position and orientation.

*Camera:* The camera provides a wide field of view as compared to the high accurate laser sensors. In this study, the images of objects captured by a fixed camera are used to calculate surface profiles around the object. Later, the surface profiles are used for the determination of sensor positions and orientations for scanning.

*Rotary Stage:* The rotary stage contributes to the sensing process of both the camera and the laser sensor. The use of the rotary stage allows the camera to capture images from all around the object to extract surface profiles. The laser profile sensor mounted at the tip of the manipulator can acquire data from all regions of the object surface with the joint operation of the rotary stage and the manipulator.

## 3    Surface Profile Guided Scan Method

The operation of the proposed SPGS method is presented in Fig. 2(a). In the first stage, object surface profiles are obtained using a horizontally positioned camera and a rotary stage are used. The object is rotated by the turntable and the 3D coordinates of the profiles are calculated by processing stereo images taken from a single camera. A motion plan is then created to move the sensor along the profiles. By moving the sensor according to the motion plan, the surface point cloud is obtained. In the next step, the holes on the surface model are searched. The NBV points are calculated to scan the holes with the sensor, and the sensor performs scanning by taking these points. The cycle of finding and scanning the holes is continued until no hole remains.

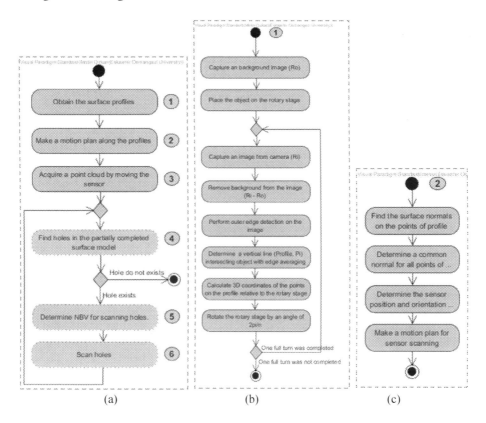

       (a)                   (b)                  (c)

**Fig. 2.** Sequence diagrams of proposed method: (a) Main sequence diagram, (b) Obtaining surface profiles, (c) Making motion plan along the profiles

### 3.1    Vertical Surface Profile Generation

The vertical surface profiles are generated by a sequential process as seen in Fig. 2(b). (i) First, a background image ($R_o$) is captured. This image is later used to separate the object from the background. (ii) Then, the object is placed onto the rotary stage. (iii) An image ($R_i$) of the object is captured to determine i$^{th}$ vertical profile from the actual view. (iv) The background image obtained in Step (i) is used to determine the binary silhouette of the object in the image using Algorithm 1. After background subtraction is completed through Gaussian mixture segmentation, median filtering is applied to eliminate noisy pixels.

| Algorithm 1: Segmenting the Object From the Background |
| --- |
| 1: function SEGOBJ( ) |
| 2:   $Im_{Bg}$ ← {Take background frame by the camera} |
| 3:   $Im_{Obj}$ ← {Take object frame by the camera} |
| 4:   $Im_{Seg}$ ← GAUSSIANMIXTURESEG($Im_{Bg}$, $Im_{Obj}$) |
| 5:   $Im_{Seg}$ ← MEDIANBLUR($Im_{Seg}$) |
| 6:   return $Im_{Seg}$ |
| 7: end function |

(v) The boundary of the silhouette of the object is extracted using edge detection, and then the convex-hull of the boundary is determined. The aim is to find a vertical line along the convex hull that will define the vertical profile of the object view. This vertical line is assumed to pass through the centroid of the convex hull, thus the x-coordinates of the points on the line is set equal to the x-coordinate of the centroid. The y-coordinates of the beginning and end points of the profile are chosen to be the maximum and minimum y-coordinates of the boundary. Once the profile line is determined, all the points on the line can be used to obtain the 3D coordinates of the profile of the object surface. However, to reduce computational load for further steps, a linear sampling is performed to choose points along the profile line (See Algorithm 2).

| Algorithm 2: Boundary Detection & Vertical Profile Definition |
| --- |
| 1: function BOUNDDETECTANDVERTPROFDEF($Im_{Seg}$) |
| 2:   $Im_{Ed}$ ← CANNYEDGEDETECTION($Im_{Seg}$) |
| 3:   $Ps_{Nz}$ ← NONZEROPIXELS($Im_{Ed}$) |
| 4:   $Ps_{CH}$ ← CONVEXHULL($Ps_{Nz}$) |
| 5:   $(x_c, y_c)$ ← CENTROID($Ps_{CH}$) |
| 6:   $\{y_l, y_u\}$ ← MINMAXY($Ps_{CH}$) |
| 7:   $Ps_{VP}$ ← LINEARSAMPLETHROUGHYAXIS $(x_c, y_l, y_u)$ |
| 8:   return $Ps_{VP}$ |
| 9: end function |

(vi) 3D coordinates of the points on the vertical profiles are determined by using a stereo vision method [15]. A single camera captures the stereo images by rotating the object on the rotary stage. The obtained vertical axis on the image plane is defined by the image points sampled on the profile line (2D space). However, it is required to obtain 3D world-coordinates to generate a motion plan for the laser sensor. The information supplied by 2D points is not sufficient to estimate corresponding 3D points. Fortunately, it is feasible to obtain another 2D point set on a different image frame (with a known transformation between the two views) and apply a stereo vision triangulation to generate the 3D points of interest. With the help of the rotary stage, the object is rotated by a predefined angle. While the object is rotating, the image frames captured by the camera and stored as long as the rotary table continues the motion. When the rotation stops, the algorithm begins to process the acquired image frames to track the 2D points in the first image (which were determined in step v) on each of the subsequent frames. Point elimination is applied for the track-fail points. This operation is handled by an optical flow algorithm. At the end of the process, the 2D points successfully tracked from the first frame to the last frame are stored as corresponding pairs (See Algorithm 3).

---

**Algorithm 3:**   Track Vertical Profile Points

```
 1: function TrackVerticalProfilePoints(Ps_VP)
 2:    Θ_RT ← { Take predefined rotary table angle }
 3:    Ims ← {}
 4:    while Rotary table is moving do
 5:        Ims ← Ims+ Capture image
 6:    end while
 7:    if Ims = ∅ then
 8:        return {}
 9:    end if
10:    RotateRotaryTable{Θ_RT}
11:    Im_prev ← Ims[0]
12:    Ps_prev ← Ps_VP
13:    Ps_new ← {}
14:    for all Im_next in Ims do
15:        {Ps_new, TState} ← OpticalFlow(Im_prev, Im_next, Ps_prev)
16:        ClearUnTrackable(TState, Ps_VP)
17:        ClearUnTrackable(TState, Ps_new)
18:        Swap(Ps_new, Ps_prev)
19:        Swap(Im_prev, Im_next)
20:    end for
21:    if count(Ps_prev) != count(Ps_VP) then
22:        return {}
23:    end if
24:    Ps_FIm ← {Ps_VP}
25:    Ps_LIm ← {Ps_prev}
26:    return {Ps_FIm, Ps_LIm}
27: end function
```

---

Then, the profile points defined on the image plane are transformed into 3D points defined with respect to the rotary stage coordinate system. The profile points on the first frame and the corresponding points on the last frame are projections of the same 3D points in the world coordinate system and the projection matrices for the first frame and the last frame are known (generated during camera calibration). Thus, a stereo vision triangulation is applicable for the acquired data to calculate the corresponding 3D points. The generated 3D points carry the position information of the vertical surface profile on the object to be scanned (See Algorithm 4).

---

**Algorithm 4:** Triangulation

1: function TRIANGULATION($Ps_{FIm}, Ps_{LIm}$)
2:     $M_{FIm} \leftarrow$ {Take projection matrix for the first frame}
3:     $M_{LIm} \leftarrow$ {Take projection matrix for the last frame}
4:     $T^{RT}_{CALIB} \leftarrow$ {Take transformation matrix between camera
                calibration coordinate system and rotary table
                coordinate system}
5:     $Ps^{CALIB} \leftarrow$ TRIANGULATE($Ps_{FIm}, Ps_{LIm}, M_{FIm}, M_{LIm}$)
6:     $Ps^{RT} \leftarrow \{\}$
7:     for all $p^{CALIB}$ in $Ps^{CALIB}$ do
8:         $Ps^{RT} \leftarrow \{Ps^{RT} + T^{RT}_{CALIB} * p^{CALIB}\}$
9:     end for
10:     return $Ps^{RT}$
11: end function

---

### 3.2  Motion Plan Generation Along the Profiles

The 3D point clouds on the surface profiles of the object are used to determine the motion plans, which the laser profile sensor will follow for scanning. The motion plan is obtained by a sequential process as given in Fig. 2(c).

We aim to generate a motion plan for the manipulator so that the sensor moves along the profile from a certain distance, i.e. the trajectory of the sensor coincides with the translated points of the surface profile. The direction of the translation is horizontal, pointing outward of the object surface and it is perpendicular to the normal of the plane that is defined by the surface profile points. The motion trajectory of the sensor, thus, will remain on the same plane with those of the surface profile points. In order to determine the normal of this plane, we estimate the normals of the 3D points on the profile through local least-square plane fitting, and calculate the vector average of these normals.

Once, the normal of the plane defined by the surface profile is determined it is rotated clockwise or counterclockwise by 90° around the z-axis to have a direction pointing out from the center of the rotary stage coordinate system. We call this vector the common normal vector of the object surface along the profile. The surface profile points are shifted by the minimum measurement distance of the laser profile sensor in the direction of this common normal vector. The view direction of the sensor during its movement along the trajectory is set to be in the opposite direction of the common normal vector, pointing towards the object surface.

The steps shown in Fig. 2(a) with a dashed line and a gray color are not presented in this paper. The interested readers may refer to [16].

## 4  Experimental Results

The proposed method was implemented by using an experimental platform. The platform consists of the components that are mentioned in the Sect. 2. We used Kawasaki's model RS005L, which is a high speed, high performance, small duty 6-DOF industrial robot. We used Allied Vision Manta G-238C, as the camera, which includes a Sony IMX174, 1/1.2" CMOS sensor with 1936x1216 pixel resolution, 50 fps, and an embedded microcontroller. The rotary stage is Standa 8MR190-2-4247, which is rotated by a step motor. It has zero backlash, high stability, and 0.01 degrees of resolution. We used a ScanControl 2900-100 laser profile sensor to collect the point clouds.

First phase of the procedure is to capture a background image and then place the object on the rotary stage. In Fig. 3(a) and (b), a captured background image and the test object on the stage are seen.

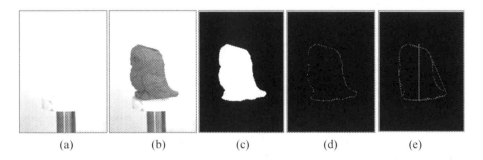

(a)            (b)            (c)            (d)            (e)

**Fig. 3.** (a) Background, (b) Object, (c) Segmented image, (d) Boundary of the object, (e) Convex hull and the vertical image plane profile, Green: convex-hull boundary, Red: vertical profile (Color figure online)

The next step is the determination of vertical profiles. The image which contains the binary mask of the segmented object is shown in the Fig. 3(c). Edge detection is applied to determine the boundary of the object and the convex-hull of the boundary is calculated as seen in Fig. 3(d) and (e). After determination of the convex hull, a vertical line is constructed to define the vertical surface profile representation in the image plane as depicted in the Fig. 3(e).

To obtain the 3D correspondences of the vertical line defined in the image plane, stereo vision triangulation process is executed. To realize the process, there is a need to obtain another frame from a different view and determine corresponding points on the other image. To obtain correspondences, a tracking procedure based on optical flow is

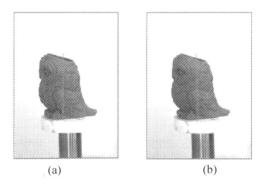

(a)                              (b)

**Fig. 4.** (a) First image and initial tracking points, (b) Last image and final position of tracked points

applied as described in the previous sections. The profile on the first image and the last image captured after 5 degrees of rotation are shown in Fig. 4(a) and (b), respectively.

Finally, the two point sets with correspondence information are used as input to the triangulation process, and the desired 3D points are estimated (Fig. 5).

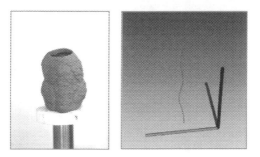

**Fig. 5.** (Left) Desired 3D surface profile, (Right) Estimated 3D profile

After estimating the 3D points on the surface profiles, a motion plan for the laser sensor is determined for scanning the surface of the object. We used a radius of 3 cm to locally estimate the normals of the profile points, then calculated the vector average to determine the normal of each plane defined by the corresponding profile points. This normal is then rotated 90° around the z-axis to obtain the common normal of the profile. Figure 6(a) shows the 3D surface points along extracted profiles of the object. The profiles each with its common normal are given in Fig. 6(b).

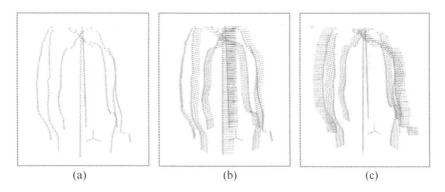

(a)                              (b)                              (c)

**Fig. 6.** (a) 3D surface points of eight surface profiles, (b) The normals of the place defined by the profiles, (c) The profiles each with a re-oriented common normal.

The normals estimated in the previous step for the points of each profile are then used to determine a common normal for the profile. The common normal is then used as the normal of all points on each profile. The common normals are then re-oriented so that the laser profile sensor has a correct line of sight during the motion plan. Figure 6(c) shows the re-oriented common normal of each profile.

24        C. Uyanik et al.

Finally, the 3D surface point cloud on the profiles and their normals are used to determine the position and orientation of the tip of the manipulator during scanning. The determined positions and orientations along with the 3D surface point cloud and the normals are shown in Fig. 7. The sensor position (blue) is found by shifting the points (green) on the profiles by the measuring range of the laser sensor in the direction of normal (black). The orientation (red) of the sensor is opposite of the normal.

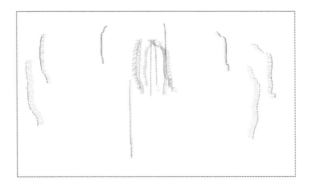

**Fig. 7.** 3D surface point clouds (green), re-oriented common normals (black), positions (blue) and orientations (red) of the tip of the manipulator during scanning. (Color figure online)

The sensor is moved by the robot manipulator along the motion plan corresponding to each profile, and the point clouds to generate the surface model are collected. Figure 8 shows the point clouds obtained by scanning along the planned trajectories.

**Fig. 8.** Point clouds obtained by scanning along three of the eight profile trajectories

To obtain the point clouds, the industrial manipulator moves the laser profile sensor according to the determined motion plans. A number of transformations are employed to define all points according to a common coordinate frame, and motion coordination between the rotary stage and robot manipulator is performed. Readers may refer to [1] for details.

Finally, complete surface model of the object is generated by merging the point clouds as seen in Fig. 9. In the first column, triangular mesh models are shown, and point cloud models are given in the second column. The surface profiles and the related sensor trajectories are indicated by dark blue color. In Fig. 10, the surface model of the object is shown in the form of a triangular mesh and a point cloud.

 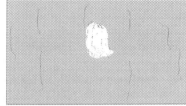

**Fig. 9.** Surface model of the object after merging all point clouds.: (First column): Mesh model, (Second column): Point cloud model. (Color figure online)

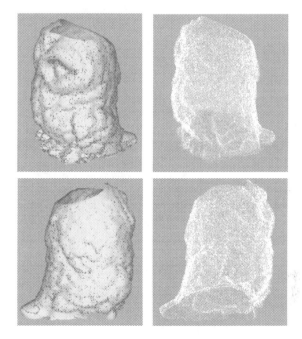

**Fig. 10.** Complete surface model of the object: (First column) Triangular mesh model, (Second column) Point cloud model

We videotaped the autonomous scanning process performed by the industrial manipulator. Sample frames from the video can be seen in Fig. 11.

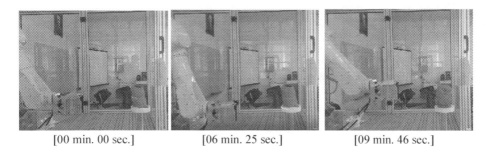

[00 min. 00 sec.]              [06 min. 25 sec.]              [09 min. 46 sec.]

**Fig. 11.** Frames captured from the application video

## 5   Conclusion

In this work, we present a novel autonomous 3D surface modeling method, consisting of an industrial manipulator and a laser profile sensor, for efficient surface reconstruction of unknown objects. The method takes advantages of both a camera with a wide angle of view and a laser profile sensor with high accurate measurement capability, so that, the surface model of any unknown object can be obtained autonomously without prior information. An experimental study is implemented using an owl-shaped pencil box as the object to be scanned. The system is able to reconstruct the complete surface model of the object without human intervention. The surface model can be further enhanced by detecting holes and determining trajectories for rescanning the corresponding object regions to complete missing information. We are currently working on the experiments to include the hole detection and scanning steps.

As future work, we will extend the experiments to scan more complex objects including concavities, and provide detailed performance analysis of the proposed method. Furthermore, we plan to use an additional camera to obtain surface profiles from the top of the object to enhance the quality of the point clouds towards the top of the object.

**Acknowledgements.** This work is supported by the Scientific and Technological Research Council of Turkey (TUBITAK) under the project number 115E374 and project title "Fully Automated 3-D Modeling of Objects by Using an Industrial Robot Manipulator".

## References

1. Mavrinac, A., Chen, X., Alarcon-Herrera, J.L.: Semiautomatic model-based view planning for active triangulation 3-D inspection systems. IEEE/ASME Trans. Mechatron. **20**(2), 799–811 (2015)
2. Lanman, D., Crispell, D., Taubin, G.: Surround structured lighting: 3-D scanning with orthographic illumination. Comput. Vis. Image Underst. **113**(11), 1107–1117 (2009)
3. Zexiao, X., Jianguo, W., Ming, J.: Study on a full field of view laser scanning system. Int. J. Mach. Tools Manuf. **47**, 33–43 (2007)

4. Hosseininaveh, A., et al.: Towards fully automatic reliable 3D acquisition: From designing imaging network to a complete and accurate point cloud. Robot. Auton. Syst. **62**, 1197–1207 (2014)

5. He, B.W., Long, Z.X., Lii, Y.F.: The research of an automatic object reconstruction method based on limit visible region of the laser-scanning vision system. Robot. Comput.-Integr. Manuf. **26**, 711–719 (2010)

6. Loriot, B., Seulin, R., Gorria, P.: Non-model based method for an automation of 3D acquisition and post-processing. Electron. Lett. Comput. Vis. Image Anal. **7**(3), 67–82 (2008)

7. Vincenzo, N., Cesare, R., Sergio, S.: A new real-time shape acquisition with a laser scanner: first test results. Robot. Comput.-Integr. Manuf. **26**, 543–550 (2014)

8. Khalfaoui, S., Seulin, R., Fougerolle, Y., Fofi, D.: An efficient method for fully automatic 3D digitization of unknown objects. Comput. Ind. **64**, 1152–1160 (2013)

9. Karaszewski, M., Sitnik, R., Bunsch, E.: On-line, collision-free positioning of a scanner during fully automated three-dimensional measurement of cultural heritage objects. Robot. Auton. Syst. **60**, 1205–1219 (2012)

10. Kriegel, S., Bodenmuller, T., Suppa, M., Hirzinger, G.: A surface-based next-best-view approach for automated 3D model completion of unknown objects. In: 2011 IEEE International Conference on Robotics and Automation, Shanghai, China, 9–13 May 2011 (2011)

11. Kjellander, J.A.P., Rahayem, M.: An integrated platform for 3D measurement with geometric reverse engineering. Comput.-Aided Des. Appl. **6**(6), 877–887 (2009)

12. Borangiu, T., Dogar, A., Dumitrache, A.: A heuristic approach for constrained real time motion planning of a redundant 7-DOF mechanism for 3D laser scanning. In: 13th IFAC Symposium on Information Control Problems in Manufacturing, vol. 13, pp. 1215–1220 (2009)

13. Kriegel, S., Rink, C., Bodenmüller, T., Suppa, M.: Efficient next-best-scan planning for autonomous 3D surface reconstruction of unknown objects. J. Real-Time Image Proc. **10**(4), 611–631 (2013)

14. Secil, S., et al.: A robotic system for autonomous 3-D surface reconstruction of objects: design and implementation. In: The 3rd International Conference on Control, Automation and Robotics (ICCAR 2017), Nagoya, Japan, 22–24 April (2017)

15. Uyanik, C., Ozkan, M.: A method for determining 3D surface points of objects by a single camera and rotary stage. In: International Conference on Computer Science and Engineering (UBMK 2017), Antalya, Turkey, 05–08 October (2017)

16. Turgut, K.: Autonomous 3-D object modeling with robot manipulator and laser profile sensor. M.Sc. thesis, Eskisehir Osmangazi University, Institute of Science (2016)

# A Modified Computed Torque Control Approach for a Master-Slave Robot Manipulator System

Ololade O. Obadina[1(✉)], Mohamed Thaha[2], Kaspar Althoefer[1], and M. Hasan Shaheed[1]

[1] School of Engineering and Materials Science, Queen Mary University of London, London, UK
o.o.obadina@qmul.ac.uk
[2] Blizard Institute, Barts and the London School of Medicine and Dentistry, Queen Mary University of London, London, UK

**Abstract.** A modified computed torque controller, adapted from the standard computed torque control law, is presented in this paper. The proposed approach is demonstrated on a 4-degree of freedom (DOF) master-slave robot manipulator and the modified computed torque controller gain parameters are optimized using both particle swarm optimization (PSO) and grey-wolf optimization algorithms. The feasibility of the proposed controller is tested experimentally and compared with its standard computed torque control counterpart. Controller tuning/optimization is carried out offline in the MATLAB/Simulink environment, and results show that the proposed controller is feasible, and performs impressively.

**Keywords:** Master slave robot · Robot manipulator
Particle swarm optimization · Grey wolf optimization
Computed torque control

## 1 Introduction

Significant growth in research has been made in developing master-slave (MS) robotic systems for various applications. Some of these areas include minimally invasive surgeries [1] and rehabilitation [2]. Limitations imposed by the majority of the existing MS robotic surgical systems include a high cost of equipment and maintenance, steep learning curve for the surgeon and the large dimension of the equipment [3, 4]. Thus, the need for smaller sized and inexpensive MS robotic systems is growing rapidly.

One of the main challenges posed with robotic systems in general is associated with developing robust controllers that are capable of handling uncertainties and disturbances in the robot's environment. The traditional proportional-integral-and-derivative (PID) controller which is widely accepted and simple to implement [5] performs poorly during high speed operations. Non-linearities in the dynamics of robot manipulators make linear feedback control techniques unsuitable for controlling the system efficiently. In most cases, the robot manipulator model is linearized and decoupled about an operating point before a linear controller can be implemented to obtain a good closed loop performance [6].

© Springer International Publishing AG, part of Springer Nature 2018
M. Giuliani et al. (Eds.): TAROS 2018, LNAI 10965, pp. 28–39, 2018.
https://doi.org/10.1007/978-3-319-96728-8_3

To meet requirements in industry, such as high speed operations of robots, several non-linear control methods have been introduced [5–8]. A particular control technique of interest is the computed torque control (CTC) which calculates torques for the robot by inverting the robot's model and feeding a signal back to cancel out non-linear effects, from a desired trajectory. The CTC scheme is conceptually easy to understand and generally performs well as long as a priori knowledge of the robot's dynamic model is known [5]. The condition of knowing the exact model, however, poses certain problems as it is difficult to model disturbances and parameter uncertainties. Song et al. [5] combines fuzzy logic control (FLC) and CTC where the FLC acts as a compensator to estimate unmodeled dynamics in robotic manipulators. To improve the accuracy and efficiency of CTC, Nguyen-Tuong et al. [9] consider two regression methods for esti-mating the dynamic model by using real data from a seven degrees of freedom (7-DOF) SARCOS robot arm. Results from both investigations show that the CTC performance using the FLC-compensation and regression-approximated model are satisfactory.

For optimal control, the performances of controllers are improved by using algo-rithms such as particle swarm optimization (PSO) and grey-wolf optimization (GWO) algorithms. The PSO algorithm, in comparison to other optimization methods, is easy to implement and only has a few adjustment parameters [10]. PSO was first developed by Eberhart and Kennedy [11], and has evolved since it was introduced over two decades ago. The PSO algorithm can be seen to minimize the cost function of an $H_\infty$ PID controller for a flexible link manipulator in [12]. Soltanpour [13] also uses the PSO algorithm to adjust the membership functions of a fuzzy sliding mode controller for a robot manipulator. The parameters of a computed torque controller for a 5-DOF robot arm are tuned using a variation of the PSO algorithm in [14] where two populations of particles were evolved simultaneously. These cited examples highlight the versatility of using the PSO algorithm for various non-linear controller types.

Another algorithm worth mentioning is the GWO algorithm, which was proposed by Mirjalili et al. [15] in 2014 and has since gained ground in research for different control applications. de Moura Oliveira et al. in [16] used the GWO algorithm to tune the PID controller gains of a single-input-single-output (SISO) 2-DOF control system. In this work, the performance of the GWO algorithm was compared with PSO and it is reported that both algorithms provided similar results. In addition, GWO algorithm with chaotic basis in [17] has been used to optimize the parameters of a higher order sliding mode controller for position control of a rigid robot manipulator. To the best of our knowledge, no research yet has reported the optimization of computed torque control parameters using GWO algorithm for robot manipulators.

This paper thus proposes a modified computed torque controller approach that has been adapted from the standard CTC scheme found in literature. The novelty of this method lies in the alteration of the standard CTC control law by making all terms in the control law equation error based. In literature, the standard CTC control law includes an angular acceleration term, which is fairly difficult to measure directly. By making all terms error based, the proposed control law is simpler and easier to implement practi-cally. Also, the gain parameters of the proposed controller are tuned using both particle swarm optimization (PSO) and grey-wolf optimization algorithms for optimum performance. Simulation results show the feasibility of the proposed controller with application to a 4-DOF master-slave robot manipulator system, and experimental investigations are limited to Joints 0 and 1 of the manipulator i.e. the base joint and shoulder joint respectively.

## 2    The Master-Slave Robotic Manipulator (MSRM) System

### 2.1    Description

The MSRM system is a laboratory prototype that was developed in Queen Mary University of London, which consists of a master manipulator, a slave manipulator and a control system (See Fig. 1). The hand movements of the user holding the master are relayed as measured position signals to the control system that then sends scaled and transformed signals to the slave manipulator. The slave then tries to track the trajectory of the master precisely in real time. With MS robot systems in general, it is fairly important that the designed controller works to keep the time delay minimal.

**Fig. 1.**  The 4-DOF master-slave robot manipulator system

Both master and slave manipulators each have 4 degrees of freedom (4-DOF) plus one for grasping at the end effector. The main difference between these manipulators is the presence of position sensors in the master, and actuators in the slave joints respectively. Only the dynamics of the slave manipulator is considered in this work.

The coordinate reference frames of the manipulator in reset position are described in Fig. 2. At reset position, all joint angles are at 0 radians.

Basically, Joint 0 is the 'base joint' which allows the slave manipulator to pivot about its base. Joint 1 is the 'shoulder joint' that supports the weight of the rest of the manipulator, while Joints 2 and 3 mimic the human wrist where the former enables the 'wrist joint' to move up and down and the latter allows a twisting rotation in the wrist joint.

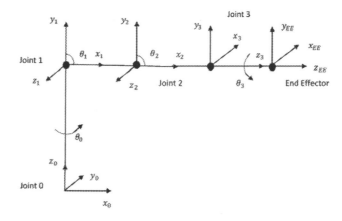

**Fig. 2.** Slave manipulator description using coordinate reference

## 2.2 Slave Manipulator Dynamics

The rigid body dynamic equations of the slave manipulator is derived from the Euler-Lagrange [18] formulation, and the dynamic equation for an N-DOF robot manipulator, written in vector form, is shown below as:

$$\tau = M(\theta)\ddot{\theta} + C(\theta,\dot{\theta}) + G(\theta) \tag{1}$$

where:

| | |
|---|---|
| $\tau$ | N × 1 vector of driving torque actuating the joints; |
| $\ddot{\theta}$ | N × 1 vector of robot's acceleration components; |
| $G(\theta)$ | N × 1 vector of gravitational components; |
| $M(\theta)$ | N × N positive definite matrix of rigid body inertia; |
| $C(\theta,\dot{\theta})$ | N × 1 vector of Coriolis and centrifugal components. |

## 3   Computed Torque Control

In control systems, the ultimate goal of a controller is to minimize tracking errors, ensure stability and robustness against uncertainties and perturbations in closed loop systems.

Computed torque control is a form of closed loop control that involves feeding back a control signal to eliminate the effects of disturbances and nonlinearities, and introduces desired torques that will ensure the error dynamics converges to zero. Some of these nonlinear terms include gravity and friction, and Coriolis and centrifugal torques.

### 3.1   Standard Computed Torque Control

The general equation of the standard CTC is described as:

$$\tau = M(\theta)\underline{V} + D(\theta, \dot{\theta}) \qquad (2)$$

where the auxiliary control input, $\underline{V}$ is given as:

$$\underline{V} = \ddot{\theta}_d + 2\zeta\omega_n\dot{e} + \omega_n^2 e \qquad (3)$$

### 3.2  Modified Computed Torque Control

The modified CTC, however, uses a similar structure as the standard CTC but incorporates the use of an integral error and omits the desired joint acceleration. The modified auxiliary control law is, thus, expressed as:

$$\underline{V} = \omega_n^2 e(t) + K_i \varepsilon + 2\zeta\omega_n\dot{e} \qquad (4)$$

Therefore, the desired computed joint torques to be inputted into the system (seen in Fig. 2) can be described mathematically as:

$$\tau = M(\theta)\left[\omega_n^2 e(t) + K_i \varepsilon + 2\zeta\omega_n\dot{e}\right] + D(\theta, \dot{\theta}) \qquad (5)$$

where

| | |
|---|---|
| $e(t)$ | Tracking error; |
| $\varepsilon$ | Integral of the tracking error; |
| $\dot{e}$ | Derivative of the tracking error; |
| $\theta$ | Actual angular position; |
| $\theta_d$ | Desired angular position; |
| $V$ | N × 1 vector of auxiliary control input; |
| $M(\theta)$ | N × N rigid body inertia matrix; |
| $D(\theta, \dot{\theta})$ | Sum of Coriolis/centrifugal and gravity terms; |
| $\omega_n, \zeta, K_i$ | Controller parameters to be tuned for each joint. |

It can be inferred that the proposed CTC approach (see Fig. 3) appears to have a similar structure to the traditional PID controller, where it uses only the tracking error, integral of error and the error derivative to form its auxiliary control law. This, therefore, gives an advantage of a controller that is simple to implement and robust enough to handle non-linearities in robotic systems.

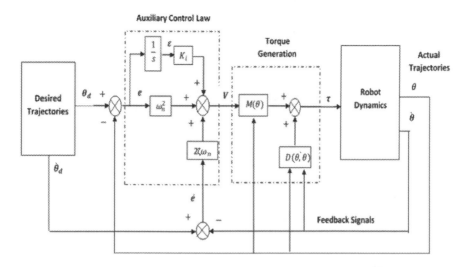

**Fig. 3.** Block diagram of computed torque approach

# 4 Controller Optimization

The gain parameters $\{\omega_n, \zeta \text{ and } K_i\}$ of the modified CTC are tuned for each joint of the MS robot system offline using both PSO and GWO algorithms in the MATLAB/Simulink environment. The objective function used for the optimization process is the mean absolute error (MAE), and it's described as follows:

$$MAE = \frac{1}{N} \sum_{i=0}^{T} |e(t)_i| \tag{6}$$

where: $e(t)_i$ is the value of tracking error per iteration, T is the total optimization time and N is the number of errors terms.

## 4.1 Particle Swarm Optimization (PSO)

Particle swarm optimization (PSO) is an evolutionary algorithm that is inspired by the behaviour of flocked species such as birds and fishes. In any given PSO problem, a search space is a set of possible solutions, where the objective of the PSO algorithm is to find the best solution among the set of possible solutions.

A particle moves through the search space by keeping track of its personal best position, which is denoted as $p_{best}$. Each particle updates its position and velocity after each iteration, and communicates with other particles in the swarm until the common best position for all particles is found [11]. This is known as the global best position, and is denoted as $g_{best}$.

The following equations governing the movement of the particles in a swarm [14], are used to compute the new position and velocity of each particle.

$$v_i^{(t+1)} = w.v_i^t + c_1.\left[p_{best} - x_i^t\right] + c_2.\left[g_{best} - x_i^t\right] \tag{7}$$

$$x_i^{(t+1)} = x_i^t + v_i^{(t+1)} \tag{8}$$

where: $w$ is the inertia weight; $c_1$ and $c_2$ are self-adjustment and social adjustment acceleration constants; $p_{best}$ is the current personal best position of $i^{th}$ particle; $g_{best}$ is the global best position of particles in the swarm; $x_i^t$ is the current position of the $i^{th}$ particle; $x_i^{(t+1)}$ is the new updated positions of the $i^{th}$ particle; $v_i^t$ is the velocity at the current location of $i^{th}$ particle; and $v_i^{t+1}$ is the velocity at the new location of $i^{th}$ particle.

### 4.2  Grey-Wolf Optimization (GWO)

The Grey-Wolf Optimization (GWO) algorithm is another swarm intelligence based algorithm that is inspired by the leadership hierarchy behaviour of Grey wolves [15] where the best candidate solution, second best and third best solutions are regarded as the 'alpha', 'beta' and 'delta' wolves respectively. The optimization is carried out in three phases, namely: hunting and searching for prey, encircling prey and, attacking prey.

For the first phase, the hunting and searching behaviour of the grey wolves are mathematical described as [15]:

$$D_\alpha = \left|\vec{C_1}.\vec{X_\alpha} - \vec{X}\right|; D_\beta = \left|\vec{C_2}.\vec{X_\beta} - \vec{X}\right|; D_\delta = \left|\vec{C_3}.\vec{X_\delta} - \vec{X}\right| \tag{9}$$

$$\vec{X_1} = \left[\vec{X_\alpha} - \vec{A_1}\right].(D_\alpha); \vec{X_2} = \left[\vec{X_\beta} - \vec{A_2}\right].(D_\beta); \vec{X_3} = \left[\vec{X_\delta} - \vec{A_3}\right].(D_\delta) \tag{10}$$

$$\vec{X_1}(t+1) = \frac{\vec{X_1} + \vec{X_2} + \vec{X_3}}{3} \tag{11}$$

The prey-encircling phase is denoted as:

$$\vec{D} = \left|\vec{C}.\vec{X_p}(t) - \vec{X}(t)\right| \tag{12}$$

$$\vec{X_1}(t+1) = \vec{X_p}(t) - \vec{A}.\vec{D} \tag{13}$$

Finally, the attacking phase is described as follows:

$$\vec{A} = 2\vec{a}.\vec{r_1} - \vec{a} \tag{14}$$

$$\vec{C} = 2\vec{r_2} \tag{15}$$

where: $\vec{X_p}$ is the position of the prey; $\vec{X}$ is the position of a grey wolf; $\vec{A}$ and $\vec{C}$ are vectors, $\vec{r_1}$ and $\vec{r_2}$ are random vectors in the range [0, 1]; $t$ indicates the current iteration; and $\vec{a}$

is a vector that decreases linearly from 2 to 0 over the course of iterations to mimic the attacking phase.

## 5 Results and Discussion

### 5.1 Comparison Between Standard CTC and Modified CTC

The feasibility of the proposed modified computed torque controller is verified by implementing the controller on two joints of the real master-slave robot system. These joints are Joints 0 and 1 denoting the base and shoulder joints respectively. The standard computed torque controller is seen to be implemented on these same joints. Using similar parameters for both types of CTCs, the controllers' performances are shown in Figs. 4 and 5.

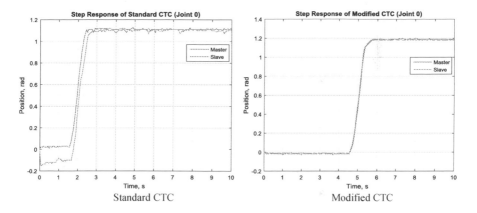

**Fig. 4.** Computed torque control performance on joint 0

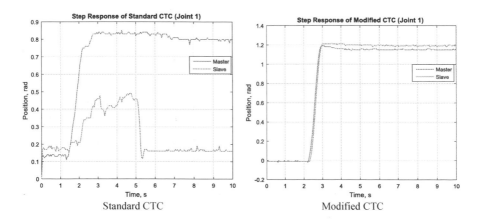

**Fig. 5.** Computed torque control performance on joint 1

The step response of the standard CTC in Joints 0 and 1 causes the slave manipulator to oscillate chaotically about its steady state while the modified CTC gives a much smoother response (see Figs. 4 and 5). A huge steady state error is also noticeable with the performance of the standard CTC on Joint 1 (Fig. 5). The offset seen in the standard CTC responses, caused by this jittery behaviour, induces a steady state error between the master and slave.

The modified CTC, however, gets rid of the offset, and the slave manipulator is seen to track the master relatively well with little or no errors. The integral action term in the modified CTC acts similarly to PID control as it is seen to eliminate steady state errors in the base joint (Joint 0) and shoulder joint (Joint 1) of the MSRM system.

## 5.2  Comparison Between PSO and GWO Algorithms

Two optimization algorithms, namely - PSO and GWO have been used to tune the parameters of the proposed controller. The optimization process is first carried out in an offline environment via MATLAB/Simulink interface, and the results are later implemented on the experimental system.

For accurate comparison, the GWO and PSO algorithms have used the same parameters for their optimization process. These parameters include: population size = 30 and maximum number of iterations = 50. The performances of PSO and GWO are compared using the percentage overshoot step response characteristic (Table 1). Also, the total computation time for each algorithm to find optimal controller gain values are presented in Table 2.

**Table 1.** Percentage overshoot comparison of modified CTC using PSO and GWO algorithms

| Modified CTC | Joint 0 | Joint 1 | Joint 2 | Joint 3 |
|---|---|---|---|---|
| % Overshoot (PSO) | 7.4 | 7.4 | 7.3 | 7.4 |
| % Overshoot (GWO) | 7.3 | 7.4 | 7.3 | 7.4 |

**Table 2.** Computation time for PSO-CTC and GWO-CTC optimization

| Computation time | PSO-CTC (in seconds) | GWO-CTC (in seconds) |
|---|---|---|
| Joint 0 | 768.9 | 741.7 |
| Joint 1 | 443.9 | 891.5 |
| Joint 2 | 782.2 | 658.9 |
| Joint 3 | 570 | 922.9 |

Figure 6 shows the iteration processes of both PSO-CTC and GWO-CTC optimization for Joints 0, 1, 2 and 3 of the MSRM system. In all cases, the PSO algorithm terminates long before the given maximum number of iterations. This shows that PSO is trapped in a minimum and the algorithm ends its iterations because it assumes it has found a global optimum for this optimization problem. On the other hand, the GWO algorithm continues its iteration process until it reaches the specified maximum number of iterations. Comparing the performances of both algorithms, GWO can be likened to a 'greedy' algorithm as it demonstrates its extensive nature in finding high quality solutions while PSO is less exhaustive in its approach.

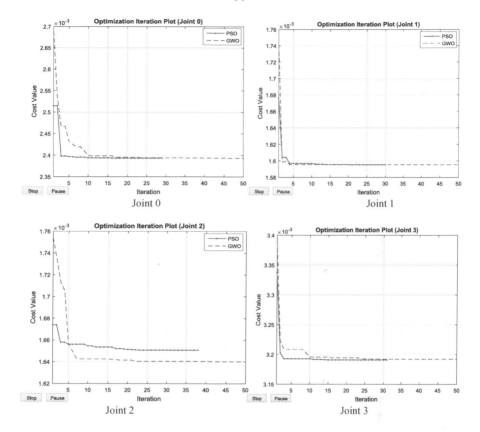

**Fig. 6.**  Iteration plots of PSO and GWO algorithms on joints 0, 1, 2 and 3.

Also, the cost objective values of both PSO and GWO algorithms at the last iteration are approximately the same across the base, shoulder and wrist-twist joints (i.e. Joints 0, 1 and 3 respectively). The GWO algorithm, however, has a lower cost objective value than the PSO algorithm during the optimization of Joint 2. The lower the cost objective value, the higher the quality of an algorithm's search results. This observation also explains the faster convergence speed of the GWO algorithm's in Table 2, and demonstrates the algorithm's better ability to find the global optimum in comparison to PSO.

With these presented results, it is safe to assume that both PSO and GWO perform similarly with respect to tuning the modified computed torque controller. In one instance (see Table 1), GWO reduces the percentage overshoot by 0.1% in comparison to PSO, which in reality, is negligible.

# 6 Conclusion

A novel modified computed torque approach is proposed and implemented on a MSRM system for position control and tracking. Obtained results show that the proposed approach is feasible, and performs better than the standard computed torque control that is popularly known in literature.

A study on the performance of two optimization algorithms – GWO and PSO with respect to tuning the modified computed torque controller, has also been carried out. Results have shown that both algorithms perform very similarly across most joints of the MSRM system in terms of step response characteristics. However, the GWO algorithm converges faster in Joint 2 and also obtains a smaller cost value compared to PSO. Results also show that the PSO algorithm terminates its iteration process prematurely while GWO algorithm reaches its maximum number of iterations before the algorithm ends. It can be inferred that GWO has a more exhaustive approach in finding higher quality solutions while PSO is less extensive.

Future work will consider improving the existing MSRM's dynamic model by identifying unknown parameters which are difficult to measure directly, using grey-box modelling techniques. This will further improve the proposed controller's performance especially when a payload is introduced at the end effector.

# References

1. Camarillo, D.B., Krummel, T.M., Salisbury, J.K.: Robotic technology in surgery: past, present, and future. Am. J. Surg. **188**(4A Suppl.), 2S–15S (2004)
2. Cortese, M., Cempini, M., Rog, P., Ribeiro, D.A., Soekadar, S.R.: A mechatronic system for robot-mediated hand telerehabilitation. IEEE/ASME Trans. Mechatron. **PP**(99), 1–12 (2014)
3. Vitiello, V.: Emerging robotic platforms for minimally invasive surgery. Biomed. Eng. IEEE Rev. **6**, 111–126 (2013)
4. Sang, H., Wang, S., Zhang, L., He, C., Zhang, L., Wang, X.: Control design and implementation of a novel master – slave surgery robot system, MicroHand A. Int. J. Med. Robot. Comput. Assist. Surg. **7**, 334–347 (2011)
5. Song, Z., Yi, J., Zhao, D., Li, X.: A computed torque controller for uncertain robotic manipulator systems: fuzzy approach. Fuzzy Sets Syst. **154**(2), 208–226 (2005)
6. Zhihong, M., Palaniswami, M.: Robust tracking control for rigid robotic manipulators. IEEE Trans. Autom. Contr. **39**(1), 154–159 (1994)
7. Bascetta, L., Rocco, P.: Revising the robust-control design for rigid robot manipulators. IEEE Trans. Robot. **26**(April), 180–187 (2010)
8. Ho, H.F., Wong, Y.K., Rad, A.B.: Robust fuzzy tracking control for robotic manipulators. Simul. Model. Pract. Theory **15**(7), 801–816 (2007)
9. Nguyen-Tuong, D., Seeger, M., Peters, J.: Computed torque control with nonparametric regression models. In: 2008 American Control Conference, pp. 212–217 (2008)
10. Geetha, M., Balajee, K., Jerome, J.: Optimal tuning of virtual feedback PID controller for a Continuous Stirred Tank Reactor (CSTR) using Particle Swarm Optimization (PSO) algorithm. In: IEEE-International Conference on Advances in Engineering, Science and Management, pp. 94–99 (2012)
11. Eberhart, R., Kennedy, J.: A new optimizer using particle swarm theory. In: Proceedings Sixth International Symposium Micro Machine and Human Science, pp. 39–43 (1995)

12. Zamani, M., Sadati, N., Ghartemani, M.K.: Design of an H∞ PID controller using particle swarm optimization. Int. J. Control Autom. Syst. **7**(2), 273–280 (2009)
13. Soltanpour, M., Khooban, M.: A particle swarm optimization approach for fuzzy sliding mode control for tracking the robot manipulator. Nonlinear Dyn. **74**(1–2), 1–12 (2013)
14. Asmara, A., Krohling, R., Hoffmann, F.: Parameter tuning of a computed-torque controller for a 5 degree of freedom robot arm using co-evolutionary particle swarm optimization. In: Proceedings 2005 IEEE Swarm Intelligence Symposium, SIS 2005, pp. 1–13 (2005)
15. Mirjalili, S., Mirjalili, S.M., Lewis, A.: Grey wolf optimizer. Adv. Eng. Softw. **69**, 46–61 (2014)
16. de Moura Oliveira, P.B., Freire, H., Solteiro Pires, E.J.: Grey wolf optimization for PID controller design with prescribed robustness margins. Soft Comput. **20**(11), 4243–4255 (2016)
17. Oliveira, J., Oliveira, P.M., Boaventura-Cunha, J., Pinho, T.: Chaos-based grey wolf optimizer for higher order sliding mode position control of a robotic manipulator. Nonlinear Dyn. **90**(2), 1353–1362 (2017)
18. Craig, J.J.: Introduction to Robotics: Mechanics and Control, 3rd edn, vol. 1, no. 3. Pearson, Upper Saddle River (2004)

# Data Synthesization for Classification in Autonomous Robotic Grasping System Using 'Catalogue'-Style Images

Michael Cheah, Josie Hughes$^{(\boxtimes)}$, and Fumiya Iida

Bio-Inspired Robotics Lab, Department of Engineering,
University of Cambridge, Cambridge, UK
michaelcheah95@gmail.com, {jaeh2,fi224}@cam.ac.uk

**Abstract.** The classification and grasping of randomly placed objects where only a limited number of training images are available, remains a challenging problem. Approaches such as data synthesis have been used to synthetically create larger training data sets from a small set of training data and can be used to improve performance. This paper examines how limited product images for 'off the shelf' items can be used to generate a synthetic data set that is used to train a that allows classification of the item, segmentation and grasping. Experiments investigating the effects of data synthesis are presented and the subsequent trained network implemented in a robotic system to perform grasping of objects.

**Keywords:** Manipulation · Learning · Data augmentation

## 1 Introduction

Robots are increasingly being required to perform automated picking and placing of objects where there is little a priori image information and the environment is cluttered and unstructured. The challenge for researchers, therefore, is to develop systems which can operate with extremely limited data-sets, minimal training time and which can function robustly in cluttered, unordered environments [2]. Deep learning computer vision techniques, specifically Convolutional Neural Networks (CNNs), have been used with considerable success [9,14] to perform classification of objects in an image. They have proven to be remarkably versatile as they are capable of learning useful features directly from the whole picture, rather than requiring heuristically defined features that tend to capture only localised data [17]. Such classification and identification methods can also be combined with robotic systems to develop automated grasping systems.

One approach to solving the classification and autonomous grasping of items is to obtain large data-sets to which deep learning methods can be used to enable classification and segmentation of images [10]. However, this is time consuming as many images of the products must be taken and requires manual or supervised labelling of the data-sets. In a warehouse or industrial setting, the large

© Springer International Publishing AG, part of Springer Nature 2018
M. Giuliani et al. (Eds.): TAROS 2018, LNAI 10965, pp. 40–51, 2018.
https://doi.org/10.1007/978-3-319-96728-8_4

number of items means that this data-set generation method is excessively time consumable and not feasible and thus a more scalable solution is required. This work explores how data synthesis can be used to generate training data sets from a very limited set of 'catalogue' style images in order to reduce the need for large data sets and extensive manual data labelling. The data systems can be used to train a CNN, and then tested in a robotic grasping system.

In this project the Mask R-CNN (Mask Regions with Convolutional Neural Networks) has been used. This provides an extension of the more commonly used Faster R-CNN by providing an object mask in addition to the bounding box provided by Faster R-CNN. As such, segmentation and classification are performed simultaneously in one step [6], offering smaller overheads as a result of the secondary branching functionality.

The Mask R-CNN is a recent development and has had limited integration and testing in real world application [13]. Previous work with Mask R-CNNs [4] has focused on using synthetically generated training data to pick objects. The training data set was mostly generated from the large scale data collection of robot experiments in simulation which allowed the easy generation of large labelled data sets. This involved 3D scanning objects and placing them into a synthetically generated images.

The objective of this research is similar to the vision required for the Amazon Robotics Challenge, where previous work has demonstrated that deep learning techniques which require only a limited data set can be used [12]. There has also been previous work investigating different data augmentation approaches [16] and similarly, prior work has been undertaken to investigate the uses of synthesizing data for neural network training [5]. Recent work has shown that networks trained on synthesised data can perform well on real test settings [3]. However, there has been little investigation into the effect of using a mix of real and synthetic background images and using product images for data synthesisation.

This work develops the vision, learning and robotic grasping systems for identifying an object in a previously unseen environment given only product 'catalogue' style images, which could potentially be found in a manufacturers database. The aim is to demonstrate that a large synthetic data set can be created using initial product images without the need for hand labelling, thus reducing the overheads in terms of data collection and labelling.

Catalogue images are defined as images on a plain clean background where there are multiple poses of the single product available. This allows for easy segmentation, no hand labelling and no additional data collection as these images form part of a product database. For this work we have generated sets of 'catalogue' like images to demonstrate the process. Using data synthesis, a is trained to allow the item to be identified and segmented in a new environment in various different conditions. The Mask R-CNN is trained only with these synthetically generated images, i.e. images which consist of a real background images and the products rendered on top of it. Data augmentation and synthesization are techniques which can be used to increase the training data available with minimal effort and overheads in order to increase robustness and reliability. We test

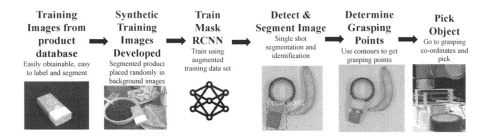

**Fig. 1.** Summary of the image identification pipeline from image acquisition to object grasping.

the hypothesis that a mix of images from the environment the picking test will be ran, termed 'real background images', and table top images from existing data sets, termed 'fake background images', improves the performance of the classifier. The real background images specifically train the network for the test environment with the addition of the fake background images to add robustness and prevent overfitting. A heuristic method for identifying grasping points, which requires only 2D images, is used with a robot arm and simple two finger gripper, enabling a start to end demonstration of the picking process. The ability to use only 2D imaging to obtain grasping points provides a simple and novel way of achieving grasping points using monocular vision.

## 2    Methods and Implementation

The overall pipeline from training data to grasping points is summarised in Fig. 1. Details about each stage of this pipeline are now discussed.

### 2.1    Training Data and Data Augmentation

The training data set consists of a small number of images (2–16) which are 'catalogue' type images. Catalogue images here is defined as images that have (1) clean backgrounds and (2) multiple poses available for a single product. These images are commonly found in product catalogues and thus could be obtained directly from the manufacturer with no further data capture required. Typically these images are from a variety of views, on a solid colour background and show only the item of interest allowing easy segmentation and labelling of data.

Data synthesis is then used to create a training data set for the neural network. First, the product is segmented using edge detection to remove the product from the solid colour background of the product image. Artefacts are cleaned up by using binary erosion with a structuring element scaled with the size of the product. While this leads to a small loss in information at the segment edges, it is offset by obtaining a cleaner segmentation of the product that still retains the product shapes and features. The procedure is shown in Fig. 2.

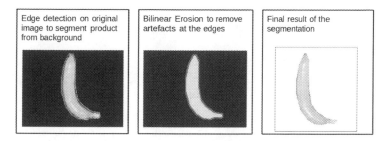

**Fig. 2.** Summary of segmentation procedure for product images

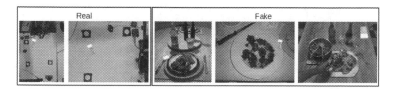

**Fig. 3.** Example images of synthetic data using real and fake backgrounds

Individual segmented images are superimposed in different base images, some of which are actual pictures from the test environment from which the object will be picked (real images), and others are images of table tops obtained from the Common Objects in Context (COCO) training set (fake background images) [11]. The COCO data set is chosen as it includes a variety of image types, and it allows for relevant backgrounds, i.e. images with tables, to be easily chosen. The addition of the fake background images should increase the robustness of the detector to assist the network in learning features that are not indicative of the products. Different ratios of real to fake background images are used to investigate the effects of increased reliability and robustness using these methods. Some examples are shown in Fig. 3.

The segmented product is placed in a background image with the position, rotation and size varied randomly to generate a synthetic training data-set. In this case, the entire data set comprises of synthetic images and requires no labelling by hand. Data synthesis is accepted as a commonly used method to reduce over-fitting of image data by artificially enlarging the data-set by using label-preserving transformations [1,8].

For this set of experiments, 500 training images were generated from 30 real and 139 fake COCO-dataset images using between 2 and 16 product images for each product. Different training data sets are generated by specifying the percentage of real to fake background images (0%–100%) and the number of product images used. The results from these experiments are discussed below.

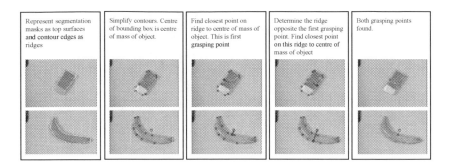

| Represent segmentation masks as top surfaces and contour edges as ridges | Simplify contours. Centre of bounding box is centre of mass of object. | Find closest point on ridge to centre of mass of object. This is first grasping point | Determine the ridge opposite the first grasping point. Find closest point on this ridge to centre of mass of object | Both grasping points found. |

**Fig. 4.** Summary of the grasping point identification process demonstrated on images of tissues and a banana.

## 2.2   Image Segmentation Using Trained

An implementation of the [6] is used for instance segmentation. Transfer learning is done using weights pretrained on the COCO-dataset. The training was performed on an NVIDIA GeForce GTX 1050 GPU. Training was carried out only on the final layer for a fixed number of steps - 20 epochs of 300 steps each, with batch size of 1, learning rate of 0.001, learning momentum of 0.9 and weight decay regularisation of 0.0001. Each training takes less than an hour to perform.

Using the trained network, image segmentation and detection can be performed. A work-space on a table has been chosen as the environment from which to grasp the object with a camera mounted directly above this. The Mask R-CNN returns binary masks for each of the segmented identified objects in the input image.

## 2.3   Grasping Point Identification

A simple algorithm for determining grasping points of table top objects, inspired by work by Richtsfeld and Vincze [15], is used here. While the top surfaces of objects used by Richtsfeld are obtained from 2.5D point clouds, our setup uses only a single 2D webcam and instead uses the segmentation masks from the to represent the top surface of the objects. The contours of these segments then represent ridges, where the two points corresponding to the two grasping points for a two fingered gripper is found that is closest to the centre of the bounding box of the object. The algorithm is summarised in Fig. 4.

There is significant work focusing specifically on the determination of grasping points from images [9], however, in this work we are focusing on the 90% of objects which can be easily picked using simple two finger grasping strategies. To achieve this we are essentially modelling the object as a box [7].

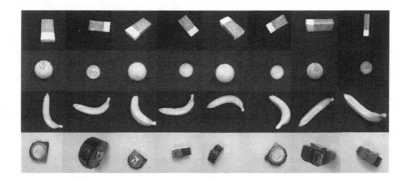

Fig. 5. Example of the product images for the three test image.

## 3    Experimental Setup

**Test Data Set.** A labelled test data set of the products was prepared in order to test the performance of the different networks trained. The validation set includes pictures of the work-space with clutter, varying lighting conditions, the test items in varying poses and additional items to test the ability of the network to avoid false positives.

A set of items to test the classification, grasping and pick and place has been chosen, namely a pack of tissues, banana, ball and measuring tape. These have been chosen as they represent a variety of sizes, forms and shapes and could be considered to be mainstream items which could be found in a picking factory environment. The items and the 'product' style images used are shown in Fig. 5.

### 3.1    Physical Hardware

To test the system developed, a pick and place setup has been developed which utilises a simple two finger manipulator for picking (Fig. 6). A UR5 robot arm is used with a work space defined within the range of arm with a camera placed above this workspace. The grasping points returned from the and edge detection algorithms are converted to real world co-ordinates using calibration parameters for the work space of the robot. Using the grasping points, the path planning of the arms is determined utilising the inverse kinematics on-board the UR5 controller. A simple two finger manipulator has been designed for picking the objects (inset Fig. 6); this has been designed to work with the generalised grasping point detection algorithm and requires only simple control. The manipulator uses a worm gear closing mechanisms utilising a DC motor with the actuator controlled over serial by an Arduino and H-bridge. A microswitch and current feedback is used on the gripper to determined when the object has been grasped and provides a simple feedback mechanism.

## 4    Experimental Results and Discussion

Two parameters for generating the synthetic data-set were studied - number of product images and percentage of real to fake background work-space images, to determine their effects on the performance of the classification and segmentation system. The testing of the classification and segmentation system has been performed on a single item, the tissues, and all networks were trained for 20 epochs. The start to end test of image identification through to grasping has been performed on all items with the success rate quantified in terms of the vision and grasping point detection and also the physical grasping success.

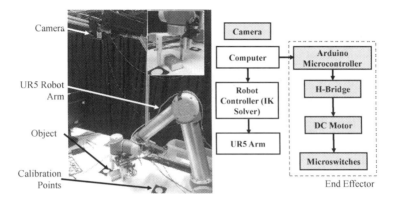

**Fig. 6.** The experimental setup development showing the robot arm, end effector and the placement area for the objects.

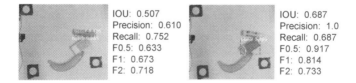

**Fig. 7.** Varying F scores for different segmentation, demonstrating that for determining grasping points achieving partial segmentation is preferable and hence $F_{0.5}$ is a more preferable performance indicator.

**Quantitative Performance Measures.** There are a number of different performance measures for quantitatively determining the performance. The precision and recall were calculated for the test data. From these the F-score and IOU was calculated which gives a measure of accuracy of the network on the test data. IOU has been chosen over mean average position as this is a more meaningful measure for grasping problems. The overall aim of this project is

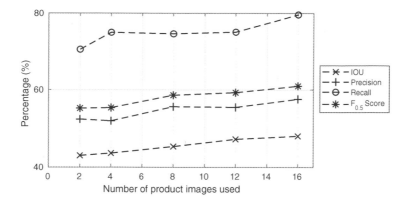

**Fig. 8.** Performance measures for the best network trained with varying numbers of tissue product images.

to identify the grasping points of an object; thus it is more desirable to obtain partial segmentation than to over-segment objects as this would lead to a higher chance of successfully determining grasping points [12]. In this case, precision should be weighted stronger than recall, therefore the $F_{0.5}$ measurement has been chosen to be used. This has been demonstrated in Fig. 7.

### 4.1   Classification and Segmentation

**Number of Product Images.** Generated data sets using varying numbers of product images were used to train the network. The performance of these networks was then tested against the labelled test data set.

Looking at the performances (Fig. 8) after 20 epochs of training, there is some marginal improvement across all performance measures as the number of product images increase. This is to be expected as the network is allowed to learn more features of the products given more instances of it to train on. In particular, Recall should be expected to increase when the network is given more product images as it is more likely to recognise the product in less common poses that networks trained with less product images are not exposed to. However, despite having many times more product images to study, the network only performs marginally better when trained on images with 16 images as compared to only 2 or 4. This may be attributed to the fact that the first images in the product database are of the more frequently observed sides, thus are more critical to object detection.

**Percentage of Real and Fake Background Images.** Using 16 training images, a varying ratio of real to synthetically created training images have been used to train the networks. The performance measures for these trained networks are given in Fig. 9.

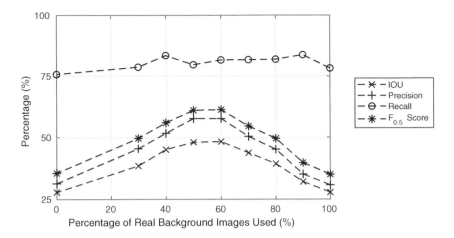

**Fig. 9.** Performance metrics for the network trained with varying numbers of product images.

The recall remains approximately constant across all percentages of training data compositions, however there is considerable drop offs in the precision when only real or synthetic backgrounds are used. When trained only on real backgrounds, the network effectively becomes a background subtractor as it learns to avoid features in the work space that are not relevant to the products, as opposed to learning features of the products that differentiate it from the background. Conversely, when trained only on synthetic backgrounds, the network does not have a chance to learn to avoid features already present in the work space that it should avoid, thus it is more susceptible to detecting false positives in the actual test. As such, it is expected that some mix of both real and synthetic backgrounds will produce an optimal result when training.

This is demonstrated by the $F_{0.5}$Score and IOU where the maximum performance is achieved with an approximately 50% mix of real and synthetic images.

## 4.2   Grasping Success

To determine the success of the pipeline from image classification, segmentation and grasping point, the grasping points have been generated for the validation set of images and the success determined manually for the grasping points generated. Situations of increasing complexity were tested, where the environment is increasingly cluttered and items were added which are similar in form to the test items were added. The results are shown in Table 1, with the grasping points and segmentation (including failure cases) shown in Fig. 10.

Additionally, the success of end-to-end grasping has been tested for the four test objects for a variety of different test scenarios. The success rate for these is also shown in Table 1.

**Table 1.** Success in determining grasping points and overall success in grasping the three test items where each is tested 10 times.

| Test item | Grasping point success (%) | Grasping success (%) |
|---|---|---|
| Tissue | 90 | 80 |
| Banana | 90 | 80 |
| Ball | 100 | 70 |
| Measuring tape | 90 | 70 |

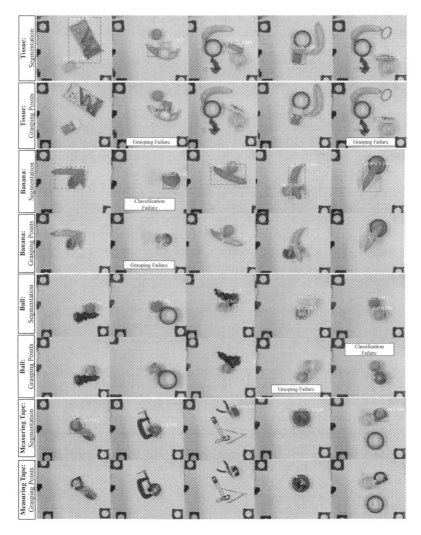

**Fig. 10.** Segmentation of the objects and the grasping points determined for a selection of the test cases. The failures are demonstrated and the reason for failure given.

Some failures can be attributed to mechanical failure in the gripping method where a two fingered approach is insufficient to grasp the item, mainly due to close proximity to the other items. In some cases, items were incorrectly identified as the test item, however, mostly the item of choice still had a higher certainty of classification so was correctly picked.

## 5   Conclusions

This work has demonstrated how product images and data synthesis can be used to create a training data set which can allow classification of items with average $F_{0.5}$Scores of greater than 0.60. This requires only a minimal data set and allows 'catalogue' style images to be used to generate classifiers for instance segmentation such that the method is scaleable. Using this method, a simple grasping system has been created which allows items to be picked in a cluttered environment with a success rate of around 80%. For the grasping experiments, the networks were only trained with 20 epochs to understand the performance in a limited time scale such that it is possible to rapidly train the network for additional items. Training the network for longer and using larger numbers of product images would enable a more optimal performance of the network to be determined.

The benefits of data augmentation and synthesisation have been demonstrated, however there is significant further work which could carried out to further improve the performance using these methods. This could include more sophisticated data augmentation methods, including the addition of occlusion and noise to the product images other background data. In these experiments a set of product 'catalogue' images was generated for each item. To further demonstrate the concept, real product images should be used, and the ability to train a variety of different items with different styles of product images should be investigated.

Further work is required to further understand the optimal ratio of real and synthetic background images and how in different test situations this varies. Additionally, testing with more items with increasingly complex or varied morphologies would further test the grasping point methodology and would further verify the results and demonstrate the benefits of the data synthesisation method presented. Integrating a more complex gripper and associated grasping point detection algorithm would allow the grasping success to improve as this would remove the failures to the mechanical system associated with using the outer contours of the object to determine grasping points.

**Acknowledgments.** With thanks to the James Dyson Foundation Undergraduate Bursary and also the EPSRC CDT in Sensor Technologies (Grant EP/L015889/1).

# References

1. Ciregan, D., Meier, U., Schmidhuber, J.: Multi-column deep neural networks for image classification. In: 2012 IEEE conference on Computer vision and pattern recognition (CVPR), pp. 3642–3649. IEEE (2012)
2. Dragan, A.D., Gordon, G.J., Srinivasa, S.S.: Learning from experience in manipulation planning: setting the right goals. In: Christensen, H.I., Khatib, O. (eds.) Robotics Research. STAR, vol. 100, pp. 309–326. Springer, Cham (2017). https://doi.org/10.1007/978-3-319-29363-9_18
3. Dwibedi, D., Misra, I., Hebert, M.: Cut, paste and learn: surprisingly easy synthesis for instance detection. ArXiv 1(2), 3 (2017)
4. Fang, K., Bai, Y., Hinterstoisser, S., Kalakrishnan, M.: Multi-task domain adaptation for deep learning of instance grasping from simulation. arXiv preprint arXiv:1710.06422 (2017)
5. Georgakis, G., Mousavian, A., Berg, A.C., Kosecka, J.: Synthesizing training data for object detection in indoor scenes. arXiv preprint arXiv:1702.07836 (2017)
6. He, K., Gkioxari, G., Dollár, P., Girshick, R.: Mask R-CNN. In: 2017 IEEE International Conference on Computer Vision (ICCV), pp. 2980–2988. IEEE (2017)
7. Huebner, K., Ruthotto, S., Kragic, D.: Minimum volume bounding box decomposition for shape approximation in robot grasping. In: IEEE International Conference on Robotics and Automation, ICRA 2008, pp. 1628–1633. IEEE (2008)
8. Krizhevsky, A., Sutskever, I., Hinton, G.E.: Imagenet classification with deep convolutional neural networks. In: Advances in neural information processing systems, pp. 1097–1105 (2012)
9. Lenz, I., Lee, H., Saxena, A.: Deep learning for detecting robotic grasps. Int. J. Robot. Res. 34(4–5), 705–724 (2015)
10. Levine, S., Pastor, P., Krizhevsky, A., Quillen, D.: Learning hand-eye coordination for robotic grasping with large-scale data collection. In: Kulić, D., Nakamura, Y., Khatib, O., Venture, G. (eds.) ISER 2016. SPAR, vol. 1, pp. 173–184. Springer, Cham (2017). https://doi.org/10.1007/978-3-319-50115-4_16
11. Lin, T.-Y., et al.: Microsoft COCO: common objects in context. In: Fleet, D., Pajdla, T., Schiele, B., Tuytelaars, T. (eds.) ECCV 2014. LNCS, vol. 8693, pp. 740–755. Springer, Cham (2014). https://doi.org/10.1007/978-3-319-10602-1_48
12. Milan, A., et al.: Semantic segmentation from limited training data. arXiv preprint arXiv:1709.07665 (2017)
13. Papandreou, G., et al..: Towards accurate multiperson pose estimation in the wild. arXiv preprint arXiv:1701.01779 (2017)
14. Redmon, J., Angelova, A.: Real-time grasp detection using convolutional neural networks. In: 2015 IEEE International Conference on Robotics and Automation (ICRA), pp. 1316–1322. IEEE (2015)
15. Richtsfeld, M., Vincze, M.: Grasping of unknown objects from a table top. In: Workshop on Vision in Action: Efficient Strategies for Cognitive Agents in Complex Environments (2008)
16. Tobin, J., Zaremba, W., Abbeel, P.: Domain randomization and generative models for robotic grasping. arXiv preprint arXiv:1710.06425 (2017)
17. Xie, L., Wang, J., Wei, Z., Wang, M., Tian, Q.: Disturblabel: Regularizing CNN on the loss layer. In: Proceedings of the IEEE Conference on Computer Vision and Pattern Recognition, pp. 4753–4762 (2016)

# BounceBot: A One-Legged Jumping Robot

James Rogers, Katherine Page-Bailey$^{(\boxtimes)}$, and Ryan Smith

School of Computing, Electronics and Mathematics, University of Plymouth, Plymouth, UK
katherine.page-bailey@students.plymouth.ac.uk

**Abstract.** This paper describes the design and development of a jumping robot made from readily available components and 3D printed parts. This robot is designed to traverse obstacles that are too large for conventional locomotion methods, utilising elastic potential energy to store and release kinetic energy at differing rates. Rapidly releasing built up energy in this manner enables a small light-weight actuator to exceed its continuous torque output. This is used to accelerate the robot vertically and jump over an obstacle up to ten times its own height. Use of soft 3D printed materials allow for the robot to resist the impact caused by landing onto/jumping into obstacles. Due to its performance and availability/cost of its parts, this prototype provides a good platform for further research into this viable yet under-developed locomotion method. As the design is open source, researchers are free to use the details contained in this report along with the documentation available online. The concept can be used in a range of situations involving locomotion over uneven terrain. Potential projects include hazardous disaster site evaluation, planet exploration, and search and rescue.

**Keywords:** Jumping robot · One-legged robot · Spring actuated · Self-righting 3D printing

## 1 Introduction

Typically, the size of ground-based robots is constrained by the terrain, notably the maximum obstacle size that is expected. The first choice is often a wheeled robot due to the simplicity and low cost of entry, but on uneven terrain they have major drawbacks. The relationship between the specified environment and wheel diameter is problematic when size/weight is constrained. If a robot needs to traverse a 1 m object, it is often not suitable to use 2 m wheels.

Jumping is a valid solution to navigation as demonstrated by its use in nature e.g. locusts [1], springtails [2], click beetles [3] and fleas [4]. In this paper, jumping is defined as the ability to briefly vertically accelerate to move on a ballistic path. This trajectory allows for navigation over obstacles. There are major difficulties in building such a robot as the energy requirements within the acceleration phase are considerable. As weight is a major factor in the performance of the robot, designing a frame that does not yield to the considerable stresses is a challenge. Equally, when the robot lands, without significant control, it could land on any part of its body. If the robot has a payload, the force exerted on the robot during landing could be substantial. Many examples that were found

© Springer International Publishing AG, part of Springer Nature 2018
M. Giuliani et al. (Eds.): TAROS 2018, LNAI 10965, pp. 52–63, 2018.
https://doi.org/10.1007/978-3-319-96728-8_5

during research did not use soft materials to overcome this problem, and instead either tried to control the landing or make the landing area soft.

A number of jumping methods have been presented, with an assortment of methods to actuate the jumping mechanism. The problems most robots experienced include righting the robot once it had landed; carrying a payload that significantly changes the robots weight and weight distribution; and getting over the barrier of a highly complex control system to guide the robot during flight. These are the issues that BounceBot has attempted to address. Existing research robots generally fit into three distinct categories: single jumpers, locomotive jumpers and running robots. Single jumpers are those that have a long reset period, often needing human interaction to reset the jump conditions – this is the category BounceBot currently fits into.

The robot closest to BounceBot in size, weight and design is SALTO, developed at Berkley. The key difference is that SALTO uses the energy of the falling robot to power the next jump in the form of a series elastic actuator made from a rubber rotational spring. SALTO also has a complex control system, using a flywheel to angle the robot in the air, allowing it to bounce off objects. SALTO aims to always land correctly, whereas BounceBot expects to have to reset itself to the jump position [5].

A group from Tel Aviv University and Ort Braude College have developed a single use jumping robot based on the design of a locust, named the TAUB. Although this robot can jump 3.35 m high, it needs a human to physically reset and there is no way to control the angle or the height of the jump. BounceBot operates in a similar manner, in which the motor winds a cable to tension the spring, then powers the jump by releasing this energy [6]. BounceBot can self-right and the jump height can be easily adjusted, plus multiple jumps can be achieved without the intervention of a human.

Researchers at EPFL have created a robot inspired by a locust that is able to jump to a height of 76 cm. This robot weighs 7 g and is only 12 cm tall. Much like the BounceBot, it is a single jumper, designed to traverse obstacles for the purpose of locomotion. EPFL also have a passive self-righting mechanism version, but this significantly limits the jumping performance [7]. There are some minor electronics on the robot, but no method of control or addition of a payload have been designed. Although BounceBot took inspiration from this robot, it is much bigger and has been designed to take heavier loads to a similar height whilst having more control during jumping. The self-righting system in BounceBot is much smaller than the overall body and adds little mass to the robot.

BounceBot is a solution with inspiration from previous designs and biological elements. A small DC motor controlled by a microcontroller winds up a cable that pulls back the leg and tensions the spring. Once the legs and spring are at the required tension the robot releases the energy in a single jumping motion, as shown in the Design Process section. The landing is softened by a set of soft 3D printed shock absorbers, designed to protect the solid chassis regardless of landing angle. Two arms are used to self-right the robot, and then the whole process can start again. This process will continue until the power is physically turned off.

The field of jumping robots is varied, with each robot trying to solve a different problem. In this paper, methods for achieving the energy requirements for this means of locomotion are investigated, using off-the-shelf components and easily accessible manufacturing techniques. In addition to the results and conclusions obtained, it is hoped that BounceBot (Fig. 1) becomes a platform for research due to its ease of construction and availability of materials.

**Fig. 1.** Final design

## 2   Design Process

### 2.1   Mechanical Process

Jumping Mechanism - The robot must be capable of rapidly accelerating itself to a sufficient vertical velocity to jump. To do so would require a very powerful yet light-weight actuator, along with a mechanism to allow said actuator to efficiently add to the robots' vertical velocity. Use of an energy storage component (such as a spring) could greatly decrease the weight of the mechanism, as kinetic energy of a smaller actuator can be stored over time and released.

Such a mechanism already exists in nature, as a locust can jump 20 times is own height [1]. This is achieved by rapidly opening its knee and hip joints from a crouched pose, accelerating its center of mass in the direction of a desired trajectory. As two joints are in motion to unfold the legs in this way, it would seem both are to be actuated to replicate such a mechanism. However, rotation in the two joints can be coupled via a parallelogram (Fig. 2), and thus can be replicated with a single actuator. The center of mass between phase 1 and 3 has been displaced vertically as the hip joint actuates, demonstrating how a single actuator can vertically accelerate a robot.

As the hip joint can now make the robot jump, the height of the jump is based on how much torque the joint can deliver. A mechanical storage medium is an intuitive solution, as a large torque is desired in short infrequent bursts. A tension spring can store the kinetic energy from a small actuator over a length of time, after which the energy can be transferred to the hip joint and released in a fraction of the winding time.

A spring is linked to the hip joint as described in Fig. 3. As the upper leg is moved from full extension to full crouch, the thread affixed to the body of the robot pulls on the spring. If released in this pose, the torque created by the tension in the thread would

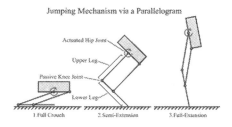

**Fig. 2.** Jumping mechanism via a parallelogram

rapidly actuate the joint to return to full extension. An added benefit to placing the spring parallel with the upper leg, is that the majority of the stresses caused by the large tension are purely compressional along the leg.

## Hip Joint Energy Storage

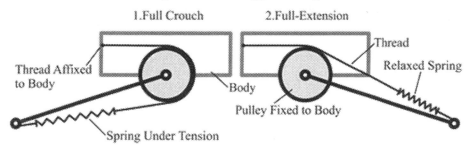

**Fig. 3.** Hip joint energy storage

To retract the legs into this crouch pose, a pulley system (Fig. 4) will apply a counter torque to the sprung joint. The hip is significantly geared down from the actuator and can be reduced further using a tackle pulley configuration.

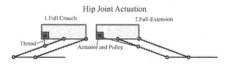

**Fig. 4.** Hip joint actuation

The hip joint has mechanical storage and can now build energy in said storage. There does not yet exist a method for releasing this energy as the actuator will most likely not be capable of unwinding in sufficient time. The solution to this is to add a cam operated latch (Fig. 5). The Pulley is connected to what is called the Reset Arm, which pivots on the same axis as the hip, yet independently. The reset arm is latched to the upper leg, allowing retraction as described in Fig. 4, building elastic potential in the hip joint. When full crouch is reached, the latch interfaces with a cam surface and releases from the reset arm. The upper leg now lacks the counter torque to remain in equilibrium with the elastic tension, and rapidly actuates to perform a jump. The reset arm can now re-open, and latch to the fully extended upper leg, completing the cycle. The reset arm must actuate in both directions; however, the pulley system can only apply torque in one. As a result, the reset arm must have a degree of elastic storage, to create torque capable of re-latching the upper leg.

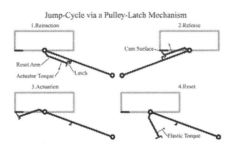

**Fig. 5.** Jump-cycle via a pulley-latch mechanism

Self-Righting Mechanism - To jump successively, the robot must recover from a landing by re-orienting itself. Self-righting is to be regardless of landing orientation, capable of righting from all stable poses (defined as the center of mass residing within the convex hull of all ground intersecting points). Two servo actuated arms are attached to the robots' sides, allowing self-righting from two of the four staple poses. As one of the stable poses is upside-down, the top of the robot is reshaped to make it unstable, rolling the robot into one of the two recoverable orientations. Figure 6 shows a forward view of the robot in a crouched/extended pose, as it recovers from landing (Fig. 7).

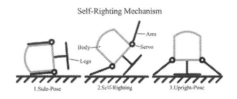

**Fig. 6.** Self-righting mechanism

**Fig. 7.** Side view of final design CAD model

# 3   Implementation

## 3.1   Final Design

The final design (Fig. 8) works around the problems that arise during physical construction. Material selection is integral to the performance of the robot, the considerable stresses on the frame from the spring and pulley mechanism must be supported. However, the more material added for support, the more mass, which greatly impacts vertical acceleration. PLA is used for the majority of the frame due to its strength to weight ratio, as well as ease of construction due to 3D printing. Where PLA is insufficient, aluminium parts were fabricated to deal with the greater stresses. This was only required on the upper leg due to the springs compressive force.

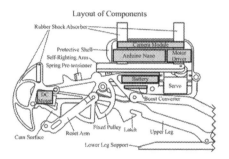

**Fig. 8.**  Layout of components

Electrical components were selected based on the loose specification in the electronic process section. Firstly, the actuator was considered, primarily searching for a good torque to weight ratio. A 6v 30 rpm DC motor and gearbox with a 986.41:1 gear ratio. This motor was selected as the actuator for the pulley retraction mechanism. To power the entire system, a 3.7v 350 mAh lithium polymer battery along with a boost converter board capable of 5 W continuous output is just within specification, whilst having a combined weight of <15 g. The servos used for the self-righting mechanism were standard 9 g servos due to their low weight as well as being within specification. All these parts are widely available, and relatively cheap. We chose the above components due to the ease of procurement, construction of the prototype and monetary/time constraints. As this robot is to demonstrate the ability to perform whilst carrying a payload, a small Wi-Fi camera module was added.

Figure 9 shows how all the parts described fit together. The majority of the electronic parts are located within close proximity to each other to reduce the weight of cabling. The camera, Arduino, and motor driver did not fit within the body and were positioned on top, as a result a light-weight protective shell of PLA encloses these components. A set of protective shock absorbers, made from NinjaFlex, encompass these sections and are designed to compress/deform during an impact to take the brunt of the force. The winding mechanism is forced to slip when it experiences sudden impacts.

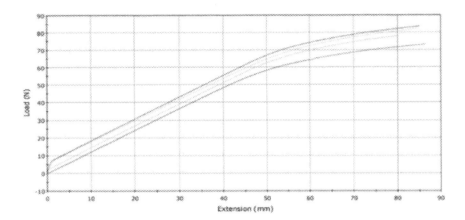

**Fig. 9.** Main jump spring tensile test

Additional design features were added after initial prototypes. Such as an extension of the lower leg forward past the knee, increasing its convex hull to be under the centre of mass, allowing the robot to stand upright in the fully extended pose. The reset arm applies a high enough torque to allow it to lock into the latch. The full crouch pose stores more energy in the spring due to the higher extension, this made testing varying spring tensions possible.

### 3.2   Operation

The on-board microcontroller is programmed to prepare a jump on start-up. At this point in time, the reset arm is latched onto the upper leg, thus actuation of the pulley will retract the robot into a crouched pose. This pose is sensed via a limit switch which is struck by the reset arm after unlatching from the upper leg. The motor controller halts actuation as the robot jumps and pauses for a length of time. Five seconds is sufficient for the robot to come to rest after landing. At this moment the servos actuate 90° to open the self-righting arms to recover to an upright position. Finally, the reset arm is opened and locked back into the upper leg latch returning the robot to its initial state prior to jumping.

## 4   Testing

### 4.1   Tensile Testing

The tensile testing was conducted in the University of Plymouth materials lab. The initial test was pulling the main leg springs to investigate its Hooke's constant. The force was recorded alongside displacement as their relationship is governed by Hooke's law. Four springs from the same batch were tested, and the results are shown in Fig. 10.

**Fig. 10.** Jumping off rubber mat

All the springs have an elastic region, followed by a region where plastic deformation takes place and Hooke's law no longer applies. According to the results, the average yield point was 50 mm. As the final design operates the spring within the linear region, plastic deformation does not occur. The spring will be subject to fatigue failure, but this will only happen after thousands of compressions, for this reason the springs have been designed to be easily replaceable. The Hooks constant of the springs was measured to be 1225, meaning the tension on each spring during use can be up to 36.75 N. As there are two springs on BounceBot, a tension of over 70 N is induced.

### 4.2   Height Testing

The basic test of a jumping robots ability is in the height it achieves. To test this, the locations of the feet were marked on both the table to ensure repeatability. A backdrop consisting of a 50 mm grid on a whiteboard was placed behind the jumping area to gauge the distance travelled in the x and y directions. The jump was then recorded by a camera at 240 fps. The camera was placed on a stand 2 m away from the jump plane and angled to be perpendicular to the board. The tests were conducted in a lab, with no air currents, at room temperature. BounceBot jumped under its own power and was caught before hitting the ground, as the tests were conducted without shock absorbers and payload to assess its maximum jumping ability.

### 4.3   Surface Friction Testing

To test the effect of surface friction, BounceBot was placed on a total of 5 different surfaces, each with a different co-efficient of friction: glass, MDF, rubber paper and a laminated desk.

Testing involved the same setup as previously detailed with the aim of investigating exactly how the flight patterns were affected by the surface it jumped from. The material was placed underneath the legs of the robot, in complete contact with the surface. The test was completed three times for each surface, recording the vertical and horizontal position at the peak height of the centre of mass; an average was taken of these three values. For each round of testing values were within 10 mm of each other hence the behaviour of the jump is related to the material, not poor repeatability. Table 1 demonstrates the impact that the surface friction has on the vertical and horizontal position of the maximum height of BounceBot.

**Table 1.**  Surface texture test results

| Surface | Vertical distance (m) | Horizontal distance (m) |
|---|---|---|
| Laminated desk | 0.86 | 0.33 |
| Rubber mat | 1.01 | 0.30 |
| MDF | 0.94 | 0.28 |
| Paper | 0.99 | 0.31 |
| Glass | 0.80 | 0.14 |

Major differences were noted in the trajectory of the robot when jumping from different surfaces. Jumps from the paper and rubber mat (Fig. 10) were the highest by far, with very similar vertical and horizontal distances. These two materials also induced the lowest rotational velocity meaning little energy was wasted on non-lateral motion. Conversely, glass produced the lowest of the jump heights, and observationally the highest rotational velocity, tumbling multiple times before landing, demonstrate that the energy released when jumping is shared between a lateral acceleration and a torque.

The experimental data reveals that this reaction force of the surface onto the robot is not purely vertical. If the reaction force is modelled as a vector and if this force vector happens to align with the robot's centre of mass, no torque is created, and the force is used purely to accelerate the robot; this is observed in the rubber/paper experiment. If the force vector is skewed so that the perpendicular distance from the centre of mass is no longer zero, a torque is induced, and a smaller component of the force accelerates the robot; as observed in the glass experiment.

It could be concluded from the data that the higher the surface friction, the higher the jump height. This is not the case as if the centre of mass was moved to align with the reaction force vector created by jumping on glass, no torque will be induced, and the jump height will be the same as the rubber experiment. However, jumping on rubber in this configuration creates a force vector out of alignment with the centre of mass, inducing a torque and a lower jump height. Thus, jump height is not improved by simply increasing the surface friction, but can be improved by selecting a friction which aligns the resulting reaction force vector with the centre of mass. Altering the position of the centre of mass will have the same affect.

### 4.4   Angled Surface Testing

To predict the behaviour when faced with a slope, BounceBot was tested in several angled positions. The slope was made from the same MDF as the surface testing section, with results found using the same method as detailed in the previous test.

As the angle increased, the robot started to slip off the MDF sheet. Table 2 shows the horizontal and vertical displacement of the peak height of the centre of mass of the robot. As expected, the horizontal displacement increased as the angle increased; more energy was used to propel the robot forward than up. From observation, the robot's rotational velocity did not noticeably change, indicating that the angle of the jump surface has insignificant effect on the rotational velocity when compared to the surface friction.

**Table 2.**  Horizontal and vertical displacements when launched at an angle

| Angle | Vertical Displacement (m) | Horizontal Displacement (m) | Angle | Vertical Displacement (m) | Horizontal Displacement (m) |
|-------|---------------------------|------------------------------|-------|---------------------------|------------------------------|
| 0° | 0.97 | 0.32 | 10.37° | 0.92 | 0.66 |
| 1.72° | 0.98 | 0.4 | 13.30° | 0.9 | 0.74 |
| 3.44° | 0.96 | 0.45 | 16.86° | 0.84 | 0.86 |
| 5.16° | 0.95 | 0.49 | 19.07° | 0.81 | 0.93 |
| 8.05° | 0.94 | 0.56 | 39.92° | 0.66 | 1.09 |

## 5   Overall Discussion

The testing of the robot shows that the jump trajectory is consistent for identical starting conditions, however more testing needs to be conducted to assess the true consistency of prolonged subsequent jumps. Further testing can be conducted to define the effects of battery voltage on both jump height and angle. Continuous use could leave the materials susceptible to fatigue. Further testing would need to be conducted to measure fatigue failure of the materials and electronic systems over time.

The jumping mechanism functions correctly in experimental conditions however, the final design is not without its flaws. During testing, there were intermittent failures with the pulley system due to the way in which the thread winds on the motors axel. During retraction the thread can wind unevenly on the pulley, increasing the axels effective diameter. Consequently, this limits the output torque of the motor below the required specification, causing a stall. However, if the motor functions correctly and allows the robot to jump, the string is wound so tightly on the axel that the inter-thread friction prevents the reset arms elastic torque from unwinding the coil. This results in a jamming of the pulley and prevents the reset arm from fully opening. Improvements could be made to this mechanism, so the robot can act autonomously.

The testing has concentrated on the workings of the jumping mechanism; however, additional testing could be conducted using different springs or different materials for the legs. The platform can be developed further with additional functionality, such as: jump angle and height control; methods for turning on the spot to allow for full navigation; and more sophisticated intelligence enabling on-board path planning. Altering the centre of mass before and during flight is a potential method for changing the jump angle and angle of the robot during flight. From these developments, BounceBot could be tested on how consistent the jump angle and jump height are.

## 6    Conclusion

This paper describes the electronic and mechanical theory and implementation of a jumping robot, which is specified to traverse obstacles greater than itself. Testing of the final design clearly demonstrates its ability to perform this task, jumping up to 10 times its crouched height. Overall, the robot acted consistently, with all height measurements under the same testing conditions falling within 25 mm. Performance testing when placed on an angled board also demonstrated the ability to jump consistently, following a good ballistic trajectory even when the horizontal distance is increased. Additional testing on functionality when launching from different surfaces revealed useful results. The robot jumped very well when launching from surfaces with higher coefficients of friction. When jumping from slippery surfaces e.g. glass, very little horizontal and vertical displacement occurred, and a very high rotational velocity was observed.

BounceBot has been made from easily accessible materials and simple construction techniques. This paper details many improvements and other tests that could be completed. All the mechanical assemblies and methods have been documented in this document and on the GitHub linked below. The performance observed during testing is impressive considering its ease of fabrication from conventional materials and off-the-shelf components. The open source nature of the project will hopefully allow researchers with limited funds access to a reliable jumping platform.

The GitHub associated with the BounceBot robot can be found at:
https://github.com/Jamesrogers221194/BounceBot

A demonstration of BounceBot in operation can be found at the following link:
https://youtu.be/hF-H4o4JICM

**Acknowledgements.** This report was created as part of the Advanced Robot Design module lead by Martin Stoelen at the University of Plymouth.

# References

1. Bennet-Clark, H.C.: The energetics of the jump of the locust Schistocerca gregaria. J. Exp. Biol. **63**(1), 53–83 (1975)
2. Brackenbury, J., Hunt, H.: Jumping in springtails: mechanism and dynamics. J. Zool. **229**, 217–236 (1993)
3. Alexander, R.M.: Principles of Animal Locomotion. Princeton University Press, Princeton (2003)
4. Gronenberg, W.: Fast actions in small animals: springs and click mechanisms. J. Comp. Physiol. A **178**(6), 727–734 (1996)
5. Haldane, D.W., Plecnik, M.M., Yim, J.K., Fearing, R.S.: Robotic vertical jumping agility via series-elastic power modulation
6. Zaitsev, V., Gvirsman, O., Hanan, U.B., Weiss, A., Ayali, A., Kosa, G.: A locust-inspired miniature jumping robot
7. Kovač, M., Schlegel, M., Zufferey, J.C., Floreano, D.: A miniature jumping robot with self-recovery capabilities. In: 2009 IEEE/RSJ International Conference on Intelligent Robots and Systems, St. Louis, MO, pp. 583–588 (2009)

# Estimating Grasping Patterns from Images Using Finetuned Convolutional Neural Networks

Ashraf Zia[✉], Bernard Tiddeman, and Patricia Shaw

Intelligent Robotics Laboratory, Department of Computer Science,
Aberystwyth University, Llandinum Building,
Aberystwyth, Ceredigion SY23 3DB, UK
{asz,bpt,phs}@aber.ac.uk

**Abstract.** Identification of suitable grasping pattern for numerous objects is a challenging computer vision task. It plays a vital role in robotics where a robotic hand is used to grasp different objects. Most of the work done in the area is based on 3D robotic grippers. An ample amount of work could also be found on humanoid robotic hands. However, there is negligible work on estimating grasping patterns from 2D images of various objects. In this paper, we propose a novel method to learn grasping patterns from images and data recorded from a dataglove, provided by the TUB Dataset. Our network retrains, a pre-trained deep Convolutional Neural Network (CNN) known as AlexNet, to learn deep features from images that correspond to human grasps. The results show that there are some interesting grasping patterns which are learned. In addition, we use two methods, Support Vector Machines (SVM) and hotelling's $T^2$ test to demonstrate that the dataset does include distinctive grasps for different objects. The results show promising grasping patterns that resembles actual human grasps.

**Keywords:** Deep learning · Transfer learning · Grasping patterns
Convolutional Neural Networks (CNN)

## 1 Introduction

Grasping objects in the way humans do is a challenging task for an intelligent robot. It depends upon successful object identification, location for reaching and stable grasping. The problem turns into an incredibly complicated situation when objects and their poses are unknown. The problem is approached with different methods. Some recent works [5,18,19,23] deal with it as a detection problem. They try to learn different joint poses and a suitable location for object grasping. Saxena et al. [18] proposes a supervised learning algorithm where the system neither builds nor requires 3d models of objects for grasping. It predicts grasping location from the images, i.e. where to grasp the object from. This method is suitable for a robotic gripper where it can successfully grasp numerous

© Springer International Publishing AG, part of Springer Nature 2018
M. Giuliani et al. (Eds.): TAROS 2018, LNAI 10965, pp. 64–75, 2018.
https://doi.org/10.1007/978-3-319-96728-8_6

new objects but not applicable for a humanoid robotic hand. Zito et al. [17] use a Gaussian Process model and tactile exploration planner to predict object shape by segmenting point cloud of the grasped object with a finger. The object surface is locally explored on all sides with the help of AtlasRRT planner. The disadvantage of exploring all sides of the object may lead to unstable grasp. Jiang et al. [5] recommend learning a novel 'grasping rectangle' representation for a 7-dimensional gripper using 3d location, orientation and opening width of the gripper. The rectangle is focused on finding the appropriate part of an image, using a two-step process, where basic features are learnt in the first step and advanced features are learned in the second step. In [6,21] three fingers grippers are used for grasping objects using images. Varley et al. [21] generates multi-fingered stable grasps using a deep learning method. The architecture is used to detect palm and fingertips locations from a partial view of the object using depth images. Levine et al. [12] used 6–14 robotic grippers to learn hand-eye coordination based on monocular images for training a CNN over a period of 2 months.

Previously, for numerous robotic tasks, hand-designed features are mostly favoured [8,13]. The issue with these methods is they are very time-consuming and complicated process where new input modalities are to be combined like RGBD images. Deep learning methods [3] have produced promising results in many visual recognition tasks [10,20]. These methods are particularly effective, due to the fact that they have capability to learn important features from both labelled and unlabelled data, preventing the necessity for hand-engineering features. However, deep learning is widely used for solving recognition tasks. Our objectives are to estimate feasible grasps and finding optimal grasp pattern for a given object. This will increase the ability of grasping efficiently for a humanoid robotic hand. The primary contribution of this work is to utilize deep learning methods for solving humanoid robotic grasping problems for generalization using images from a camera. This is done with training a deep CNN with images of various objects and the associated measured grasping patterns as a regression problem (see Fig. 1).

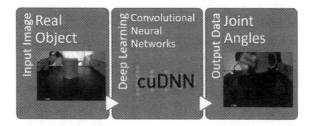

**Fig. 1.** A high-level model of the system where input image of the object is used to train the deep CNN, features are extracted and learned by the CNN, and as an output 22 joint angles are produced.

In this paper, we are using the well-known AlexNet [9] object recognition model for fine-tuning, to work as a joint regressor for estimating grasping patterns from images. The proposed technique uses a supervised learning method which takes a raw frame of an image as input, and generates hand joint angles. There are multiple advantages of such formulation. First, CNN models are end-to-end trainable which could learn representations of hierarchical features. Secondly, more abstract concepts can be learned from the deeper layers using raw inputs that allows joints regressor to encapsulate context information from input images. The major disadvantage of deep learning models is that they require large amount of training data in order to produce desired behaviour for generalization.

## 2    Related Work

### 2.1    Grasping with Hand's from RGB Images

In our literature review we could not find any previous work on estimation of joints angles from 2D images using deep learning or Convolutional Neural Networks (CNN) for a human hand. This is the first work of its kind where we try to predict various grasping patterns for different objects using fine-tuned deep learning network. The other subsequent section describes grasping with grippers from RGBD images.

### 2.2    Grasping with Grippers from RGBD Images

Rogez et al. [16] investigate classifying grasp shape in various standard hand-held manipulation of objects with different parameters. For a fine-grained grasp classification of everyday objects, force, contact point and object estimations are the parameters that are analysed alongside an image of objects. A solution is proposed for considering the continuous prediction task on the high-dimensional data as a discrete functional grasp classification problem. The dataset is obtained from an egocentric perspective with RGBD images. The study examines depth information as an essential part of detection and segmentation. On the other hand, extended RGB features help in predicting superior grasp recognition.

Grasping objects from RGBD images with the help of two finger robotic grippers are the most common practices currently in use. Lenz et al. [11] applied a deep learning method to solve the problem of identifying robotic grasps from RGBD images for different objects. The method has the benefit of saving time for hand-engineering features of various objects. For fast and robust detection, two deep neural networks were presented in a cascaded system, where the second network re-evaluates the best detection from the first. A novel feature learning algorithm is presented for learning multimodal data depending on group regularization. In comparison to the existing deep learning methods for multimodal data, the algorithm developed better features by using exhaustive experiments for grasp detection of the robot. Experimental results demonstrate that the two-stage deep learning algorithm both on real and offline robotic platforms has the capability to detect grasps for a broad range of objects efficiently. The robot can recognize grasps for objects which are not seen by the system before, but relied on a depth camera and was only applied to a 2 finger gripper.

Yu et al. [22] present a novel system for recognizing object and estimating their poses using deep learning methods. A robotic vision based system is introduced for determining how to grasp with various poses. The model can learn hierarchical features that improve the recognition process. Distinct classes are assigned to various poses in the Max-pooling CNN. The deep network is trained with a database of five image objects with different poses. The dataset is divided into training and testing parts on which the deep CNN model is applied. Experimental results show promise for achieving greater accuracy on object recognition and pose estimation. Distinct objects with various poses can also be successfully grasped. There is a limitation for successful recognition and grasping of objects with complex backgrounds. Kopicki et al. [7] use a two-step process to learn stable grasps, for grasping novel objects using under-actuated hands. In the training phase inside simulator, based on trial and error, different objects are grasped by a humanoid robotic hand until a stable grasp is found in the equilibrium state. System is trained on different grasp types against distinct objects for generalization. Accuracy can be increased by training the system with more objects and grasp types.

# 3  Methodology

In this section we describe the methodology adopted for sampling data and structure of CNN. We are using data from the TUB Dataset [15], produced using a CyberGloveII, having 22 sensors, 3 on each finger, 4 abduction sensors on the palm and 3 sensors on the wrist. Data from the TUB dataset is first pre-processed. Images are re-scaled and joint angles are normalized, as the joint sensor values are between 0 and 255. Each image file is then associated with the joint angle values where training and testing datasets are created. The deep CNN is then trained and tested with the respective datasets.

## 3.1  Data Generation

Training a deep CNN is an optimization problem concerning numerous parameters. While using a supervised learning algorithm, massive amounts of labelled data is required for better training and managing the effect of over-fitting to accomplish an acceptable generalization. Collecting data for human hand pose estimation, for training using robotic vision and related problems is an expensive process. It not only involves capturing hand actions in front of RGB camera and sensors but also requires great amount of time, effort and resources to train. Additionally, obtaining accurate values for joint angles using ground truth labels is also a challenging task. Therefore, we use the dataset presented in [15] as our primary source of training and testing data.

## 3.2   Technical University of Berlin (TUB) Dataset

In this paper, we examine individual learning of grasping a single object placed from a table-top scenario. We use the TUB dataset [15] for our experiments where 25 different objects of 6 categories are grasped by 18 human subjects using CybergloveII.[1] Grasping categories are distinct to each other in order to train the CNN for better generalization. We discarded some objects from the dataset because they were difficult to grasp and subjects failed to grasp them in their first attempt. Moreover, subjects end up grasping those objects by dragging on the table surface, adding noisy information to the dataset (see Fig. 2).

Discarded objects are: book, cd, credit card, key, button, french chalk, game card, screw, match and rubber band.

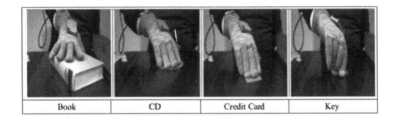

**Fig. 2.** Some of the discarded objects from the dataset.

The final dataset used for the experiments includes observations from 18 different subjects accomplishing the task of grasping over 16 objects. The sampled data is pre-processed before being given to the neural network. The joint sensor values for each angle are between 0 and 255, therefore, they are normalized between 0 and 1 as follows:

$$NormValue_i = \frac{x_i - min(x)}{max(x) - min(x)} \tag{1}$$

where $x = (x_1, \ldots, x_n)$ and $NormValue_i$ is the $i^{th}$ normalized data.

## 3.3   Frame Extraction, Segmentation and Labelling

We have extracted frames from all videos of subjects grasping different objects, except the discarded ones. Particularly, we select the grasping joints data from frames identified by an expert user. When the object is grasped (Fig. 3(c)), in a specific frame, the joint angles, are selected from the timeline (Fig. 3(d)). By cropping and rescaling the input images to 227 × 227 they are made suitable for AlexNet's network architecture. Next, images are associated with 22 joint sensor angles normalized in the range (0–255).

---

[1] In the description of the TUB dataset 17 subjects are mentioned. However, data is recorded from 18 subjects in the real dataset.

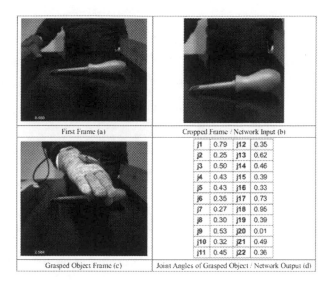

| | | | | |
|---|---|---|---|---|
| First Frame (a) | | Cropped Frame / Network Input (b) | | |

| j1 | 0.79 | j12 | 0.35 |
|---|---|---|---|
| j2 | 0.25 | j13 | 0.62 |
| j3 | 0.50 | j14 | 0.46 |
| j4 | 0.43 | j15 | 0.39 |
| j5 | 0.43 | j16 | 0.33 |
| j6 | 0.35 | j17 | 0.73 |
| j7 | 0.27 | j18 | 0.95 |
| j8 | 0.30 | j19 | 0.39 |
| j9 | 0.53 | j20 | 0.01 |
| j10 | 0.32 | j21 | 0.49 |
| j11 | 0.45 | j22 | 0.36 |

Grasped Object Frame (c)  |  Joint Angles of Grasped Object / Network Output (d)

**Fig. 3.** The top left is the original image (640 × 480) from the TUB dataset. Next to it is the cropped and re-scaled image (227 × 227) where object is magnified, given as input to the network. Bottom left has the grasped object frame while bottom right contains a table of the joint angles from the grasped object frame, learned as output of the network.

## 3.4    Architecture of the CNN

The architecture of the Fine-tuned Alexnet [9] is presented in Fig. 4. A grey scale image which is re-scaled to 227 × 227 × 3, is given as input to the network, to generate 22 real valued joint angles for the grasp pattern. There are 5 convolutional layers followed by pooling layers. Each convolutional layer, its parameters have a different number of strides and padding. The last two fully connected layers are retrained with our own data and two drop out layers are added to minimize over-fitting of the model.

## 3.5    Fine Tuning or Transfer Learning

Fine tuning or transfer learning is the idea of retraining a pre-trained deep CNN model with your own customized data (see Fig. 4). However, the rate of success depends upon the degree of similarity between actual data with which the model was originally trained and the current problem. Initially, our data is in grey scale, so we spread it over 3 channels to match the AlexNet input. AlexNet was trained on the ImageNet [4] dataset and the deeper layers are searching for generic features in which we are not interested. To tackle this problem, a variable learning rate is implemented on each layer for better management. Specifically, for the first three layers, a fixed learning rate of 0.001 is applied whereas 0.005 is used for the continuing layers and in the final layer of regression module, a highest learning rate of 0.01 is implemented. The stochastic gradient descent

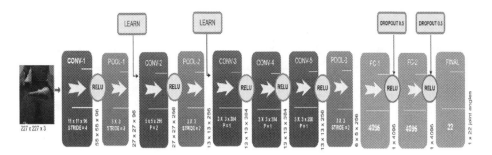

**Fig. 4.** Architecture of the fine-tuned Alexnet [9] with addition of two dropout layers.

algorithm is used for optimization. A batch size of 200 and momentum of 0.9 is used. The model is fine-tuned for 100 epochs on NVIDIA 1060 GTX GPU. The AlexNet model is retrained in the tensorflow [2] framework, where an image of $227 \times 227 \times 3$ pixels, is given to the model as an input and joints poses (real values) are estimated as outputs. The intended model is trained on 1910 images and validated on a set of 950 testing images.

## 4   Experiment Results

This section describes various results obtained from training/testing sets of the neural network. The network is trained with data from 12 subjects and tested with data from 6 subjects.

### 4.1   Results

The deep CNN is showing promising results for estimation of 22 different joint angles. It is clear from Fig. 6 that there is minimum standard deviation error between the joints except joint number 18 of the human hand that are sufficient enough to approximately recreate the human hand grasp pattern. This has been discussed subsequently in the later section.

### 4.2   Learning Curve and Per-Joint Analysis

We have experimented with different parameters such as learning rate, batch size and momentum for training the network and the results appear to be stable. Figure 5, shows a typical run of the training with training and testing errors shown. Error rate is decreasing with the increasing number of epochs. Variations in the training curve are due to batch size of the input data.

Figure 6 shows per-joint analysis of each finger associated with its respective joint. After training the network, joint 18 has the highest standard deviation error of 0.12. This refers to the little finger top joint. Except joint 18 standard deviation of every other joint is less than 0.1.

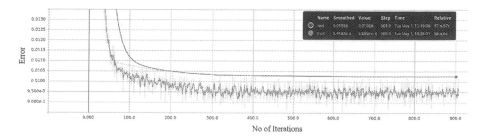

**Fig. 5.** Learning curves for training the deep network model.

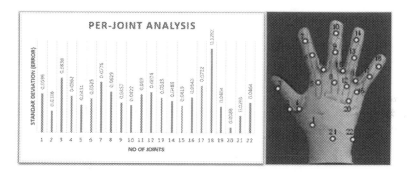

**Fig. 6. Leftmost image:** Per-joint analysis of hand with standard deviation error against the number of joints. **Rightmost image:** CyberGlove mapping of sensors onto the fingers.

## 4.3   Calibration for Visualization

The experimental results from the deep network are visualized on a simulator having a humanoid hand. For this purpose we have used the GraspIt [14] simulator which can take input from the CyberGlove [1] human hand. The mapping must be calibrated in order to map the joint angles from the dataglove onto the Graspit hand (Fig. 7).

The TUB dataset in not shipped with calibration data. Typically this would be needed per subject to account for varying hand shapes. For simplicity, we estimate a single set of calibration parameters for mapping onto the model hand. Calibration of joint values is very important for applying the tracked data to a robotic hand. In this paper we are not trying to do that, but demonstrate the feasibility by visualizing results and robotic hand simulation. There are 22 sensors in the CyberGloveII [1], each having a raw value between 0–255. In order to map joint values from the network, we first reproduced original grasping patterns of various objects by manually adjusting the GraspIt joint angles to match the visual appearances of the hand. Therefore, the results that we get after training the deep network, should resemble the average grasping patterns generated by all subjects.

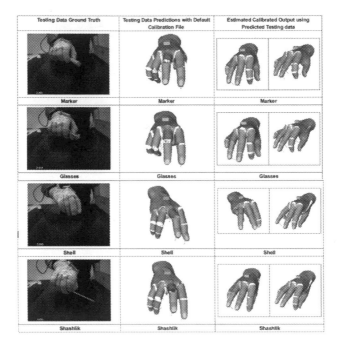

**Fig. 7.** This figure shows the estimated calibrated results on different objects using GraspIt simulator default and estimated calibration files for the hand.

## 5    Data Analysis

Although the network appears to be learning well, we considered the possibility that the data may not show much variety or consistency of grasp shape for different objects. We performed two tests, SVM and Hotelling's $T^2$ test, in order to analyse the data. An SVM (Support Vector Machine) is used to predict the objects from the grasp patterns and Hotelling's $T^2$ test is used to compare different groups of objects grasp patterns, to assess if they are drawn from different distributions.

### 5.1    Support Vector Machine

In the SVM, we try to predict the object from the grasp pattern. We performed cross-validation, where the training and testing split is 70% and 30%. In the following confusion matrix table we have 31% misclassification rate for the cross-validation of the dataset. The objects that are most often correctly classified are coffeemug, bowl and glasses whereas the objects which are often incorrectly classified are toy, tape and cigarette. These results indicate that different graps are used for different objects with some overlapped grasp shape (Table 1).

**Table 1.** Confusion Matrix for SVM

| pred | bowl | chestnut | cigarette | coffeemug | comb | frenchchalk | glasses | marker | matchbox | plate | saltshaker | screwdriver | shashlik | shell | tape | toy |
|---|---|---|---|---|---|---|---|---|---|---|---|---|---|---|---|---|
| bowl | 107 | 0 | 0 | 0 | 0 | 1 | 5 | 2 | 0 | 8 | 0 | 0 | 0 | 0 | 1 | 0 |
| chestnut | 0 | 81 | 0 | 1 | 2 | 2 | 3 | 3 | 2 | 0 | 8 | 8 | 0 | 2 | 22 | 2 |
| cigarette | 0 | 1 | 79 | 1 | 2 | 5 | 6 | 13 | 3 | 0 | 2 | 2 | 5 | 7 | 5 | 4 |
| coffeemug | 1 | 0 | 1 | 106 | 1 | 0 | 1 | 0 | 2 | 2 | 0 | 2 | 0 | 1 | 1 | 1 |
| comb | 0 | 0 | 5 | 0 | 89 | 8 | 1 | 4 | 1 | 3 | 0 | 0 | 15 | 2 | 0 | 0 |
| frenchchalk | 0 | 4 | 3 | 0 | 2 | 65 | 4 | 1 | 4 | 0 | 7 | 1 | 3 | 2 | 9 | 3 |
| glasses | 0 | 1 | 2 | 0 | 2 | 1 | 62 | 2 | 0 | 2 | 0 | 2 | 3 | 0 | 2 | 0 |
| marker | 1 | 0 | 6 | 1 | 4 | 0 | 6 | 73 | 0 | 4 | 1 | 2 | 0 | 0 | 0 | 1 |
| matchbox | 0 | 4 | 8 | 1 | 4 | 1 | 2 | 0 | 94 | 1 | 9 | 3 | 2 | 0 | 7 | 0 |
| plate | 6 | 1 | 1 | 1 | 1 | 0 | 2 | 6 | 0 | 99 | 0 | 3 | 0 | 0 | 0 | 0 |
| saltshaker | 2 | 1 | 0 | 2 | 0 | 9 | 3 | 2 | 2 | 0 | 77 | 2 | 1 | 3 | 3 | 5 |
| screwdriver | 0 | 3 | 0 | 0 | 1 | 1 | 3 | 3 | 0 | 0 | 1 | 73 | 2 | 2 | 2 | 2 |
| shashlik | 0 | 0 | 3 | 0 | 9 | 4 | 1 | 1 | 0 | 0 | 0 | 0 | 85 | 1 | 0 | 0 |
| shell | 1 | 3 | 5 | 2 | 1 | 9 | 8 | 1 | 0 | 0 | 6 | 0 | 1 | 65 | 7 | 7 |
| tape | 0 | 14 | 4 | 0 | 0 | 5 | 3 | 6 | 9 | 0 | 2 | 17 | 1 | 8 | 55 | 3 |
| toy | 1 | 7 | 3 | 3 | 1 | 9 | 9 | 2 | 2 | 1 | 6 | 5 | 2 | 26 | 5 | 92 |

## 5.2 Hotelling's $T^2$ Test

Since our data is multi-dimensional having 22 different dimensions (joints), therefore, in order to compare the means of two individual groups (objects) we performed Hotelling's $T^2$ Test for two-independent samples (see Fig. 8). The statistical test shows us that all the groups are statistically significantly different having p-values less than 0.05, therefore we reject the null hypothesis that the grasp shapes are the same. On the x-axis we have number of pairs of different objects while p-values (probabilities) are on the y-axis. We used Bonferroni correction to account for the higher likelihood of finding a specious difference with a

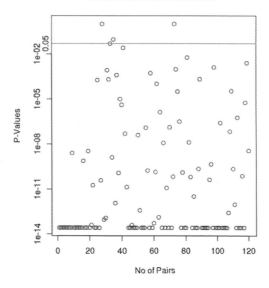

**Fig. 8.** Bonferroni error correction.

large number of pairs. Furthermore, the Bonferroni correction reveals that only three pairs 28, 34 and 73 are not statistically different therefore, we fail to reject the null hypothesis for these three different pairs, where pair 28 is (chestnut, tape), pair 34 is (cigarette, marker), and pair 73 is (frenchchalk, shell). Again, this shows that distinctive grips are used for different grasps.

## 6    Conclusion and Future Work

In this paper, we presented a deep learning model for estimating grasping patterns from raw images. We used deep CNN joints regression model for training and estimating human grasping pose. Dropout layers are introduced to prevent the model from over-fitting. Regression error could be reduced by augmenting different noise models in the future. We are also looking at better representation schemes that enhances the input signal to the deep network. Experimental results demonstrate that a general deep learning model (AlexNet) which had been trained for solving visual classification problems can be used to perform joints estimation by transferring knowledge from the existing trained model.

Current experimental work focuses on training a deep CNN with images which are not from the egocentric perspective. In future work, we would like to train a deep CNN with images from an egocentric perspective of the robot or human. Furthermore, we would consider increased variation in image/object appearance with other robotic aspects (hand location/orientation, kinematics, forces, slip etc.). Moreover, we will try to implement the predicted results on a real humanoid robot like the iCub for grasping different objects.

## References

1. Cyberglove ii cyberglove systems llc. http://www.cyberglovesystems.com/cyberglove-ii/. Accessed 12 Oct 2007
2. Abadi, M., et al.: TensorFlow: large-scale machine learning on heterogeneous distributed systems. arXiv preprint arXiv:1603.04467 (2016)
3. Bengio, Y., et al.: Learning deep architectures for AI. Found. Trends® Mach. Learn. $2$(1), 1-127 (2009)
4. Deng, J., Dong, W., Socher, R., Li, L.J., Li, K., Fei-Fei, L.: ImageNet: a large-scale hierarchical image database. In: CVPR 2009 (2009)
5. Jiang, Y., Moseson, S., Saxena, A.: Efficient grasping from RGBD images: learning using a new rectangle representation. In: 2011 IEEE International Conference on Robotics and Automation (ICRA), pp. 3304–3311. IEEE (2011)
6. Kappler, D., Bohg, J., Schaal, S.: Leveraging big data for grasp planning. In: 2015 IEEE International Conference on Robotics and Automation (ICRA), pp. 4304–4311. IEEE (2015)
7. Kopicki, M., Rosales, C.J., Marino, H., Gabiccini, M., Wyatt, J.L.: Learning and inference of dexterous grasps for novel objects with underactuated hands. arXiv preprint arXiv:1609.07592 (2016)
8. Kragic, D., Christensen, H.I.: Robust visual servoing. Int. J. Robot. Res. $\mathbf{22}$(10–11), 923–939 (2003)

9. Krizhevsky, A., Sutskever, I., Hinton, G.E.: Imagenet classification with deep convolutional neural networks. In: Advances in neural information processing systems, pp. 1097–1105 (2012)

10. Le, Q.V.: Building high-level features using large scale unsupervised learning. In: 2013 IEEE International Conference on Acoustics, Speech and Signal Processing (ICASSP), pp. 8595–8598. IEEE (2013)

11. Lenz, I., Lee, H., Saxena, A.: Deep learning for detecting robotic grasps. Int. J. Robot. Res. **34**(4–5), 705–724 (2015)

12. Levine, S., Pastor, P., Krizhevsky, A., Ibarz, J., Quillen, D.: Learning hand-eye coordination for robotic grasping with deep learning and large-scale data collection. Int. J. Robot. Res. **37**, 421–436 (2016). https://doi.org/10.1177/0278364917710318

13. Maitin-Shepard, J., Cusumano-Towner, M., Lei, J., Abbeel, P.: Cloth grasp point detection based on multiple-view geometric cues with application to robotic towel folding. In: 2010 IEEE International Conference on Robotics and Automation (ICRA), pp. 2308–2315. IEEE (2010)

14. Miller, A.T., Miller, A.T.: Graspit!: a versatile simulator for robotic grasping. IEEE Robot. Autom. Mag. **11**, 110–122 (2004)

15. Puhlmann, S., Heinemann, F., Brock, O., Maertens, M.: A compact representation of human single-object grasping. In: 2016 IEEE/RSJ International Conference on Intelligent Robots and Systems (IROS), pp. 1954–1959. IEEE (2016)

16. Rogez, G., Supancic, J.S., Ramanan, D.: Understanding everyday hands in action from RGB-D images. In: Proceedings of the IEEE International Conference on Computer Vision, pp. 3889–3897 (2015)

17. Rosales, C., Spinelli, F., Gabiccini, M., Zito, C., Wyatt, J.L.: Gpatlasrrt: a local tactile exploration planner for recovering the shape of novel objects. Int. J. Humanoid Robot. **15**(01), 1850014 (2018)

18. Saxena, A., Driemeyer, J., Kearns, J., Ng, A.Y.: Robotic grasping of novel objects. In: Advances in neural information processing systems, pp. 1209–1216 (2007)

19. Saxena, A., Wong, L.L., Ng, A.Y.: Learning grasp strategies with partial shape information. In: AAAI, vol. 3, pp. 1491–1494 (2008)

20. Sohn, K., Jung, D.Y., Lee, H., Hero, A.O.: Efficient learning of sparse, distributed, convolutional feature representations for object recognition. In: 2011 IEEE International Conference on Computer Vision (ICCV), pp. 2643–2650. IEEE (2011)

21. Varley, J., Weisz, J., Weiss, J., Allen, P.: Generating multi-fingered robotic grasps via deep learning. In: 2015 IEEE/RSJ International Conference on Intelligent Robots and Systems (IROS), pp. 4415–4420. IEEE (2015)

22. Yu, J., Weng, K., Liang, G., Xie, G.: A vision-based robotic grasping system using deep learning for 3D object recognition and pose estimation. In: 2013 IEEE International Conference on Robotics and Biomimetics (ROBIO), pp. 1175–1180. IEEE (2013)

23. Zhang, L.E., Ciocarlie, M., Hsiao, K.: Grasp evaluation with graspable feature matching. In: RSS Workshop on Mobile Manipulation: Learning to Manipulate (2011)

# Soft and Bioinspired Robotics

# Easy Undressing with Soft Robotics

Tim Helps[1,2(✉)], Majid Taghavi[1,2], Sarah Manns[3], Ailie J. Turton[4], and Jonathan Rossiter[1,2]

[1] Department of Engineering Mathematics, University of Bristol, Bristol, BS8 1UB, UK
tim.helps@bristol.ac.uk
[2] Bristol Robotics Laboratory, Bristol, BS16 1QY, UK
[3] Faculty of Health and Applied Sciences, University of the West of England, Bristol, BS16 1DD, UK
[4] Department of Allied Health Professions, University of the West of England, Bristol, BS16 1DD, UK

**Abstract.** Dexterity impairments affect many people worldwide, limiting their ability to easily perform daily tasks and to be independent. Difficulty getting dressed and undressed is commonly reported. Some research has been performed on robot-assisted dressing, where an external device helps the user put on and take off clothes. However, no wearable robotic technology or robotic assistive clothing has yet been proposed that actively helps the user dress. In this article, we introduce the concept of Smart Adaptive Clothing, which uses Soft Robotic technology to assist the user in dressing and undressing. We discuss how Soft Robotic technologies can be applied to Smart Adaptive Clothing and present a proof of concept study of a Pneumatic Smart Adaptive Belt. The belt weighs only 68 g, can expand by up to 14% in less than 6 s, and is demonstrated aiding undressing on a mannequin, achieving an extremely low undressing time of 1.7 s.

**Keywords:** Healthcare · Adaptive clothing · Soft robotics · Wearable robotics

## 1 Introduction

Limitations in dexterity affect a large number of older adults and people with a disability: in the UK, 21% of men and 30% of women aged 65 and over need help with at least one Activity of Daily Living (ADL) [1], and 27% of people with a disability report dexterity impairments [2]. During focus groups discussing wearable robotic technology with older adults and people with a disability [3], one commonly reported requirement was that clothing should be easy to put on and take off (Fig. 1). For example, people who have had strokes often experience difficulty dressing: one study found 36% of patients could not dress independently 2 years after a stroke [4]. In addition to being challenging, dressing and undressing can be a source of pain, such as in patients who suffer from rheumatoid arthritis [5]. For people living with dexterity impairments, shortening the time taken to undress can be especially important given the increased complexity of other urgent tasks, such as going to the toilet.

© Springer International Publishing AG, part of Springer Nature 2018
M. Giuliani et al. (Eds.): TAROS 2018, LNAI 10965, pp. 79–90, 2018.
https://doi.org/10.1007/978-3-319-96728-8_7

**Fig. 1.** One of several illustrations drawn to capture views expressed during focus groups with older adults and people with a disability. For assistive technology, ease of putting on and taking off was a regularly reported necessity. Illustrations by local artist Bethan Mure http://www.bmurecreative.co.uk/

Usually, independence when performing personal activities can be improved through occupational therapy [6]. However, independence may also be improved through Soft Robotic technology: for example, the well-known McKibben pneumatic artificial muscle was originally invented in the late 1950s by Joseph L. McKibben for his daughter Karen McKibben, who was paralyzed with polio [7, 8]. Many robotic products have since been proposed to assist the ageing population, however these are often not well matched to that population's desire for accessible and easy-to-use technology [9].

Some research has been conducted in terms of robotic assistance in dressing and undressing. Upper body dressing has been demonstrated using a dual-arm humanoid robot [10], and lower body dressing has been performed using a life-sized humanoid robot [11]. Sensing during dressing has also been studied [12].

Wearable robotic assistive devices have also garnered considerable interest in recent years. McKibben pneumatic artificial muscles have been included in orthotics for ankle flexion [13], knee assistance [14] and even whole lower body assistance to augment normal muscle function in healthy users [15]. Flat pneumatic artificial muscles have been included in a knee orthotic [16], and shape-memory alloy wire has been proposed as an actuation technology to assist with ankle and knee movement [17]. A knee extension orthotic has also been described using PVC gel actuators [18].

A common solution is to use DC motors, which are either mounted on an immobile base [19], mobile trolley [20], or in a bulky backpack. Rather than deliver power directly to the joints as in an exoskeleton, power can be transmitted using Bowden cables, to achieve post-stroke shoulder rehabilitation [21], ankle extension [22], and hip extension [23]. Another design uses DC motor driven drums, which spool fabric ribbons to provide power for hip extension [24].

In all of these examples, the wearable robotic assistive device is designed to exert forces upon the body, usually to provide additional power to joints and limbs. Some research has been done on making adaptive fabrics, which can controllably change either their shape [25] or their stiffness [26], however we were unable to find any examples of soft robotic clothing that adjusted its fit to promote ease of dressing in those with limited dexterity. Although adaptive clothing has been explored in fiction (Marty McFly's shoes in Back to the Future Part II) and fashion (Nike MAG), it has yet to garner serious academic or healthcare attention. This is especially noteworthy because easy dressing and undressing was so often described as an essential capability for mechanically assistive clothing in focus groups. Inevitably, some users will have sufficient dexterity that non-robotic solutions (such as elasticated clothing with magnetic or hook-and-loop mechanisms) are sufficient. However, for users with severe dexterity impairments even these may be challenging and painful to use. These users require clothing that can easily be put on and taken off without direct physical interaction.

To address this need, we introduce the concept of Smart Adaptive Clothing, able to independently adjust its fit to help with dressing and undressing. We discuss some ideal qualities of the clothing and describe how the desired behaviors might be achieved. In each case, we refer to existing Soft Robotic technology that could be exploited to achieve the desired behavior. Finally, we present a proof of concept study and demonstrate an assistive belt powered by expanding pneumatic artificial muscles, capable of rapidly increasing its diameter, promoting simple, fast and comfortable dressing and undressing.

## 2    Easy on, Easy off

Figure 2 shows the fundamental Smart Adaptive Clothing concept. The clothing should be capable of switching between two states – a loose fitting state and a tight-fitting state. During dressing, the user can more easily put on the loose-fitting clothing (a), before initiating its transition from a loose-fitting (b) to a tight-fitting (c) state. During undressing, transitioning the clothing to its loose-fitting state should allow for rapid undressing.

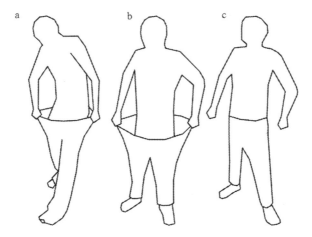

**Fig. 2.** Concept drawings for Smart Adaptive Clothing. (a) Putting on adaptive clothing while in a loose-fitting state. (b) Ready to tighten adaptive clothing. (c) Smart Adaptive Clothing tightens to a comfortable diameter.

To achieve this behavior, the clothing requires one or more circular elements that are able to increase or decrease their diameter, which surround parts of the body, such as waist, legs or arms. A greater change in diameter will be more beneficial up to a point, beyond which the loose-fitting diameter might be too large, and the clothing might become unwieldy and too hard to use. The exact change in diameter required will vary depending upon the user's preference.

The energy cost of changing fit is also an important performance metric; for clothing with on-board power, it will determine time-between-charges for the clothing.

We propose two separate behaviors that could be exploited to achieve Smart Adaptive Clothing: variable stiffness structures and artificial muscles. In the case of variable stiffness structures, the compliance of the clothing can be controlled. When the clothing is in a compliant state, the user will easily be able to stretch it to a large diameter. Once the user is ready, transitioning to the stiff state will cause the clothing to tightly fit the body. In the case of artificial muscles, the clothing will contain one or more actuators that can extend or shorten, directly controlling the fit of the clothing based on the user's requirements.

## 3  Variable Stiffness Clothing

### 3.1  Active Stiffening

We will first consider technology that becomes stiffer upon activation. Variable stiffness technology may be less attractive to users compared with actuated clothing, since no mechanical work is done by the technology and the user must adjust the fit of their clothing themselves; however, this can mean that the energy costs associated with state change are lower. With active stiffening clothing, the technology must be activated for the clothing to transition to a tight-fitting state.

In magnetorheological or electrorheological fluids, an applied magnetic or electric field can increase stiffness [27]. Similarly, electroadhesive structures can adhere to surfaces [28] or between layers [29] allowing an almost forty-fold increase in stiffness. However, the magnetic or electric field would need to be maintained while the clothing is in its stiff (tight-fitting) state, implying a continuous power requirement while the clothing is worn.

Granular jamming, whereby applied negative pressure results in a granular media (such as coffee grains) "locking" together [30] could provide a similar effect, and it should be possible to maintain the negative pressure at no power cost by closing a valve. However, clothing filled with granular media (or magneto- or electrorheological fluids) may not be comfortable to the user or aesthetically pleasing.

### 3.2 Active Softening

Active softening variable stiffness materials will become less stiff when activated, allowing the user to easily dress and undress. These may be advantageous over active stiffening materials since the material only needs to be active during short dressing and undressing periods.

Many materials become softer when heated, however some materials can exhibit a considerable and reversible stiffness change by being heated above their glass-transition temperature. At this temperature, they transition from a hard, brittle glass state to a soft, rubbery amorphous state. This process can be achieved by joule heating of embedded electrically conductive materials [31]. Glass transition materials could be quite suitable for embedding within Smart Adaptive Clothing, although the requirement for thermal activation can result in longer heating times compared with electroactive materials, making them less suitable for rapid dressing and undressing.

## 4 Mechanically Active Clothing

Current artificial muscle technologies also show great potential as the active materials in Smart Adaptive Clothing. Most artificial muscles exhibit tensile shortening and so could be embedded in the waistline of a lower body garment to form a ring that would tighten upon the muscle's activation.

### 4.1 Active Tightening

Coiled polymer actuators are a recent thermoactive artificial muscle technology, whereby twisted and coiled polymer fibers reversibly untwist when heating, resulting in large strokes and forces [32]. Homochirally wound coils (where the direction of coiling matches the direction of twisting) can contract by up to 49% when heated. Coiled polymers can be made from synthetic fibres such as nylon and therefore are well suited for inclusion in clothing – they could be easily integrated into the waistband of a lower body garment and heated to tighten the garment's fit. Shape-memory alloys actuators behave similarly, shortening when heated, and could be integrated in the same way [33]. The fibers may need shielding from the user's skin to prevent discomfort or burns if the temperature of operation is high; in [32] they were heated above 100 °C, which would necessitate thick insulation. However, such high temperatures may not be necessary if lower contraction ratios are permissible.

As with active stiffening variable stiffness technology, both solutions would need the technology to be active all the while the garment was worn. Given that coiled polymers and shape-memory alloys are thermally driven, this could imply high energy costs and discomfort associated with long term heating.

Various fluidic artificial muscles, such as McKibben, pleated [34], Pouch motors [35], Peano muscles [36], vacuum-actuated muscle-inspired pneumatic structures (VAMPs) [37] and fluid-driven origami-inspired artificial muscles (FOAMs) [38] can contract when a positive or negative pressure is applied and could be included around the waist to contract and tighten the fit when activated. Those driven by positive pressure (McKibben, Pouch motor and Peano muscles) have the added advantage of fattening laterally when activating, which would further tighten the fit. With fluidic systems, valves can be used to close off the tightening structure while the garment is worn, resulting in zero energy costs while wearing the clothing.

## 4.2  Active Loosening

Active loosening technology seems best suited for the Smart Adaptive Clothing. Clothing containing these materials would be tight while passive, and the actuators only need be activated during dressing and undressing, keeping energy costs low. Furthermore, in contrast with actively softening variable stiffness technology, here the actuators do the work required to loosen the garment, maximizing the convenience to the user, who may only have full use of one arm, as is common in the case of people who have had strokes.

Heterochirally coiled polymer muscles, in which the chiralities of coils and twisted fibers are opposed, expand by up to 67% during heating [32]. These could be readily integrated into Smart Adaptive Clothing. Two-way shape-memory alloy structures can also be programmed such that they elongate by heating and contract upon cooling. For example, shape-memory alloy springs can reversibly expand by over 90% of their initial length when heated to 65 °C [39].

Various bellows-like soft actuators expand longitudinally and contract laterally when they are inflated by air, so could be used for as loosening structures around the waistline [40]. In all fluidic actuators, replacing the working gas with a liquid will reduce the volume required to achieve a desired output force (assuming incompressibility), and can also allow for sensing of expansion and contraction [41]. Similar to bellows actuators, fiber wound inverse pneumatic artificial muscles (IPAMs) have been shown to exhibit up to 300% expansion when filled with high pressure fluid [42]. IPAMs are especially suited for Smart Adaptive Clothing because of their high strain, small cross-sectional area, and fast response time.

## 5    Case Study: Pneumatic Smart Adaptive Belt

In this section, we present a Pneumatic Smart Adaptive Belt powered by inverse pneumatic artificial muscle technology. As in the rest of the article, the desire is to design a device that can transition between a tight-fitting and loose-fitting state, speeding up and simplifying dressing and undressing.

We based the design of the Smart Adaptive Belt upon the inverse pneumatic artificial muscle. To construct the belt, we began with a length of 10 mm diameter, 1 mm wall thickness silicone tubing (T10X1ST60, Polymax Ltd, UK). Using this tubing alone, application of pressurized air induces axial lengthening but also radial expansion, and the tubing is liable to burst before large axial lengthening has occurred. To prevent radial expansion and raise failure pressure, the tubing was wrapped with 0.08 mm diameter braided fishing line (6LB SeaKnight Classic Line Braid x 4, SeaKnight, China). During inflation, as the belt lengthens axially, the gap between adjacent bindings increases; to ensure radial expansion was limited even at high pressures, we pre-stretched the silicone tubing by 40% prior to binding. The tubing was wrapped twice, once in each direction, and the bindings were held in place using a thin silicone adhesive coating (Sil-Poxy, Smooth-On, US). The bound tubing was cut to length and connected to a pneumatic T-connector using hose clamps to form the Smart Adaptive Belt. The belt mass was 68 g.

Figure 3 shows results from characterization experiments with the belt. The pressure was recorded using a pressure sensor (HSCSAAD060PDAA5, Honeywell, US), and the average diameter (based on maximum and minimum diameter) was determined from images using MATLAB image processing commands. Pressure was applied using a

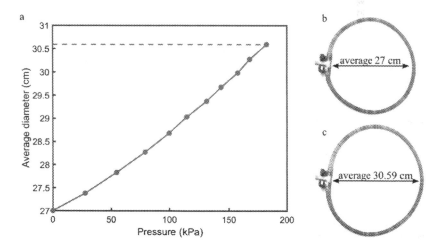

**Fig. 3.** Pressure induced expansion of the Pneumatic Smart Adaptive Belt. (a) Average diameter variation with applied pressure. (b) The belt at rest, with an average diameter of 27 cm. (c) 13% expansion was achieved by application of ~180 kPa.

small 12 V vacuum pump (ROB-10398, SparkFun, US). Repeatable 13% circumferential expansion was achieved at an applied pressure of ~180 kPa. In imperial units, the belt circumference increased from 33.39 to 37.84 inches, an increase of roughly two standard clothes sizes.

Figure 4 shows results from experiments to determine the expansion and relaxation speeds of the Pneumatic Smart Adaptive Belt. In these experiments pressure was not recorded, and diameter was determined from captured video using MATLAB. 14% expansion was achieved after 5.5 s of inflation (Fig. 4a), while in relaxation experiments, the belt returned to 1% greater than at-rest diameter after 0.37 s and relaxed fully after 2.7 s.

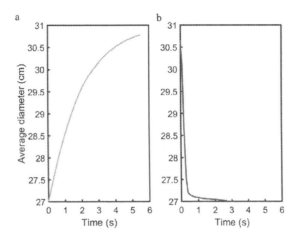

**Fig. 4.** Results from expansion (a) and relaxation (b) experiments with the Pneumatic Smart Adaptive Belt. 14% expansion was achieved after 5.5 s of inflation. Relaxation to 1% greater than at-rest diameter was achieved after 0.37 s, and full relaxation to at-rest diameter after 2.7 s.

Finally, we performed experiments using the Pneumatic Smart Adaptive Belt worn by a wooden mannequin (Fig. 5). The fit of belt was tight enough to secure a pair of jogging bottoms to the mannequin (the resting diameter of the belt will determine its tightness of fit). Upon application of pressure, the Smart Adaptive Belt's diameter increased, and the jogging bottoms fell to the floor. The undressing time (from initiation of inflation to the garment falling to the floor) was 1.7 s, which should be sufficient for even urgent tasks such as going to the toilet.

Being an active-loosening prototype, the Smart Adaptive Belt has the advantage of only consuming energy when being put on or taken off. It has a high expansion coefficient, allowing a large difference in tightness between its tight- and loose-fitting states, and it can change its fit rapidly. Disadvantages include the fact that it will assume a circular cross section when inflated, making it less like a belt, which may put off users. Additionally, inflating the belt with a pump or air supply produces an audible (though not loud) noise, which may be undesirable for some users.

Future work will involve improving the maximum expansion of the belt and minimizing the air supply and control systems so that they can be mounted on-board.

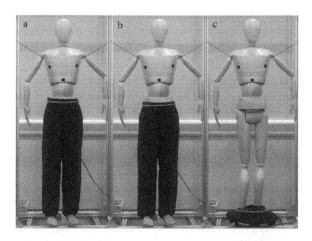

**Fig. 5.** Snapshots from video taken during experiments with the Pneumatic Smart Adaptive Belt on a wooden mannequin.

We are currently developing a portable air supply for the belt driven by a 12 g $CO_2$ cartridge and valve which has a combined weight of less than 100 g. Because the compressed air is delivered by the $CO_2$ cartridge, the electrical power requirements are very low; the 3 V valve (S070C-RBG-32, SMC, Japan) consumes 0.35 W (~117 mA) while open, so a tiny 2.65 g 110 mAh lithium polymer battery can provide roughly one hour's worth of valve operation, or ~650 inflations (14% expansion was achieved after 5.5 s of inflation). We have not yet tested how many times a single CO2 cartridge can inflate the belt, however given the quantity of gas stored within the cartridge and comparatively low pressure requirement of the belt, we anticipate it will be high.

The Pneumatic Smart Adaptive Belt secured the jogging bottoms tightly on the wooden mannequin, however in future we plan to integrate the belt into a custom garment. This device will adhere to health and safety guidelines and will be used in studies with real users to provide feedback for future generations of Smart Adaptive Clothing.

**Acknowledgements.** Research supported by UK Engineering and Physical Sciences Research Council grants EP/M020460/1 and EP/M026388/1. Local graphic facilitator Bethan Mure was responsible for illustrations during focus groups described in [3]. More of Bethan's work can be found at www.bmurecreative.co.uk

# References

1. Age UK: Later Life in the United Kingdom (2017)
2. Office for National Statistics: Family Resources Survey (2017)
3. Manns, S., Turton, A.: The occupational therapist, the doctor, the researcher, the roboticist, and the artist. BMJ Open, **7** (2017). https://doi.org/10.1136/bmjopen-2017-016492.23

4. Walker, M.F.: Stroke rehabilitation: evidence-based or evidence-tinged? J. Rehabil. Med. **39**, 193–197 (2007). https://doi.org/10.2340/16501977-0063
5. Azher, N., Saeed, M., Kalsoom, S.: Adaptive clothing for females with arthritis Impairment. Institute of Education and Research, University of the Punjab, Lahore (2012)
6. Legg, L., Drummond, A., Leonardi-Bee, J., et al.: Occupational therapy for patients with problems in personal activities of daily living after stroke: systematic review of randomised trials. BMJ **335**, 922 (2007). https://doi.org/10.1136/bmj.39343.466863.55
7. LIFE writers: Artificial Muscle. LIFE Mag. pp. 87–88 (1960)
8. Agerholm, M., Lord, A.: The "Artificial Muscle" of Mckibben. Lancet **277**, 660–661 (1961). https://doi.org/10.1016/S0140-6736(61)91676-2
9. Forlizzi, J.: Robotic products to assist the aging population. Interactions **12**, 16 (2005). https://doi.org/10.1145/1052438.1052454
10. Gao, Y., Chang, H.J., Demiris, Y.: User modelling for personalised dressing assistance by humanoid robots. In: IEEE International Conference on Intelligent Robots Systems, pp. 1840–1845 (2015). https://doi.org/10.1109/iros.2015.7353617
11. Yamazaki, K., Oya, R., Nagahama, K., et al.: Bottom dressing by a dual-arm robot using a clothing state estimation based on dynamic shape changes. Int. J. Adv. Robot. Syst. **13**, 5 (2016). https://doi.org/10.5772/61930
12. Kapusta, A., Yu, W., Bhattacharjee, T., et al: Data-driven haptic perception for robot-assisted dressing. In: IEEE International Symposium on Robot and Human, RO-MAN 2016, pp. 451–458 (2016). https://doi.org/10.1109/roman.2016.7745158
13. Park, Y.L., Chen, B.R., Young, D., et al.: Bio-inspired active soft orthotic device for ankle foot pathologies. In: IEEE International Conference on Intelligent Robots and Systems, pp. 4488–4495 (2011). https://doi.org/10.1109/IROS.2011.6048620
14. Park, Y.L., Chen, B.R., Majidi, C., et al.: Active modular elastomer sleeve for soft wearable assistance robots. In: IEEE Conference on Intelligent Robots and Systems, pp. 1595–1602 (2012). https://doi.org/10.1109/IROS.2012.6386158
15. Wehner, M., Quinlivan, B., Aubin, P.M., et al.: A lightweight soft exosuit for gait assistance, pp. 3347–3354 (2013). https://doi.org/10.1109/icra.2013.6631046
16. Park, Y.L., Santos, J., Galloway, K.G., et al.: A soft wearable robotic device for active knee motions using flat pneumatic artificial muscles. In: Proceedings of IEEE International Conference on Robotics and Automation, pp. 4805–4810 (2014). https://doi.org/10.1109/ICRA.2014.6907562
17. Stirling, L., Yu, C.H., Miller, J., et al.: Applicability of shape memory alloy wire for an active, soft orthotic. J. Mater. Eng. Perform. **20**, 658–662 (2011). https://doi.org/10.1007/s11665-011-9858-7
18. Li, Y., Hashimoto, M.: Development of a lightweight walking assist wear using PVC gel artificial muscles. In: Proceedings of IEEE RAS EMBS International Conference on Biomedical Robotics and Biomechatronics, July 2016, pp. 686–691 (2016). https://doi.org/10.1109/biorob.2016.7523706
19. Lee, S., Crea, S., Malcolm, P., et al.: Controlling negative and positive power at the ankle with a soft exosuit. In: Proceedings of the 2016 IEEE International Conference on Robotics and Automation (ICRA), pp 3509–3515 (2016). https://doi.org/10.1109/icra.2016.7487531
20. Bae, J., De Rossi, S.M.M., O'Donnell, K., et al.: A soft exosuit for patients with stroke: feasibility study with a mobile off-board actuation unit. In: IEEE International Conference on Rehabilitation Robotics, pp. 131–138, September 2015. https://doi.org/10.1109/icorr.2015.7281188

21. Galiana, I., Hammond, F.L., Howe, R.D., Popovic, M.B.: Wearable soft robotic device for post-stroke shoulder rehabilitation: identifying misalignments. In: IEEE International Conference on Intelligent Robots and Systems, pp. 317–322 (2012). https://doi.org/10.1109/IROS.2012.6385786
22. Asbeck, A.T., Dyer, R.J., Larusson, A.F., Walsh, C.J.: Biologically-inspired soft exosuit. In: IEEE International Conference on Rehabilitation Robotics (2013). https://doi.org/10.1109/ICORR.2013.6650455
23. Asbeck, A.T., Schmidt, K., Galiana, I., et al.: Multi-joint soft exosuit for gait assistance. In: Proceedings of IEEE International Conference on Robotics and Automation, pp. 6197–6204, June 2015. https://doi.org/10.1109/icra.2015.7140069
24. Asbeck, A.T., Schmidt, K., Walsh, C.J.: Soft exosuit for hip assistance. Robot. Auton. Syst. **73**, 102–110 (2015). https://doi.org/10.1016/j.robot.2014.09.025
25. Yuen, M., Cherian, A., Case, J.C., et al.: Conformable actuation and sensing with robotic fabric. In: IEEE International Conference on Intelligent Robots and Systems, pp. 580–586 (2014). https://doi.org/10.1109/IROS.2014.6942618
26. Chenal, T.P., Case, J.C., Paik, J., Kramer, R.K.: Variable stiffness fabrics with embedded shape memory materials for wearable applications. In: IEEE International Conference on Intelligent Robots and Systems, pp. 2827–2831 (2014). https://doi.org/10.1109/IROS.2014.6942950
27. Yalcintas, M., Dai, H.: Magnetorheological and electrorheological materials in adaptive structures and their performance comparison. Smart Mater. Struct. **8**, 560 (1999). https://doi.org/10.1088/0964-1726/8/5/306
28. Shintake, J., Rosset, S., Schubert, B., et al.: Versatile Soft grippers with intrinsic electroadhesion based on multifunctional polymer actuators. Adv. Mater. **28**, 231–238 (2016). https://doi.org/10.1002/adma.201504264
29. Imamura, H., Kadooka, K., Taya, M.: A variable stiffness dielectric elastomer actuator based on electrostatic chucking. Soft Matter **13**, 3440–3448 (2017). https://doi.org/10.1039/C7SM00546F
30. Brown, E., Rodenberg, N., Amend, J., et al.: Universal robotic gripper based on the jamming of granular material. Proc. Natl. Acad. Sci. **107**, 18809–18814 (2010). https://doi.org/10.1073/pnas.1003250107
31. Taghavi, M., Helps, T., Huang, B., Rossiter, J.: 3D-printed ready-to-use variable-stiffness structures. IEEE Robot. Autom. Lett. **3**, 2402–2407 (2018). https://doi.org/10.1109/LRA.2018.2812917
32. Haines, C.S., Lima, M.D., Li, N., et al.: Artificial muscles from fishing line and sewing thread. Science **343**, 868–872 (2014). https://doi.org/10.1126/science.1246906
33. Madden, J.D.W., Vandesteeg, N.A., Anquetil, P.A., et al.: Artificial muscle technology: physical principles and naval prospects. IEEE J. Ocean. Eng. **29**, 706–728 (2004). https://doi.org/10.1109/JOE.2004.833135
34. Daerden, F., Lefeber, D., Verrelst, B., Van Ham, R.: Pleated pneumatic artificial muscles: compliant robotic actuators. In: Proceedings of 2001 IEEE/RSJ International Conference on Intelligent Robots and Systems, vol. 4, pp. 1958–1963 (2001). https://doi.org/10.1109/iros.2001.976360
35. Niiyama, R., Rus, D., Kim, S.: Pouch motors: printable/inflatable soft actuators for robotics. In: Proceedings of 2014 IEEE International Conference on Robotics and Automation, pp. 6332–6337 (2014). https://doi.org/10.1109/icra.2014.6907793
36. Veale, A.J., Anderson, I.A., Xie, S.Q.: The smart Peano fluidic muscle: a low profile flexible orthosis actuator that feels pain. vol. 9435, p. 94351V (2015). https://doi.org/10.1117/12.2084130

37. Yang, D., Verma, M.S., So, J.-H., et al.: Buckling pneumatic linear actuators inspired by muscle. Adv. Mater. Technol. **1**, 1600055 (2016). https://doi.org/10.1002/admt.201600055
38. Li, S., Vogt, D.M., Rus, D., Wood, R.J.: Fluid-driven origami-inspired artificial muscles. Proc. Natl. Acad. Sci. **114**, 13132–13137 (2017). https://doi.org/10.1073/pnas.1713450114
39. Wang, J., Wang, J.: Shape memory effect of TiNi-based springs trained by constraint annealing. Met. Mater. Int. **19**, 295 (2013). https://doi.org/10.1007/s12540-013-2025-y
40. Belforte, G., Eula, G., Ivanov, A., Visan, A.L.: Bellows textile muscle. J. Text. Inst. **105**, 356–364 (2014). https://doi.org/10.1080/00405000.2013.840414
41. Helps, T., Rossiter, J.: Proprioceptive flexible fluidic actuators using conductive working fluids. Soft Robot. **5**, 175–189 (2018). https://doi.org/10.1089/soro.2017.0012
42. Hawkes, E.W., Christensen, D.L., Okamura, A.M.: Design and implementation of a 300% strain soft artificial muscle, pp. 4022–4029 (2016). https://doi.org/10.1109/icra.2016.7487592

# Biomimetic Knee Design to Improve Joint Torque and Life for Bipedal Robotics

Alexander G. Steele[1(✉)], Alexander Hunt[1], and Appolinaire C. Etoundi[2]

[1] Department of Mechanical Engineering, Portland State University (PSU), Portland, OR, USA
{ajmar,ajh26}@pdx.edu
[2] Department Engineering Design and Mathematics, Bristol Robotics Laboratory,
University of the West of England, Bristol, UK
Appolinaire.Etoundi@uwe.ac.uk

**Abstract.** This paper details the design, construction, and performance analysis of a biologically inspired knee joint for use in bipedal robotics. The design copies the condylar surfaces of the distal end of the femur and utilizes the same crossed four-bar linkage design the human knee uses. The joint includes a changing center of rotation, a screw-home mechanism, and patella; these are characteristics of the knee that are desirable to copy for bipedal robotics. The design was calculated to have an average sliding to rolling ratio of 0.079, a maximum moment arm of 2.7 in and a range of motion of 151°. This should reduce wear and perform similar to the human knee. Prototypes of the joint have been created to test these predicted properties.

**Keywords:** Condylar hinge joint · Knee biomechanics · Bipedal robot
Adaptive robotics · Knee joint · Screw-home mechanism · Four bar linkages

## 1   Introduction

Current articulated robotics systems use common rotational joining techniques through the use of revolute joints, also known as hinge or pin joints. There are several different examples of these joints, but they all have similar properties [1]. This class of joints has a single degree of freedom, rotation about the pin. Typically, the two rigid parts have a pinned center that enables the rotation of the joint. Due to their simplicity to elaborate and drive, the single degree of freedom offered by pin joints makes them desirable for control purposes. Additionally, they offer a low cost and easy to replace option.

However, due to the high shear stress that can be applied to the joint through normal operations, the joints wear quickly [1]. Clamping forces applied to the pin, or preload, also causes joint fatigue, which can lead to premature wearing as it introduces tensile forces, and can induce creep. At the hole, where bearing forces apply and stress concentration occur, the ratio between the diameter of that hole and the edge of the material to the edge of the hole has a direct effect on the wear and failure of the joint. Furthermore, since the joint is a single pin without added supports to strengthen its overall structure, which leads it to cause serious damage within the system it, is placed in when failure occur.

© Springer International Publishing AG, part of Springer Nature 2018
M. Giuliani et al. (Eds.): TAROS 2018, LNAI 10965, pp. 91–102, 2018.
https://doi.org/10.1007/978-3-319-96728-8_8

In recent years, biomimetic design has led to several different attempts to model and design a mechanical joint similar to the human knee like the one shown in Fig. 1. These designs have looked at different aspects of the knee and attempted to mimic them. Several of these designs include a screw-home mechanism and patellar analogs [2–6].

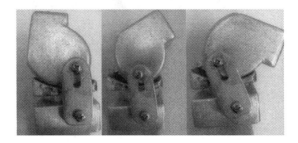

**Fig. 1.**  Previous biomimetic knee design [7]

For most of these designs, the biomimetic approach involves the utilization of the four-bar linkage design when modeling the human knee. In theory, this design should have kinematics close to the human knee. However, the designs that have been put forth are "floating designs" or complex linkage designs that do not have contacting surfaces such their human counterparts [8]. This predominately places load onto the pin connections and while the force profile over the entire range of motion differs, the pin joints have to carry the weight just as the solitary pin joint design first mentioned.

Hobon et al. [9] modeled the benefits of using what they termed as a rolling knee (RK). This joint, shown in Fig. 2, consists of two rolling cylinders joined by a solid link, which has a pin joint at the center of either cylinder. This design eliminates a portion of the force placed on the pin joint by applying it through the contact point of the cylinders. The RK design was developed to be a better solution than pin joints in regards to energy consumption during walking gait.

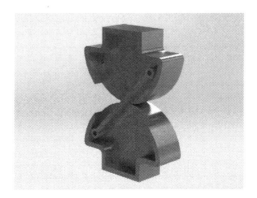

**Fig. 2.**  Rolling knee (RK) model [9]

While the authors state this is a quasi-optimal solution for energy consumption in a walking gait, wear of the joint has not been addressed. By using the RK solution, the force from the weight of the robot is applied at a one-dimensional line across the cylinder, this force can cause premature wearing, and an impact load could lead to permanent deformation of the cylinders. Since there is no locking mechanism, energy is needed to keep the robot upright when standing. When fully flexed, the weight of the robot is still applied to the pin joints used to attach the two cylinders, which carries the same problems as the previously discussed pin joint design.

All of these designs fail in some way to maximize joint life because they still place weight primarily on pinned connections. We propose that further analysis of the human knee kinematics and biology can further improve these designs and lead to a better design.

## 2 Anatomy and Physiology of the Human Knee

The knee joint is significantly more complex than initial observations would reveal. It is also the largest joint in the body. While the motion of the knee looks simple, it has a degree of freedom of six, three rotational and three translational shown in Fig. 3, its movement is constrained by four main ligaments. Although there is some translation occurring in the knee, it is not significant and the dominating movements are rotational: these are flexion/extension, medial rotation, and lateral rotation. The range of motion of the knee during flexion and extension has been found to be between 120 and 150°, with about 10° of rotation medially when the knee is flexed and about 30 to 40° of lateral rotation [10].

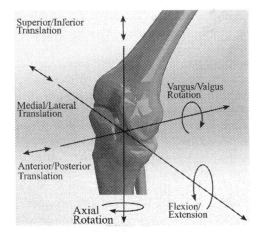

**Fig. 3.** The degree of freedom is 6 for the human knee [8]

When fully extended, the knee has a locking mechanism called the screw home mechanism. When the tibial head rotates relative to the distal end of the femur, an oblique pull of the ligaments during the last 30 to 35° of extension increase joint stability, resisting forces applied laterally to the body. Once in this locked position, the knee requires little external force to remain locked and in the fully extended position.

At the knee joint, where the femur and tibia meet, sits the patella (also known as the kneecap) that protects the articular surfaces. The primary role of the patella is assisting in knee extension by increasing the angle in which the patellar tendon acts. This increases the leverage the tendon can exert on the joint by 20 to 30% [11, 12]. The quadriceps tendon attaches the top of patella to the quadriceps femoris muscle, the main muscle responsible for extension of the knee. To resist lateral dislocation, the patella is stabilized by the large size of the lateral femoral that can be seen in Fig. 4.

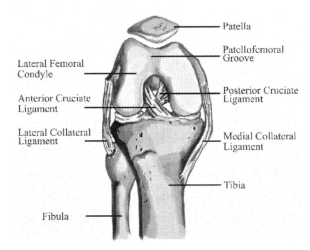

**Fig. 4.** Anatomy of the human left knee as seen from the front bent at 90°. The patella resists dislocation due in part to the patellofemoral groove. [13]

While the knee has six main ligaments, the focus of this work is on the anterior cruciate ligament (ACL) and the posterior cruciate ligament (PCL). The ACL and PCL are two bundles of bands made up of dense connective tissue located intracapsular to the joint. The ACL resists anterior tibial translation and rotational loads, while the PCL resists posterior translation and shearing forces.

## 3    Methods: Knee Development

### 3.1    Instantaneous Center of Rotation of the Patellofemoral Joint

Our design utilizes the same four-bar cross-link configuration found in the human knee so determining the location of the instantaneous center of rotation (ICR) is important because it determines the length of the moment arm. The further away the instantaneous center of rotation is from the line of action produced by the muscle, the less force required to produce the needed amount of torque to create movement.

Figure 5 shows the linkage configuration used in the construction as well as the link designation, angle designation, and coordinate system for the following equations.

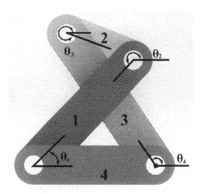

**Fig. 5.** Four-bar linkage used in the proposed design

For n number of moving bodies, there are N number of instantaneous centers of rotation such that

$$N = \frac{n(n-1)}{2} \tag{1}$$

From Eq. 1, a four-bar linkage has six ICR, four of which are the joints where two links meet. This leaves two ICR that are not explicitly formed at joints; however, we are only interested in one of these ICR. This is the ICR formed by the intersection of the lines created from links 1 and 3, where link 1 is the PCL, link 3 represents the ACL, and links 2 and 4 represent the fibular end and tibial head respectively; this closed link configuration can be defined as four vectors in a closed polygon where the sum is zero, written as

$$\overrightarrow{AB} + \overrightarrow{BC} + \overrightarrow{CD} + \overrightarrow{DA} = 0 \tag{2}$$

However, because $\overrightarrow{DA}$ is parallel to the origin it can be reduced to just the length $L_4$. Then vector equation may be rewritten in complex-number form such that

$$L_1 e^{i\theta_1} + L_2 e^{i\theta_2} + L_3 e^{i\theta_3} + L_4 \tag{3}$$

Next Eq. 3 is separated into the real and imaginary parts

$$L_1 cos(\theta_1) = L_3 \cos(\theta_4) + L_2 \cos(\theta_3) + L_4 \tag{4}$$

$$L_3 \sin(\theta_1) = L_3 \sin(\theta_4) + L_2 sin(\theta_3) \tag{5}$$

Solving to find the intersection of the two links, we obtain the set of equations for the instantaneous center of rotation given in x and y coordinates.

$$x = L_4 \frac{\tan\left(\theta_4\right)}{\tan\left(\theta_4\right) - \tan\left(\theta_1\right)} \tag{6}$$

$$y = L_4 \frac{\tan\left(\theta_4\right) * \tan\left(\theta_1\right)}{\tan\left(\theta_4\right) - \tan\left(\theta_1\right)} \tag{7}$$

### 3.2 Design Modification for Screw-Home Mechanism Analog

Another important feature of the knee is the screw-home mechanism. An analog to the screw-home mechanism is achieved using the geometry of the linkage because the design uses a solid and crossed 4-bar linkage design. Figure 6 shows how by limiting the forward movement of link 1 through modification of the condylar surface of the tibial head creates a mechanical stop that prevents any additional forward movement.

**Fig. 6.** Modification of the proposed tibial head preventing flexion or over extension when forces are applied superiorly

Once the joint is in the upright position, the modification to the tibial head creates a locking mechanism such that any amount of loading force applied to the knee – for example a standing position – cannot induce a rotation of the joint due to the placement of the ICR at full extension. The design directs weight through the condylar surfaces of the distal end of the femur and the tibial head instead of the connecting links of the joint. This broad surface contact spreads out the load and reduces this source of premature wear and failure.

### 3.3 Patellar Design for Effective Moment Arm Increase

One of the first considerations for approximating the patella in the design was the contact faces. Contact needs to be maximized to reduce the wear of the surfaces. Additionally, in order to maximize the torque about the joint applied by the quadriceps muscles the force vector applied by the patella to the joint should point perpendicularly to the moment arm. Figure 7 shows how the forces are applied to the knee joint, where the resultant force $F(\theta)$ passes through the instantaneous center of rotation and is calculated by

$$F(\theta) = 2Q * \cos\left(\frac{\theta}{2}\right) \tag{8}$$

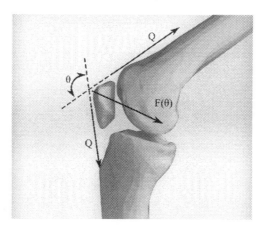

**Fig. 7.** Force applied to the knee through the patella as seen from the side

The angle $\theta$ is the angle between the quadriceps tendon and the patellar tendon. Because the ICR curve of the designed joint is flattened, the resultant force can be directed perpendicularly to the moment arm and through the ICR longer than an ICR curve that was more convex. By correctly angling the patellar using Eq. 8, the resultant force from the actuator can be maximized through the entire extension of the joint.

### 3.4   Designing the Condylar Surfaces to Ensure Contact Throughout Joint Motion

Design of the distal end of the femur and the tibial head were done to ensure that the condylar surfaces made contact throughout the entire range of motion of the joint. By doing this we can redirect the forces from the linkage to the condylar surfaces, this will reduce wear and reduce the risk of catastrophic failure.

However, because the linkages we are using are solid and the linkages of the human knee are flexible, the contacting surfaces of the knee could not be copied outright; instead a new design for the tibial contact surfaces had to be designed to reduce sliding while still being compact. For that reason, the curve of the medial condyle, the larger of the two condyles, was chosen for both the contact surfaces of the distal end of the femur.

The tibial head had to be designed so that when the end of the femur is constrained to the crossed four-bar linkage it maintained contact throughout the range of motion. In order to do this, the shape of the curve created by the femur when constrained by the four-bar linkage was calculated and then used to create a 2-dimensional profile that would be used to create the contact surfaces of the tibia.

This curve was then turned into the profile of the tibial contact surface using Solid-Works. The rest of the tibial head was then designed around the movement of the linkage so that it would not interfere with the range of motion.

## 3.5  Modification of the Tibial Head to Eliminate Deflection from Out-of-Plane Forces

When using the basic four-bar link design, out-of-plane forces applied at full flexion caused unwanted twisting and bending to the joint. This bending puts the linkages in a high stress condition, which could cause premature wear or failure.

To eliminate this, an extension was added and designed to lock into the distal end of the femur, which can be seen in Fig. 8. This addition removes the force applied to the links at full flexion, applying it directly to the back of the tibial head.

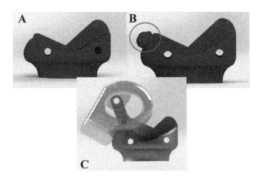

**Fig. 8.** Tibial head seen laterally (A) prior to modification, (B) post modification, change highlighted in red circle, and (C) tibial head locked with the distal end of the femur for reference. (Color figure online)

## 3.6  Joint Sliding-Rolling Ratio

To maximize the life of the joint, it is desirable to have a sliding- rolling ratio as close to zero as possible, this would indicate that the joint is in a pure rolling condition. Alternatively a sliding to rolling ratio of one would indicate that the joint is in a pure sliding condition, which leads to premature wear [14]. Using SolidWorks, we created a motion study to determine the sliding to rolling ratio of the joint. Figure 9 shows how the ratio is determined. First, the travel arc length of the tibia ($\Delta L_T$) and the travel arc length of the femur ($\Delta L_F$) are defined as

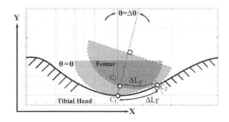

**Fig. 9.** Kinematics of sliding to rolling ratio from initial contact point $C_1$ to $C_2$

$$\Delta L_T(\theta) = C_{Tf}(\theta) - C_{Ti}(\theta) \tag{9}$$

$$\Delta L_F(\theta) = C_{Ff}(\theta) - C_{Fi}(\theta) \tag{10}$$

Where $C_{Ti}$ and $C_{Fi}$ are the initial contact points and $C_{Tf}$ and $C_{Ff}$ are the final contact points of the tibia and femur given an incremental flexion angle ($\theta$). Once the travel arc length is calculated, the sliding to rolling ratio (SR) is calculated by

$$SR(\theta) = \frac{\Delta L_T(\theta) - \Delta L_F(\theta)}{\Delta L_T(\theta)} \tag{11}$$

### 3.7  Joint Construction

Figure 10 shows the physical joint that will be used for future testing. Construction of this test joint was done using a 3D printer that has the ability to inlay continuous carbon fiber into the print. This imbues the part with exceptional strength. Metal fasteners were placed directly into the print so that metal shafts and lubricated sleeve bearings could be added to reduce friction at the joint connections. By adding the fasteners directly into the print, a clamping force is not required to keep the link on the shaft. This ensures that the link cannot physically become separated from the shaft and eliminates one factor of joint wear.

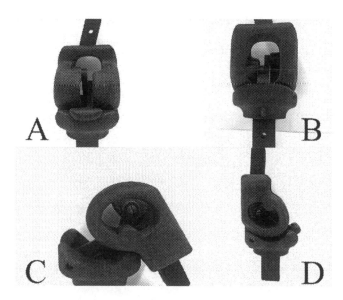

**Fig. 10.** Constructed joint (A) rear view, (B) front view, (C) full flexion, and (D) full extension

# 4    Results

## 4.1    Instantaneous Center of Rotation

The length of the links which correspond to our designed joint are [L1, L2, L3, L4] = [1.85, 0.92, 2.03, 1.57] given in inches. A plot of the changing moment arm as the knee as it goes from fully extended to fully flexed is shown in Fig. 11. The ICR only moves ± 0.2 in out of plane from the desired line of action and has a maximum overall moment arm of 2.7 in prior to the addition of a patella.

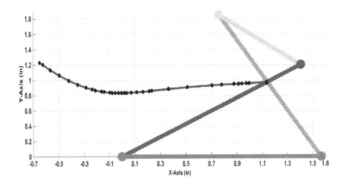

**Fig. 11.**    Instantaneous center of rotation plot of proposed joint for the full range of motion.

The designed joint is only 2.8 in wide and has a range of motion of 151°; this roughly the same size and range of motion of the human knee. In a fully extended position, such as when standing, the joint locks so that no extra energy is needed to keep the joint in that position, this feature in conjunction with the large moment arm should greatly reduce the energy requirements of a robot when compared to one with a pin joint.

## 4.2    Sliding to Rolling Ratio

Figure 12 is the SolidWorks Motion Analysis results for the sliding to rolling simulation with regard to flexion calculated at 0.5° intervals through the full range of motion of the joint. The ratio of sliding to rolling of the proposed joint, on average is 0.079 with a minimum value of 0.018 and a maximum value of 0.28. Because a sliding to rolling ratio close to zero is desirable for wear, the low average and maximum values should give the joint an exceptionally high lifetime when compared to revolute joints.

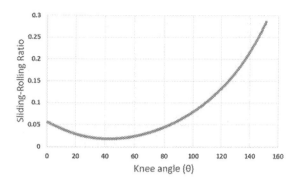

**Fig. 12.** Sliding to rolling ratio over the designed joints range of motion where 0 is a pure rolling condition and 1 is a pure sliding condition, which increases wear.

## 5 Discussion

Comparison of the ICR curve with one developed by Fekete [15] demonstrate that the placement of the curve is similar to the placement of the ICR curve of the human knee. Due to the compliance of tendons in the human knee, unlike the solid links used in the current design, the ICR curve of a human knee is more convex than the ICR curve of the designed knee. However, the placement of the curve is similar to the placement of the ICR curve of the human knee and the flattened ICR curve of the designed joint has desirable properties with respect to the force requirements to create motion.

There are too many variables to determine the sliding to rolling ratio of the human knee in vivo so we cannot confidently include a graphical comparison. However, current research on the subject suggests the sliding to rolling ratio of the human knee is between 0.3–0.46 [8, 14].

By mimicking the design of the human knee, the designed joint is comparable in size while having several of the knees' desirable properties. This is in part due to the complex geometry that was obtained from 3D printing instead of using traditional methods. 3D printing also reduced the time of construction to just over one day as compared to potentially weeks of traditional machining.

Because the joint is made primarily from a nylon and carbon fiber chop and has a continuous carbon fiber inlay, the joint has exceptional strength and can be used functionally, but weighs just 0.66 lb. Furthermore, the majority of the weight of the joint is due to the steel fastening hardware added internally to the design mid-print and not from the print material itself.

One of the goals in the design of our knee joint was to reduce wear, with an average sliding to rolling ratio of 0.079, the joint has a significantly lower sliding to rolling ratio than the human knee. By having continuous contact of the loading faces, the load applied to the pins is minimized and the addition of the locking extension on the rear of the tibia transfers a majority of the forces that would be placed on the pins at full flexion. By removing most of the loading forces from the pin connections, the joint will be less likely to suffer from a catastrophic failure and should last significantly longer than the traditional pin joint.

**Acknowledgments.** The authors acknowledge the support of the Mechanical and Materials Engineering Department in the Maseeh College of Engineering at Portland State University and the support of the UK Engineering and Physical Sciences Research Council (EPSRC) under grant reference EP/P022588/1.

# References

1. Mukras, S., Kim, N.H., Mauntler, N.A., Schmitz, T.L., Sawyer, W.G.: Analysis of planar multibody systems with revolute joint wear. Wear **268**, 643–652 (2010)
2. Asano, Y., et al.: Achievement of twist squat by musculoskeletal humanoid with screw-home mechanism. In: IEEE RSJ International Conference on Intelligent Robots and Systems (2013)
3. Etoundi, A.C.: A bio-inspired condylar hinge joint for mobile robots. In: International Conference on Intelligent Robots and Systems (2011)
4. Burgess, S.C., Etoundi, A.C.: Performance maps for a bio-inspired robotic condylar hinge joint. J. Mech. Des. **136**, 115002–115007 (2014)
5. Khan, H., Featherstone, R., Caldwell, D.G., Semini, C.: Bio-inspired knee joint mechanism for a hydraulic quadruped robot. In: 2015 6th International Conference on Automation, Robotics and Applications (ICARA), pp. 325–331 (2015)
6. Etoundi, A., Burgess, S., Vaidyanathan, R.: A bio-inspired condylar hinge for robotic limbs. J. Mech. Robot. **5**, 8 (2013)
7. Steele, A.G., Hunt, A., Etoundi, A.C.: Development of a bio-inspired knee joint mechanism for a bipedal robot. In: Mangan, M., Cutkosky, M., Mura, A., Verschure, Paul F.M.J., Prescott, T., Lepora, N. (eds.) Living Machines 2017. LNCS (LNAI), vol. 10384, pp. 418–427. Springer, Cham (2017). https://doi.org/10.1007/978-3-319-63537-8_35
8. Masouros, S.D., Bull, A.M.J., Amis, A.A.: Biomechanics of the knee joint. Orthop. TRAUMA. **24**, 84–91 (2010)
9. Hobon, M., Elyaaqoubi, N.L., Abba, G.: Quasi optimal sagittal gait of a biped robot with a new structure of knee joint. Robot. Auton. Syst. **62**, 436–445 (2014)
10. Soucie, J.M., et al.: Range of motion measurements: reference values and a database for comparison studies. Haemophilia **17**, 500–507 (2011)
11. Fox, A.S.J., Wanivenhaus, F., Rodeo, S.A.: The basic science of the patella: structure, composition, and function. J. Knee Surg. **25**, 127–141 (2012)
12. Halonen, K.S., et al.: Importance of patella, quadriceps forces, and depthwise cartilage structure on knee joint motion and cartilage response during gait. J. Biomech. Eng. **138**, 071002 (2016)
13. Abulhasan, J.F., Grey, M.J.: Anatomy and physiology of knee stability. J. Funct. Morphol. Kinesiol. **2**, 34 (2017)
14. Fekete, G., et al.: Sliding-rolling ratio during deep squat with regard to different knee prostheses. Acta Polytech. Hung. **9**, 20 (2012)
15. Fekete, G.: Kinetics and kinematics of the human knee joint under standard and non-standard squat movement (2013)

# Evaluating the Radiation Tolerance of a Robotic Finger

Richard French, Alice Cryer, Gabriel Kapellmann-Zafra,
and Hector Marin-Reyes$^{(\boxtimes)}$

The University of Sheffield, Western Bank, Sheffield S10 2TN, UK
h.marin-reyes@sheffield.ac.uk

**Abstract.** In 2024, The Large Hadron Collider (LHC) at CERN will
be upgraded to increase its luminosity by a factor of 10 (HL-LHC). The
ATLAS inner detector (ITk) will be upgraded at the same time. It has
suffered the most radiation damage, as it is the section closest to the
beamline, and the particle collisions. Due to the risk of excessive radiation doses, human intervention to decommission the inner detector will be
restricted. Robotic systems are being developed to carry out the decommissioning and limit radiation exposure to personnel. In this paper, we
present a study of the radiation tolerance of a robotic finger assessed in
the Birmingham Cyclotron facility. The finger was part of the Shadow
Grasper from Shadow Robot Company, which uses a set of Maxon DC
motors.

**Keywords:** Radiation · Robotic grasping system
Radioactive environment

## 1  Introduction

The Large Hadron Collider (LHC) at CERN in Geneva, Switzerland is the largest
particle accelerator in the world. It collides high-energy hadrons to create sub-
atomic particles, which are detected and studied by the 4 main experiments
along the beamline. One of these is ATLAS, a large multipurpose detector which
is formed of multiple sub-detectors, each devoted to particle identification and
tracking [6]. In 2024, the LHC will be upgraded to increase its luminosity by a
factor of 10 (HL-LHC). The ATLAS inner detector (ITk) will be upgraded at
the same time. As it is the section closest to the beamline, and therefore the
particle collisions, it has suffered the most radiation damage. The detector is
anticipated to emit $1.1\,\mathrm{mSv/h}$ at $10\,\mathrm{cm}$ from the beamline at shutdown [9,11].

This project has been funded by Innovate-UK under their "Energy Game Changer"
collaborative research and development programme.

This project has received funding from the European Union's Horizon 2020 Research
and Innovation programme under Grant Agreement no. 654168.

Robotic grasping systems and end effectors are an important element of a decommissioning robot. For the future decommissioning of the ATLAS inner detector, a robotic manipulator composed of three complex fingers is required to have a certain amount of dexterity. This to prevent any type of damage to the outer detector components. A finger from a human-like robotic hand has been previously assessed for their radiation tolerance, and are an ongoing area of R&D for our industrial collaborator, the Shadow Robot Company [9,11]. In this paper we focus on a finger from their more robust and industrial-like robotic manipulator.

## 2    Related Work

Complementary Metal Oxide Semiconductor (CMOS) chips seem to have definitively overtaken CCDs in the semi-conductor industry. However scaling circuitry complexity and density leaves electronics increasingly susceptible to radiation damage. Total Ionizing Dose (TID) effects occur when incident radiation ionizes atoms in the target material. Electron-hole pairs are generated, either by the initial interaction, or by secondary particles. The build-up of these pairs at interfaces within the semiconductor layers changes the behaviour of the switches by increasing leakage current and the 1/f noise in a CMOS device [3]. The change in performance from a compromised CMOS has detrimental knock on effects in the rest of the circuitry. As the devices are scaled down, the layers susceptible to damage get thinner, exacerbating the problem [3].

Many different applications for robotic systems have been identified in the nuclear industry. Radiation hardened robotics has gained a lot of interest as robots involvement in radioactive environments are more complex to those in other industries [17]. Mainly because of legal and ethical limitations on radiation exposure, as a consequence, robotic systems are more in need to be deployed in radioactive environments [2,16].

Space instrumentation conducts an extensive amount of research into how radiation affects electronics, however the levels of radiation between the space and nuclear environments differ by orders of magnitude [16]. Multiple attempts to test robotic systems under radioactive conditions have been reported through literature. The Quince rescue robotic platform was tested under similar conditions to the Fukushima power plant [15]. Development and testing of a tele-operated underwater maintenance robot for inspecting reactor coolant demonstrated to work under 30 m of water, and accomplish small maintenance tasks such as would be expected inside a nuclear cooling system [12]. However, it was never tested while working with radioactive materials. A bridge transported servo-manipulator with individual motor modules which could be remotely repaired is proposed as a long term solution [10]. Even multi-robot systems have been proposed to help detect radiation sources [4]. Nevertheless, tests have always been performed over full systems instead of focusing on testing and perfecting particular modules and components.

On the other hand, when testing electronic systems, it is less common for entire circuit boards to be irradiated, instead concentrating on the characterization of sensors and other electronic 'weak spots'.

Decommissioning projects often use commercial-off-the-shelf (COTS) components. Without the need for bespoke parts, the costs are lower and enables the system to be easily repaired. Fail-safe components such as a voltage regulators have been explored. It was found that the degradation of micro-controllers in the environment was predictable [18]. Similar to electronics, the study and testing of hardware should be also focused on the 'weak spots' of a robotic system.

## 3    Experimental Setup

The irradiation facility in the Medical Physics Dept of the University of Birmingham uses a Scanditronix MC40 cyclotron to produce a beam of protons of energy up to 40 MeV. It was commissioned to create Krypton radio nuclides for UK hospitals. Now it is also used to evaluate radiation tolerance for detector components for the ATLAS detector upgrade, as well as for industry hardware [7,8,14]

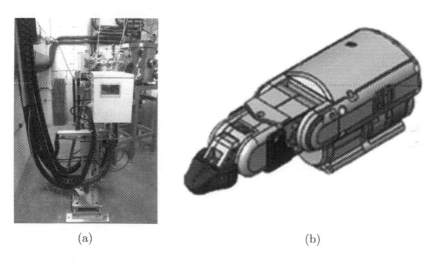

(a)                                                            (b)

**Fig. 1.** (a) The Birmingham cyclotron test box setup over a robotic scanner. (b) CAD model of the shadow grasper finger.

The tested robotic finger was part of a robotic manipulator called the Shadow Smart Grasping System by the Shadow Robot Company. It is composed of three similar fingers and a base. It was placed inside a box located in the cyclotron beam (see Fig. 1a). It was programmed with a constant routine to keep it in motion. This to facilitate the detection of any faults during the irradiation. The routine involved the movement of two of three Maxon motors (see Fig. 3), and within this study the beam was targeted to only one specific motor (Maxon 18 V DC). The box had no cooling, as during the experiment a webcam was used to observe the finger's movement routine (see Fig. 1b). The window where the beam enters the box is visible in Figs. 2a and b. Gafchromic film was used to show where the beam had struck the finger.

The static proton beam area was of $1\,cm^2$ and its intensity has a penetration limit of 8 mm (measured with water). The stopping power and average density of the finger were calculated in order to calculate how long the finger would need in the beam.

The approximate stopping power of a compound material is calculated by summing the stopping power of the component materials multiplied by their fractional weight [13]. The values for the stopping power of the component materials were taken from the NIST database [5].

$$\left(-\frac{dE}{d\chi}\right)_{comp} = \sum_i w_i \left(-\frac{dE}{d\chi_i}\right)_i \qquad (1)$$

(a)                                                          (b)

Fig. 2. Webcam images of the finger (a) The first orientation, the finger applies pressure on the block below (b) Second orientation showing gafchromic film, the finger applies pressure on block below.

Due to the thickness of the finger case creating a high resistance to the beam, two orientations of the finger were assessed. Figure 2a shows the orientation of the first irradiation and Fig. 2b the second. During the first orientation (Fig. 3), the beam was directed through the length of the finger. This so that the finger movement would cause it to move in and out of the beam. The second orientation had the beam perpendicular to the base (Fig. 4).

The finger's routine was 15 s long and had to be continuous at all times to facilitate the detection of any fault. First the main body joint twists, followed by the curl of the phalanges' joint to form a hook (see Figs. 3b and 4b). The system then moves back to the original position following the same trajectory, where the fingertip applies pressure to a representative block of plastic directly underneath (see Figs. 3c and 4c). This was implemented to observe how the pressure sensor reacted in the radiated environment. After that, the finger relaxes the pressure on the block and commences the routine again.

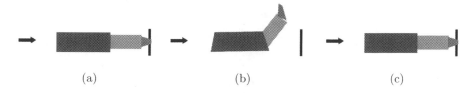

**Fig. 3.** (a) The finger starting position. (b) The finger rotates sideways and curls perpendicular to the beam. (c) The finger uncurls and applies pressure to the block below.

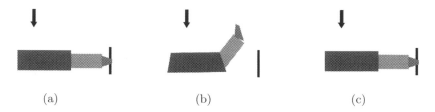

**Fig. 4.** (a) The finger starting position. (b) The finger rotates sideways and curls into the beam. (c) Finger uncurls and applies pressure to the block below.

## 4    Results

For the first irradiation the finger was orientated as in Fig. 2a, it was irradiated with the beam set at 23 MeV protons at 10 nA. It spent two-thirds of the total irradiation time within the beam. Because the casing was 8 mm thick, some gafchromic film was placed between the casing and the interior to verify penetration of the beam. This irradiation lasted 18 min where the beam traced over an area of 7 cm x 1 cm. The localized area received a targeted total dose of 24.2 kGy with no apparent loss of casing integrity. The dose calculation was adjusted to reflect that the beam did not penetrate through the casing, which is PA12 Nylon. In total, the irradiated dose of the whole finger at this point is 727 Gy.

In the second irradiation the finger was orientated as in Fig. 2b, it was irradiated with the beam set at 23 MeV protons at 5 nA (this was due to a current drift of the cyclotron beam). It spent one third of the total radiation time in the beam. In this new orientation, the casing was 2 mm thick, and the beam remained static and was aimed directly at a finger motor driver. The finger stopped working after 9 min. It received 2.1 kGy at this 7 cm x 1 cm specific area irradiation. This was calculated using the stopping power for the whole finger. After this irradiation the TID of the finger was 91 Gy. At failure, the total irradiated dose of the entire device was 818 Gy.

This is significantly more than the radiation dose expected for the ATLAS decommissioning, which was estimated to be around 1 mSv/h [9]. A human radiation worker's dosage is limited by the ICRP in 2007 to 50 mSv/year maximum, and 20 mSv average over 5 years. The weighting factor for protons is set at $W = 2$, so the robotic manipulator was irradiated with 1.6 kSv, orders of magnitude higher than acceptable human exposure [1].

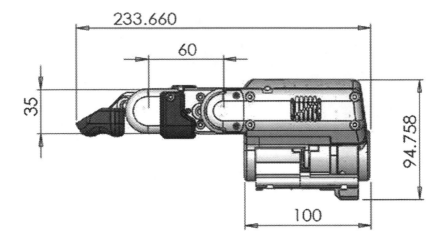

**Fig. 5.** Side view of the finger

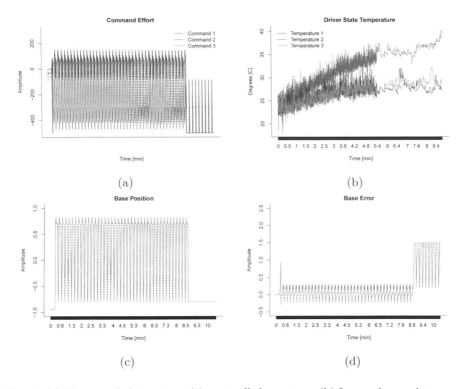

**Fig. 6.** (a) Commanded target positions to all the motors. (b) Internal sensed temperatures of the motors. (c) Sensed position of the finger base motor. (d) Error measured between the targeted position and the real position of the finger base motor.

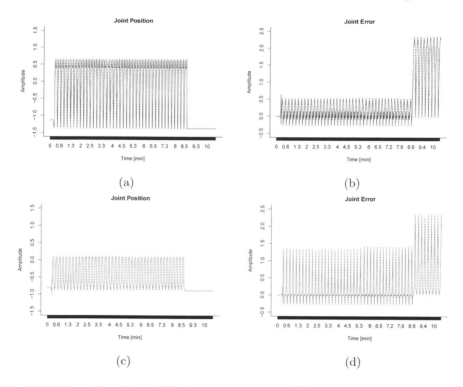

**Fig. 7.** (a) Sensed position of the finger joint motor. (b) Error measured between the targeted position and the real position of the finger joint motor. (c) Sensed position of the finger tip motor. (d) Error measured between the targeted position and the real position of the finger tip motor.

Figure 5 shows a side view of the finger. The three segments are clearly visible. The base is 100 mm, and its joint rotates out of the page. The second segment is 60 mm long and the joint rotates on the plane of the page. The final segment is 73.66 mm, and the joint rotates on the plane of the page

Figure 6 presents the logged data from the finger's base motor and Fig. 7 presents the logged information of the finger's joint and tip. Except for Fig. 6a which presents the commands and target positions sent to all the fingers' motors, and Fig. 6b which presents the fingers' internal sensed temperature for each joint, the rest of the figures show a disruption at 9 min.

Figure 6b presents the temperature of the three motors through the 10 min of the second irradiation. It is evident that motor 1 (the base motor) was the one being irradiated. This graph shows a clear rise of the motors' temperature as time passes. We suspect that around minute 5, the sensing hardware or communication drivers were also affected, as the temperature readings change abruptly. The temperature sensors are analog based, this could mean that the ADC could have suffered some damage. However, we do not have enough evidence to declare what exactly affected the readings. This, of course, will be further investigated.

Figure 6c presents the measured position of the finger base motor and Fig. 6d presents the error measured between the current position and the desired targeted position. After 9 min it is possible to see that the sensor stopped detecting a change of position, and through webcam feedback we could see that the finger had stopped moving, most likely meaning that the chip driving the motor had been damaged. As expected, the error became big when the motor stopped moving.

Figure 7a presents the measured position of the finger joint and Fig. 7b presents the error regarding the joints' position. Similarly, Fig. 7c presents the measured position of the fingertip and Fig. 7d presents its error. These graphs show a total stop of motion from the joint and tip motors. This happened due to the continuous routine constraint. The program was set to wait for the base motor to reach to a certain position before moving the other sections of the finger. Because the base motor had failed and was no longer moving, the other motors could not start their programmed motion.

## 5  Conclusion

After a total irradiated dose of 818 Gy to the entire device, the Shadow Grasper manipulator proved to be significantly resistant to radiation, and would be suitable for use in radioactive environments. A sample area of casing was irradiated to 24.2 kGy with no apparent loss in integrity. A second irradiation experiment within the cyclotron vault has been proposed. Further tests are needed to detect weak areas of the electronic design, and to assess the manipulator's resistance to a broader range of radiation. As well, working routines need to be better designed to prevent the system from blocking itself.

**Acknowledgments.** We are very grateful to Shadow Robot Company, especially Annagiulia Morachioli, Gavin Cassidy and James Southall-Andrews for their invaluable support. We also thank the University of Birmingham, especially Tony Price, Laura Gonella and Philip Allport for setting up the proton beam and for their help in installing our apparatus.

## References

1. P103: The 2007 recommendations of the international commission on radiological protection. Ann. ICRP **37**(2–4) (2007)
2. Alexandre, J.M.: Electronic system operating under irradiation, process for designing such a system and application thereof to the control of a mobile robot, uS Patent 6,812,476, 2 November 2004
3. Barnaby, H.: Total-ionizing-dose effects in modern cmos technologies. IEEE Trans. Nucl. Sci. **53**(6), 3103–3121 (2006)
4. Bashyal, S., Venayagamoorthy, G.K.: Human swarm interaction for radiation source search and localization. In: IEEE 2008 Swarm Intelligence Symposium, SIS 2008, pp. 1–8. IEEE (2008)

5. Berger, M.J., Chang, J.: ESTAR, PSTAR, and ASTAR: computer programs for calculating stopping-power and range tables for electrons, protons, and helium ions (version 1.2.3). http://physics.nist.gov/Star
6. The ATLAS Collaboration: The ATLAS experiment at the CERN large hadron collider. J. Instrum. **3**(08), S08003 (2008). http://stacks.iop.org/1748-0221/3/i=08/a=S08003
7. Dervan, P., et al.: Upgrade to the birmingham irradiation facility. Nucl. Instrum. Methods Phys. Res. Sect. A **796**, 80–84 (2015)
8. Dervan, P., French, R., Hodgson, P., Marin-Reyes, H., Wilson, J.: The Birmingham irradiation facility. Nucl. Instrum. Methods Phys. Res. Sect. A **730**, 101–104 (2013)
9. French, R., Marin-Reyes, H., Kourlitis, E.: Usability study to qualify a dexterous robotic manipulator for high radiation environments. In: 2016 IEEE 21st International Conference on Emerging Technologies and Factory Automation (ETFA), pp. 1–6. IEEE (2016)
10. Jik Lee, H., Kwang Lee, J., Suk Park, B., Sup Yoon, J.: Bridge transported servo manipulator system for remote handling tasks under a radiation environment. Ind. Robot: Int. J. **36**(2), 165–175 (2009)
11. Kourlitis, E., French, R., Marin-Reyes, H.: Radiation exposure assessment of a robot hand system, Chap. 7, pp. 356–365. World Scientific (2016)
12. Lee, S.U., Choi, Y.S., Jeong, K.M., Jung, S.: Development of a tele-operated underwater robotic system for maintaining a light-water type power reactor. In: 2006 SICE-ICASE International Joint Conference, pp. 3017–3021, October 2006
13. Leroy, R.: Electromagnetic interaction of charged particles in matter, chap. 2, p. 74. World Scientific (2016)
14. Marin-Reyes, H., French, R., Hodgson, P., Parker, K., Wilson, J., Dervan, P.: Pre-configured XY-axis Cartesian robot system for a new ATLAS scanning facility, Chap. 8, pp. 477–483. World Scientific (2014)
15. Nagatani, K., et al.: Gamma-ray irradiation test of electric components of rescue mobile robot quince. In: 2011 IEEE International Symposium on Safety, Security, and Rescue Robotics (SSRR), pp. 56–60. IEEE (2011)
16. Nancekievill, M., Watson, S., Green, P.R., Lennox, B.: Radiation tolerance of commercial-off-the-shelf components deployed in an underground nuclear decommissioning embedded system. In: 2016 IEEE Radiation Effects Data Workshop (REDW), pp. 1–5, July 2016
17. Sharp, R., Decreton, M.: Radiation tolerance of components and materials in nuclear robot applications. Reliab. Eng. Syst. Saf. **53**(3), 291–299 (1996)
18. Weide-Zaage, K., Eichin, P., Chen, C., Zhao, Y., Zhao, L.: Cots - radiation effects approaches and considerations. In: 2017 Pan Pacific Microelectronics Symposium (Pan Pacific), pp. 1–8, February 2017

# Soft Pneumatic Prosthetic Hand

Jan Fras$^{(\boxtimes)}$ and Kaspar Althoefer

Centre for Advanced Robotics @ Queen Mary (ARQ),
Faculty of Science and Engineering, Queen Mary University of London,
London, UK
{j.fras,k.althoefer}@qmul.ac.uk

**Abstract.** Conventional prosthetic devices are heavy, expensive and rigid. They are complex, fragile and require sophisticated control strategies in order to deal with the grasping and manipulation tasks. In this paper we propose a new pneumatic soft prosthetic hand that is very simple to control due to its compliant structure and cheap in production. It is designed to be easily reshaped and resized to adapt easily to each individual user preferences. It is designed to be frequently changed whenever a child patient require a bigger size or whenever the old one is worn out or broken. Since it is soft and compliant it can be safely used even by small children without a risk of harmful mechanical interaction.

## 1  Introduction

Human hand is a very complex structure that contains 27° of freedom. It is strong but precise, compliant and dexterous. For that reason the conventional prosthetic hands are complex and expensive devices. They contain sophisticated electrical motors and require complex controllers. They are heavy and incontinent. They are made of rigid components, so any compliance is ensured with even more complex controller or with more advanced actuators. Taking all the drawbacks of traditional rigid prosthetics into account, soft robotics seems to be an promising approach to introduce a significant improvement into that area. Soft hands can be significantly cheaper as they are made of simple and affordable materials. Since soft devices are compliant they adapt easily to the environment and thus reduce the complexity of the controller. That reduces the costs further, as for many grasps even one degree of actuation is sufficient. For that reason they can be considered as more suitable for children users as they require frequent prosthetic change due to their body growth. In recent years a number of soft and compliant hand designs has been presented. Pisa/IIT Soft Hand [1] uses only one motor to actuate all the joints which significantly simplifies the control. In [2] a soft hand composed of pneumatic PneuFlex actuators is proposed. In that particular design, each finger is made of individually controlled pneumatic actuator. Other soft pneumatic hand is proposed in [3]. Its mechanics is quite similar to [2] but have sensors integrated. There are various designs utilizing different number of actuators driven by tendons or pressure [4–6]. All of those designs propose a morphology that is similar to a human hand, however, they

© Springer International Publishing AG, part of Springer Nature 2018
M. Giuliani et al. (Eds.): TAROS 2018, LNAI 10965, pp. 112–120, 2018.
https://doi.org/10.1007/978-3-319-96728-8_10

differ a lot form the actual human limb in terms of shape and appearance, which is a significant factor when the device is considered as a prosthetic [7]. In this paper we propose a pneumatic prosthetic that has truly anatomical shape and is much more human-like than other pneumatic designs presented so far. The hand provides six degrees of actuation that can be controlled separately or connected together. The thumb in the proposed device is designed to work in both the apposition and opposition modes.

The hand dimensions, proportions and configuration can be easy adjusted for each and every individual user by adapting the external shape of the device or simply resizing the moulds. It is made of soft and compliant materials and due to that it is safe and adapts easily to the handled object. It is designed to be a low cost in order to make it affordable for a wide range of patients and in particular to make it easily changeable for children patients that require a frequent prosthetic change due to their body growth. It is designed to use simple materials and common techniques in order to allow a low qualified user to manufacture it to make it even more accessible. The manufacturing process utilizes 3D printing and silicone casting techniques.

## 2   Design

The hand is made out of soft materials. The palm and inner side of fingers is made of relatively stiff silicone SmoothSill 940 (Shore A 40). The actuators embedded in fingers are made of soft silicone EcoFlex 0050 (Shore 00 50) and a polyester thread. Combination of materials with different mechanical properties enables to achieve required bending motion. The design is derived from soft industrial grippers presented in [8]. Previous research shown that proposed approach can be efficiently used in grasping and manipulation tasks, see Fig. 1.

### 2.1   Hand Structure

In order to make the prosthetic as bio-mimicking as possible its design is based on a 3D scan of real human hand. Such an approach ensures proper ratio of the fingers and the palm which make the device look more natural. The dimensions of the described prototype are shown in Fig. 2 The fingers are driven with soft fluidic actuators, one per finger and two for the thumb. The actuators are hollow chambers reinforced with polyester thread. The thread constrains the fingers radial expansion but does not affect their elongation capabilities. The stiff silicone creates an exoskeleton that defines the hand shape and affects the deformation of the actuators, Fig. 2. Since the exoskeleton is made of stiff silicone it tends to elongate less than the actuator itself and thanks to that the translational motion of the actuators is transformed into the bending motion of the finger. The exoskeleton structure is designed to constrain the actuators deformation more in the areas that correspond with the bones and to emphasize the bending in the areas corresponding with the joints of the real human fingers.

**Fig. 1.** Soft industrial gripper [8].

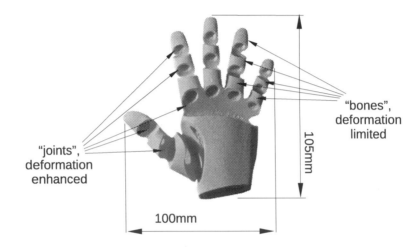

**Fig. 2.** Exoskeleton (in blue) defines the hands' shape and generates bending motion. (Color figure online)

One actuator is used for each finger except the thumb that is controlled with two actuators. Thanks to that its configuration can be changed between opposition and opposition mode.

Despite the fact exoskeleton constrains the motion of the actuators and reduces it in the link areas, the whole design is soft and compliant. For that reason the fingers' motion is not limited to discrete joints but is distributed on along their lengths. In previous research we have shown that finite rotary joints can be made using only soft materials [9], but we found such a solution not applicable in that case due to excessive size and the need of using separate actuator for each joint. Using such actuators would make the design and the manufacturing unnecessarily too complex (Fig. 3).

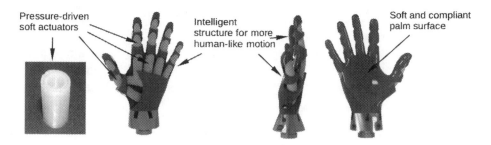

**Fig. 3.** Structure of the hand

## 2.2  Actuator

The cross-section of the actuator is circular that ensures its consistency during the actuation process. Any other cross-section geometry would be affected by the internal pressure [9]. The actuators are pneumatic flexible cylinders that contains helical reinforcement into their walls [10]. They are driven with pneumatic pressure that causes them to expand. Since the reinforcement constrains any radial deformation they expand only in longitudinal direction. Such elongation is then converted into bending motion by the exoskeleton structure [8]. We have already successfully embedded similar actuators for grasping, manipulation and locomotion [8–10]. Each actuator can be controlled independently but due to their flexibility and compliance they can also efficiently work in groups. Such a property makes the dexterous manipulation less complex in terms of control and allows the hand structure to take over part of the controller's effort.

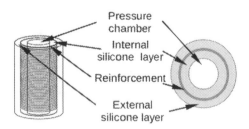

**Fig. 4.** Structure of the actuator

The actuator's structure is presented in Fig. 4. It contains internal wall that surrounds the actuation volume and creates the actuation chamber. The force generated by internal pressure is transferred by this wall on a surrounding reinforcement. The reinforcement is made with single polyester thread that forms a helix around the pressure chamber. Small thread pitch angle guarantees that the reinforcement does not affect the longitudinal actuator properties, but efficiently constrains radial deformation [10]. The external wall of the actuator enforces the reinforcement to stay in desired shape and to not detach from the actuation chamber. The tip and the bottom of the actuator is sealed with stiffer material (same as used for the exoskeleton structure). Bottom of the actuator contains small, 1.2 mm wide channel that is used to connect the pressure pipes.

## 2.3    Mechanical Interface

As a prosthetic, the hand requires a proper mechanical user interface to be attached to the patients arm. The hand itself is designed to be easily detached from such an interface (e.g. for the replacement purpose) and to enable rotation corresponding to the wrist joint. Since the hand is soft, it can not be easily attached to the interface with screws. We don't want it also to be glued, since such an connection would be permanent. For that reason a connector has been designed. The connector is based on spline and flange joints. Such an approach provides reliable but flexible connection that can be easily detached whenever required. On the other side of the connector there is a rotational joint that enables to change the whole hand orientation, Fig. 5. The connector is hollow, so that the pressure pipes can be easily guided inside.

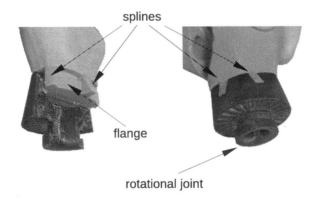

**Fig. 5.** Rotational hand connector.

## 3    Manufacturing

The manufacturing process is very much similar to the process described in [8–10]. It involves several silicone moulding steps and utilizes a set of 3D printed moulds made of ABS filament. The materials used are two silicones of different stiffness and polyester thread for the reinforcement.

### 3.1    Actuators

The process starts with preparing the thread to be embedded into the actuators structure. The thread is winded tightly onto long conical cores. When wrapped the cores are enclosed within the mould and cast with soft silicone. The mould keeps them centered and creates a thin and uniform layer of silicone that forms the external actuator wall and bounds the reinforcing thread. As the internal rods' diameter decrease with its length, the silicone layer with the thread inside can be easily removed from the rods towards the thinner end of the core, Fig. 6. In case of cylindrical design the internal rods are very difficult to remove due to high friction between the rods and the cores. The dimensions of the actuators are as follows: 10 mm and 6 mm external diameters at the base and at the tip respectively (index, middle, and ring fingers), 8 mm and 5 mm in diameter at the base and the tip respectively (pinky finger) and 12 mm and 9 mm in the base and the tip respectively (the thumb). The thickness of the actuator wall is 1 mm.

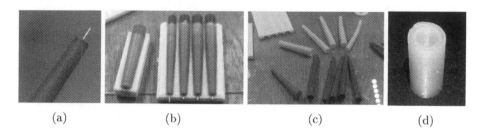

(a)            (b)            (c)            (d)

**Fig. 6.** Actuators manufacturing: reinforcement, external layer, cross-section - reinforcement and internal layer visible.

Such a conical tubes with the helical thread structure attached to the internal side of are filled with new portion of silicone and inserted into the same mould again to create another layer of silicone. The difference is that in this step smaller rods are inserted, so that a certain distance inside the winding is preserved for the uncured silicone. While the silicone cures it creates a layer on the internal side of the reinforcement. The purpose of this layer is to protect the thread from detaching the chamber surface when pressurized. Once the conical tubes are finished (Fig. 6c), they are sealed on both ends to create the ready to use actuators. For that the stiff silicone is used. The wider end of each actuator, that is its base, contains small hole for the pressure inlet. For those holes 1.2 mm

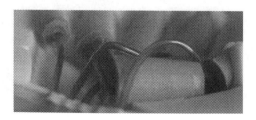

**Fig. 7.** Fingers bases with pressure pipes connected. The actuators' pressure inlets are 1.2 mm in diameter, the pipes' diameter is 2 mm.

needle is inserted into the mould that creates the actuators enclosure. Such a diameter of the hole combined with 2 mm diameter flexible pipe creates airtight and reliable connection that does not require gluing. However the tubes are glued in order to prevent them to be pulled out from the actuator, Fig. 7.

## 3.2    Hand

Once the set of actuators is ready, they are arranged in the mould that forms the hands' final shape. The mould ensures the joints to not be covered with the stiff silicone on the outer side that finally makes them to bend into the desired direction. This is crucial to not cover the external side of the joints, otherwise the expansion of the actuators would be constrained in the whole volume in the same way and no bending would be generated. This functionality is provided by especially designed sockets that protect the crucial areas of the actuators, Fig. 8.

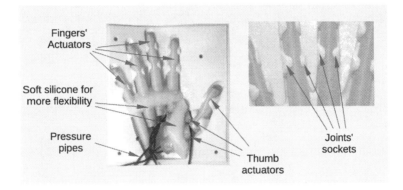

Fig. 8.

The auxiliary structures made of soft silicone help to provide more flexibility where required (e.g. in between the base - metacarpophalangeal - joint of each finger and the palm surface). The auxiliary structures are made with soft silicone. As they are placed into the mould before injection of the stiffer material, they ensure the crucial areas are flexible enough to provide the required motion. Before injecting of the stiff silicone all the arranged parts are glued to the mould using the same soft silicone, so they attach tightly to the mould. Thanks to that risk of penetration of the undesired areas by the stiff silicone is dramatically decreased.

When all the above is done, the mould is closed and the stiff silicone is injected into it that is the last manufacturing step. The filled mould and the hand taken out from the mould is presented in Fig. 9.

After cutting off the silicone that filled the canals in the mould the hand is ready to use.

**Fig. 9.**

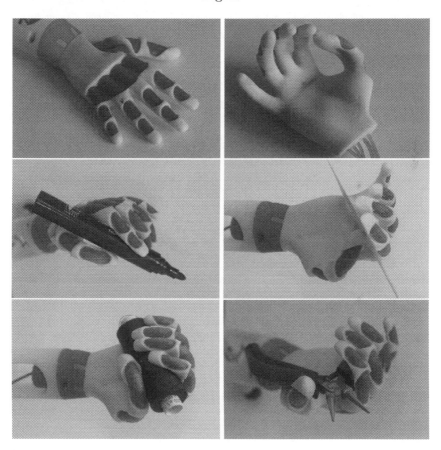

**Fig. 10.** Soft prosthetic hand

## 4    Conclusions

In this paper we propose a soft prosthetic hand that is cheap and easy to manufacture. It is designed to be easily adjusted for individual needs of the patient and to be easily replaced in case of damage or whenever bigger size is needed. For those reasons is especially suitable for children patients as it is affordable and safe. The proposed design show a great potential and received very positive feedback (during number of exhibitions) regarding its appearance and features. Initial tests show it provides sufficient grasping capabilities to perform simple tasks. Work presented in this paper is an early prototype and has not been extensively tested yet. In the nearest future we plan to extensively test the forces and bending angles generated by individual fingers as functions of pressure as well as the grasping and manipulation capabilities. We also consider hydraulic and pneumatic actuation. We also investigate the 3D printing as a potential technology for manufacturing of parts or whole device. Exemplary grasped objects and gestures are presented in Fig. 10.

# References

1. Catalano, M.G., Grioli, G., Farnioli, E., Serio, A., Piazza, C., Bicchi, A.: Adaptive synergies for the design and control of the Pisa/IIT SoftHand. Int. J. Robot. Res. **33**(5), 768–782 (2014)
2. Deimel, R., Brock, O.: A novel type of compliant and underactuated robotic hand for dexterous grasping. Int. J. Robot. Res. **35**(1–3), 161–185 (2016)
3. Zhao, H., O'Brien, K., Li, S., Shepherd, R.F.: Optoelectronically innervated soft prosthetic hand via stretchable optical waveguides. Sci. Robot. **1**(1), eaai7529 (2016)
4. Schulz, S., Pylatiuk, C., Bretthauer, G.: A new ultralight anthropomorphic hand. In: 2001 Proceedings of the IEEE International Conference on Robotics and Automation, ICRA 2001, vol. 3, pp. 2437–2441. IEEE (2001)
5. Tavakoli, M., de Almeida, A.T.: Adaptive under-actuated anthropomorphic hand: ISR-SoftHand. In: 2014 IEEE/RSJ International Conference on Intelligent Robots and Systems (IROS 2014), pp. 1629–1634. IEEE (2014)
6. Carrozza, M.C., et al.: A cosmetic prosthetic hand with tendon driven underactuated mechanism and compliant joints: ongoing research and preliminary results. In: Proceedings of the 2005 IEEE International Conference on Robotics and Automation, ICRA 2005, pp. 2661–2666. IEEE (2005)
7. Kaczkowski, M.: Cosmesis is much more than appearance... It's function. inMotion **9**, 1–48 (1999)
8. Fraś, J., Maciaś, M., Czubaczyński, F., Sałek, P., Główka, J.: Soft flexible gripper design, characterization and application. In: Szewczyk, R., Kaliczyńska, M. (eds.) SCIT 2016. AISC, vol. 543, pp. 368–377. Springer, Cham (2017). https://doi.org/10.1007/978-3-319-48923-0_40
9. Fras, J., Noh, Y., Wurdemann, H., Althoefer, K.: Soft fluidic rotary actuator with improved actuation properties. In: International Conference on Intelligent Robots and Systems. IEEE (2017)
10. Fras, J., Czarnowski, J., Macias, M., Glowka, J., Cianchetti, M., Menciassi, A.: New STIFF-FLOP module construction idea for improved actuation and sensing. In: International Conference on Robotics and Automation, pp. 2901–2906. IEEE (2015)

# Path Planning and Autonomous Vehicles

# Tabu Temporal Difference Learning for Robot Path Planning in Uncertain Environments

Changyun Wei[✉] and Fusheng Ni

College of Mechanical and Electrical Engineering, Hohai University,
NO. 200 Jinling Bei Road, Changzhou 213022, Jiangsu Province, China
weichangyun@hotmail.com

**Abstract.** This paper addresses the robot path planning problem in uncertain environments, where the robot has to avoid potential collisions with other agents or obstacles, as well as rectify actuation errors caused by environmental disturbances. This problem is motivated by many practical applications, such as ocean exploration by underwater vehicles, and package transportation in a warehouse by mobile robots. The novel feature of this paper is that we propose a Tabu methodology consisting of an Adaptive Action Selection Rule and a Tabu Action Elimination Strategy to improve the classic Temporal Difference (TD) learning approach. Furthermore, two classic TD learning algorithms (i.e., Q-learning and SASRA) are revised by the proposed Tabu methodology for optimizing learning performance. We use a simulated environment to evaluate the proposed algorithms. The results show that the proposed approach can provide an effective solution for generating collision-free and safety paths for robots in uncertain environments.

**Keywords:** Reinforcement learning · Path planning
Uncertain environments · Performance

## 1 Introduction

The path planning problem has been extensively studied in the robot domain, where the robot has to generate a collision-free path with some given criteria in an environment [1,2]. In this work, we seek to address the path planning problem in uncertain, dynamic environments. In such an environment, the challenge issues for path planning involve how to avoid collisions with other agents/obstacles, as well as how to reduce the influences of actuation errors caused by environmental disturbances. The former issue indicates that offline planning approaches cannot be applied to solve such a problem anymore since the environment is not static, and the robot does not have accurate knowledge about the environment. The latter issue implies that typical collision-free paths cannot ensure the success of path execution. This is because the robot's motion can be seriously disturbed by uncertain environmental factors (e.g., ocean currents) that will amplify actuation

© Springer International Publishing AG, part of Springer Nature 2018
M. Giuliani et al. (Eds.): TAROS 2018, LNAI 10965, pp. 123–134, 2018.
https://doi.org/10.1007/978-3-319-96728-8_11

errors of an underwater robot [3]. Aa a result, the robot cannot execute a planned trajectory with high precision towards its destination. For safety reasons, the robot is required to stay away from obstacles or unsafe areas as far as possible.

Most path planning solutions ignore uncertainty, and thus a global planner is usually employed to guide the robot towards its destination [4], such as Dijkstra, Bellman-Ford, Floyd-Warshall, A-star and its variants [5–7]. Taking account of uncertainty, the robot typically works in a dynamic, stochastic environment where it needs to avoid potential collisions with dynamic obstacles or other moving robots. In such a problem, a scheduled path should be redefined based on local information so that the robot can keep away from nearby obstacles or other robots. The common method that tries to push the robot away from obstacles or unsafe areas is based on Artificial Potential Fields (APFs) [8,9]. The basic idea is that the path planner needs to generate repulsive forces for obstacles/agents and attractive forces for the destination. To this end, many heuristic functions (e.g., the work [9]) are developed to realize the potential fields of repulsion and attraction. However, an inherent disadvantage of APFs is the tendency to get stuck in local minima of potential functions, especially when generating paths in crowed areas.

Evolutionary algorithms are also popular to solve the pathfinding problem in an environment with complex configurations. For example, the work [10] proposes a genetic algorithm to find optimal paths in road networks with time-dependent stochastic travel times. The work [11] introduces a genetic algorithm to minimise travel distance and maximise path safety. Particle swarm optimization [12] is applied for a robot to navigate in an environment with various danger sources. In [13], a swarm intelligence algorithm based on the flashing behavior of fireflies is discussed to generate the optimal path in a static environment. Most of the evolutionary algorithms focus on the complexity of environmental configurations, but for a dynamic environment, it is still a challenge to generate the optimal path in an efficient manner.

Learning is an effective way for guiding a robot towards its goal. Early research [14] has employed supervised learning to train a robot in a given map for deciding its next optimal position. However, a small change in the environment can lead to the failure of executing a planned path. Reinforcement learning is an alternative learning framework, in which a learning agent can adapt its parameter based on feedbacks from the environment [15]. Thus, the primary advantage of reinforcement learning lies in the inherent capability of dealing with the changes of the environment. For example, Q-learning is a popular algorithm for guiding a robot across obstacle areas [16,17]. In RL algorithms, a learning agent has to decide whether to search for new information or to apply its current knowledge so as to select the action that leads to the maximal reward. Of course, the learning agent is expected to find the optimal policy in as few actions as possible. However, for a specific learning task it is impracticable to directly reach a conclusion on which *action selection strategy* will perform the best. The action selection strategy is also called exploration strategy in some literature [18]. Typically, the set of learning parameters will be adjusted throughout hand-tuning for determining the appropriate parameters. In this work, we also seek to investigate an *online* method for adjusting the set of learning parameters so that the optimal policy for pathfinding can be obtained in as few steps as possible.

This work focuses on the robot path planning problem in an initially unknown, uncertain environment. The main contribution of this work is that we propose a Tabu methodology with the aim of improving learning performance of the classic temporal difference learning approach. Furthermore, we systematically evaluate the classic Q-learning and SARSA algorithms with the revised algorithms proposed in this paper in a simulated environment. The results and findings of this work can provide an usefully reference for the design of robotic control systems.

The paper is structured as follows. We discuss the preliminaries of the reinforcement learning framework in Sect. 2. Then we introduce the proposed Tabu temporal difference approach for the robot path planning problem in Sect. 3. In Sect. 4, we use a simulated environment to compare the relative performance of the classic temporal difference approach with the revised approach proposed in this work. Finally, Sect. 5 concludes this work.

## 2   Preliminaries of Reinforcement Learning

Reinforcement Learning is a formal framework that emphasizes learning by an agent through trial-and-error interactions with its environment. The standard reinforcement learning framework is modeled by the Markov Decision Process (MDP) that can be defined as a tuple $\langle S, A, P, R, \gamma \rangle$. In a MDP, the state spaces $S$ contains the set of all possible states $s$, the action space $A$ contains the set of all possible actions $a$, the transition probability function $P_{ss'}^{a}$ represents the conditional probabilities $p(s'|s, a)$. The transition probability function specifies the next state distribution $s'$ when the agent performs action $a$ in state $s$. The reward function $R_{ss'}^{a}$ specifies the expected immediate reward for a given state transition to state $s'$ after taking action $a$ in state $s$.

In reinforcement learning, the learning agent interacts with its environment via perceptions and actions. At each time step $t$, the agent perceives its current *state* $s_t \in S$ of the environment, and then selects an *action* $a_t \in A$ to execute, which can change the state of the environment to $s_{t+1}$ at the next time step $t+1$. At the same time, the agent gets a feedback signal from the environment, called *reward* $r_{t+1} \in R$. The reward function only captures the immediate impact of taking an action. A *policy* $\pi : S \mapsto A$ is defined to map the states of the environments to the actions taken in those states, determining how the agent chooses an action in any given state.

The goal of the agent in reinforcement learning is to find the optimal policy that maximizes the long-term sum of discounted rewards from any initial state $s$. This long-term sum of discounted rewards is captured in a *value function* $V^{\pi} : S \mapsto \mathbb{R}$, which is defined as:

$$V^{\pi}(s) = \sum_{t=0}^{\infty} \gamma^{t} r_{t+1}, \tag{1}$$

where $\gamma \in [0,1)$ is the discount factor that determines the importance of future rewards, and $V^\pi(s)$ is the expected return from state $s$ when following policy $\pi$. Given a fixed policy $\pi$, the value function $V^\pi$ satisfies the Bellman equation [15]:

$$V^\pi(s) = \max_{a \in A} \gamma \sum_{s' \in S} P^a_{ss'}[R^a_{ss'} + V^\pi(s')]. \tag{2}$$

The idea of dynamic programming can be used to iteratively update the value function. If the optimal value function is defined as $V^*(s) = \max_\pi V^\pi(s)$, then we can get a version of Bellman's equations for the optimal value function:

$$V^*(s) = \max_{a \in A} \gamma \sum_{s' \in S} P^a_{ss'}[R^a_{ss'} + V^*(s')]. \tag{3}$$

Value-based reinforcement learning algorithms [19] are frequently used to maximizes the long-term sum of discounted rewards. In addition to the value function $V^\pi(s)$, the action-value function $Q^\pi(s, a)$ can also iteratively update the value estimates for the agent's current policy. The difference is that $Q^\pi(s, a)$ specifically captures the expected return after choosing action $a$ in state $s$ when following policy $\pi$, whereas $V^\pi(s)$ does not explicitly say anything about an action.

## 3    Tabu Temporal Difference Learning for Path Planning

In reinforcement learning, if the *model* that predicts the behaviour of the environment is known, the state transition function $P$ and reward function $R$ are available for the agent to predict the next state and immediate reward. In this case, the value function can be obtained by performing a full-width lookahead over all possible actions and state transitions, and thus model-based algorithms such as dynamic programming can be used to update the value function by a full backup. In contrast, if the model is unknown, the agent needs to interact with the environment to learn the model, and then the value function is updated from sampled experience.

In this paper, as the environment is uncertain and dynamic, we focus on the model-free reinforcement learning task in which the robot needs to learn the state transition and reward from sampled experience. Temporal Difference (TD) learning is one of the model-free reinforcement learning methods that can directly learn from experience without the model of environment's dynamics.

### 3.1    Classical Temporal Difference Learning

TD learning can directly estimate the action-value function (or called Q-value) $Q(s, a)$, and the policy is updated by selecting the action that maximizes the Q-value. *Q-learning* and *SARSA* are the popular TD learning algorithms, in which the Q-value is updated as follows:

$$Q(s,a) \leftarrow Q(s,a) + \alpha\delta$$
$$\delta_Q = R_{ss'}^a + \gamma \max_{a'} Q(s',a') - Q(s,a) \qquad (4)$$
$$\delta_{SARSA} = R_{ss'}^a + \gamma Q(s',a') - Q(s,a)$$

where $\alpha$ is the learning rate, $\gamma$ is the discount factor, and $\delta$ is the TD error. The Q-learning and SARSA algorithms have difference formulas to calculate the TD error. The pseudocodes of the Classical TD approach (i.e., Q-learning and SARSA) are described in Algorithm 1.

---

**Algorithm 1.** Classical Temporal Difference Learning.

1: Initialize $Q(s,a)$ for all $s \in S, a \in A$ arbitrarily;
2: **repeat** (for each episode):
3:     Initialize $s$;
4:     **repeat** (for each step of episode):
5:         Select action $a$ in state $s$ based on $\varepsilon$-greedy policy;
6:         Execute action $a$, observe next state $s'$, and receive reward $R_{ss'}^a$;
7:         Calculate TD error:
8:             $\delta_Q = R_{ss'}^a + \gamma \max_{a'} Q(s',a') - Q(s,a)$,         ▷ Q-learning.
9:             $\delta_{SARSA} = R_{ss'}^a + \gamma Q(s',a') - Q(s,a)$;         ▷ SARSA.
10:        Update the table entry: $Q(s,a) \leftarrow Q(s,a) + \alpha\delta$;
11:        $s \leftarrow s'$;
12:    **until** $s$ is terminal.
13: **until** end of the episodes.

---

We can see from the pseudocodes that the TD error of Q-learning is corrected by $\gamma \max_{a'}(Q(s',a'))$ that is the maximum possible reward in the following state. Comparatively, the TD error of SARSA is updated by the Q-values of the actually selected action that depends on the executed policy. It is obvious that both of the TD learning algorithms only need one time step to backup the Q-value, and thus they are considered as *on-line* learning methods. For this reason, we can claim that the learning agent has the capability of making real-time adjustments based on dynamic situations of the environment.

### 3.2   Tabu Temporal Difference Learning

For the path planning problem in an initially unknown and dynamic environment, the learning agent first needs to learn the Q-values in order to generate an optimal path. In learning periods, the agent must try out available actions in each state and learn from the experiences over time. According to temporal difference learning, the robot needs to select an action in each state according to a particular policy to update the Q-values. For the robot path planning problem, the classical temporal difference learning algorithms still need to thoroughly examine the following issues:

– The trad-off dilemma between exploitation and exploration, i.e., finding a good balance between exploiting current knowledge to generate the best known collision-free path, or exploring new actions in the hope of finding a shorter path.
– The avoidance of cycling exploration in an episode for improving online performance, i.e., preventing the learning agent aimlessly wandering in the local area when enough experience has not yet been acquired.

In order to address the above issues in this work, we come up with a *Tabu methodology* that consists of an *Adaptive Action Selection Rule (AASR)* and a *Tabu Action Elimination Strategy (TAES)* to revise the classic temporal difference learning. The AASR is used to ensure that observed best actions will progressively receive more trials, while the TAES utilizes the memory of search history to avoid blind randomization of choosing the next action in a local area.

**Adaptive Action Selection Rule (AASR).** In TD learning, the *greedy action selection* rule always tries to exploit the current knowledge to maximize the immediate reward, which is achieved by selecting the action with highest value. However, the uncertainty of the environment implies that at least one of the other available actions may lead to better rewards than the greedy action. Thus, in TD learning the $\varepsilon$-greedy is a popular action selection rule:

$$\pi(s) = \begin{cases} \arg\max_a Q(s,a) & \text{with probability } 1 - \varepsilon \\ a_{random} & \text{with probability } \varepsilon. \end{cases} \tag{5}$$

According to the standard $\varepsilon$-greedy rule, the action with highest value will be selected at the most time with probability $1 - \varepsilon$, whereas the other actions will be selected randomly with small probability $\varepsilon$.

A disadvantage of the standard $\varepsilon$-greedy rule is that with the increase of the number of exploration all the non-greedy actions are always tried with equal probability. However, in order to enhance learning performance, we hope that observed best actions should progressively receive more trials instead of with a fixed probability $1 - \varepsilon$. In this work, we improve the standard $\varepsilon$-greedy action selection rule by iteratively updating the $\varepsilon$ according to the learning episodes:

$$\varepsilon \leftarrow \varepsilon - \frac{N_{current\_episode}}{N_{maximum\_episode}} * \varepsilon \tag{6}$$

where $N_{current\_episode}$ indicates the current learning episode, and $N_{maximum\_episode}$ is the upper bound of the learning episodes. Such an adaptive action selection rule can ensure that the robot will initially explore the environment with high possibility by selecting the non-greedy actions, but the preference of exploration will decay with the increase of knowledge about the environment. Consequently, the action with the best value can progressively receive more trials, which is in line with the expectations of path planning in uncertain environments.

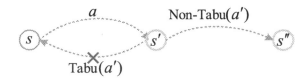

**Fig. 1.** Graphical description of the Tabu Action Elimination Strategy.

**Tabu Action Elimination Strategy (TAES).** The TAES is developed to avoid cycling search in a learning episode and consequently speed up learning performance. The graphical description of the TAES is shown in Fig. 1. The general idea is that when action $a$ is selected in state $s$ at time step $t$, then the TAES will not allow the learning agent at time step $t + 1$ in state $s'$ to choose an action that guides the agent towards the previous sate $s$. To this end, the TAES utilizes the memory of search history to avoid blind randomization of choosing the next action. The strategy is realized by setting the action leading to the previous state into a Tabu list. Of course, the Tabu list should be updated online for each state. In this work, the tenure of the tabu list will disappear after one step restriction.

**Tabu Temporal Difference Learning Algorithms.** As discussed above, we have proposed the Tabu methodology, consisting of the Adaptive Action Selection Rule and the Tabu Action Elimination Strategy, to revise the classic temporal difference learning algorithms. In this work, the revised TD learning algorithms are named as *Tabu Q-learning* and *Tabu SARSA*, respectively. The pseudocodes of the Tabu Q-learning and Tabu SARSA are shown in Algorithm 2.

---

**Algorithm 2.** Tabu Q-learning/SARSA for robot path planning.

---

1: Initialize $Q(s, a)$ for all $s \in S, a \in A$ arbitrarily;
2: **repeat** (for each episode):
3:     Initialize $s$;
4:     Update the exploration rate $\varepsilon$;                      ▷ According to Eq. 6.
5:     Reset the TabuList;
6:     **repeat** (for each step of episode):
7:         Select action $a$ from non-TabuList in state $s$ based on $\varepsilon$-greedy policy;
8:         Execute action $a$, observe next state $s'$, and receive reward $R_{ss'}^a$;
9:         Calculate TD error:
10:            $\delta_Q = R_{ss'}^a + \gamma \max_{a'} Q(s', a') - Q(s, a),$                  ▷ Q-learning.
11:            $\delta_{SARSA} = R_{ss'}^a + \gamma Q(s', a') - Q(s, a);$                  ▷ SARSA.
12:         Update the table entry: $Q(s, a) \leftarrow Q(s, a) + \alpha \delta$;
13:         $s \leftarrow s'$;
14:         Update the TabuList according to the criteria.                  ▷ based on TAES.
15:     **until** $s$ is terminal.
16: **until** end of the episodes.

---

In this revised TD learning approach, the exploration rate $\varepsilon$ is updated online for each episode based on the learning progress (line 4). Since the TAES aims at preventing cycling trajectory of steps in each episode, the list of Tabu actions will be reset for each episode (line 5). When selecting an action, the Tabu actions must be eliminated first from the list of potential actions (line 7). The TD errors for Q-learning (line 10) and SARSA (line 11) are calculated in each step as usual. The difference is that after moving to the next state, the Tabu action list will be updated accordingly based on the Tabu Action Elimination Strategy (line 14).

# 4    Experiments and Results

## 4.1    Experiment Setup

In order to evaluate the performance of the revised TD learning algorithms, we carry out an empirical study. The experiments are performed in a simulated environment that uses grid maps with size $28 \times 36$. The robot needs to start from the upper left corner of the map, and then move towards its destination located at the lower right corner of the map by following a collision-free path. The other gray cells represent the obstacles. The obstacle distribution is pre-designed and the same for all simulation runs, but the learning agent does not have the map information in advance. For the path planning problem in uncertain environments, the robot may be at risk if its trajectory points are too close to those gray cells.

In the experiments, we evaluate four algorithms: classic Q-learning, classic SARSA, Tabu Q-learning, and Tabu SARSA. The learning parameters for all algorithms are the same for each simulation run. As the environment is initially unknown, the state transition function and reward function are not available in advance for directly generating a feasible path. Instead, the learning agent has to interact with the environment to learn the model the environment during the learning process. Gradually, the Q-value of selecting an action in each state is updated from experience. We set the upper bound of the learning episodes to 2000 in the experiment. In the learning periods, the Q-table is obtained by these algorithms. After learning is over, the optimal path is generated from the robot's starting location towards the destination. Each simulation has been run for 10 times to reduce variance and filter out random effects.

## 4.2    Results

**Classic Q-Learning vs. Tabu Q-Learning.** We first compare the relative performance of the Classic Q-learning and Tabu Q-learning algorithms. The generated optimal paths by these two algorithms are shown in Fig. 2(a), (b), and the learning performance is shown in Fig. 2(c). We can see that when the learning process is over, both of the algorithms can successfully generate a collision-free path. With respect to learning performance, in the early stage of learning both of the algorithms cannot show significant differences. However, in the later stage of learning, the Tabu Q-learning algorithm gradually needs fewer steps for each episode than the Classic Q-learning algorithm. This is because the Classic Q-learning applies a fixed $\epsilon$-greedy rule, and, thus, the learning agent always selects the action with the highest value with probability $1 - \epsilon$ in all learning episodes. Therefore, at the end of the learning process, the agent still has the tendency to explore the non-optimal actions with probability $\epsilon$. Comparatively, according to the Adaptive Action Selection Rule of Tabu Q-learning, the parameter $\epsilon$ will adapts itself according to the number of learning episodes. It will approach zero at the end of the learning process, so the learning agent will select the optimal action in a greedy manner. Thus, we can say that in the early stage of learning both of the algorithms cannot show significant differences. However, in the later stage of learning, the Tabu Q-learning algorithm gradually needs fewer moving steps for each episode and finally converge to the optimal policy in the end.

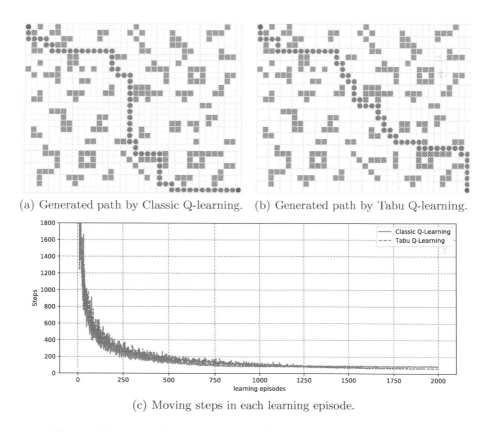

(a) Generated path by Classic Q-learning.    (b) Generated path by Tabu Q-learning.

(c) Moving steps in each learning episode.

**Fig. 2.** Relative performance of classic Q-learning and Tabu Q-learning.

**Classic SARSA vs. Tabu SARSA.** We compare the relative performance of the Classic SARSA and Tabu SARSA algorithms in Fig. 3. The generated optimal paths are shown in Fig. 3(a), (b), and the learning performance is shown in Fig. 3(c). With regard to generating feasible paths, both of the algorithms are competent. However, we can clearly see that the curve of moving steps for each episode of the Classic SARSA algorithms fluctuates wildly, in comparison with the proposed Tabu SARSA algorithm. This means that the Classic SARSA algorithms cannot properly deal with cycling exploration in an episode, and the learning agent puts in a great deal of effort to explore the state space during the learning process in a somewhat aimless manner. In contrast, the Tabu SARSA algorithm can encourage the learning agent to explore the state space in the beginning, and it can converge to the optimal policy at the end of the learning process.

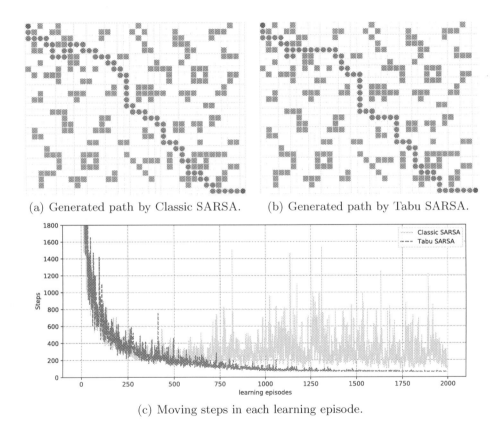

(a) Generated path by Classic SARSA.    (b) Generated path by Tabu SARSA.

(c) Moving steps in each learning episode.

**Fig. 3.** Relative performance of classic SARSA and Tabu SARSA.

**Tabu Q-Learning vs. Tabu SARSA.** For the robot path planning problem studied in this paper, we can compare the proposed Tabu Q-learning and SARSA algorithm with respect to safety concerns. As mentioned above, an idea path is expected to push the robot away from the unsafe areas as far as possible because the robot can be drifted away from the generated path by environmental disturbances. As shown in Figs. 2(b), 3(b), although both of them can produce collision-free paths, we still can conclude that the Tabu SARSA algorithm generates more safer paths than the Tabu Q-learning algorithm. This is because the Tabu SARSA algorithm, moreover, tries to push the robot away from obstacles as far as possible.

## 5   Conclusion

In this paper, we proposed a Tabu TD learning approach, consisting of an Adaptive Action Selection Rule and a Tabu Action Elimination Strategy, to the robot path planning problem in an initially unknown and uncertain environment. We evaluated theses algorithms in a simulated environments. The results can show that the revised Tabu Q-learning and Tabu SARSA algorithms outperform the corresponding classic ones. In particular, the Tabu SARSA algorithm can provide a reliable and safety path for the robot in an uncertain environment. In future, we would like to investigate the reinforcement learning approach to solving multiple conflicting objectives, as well as the path planning approach in large or continuous state-space.

**Acknowledgments.** This research is supported by the National Natural Science Foundation of China (Grant No. 61703138), and Natural Science Foundation of Jiangsu Province (Grant No. BK20170307).

## References

1. Hossain, M.A., Ferdous, I.: Autonomous robot path planning in dynamic environment using a new optimization technique inspired by bacterial foraging technique. Robot. Auton. Syst. **64**, 137–141 (2015)
2. Berenson, D., Abbeel, P., Goldberg, K.: A robot path planning framework that learns from experience. In: 2012 IEEE International Conference on Robotics and Automation (ICRA), pp. 3671–3678. IEEE (2012)
3. Lolla, T., Ueckermann, M.P., Yigit, K., Haley, P. J., J.: Path planning in time dependent flow fields using level set methods. In: IEEE International Conference on Robotics and Automation, pp. 166–173 (2012)
4. Du Toit, N., Burdick, J.: Robot motion planning in dynamic, uncertain environments. IEEE Trans. Rob. **28**(1), 101–115 (2012)
5. Ducho, F., Babinec, A., Kajan, M., Beo, P., Florek, M., Fico, T., Juriica, L.: Path planning with modified a star algorithm for a mobile robot. Procedia Eng. **96**, 59–69 (2014)
6. Wang, C., et al.: Path planning of automated guided vehicles based on improved a-star algorithm. In: IEEE International Conference on Information and Automation, pp. 2071–2076 (2015)
7. Chaari, I., Koubaa, A., Bennaceur, H., Ammar, A., Alajlan, M., Youssef, H.: Design and performance analysis of global path planning techniques for autonomous mobile robots in grid environments. Int. J. Adv. Robot. Syst. **14**(2), 1729881416663663 (2017)

8. Chiang, H.T., Malone, N., Lesser, K., Oishi, M.: Path-guided artificial potential fields with stochastic reachable sets for motion planning in highly dynamic environments. In: IEEE International Conference on Robotics and Automation, pp. 2347–2354. (2015)

9. Amiryan, J., Jamzad, M.: Adaptive motion planning with artificial potential fields using a prior path. In: RSI International Conference on Robotics and Mechatronics, pp. 731–736 (2016)

10. Rajabi-Bahaabadi, M., Shariat-Mohaymany, A., Babaei, M., Chang, W.A.: Multi-objective path finding in stochastic time-dependent road networks using non-dominated sorting genetic algorithm. J. Expert Syst. Appl. **42**(12), 5056–5064 (2015)

11. Ahmed, F., Deb, K.: Multi-objective optimal path planning using elitist non-dominated sorting genetic algorithms. Soft. Comput. **17**(7), 1283–1299 (2013)

12. Zhang, Y., Gong, D.W., Zhang, J.H.: Robot path planning in uncertain environment using multi-objective particle swarm optimization. Neurocomputing **103**(2), 172–185 (2013)

13. Hidalgo-Paniagua, A., Vega-Rodrguez, M.A., Ferruz, J., Pavn, N.: Solving the multi-objective path planning problem in mobile robotics with a firefly-based approach. Soft Comput. **21**(4), 1–16 (2015)

14. Antonelo, E.A., Schrauwen, B.: Supervised learning of internal models for autonomous goal-oriented robot navigation using reservoir computing. In: IEEE International Conference on Robotics and Automation, pp. 2959–2964 (2010)

15. Sutton, R.S., Barto, A.G.: Reinforcement learning: an introduction, Bradford book. Mach. Learn. **16**(1), 285–286 (2005)

16. Babu, V.M., Krishna, U.V., Shahensha, S.K.: An autonomous path finding robot using q-learning. In: International Conference on Intelligent Systems and Control (2016)

17. Kong, Y.H., Lee, W.C.: Dynamic obstacle avoidance and optimal path finding algorithm for mobile robot using q-learning. J. Korean Inst. Inf. Technol. **15**(9), 57–62 (2017)

18. Hester, T., Lopes, M., Stone, P.: Learning exploration strategies in model-based reinforcement learning. In: International Conference on Autonomous Agents and Multi-Agent Systems, pp. 1069–1076 (2013)

19. Zhang, B., Mao, Z., Liu, W., Liu, J.: Geometric reinforcement learning for path planning of UAVs. J. Intell. Robot. Syst. **77**(2), 391–409 (2015)

# Modelling and Predicting Rhythmic Flow Patterns in Dynamic Environments

Sergi Molina[1](✉), Grzegorz Cielniak[1], Tomáš Krajník[2], and Tom Duckett[1]

[1] Lincoln Center for Autonomous Systems, University of Lincoln, Lincoln, UK
{smolinamellado,gcielniak,tduckett}@lincoln.ac.uk
[2] Faculty of Electrical Engineering, Czech Technical University, Prague, Czechia
tomas.krajnik@fel.cvut.cz

**Abstract.** We present a time-dependent probabilistic map able to model and predict flow patterns of people in indoor environments. The proposed representation models the likelihood of motion direction on a grid-based map by a set of harmonic functions, which efficiently capture long-term (minutes to weeks) variations of crowd movements over time. The evaluation, performed on data from two real environments, shows that the proposed model enables prediction of human movement patterns in the future. Potential applications include human-aware motion planning, improving the efficiency and safety of robot navigation.

**Keywords:** Mobile robots · Long-term autonomy · Human activities

## 1 Introduction

Robotic automation has been happening in industry for many years in structured environments. Modern factory floors are changing to work in a more flexible way, where robots such as AGVs or forklifts have to share the same environment with people in a collaborative manner. To improve the efficiency of mobile robot navigation in human-populated areas, a robot should take into account the general flow of the people in the environment [1]. However, the flows of people movement are not constant over time, but are constantly changing.

This work considers building spatio-temporal models of human flow to improve the efficiency of long-term robot operation, assuming that the observed direction of motion follow underlying patterns due to the rhythmic nature of human activities. We model the temporal dimension of activities using periodic functions at different time scales, going from minutes to days. By learning typical motion patterns, the robot can either avoid areas with high density of people movement, or move among the crowd with the expected dominant direction of flow, thus blending better with its surroundings.

Our model applies the Frequency Map Enhancement (FreMEn [2]) to a grid-based discretized representation of space, where each cell contains several hypothesis of people movement direction. To evaluate the proposed model, we

© Springer International Publishing AG, part of Springer Nature 2018
M. Giuliani et al. (Eds.): TAROS 2018, LNAI 10965, pp. 135–146, 2018.
https://doi.org/10.1007/978-3-319-96728-8_12

performed experiments using two datasets gathered over the course of several weeks: one from a shopping center in Japan [3], and one at University of Lincoln, UK. The experiments show that the proposed model can learn the flow patterns and predict people movement at a given time in the future.

## 2 Related Work

Recently, a number of approaches for mapping environment dynamics have been proposed. One general approach is to store past observations in a compressed way, as in Arbuckle et al. [4] and Mitsou and Tzafestas [5], without the actual intention of using the past observations for predictions of future states. Other approaches learn generative models, which can predict people motion direction in order to improve collision avoidance. While these approaches use long-term data for training, they are aimed at short term prediction of people movement based on current observations [6–8]. Works like Wang et al. [9], Kucner et al. [10], and Saarinen et al. [11] treat dynamics as a change of occupancy in grid map cells, which allows to represent characteristic motion patterns at given areas. [10] proposed to model how the occupancy likelihood of a given cell in a grid is influenced by the neighbouring cells and showed that this representation allows to model object movement directly in an occupancy grid. Similarly in [9, 11] the direction of traversal for each cell is obtained using an input-output hidden Markov model and a Markov chain, respectively. The aforementioned works assume that the typical motion patterns are constant in time, which might not be typical, e.g. human flows at an entrance of an office building at the start and end of a work-day are likely to be in opposite directions.

Thus, one should take into account the temporal domain, which is important in human-populated environments. For example, Dayoub et al. [12] and Rosen et al. [13] used statistical methods modelling short and long-term to create persistence models and reasoned about the stability of the environmental states over time. Tipaldi et al. [14] proposed to represent the occupancy of cells in a traditional occupancy grid with a hidden Markov model for improving robot localisation over the traditional approaches. The idea of identifying periodic patterns in the measured states and using them for future predictions was presented in Krajník et al. [2]. These approaches demonstrated that by considering temporal aspects such as periodicities in the environment, robotic capabilities including localisation, planning and exploration can be improved [14–16].

Inspired by the cell models to represent dynamics and the power of spectral analysis to create spatio-temporal models capable of long-term predictions, we have developed a model which is able to predict crowd movements. Similar to the work by Jovan et al. [17] based on counting human trajectories during intervals of time, in our approach we count the number of people walking in certain directions in a grid-based representation of the environment.

# 3   Spatio-Temporal Model

The aim of this work is to create a model of human motion which is able to predict the flow patterns of people over time, as well as where and when these flows are happening. The underlying geometric space is represented by a grid, where each cell contains $k$ temporal models, which correspond to $k$ discretized orientations of people motion through the given cell over time. Since the total number of temporal models, which are of a fixed size, is $k \times$ the number of cells (n), the spatio-temporal model does not grow over time regardless of the duration of data collection. This makes the model not only memory efficient, but also allows to make probabilistic predictions of the likely flow of people in a certain direction for a given cell at any instant of time.

## 3.1   Temporal Framework - FreMEn

The temporal models, which can capture patterns of people movement, are based on the FreMEn framework [2]. FreMEn is a mathematical tool based on the Fourier Transform, which considers the probability of a given state as a function of time and represents it by a combination of harmonic components. The model not only allows representation of environment dynamics over arbitrary timescales with constant memory requirements, but also prediction of future environment states based on the patterns learned.

To illustrate the basic principles of FreMEn, let us consider a binary state such as the presence or absence of a visual feature (see Fig. 1). Treating the measured state as a signal, we decompose it by means of the Fourier Transform, obtaining a frequency spectrum with the corresponding amplitudes, frequencies and phase shifts. Then, transferring the most prominent spectral components to the time domain provides an analytic expression representing the probability of the feature being visible at a given time in the past or future.

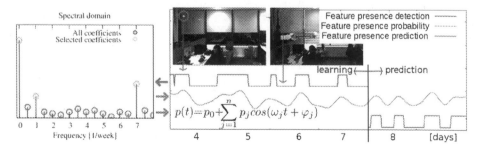

**Fig. 1.** Example of the FreMEn applied in a binary state [2].

Assuming the direction of people movement is affected by patterns that might be periodic, we apply the FreMEn concept to discretised directions of people movement through a particular cell.

### 3.2  Building the Model

Our model assumes that it is provided with people detection data, containing person position and orientation $(x, y, \alpha)$. At the beginning of the model construction, we associate each cell with $k$ bins, corresponding to the discretised orientation of people motion and to the $k$ temporal models. When building the model, the $x, y$ positions are discretised and assigned to a corresponding cell and the orientation $\alpha$ is assigned to one of the $k$ bins, whose value is incremented by 1. In other words, we count the number of people detections occurring in each orientation bin and cell. After a predefined interval of time, we normalise the bins, and use the normalised values to update the spectra of the temporal models by the scheme described in [2]. Then, we reset the bin values to 0 and start the counting again. Notice that the number of people detected in a particular cell is not a determining factor since we aim to model the relative amount of occurrences among all $k$ orientations.

### 3.3  Making Predictions

To predict the orientation of a human movement through a cell at a future time $t$, we first calculate the probability for each discretised orientation $\theta$, ($\theta = i\frac{2\pi}{k}$ and $i \in \{0, 1, \ldots, k-1\}$), associated to that cell as

$$p_\theta(t) = p_0 + \sum_{j=1}^{m} p_j cos(\omega_j t + \varphi_j), \tag{1}$$

where $p_0$ is the stationary probability, $m$ is the number of the most prominent spectral components, and $p_j$, $\omega_j$ and $\varphi_j$ are their amplitudes, periods and phases. The spectral components $\omega_j$ are drawn from a set of $\omega_s$ that, in our case, we have selected to cover periodicities ranging from 20 min to 1 day with the following distribution:

$$\omega_s = 2\pi \frac{1+s}{24 \cdot 3600}, \qquad s \in 0, 1, 2, 3, 4, \ldots, 72. \tag{2}$$

After computing the probabilities for every single orientation, we conclude that the dominant orientation within that cell for that instant of time, $t$, corresponds to the orientation with the highest predicted probability:

$$cell_\theta = argmax(p_\theta(t)), \qquad \theta \in i\frac{2\pi}{k}, \quad i \in \{0, 1, \ldots, k-1\}. \tag{3}$$

## 4  Evaluation Datasets

In order to evaluate the model, we have run experiments using two datasets. The first one is from the ATC shopping center in Japan [3], and the second one is a dataset recorded in the corridors of our offices at the University of Lincoln, UK (UoL). Both of them provide an environment with complex movements and enough days to the train the models in the long-term, although ATC covers a larger area than UoL. The people detections inside the environment are given in $x$, $y$ coordinates together with the angle of movement $\alpha$ for every timestamp.

## 4.1   ATC Dataset

The first one is a pedestrian tracking dataset recorded at the ATC shopping center in Osaka, Japan [3]. The perception system consists of multiple 3D range sensors (36 × Panasonic D-Imager, 11 × Asus Xtion PRO and 2 × Velodyne HDL-32E), covering an area of approximately 900 m$^2$ (Fig. 2), able to detect and track all the people around the place in every instant of time. The data provided was recorded on every Wednesday and Sunday between October 24$^{th}$, 2012 and November 29$^{th}$, 2013, resulting in a total of 92 days. From all these data, we selected the first 17 Wednesdays and 17 Sundays, using 15 of each as our training set and the other 4 days as testing data. The recording of each day provides people trajectories starting from approximately 09:00 until 21:00, so for the rest of day we assume there are no occurrences of people, simulating the shopping center being closed.

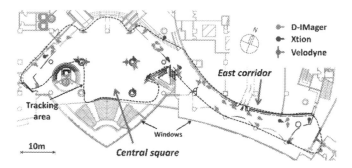

**Fig. 2.** Shopping center map with the location of all the sensors and the two main zones.

## 4.2   UoL Dataset

The second dataset was collected at one of corridors in the Isaac Newton Building building at the University of Lincoln (UoL). The data collection was performed by a stationary robot equipped with a Velodyne VLP-16 and a 2D laser. The robot was placed in one of the T-shaped junctions in a way that allowed its sensors to scan the three connecting corridors simultaneously, covering a total area of approximately 64 m$^2$ (see Fig. 3). To detect and localize people in the 3D point cloud provided by the lidar, we used an efficient and reliable person detection method developed by Yan et al. [18]. Our dataset spanned from mornings to late evenings for 14 days, sparsely recorded over a four week period. From these, 13 days were used for training and the remaining one was used to evaluate the model.

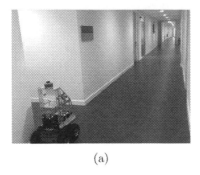
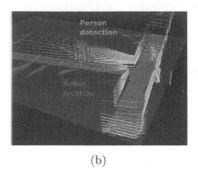

(a)                                            (b)

**Fig. 3.** UoL dataset: robot location in the corridor (a) and example of a person walking seen by the Velodyne scans (b).

## 5    Experiments

In our experiments, we discretised the space into $1 \times 1$ m cells for the ATC dataset and $0.5 \times 0.5$ m cells for the UoL one, which results in a total of $n = 1200$ and $n = 400$ active cells, respectively. Regarding the dynamics, works presented in [9,10] treat them by means of cell-to-cell transitions. However experiments in our previous work (Molina et al. [19]) showed that the diagonal cell transitions tend to be less likely than the 4 cardinal directions (N/S/E/W). So in order to ensure that all the orientations are treated the same way, we have instead discretized the angles of people traversing a particular cell into a finite set of directions ($k = 8$) as in Fig. 4a. There is no theoretical limit on how coarse the granularity of the spatial and angular discretization can be, apart from the increased computational cost. However, setting it too high could lead to not have enough data to fill all states and a loss of generality, while on the other hand, setting it too low could increase the accuracy but result in a much lower model resolution in exchange.

Moreover, the interval used for creating the histograms, used as the input for the model in the training phase, was 10 min. Figure 4b shows an example of a situation where during a random 10-minute interval in a random cell, a total of 61 people detections occurred within the boundaries of that cell. The distribution of detections shown in the histogram states that for those 10 min, the people traversing that cell tend to walk at angles in the range of the bin corresponding to $\theta_2$ (i.e. between 67.5 and 112.5°).

### 5.1    Comparing Ground Truth Against Predicted Values

To estimate the optimal number of model components ($m$) to be taken into account for predictions, we need to compare the predictions obtained from the model against the real data. We have defined the error as a percentage ratio between the cells predicted with the wrong orientation when compared with the ground truth and the total number of cells.

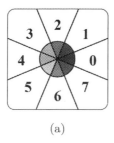

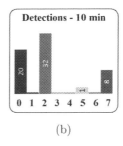

(a)                                                       (b)

**Fig. 4.** (a) 8 bins discretizing every 45° the full circumference. (b) Histogram of detections, before normalizing, obtained in a cell during an interval of 10 min.

However, predicting the dominant orientation with the real data at a single point in time $t$ is not possible, since for a single instant we cannot count enough detections to determine which orientations obtain the highest number. Instead, the idea is to compare the most dominant orientation obtained during a particular interval of time ($\Delta t$). For the real data we chose the orientation in each cell with the higher number of occurrences over the time interval, the same as we did during model building. For the model prediction, we compute the cumulative probability values in the same interval for all the orientations and pick the one with the highest number.

$$cell_\theta = argmax(\int_{\Delta t} p_\theta(t)), \qquad \theta \in i\frac{2\pi}{k}, \quad i \in \{0, 1, \dots, k-1\}. \qquad (4)$$

## 5.2   Results

In order to evaluate the model we have calculated the error for both testing sets using multiple values of modelled periodicities $m$, going from 0, which corresponds to a stationary model, to 4, and for different time intervals: of 0.5, 1, 2, 3, 4 and 6 h. Since there was no movement of people during night-time in both datasets, we calculated the error only for half a day, i.e. 09:00–21:00 at ATC and 8:00–20:00 at UoL. Since for the ATC dataset we have used 4 days for evaluation, the results shown are the average over all days. The error results for all the combinations of model orders (number of periodicities) and time intervals for both datasets are summarized in Table 1.

It is clear that for the ATC dataset, modeling the time domain with at least one periodicity (i.e. model component) provides us with significantly more accurate prediction of the people movement. For the UoL dataset, the improvement in accuracy of the higher order model over the static one (with $m = 0$) is not as prominent as in the ATC case, but it is still statistically significant. This difference is caused by the lack of clear periodicities present in the environment at UoL as shown in Figs. 9 and 10.

In both cases, the models with between 2 and 4 periodicities obtain the best results, each having a similar performance. However, when choosing the optimal value $m$, if there is no substantial change when adding more periodicities, it is better to stay with lower values so the model remains simpler and faster to calculate. So for this case staying with order 2, or even 1, would be the best choice, which is in accordance with the results in Krajnik et al. [2].

Looking at the interval parameter, it is clear that for both datasets, going for higher intervals times means obtaining lower error values, but in return we suffer from bigger temporal granularity, as the predictions also span longer time intervals.

**Table 1.** Model errors for both datasets using different order models and time intervals [%]

| Interval [h] | ATC dataset | | | | | | UoL dataset | | | | | |
|---|---|---|---|---|---|---|---|---|---|---|---|---|
| | 0.5 | 1 | 2 | 3 | 4 | 6 | 0.5 | 1 | 2 | 3 | 4 | 6 |
| Order 0 | 45.0 | 44.2 | 40.8 | 38.5 | 37.2 | 34.6 | 40.1 | 37.5 | 34.3 | 32.5 | 32.6 | 30.6 |
| Order 1 | 42.3 | 40.7 | 36.9 | 34.5 | 33.4 | 30.9 | 38.2 | 36.4 | 33.4 | 31.2 | 31.9 | 29.2 |
| Order 2 | 42.0 | 40.3 | 36.7 | 34.0 | 32.1 | **29.8** | 39.8 | 37.6 | 34.0 | 31.5 | 31.3 | **28.0** |
| Order 3 | 42.1 | 40.2 | 36.7 | 34.1 | 32.4 | 30.0 | 38.8 | 36.2 | 33.6 | 31.3 | 30.7 | 28.1 |
| Order 4 | 41.9 | 39.8 | 36.2 | 33.5 | 32.0 | 29.8 | 38.5 | 36.5 | 33.3 | 31.2 | 30.8 | 28.4 |

## 5.3  Qualitative Evaluation

To better understand the approach and results obtained, we have drawn the orientations for the ground truth and the model predictions for both datasets.

For better visualization and due to space constraints, for the ATC dataset we have plotted the grid only for the central square, although the east corridor also contains relevant flow patterns. The model chosen for presentation in Fig. 6 is of order 2, meaning we are taking the two most prominent FreMEn components (corresponding to 24 and 12 h). The interval time selected is 4 h, so the ground truth and predictions are calculated from 09:00 to 13:00, from 13:00 to 17:00, and from 17:00 to 21:00. Looking at the ground truth (Fig. 5) one quickly notices that the central area of the square presents a noticeable change in the flow during the day. The flow of people changes from the "West" direction (green) in the morning to the "East" direction (dark blue) in the afternoon. Checking the same intervals for the orientations predicted (Fig. 6), the model was able to capture and learn the periodicities occurring, being capable to predict those changes with a high degree of fidelity for future states.

To understand how the internal representation of a cell works, in Figs. 7 and 8 there are examples of two different cells, one placed in a changing environment like the central square (Fig. 8) and the other one in a location with a constant flow in the same direction during the whole day (Fig. 7), both marked with black circles in Figs. 5 and 6. The plot shows the probabilities calculated for all the orientations of the cell during the day (00:00 to 24:00), taking the same two periodicities

**Fig. 5.** ATC - ground truth for the intervals (left to right) 09:00 to 13:00, 13:00 to 17:00 and 17:00 to 21:00. (Color figure online)

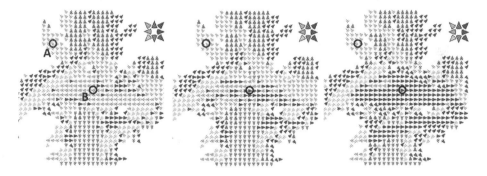

**Fig. 6.** ATC - model predictions for the intervals (left to right) 09:00 to 13:00, 13:00 to 17:00 and 17:00 to 21:00. (Color figure online)

in the model as for the representation of the environment. In the dynamic cell, the two predominant orientations which alternate during the day obtain higher probability values than the rest. The "West" one tends to be more likely to occur during the morning, while the "East" orientation overrides the previous one as time passes. This indicates that in the morning the number of people entering the mall tends to be higher than of those leaving, hence the arrows in one direction, but in the afternoon the situation changes to the opposite. However, taking a look at the static cell only one orientation ("North-West") obtained higher probabilities compared with the rest, due to the cell belonging to a location used mainly as an exit corridor.

For the UoL dataset we have chosen to plot also the results taking two periodicities, but in this case picking an interval of 6 h, obtaining two predictions during the day, from 08:00 to 14:00 and from 14:00 to 20:00. The UoL Figs. 9 and 10 do not show a clear rhythmic flow as occurred in the previous dataset, hence the lower increase in performance when going from a static model to one taking into account some periodicities. Despite that fact, our approach is still able to recognize the main flows in the different areas of the corridor where we recorded the dataset.

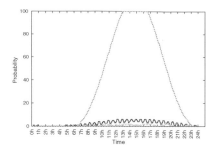

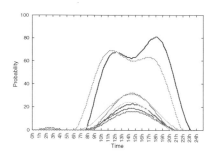

**Fig. 7.** Probabilities of the 8 orientations for a cell in a corridor with constant flow orientation (cell A in Figs. 5 and 6) during one day.

**Fig. 8.** Probabilities of the 8 orientations for a cell in the central area with changing flow orientation (cell B in Figs. 5 and 6) during one day.

**Fig. 9.** UoL - ground truth for the intervals (left to right) 08:00 to 14:00, and 14:00 to 20:00.

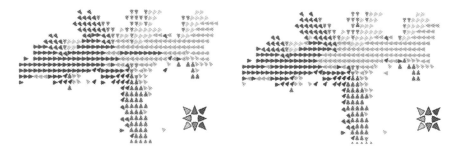

**Fig. 10.** UoL - model predictions for the intervals (left to right) 08:00 to 14:00, and 14:00 to 20:00.

## 6    Conclusion

We have proposed an approach to model the dynamics of human motion in an indoor environment from a long-term perspective. The approach can generate predictions of future crowd movement directions at any given time. The model assumes that human activities are influenced by human habits which follow certain routines. This allows to represent part of the temporal dynamics by means of a combination of harmonic functions. The experiments showed that although not all the dynamics are periodic, taking into account the periodic patterns allows to calculate more accurate predictions of people movement compared to models that neglect the temporal domain.

However, one of the limitations of the developed model lies in the fact that once the number of periodicities $m$ is chosen, all the cells in the map are predicted using the same $m$. It is unlikely that all cells will experience the same rhythm of activities, so it would be relevant to analyze all the cells individually and choose for each one the best model order to fit the data. This could also be used to cluster the cells into semantic categories according to the types of activities observed.

From a robotics perspective, this representation could be used to take the predicted human motion into account when planning the robot movement as presented in [1]. A navigation algorithm taking into account the people movement would result in more natural and harmonious movement with respect to the crowd, moving with the flow and obtaining fewer face-to-face encounters.

For the experiments presented in this paper, we assumed that the environment is fully observable. However, we know this is unlikely in a real-world scenario, where we would only observe the immediate vicinity of the robot through the robot's own sensors. The capability of FreMEn to work with sparse data [2] allows us to update our models only with the data actually observed by the robot. However, this requires that the robot actively gathers data at locations and times that provide new information to update the spatio-temporal model. Thus, we plan to study robot exploration strategies, which would actively maintain the spatio-temporal representations to keep them up-to-date. Future work will also include testing the model in other scenarios such as warehouse operations to check the method's generalization capabilities.

**Acknowledgement.** This work has been supported within H2020-ICT by the EC under grant number 732737 (ILIAD), by CSF grant no. 17-27006Y and OP VVV Research Center for Informatics no. CZ.02.1.01/0.0/0.0/16_019/0000765.

# References

1. Palmieri, L., Kucner, T.P., Magnusson, M., Lilienthal, A.J., Arras, K.O.: Kinodynamic motion planning on Gaussian mixture fields. In: IEEE International Conference on Robotics and Automation (ICRA), pp. 6176–6181. IEEE (2017)
2. Krajník, T., Fentanes, J.P., Santos, J., Duckett, T.: FreMEn: frequency map enhancement for long-term mobile robot autonomy in changing environments. IEEE Trans. Robot. (2017)
3. Brscic, D., Kanda, T., Ikeda, T., Miyashita, T.: Person position and body direction tracking in large public spaces using 3D range sensors. IEEE Trans. Hum.-Mach. Syst. **43**(6), 522–534 (2013)
4. Arbuckle, D., Howard, A., Mataric, M.: Temporal occupancy grids: a method for classifying the spatio-temporal properties of the environment. In: IEEE/RSJ International Conference on Intelligent Robots and Systems (IROS) (2002)

5. Mitsou, N., Tzafestas, C.: Temporal occupancy grid for mobile robot dynamic environment mapping. In: Mediterranean Conference on Control Automation (2007)
6. Sun, L., Yan, Z., Molina, S., Hanheide, M., Duckett, T.: 3DOF pedestrian trajectory prediction learned from long-term autonomous mobile robot deployment data. In: IEEE International Conference on Robotics and Automation (2018)
7. Rudenko, A., Palmieri, L., Arras, O.: Joint long-term prediction of human motion using a planning-based social force approach. In: IEEE International Conference on Robotics and Automation (ICRA) (2018)
8. Bennewitz, M., Burgard, W., Cielniak, G., Thrun, S.: Learning motion patterns of people for compliant robot motion. IJRR **24**(1), 31–48 (2005)
9. Wang, Z., Ambrus, R., Jensfelt, P., Folkesson, J.: Modeling motion patterns of dynamic objects by IOHMM. In: 2014 IEEE/RSJ International Conference on Intelligent Robots and Systems (IROS 2014), pp. 1832–1838. IEEE (2014)
10. Kucner, T., Saarinen, J., Magnusson, M., Lilienthal, A.J.: Conditional transition maps learning motion patterns in dynamics environments. In: IEEE International Conference on Intelligent Robots and Systems (2013)
11. Saarinen, J., Andreasson, H., Lilienthal, A.J.: Independent Markov chain occupancy grid maps for representation of dynamic environment. In: IEEE Intelligent Robots and Systems, pp. 3489–3495. IEEE (2012)
12. Dayoub, F., Cielniak, G., Duckett, T.: Long-term experiments with an adaptive spherical view representation for navigation in changing environments. Robot. Auton. Syst. **59**, 285–295 (2011)
13. Rosen, D.M., Mason, J., Leonard, J.J.: Towards lifelong feature-based mapping in semi-static environments. In: International Conference on Robotics and Automation (ICRA), pp. 1063–1070. IEEE, May 2016
14. Tipaldi, G.D., Meyer-Delius, D., Burgard, W.: Lifelong localization in changing environments. IJRR **32**, 1662–1678 (2013)
15. Fentanes, J.P., Lacerda, B., Krajník, T., Hawes, N., Hanheide, M.: Now or later? Predicting and maximising success of navigation actions from long-term experience. In: International Conference on Robotics and Automation, pp. 1112–1117, May 2015
16. Santos, J.M., Krajnik, T., Fentanes, J.P., Duckett, T.: Lifelong information-driven exploration to complete and refine 4D spatio-temporal maps. Robot. Autom. Lett. **1**, 684–691 (2016)
17. Jovan, F., et al.: A poisson-spectral model for modelling temporal patterns in human data observed by a robot. In: 2016 IEEE/RSJ International Conference on Intelligent Robots and Systems (IROS), pp. 4013–4018, October 2016
18. Yan, Z., Duckett, T., Bellotto, N., et al.: Online learning for human classification in 3D LiDAR-based tracking. In: International Conference on Intelligent Robots and Systems (IROS) (2017)
19. Molina, S., Cielniak, G., Krajnik, T., Duckett, T.: Modelling and predicting rhythmic flow patterns in dynamics environments. In: Robotics and Autonomous Systems: Robots Working for and Among Us (2017)

# Extending Deep Neural Network Trail Navigation for Unmanned Aerial Vehicle Operation Within the Forest Canopy

Bruna G. Maciel-Pearson$^{(\boxtimes)}$, Patrice Carbonneau$^{(\boxtimes)}$, and Toby P. Breckon$^{(\boxtimes)}$

Durham University, Durham, UK
{b.g.maciel-pearson,patrice.carbonneau,toby.breckon}@durham.ac.uk

**Abstract.** Autonomous flight within a forest canopy represents a key challenge for generalised scene understanding on-board a future Unmanned Aerial Vehicle (UAV) platforms. Here we present an approach for automatic trail navigation within such an unstructured environment that successfully generalises across differing image resolutions - allowing UAV with varying sensor payload capabilities to operate equally in such challenging environmental conditions. Specifically, this work presents an optimised deep neural network architecture, capable of state-of-the-art performance across varying resolution aerial UAV imagery, that improves forest trail detection for UAV guidance even when using significantly low resolution images that are representative of low-cost search and rescue capable UAV platforms.

**Keywords:** Deep learning · Trail detection · Autonomous UAV
Unstructured environment

## 1 Introduction

Challenging activities such as Search and Rescue (SaR) missions [14], visual exploration of disaster areas [1,2] aerial reconnaissance and surveillance [6,13], assessment of forest structure or riverscape [4,10,12] have one thing common: an unstructured environment within which a Unarmed Aerial Vehicle (UAV) could be deployed for autonomous navigation. In most scenarios UAV are manually controlled and it is the pilot who defines and navigates the flight. Growing interest in solving this challenge has motivated researchers to investigate the use of Deep Neural Networks (DNN) to identify trail images for UAV navigation. Within such unstructured environments, a trail represents an existing loosely defined navigation pathway (thoroughfare) used by humans and animals that have transited the environment previously. As such, trails tend to facilitate semi-efficient point-to-point transit routes with lesser obstacle occurrence, hence making them key elements of any effective autonomous navigation in these environments. However, in order to train such a DNN for the trail navigation task, a large volume of labelled data is required, which is challenging to obtain due to the nature of the target task in hand (i.e. sub-canopy UAV operation).

Creative ways to address this data collection issue include gathering data with a head-mounted rig [7], a wide-baseline rig [15], flying the UAV into obstacles [5] and the use of simulated environments [9,11]. Under any such situation, the generalisation of the resulting DNN model remains constrained due to the fact that only one domain have being used in training.

The data gathered from multiple mounted cameras often entails a high level of discrepancy in illumination between images as we can observe from an image triplet retrieved simultaneously during data gathering of the IDSIA dataset (Fig. 1). When comparing the three images from the top row (Fig. 1), we can observe that the *forward* camera tends to capture a much clearer view of the trail, with better illumination than the sideways camera. A similar pattern is also observed on the bottom row and although varied illumination conditions may facilitate the distinction from the *left* and *right* images to the *center* it is not an accurate representation of the real environment experienced by an UAV in flight (Fig. 1). Additionally, the features characterizing a trail are typically present in the triplet set with the only discrepancy being the extent of sideways vegetation/obstacle that is found in each image (illustrated by Fig. 1). As a result, for a classification problem we observe that any DNN is essentially only learning how to identify where the UAV is positioned within the environment as opposed to finding the position of the trail (Fig. 1).

**Fig. 1.** Example from the IDSIA dataset [7] of varied luminance condition often present when using multiple mounted cameras for image data collection within the forest canopy.

In this scenario the steering decision is usually made by identifying wherever the UAV is flying too close to the vegetation/obstacles which are commonly found on the *left* or *right* side of the trail. Based on this information the UAV position can be adjusted by calculating the turning angle [7,15], which tends to lead to a new orientation (of the UAV) towards the center of the trail.

By contrast to early work of [5,7,15] that use a multiple camera approach, our work demonstrates that the same trail direction required for autonomous UAV navigation can be acquired by using imagery gathered by a single forward-facing camera (Fig. 2). This is due the fact that the center of the forward-facing camera usually shows the trail ahead, for a correctly oriented UAV relative to the trail direction (Fig. 2 - centre). Additionally, we demonstrate that a trail can be identified in unseen trail examples by training the model with data gathered across varying devices, camera resolutions and forest locations. This not only facilitates more general data gathering but also eliminates the need for synthetic data and augmentation. As result, the same model can be used by UAV with differing sensor payload capabilities.

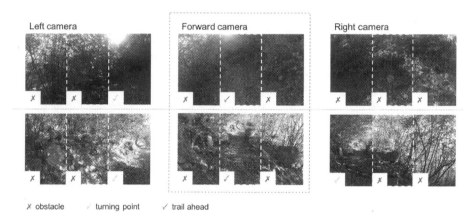

**Fig. 2.** Abstraction of three way image cropping performed on varied camera view (IDSIA dataset [7])

In summary in this work we present a method that both simplifies data gathering and allows real-time labelling of data examples for this trail navigation task, increasing generality in the resulting DNN solution. In addition we present an optimized DNN that learns the position of the trail and a public available dataset (http://dx.doi.org/10.15128/r1st74cq45z) gathered localy (Durham/UK) which allows easy reproductibility of this work.

## 2  Related Work

Scene understanding within unstructured environments with varying illumination conditions are critical for autonomous flight within the forest canopy. Significant advancement towards this goal was achieved by [7] which provided a dataset gathered by a human trail walker using a head-mounted rig with three cameras, allowing their proposed DNN architecture to identify the direction of the trail in a given view - $\{left, right, forward\}$. A similar approach is followed by [15] whereby a wide-baseline rig is used, also with three cameras, to gather data which they used to augment the dataset of [7] (denoted: IDSIA dataset). As a result, the approach presented by [15] is capable of estimating both lateral offset and trail direction. In both cases [7,15], the authors, follow the common practice of dataset augmentation, via affine image transformations, which adds extra computation without any improved performance guarantees.

Alternatively, synthetic data, from virtual environment models, could potentially replace or at least supplement hard-won real environment data [9,11,18]. However, the significant discrepancy between synthetic data and real-world data often results in models that are trained only on synthetic environment examples not being able to directly transfer this knowledge to real-world operating tasks [3,5,9,16].

Even when training a DNN using only real-world data, it must be noted that the models trained on a limited domain-specific dataset often fail to generalise successfully. In addition, since common DNN architectures require the dataset to be formed from fixed resolution images [8], models commonly fail to generalize across domains. Recent work of [17] investigated the use of reinforcement learning applied in conjunction with Q-learning and adversarial learning frameworks, which could potentially improve the generalisation of the model to different domains. Although encouraging results have been found, which were primarily achieved in a semi-structured environment (roadway), the suitability of this approach in a dynamic and complex environment such as sub forest canopy remains debatable. Instead of only focusing in improving generalisation across domains, our work also investigates the generalisation across varying resolution aerial UAV imagery, by combining a dataset of high-resolution images with a much lower resolution image dataset which better represents UAV with low payload capabilities. Furthermore, we demonstrate a simpler method to data gathering, inspired by the work of [7] that can improve the identification of trails or similar thoroughfares on unstructured environments.

## 3   Approach

Here we are primarily motivated by the three class problem presented by [7] in which an estimation of the trail direction, $\{left, right, forward\}$, is achieved by processing an image triplet of left/right/forward camera views via a DNN. In contrast to [7,15], our approach uses only a single forward facing camera view which is more representative of an operational UAV scenario (i.e. a single forward facing camera; minimal size, weight and power). This image view is then itself cropped into $\{left, right, forward\}$ which can be labelled for trail presence/absence (Fig. 2).

Using the architecture of [7] (illustrated in Fig. 3), we evaluate varying image resolution, the use of additional data augmentation (DA) and activation function $(tanh()/ReLU())$. As illustrated in Fig. 3 the network is composed of 10 layers that are subdivided into four convolution and four pooling layers, followed by a fully connected layer and a softmax layer. The result of each convolution layer

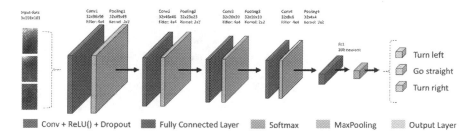

**Fig. 3.** An outline of our DNN architecture - based on [7]

is fed into a maximum pooling layer. A final *softmax* layer outputs maps to an associated probability for our three class labels {*left, center, right*} from which navigation decisions are then made.

The DNN training uses a gradient descent optimiser, random weight initialisation with zero node biases and is performed over 90 epochs with a 0.05 reduction in learning rate per epoch (decay rate: 0.95). For both training and testing we use the high-resolution (752 × 480) IDSIA dataset (from [7]; denoted H in results of Table 1) and a low-resolution (320 × 240) Urpeth Burn (UB) dataset, gathered locally (County Durham, UK; denoted L in results of Table 1). For training 36,078 high-resolution and 32,017 low-resolution image were used, while for testing 12,252 high-resolution and 5,152 low-resolutions images were used. All DNN training is performed on a Nvidia 1060 GPU.

Further data augmentation (mirror, translation & rotation) was performed on a copy of this original dataset, resulting in a total data set size of 72,135 high-resolution image. For simplicity of reporting, we define *NA* as non-augmented data obtained results and *DA* as data augmented obtained results (Table 1).

Our approach allows image labelling to be performed in automatically since the retrieved image, captured facing forward with the trail in the centre, is simply cropped in 3 equal sizes; for each side, a label is associated as follow: *C* - center (trail), *L* - left (no trail) and *R* - right (no trail).

Our DNN model thus learns the signature of a trail associated to class *C* and non-trail associated to classes *L* and *R*. These class labels are returned based on the contents of the left, right or center image crop independently of its actual origin from the full sized image. As a result, the presence of class *C* within the image can be directly correlated to trail presence (Fig. 4).

Based on the output certainty from the final *softmax* layer in the DNN for class *C*, the presence of a trail in each of the {*left, right, center*} cropped image regions can be determined facilitating a second labelling for trail presence/absence to be performed. As a result we arrive at a set of six possible classes {$L - TF, L - NT, R - TF, R - NT, C - TF, C - NT$} for our original set of image regions, {*left, right, centre*} with either a Trail Found (TF) or No Trail (NT) label. Within our exploratory formulation, we envisage the navigation decision being taken based on the direction (image region) with the highest level of confidence for trail presence (TF in Fig. 4).

**Fig. 4.** Illustration of level of confidence outputed by the DNN for each image crop.

## 4  Results

Our experimental results are divided into three sets:- (1) image triplet approach of [7] with differing activation functions ($tanh()/ReLU()$ - Table 1, upper two divisions), (2) our proposed approach (single forward view image, split into three views - Table 1, middle division, bold) and (3) the impact of high/low/varied image resolutions on performance (Table 1, lower division). Due to the variety of resolution and demographic distribution in the dataset, a 10-fold cross validation was performed across the range of proposed methods (Table 1). The testing dataset (unseen data) was processed by each model, generated during training and its performance can be observed in the blox plot Fig. 5, which includes median values and outliers for each fold.

**Table 1.** Results performance for testing in high ($H$) and low ($L$) image dataset combinations, computed for each class ($C$ - Center, $R$ - Right, $L$ - Left)

| Approach | DA | Activation function | Training | Testing | Mean accuracy ($\pm std$) | Precision | | | Recall | | | F1 | | |
|---|---|---|---|---|---|---|---|---|---|---|---|---|---|---|
| | | | | | | C | R | L | C | R | L | C | R | L |
| Giusti et al. [7] | ✓ | tanh() | H | H | 0.46 (±0.06) | 0.50 | 0.53 | 0.38 | 0.98 | 0.04 | 0.37 | 0.67 | 0.07 | 0.38 |
| Giusti et al. [7] | ✗ | tanh() | H | H | 0.73 (±0.08) | 0.97 | 0.72 | 0.62 | 0.62 | 0.77 | 0.81 | 0.76 | 0.74 | 0.70 |
| Giusti et al. [7] | ✓ | ReLU() | H | H | 0.40 (±0.06) | 0.44 | 0.89 | 0.29 | 0.99 | 0.03 | 0.20 | 0.41 | 0.60 | 0.06 |
| Giusti et al. [7] | ✗ | ReLU() | H | H | 0.66 (±0.07) | 0.97 | 0.69 | 0.54 | 0.49 | 0.69 | 0.82 | 0.65 | 0.69 | 0.66 |
| **Our approach** | ✓ | **ReLU()** | **H** | **H** | **0.93(±0.09)** | **0.99** | **0.90** | **0.94** | **0.86** | **0.98** | **0.96** | **0.92** | **0.94** | **0.96** |
| **Our approach** | ✗ | **ReLU()** | **H** | **H** | **0.92(±0.09)** | **0.97** | **0.88** | **0.93** | **0.83** | **0.98** | **0.97** | **0.89** | **0.93** | **0.96** |
| High resolution | ✗ | ReLU() | H | L | 0.51 (±0.09) | 0.61 | 0.49 | 0.49 | 0.05 | 0.73 | 0.70 | 0.09 | 0.59 | 0.57 |
| Low resolution | ✗ | ReLU() | L | L | 0.73 (±0.06) | 0.80 | 0.74 | 0.66 | 0.57 | 0.77 | 0.82 | 0.67 | 0.76 | 0.73 |
| Varied resolutions | ✗ | ReLU() | H+L | L | 0.74 (±0.06) | 0.80 | 0.76 | 0.67 | 0.60 | 0.78 | 0.82 | 0.68 | 0.77 | 0.74 |
| **Varied resolutions** | ✗ | **ReLU()** | **H+L** | **H** | **0.93(±0.02)** | **0.97** | **0.91** | **0.91** | **0.84** | **0.97** | **0.98** | **0.90** | **0.94** | **0.94** |

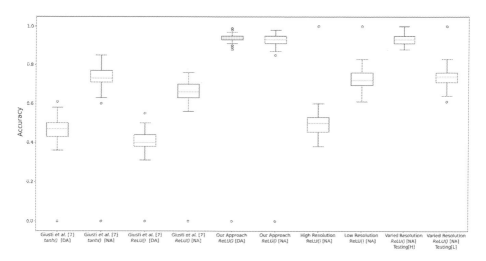

**Fig. 5.** Comparison of performance from the highest accuracy model for each approach, based on 10-fold cross validation.

Overall we see what the use of the *ReLU()* activation outperforms *tanh()* and our approach gives high levels of mean accuracy without the need for data augmentation outperforming the prior reported results in [7] (*in fact no significant improvement was achieved by data augmentation*).

Although our approach fails to generalise when trained with high-resolution images on to low resolution images, it achieves 93% mean accuracy when low-resolution images are added to the training dataset and achieves 73% mean accuracy for training and testing on low-resolution images only (Table 1, lower division).

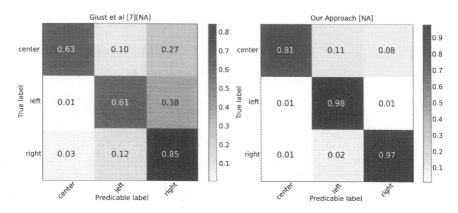

**Fig. 6.** Comparison of performance of Giust et al. [7] [NA] (left) versus when our approach [NA] (right).

Further analyse of the testing dataset (Table 1) also highlights that augmenting the data, specifically for this scenario, does not improve the classification of the view direction. By looking at the distribution of each approach (Fig. 5) we can observe that combining different image resolutions during training is advantageous regardless of the resolution of the testing image.

When analysing the confusion matrix (Fig. 6 - left) showing the test results derived from a model trained using Giusti et al. [7] approach, we can observe that since each frame usually contains both trail and vegetation, it is harder for the model to correct distinguish between the classes. In contrast the model trained using our approach (Fig. 6 - right) can easily classify each side.

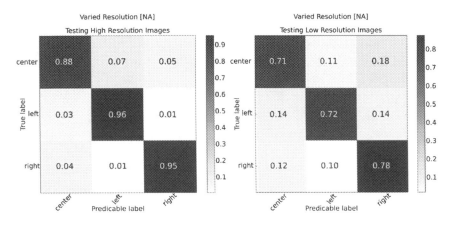

**Fig. 7.** Comparison of how our approach [NA] classifies images with low (right) and high (left) resolution.

Regardless of the image resolution in the testing dataset, the same pattern can be observed when comparing the confusion matrix (Fig. 7) of a model trained with a dataset containing split images of varied resolution.

These findings can be also observed on the qualitative results presented on Figs. 8 and 9, whereby we demonstrate a second labelling for tail presence/absence. Currently we can not quantify the accuracy of this extended labelling without manually checking each one. Due to that the qualitative results shown on Figs. 8 and 9 are based on a hand picked selection of the most challenging scenarios from the testing dataset. These scenarios are then evaluated by different models and the level of accuracy is compared accordingly.

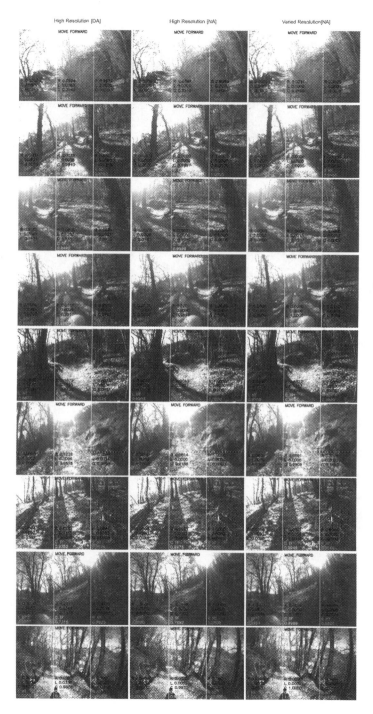

**Fig. 8.** Comparison of performance of different models when tested on high resolution images (IDSIA dataset [7]).

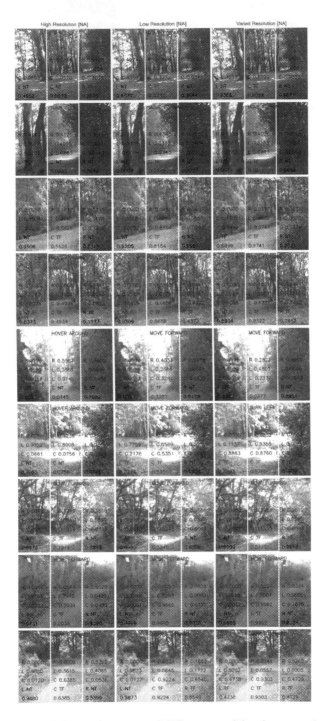

**Fig. 9.** Comparison of the performance of different models when tested on low resolution images.

# 5    Conclusion

In this paper, we present an alternative method to gather and process UAV imagery that improves the level of accuracy for trail navigation under forest canopy based on the use of a single forward facing camera view instead of the multiple camera approach of [7, 15]. Our approach also performs well across varying image resolutions and increases the capability of low-cost UAV platforms with limited payload capacity. Future work will include additional aspects of UAV perception and control targeting end-to-end autonomy across this and other challenging operating environments.

# References

1. Apvrille, L., Tanzi, T., Dugelay, J.L.: Autonomous drones for assisting rescue services within the context of natural disasters. In: General Assembly and Scientific Symposium, pp. 1–4. IEEE (2014)
2. Câmara, D.: Cavalry to the rescue: drones fleet to help rescuers operations over disasters scenarios. In: Conference on Antenna Measurements & Applications, pp. 1–4. IEEE (2014)
3. Christiano, P., et al.: Transfer from simulation to real world through learning deep inverse dynamics model. arXiv preprint arXiv:1610.03518 (2016)
4. Dietrich, J.T.: Riverscape mapping with helicopter-based structure-from-motion photogrammetry. Geomorphology **252**, 144–157 (2016)
5. Gandhi, D., Pinto, L., Gupta, A.: Learning to fly by crashing. arXiv preprint arXiv:1704.05588 (2017)
6. Gaszczak, A., Breckon, T.P., Han, J.: Real-time people and vehicle detection from UAV imagery. In: Intelligent Robots and Computer Vision XXVIII: Algorithms and Techniques, vol. 7878, pp. 78780B. International Society for Optics and Photonics (2011)
7. Giusti, A., et al.: A machine learning approach to visual perception of forest trails for mobile robots. IEEE Robot. Autom. Lett. **1**(2), 661–667 (2016)
8. He, K., Zhang, X., Ren, S., Sun, J.: Spatial pyramid pooling in deep convolutional networks for visual recognition. In: Fleet, D., Pajdla, T., Schiele, B., Tuytelaars, T. (eds.) ECCV 2014. LNCS, vol. 8691, pp. 346–361. Springer, Cham (2014). https://doi.org/10.1007/978-3-319-10578-9_23
9. Kelchtermans, K., Tuytelaars, T.: How hard is it to cross the room?-training (recurrent) neural networks to steer a UAV. arXiv preprint arXiv:1702.07600 (2017)
10. Koh, L.P., Wich, S.A.: Dawn of drone ecology: low-cost autonomous aerial vehicles for conservation. Trop. Conserv. Sci. **5**(2), 121–132 (2012)
11. Mueller, M., Casser, V., Smith, N., Ghanem, B.: Teaching UAV to race using UE4Sim. arXiv preprint arXiv:1708.05884 (2017)
12. Paneque-Gálvez, J., McCall, M.K., Napoletano, B.M., Wich, S.A., Koh, L.P.: Small drones for community-based forest monitoring: an assessment of their feasibility and potential in tropical areas. Forests **5**(6), 1481–1507 (2014)
13. Puri, A.: A survey of unmanned aerial vehicles (UAV) for traffic surveillance. Department of computer science and engineering, University of South Florida, pp. 1–29 (2005)

14. Rémy, G., Senouci, S.-M., Jan, F., Gourhant, Y.: Sar drones: drones for advanced search and rescue missions. Journées Nationales des Communications dans les Transports **1**, 1–3 (2013)
15. Smolyanskiy, N., Kamenev, A., Smith, J., Birchfield, S.: Toward low-flying autonomous MAV trail navigation using deep neural networks for environmental awareness. In: 2017 IEEE/RSJ International Conference on Intelligent Robots and Systems (IROS), Vancouver, BC, pp. 4241–4247 (2017)
16. Tai, L., Liu, M.: Deep-learning in mobile robotics-from perception to control systems: a survey on why and why not. arXiv preprint arXiv:1612.07139 (2016)
17. Yoo J, Hong Y, Yoon S.: Autonomous UAV navigation with domain adaptation. arXiv preprint arXiv:1712.03742 (2017)
18. Zhang, T., Kahn, G., Levine, S., Abbeel, P.: Learning deep control policies for autonomous aerial vehicles with MPC-guided policy search. In: 2016 International Conference on Robotics and Automation 2016, pp. 528–535. IEEE (2016)

# Virtual Environment for Training Autonomous Vehicles

Jerome Leudet[1,2], Tommi Mikkonen[1], François Christophe[1(✉)], and Tomi Männistö[1]

[1] Department of Computer Science, University of Helsinki,
Gustaf Hällströmin katu 2b, Helsinki, Finland
{tommi.mikkonen,francois.christophe,tomi.mannisto}@helsinki.fi
[2] AILiveSim, Helsinki, Finland
jerome.leudet@AILiveSim.com
http://www.ailivesim.com

**Abstract.** Driver assistance and semi-autonomous features are regularly added to commercial vehicles with two key stakes: collecting data for training self-driving algorithms, and using these vehicles as testbeds for these algorithms. Due to the nature of algorithms used in autonomous vehicles, their behavior in unknown situation is not fully predictable. This calls for extensive testing. In this paper, we propose to use a virtual environment for both testing algorithms for autonomous vehicles and acquiring simulated data for their training. The benefit of this environment is to able to train algorithms with realistic simulated sensor data before their deployment in real life. To this end, the proposed virtual environment has the capacity to generate similar data than real sensors (e.g. cameras, LiDar, ...). After reviewing state-of-the-art techniques and datasets available for the automotive industry, we identify that dynamic data generated on-demand is needed to improve the current results in training autonomous vehicles. Our proposition describes the benefits a virtual environment brings in improving the development, quality and confidence in the algorithms.

**Keywords:** Virtual reality · Simulators · Sensor data synthesis
Game physics engine · Machine vision · Neural networks · Datasets

## 1 Introduction

The race towards self-driving vehicles is creating a momentum in the transportation industry as bigger players on this market achieve important milestones [15]. For instance, automatic driver assistants are already in production, and fully autonomous vehicles are being tested on the roads in several countries. SAE, an association developing standards (http://www.sae.org/), has defined different levels of driver assistance [20], the fifth being fully autonomous driving. It

---

T. Männistö—This article was written under the funding of TEKES/DIMECC program with the project Design for Value (D4V).

© Springer International Publishing AG, part of Springer Nature 2018
M. Giuliani et al. (Eds.): TAROS 2018, LNAI 10965, pp. 159–169, 2018.
https://doi.org/10.1007/978-3-319-96728-8_14

is assumed that achieving this level could result in safer roads [22], better efficiency and less energy consumption thanks to the change in usage of personal cars [4,16]. However, this remains to be seen, as autonomous vehicles could also increase the overall traffic resulting in higher global energy consumption. Anyhow, it is certain that this technology will transform deeply the means of transportation.

However, manufacturers are still facing various safety and legal concerns [1], as legislation is being introduced to allow autonomous vehicles. The ISO 26262 [25] addresses the need for an international standard that promotes testing of safety critical components. A critical goal of this standard it to guarantee the required quality of the vehicles and its subsequent system updates. New approaches are needed to answer this question and we address it here with the use of a simulation environment to help in developing and testing autonomous vehicles. We propose an interactive simulation environment where the behaviour of autonomous vehicles can be simulated while virtual sensors are used to emulate real input data. Our approach consists of giving the possibility to build a virtual twin of software used in autonomous vehicles and also the possibility to generate on-demand data that can be used to train, test, or develop autonomous systems. With this approach, we analyze the difference between developing such simulation environment and directly working on the development of the real autonomous system. What are the necessary features from such environment in order to make the development process shorter but also increase the performance of algorithms. In short, what makes it worth the effort?

This paper proceeds as follows. After reviewing the state-of-the-art techniques available to the automotive industry, we identify the need for a simulation environment and the production of synthetic data generated on-demand. Our proposition describes the benefits of a simulation environment, i.e. improving development, quality and confidence in the algorithms.

## 2   Machine Vision Used for Autonomous Vehicles

Techniques used to implement both driver assists and autopilots have relied on Computer Vision [9]. Traditionally, hand-crafted analytic techniques to detect specific features in the image have been used, but more recently machine learning with deep convolutional neural networks have taken a crucial role in Computer Vision. Neural Networks are usually trained on a large amount of data. The quality of the data used to train the algorithms is of critical importance and also the limiting factor of the current methods [10]. Data must provide enough diversity [17] to prevent the algorithm from over-fitting to the specific data used during training. When using supervised learning, the dataset must also provide a ground truth for part of the data. For example it can take the form of labels or pixel level segmentation [12,21]. Depending on the way they are created, datasets all have biases [26] that result in practical limitations.

**How Machine Vision Techniques have Improved.** When reviewing the history of neural networks, improving the results at some tasks either comes from a structural change in the network architecture, an improvement in the training mechanism, or improvements in the training data that is used to tune the parameters of the network. For example looking at results of classification of images from Imagenet, to improve from AlexNet [12], the VGG resulted from a simplification of the network reducing the number of parameter, allowing the network to be simpler to train while increasing the number of layers [21]. Furthermore, ResNet and GoogLeNet used tricks to make very deep network training possible. GoogLeNet introduced the inception module [24] that included $1 \times 1$ convolution to reduce the dimensionality, and ResNet created Residual blocks that allowed for the input to go through the network [8]. In practice, architectures trained on bigger dataset exhibit better performance. In many cases, techniques of dataset augmentation are used to create more data by altering the existing data. Large networks have a high entropic capacity, and therefore they will require a large amount of data to avoid over-fitting, or, in other words, the situation that takes place when the network has learned all the training data and looses the ability to generalize to new data. To train on smaller datasets, regularization techniques like Dropout [23] have been proposed. Yet training takes a long time even on clusters of GPUs, and therefore improving the speed of convergence of the networks is also an active area of research. Techniques like FreezeOut [2], or Self-Normalizing Neural Networks [11] proposed a way to avoid vanishing or exploding gradients by choosing a specific activation function.

**Need for Datasets Improvement.** To create datasets for autonomous vehicles, we can observe a lot of empirical approaches where a car equipped with a set of plausible sensors is driving through real-life situations. They will not guarantee an optimal distribution on the situations encountered, and, in particular, they will not guarantee the dataset to be balanced.

Capturing sufficient diversity in a dataset is a challenge. Therefore, we often see datasets that are restricted to a selected subset of cases, each dataset tackling one small part of the whole set of possible environments and conditions: for example, KITTY [7] and CityScapes [5] are collected only in Germany, or Oxford Dataset [14] is collected only in Oxford, meaning that those examples are geographically restricted. Because of the amount of human labor required for labeling data, creative approaches have been tried, such as crowd sourcing, gamification, semi-supervised learning, or per-label payments using Mechanical Turk, i.e. an online crowdsourcing marketplace platform [27]. This leads to variable level of quality in labeled data. Some datasets are used by different teams to benchmark and compare results, but they are also tailored for specific problems. If gathering a dataset is hard, it might possibly limit or delay the study of new idea that would require a new dataset.

To circumvent the biases of datasets, Multi-Domain Road Scene Semantic Segmentation proposes to train the algorithms using six different datasets and two more to test their capacity to generalize [19]. This is technically cumbersome, because each dataset presents the data with its own format and uses a different subset of sensors, causing a significant overhead for anyone wanting to use a dataset for the first time. The absence of standards is justified by the wide variety of applications, sensors and teams, but makes it difficult to re-use. Different tasks will require different types of ground truth to train upon. Each dataset will only provide a fixed set of ground truth information, thus restricting the use of this dataset to certain tasks. So teams might have to create new datasets because none of the existing ones could provide the ground truth information that suits their needs.

**Datasets from Synthetic Data.** An example of data generated from a virtual environment is the SYNTHIA dataset. SYNTHIA is a dataset gathered from a simulator [17], a virtual city built with the Unity game engine. The simulator can generate additional information needed for supervised learning automatically, without any human manual labeling. A specific dataset was created, but the simulator itself has not been released at the time of writing this paper.

Virtual data has been used to train neural networks at segmentation tasks using well-known NN architectures [18], and the results were benchmarked against 4 different datasets (Kitti, CamVid, U-labelMe, and CBCL) [3,7,10,13]. These reports conclude that augmenting the dataset with synthetic images from SYNTHIA would consistently improve performances of the architecture on the benchmark. According to [10], a training approach only based on simulation is also viable for the classification of real world images.

**Learning Scenarios.** The study in [6] shows how the use of virtual reality decreases the number of real-world samples. This study also develops an approach that gradually increases the fidelity simulation allowing the learning agent to learn quicker on the lowest simulation fidelity levels, while still finding near-optimal policies in a physical robot domain with fewer expensive real-world samples than previous transfer approaches or learning without simulators.

Even looking outside supervised learning where the ground truth is always accessible and used to tune the network prediction, reinforcement techniques are applied in [28] learning and imitating learning and proposed an approach that they have tested in the TORCS simulator [3]. A neural network to switch between the primary trained policy and a reference safe policy was trained in this paper, allowing the data collection phase to train on progressively difficult situations. Their proposed network effectively creates an automatic curriculum and that drastically speeds up the convergence of the driving network.

# 3 Proposed Virtual Environment

In this section, we present the development of our virtual environment for simulating autonomous driving algorithms in specific situations. This environment is based on the unreal engine[1] and offers detailed control on the content of the environment and the situations that are simulated. An ego vehicle can be equipped with virtual sensors and its control commands can be simulated. In this specific case, we considered autonomous car driving but the same solution could be used for training and testing other autonomous systems too (e.g. ships,

---

[1] https://www.unrealengine.com/.

drones, robots). The demonstration presented in this section is also available as video[2]. The following sub-sections presents an overview of the benefits in using this environment.

**Augmenting Datasets with Synthetic Data.** The ability to generate an arbitrary number of training samples allows to train a neural net up to its full potential without being limited by the size of the dataset. For example, the top performing implementations on KITTI or CityScapes could be improved by augmenting them with more images from our proposed simulator. In Fig. 1 we have configured multiple cameras with different specs attached to the vehicle. We have one wide angle camera on the rooftop, two cameras on the front bumper and two fisheye cameras on the rear mirror.

**Fig. 1.** Different viewpoints from cameras embedded in the virtual autonomous car

**Possibility to Create Datasets on Demand.** Generating training data on demand from a virtual environment brings the significant advantage of not having to define parameters of configuration in advance. This can be used to replicate real life configurations or create new configuration with sensors that might not be available in real life. For example the sensors with chosen specs might not be available at hand or might not yet be commercially available yet. Figure 2. Having control over sensors specs also enables co-designing algorithms together with the needed amount and quality of input sensors for optimal results.

**Crafting Ground Truth Based on Parameters.** Ground-truth information represents meta data about what the sensor data captures, e.g. labels of objects contained in a picture represent a ground truth for classifying these pictures according to what they contain. For example, ground-truth can be used to measure the accuracy of the algorithms that analyze sensor data, or to train neural

---

[2] https://youtu.be/dUX-A6sag-s.

**Fig. 2.** Production of data on-demand from sensors: Lidar, GNSS, IMU

networks using regression. Having access to the internal representation of the world in the game engine allows us to craft the ground truth for the purpose of the problem we are currently trying to solve. For example, we can extract bounding boxes out of objects of a specified class, or retain the information about what every pixel is representing. This information can be collected for each sensor or at a more abstract level represent the state of the world. This systematic approach to ground truth is much more reliable than manually annotating images, as even partially or totally obstructed objects are known. As can be seen from Fig. 3, the ground truth does not have to be limited to the visibility, and we can collect any other information that is available in the world state representation in the game. For example, we can extract information about the intent or state of different actors in the scene that would be very hard to get out of data captured in real life.

**Fig. 3.** Examples of ground truth configurations

## 4   Lessons Learned from Using a Virtual Environment

As identified from our background study, there is a clear need for improving datasets used for training autonomous vehicles. In this section, we analyze the advantages and limitations of our proposed virtual environment in covering this need. First, the use of a virtual environment presents a clear relevance in improving the quality of data and balancing datasets to avoid over-fitting. Second, a question about trade-off between developing a "dummy" model and the development of an actual virtual twin of an autonomous vehicle emerged when developing this environment. While the former, fast to implement, is used to collect data by driving a predefined path, the later presents more reactivity to the dynamic events happening in the environment but takes a longer time to develop. Third, another aspect relevant to virtual environment is related to testing capability. We develop these three points further in the corresponding sub-sections.

**Balanced Datasets and Quantity of Data.** When training neural networks with unbalanced datasets, one option is to artificially augment the dataset either by altering existing images or by adding completely new images. This is usually done by adjusting luminosity or applying distortion on the existing real-life images. With parametric simulation, we can create plausible variations of the images that are sampled, thus making the augmentation operation much more meaningful than classic methods. We can modify environmental parameters, collect images at a different time of day, on different seasons, with different weather as presented in Fig. 4. We can also change the sensor that is used to collect the data and its position in the world. By procedurally generating new environments, we can even create scenes that meet a set of constraints but always have significant variation in them.

**Fig. 4.** Various configurations for types of vehicles, weather and time of the day

To our knowledge, there are no metrics to assess the quality of a dataset to perform a given task. However, we expect that, in order to meet the demanding ISO 26262, a test set will have to include a wide variety of cases. There are cases that are particularly difficult to reproduce in real life, yet that can lead to fatal accidents. Cases that would endanger the safety or integrity of poeple involved for example. Yet testing those cases would be important as doing the right things in those cases can have a direct impact on human lives. Those cases are sparse in datasets captured in real life just because they are rare. But we can procedurally create multiple variations on demand in the simulation. This would allow us to create more instances of test cases that are identified as not sufficiently represented.

The main issue with data produced from virtual environments relies on the question of balancing between practicality and realism. Synthetic data needs to be comparable to data from real life but only to a degree that allows generalization from algorithms, e.g. recognizing between different roadsigns based on their shapes. This issue affects the amount of time spend to improve the quality of objects and textures in the environment. With the current environments, it is possible to achieve high quality images and sensor data, however the aspect of practicality needs to be tested during the execution of machine vision algorithms, in order to produce content at the right level of quality.

**Improve Development Iteration Time.** We have seen in background study that some of the architectures currently used in machine vision tasks are composite solutions reusing other networks. The total training of all the networks is a time consuming task. Luckily, networks can be retrained from previous generations if needed, or sub-networks can be trained in isolation to simplify the training and to limit it to the subsystem that is believed to be faulty. The benefit of such approach is to be able to launch system directly and have fast feedback form users. However, this also implies a development process where testing is disconnected from training and recalls for retraining are necessary. In order to tackle this issue, simulation models could be used for testing networks early during training phases.

Simplifying the simulation models at first could force the learning of important features first, and then learn to ignore details when gradually increasing the level of realism of the data presented. For example, we can decide to first learn in sunny conditions on clean environments, and then add other weather conditions, seasons and light. We could also go further and choose a strategy using low level of details in the object representation or in the textures used. Our intuition is that it could allow for better generalization and require less training sample overall thus saving some time in the development.

**Tests Using Dynamic Simulation.** In addition, an important lesson learned during the development of this environment is that the virtual environment should give the possibility to deploy software tested from the virtual twin into the real system without effort. This is a critical capability the training in the simulation is irrelevant. Several solutions can be used. A domain adaptation step can be added to transfer what has been learned in the virtual world to the real world. Generative or style transfer algorithms could be used to make the data from virtual sensors look more like the real data.

## 5    Conclusions

In this paper we proposed the use of a virtual environment integrated in the training of software for autonomous vehicles. This integration has the principal benefits of giving the possibility to test and validate early the performance of software during the design of an autonomous system, and the possibility to procedurally generate data on demand for the training of these systems. From a proof-of-concept, we conclude that a virtual environment has three main benefits. First, it helps to balance datasets by providing the specific data they are missing, like samples from critical situations. Current game engines make it possible to achieve a sufficient level of realism, while generating a large amount variations in time of day, season or level and amount of detail. Second, when integrated in the early development phases, the number of development iterations should decrease as the quality of simulation models and autonomous software increases. Third, such environment provides a mean to systematically test autonomous driving software with the use of dynamic simulations. As a limitation, such environment requires to be capable of deploying the model of the virtual twin into the real system in order to increase the efficiency of the development process of such autonomous system. Finally, using simulators for testing and validating decisions of autonomous vehicles seems like a sensible step towards making those systems more performant and might contribute to make them safer when driving amongst us, so we will continue to study those topics further.

# References

1. Ackerman, E., Pratt, G.: Toyota's Gill Pratt on Self-Driving Cars and the Reality of Full Autonomy. IEEE Spectrum (2017)
2. Brock, A., Lim, T., Ritchie, J.M., Weston, N.: FreezeOut: accelerate training by progressively freezing layers (2017)
3. Brostow, G.J., Fauqueur, J., Cipolla, R.: Semantic object classes in video: a high-definition ground truth database. Pattern Recogn. Lett. **30**(2), 88–97 (2009)
4. Contestabile, M., Alajaji, M., Almubarak, B.: Will current electric vehicle policy lead to cost-effective electrification of passenger car transport? Energy Policy **110**, 20–30 (2017)
5. Cordts, M., Omran, M., Ramos, S., Rehfeld, T., Enzweiler, M., Benenson, R., Franke, U., Roth, S., Schiele, B.: The Cityscapes dataset for semantic urban scene understanding. In: CVPR, pp. 3213–3223 (2016)
6. Cutler, M., Walsh, T.J., How, J.P.: Real-world reinforcement learning via multifidelity simulators. IEEE Trans. Robot. **31**(3), 655–671 (2015)
7. Geiger, A., Lenz, P., Stiller, C., Urtasun, R.: Vision meets robotics: the KITTI dataset. Int. J. Robot. Res. **32**(11), 1231–1237 (2013)
8. He, K., Zhang, X., Ren, S., Sun, J.: Deep residual learning for image recognition. Arxiv.Org **7**(3), 171–180 (2015)
9. Janai, J., Güney, F., Behl, A., Geiger, A.: Computer vision for autonomous vehicles: problems, datasets and state-of-the-art (2017)
10. Johnson-Roberson, M., Barto, C., Mehta, R., Sridhar, S.N., Rosaen, K., Vasudevan, R.: Driving in the matrix: can virtual worlds replace human-generated annotations for real world tasks? (2016)
11. Klambauer, G., Unterthiner, T., Mayr, A., Hochreiter, S.: Self-Normalizing Neural Networks (2017)
12. Krizhevsky, A., Sutskever, I., Hinton, G.E.: ImageNet classification with deep convolutional neural networks. In: Advances in Neural Information Processing Systems, pp. 1–9 (2012)
13. Leibo, J.Z., Liao, Q., Poggio, T.: Subtasks of unconstrained face recognition. In: International Joint Conference on Computer Vision Theory and Applications, pp. 1–9 (2013)
14. Maddern, W., Pascoe, G., Linegar, C., Newman, P.: 1 year, 1000 km: the Oxford Robotcar dataset. Int. J. Robot. Res. **36**, 3–15 (2016)
15. Muoio, D.: These 19 companies are racing to build self-driving cars in the next 5 years. Business Insider Nordic (2017)
16. Palmer, K., Tate, J.E., Wadud, Z., Nellthorp, J.: Total cost of ownership and market share for hybrid and electric vehicles in the UK, US and Japan. Appl. Energy **209**, 108–119 (2018)
17. Ros, G., Sellart, L., Materzynska, J., Vazquez, D., Lopez, A.M.: The SYNTHIA dataset: a large collection of synthetic images for semantic segmentation of urban scenes (2016)

18. Ros, G., Sellart, L., Materzynska, J., Vazquez, D., Lopez, A.M.: The SYNTHIA dataset: a large collection of synthetic images for semantic segmentation of urban scenes. In: 2016 IEEE Conference on Computer Vision and Pattern Recognition (CVPR), pp. 3234–3243. IEEE (2016)
19. Ros, G., Stent, S., Alcantarilla, P.F., Watanabe, T.: Training constrained deconvolutional networks for road scene semantic segmentation. In: IEEE Conference on Computer Vision and Pattern Recognition (2016)
20. SAE: Taxonomy and definitions for terms related to driving automation systems for on-road motor vehicles. Glob. Ground Veh. Stand. (J3016), 30 (2016)
21. Simonyan, K., Zisserman, A.: Very deep convolutional networks for large-scale image recognition. In: International Conference on Learning Representations (ICRL), pp. 1–14 (2015)
22. Singh, S.: Critical reasons for crashes investigated in the national motor vehicle crash causation survey. Technical report, Department of Transportation - NHTSAs National Center for Statistics and Analysis, Washington, DC, USA (2015)
23. Srivastava, N., Hinton, G., Krizhevsky, A., Sutskever, I., Salakhutdinov, R.: Dropout: a simple way to prevent neural networks from overfitting. J. Mach. Learn. Res. **15**, 1929–1958 (2014)
24. Szegedy, C., Liu, W., Jia, Y., Sermanet, P., Reed, S., Anguelov, D., Erhan, D., Vanhoucke, V., Rabinovich, A.: Going deeper with convolutions. In: 2015 IEEE Conference on Computer Vision and Pattern Recognition (CVPR), pp. 1–9. IEEE (2015)
25. Technical Committee ISO/TC 22: ISO1:2011(en), Road vehicles Functional safety Part 1: Vocabulary (2011)
26. Torralba, A., Efros, A.A.: Unbiased look at dataset bias. In: Proceedings of the IEEE Computer Society Conference on Computer Vision and Pattern Recognition, pp. 1521–1528 (2011)
27. Von Ahn, L., Liu, R., Blum, M.: Peekaboom: a game for locating objects in images. In: Proceedings of the SIGCHI conference on Human Factors in computing systems - CHI 2006, p. 55 (2006)
28. Zhang, J., Cho, K.: Query-efficient imitation learning for end-to-end autonomous driving (2016)

# Comparing Model-Based and Data-Driven Controllers for an Autonomous Vehicle Task

Erwin Jose Lopez Pulgarin[1]($\boxtimes$)(iD), Tugrul Irmak[1], Joel Variath Paul[1],
Arisara Meekul[1], Guido Herrmann[1]($\boxtimes$)(iD), and Ute Leonards[2]($\boxtimes$)(iD)

[1] Mechanical Engineering, University of Bristol, Bristol, UK
{erwin.lopez,g.herrmann}@bristol.ac.uk
[2] Experimental Psychology, University of Bristol, Bristol, UK
ute.leonards@bristol.ac.uk

**Abstract.** The advent of autonomous vehicles comes with many questions from an ethical and technological point of view. The need for high performing controllers, which show transparency and predictability is crucial to generate trust in such systems. Popular data-driven, black box-like approaches such as deep learning and reinforcement learning are used more and more in robotics due to their ability to process large amounts of information, with outstanding performance, but raising concerns about their transparency and predictability. Model-based control approaches are still a reliable and predictable alternative, used extensively in industry but with restrictions of their own. Which of these approaches is preferable is difficult to assess as they are rarely directly compared with each other for the same task, especially for autonomous vehicles. Here we compare two popular approaches for control synthesis, model-based control i.e. Model Predictive Controller (MPC), and data-driven control i.e. Reinforcement Learning (RL) for a lane keeping task with speed limit for an autonomous vehicle; controllers were to take control after a human driver had departed lanes or gone above the speed limit. We report the differences between both control approaches from analysis, architecture, synthesis, tuning and deployment and compare performance, taking overall benefits and difficulties of each control approach into account.

## 1 Introduction

Current trends in automotive driver-assist systems indicate an increase in vehicle autonomy, making cars more like robots. Even when considering current robotics standards for personal robots like ISO 13482:2014 [7], semi-autonomous and autonomous vehicles fall into the categories of Person Carrier Robots.

Autonomous and semi-autonomous vehicles are areas of relevant commercial interest, with a multitude of ethical and technical challenges yet to be solved. One issue that remains unsolved is how to create controllers that integrate a large amount of heterogeneous sensor data (e.g. cameras, range sensors, vehicle

© Springer International Publishing AG, part of Springer Nature 2018
M. Giuliani et al. (Eds.): TAROS 2018, LNAI 10965, pp. 170–182, 2018.
https://doi.org/10.1007/978-3-319-96728-8_15

sensors and driver sensors) and that are able to deal with highly complex and changing environments.

A large variety of control algorithms and approaches has been proposed to solve this problem in both real and simulated environments [12,18,21]. We can divide them into two categories, model based and data-driven. The former category belongs to a classical approach for industrial control; it uses a plant model and represents a mathematical description of the dynamics surrounding the system with a controller shaping those dynamics to meet a set of predefined requirements. The latter is based on an approach from computer science inspired by the human process of learning, subsequent decisions [6] and actions, i.e. the current artificial intelligence paradigm; available measurements or estimations are used to create a relation between the way we can manipulate the system (actions) and its measurements (states) by rewarding or punishing certain behaviours, with limited to no knowledge about the system itself.

In the domain of autonomous and semi-autonomous systems, some of the prominent algorithms used in each category are Model Predictive Control (MPC) [9,14] for the model-based and Reinforcement Learning [2,17] by actor-critic algorithms like Deep Deterministic Policy Gradients (DDPG) for the data-driven models.

Both approaches have their own benefits and hindrances during the possible stages of control design (i.e. analysis, architecture design, synthesis, tuning and deployment), requiring sets of skills and resources (e.g. computational time); yet to the best of our knowledge, they have never been directly compared for a set of identical tasks related to autonomous vehicles. Automatic control of the speed of a vehicle (i.e. cruise control) and maintaining a vehicle in the centre of the lane (i.e. lane keeping) are typical common tasks for autonomous vehicles and subsequent advanced driver assistance systems (ADAS). For automatic control systems, it is often the case that initialisation time is prohibitively long as in the range of seconds. For vehicle control and ADAS, it means that the controllers need to be run in parallel whilst the human is driving, and control be switched either manually or automatically. Switching between controllers is not a trivial task. The transients caused by controller switching can produce instabilities. The non-responsiveness of the vehicle to the ADAS inputs while the human driver is in control could cause actuator saturation. An abrupt handover of control to the ADAS could result in a violent response of the vehicle such as a spin, collision or loss of control. Speed has been linked to switching performance in autonomous vehicles scenarios [21].

In this paper, we applied separately MPC and DDPG to a cruise control and lane keeping task for a semi-autonomous vehicle or Advanced Driver Assist System (ADAS) [8]. Specifically, the task requires to switch control from a human driver to an automatic controller based on a performance metric. Here we present a one-on-one comparison between the two design methodologies during the different steps of the process and analyse the obtained performance; comments and ideas on how to improve each controller are also provided. Concepts around control design, the different control design approaches, algorithms and simulation models are explained in Sects. 2 and 3. Section 4 analyses and compares the results, and Sect. 5 talks about conclusions and future work.

## 2    Simulation Environment

The Open Car Racing Simulator [1] (TORCS) is an open source software. It allows to create its own artificial "drivers" that use virtual sensors to gather information about the road and the state of the vehicle; it also enables customized tracks and to connect to it through third party software (e.g. Python, MATLAB) with external pluggins, facilitating testing and prototyping.

The artificial driver controls steering wheel angle, throttle and brake commands. It implements a rich set of virtual measurements as sensor input. The sensors provide translational velocity in all 3 axis, 4 sensor readings of rotational wheel speed, number of engine cycles per minute, normalised position on track with regard to track width, angle of the long axis of the car relative to centre line of track and 19 sensor readings of track edge and car (i.e. laser radar).

Only the data-driven controller required the laser sensor input to work, whereas the model-based controller could work without it.

We used a variety of tracks with different difficulty levels (i.e. more aggressive geometry and thinner track width) to estimate the reliability of our two systems. Twelve different tracks were used in the experiment, with track widths ranging from 10 to 15 m, track length ranging from 2000 to 6000 m and curvatures ranging in average from 0.0016 to $0.02\,m^{-1}$ with a maximum of $0.087\,m^{-1}$.

## 3    Control Design Approaches

Creating a control system is a complex process that involves several stages from the study and comprehension of the problem to the implementation of the obtained solution using a mathematical representation. The necessary steps will be taken as the important criteria for our comparison between the two different control approaches:

**Analysis** deals with understanding the system through looking at specific objectives (e.g. reference tracking, regulation control) and the requirements at hand. Both, system actions and system states (i.e. sensed or estimated system variables), respectively, are examined as well as the relationship between them.

**Architecture Design** has to do with selecting the structure of the proposed algorithm that meets the desired requirements. This step might involve the control law that will be implemented by the controller, and any or all initial parameter values for the control architecture (e.g. weights, starting point, look ahead time).

**Synthesis** deals with creating the controller with the architecture selected, generating a functional model that can enforce the control objective and requirements, to test and validate its performance.

**Tuning** involves the evaluation of the synthesized controller and the optimization of its performance. It deals with improving the controller in individual or all its performance requirements by means of tuning optimizing any value that does not change the architecture of the controller (e.g. weights, factors).

**Deployment** deals with taking the designed controller into the real application and establish how it can be best used with both sensors, actuators and an automatic computer.

### 3.1   Model Predictive Controller

Model Predictive Control (MPC) is an advanced technique that deals with a short term optimal target problem by combining a prediction and a control strategy. It approximates future behaviours of the target plant, compares the predicted state of the plant with a set of predefined objectives and computes the optimal control inputs to achieve the objectives, whilst respecting the plant's constraints.

MPCs have been successful in semi-autonomous and autonomous vehicles, as they can handle Multi-Input-Multi-Output (MIMO) systems with controller input and state variable constraints while considering the non-linear dynamics of vehicles [16].

They use an explicit internal model which is often a simplification of the actual system/plant dynamics to predict the outputs at future time instances (prediction horizon). The dynamics of any given system in discrete time can be expressed in the state-space form as:

$$x_{k+1} = Ax_k + Bu_k \tag{1}$$

$$y_{k+1} = CAx_k + CBu_k + d_{k+1} \tag{2}$$

$x$ is the state vector of system variables, $A$ the system matrix, $y$ the output vector of observed variables, $B$ the input matrix, $u$ the control input vector, $C$ the output matrix, $k$ the time step and $d$ the disturbance matrix.

At each control interval, the prediction horizon is shifted towards the future and a new set of predictions is made. Further details can be seen in [15].

For situations where time-varying plant characteristics exist, two of the many approaches for MPC implementation are: Implicit MPC with a linearised model around an operating model and Adaptive MPC with a model being updated at run time [10].

Published MPC algorithms for autonomous vehicles are often adaptive and use dynamic vehicle models (LPV) with a non-linear tyre model. Still, the use of kinematic models (i.e. linearised models around an operating point) for lateral control has been proposed and studied [11], showing that kinematic models with discretization time of 200 ms show similar performance to dynamic models with discretization time of 100 ms.

**Bicycle Model.** The dynamics of a road vehicle are complex [11], involving 3 translational and 3 rotational degrees of freedom (DOF's), which are often interdependent due to the nature of the vehicle's suspension. The coordinate system used during our modelling of the vehicle followed the 'SAE International: Vehicle Dynamics Terminology J670E' [19]. The non-linear nature of the suspension system, the effects of aerodynamic drag and lift forces and the nature of contact condition between the tyres and the road surface add additional complexity. The vehicle dynamics for the purposes of this project can be de-coupled in the longitudinal and lateral directions to produce independent mathematical models of either kinematic or dynamic nature.

**Lateral dynamics** of the vehicle can be simplified by approximating them to a 2 DOF bicycle model representing the lateral and yaw motions. A few assumptions are made for the application of this simplified model, like constant longitudinal velocity, small slip angles (i.e. tyres operate in the linear region), no aligning moments in the tyres, no road gradient or bank angles, no lateral or longitudinal load transfer and no rolling or pitching motions. These assumptions are only valid at low speeds as the tyres experience significant slip and load transfers when cornering at high speeds.

Modelling the front pair of wheels as a single unit assumes that the steering angles on the left and right sides of the vehicle are the same. Automobiles in general use Ackerman geometry to ensure that the steering angles of the left and right wheels are such that they arc around a common instantaneous rolling centre for the vehicle. During cornering, the tyre's velocity has a component normal to the tyre plane, in addition to the component in the direction of motion. This is because the tyre experiences deformation and slip in the lateral direction. The angle between the direction of heading and the direction of travel (or ratio of lateral and longitudinal components of velocity) is known as slip angle. The cornering stiffness is defined as the ratio of change in lateral force and the change in slip angle. In commercial vehicles, the cornering stiffness of the front wheels is greater than that of the rear wheels, as it is implemented in this model. Further details available in [3].

**Longitudinal dynamics** govern the forward motion of the vehicle, constrained in the XZ plane. The longitudinal motion of the chassis accounts for aerodynamic drag and variations in the road incline to obtain a force balance like:

$$F_{forward} = M\frac{d}{dt}V_x + F_{aerodynamic} + F_{rolling} + F_{gravitational} + F_{friction} \quad (3)$$

$F_{aerodynamic}$ is aerodynamic drag, $F_{rolling}$ rolling resistance, $F_{gravitational}$ gravitational forces at slopes and $F_{friction}$ are frictional forces due to other mechanical losses of energy in the system. Vehicle parameters include mass $M = 1150\,\text{kg}$, density of air $\rho = 1.225\,\text{kg/m}^3$, drag coefficient $C_D = 0.8$, equivalent frontal area $A_F = 1.92\,\text{m}^2$, rolling resistance coefficients $C_{r0}/C_{r1} = 10^{-2}/10^{-4}$, coefficient of frictional damping $C_v = 7$, cornering stiffness of front tyre $C_f = 27\,\text{kN/rad}$, cornering stiffness of rear tyre $C_r = 21\,\text{kN/rad}$, distance of front and rear tyres (from centre of gravity) $l_f = l_r = 1.9\,\text{m}$ and moment of inertia about z-axis $I_z = 960\,\text{kgm}^2$.

**Control Structure.** An Implicit MPC for lateral and an Adaptive MPC for longitudinal motion were created to control the vehicle.

For **lateral control**, the expression of the lateral force balancing equations in terms of lateral error $y_e$ and heading error $\psi_e$ produce:

$$
\begin{bmatrix} \dot{y}_e \\ \ddot{y}_e \\ \dot{\psi}_e \\ \ddot{\psi}_e \end{bmatrix} = \begin{bmatrix} 0 & 1 & 0 & 0 \\ 0 & -\frac{(C_f+C_r)}{MV_x} & 0 & -V_x - \frac{C_f l_f - C_r l_r}{MV_x} \\ 0 & 0 & 0 & 1 \\ 0 & -\frac{C_f l_f - C_r l_r}{I_z V_x} & 0 & -\frac{C_f l_f^2 + C_r l_r^2}{I_z V_x} \end{bmatrix} \begin{bmatrix} y_e \\ \dot{y}_e \\ \psi_e \\ \dot{\psi}_e \end{bmatrix} + \begin{bmatrix} 0 \\ \frac{C_f}{M} \\ 0 \\ \frac{C_f l_f}{I_z} \end{bmatrix} \delta_f \qquad (4)
$$

The obtained expression is a function of the longitudinal velocity of the car $V_x$. An Implicit MPC with a linearised model and an Adaptive MPC were tested. The Implicit MPC was linearised about an operating point of 10 m/s with a set of bounds for the manipulated variables (MV). Both controllers performed almost identically. Adaptive MPC is computationally intensive and runs into numerical errors at high velocities (>90 km/h). As there is no significant performance advantage in switching to an adaptive controller, the implicit MPC is selected [10].

The used control parameters were: Prediction Horizon ($H_p = 30$), Control Horizon ($H_c = 5$) and Sampling time ($T_s = 20$ ms). The used tuning parameters were: MV min/max = $-0.66/0.66$ rad, MV Rate min/max = $-0.8/0.8$ rads/s, MV Scale factor = 8, $Q_n = diag[1\ 0.5]$, $R_n = 2$.

The **longitudinal controller** regulates the throttle and brakes to achieve its desired forward velocity. Both Implicit MPC and Adaptive MPC were tested, with the former having limited accuracy obtained due to not accommodating the variance of throttle demand with road terrain. The Adaptive MPC implements a dynamic model of the forward dynamics incorporating gravitational, aerodynamic and rolling resistances. The Linear Parameter-Varying Model (LPV) used depends on Angle of incline (Slope) $\alpha$, Pedal constant $F_p$, Gear ratio $G_r$, Throttle input $u$, Longitudinal velocity $V_x$ and the other longitudinal parameters. It can be expressed as:

$$
[\dot{V}_x] = \left[ -\left( \frac{g(sin(\alpha)+C_{r0})}{Vx} + \frac{(\rho C_D A_F V_x + 2C_v)}{2M} \right) \right] [V_x] + [F_p G_r] u_f \qquad (5)
$$

To reduce cornering tendencies due to turning whilst maintaining a stable cruise velocity, a strategy to adapt the velocity output demand was implemented. Road curvature is used to reduce the velocity whilst turning to improve vehicle handling. The minimum value between the cruise velocity and a threshold is used as a final cruise velocity. Empirical testing revealed that a threshold of $0.3/abs(RoadCurvature)$ produced the best results.

## 3.2   Reinforcement Learning

Reinforcement Learning is based on the idea that reinforcement, if given in the form of a reward or punishment, will help to optimise a behavioural response.

This process of behavioural adaptation (learning) aims to maximise the cumulative reward extracted from the environment. The agent is said to navigate a Markov decision process (MDP) [20], as defined by the five tuple $\langle S, A, R, P, \gamma \rangle$: $S$ is the set of states, $A$ is the set of actions, $R$ is the expected reward given a state action pair, $R_s^a = \mathbb{E}[r_t \mid S_t = s, A_t = a]$, $P$ is the state transition probability matrix $P_{ss'}^a = \mathbb{E}[S_{t+1} = s' \mid S_t = s, A_t = a]$ and $\gamma$ is the discount factor in domain $[0,1]$.

The goal of the agent is to extract the most reward from the MDP by deciding on the best action, given the state it is in. The actions of an agent, given the state it is in, are determined by the agent's policy. MDPs are time invariant and depend only on the current state and not the state history. Solving an MDP means finding an optimal policy which yields the optimal value. Policy evaluation can be done by Monte-Carlo (MC) Backup and Temporal Difference (TD) Backup [20]. Policy control, the process of iteratively finding a better policy, can be done by algorithms such as SARSA or Q-learning [22], which creates a Q-value $Q$ that relates actions $a$ and states $s$ through a reward.

As the number of states and actions increases, the number of table entries required increases exponentially. Physical systems are controlled in a continuous state action space, creating the need for continuous function approximators.

For physical systems, the idea of actor-critic was introduced [23]. The actor is the policy which is updated every iteration. The critic is the Q value, which is updated every iteration. Initial implementations also had the critic being updated by minimising the mean square difference between the approximation and the computed evaluated values. The actor is a Gaussian distribution over actions, given state where the mean and standard deviation is parametrised by a linear sum of weighted features.

The policy parameters are updated to maximise the cumulative reward extracted from the MDP, where each state transition yields a reward. The magnitude of this reward is determined by the reward function. Therefore, the reward function implicitly describes the optimal behaviour. Poorly designed reward functions can lead to oscillations in policy and convergence to poor policies. Generally, reward functions which give continuous reward are better behaved than those that have a large delay. An example of this is chess. A move in mid game can lead to victory later, but it may not be easy to identify the utility of this singular move among the whole trajectory.

**Control Structure.** An actor critic reinforcement learning (RL) technique was used to develop a continuous state-action controller. The method used was based on deep deterministic policy gradient (DDPG) algorithm [13], integrating an additional Proportional-Integral loop to improve tracking performance.

The action value (critic) function and the policy (actor) are both approximated by two neural networks (NN) with two hidden layers each and a linear rectifier (relu) activation function. For the first and second hidden layer, 300 and 600 nodes were selected respectively based on improvements done on the original implementation [13]. The algorithm uses all 29 sensor inputs. The critic input to the first layer is the state and to the second layer is the action. The output is the action value. The matrice's weights are initialized using Xavier [4] initialisation. Policy parameters are tuned online using stochastic gradient descent.

The vehicle was trained on the track with the widest variety of turns (i.e. straight, cambered, inclined and sharp). This increases the generality of the trained algorithm to other tracks. The aim of the DDPG is to control a vehicle to safely travel at a user specified cruising velocity, $V_t$ whilst reducing the lateral distance from the centreline of the track, $|y_e|$.

The reward function [13] $R(s) = V_l(\cos\theta - |\sin\theta| - |y_e|)$ was used. $V_l$ is the component of the vehicle's longitudinal velocity in the direction of the track. $\theta$ is the yaw angle. Additionally, a negative reward was given if the vehicle left the track. Lastly, the simulation was reset if no progress was made after 500 simulation steps. Only 2 of every 3 controllers synthesized had good performance (i.e. algorithm converged).

The DDPG allows for the development of a robust model-free controller for a high speed racer. However, it does not yield well to constraining the cruising speed to a user reference. To tackle this, the DDPG+PI controller was developed which uses both reinforcement learning and classical proportional-integral control to overcome the limitations of both methods. A proportional gain of 8 and an integral gain of 0.05 were empirically obtained for the PI component. This allows good levels of robust tracking of the velocity and track demand.

## 4    Comparative Evaluation

The obtained compliant controllers showed similar nominal performance, following different design methodologies and taking different amounts of effort and resources in each stage.

### 4.1    Design Procedure Comparison

For the model-based controller or MPC:

- **Analysis:** A great deal of effort must be put into a mathematical model of the car and its movement in a dynamic framework. This is a time-consuming task, requiring a great amount of specialized knowledge.
- **Architecture:** Changes are restricted to the type of MPC being implemented (e.g. MPC, optimal MPC) and its parameters, which are generally not many.
- **Synthesis:** Time and computational resources are linked to the complexity of the mathematical formulation. It deals with automatically generating a code that solves a mathematical equation inside the control loop. The code could be too large and the equation too slow or unfeasible to be solved; Nonetheless, this can be included and validated before synthesis and dealt with.
- **Tuning:** Parameters can be manually tuned and are intuitive to the problem being solved, as they increase or decrease the size of the equation to be solved.

– **Deployment:** It needs a solver for an equation to be run inside the control loop, which could be difficult or unfeasible to do in a final implementation. Our implementation did not suffer of these problems, but running two MPCs simultaneously was computationally intensive.

For the data-driven controller or DDPG+PI:

– **Analysis:** No great amount of previous knowledge or expert knowledge is required. Just a small amount of information about the situation itself and how the states could be related is necessary to formulate a reward function.
– **Architecture:** After choosing a control architecture, no further work is necessary, and the algorithm can be implemented. The architecture itself allows for integration of any input into the controller. Yet, the selection of control structure is closely intertwined with a successful synthesis process. Careful iterative tests are needed to augment the right input signals and add any necessary control structures (e.g. additional PID blocks).
– **Synthesis:** Takes a large amount of time and computational power, as training requires replay and repetition of the driving scenario.
– **Tuning:** Takes a large amount of time, mainly due to the time it takes to synthesise each controller. Tuning of the parameters is not intuitive, and a rework of the reward function could be unpredictable in terms of design time and obtained performance.
– **Deployment:** It only needs to use the matrix weights, with sequential multiplication of the sensor inputs to create the control rule inside the control loop. Hence, the controller was easily portable between Python and MATLAB.

MPC does not have a native way of dealing with a great number of sensors, if the model does not incorporate them. RL can accommodate these sensors as part of the architecture. RL cannot accommodate big tracking errors or adapt to very different scenarios from the one the training was done, reason why adhoc methods like the PI controller improve the nominal performance.

Initial tests led to both controllers producing instabilities when control was given to them from human driving. As suggested in previous studies [21], a speed-dependent transition window (e.g. faster switching at higher speeds) with a 1st order transfer function was implemented. Smooth transitions were generated, and instabilities were avoided.

## 4.2    Speed Limit Violation

The vehicle is driven over a speed limit by a human driver past 2 different pre-defined maximum velocities (100 km/h and 110 km/h), with the controllers taking over and reducing the speed to 70 km/h and 90 km/h respectively.

Both controllers manage to take the speed down successfully. Figures 1a and 2a show the change in throttle control signal when controllers take over. Figures 1b and 2b show the resulting change in velocity. Controllers taking-over happen around a time of 10 s. MPC shows a smoother deceleration in all cases.

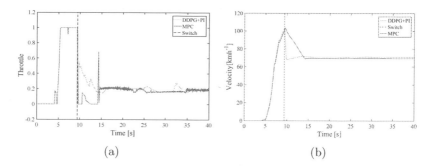

**Fig. 1.** Controllers takeover from driver due to over speeding at $100\,\mathrm{kmh}^{-1}$ (dotted black line). Throttle (a) and Vehicle velocity (b)

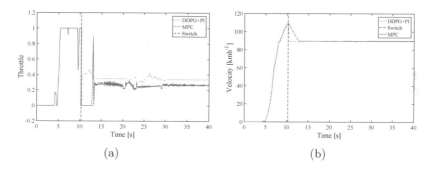

**Fig. 2.** Controllers takeover from driver due to over speeding at $110\,\mathrm{kmh}^{-1}$ (dotted black line). Throttle (a) and Vehicle velocity (b)

This is due to the action constraints applied on the rates of throttle and brake usage for MPC, compared to the possible integral term winds up as the over-speed value is reached for the RL controller.

### 4.3 Lane Departure

The vehicle is driven off track by a human driver at two different velocities (60 km/h and 110 km/h), with the controllers taking over once the lateral error increases over a threshold.

Both controllers take the vehicle back on track. Figures 3a and 4a show the change in steering wheel control signal when controllers take over. Figures 3b and 4b show the resulting change in lateral error. Different performance traits between controllers and between nominal speeds were obtained, which complies to the intuitive idea that a car is more difficult to control at higher speeds. The RL controller shows higher oscillatory behaviour for the steering control, especially for the low speed case. The MPC controller shows consistently smooth steering control in both cases, but a more aggressive corrective manoeuvring for high speeds, which may lead to the vehicle spinning out of control.

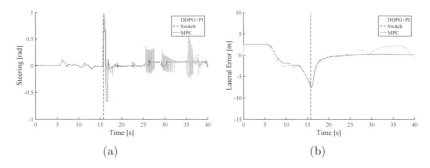

**Fig. 3.** Controller takeover from driver due to lane departure at $60 \, \mathrm{kmh}^{-1}$ (dotted black line). Steering wheel angle (a) and Vehicle lateral error (b)

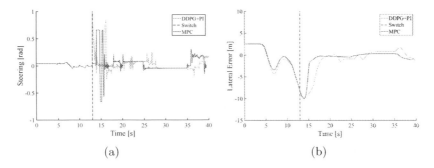

**Fig. 4.** Controller takeover from driver due to lane departure at $110 \, \mathrm{kmh}^{-1}$ (dotted black line). Steering wheel angle (a) and Vehicle lateral error (b)

The difference in behaviour could be linked to both controllers' architectures. The RL controller had a PI controller added on top to overcome its limitations with regards to error tracking, which allowed for better performance, especially at high speeds, but reduced performance for low speeds; as the RL controller was trained with higher speeds, tracking low speeds is specially challenging for it. The MPC controller allows to minimise the magnitude and frequencies of the lateral and longitudinal acceleration, resulting in smoother rides at all speeds, but reduced performance at high speeds due to the limitations of its internal model.

## 5    Conclusions

The design process for a controller used in semi-autonomous vehicles was presented, using two different design approaches (one model-based, the other data-driven). The controllers were directly compared with each other based on their performance when used to correct a speed limit violation or lane departure situation created by a human driver.

Both approaches were successful in producing a controller that keeps the vehicle in the lane and under a certain speed limit. Each had different benefits due to the design process, mainly with the MPC controller having direct ways to define control requirements and constraints, intuitive tuning and reduced synthesis time, and with the RL needing no expert knowledge about the model, support of large number of sensors and the high speed that its final implementation runs on.

For Lane departure correction, the RL controller seemed to perform better than the MPC controller as it changed vehicle position more gradually, resulting in a less aggressive return to the centreline. For the speed correction, however, the MPC controller seemed to perform better due to its control constraints, allowing a gentle deceleration.

The speed-dependent window smoothed the transition between manual human control and automatic controller; yet the controllers could generate discomfort to a human driver which should be considered when designing the controller. Restricting the vehicle's acceleration in the xy plane would reduce the possibility of inducing motion sickness or discomfort [5].

The fact that the model-based controller showed similar performance to the data-driven controller using less sensors is worth mentioning. This could be related to the predictive nature of the MPC, which achieves an estimation of the state of the vehicle further ahead in the track without the laser sensor; this estimation would not consider sudden changes, evidenced of that is the reduced performance of the controller when cornering at high speeds.

# References

1. Wymann, B., Coulom, R., Dimitrakakis, C., Espié, E.: Andrew Sumner: TORCS, The Open Racing Car Simulator (2014). http://www.torcs.org
2. Chen, C., Seff, A., Kornhauser, A., Xiao, J.: Deepdriving: learning affordance for direct perception in autonomous driving. In: 2015 IEEE International Conference on Computer Vision (ICCV), pp. 2722–2730. IEEE (2015)
3. Gillespie, T.D.: Vehicle Dynamics. Warren dale (1997)
4. Glorot, X., Bengio, Y.: Understanding the difficulty of training deep feedforward neural networks. In: Proceedings of the Thirteenth International Conference on Artificial Intelligence and Statistics, pp. 249–256 (2010)
5. Griffin, M.J.: Handbook of Human Vibration. Academic press, Cambridge (2012)
6. Haddadin, S., Haddadin, S., Khoury, A., Rokahr, T., Parusel, S., Burgkart, R., Bicchi, A., Albu-Schäffer, A.: On making robots understand safety: embedding injury knowledge into control. Int. J. Robot. Res. **31**(13), 1578–1602 (2012). http://ijr.sagepub.com/content/31/13/1578
7. ISO: ISO 13482:2014: Robots and robotic devices - Safety requirements for personal care robots. International Organization for Standardization, Geneva, Switzerland (2011)
8. Jacobs, M.: videantis ≫ Handy list of automotive ADAS acronyms. http://www.videantis.com/handy-list-of-automotive-adas-acronyms.html
9. Keviczky, T., Falcone, P., Borrelli, F., Asgari, J., Hrovat, D.: Predictive control approach to autonomous vehicle steering. In: American Control Conference, 2006, p. 6-pp. IEEE (2006)

10. Kim, J.S.: Recent advances in adaptive MPC. In: ICCAS, vol. 2010, pp. 218–222 (2010)
11. Kong, J., Pfeiffer, M., Schildbach, G., Borrelli, F.: Kinematic and dynamic vehicle models for autonomous driving control design. In: 2015 IEEE Intelligent Vehicles Symposium (IV), pp. 1094–1099. IEEE (2015)
12. Lefevre, S., Carvalho, A., Borrelli, F.: A learning-based framework for velocity control in autonomous driving. IEEE Trans. Autom. Sci. Eng. **13**(1), 32–42 (2016)
13. Lillicrap, T.P., Hunt, J.J., Pritzel, A., Heess, N., Erez, T., Tassa, Y., Silver, D., Wierstra, D.: Continuous control with deep reinforcement learning, September 2015. arXiv:1509.02971 [cs, stat]
14. Lima, P.: Predictive control for autonomous driving. Ph.D. thesis, KTH, 2016. Unpublished thesis (2016)
15. Maciejowski, J.M.: Predictive Control: With Constraints. Pearson education, London (2002)
16. Morari, M., Lee, J.H.: Model predictive control: past, present and future. Comput. Chem. Eng. **23**(4–5), 667–682 (1999). http://www.sciencedirect.com/science/article/pii/S0098135498003019
17. Pomerleau, D.A.: Efficient training of artificial neural networks for autonomous navigation. Neural Comput. **3**(1), 88–97 (1991)
18. Shia, V., Gao, Y., Vasudevan, R., Campbell, K., Lin, T., Borrelli, F., Bajcsy, R.: Semiautonomous vehicular control using driver modeling. IEEE Trans. Intell. Transp. Syst. **15**(6), 2696–2709 (2014)
19. Standard, S.A.: Vehicle Dynamics Terminology: J670E. SAE International (1976)
20. Sutton, R.S., Barto, A.G.: Reinforcement Learning: An Introduction, vol. 1. MIT press, Cambridge (1998)
21. VENTURER: VENTURER Trial 1: Planned handover. Technical report, May 2017
22. Watkins, C.J., Dayan, P.: Q-learning. Mach. Learn. **8**(3–4), 279–292 (1992)
23. Williams, R.J.: Simple statistical gradient-following algorithms for connectionist reinforcement learning. In: Sutton, R.S. (ed.) Reinforcement Learning, pp. 5–32. Springer, Boston (1992). https://doi.org/10.1007/978-1-4615-3618-5_2

# An Improved Robot Path Planning Model Using Cellular Automata

Luiz G. A. Martins[1]([✉]), Rafael da P. Cândido[1], Mauricio C. Escarpinati[1], Patricia A. Vargas[2], and Gina M. B. de Oliveira[1]

[1] Bio-inspired Computing Laboratory, Faculty of Computing,
Federal University of Uberlândia, Uberlândia, Brazil
{lgamartins,mescarpinati,gina}@ufu.br, rcandidop@gmail.com
[2] Robotics Laboratory, School of Mathematical and Computer Sciences,
Heriot-Watt University, Edinburgh, UK
p.a.vargas@hw.ac.uk

**Abstract.** Bio-inspired techniques have been successfully applied to the path-planning problem. Amongst those techniques, Cellular Automata (CA) have been seen a potential alternative due to its decentralized structure and low computational cost. In this work, an improved CA model is implemented and evaluated both in simulation and real environments using the e-puck robot. The objective was to construct a collision-free path plan from the robot initial position to the target position by applying the refined CA model and environment pre-processed images captured during its navigation. The simulations and real experiments show promising results on the model performance for a single robot.

**Keywords:** Autonomous robotics · Cellular Automata · Path-planning

## 1 Introduction

Path-planning is one of the most investigated problems in autonomous robotics [1]. In the past twenty years, Cellular Automata (CA) have been successfully applied to robot path-planning [2–8]. Its unique decentralized architecture allows the generation of highly distributed solutions to the path-planing problem even in complex scenarios.

This work proposes an improvement to the CA path-planning models for a single robot introduced in [9,10] by using environmental cues while navigating through an environment. Behring et al. [9] and Oliveira et al. [10] propose a model in which the robot finds the best trajectory between two cells (or positions), an initial cell and an target cell, while avoiding collisions. In order to calculate the optimal path, the robot must identify its current position (initial cell), the obstacles' cells and the target cell. This could be obtained via a pre-processed image captured from a bird eyes' view camera at each $n$ moving steps. The processed image generates a lattice map (i.e., cross-linked) of the environment. At each generated map, a new optimised path plan is created based on CA

© Springer International Publishing AG, part of Springer Nature 2018
M. Giuliani et al. (Eds.): TAROS 2018, LNAI 10965, pp. 183–194, 2018.
https://doi.org/10.1007/978-3-319-96728-8_16

distance diffusion technique, which would guide the robot from its current cell to the target cell. CA rules are used to define a numerical value for each free cell from the point of origin to the endpoint. The robot task is then to move to the next neighbour cell with the lowest value.

The main contributions of this work are the creation of a new refined navigation model and the use of an alternative method to reduce odometry inaccuracy. Firstly, the cell dimensions were changed to match the size of the robot. The major reason to do this is to improve the precision of the actual robot trajectory making possible the robot navigate between narrow spaces and more complex arrangements of obstacles. Secondly, a method proposed in [11] for odometry calibration was implemented, which improved the path-planning. Finally, a new method for trajectory correction was proposed aiming to keep the robot placed in the central position of a cell. The new improved navigation model was tested both in simulation using the Webots platform [12] and with real e-puck robots [13]. A better performance was observed both in simulation and in the experiment with real robots.

The remainder of this paper is organised as follows. Section 2 introduces CA basic concepts and highlights its main use in robot path-planning. Section 3 focuses on the path-planning process and revisits previous models [9,10]. Section 4 describes in details the implemented changes to the previous models. Experiments and results are discussed in Sect. 5. Section 6 presents the conclusion and suggests future work.

## 2    Cellular Automata and Path Planning

Cellular Automata (CA) are dynamical systems, highly decentralised made of simple components and local interactions. These systems are capable of presenting complex functions with elevated robustness and efficiency, similar to the behaviour found in many complex systems in nature. Usually CA are composed of two parts: the cellular space and the transition rule. The cellular space is a $d$-dimensional lattice with $N$ cells. These cells follow the same connection pattern with its close neighbours (local connections). CA are mostly characterised by the transition rule, which will determine the next configuration of the lattice at each step. Therefore, the cells interact with others in a local and synchronous way. For instance, the cell state $i$ at time step $t + 1$ relies only on its own state and the state of its close neighbours at time step $t$. CA could be represented on a bidimensional space where the lattice is a 2D matrix and the most common neighbourhood rules adopted are von Neumann and Moore [10]. The von Neuman neighbourhood is composed by the central cell and its four neighbours in cardinal direction from it. In the Moore neighbourhood, the diagonal cells are also included, summing up to 9 cells in total. In this present work we adopt the Moore neighbourhood.

The main objective of a path-planning strategy is to optimise the path between a point of origin and a target point. Traditional approaches to path-planing are route-maps [14], cell decomposition [15] and field potential [16].

Nonetheless, CA have also been successfully applied to path-planing problems and many CA models could be found in the literature [2–4,6,9,10,17].

CA-based models for path-planning can be classified into six distinct approaches [6]: power diffusion; distance diffusion; goal attraction; Voronoi's diagram; local decision making; and message sending. The new refined model presented in this work belongs to the distance diffusion approach [9,10]. In this approach, the planning consists of a CA rule that is used to calculate the distance between the free cell and the target point. The new proposed model was inspired on the model described in [10], and it will be described into further details in Sect. 4.

## 3    Previous CA Models

The fist model [9] uses distance diffusion algorithm and it is divided into phases. Initially, all obstacles are virtually enlarged to avoid collisions. The level of obstacle enlargement is a pre-defined parameter. After that, the distance of each free cell from the target cell is calculated using the CA transition rule. This process of path-planning is illustrated in Fig. 1. The black cells represent the obstacles, the white cells represent the free cells and the gray cells represent the robot position (I) and the target cell (G), respectively. Figure 1(a) shows the environment mapping (grid) after the $13^{th}$ iteration of the distance diffusion is applied. Figure 1(b) depicts the path obtained after the CA rule application. By using this strategy, the robot always chose the shortest path to the target.

(a) Environment mapping                    (b) Calculated path

**Fig. 1.** Example of a path-planning.

The model proposed by [10] is an improvement to [9]. In [10], the distance diffusion is calculated at each $n$ steps and not only at the beginning. Using this approach, the authors show that a new path is redefined at each $n$ steps. This modification makes it possible to approximate the actual path performed by the robot to the ideal route calculated in the initial position, turning its final position closest to the goal. The second major change observed in [10] is related to the obstacle enlargement cells, which may cause a deadlock depending on the current position of the robot. The authors proposed a distance diffusion in which two metrics are calculated for the enlarged obstacle cells: the Next Free Cell Distance (NFCD) and the Next True Obstacle Distance (NTOD). Two CA rules are employed to diffuse the new distances, which are used to help the robot to escape from regions near to obstacles. With this strategy, deadlocks were avoided, the robot rapidly moves from the enlarged area to a free cell, and the robot moved as far as possible from the obstacles.

We started our investigation by reproducing these previous models, confirming that the path recalculation proposed in [10] could improve the robot's navigation by approximating the real trajectory from the planned path when starting from its initial position. However, after we perform the cell size reduction (from 14 cm to 7 cm), it was possible to observe that the path recalculation is not enough to guarantee a suitable navigation and several times we still observe collisions during robot's navigation. It was possible to observe that although this cell dimension reduction enable the robot to try more complex trajectories passing by narrow spaces, this capability demands a more accurate model for navigation and positioning. In the next section we describe the major modifications proposed in this model to achieve such capability.

## 4    New Refined CA Model

Two major changes were made to the model in [10]. First, the *University of Michigan Benchmark test (UMBMark)* [11] odometry calibration method was used to reduce the odometry inaccuracy. Although the odometry error was mitigated, it was observed that the robot did not always stop at the center of the cell during the path recalculation. This caused an incremental error in the final localization of the robot, which was distant from the target cell. In order to solve this problem, the second major improvement was the proposition of a new method to make an online correction of the robot's trajectory, trying to keep the robot placed in the center of the planned cell.

We called this method as OPC (Online Positioning Correction). The development of the proposed method was motivated by the perception that, in the previous models, it is considered that the robot is always in the center of the cell to determine the next robot's step. However, most of the time the robot is displaced in its current cell as a result of non-systematic errors (e.g., wheel slip and/or inaccurate rotations). Thus, the movement of the robot towards the next cell is performed without considering such error, causing its propagation and, consequently, its accumulation along the path. OPC is based on the direction the robot must take to reach the next cell considering the path previously calculated by the CA rule. OPC is divided into two possible situations related to the direction of the next cell: cardinal and collateral points. For each situation, the method will use a different approach to make the correction calculus. They are illustrated in Fig. 2 and are explained following.

The possible cardinal points of direction are north, south, east and west. The approach to made the correction calculus in such situation is illustrated in

Fig. 2(a), where point (1) represents the center of the current cell, the several points (2) represent the center of the tentative cells to where the robot could move to and the several points (A) represent the possible actual positions of the robot within the current cell. From the coordinates of points (1), (2) and (A) corresponding to the current situation, the angle $\theta$ and the distance $P$ are calculated. $\theta$ is the angle that the robot should rotate and $P$ the distance that must be traveled for it to reach the center of the next desired cell (point (2)).

Figure 2(b) illustrates the approach for the collateral points, i.e. northeast, southeast, southwest, northwest. It is similar to the approach explained for cardinal points. However, now we also need to calculate point (3), which is used to adjust the computation of the distance to be traveled through a translation operation. The $\theta$ angle is formed by the segment lines (A-3) and (A-2). As shown in Fig. 2(c), to determine the rotation angle $\theta$, it was used the equation of the line that connects (1) and (2). The distance $P$ is given by the segment (A-2).

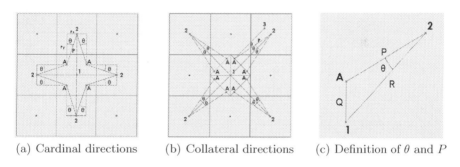

(a) Cardinal directions     (b) Collateral directions     (c) Definition of $\theta$ and $P$

**Fig. 2.** Online positioning correction (OPC).

The navigation model used in this work is based on CA rules and thus the environment is discretized in a lattice of cells. Therefore, When the robot moves from its current cell to an adjacent one, this is considered a discrete step of the robot's trajectory. The proposed correction is not applied at each step since the image acquisition and processing can make the model computationally expensive. Hence, the correction method proposed here is also applied at each $n$ steps when the robot receives the processed image, i.e., in the same step that the image is used to recalculate the path. Using this approach, a new path is recalculated at each $n$ steps and the next step of this path is also calibrated to make the robot move towards to the center of the next cell. As a result we developed a lighter processing navigation model where the robot moves from one cell to the other and has its path and position corrected at the same $n$ interval of steps.

## 5    Experiments and Results

In order to evaluate the effectiveness of the proposed modifications, we run simulations and real experiments using the CA model for the navigation of a e-puck robot [13]. Initially, simulated experiments described in the next subsection were performed aiming to evaluate the effect of the cell size reduction in the previous models. New simulations were run using different combinations of the 3 methods: *UMBMark*, path recalculation (PR) and the online positioning correction (OPC). The trajectories resulted from the tested approaches were used to analize their performances (Sect. 5.2). Finally, in order to validate the observed behavior, we performed experiments using a real e-puck (Sect. 5.3).

All simulations were run using the *Webots* platform [12]. Two scenarios were used in the simulated experiments reported here, which are shown in Fig. 3(a) and (b). Both of them are lattices with 9 columns × 18 rows of cells being that the size of each cell is 7 × 7 cm. Ten cells are obstacles (in black) that must be avoided and one cell is the goal (in red). The gray cells represent the enlarged obstacles. The robot is not allowed to traverse in this area when calculating the shortest path. However, the robot eventually passes through these areas due to the lack of precision of navigation. Although it is not considered a navigation fault (just the collisions with obstacles are errors), a good trajectory must avoid this kind of incursion. Figure 3 also shows the robot's initial position in each scenario and the path calculated using the CA-model proposed in [9] to propagate the smallest distances to the goal before the robot starts its navigation.

Later, the simulated scenarios were replicated to perform experiments using a real e-puck robot. Therefore, an arena with 63 × 126 cm was prepared for each scenario: a cover paper was elaborated for each one, plotting a grid with 7 × 7 cm cells. The obstacle and the goal cells were collored in the same positions of the simulated scenarios. Figure 3(c) shows the arena prepared for first scenario.

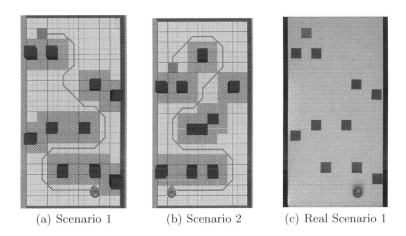

(a) Scenario 1          (b) Scenario 2          (c) Real Scenario 1

**Fig. 3.** Simulated and real scenarios used in the experiments. (Color figure online)

In the real experiments, a bird's eye view camera is used to give visual information to e-pucks. In simulations, a numeric matrix gives all the inputs to the robot (current position, obstacles positions and goal position) to calculate the planned path and to start its navigation. After the navigation starts, its online position is given by a GPS slot, which is an available component of the e-puck architectures in Webots that could give both position and rotation with the adequate precision in a scenario with this dimension (63 cm x 126 cm). However, in the real world, this component is not available in the standard e-puck. Besides, a GPS component with the needed precision is a high cost element. Therefore, all the initial information and the robot's online position and angle are captured by the bird's eye view camera, which was placed in the middle of the arena. Figure 3(c) shows the image captured by the camera.

As the real robot needs to have available the new environment configuration in order to recalculate the path and to correct the robot position, a dedicated image processing algorithm, with a very low computational cost, was used at each $n$ steps. This algorithm consists of taking an image of the arena, and then applying the Otsu technique [18] in order to binarize the image. After that, the edges of the arena are mapped using the Hough Transform [18], which allows for the constructing of a virtual grid format that is produced to a pre-established size, and the objects in each cell are identified. Thus, at the end of the process an ASCII file is recorded as output data, informing the position and the content of each occupied cell. This strategy guarantees a low cost image processing as well as a low cost data output.

Three performance metrics were used to evaluate the efficiency of the model: the final positioning error, the time required for the navigation and the distance traveled. The former metric (final error) has a higher degree of relevance.

### 5.1    Cell Size Reduction in the Previous Models

Figure 4 shows the application of the previous models after the cell dimension was reduced from 14 cm (used in [10]) to 7 cm (equivalent to epuck's dimension). They were applied in the *Scenario 1* shown in Fig. 3(a), which shows the desired path for this scenario, calculated through CA diffusion starting from the robot's initial position. The simulated robot's trajectories resulted from the previous models ([9,10]) are shown in Fig. 4(a) and (b), respectively.

It could be observed that the robot could not reach its target cell in the first model (Fig. 4(a)) but it reaches in the second model (Fig. 4(b)). Therefore, the performance using the model from [10] is better than [9]. Nonetheless, there was still collision in both cases. Arrows indicate collision points in Figs. 4(a) and (b). The collisions observed using the model from [10] is due to the cell dimension reduction.

### 5.2    Simulated Experiments with the Proposed Modifications

This section presents the results of simulations of the navigation model using different combinations of the 3 methods: *UMBMark* for odometry calibration, the path recalculation (PR), and the proposed online positioning correction (OPC). It was empirically determined that for the path recalculation the best $n$ is 5 steps. In these experiments, *Scenario 1* (Fig. 3(a)) was also used. After the application

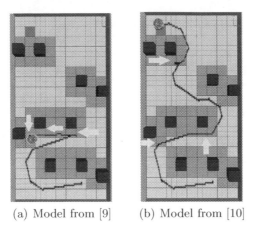

(a) Model from [9]     (b) Model from [10]

**Fig. 4.** Simulated experiments using previous models.

of the *UMBMark* method, it was observed a better robot's performance, both in its localization throughout the experiment and also with the proximity to the target cell at the end of the simulation.

The simulated experiment where there was no calibration of the *UMBMark* method but there was the path recalculation at each 5 steps was previously shown in the last subsection (Fig. 4(b)). The distance error at the end of the simulation was 3.1156 cm and the robot moved 2.46 m in 2 min and 16 s. Nonetheless, the robot had collisions.

In the simulation presented in Fig. 5(a), there is calibration of *UMBMark* method but there is no path recalculation. Results indicate that the final error to the goal was 5.1802 cm and the robot moved 2.05 m in 2 min and 3 s. Therefore, the final overall error using the *UMBMark* was larger than using the path recalculation. However, the calibration was better to keep the robot far from the obstacles and no collision was observed. This result makes us hypothesize that the best solution for the odometry inaccuracy is the use of the *UMBMark* calibration method together with the path recalculation (PR) at each 5 steps. Thus, we simulate the robot's navigation when an approach combining both methods (*UMBMark* and PR) is used.

Figure 5(b) shows the results trajectory using this approach in the *Webots* platform. It was possible to observe that the robot reached the target cell with 1.4940 cm distance and the robot moved for 1.98 m in 1 min and 56 s. Therefore, this combined approach returned a better trajectory, returning a smaller final error and a shorter path with no collision. However, the final path was not ideal. It is possible to observe in Fig. 5(b) that the robot breaks into obstacle enlarged areas in some parts of the trajectory and it is still different from the ideal path shown in Fig. 3(a) for this scenario.

The analytical method OPC described in Sect. 4 was used to mitigate the error at each path calculation. The results for the approach that combines the three methods (*UMBMark*, PR and OPC) can be seen in Fig. 5(c). It is clear the improvement in the robot performance approximating the real trajectory from the ideal path. The final distance error on Fig. 5(c) was 0.6682 cm, smaller than the final error in Fig. 5(b). However, the robot moved for 2.11 m in 2 min and 7 s using the approach that combines the three methods. Therefore, the distance and time it took the robot to move from the point of origin to the target cell in Fig. 5(b) were smaller than Fig. 5(c). This happens because in the last figure, the robot used an almost ideal path, therefore it would be a longer one for no shortcuts were used.

Summing up, in the simulations, the new CA path-planning model using the three methods assisted the robot not only to reach its target reducing the final error, but also to follow an almost ideal path.

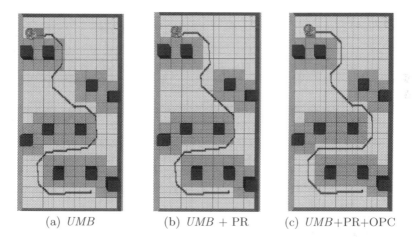

(a) *UMB*            (b) *UMB* + PR            (c) *UMB*+PR+OPC

**Fig. 5.** Simulations experiments using the odometry calibration with *UMBMark* method, path recalculation and OPC approaches.

## 5.3   Experiments with Real Robots

Finally, we performed the experiments with the real robot aiming to confirm the simulated results and to analyse the performance of the new model in real scenarios with the e-puck. Initially, two different approaches were applied using the arena prepared for the *Scenario 1*: one where no method was applied with just the distance diffusion as in [9] and one where only the *UMBMark* method was used. It was observed in the first experiment that the robot made a turn to avoid the first three obstacles but then it went on a straight line into the other obstacles. Figure 6(a) shows the moment when the robot hit the obstacle. During the second experiment, the robot was capable of avoiding more obstacles. However, as it can be observed in Fig. 6(b), the robot passed the arena borderline thus colliding three cells away where it should be. We believe that this inappropriate behavior of the robot even with the calibration is due to the robot's stronger skidding in the real environment.

Starting from this point, the real experiments made use of the bird's eye view camera in order to recalculate the path. In the third experiment using the *Scenario 1*, the robot recalculates and fixes the path at each 5 steps. Using path recalculation and *UMBMark*, the robot was able to navigate almost until the goal (Fig. 6(c)). However, it collides with an obstacle.

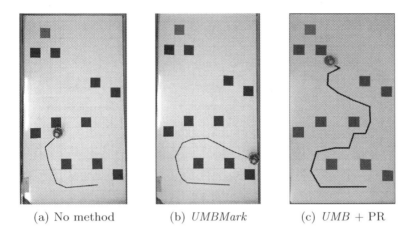

(a) No method          (b) *UMBMark*          (c) *UMB* + PR

**Fig. 6.** Real experiments with the *Scenario 1* using preliminar approaches.

The last experiment with *Scenario 1* was performed by including the online positioning correction (OPC). Using the complete and final approach (UMB+PR+OPC), the robot could finally reached the goal with no collisions (Fig. 7(a)). Overall the results obtained in simulation were successfully replicated on a real scenario. Moreover, only using the combined approach (*UMBMark*, PR

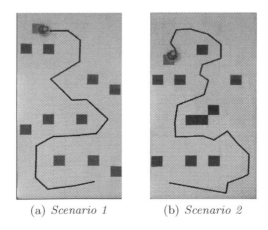

(a) *Scenario 1*          (b) *Scenario 2*

**Fig. 7.** Real experiments using the final combined approach (UMB+PR+OPC).

and OPC) the robot was able to achieve the goal, highlighting the importance of online trajectory corrections to guarantee a successful navigation. The experiments took place in two distinct scenarios to reassure the robustness of the approach. Figure 7(b) shows the robot's trajectory obtained in the second scenario. The robot successfully completed the path and reached its target. Videos of the experiments can be found at [19].

## 6    Conclusion and Future Work

This work implemented and successfully tested, in simulation and with real robots, a new improved CA model for path-planning. The model comprises of three methods, one is the odometry calibration using *UMBMark*, the second is the path recalculation, and the third is the online positioning correction (OPC) proposed here. The first method proved efficient in mitigating the odometry inaccuracy. The second method and third methods are applied at each $n$ steps and together with the first one, assisted the robot to have an excellent performance in all scenarios, simulated and real, proving the efficiency of the refined CA model.

Although path recalculation was previously proposed in [10], it is the first time that it was investigated using real robots. The results reported here show that this approach alone is not enough to guarantee a real trajectory close to the planned path. A better method for positioning the robot in the center of the cell and an odometry correction are also needed to reach the goal with no collisions. Moreover, even in the simulated experiments, the results show that if the cell size is reduced to enable the robot to navigate through narrow spaces the path recalculation is not enough to guarantee an adequate trajectory and collisions were observed. When applying the *UMBMark* correction together with path recalculation, the robot could reach the goal in the simulated scenarios without collisions. However, by also including the OPC method, the final overall error was reduced in approximately 50%. Despite of presenting here a single run for each model variation (simulation and real experiment), different executions were performed in each case and we can affirm that the chosen runs represent the typical robot behavior. In the future, we intend to do a more detailed statistical analysis that better characterizes the average behavior.

Future work includes further analysis of the robot odometry errors and also the development of a new path-planning model, which could investigate the use of possible robot rotations at each recalculation step. Searching for not only the shortest path, but also for the best angle. Likewise, an evolutionary robotics approach [20] could be combined with the CA approach to create a hybrid path-planning model which would overcome all main issues found so far. Future experiments could also make use of the e-puck robot's camera and the infrared sensors in addition to bird's eye view camera. This would give the robot more flexibility and robustness to face dynamic and unknown environments.

**Acknowledgment.** The authors thank FAPEMIG, CAPES and CNPq for the financial support, and Hugo Sardinha for their assistance in formatting of the paper.

# References

1. Arkin, R.C.: Behavior-Based Robotics. MIT press, Cambridge (1998)
2. Tzionas, P.G., Thanailakis, A., Tsalides, P.G.: Collision-free path planning for a diamond-shaped robot using two-dimensional cellular automata. Trans. Robot. Autom. **13**(2), 237–250 (1997)
3. Marchese, F.M.: A directional diffusion algorithm on cellular automata for robot path-planning. Future Gener. Comput. Syst. **18**(7), 983–994 (2002)
4. Ioannidis, K., Sirakoulis, G., Andreadis, I.: A cellular automaton collision-free path planner suitable for cooperative robots. In: Panhellenic Conference on Informatics, pp. 256–260 (2008)
5. Akbarimajd, A., Hassanzadeh, A.: A novel cellular automata based real time path planning method for mobile robots. J. Eng. Res. Appl. **1**(4), 1262–1267 (2011)
6. Ferreira, G.B.S., Vargas, P.A., Oliveira, G.M.B.: An improved cellular automata-based model for robot path-planning. In: Mistry, M., Leonardis, A., Witkowski, M., Melhuish, C. (eds.) TAROS 2014. LNCS (LNAI), vol. 8717, pp. 25–36. Springer, Cham (2014). https://doi.org/10.1007/978-3-319-10401-0_3
7. Lima, D.A., Oliveira, G.M.B.: A cellular automata ant memory model of foraging in a swarm of robots. Appl. Math. Model. **47**, 551–572 (2017)
8. Tinoco, C.R., Lima, D.A., Oliveira, G.M.: An improved model for swarm robotics in surveillance based on cellular automata and repulsive pheromone with discrete diffusion. Int. J. Parallel Emerg. Distrib. Syst. 1–25 (2017)
9. Behring, C., Bracho, M., Castro, M., Moreno, J.: An algorithm for robot path planning with cellular automata. In: Bandini, S., Worsch, T. (eds.) International Conference on Cellular Automata for Research and Industry (2000), pp. 11–19. Springer, Heidelberg (2000). https://doi.org/10.1007/978-1-4471-0709-5_2
10. Oliveira, G., Vargas, P., Ferreira, G.: Investigating a cellular automata model that performs three distance diffusion on a robot path planning. In: Proceedings of the European Conference on Artificial Life, pp. 271–278 (2015)
11. Borenstein, J., Feng., L.: Umbmark a method for measuring, comparing, and correcting dead-reckoning errors in robots. Technical report, University of Michigan (1994)
12. Webots: Robot simulator (2017). https://www.cyberbotics.com/overview/
13. E-puck: Robot (2017). http://www.e-puck.org
14. Zhang, Y., Fattahi, N., Li, W.: Probabilistic roadmap with self-learning for path planning of a mobile robot in a dynamic and unstructured environment. In: Conference on Mechatronics and Automation, pp. 1074–1079 (2013)
15. Ramer, C., Reitelshofer, S., Franke, J.: A robot motion planner for 6-DOF industrial robots based on the cell decomposition of workspace. In: Symposium on Robotics, pp. 1–4 (2013)
16. Jianjun, Y., Hongwei, D., Guanwei, W., Lu, Z.: Research about local path planning of moving robot based on improved artificial potential field. In: Chinese Control and Decision Conference, pp. 2861–2865 (2013)
17. Parker, L.E., Birch, B., Reardon, C.: Indoor target intercept using an acoustic sensor network and dual wavefrontpath planning. In: Proceedings of IEEE International Symposium on Intelligent Robots and Systems, pp. 278–283 (2003)
18. Gonzalez, R.C., Woods, R.E.: Digital Image Processing. Prentice Hall, Upper Saddle River (2007)
19. Videos: Bio-inspired computing lab (2018). https://www.youtube.com/channel/UC4uDX-7nXDGYl4Hu5IVCJdw?disable_polymer=true
20. Vargas, P.A., et al.: The Horizons of Evolutionary Robotics. MIT press, Cambridge (2014)

# Robotics Vision and Teleoperation

# Colias IV: The Affordable Micro Robot Platform with Bio-inspired Vision

Cheng Hu$^{(\boxtimes)}$ (iD), Qinbing Fu (iD), and Shigang Yue (iD)

Lincoln Centre for Autonomous Systems Research, University of Lincoln, Lincoln, UK
{chu,qifu,syue}@lincoln.ac.uk

**Abstract.** Vision is one of the most important sensing modalities for robots and has been realized on mostly large platforms. However for micro robots which are commonly utilized in swarm robotic studies, the visual ability is seldom applied or with reduced functions/resolution, due to the high demanding on the computation power. This research has proposed the low-cost micro ground robot Colias IV, which is particularly designed to meet the requirements to allow embedded vision based tasks on-board, such as bio-inspired collision detection neural networks. Numerous of successful approaches have demonstrated that the proposed micro robot Colias IV to be a feasible platform for introducing visual based algorithms into swarm robotics.

**Keywords:** Micro robot · Bio-inspired · Vision · Collision detection
Low-cost

## 1 Introduction

Vision is one of the most important sensing modalities for autonomous robots since it provides the abundant and reliable information about the surrounding environment. Thanks to the development in computer vision technology, many large-scale robots are taking advantage from vision sensors and also the most advanced vision algorithms [1].

On the other hand, small-scale robots, especially micro robots that are usually employed in the swarm robotic research, can hardly benefit from visual sensing. Even though the growth of interest in swarm robotics has brought us a wide range to choose from [2–6], there is still no optimal design for all desires. One of the greatest challenges is the trade-off between limited computational resources on-board and the requirements for image processing in real-time. The lack of vision inputs for swarm robotics has become a major concern for researchers recently. For example, the *E-puck* [2], *Swarm-bot* [3] or *mROBerTO* [4] are short of RAM size or sufficient CPU frequency. On the other hand, for those robots whose CPU are strong enough, they are usually oversized for swarm scenarios, such as *Kobot* [5], *Wolfbot* [6] and *Khepera III*. The comparison of related robot platform are illustrated in Table 1.

© Springer International Publishing AG, part of Springer Nature 2018
M. Giuliani et al. (Eds.): TAROS 2018, LNAI 10965, pp. 197–208, 2018.
https://doi.org/10.1007/978-3-319-96728-8_17

**Table 1.** The compare of cutting-edge robot platforms with image sensors

| | Kobot | KheperaIII | E-puck | Swarm-Bot | mROBerTO | Colias IV |
|---|---|---|---|---|---|---|
| CPU (MHz) | 200 | 600 | 64 | 40 | 16 | 180 |
| RAM | 32M | 32M | 8K | 648K | 32K | 256K |
| Cost (£) | 800 | 2000 | 580 | 500 | 50* | 80* |
| Diameter (cm) | 12 | 7 | 7.5 | 12.7 | 2.2 | 4 |
| Sensor types | 4 | 7 | 4 | 4 | 7 | 6 |
| Autonomy (h) | 10 | 1 | 1 | 3 | 1.5–6 | 1.5 |
| Remarks | Undeveloped | Discontinue | | | *parts | *parts |

For micro robots, suitable vision based algorithms should be selected and applied [2,7]. For example, the bio-inspired collision detection model Lobular Giant Movement Detector (LGMD) inspired from locust visual neurons [8,9]. Recently, the LGMD neuron has been modelled into computational algorithms for autonomous vehicles [10–12]. However, due to the requirements on hardware resources for image processing, the available robotic platforms or workaround approaches are unsatisfactory: either too large [10], too expensive [11], or can't get rid of the connecting with a host device (wire or wirelessly) to process the vision model [12]. These inconveniences prevent this promising visual model to be applied in swarm robotic researches for further study. An affordable micro robot platform that is small enough and can work independently is necessary.

In this paper, we propose a novel design of micro robot *Colias IV* to satisfy mentioned requirements, which is an affordable hardware platform mainly deals with visual tasks. As an upgrade version of previously develop micro robot *Colias* [13] that is a differential driven ground robot with modular design, the circular footprint occupies only 40 mm in diameter. The new *Colias IV* is additionally featured with an strong ARM Cortex M4 processor, a tiny VGA camera, two digital microphones, one 9-axis motion sensors and various of other sensing modules. To develop algorithms on the platform easily, software packages are provided, including the motion planning and controlling strategies, a friendly embedded programming environment and remote user accessibility through extension modules. The bio-inspired collision detection algorithm called Embedded-LGMD (ELGMD) and other related visual neural networks have been successfully realized on this micro robot, which shows its practicability on conducting vision based tasks autonomously.

## 2    The Assembly of Colias IV

The designed micro robot platform is based on three primary objectives: (1) to realize middle-strength computation tasks including low-level image processing autonomously, (2) to achieve better modularity so that each part has certain features and functions that can work independently, and (3) to maximize the use of space to save as much space occupation as possible.

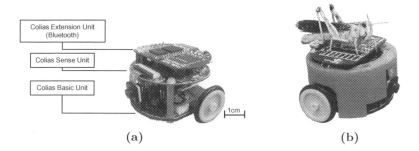

**Fig. 1.** (a) The *Colias IV* robot with CEU (Bluetooth) board attached, showing the modules' connections. The battery is located between the CSU and CBU; (b) A *Colias IV* coated with a 3D-printed shell and CEU (USB-serial). An adult locust is standing on the robot to compare the size.

As a result of the objectives, the robot is composed of three modularized layers that provide different functions, namely the Colias Basic Unit (CBU), the Colias Sensing Unit (CSU) and the Colias Extension Units (CEU) (Fig. 1). The CBU serves preliminary robot features such as motion, power management and some basic sensing. The CSU provides the high-level sensors such as motion sensors and camera towards better programming environment with image processing. Robot formed by CBU and CSU is sufficient for most of the experiments. Furthermore, CEU provides specialized features such as connectivity and illumination. The overall weight of *Colias IV* is 40–60 g, varied according to different extensions. The hardware architecture of *Colias IV* is illustrated in Fig. 2.

## 2.1    The Colias Basic Unit (CBU)

The Colias basic unit (CBU) is a upgraded version of previous *Colias* robot started in 2013 [13], which is a light weight robot designed for swarm applications. It is one of the smallest and cheapest micro-robots in this field. CBU employs a circular platform with a diameter of 40 mm. It serves basic sensing, motion generation and power management. The schematic design of the CBU is illustrated in Fig. 2, and a photograph of CBU is shown in Fig. 3.

**Micro Processor.** The purpose of CBU is basic motion control and sensing, thus the primary consideration for choosing the processor is more of stability and power-efficiency but not computation speed. The AVR series micro-controller ATMega168P from Atmel is selected to meet these requirements. It is an 8-bit micro-controller running at 8 MHz, equipped with 16 KBytes Flash, 1 KByte RAM. It has 24 IO pins supporting analog-digital converter and serial ports.

The application program inside the CBU's is arranged with an infinite loop. In the determined duty cycle of approximately 2 ms, the micro controller manages to update a specific area of RAM as a register map. The register map maintains the CBU's system status including sensor data, LED configuration,

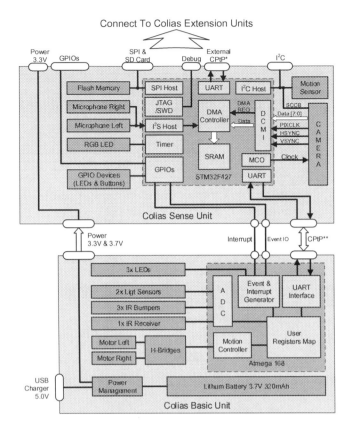

**Fig. 2.** The *Colias IV* block diagram, showing the CBU and CSU architecture. *CPtP is a reliable data transmission protocol that utilizing the UART as the physical layer.

motion configuration and also system information. There is a separate interrupt handle to decode and response to incoming control messages from CSU or other higher level modules.

**Environment Sensors.** The CBU is equipped with three kinds of sensors, which are short range infra-red (IR) proximity sensors facing front, ambient light sensors facing ground, and one long range IR receiver towards back.

The short range IR sensors (bumpers) are commonly used to indicate real collisions. Each bumper has a IR emitter and a receiver towards the same direction. Confirmation of collision is relied on the strength of received signal. There are three bumper sensors facing front separated by 30°. Their average detection distance is 20 mm, which is also influenced by the light absorbing character of the obstacle (Fig. 4a). The ambient light sensors are responsible to measure light intensity within the spectrum of visible light with a photo-transistor. They are mounted towards the ground on both sides of the robot, which enable the robot to follow patterns on the ground, or react to the surrounding illumination

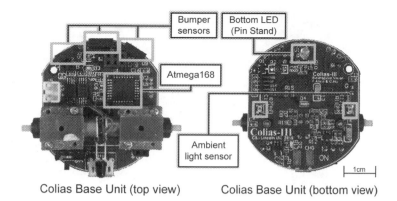

Colias Base Unit (top view)    Colias Base Unit (bottom view)

**Fig. 3.** The photo of CBU from both sides with wheels and battery removed, indicating several major components. In the bottom view, notice that the bottom LED that also acts as the front pin stand.

status. There is a long range IR receiver mounted to the back, which is applied to receive signals from IR remote controller and trigger actions accordingly. This feature improves the efficiency when conducting experiments on multiple robot agents.

**Locomotion.** The *Colias IV* employs differential driving method with two mini geared DC motors. Each motor is driven through a H-bridge using pulse width modulation (PWM) for power tuning. To support the robot with only two wheels, the front LED is used as auxiliary fixed point stand, as indicated in Fig. 3. The tested performance of speed tuning is shown in Fig. 4b with battery conditions of full charged and normal levels. Due to the compact design that prohibits encoders to be mounted on-board, the rotation speed of wheels can not be measured directly. However the attitude of the robot can be estimated through motion sensors described in Sect. 2.2.

Contributed by the high gear ratio (136:1) and lightweight of the robot load (50 g), the acceleration process could be achieved in several milliseconds. The dynamics of the motor is normally not taken into consideration when modelling the motion. The kinematics of the robot motion is described as a simple differential driven model. Let $v_l$ and $v_r$ donate to the left and right wheel velocities, we got the equation to represent the desired motion at any moment:

$$\omega(R + \frac{l}{2}) = v_l \tag{1}$$

$$\omega(R - \frac{l}{2}) = v_r \tag{2}$$

where $\omega$ is the angular velocity of the robot body, $l$ is the distance between the wheels and $R$ donates the distance between the midpoint of the wheels and Instant Centre of Rotation ($ICR$).

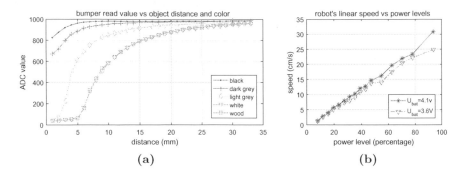

(a)                                              (b)

**Fig. 4.** Tests on some of the CBU features. (a) The short range bumper read-out value against object distance with different colour. The white object: normal white paper; the light grey to black: printing with 25%, 75% and 100% densities; wood: pine wood surface; (b) The robot's linear moving speed (forward motion) vs PWM controlled power level in battery conditions: full battery (4.1 V) and nominal battery level (3.6 V).

The robot can be operated with open-loop movement control when precise motion is not required. It can also achieve close-loop motion control by build-in PID controllers when the motion sensor (gyroscope) is used to estimate the attitude of the robot itself. The PID controllers are available for either turning speed or the heading angle servo, as well as their combination that forms a cascade controller to increase the overall dynamic response.

**Power Management.** The robot is powered by a Li-Ion battery with the capacity of 320 mAh (milliamp Hours) which provides an autonomy of approximately 1.5 h for the robot. The nominal voltage is 3.7 V. The battery charging process, which is managed by a charging monitor chip TP4054, can be supplied through either an USB-micro port or a pair of charging shoes at the bottom of the board at 5 V. The whole robot is powered by this battery through a linear regulator at 3.3 V except the motors, which are directly powered by the battery. The power consumption of typical components are listed in Table 2. The power consumption of the robot under normal conditions (in a basic arena with only walls) and short-range communication (low-power IR emitters) is about 150 mW. However, it can be reduced to approximately 30 mW when IR emitters are turned off occasionally.

## 2.2   The Colias Sense Unit (CSU)

The Colias Sense Unit (CSU) is the most important layer in the platform. It processes the main sensing task and most of the computation tasks. The earlier version of CSU was described as the *extension vision module* attaching to the formal *Colias* robot in previous research [14,15], which has only the camera sensor installed. The redesigned CSU now provides variety of sensors including the CMOS camera, two Microelectromechanical systems (MEMS) microphones

**Table 2.** The power consumptions of major components

| Module name & description | Typical | Max | Unit |
|---|---|---|---|
| Processor I active * | 2.5 | 8 | |
| Processor II standby ** | 2.5 | | |
| Processor II active | 95 | 130 | |
| Camera active | 12 | 18 | mA |
| IR Sensors x3 | 9 | 45 | |
| Motion Sensor | 2 | 4.7 | |
| DC Motor x2 | 80 (10 cm/s) | 300 (30 cm/s) | |

*This is the AVR chip in Colias Basic Unit.
**This is the STM32F427 chip in Colias Sensing Unit.

with digital outputs and a 9-DOF (domain of freedom) motion sensor. All the sensors are connected to the powerful ARM processor. The CSU is also equipped with an external Flash chip with up to 256 Mbits for permanent data storage. With external sockets for multiple interfaces, extension modules can be mounted to the CSU, providing features such as inter-robot long range communication, illumination or even physical grippers. The photograph of CSU is shown in Fig. 5, and the schematic of CSU is shown in Fig. 2. The CSU is connected to the CBU with three group of pin headers for power supply and communication. A reliable communication protocol is designed and applied here for exchanging message between the two units.

**Main Processor.** An ARM Cortex-M4F core micro controller is deployed as the main processor in the CSU that can handle intensive image processing and monitoring all other modules including the camera, CBU and other sensors. The 32-bit Micro Control Unit (MCU) STM32F427 is an upgraded version of which previously deployed in [14,15] (STM32F407). Several features make the STM32F427 chip an ideal platform for the designed objectives. For example, the high-performance processor with Reduced Instruction Set Computer(RISC) technology and the floating processing units (FPU) running at a high speed of 180 MHz donate for effectiveness and low power consumption; the 256 KByte SRAM and 2 MByte Flash provide the necessary storage space for image buffering; the on-board peripheral digital camera interface (DCMI), which is a high speed data interface for receiving camera data, frees the CPU from the hard burdens of managing large amount of data transferring. Moreover, the package size of STM32F427 is only 14 mm × 14 mm with quad-flat-package (QFP) footprint. Comparing to stronger chips that is often packed as Ball Grid Array (BGA), QFP is more favourable in two-layer PCB layout design, which is cost-efficient for manufacturing and testing.

The major part of implemented algorithms are realized in embedded C/C++. Since there are lots of tasks to be managed asynchronously and periodically, the recommended software architecture is the "interrupt-controlled loop" to ensure minimum latency and memory occupation on tasks dispatching. To provide a friendly programming environment for developers so that background tasks are isolated from the user codes, a supporting package is designed to manipulate peripheral devices and communication interfaces as a brunch of handles, including the camera driver, the motion sensory data calculation, I/O devices and the CBU commands. The organization of this package is compatible and inheritable with the hardware abstract layer (HAL) drivers package provided by STMicro-electronics.

**Camera.** A low voltage CMOS image sensor OV7670 module is utilised in CSU, as it is a low-cost camera with a compact package size of $8 \times 4 \, \text{mm}^3$ with flexible flat fable (FFC) connector. The power supply is 3.3 V with active power consumption of up to 60 mW. The camera is capable of operating up to 30 frames per seconds (fps) in VGA mode with output support for various colour formats. The horizontal viewing angle is approximately $70°$. As a trade-off for image quality and memory space, the resolution is configured at $72 \times 99$ pixel on 30 fps, with output format of 8-bit YUV422. This image format separates each pixel's colour channels from the brightness channel, thus no additional colour transforming operations are required when only brightness information is required in further processing. The camera is connected to the MCU with two groups of interfaces, which are a serial camera control bus (SCCB) for camera configuration, and a group of image data/synchronization signals through DCMI interface, as shown in Fig. 2.

**Other Sensor.** One 9-DoF (degrees of freedom) motion sensor MPU9250 which contains a gyroscope, an accelerometer and a magnetometer is installed in the CSU which enables Colias to detect its attitude. The motion sensor is connected to the MCU via $I^2C$ interface with the refresh rate of 20 Hz. The robot's orientation is periodically estimated by a differential equation:

$$\begin{bmatrix} \dot{\gamma}_{t+1} \\ \dot{\theta}_{t+1} \\ \dot{\psi}_{t+1} \end{bmatrix} = \frac{1}{\cos \theta_t} \begin{bmatrix} \cos \theta_t & \sin \gamma_t \sin \theta_t & \cos \gamma_t \sin \theta_t \\ 0 & \cos \theta_t \cos \gamma_t & -\sin \gamma_t \cos \theta_t \\ 0 & \sin \gamma_t & \cos \gamma_t \cos \theta_t \end{bmatrix}^{-1} \cdot \begin{bmatrix} \omega_t^{EbX} \\ \omega_t^{EbY} \\ \omega_t^{EbZ} \end{bmatrix} \quad (3)$$

where the left part is refreshed robot's orientation, represented by Euler angles (roll, pitch and yaw) and the right part is the estimated orientation last time. $\omega_t^{EbX}$, $\omega_t^{EbY}$ and $\omega_t^{EbZ}$ are acquired rotation speed around three axes from the IMU sensor. In this attitude estimation approach, there is a zero point shifting problem caused by the nature of gyroscope, leading to an increasing accumulated error. According to our tests, this error is less than $2°$ per minute, yet acceptable enough for simple behaviour generation in our experiments.

Two MEMS microphones are also applied in the CSU. Each microphone has the frequency response of 60-15 kHz with sensitivity up tp $-26$ dBFS. The omnidirectional microphones are placed with a distance of 33 mm, connected with the main processor through $I^2S$ interface. The power consumption is 1.4 mA

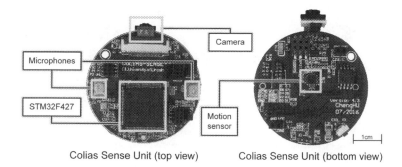

Colias Sense Unit (top view)          Colias Sense Unit (bottom view)

**Fig. 5.** The photo of CSU from both sides. Showing some major components.

each. The microphones are reserved for future applications. For example, by analysing the phase delay between the pair of microphones from a single sound source, the source localization and tracking tasks could be achieved.

### 2.3   The Colias Extension Units (CEU)

We have inserted as many peripherals into the tiny boards of CBU and CSU, enabling *Colias IV* to perform most of the experiments independently. Yet some further features which consume large space but not required by all experiments, or only required for debugging sessions such as USB interface, Bluetooth data transmitter, wireless first person view transmitter [16] or other local communication oriented sensors, are achieved by removable extension units connected to CSU through the extension sockets.

Currently we have realized four different types of CEUs. The USB module and Bluetooth module are used in the research mostly. The USB extension module serves the main purpose of debugging, downloading binary program into the CSU, and transmit massive data like a frame of image through an USB cable. The maximum bandwidth is 3 MBit/s. The Bluetooth extension module enables the *Colias IV* to communicate with a remote host device such as a laptop or a smart-phone, receiving motion commands or sending sensor data. The maximum bandwidth is 512 KBit/s. Both USB and Bluetooth extension modules are equipped with an SD card slot and eight LEDs, which are extremely useful in experiments with multiple robots that temporary data storage is needed.

## 3   Bio-inspired Visual Motion Sensing: Case Studies

Benefiting from the friendly developing environment, several successful bio-inspired visual motion sensing model such as the LGMD1 [16,17], LGMD2 [15] and DSN [18] could be realized inside the *Colias IV* robot, enabling them to work independently to recognize fast approaching objects and trigger maneuver commands such as collision avoidance (Fig. 6).

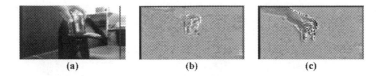

**Fig. 6.** The sample of LGMD1 layers during a single process. (a) shows the original input image, that a can of beer is waving in front of the robot; (b) shows the result of summing layer (the sum of the excitation layer and the inhibition layer) that filters out stationary background; (c) shows the grouping layer, which enhancing the filtered moving foregrounds. (figure adapted from [17])

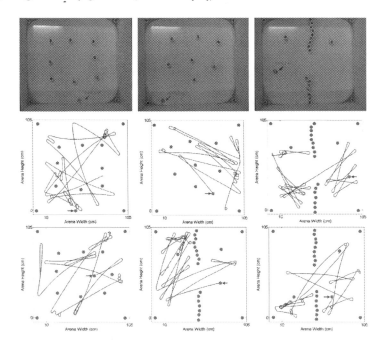

**Fig. 7.** The experiment of a *Colias IV* robot with embedded LGMD2 model to detect imminent collisions. The robot is allowed to wander inside the arena with distributed obstacles. The red dots indicate the obstacles. (figure adapted from [15]) (Color figure online)

The embedded LGMD1 model (also called the ELGMD) is a layered neural model formed by five layers with lateral inhibition mechanism and two single cells [17]. The computational model contains only low-level image processing such as excitation transferring and neighbouring operations. With latest optimizations for the embedded processor, it can achieve CPU time occupation of 7–10 ms, and the RAM occupation of around 38 KBytes. In previous experiments with embedded LGMD1, the robot is able to run autonomously inside an square arena full of obstacles for more than 10 min without collisions. Details of the structure of ELGMD, its realization on *Colias IV* and the experiments are available in [17].

In locust, the LGMD2 is a neighbouring neural model identified next to the LGMD1. They share lots of similarities on structure and neural responses towards approaching objects. The difference is that the LGMD2 does little or no response to bright approaching objects in front of dark background [19]. This special mechanism which enhance the model's foreground selectivity is also realized in the embedded LGMD2 model with the *Colias IV* robot [15]. Their different responses towards visual looms are also demonstrated and analysed in arena experiments with several robots equipped with both the LGMD1 and LGMD2 model, but their input visions are two overlapping parts from a single frame [16]. The example of these experiments are represented in Fig. 7.

All these embedded visual models are developed on the *Colias IV* robot platform, which demonstrates its feasibility and further potential for researching bio-inspired visual models, or other computational demanding models on-board when multi sensory data is required.

## 4 Summary

A miniature ground mobile robot *Colias IV* occupying footprint of 4 cm in diameter is developed to study computational intensive embedded models. Featured by a strong ARM processor, variety of sensors including a tiny camera and two digital microphones, and enormous capabilities of connectivity, this micro robot can realize bio-inspired visual detecting model such as LGMD1 and other related neural models on-board in real time, which have been tested and studied by a series of experiments.

Even though with compact size and low cost, the developed robot *Colias IV* has shown potential for further research based on multi-agent experiments such as the aggregation behaviours in robot swarms. But challenges still exist, for example, to coordinate a group of robots spontaneously, the required communication among each other is difficult to be accomplished without global synchronization. This could be solved by utilizing an extension board with additional communication modules, relying on either RF or optical approaches.

**Acknowledgement.** This work was supported by the EU FP7 project HAZCEPT (318907) and Horizon 2020 project STEP2DYNA (691154).

## References

1. Kostavelis, I., Gasteratos, A.: Semantic mapping for mobile robotics tasks: a survey. Robot. Auton. Syst. **66**, 86–103 (2015)
2. Chen, J., Gauci, M., Li, W., Kolling, A., Groß, R.: Occlusion-based cooperative transport with a swarm of miniature mobile robots. IEEE Trans. Robot. **31**(2), 307–321 (2015)

3. Dorigo, M.: SWARM-BOT: an experiment in swarm robotics. In: 2005 Swarm Intelligence Symposium, Proceedings 2005 IEEE. SIS 2005, pp. 192–200. IEEE (2005)
4. Kim, J.Y., Colaco, T., Kashino, Z., Nejat, G., Benhabib, B.: mROBerTo: a modular millirobot for swarm-behavior studies. In: 2016 IEEE/RSJ International Conference on Intelligent Robots and Systems (IROS), pp. 2109–2114. IEEE (2016)
5. Turgut, A.E., Gokce, F., Celikkanat, H., Bayindir, L., Sahin, E.: Kobot: a mobile robot designed specifically for swarm robotics research. METUCENG-TR Technical report Middle East Technical University, Ankara, Turkey, vol. 5, p. 2007 (2007)
6. Betthauser, J., et al.: Wolfbot: a distributed mobile sensing platform for research and education. In: 2014 Zone 1 Conference of the American Society for Engineering Education (ASEE Zone 1), pp. 1–8. IEEE (2014)
7. Fu, Q., Yue, S., Hu, C.: Bio-inspired collision detector with enhanced selectivity for ground robotic vision system. Trans. Neural Netw. **17**(3), 705–716 (2016)
8. Rind, F.C., Simmons, P.J.: Orthopteran DCMD neuron: a reevaluation of responses to moving objects. i. selective responses to approaching objects. J. Neurophysiol. **68**(5), 1654–1666 (1992)
9. Hatsopoulos, N., Gabbiani, F., Laurent, G.: Elementary computation of object approach by a wide-field visual neuron. Science **270**(5238), 1000 (1995)
10. Meng, H.Y., et al.: A modified model for the lobula giant movement detector and its FPGA implementation. Comput. Vis. Image Underst. **114**(11), 1238–1247 (2010)
11. Yue, S., Rind, F.C.: Collision detection in complex dynamic scenes using an LGMD-based visual neural network with feature enhancement. IEEE Trans. Neural Netw. **17**(3), 705–716 (2006)
12. i Badia, S.B., Bernardet, U., Verschure, P.F.: Non-linear neuronal responses as an emergent property of afferent networks: a case study of the locust lobula giant movement detector. PLoS Comput. Biol. **6**(3), e1000701 (2010)
13. Arvin, F., Murray, J., Zhang, C., Yue, S.: Colias: an autonomous micro robot for swarm robotic applications. Int. J. Adv. Robot. Syst. **11**, 1 (2014)
14. Hu, C., Arvin, F., Yue, S.: Development of a bio-inspired vision system for mobile micro-robots. In: 2014 Joint IEEE International Conferences on Development and Learning and Epigenetic Robotics (ICDL-Epirob), pp. 81–86. IEEE (2014)
15. Fu, Q., Yue, S.: Modelling LGMD2 visual neuron system. In: IEEE 25th International Workshop on Machine Learning for Signal Processing (MLSP), pp. 1–6. IEEE (2015)
16. Fu, Q., Hu, C., Liu, T., Yue, S.: Collision selective LGMDs neuron models research benefits from a vision-based autonomous micro robot. In: 2017 IEEE/RSJ International Conference on Intelligent Robots and Systems (IROS), pp. 3996–4002, September 2017
17. Hu, C., Arvin, F., Xiong, C., Yue, S.: Bio-inspired embedded vision system for autonomous micro-robots: the LGMD case. IEEE Trans. Cogn. Dev. Syst. **9**(3), 241–254 (2017)
18. Yue, S., Fu, Q.: Modeling direction selective visual neural network with on and off pathways for extracting motion cues from cluttered background. In: 2017 International Joint Conference on Neural Networks (IJCNN), pp. 831–838, May 2017
19. Rind, F.C., et al.: Two identified looming detectors in the locust: ubiquitous lateral connections among their inputs contribute to selective responses to looming objects. Scientific reports, vol. 6 (2016)

# ResQbot: A Mobile Rescue Robot with Immersive Teleperception for Casualty Extraction

Roni Permana Saputra[1,2(✉)] and Petar Kormushev[1]

[1] Robot Intelligence Lab, Dyson School of Design Engineering,
Imperial College London, London, UK
{r.saputra,p.kormushev}@imperial.ac.uk
[2] Research Centre for Electrical Power and Mechatronics,
Indonesian Institute of Sciences - LIPI, Jakarta, Indonesia
https://www.imperial.ac.uk/robot-intelligence/

**Abstract.** In this work, we propose a novel mobile rescue robot equipped with an immersive stereoscopic teleperception and a teleoperation control. This robot is designed with the capability to perform safely a casualty-extraction procedure. We have built a proof-of-concept mobile rescue robot called ResQbot for the experimental platform. An approach called "loco-manipulation" is used to perform the casualty-extraction procedure using the platform. The performance of this robot is evaluated in terms of task accomplishment and safety by conducting a mock rescue experiment. We use a custom-made human-sized dummy that has been sensorised to be used as the casualty. In terms of safety, we observe several parameters during the experiment including impact force, acceleration, speed and displacement of the dummy's head. We also compare the performance of the proposed immersive stereoscopic teleperception to conventional monocular teleperception. The results of the experiments show that the observed safety parameters are below key safety thresholds which could possibly lead to head or neck injuries. Moreover, the teleperception comparison results demonstrate an improvement in task-accomplishment performance when the operator is using the immersive teleperception.

**Keywords:** Mobile rescue robot · Immersive teleperception
Casualty extraction · Loco-manipulation

## 1 Introduction

Catastrophic events, disasters, or local incidents generate hazardous and unstable environments in which there is an urgent need for timely and reliable intervention, mainly to save lives. A multi-storey building fire disaster—such as the recent Grenfell Tower Inferno in London, United Kingdom [1]—is an example of such a scenario. Responding to such situations is a race against time—immediate

© Springer International Publishing AG, part of Springer Nature 2018
M. Giuliani et al. (Eds.): TAROS 2018, LNAI 10965, pp. 209–220, 2018.
https://doi.org/10.1007/978-3-319-96728-8_18

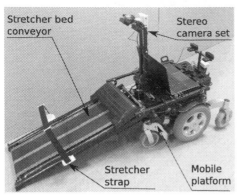 

(a) ResQbot robot platform          (b) Teleoperating ResQbot

**Fig. 1.** Proposed mobile rescue robot with immersive stereoscopic teleperception: (a) The ResQbot platform comprising a motorised stretcher bed conveyor attached to a differential-drive mobile base, a stretcher strap module and a stereo camera rig, (b) Operator provided with teleperception via HTC-Vive headset.

action is required to reach all potential survivors in time. Such responses, however, are limited to the availability of trained first responders as well as prone to potential risks to their lives. The high risk to the lives of rescue workers means that, in reality, fast response on-site human intervention may not always be a possibility.

Using robots in search-and-rescue (SAR) missions offers a great alternative by potentially minimising the danger for the first responders. Moreover, it is more flexible—the number of these robots can be expanded to perform faster responses. Thus, various robotic designs have been proposed to suit several specific SAR applications [2,3]. These robots are designed to assist with one or sometimes multiple tasks as part of a SAR operation—including reconnaissance, exploration, search, monitoring, and excavation.

Our aim in this study is to develop a mobile rescue robot system (see Fig. 1a) that is capable of performing a casualty-extraction procedure. This procedure includes loading and transporting a human victim—a.k.a. casualty—smoothly, which is essential for ensuring the victim's safety, via teleoperation mode. We also aim to develop more immersive teleperception for the robot's operators to improve their performance and produce higher operation accuracy and safer operations.

## 2   Related Work

Wide-ranging robotics research studies have been undertaken in the area of search, exploration, and monitoring, specifically with applications in SAR scenarios [4–6]. Despite the use of the term 'rescue' in SAR, little attention has been given to the development of a rescue robot that is capable of performing a physical rescue mission, including loading and transporting a victim to a safe zone—a.k.a. casualty extraction.

Several research studies have been conducted to enable the use of robots in the rescue phase of SAR missions. The majority of these studies focused on developing mobile robots—mainly tracked mobile robots—with mounted articulated manipulators [7,8] or other novel arm mechanisms, such as elephant trunk-like arms [9] or snake-like arms [3]. Such designs enable the mobile robots to move debris by using their manipulators and also perform other physical interventions during the rescue mission, such as a casualty-extraction procedure.

Battlefield Extraction Assist Robot (BEAR) is one of the most sophisticated robot platforms designed and developed specifically for casualty-extraction procedures [2,10]. This robot was developed by Vecna Technologies and intended for the U.S. Army [11]. It has a humanoid form with two independent, tracked locomotion systems. It is also equipped with a heavy-duty, dual-arm system that is capable of lifting and carrying up to 227-kg loads [12]. This robot is capable of performing casualty-extraction procedures by lifting up and carrying the casualty using its two arms. However, such a procedure could cause additional damage to the already injured victim—such as a spinal or neck injury from the lack of body support during the procedure.

Several investigations have been conducted on the development of rescue robots capable of performing safer and more robust casualty-extraction routines. These robots were designed to be more compact by using stretcher-type constructions or litters [13–16]. The robots presented in these studies are intended for performing safe casualty extractions with simpler mechanisms compared to arm mechanisms. The use of the stretcher-type design on this robot also ensures the victim's safety during transportation.

The mobile rescue robot demonstrated by the Tokyo Fire Department is one of the robots that uses this design concept [17,18]. This robot is equipped with a belt-conveyor mechanism and also a pair of articulated manipulators. It uses its manipulators to lift up the casualty and place it onto the conveyor during the casualty-extraction procedure [19]. Then the belt conveyor pulls up the casualty into the container inside the robot for safe transportation. Compared to BEAR, this robot offers a safer casualty-transportation process. However, lifting up the casualty during the loading process is still a procedure that is highly likely to cause additional damage to the victim.

Iwano et al. in [13–15] proposed a mobile rescue robot platform capable of performing casualty extraction without a "lifting" process. This robot loads the casualty merely using a belt-conveyor mechanism. This belt conveyor pulls the casualty from the ground onto the mobile platform, while the mobile platform synchronises the movement toward the body [15]. Since there is no "lifting" process during the casualty-extraction procedure, this method is expected to be safer than the methods applied in BEAR and the Tokyo Fire Department's robot. However, to the best of our knowledge, no safety evaluation of performing this extraction method has been published.

In terms of controlling method, these robots are still manually operated or teleoperated by human operators. The BEAR robot and the rescue robot demonstrated by the Tokyo Fire Department are teleoperated by human operators using a conventional teleoperation control setup [18]. On the other hand, based on the reports presented in [13–15], the rescue robot developed by Iwano et al. still requires human operators to be present on the scene to perform casualty-extraction procedures.

## 3  Research Contributions

In this work, we present a mobile rescue robot we developed that is capable of performing a casualty-extraction procedure using the method presented in [14]. Moreover, we equip this robot with teleoperation control and an immersive stereoscopic teleperception. As a proof of concept, we have designed and built a novel mobile rescue robot platform called ResQbot [20] shown in Fig. 1. This robot is equipped with an onboard stereoscopic camera rig to provide immersive teleperception that is transmitted via a virtual-reality (VR) headset to the operator.

The contributions to this work are:

1. Proof-of-concept ResQbot, including teleoperation mode with immersive teleperception via HTC Vive[1] headset;
2. Preliminary evaluation of loco-manipulation-based casualty extraction using the ResQbot platform, in terms of task accomplishment and safety;
3. Evaluation of the proposed immersive teleperception compared with the other teleperception methods, including the conventional teleperception setup and direct observation as a baseline.

## 4  Casualty Extraction via Loco-Manipulation Approach

To perform a casualty-extraction procedure using the ResQbot platform, we propose using a loco-manipulation approach. By using this approach, the robot can implicitly achieve a manipulation objective—which is loading of a victim onto the robot—through a series of locomotive manoeuvres. We utilise the conveyor module mounted on the mobile robot base to create a simple mechanism for the loading of a victim onto the conveyor surface by solely following a locomotive routine.

Figure 2 illustrates the proposed casualty-extraction operation using the loco-manipulation technique. By removing the need for high-complexity robotic manipulators or mechanisms, this technique greatly simplifies the underlying controls required for conducting complex casualty extraction in rescue missions. This simplicity is highly beneficial for intuitive teleoperation by human operators.

This casualty-extraction procedure involves four major phases:

1. **Relative pose adjustment**: the robot aligns its relative pose with respect to the victim in preparation for performing the loco-manipulation routine.

---

[1] Virtual Reality Head Mounted Display by VIVE: https://www.vive.com/.

2. **Approaching**: the robot gently approaches the victim to safely make contact with the victim's head for initiating the loading process.
3. **Loading**: by using a balance between the locomotion of the base and the motion of the belt conveyor, the robot smoothly loads the victim onboard. Smooth operation at this stage is crucial in order to minimise traumatic injury caused by the operation. The victim is fully onboard when the upper body is fully loaded onto the stretcher bed. We consider the upper body to be from the head to the hip, thus protecting the critical parts of the body, including the head and spinal cord.
4. **Fastening**: once the victim is fully onboard, the strapping mechanism fastens the victim using a stretcher-strap mechanism in preparation for safe transportation. The conveyor surface serves as a stretcher bed for transporting the victim to a safe zone where paramedics can provide further medical care.

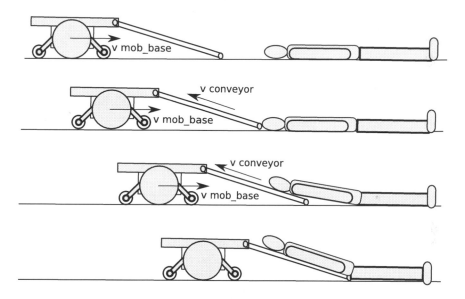

**Fig. 2.** Illustration of casualty extraction via loco-manipulation technique. From the top to the bottom: (1) ResQbot gently approaching the victim, (2) the belt conveyor on the stretcher bed moving at the synchronized speed of the mobile base, (3) the belt conveyor pulling the victim onto stretcher bed while the mobile base move to the opposite direction, (4) the victim fully onboard the stretcher bed.

## 5   Robot Platform

We have designed and built a novel mobile rescue robot platform called ResQbot as a proof of concept for the implementation of the proposed casualty-extraction procedure. Figure 1a shows the ResQbot platform that has been developed in this project. This platform is designed to be able to perform a casualty-extraction task based on the proposed loco-manipulation approach. This platform consists of two main modules: a differential-drive mobile base and a motorised stretcher-bed conveyor module. The platform is also equipped with a range of perception devices, including an RGB-D camera and a stereoscopic camera rig; these devices provide the perception required during the operation. We used an Xbox joystick controller for the operator interface to control the robot. We also proposed an immersive teleperception interface for this mobile robot using an HTC Vive virtual reality headset. This headset will provide teleperception for the operator by displaying a real-time visual image sent from the onboard stereo camera of the mobile robot. Figure 1b shows the operator teleoperates ResQbot using the proposed teleoperation and teleperception devices.

## 5.1   Mobile Base Module

The mobile base module used for the ResQbot platform is a differential drive module. This platform is a customised version of a commercially available powered wheelchair—Quickie Salsa-M—manufactured by Sunrise Medical[2]. This mobile base is chosen for its versatile design and stability owing to its original design purpose, which was to carry the disabled both indoors and outdoors. This platform has a compact turning circle while ensuring stability and safety through its all-wheel independent suspension and anti-pitch technology over rough or uneven terrain. Its mobile base is also capable of manoeuvring through narrow pathways and confined spaces, due to its compact design (only 600 mm in width).

## 5.2   Motorised Stretcher Bed Module

ResQbot is equipped with an active stretcher-bed module that enables active pulling up of the victim's body while the mobile platform is moving. This module is mounted at the back of the mobile base via hinges allowing it to fold (for compact navigation) or unfold (for loading and transporting the victim) on demand. This stretcher bed is composed of a belt-conveyor module that is capable of transporting a maximum payload of 100 kg at its maximum power. This belt conveyor is powered by a 240 VDC motor with 500 W maximum power. The motor is controlled through a driver module powered by a 240 VAC onboard power inverter, and the pulse-width modulation (PWM) control signal is used to control the motor's speed.

During loading of the victim's body, the active-pulling speed of the belt conveyor has to be synchronised with the locomotion speed of the mobile platform. Therefore, this module is equipped with a closed-loop speed control system to synchronise the conveyor speed and the mobile base locomotion speed. An incremental rotary encoder connected to the conveyor's pulley is used to provide speed measurements of the belt conveyor as feedback to the controller. Another incremental rotary encoder is connected to an omnidirectional wheel attached to the

[2] Quickie Salsa-M powered wheelchair by Sunrise Medical: www.sunrisemedical.co.uk.

floor. This encoder provides measurements of the mobile base linear speed. The measured mobile base linear speed is used for the speed reference of the conveyor controller.

For a safe transportation process, the victim has to be safely placed onboard the stretcher bed. Thus, this stretcher-bed module is also equipped with a motorised stretcher strap to enable fastening of the victim on the bed as a safety measure. This stretcher-strap module is powered by a 24 VDC motor. The motor is controlled to fasten and unfasten the stretcher strap during the casualty-extraction procedure.

## 6    Experimental Setups and Results

**Experimental Setting.** We have conducted a number of experimental trials to evaluate our proof-of-concept mobile-rescue-robot platform, ResQbot, in terms of task accomplishment, safety and teleperception comparison. In these experiments, we conducted a mock casualty-extraction procedure using ResQbot by teleoperation with three different teleperception modalities:

- **Direct mode (baseline)**: user controls the robot while being present at the scene;
- **Conventional mode**: user receives visual feedback provided by a monocular camera through a display monitor;
- **Immersive mode**: the user receives stereoscopic vision provided by an onboard stereoscopic camera module and through a virtual reality headset.

Ninety series of trials in total were conducted, with 30 series for each teleperception modality. We conducted this number of trials to capture any possible problems encountered during the trials. For the whole experiment, we used the same setup of the victim and its relative position and orientation with respect to the ResQbot. These various victim positions are inside the area of the ResQbot perception device's field of view.

To evaluate the safety of the proposed casualty-extraction procedure using the ResQbot platform, we conducted the trials using a sensorised dummy as the casualty. This dummy was equipped with an inertial measurement unit (IMU) sensor placed on its head. We used 3DM-GX4-25[3] IMU sensor, with resolution $< 0.1$ mg and bias instability $\pm 0.04$ mg. During the trials, we recorded the data from this sensor at 100 Hz sampling frequency.

**Task Accomplishment.** In general, we achieved successful task accomplishment of the casualty-extraction procedure in every trial. Screenshot images in Fig. 3 demonstrate the procedure applied during the casualty-extraction operation performed by ResQbot in the experiments.

---

[3] LORD MicroStrain IMU: http://www.microstrain.com/inertial/3dm-gx4-25.

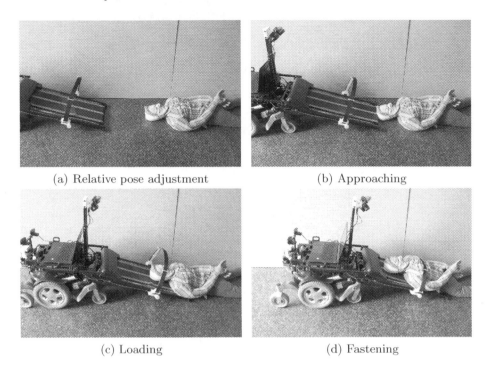

(a) Relative pose adjustment                    (b) Approaching

(c) Loading                                      (d) Fastening

**Fig. 3.** A sequence of images showing the progress of the casualty extraction task in the simulated rescue mission scenario in our experiments.

**Safety Evaluation.** In this experiment, we observed the impact applied to the dummy's head during the casualty-extraction procedure. This impact caused force and displacement of the dummy's head. The observation was focused on the part during the loading phase when the robot—i.e. the stretcher-bed conveyor—made first contact with the dummy's head. Two extreme cases were selected (i.e. roughest and smoothest operation, respectively) for this safety evaluation. These two cases represent the largest and the smallest maximum instant acceleration of each test within the whole experiment.

Figure 4 shows the dummy's head displacement, speed and acceleration during the loading process caused by the robot's first contact. Two extreme cases are presented; one is the smoothest trial (in blue), and the other one is the roughest trial (in red). The dashed vertical line (in green) indicates the time-step at which the contact was initiated during the loading process.

The forces applied to the dummy's head can be estimated based on these measured accelerations from the IMU, and it can be calculated via:

$$F_i = ma + F_s$$

in which, $F_i$ corresponds to the estimated instantaneous force applied to the dummy's head, and $F_s$ corresponds to the static friction force between the dummy's head and the ground [21]. The estimated force was calculated based on

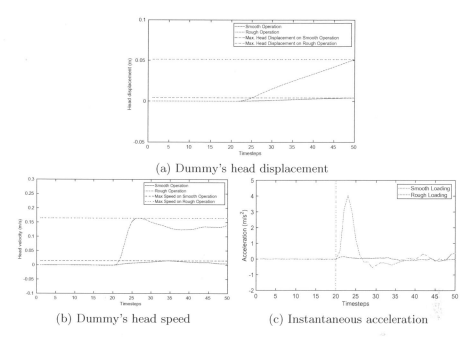

(a) Dummy's head displacement

(b) Dummy's head speed      (c) Instantaneous acceleration

**Fig. 4.** The observation of two extreme cases of casualty extraction trial, (1) the smoothest trial (in blue) and (2) the roughest trial (in red). The dashed vertical line (in green) indicates the time-step at which the contact is initiated. (Color figure online)

the measured maximum instant acceleration (a) during the operation and the approximated mass of the dummy's head (m). Table 1 summarises the observations of the two significant cases—i.e. smoothest and roughest trial—during the experiment. These cases correspond to the maximum instantaneous accelerations of the dummy's head caused by the robot during the casualty-extraction procedure.

We compared the results presented in Table 1 with several key safety thresholds—which were reported in the literature as possible causes of head or neck injuries to the casualty [22,23]. Figure 5 illustrates the comparison between the trial results and the thresholds from the literature. It can be seen that all evaluated parameters in the experiments are relatively small and below the threshold. Even though not conclusive yet, these preliminary results show high safety promise for the proposed platform of the casualty-extraction procedure, and for further development. Thus it also motivates more elaborate safety evaluations for the practical deployment of the platform.

**Teleperception Comparison.** In this work, we proposed immersive teleperception via an HTC Vive headset to provide visual perception for the operator when operating the ResQbot platform. We evaluated this proposed teleperception modality by comparing it to the conventional teleperception setup

**Table 1.** The summary of two significantly different trials—i.e. smooth and rough operation—performed during the experiment.

|  | Smooth trial | Rough trial |
|---|---|---|
| Max. instant acceleration ($m/s^2$) | $\approx 0.154$ | $\approx 4.042$ |
| Max. Velocity ($m/s$) during initial contact | $\approx 0.015$ | $\approx 0.16$ |
| Victim's head displacement ($m$) | $\approx 0.004$ | $\approx 0.051$ |
| Max. impact force ($N$) | $\approx 23.63$ | $\approx 41.12$ |

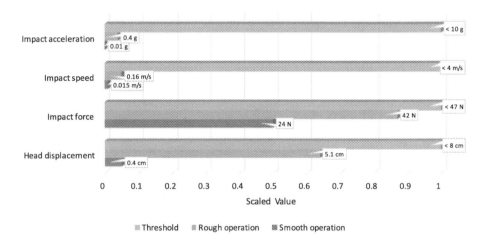

**Fig. 5.** The comparison between the trial results and the thresholds from the literature.

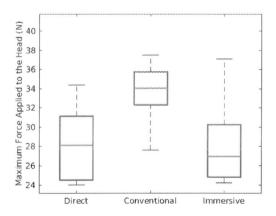

**Fig. 6.** The distribution of the estimated maximal forces in the three different perception modes during the experiments.

(i.e. providing visual perception via single monitor) and the direct-observation scenario as a baseline (i.e. controlling the robot while being present at the scene).

We compared these three perception modes in terms of the smoothness of the casualty-extraction procedure, which is represented by the maximum force applied to the dummy's head during the experiment in both cases. Figure 6 shows a box plot of the distribution of the estimated maximal forces in the three different perception modes during the experiments. According to Fig. 6, in terms of the smoothness of the procedure, we observed that the VR mode (i.e. immersive) results in a higher population of smoother trials than the conventional mode. In fact, the VR mode achieves smooth operations with low maximal estimated forces under 28 N for approximately 50% of its trials, similar to the direct-observation mode, in which the operator has direct access to observe the scene during the operation.

## 7   Conclusion

In this paper, we presented a proposed mobile rescue robot system that is capable of safely loading and transporting a casualty. We proposed an immersive stereoscopic teleperception modality via an HTC Vive headset to provide the teleoperator with more realistic and intuitive perception information during the operation. As a proof of concept of the proposed system, we designed and built a novel mobile rescue robot called ResQbot, which is controlled via teleoperation. We evaluated the proposed platform in terms of task accomplishment, safety and teleperception comparison for completing a casualty-extraction procedure. Based on the results of our experiments, the proposed platform is capable of performing a safe casualty-extraction procedure and offers great promise for further development. Moreover, the teleperception comparisons highlight that the proposed immersive teleperception can improve the performance of the teleoperator controlling the mobile robot's performance during a casualty-extraction procedure.

**Acknowledgement.** Roni Permana Saputra would like to thank Indonesia Endowment Fund for Education - LPDP, for the financial support of the PhD program. The authors would also like to show our gratitude to Arash Tavakoli and Nemanja Rakicevic for helpful discussions and inputs for the present work.

## References

1. The Telegraph News: Grenfell Tower inferno a 'disaster waiting to happen' as concerns are raised for safety of other buildings. http://www.telegraph.co.uk/news/2017/06/14/grenfell-tower-inferno-disaster-waiting-happen-concerns-raised/
2. Yoo, A.C., Gilbert, G.R., Broderick, T.J.: Military robotic combat casualty extraction and care. In: Rosen, J., Hannaford, B., Satava, R. (eds.) Surgical Robotics, pp. 13–32. Springer, Boston (2011). https://doi.org/10.1007/978-1-4419-1126-1_2
3. Murphy, R.R., et al.: Search and rescue robotics. In: Siciliano, B., Khatib, O. (eds.) Springer Handbook of Robotics, pp. 1151–1173. Springer, Heidelberg (2008). https://doi.org/10.1007/978-3-540-30301-5_51

4. Shen, S., Michael, N., Kumar, V.: Autonomous indoor 3D exploration with a micro-aerial vehicle. In: 2012 IEEE International Conference on Robotics and Automation (ICRA), pp. 9–15. IEEE (2012)
5. Waharte, S., Trigoni, N.: Supporting search and rescue operations with UAVs. In: 2010 International Conference on Emerging Security Technologies (EST), pp. 142–147. IEEE (2010)
6. Goodrich, M.A., et al.: Supporting wilderness search and rescue using a camera-equipped mini UAV. J. Field Robot. **25**, 89–110 (2008)
7. Gearin, M.: Remote-controlled robots. http://www.telerob.com/en/products/remote-controlled-robots
8. Schwarz, M., et al.: NimbRo rescue: solving disaster-response tasks with the mobile manipulation robot momaro. J. Field Robot. **25**, 89–110 (2017)
9. Wolf, A., Brown, H.B., Casciola, R., Costa, A., Schwerin, M., Shamas, E., Choset, H.: A mobile hyper redundant mechanism for search and rescue tasks. In: 2003 IEEE/RSJ International Conference on Intelligent Robots and Systems, (IROS 2003). Proceedings, vol. 3, pp. 2889–2895. IEEE (2003)
10. Theobald, D.: Mobile extraction-assist robot. U.S. Patent No. 7,719,222. Washington, DC: U.S. Patent and Trademark Office (2010)
11. Vecna Robotics: The BEAR Battlefield Extraction-Assist Robot (2010)
12. Quick, D.: Battlefield Extraction-Assist Robot to ferry wounded to safety. https://newatlas.com/battlefield-extraction-assist-robot/17059/
13. Iwano, Y., Osuka, K., Amano, H.: Development of rescue support stretcher system with stair-climbing. In: 2011 IEEE International Symposium on Safety, Security, and Rescue Robotics (SSRR), pp. 245–250. IEEE (2011)
14. Iwano, Y., Osuka, K., Amano, H.: Development of rescue support stretcher system. In: 2010 IEEE International Symposium on Safety, Security, and Rescue Robotics (SSRR), pp. 1–6. IEEE (2010)
15. Iwano, Y., Osuka, K., Amano, H.: Evaluation of rescue support stretcher system. In: 2012 IEEE RO-MAN: The 21st IEEE International Symposium on Robot and Human Interactive Communication, pp. 245–250. IEEE (2012)
16. Sahashi, T., Sahashi, A., Uchiyama, H., Fukumoto, I.: A study of operational liability of the medical rescue robot under disaster. In: 2011 IEEE/SICE International Symposium on System Integration (SII), pp. 1281–1286. IEEE (2011)
17. Ota, K.: RoboCue, the Tokyo Fire Department's Rescue-Bot. Popular Science Magazine, pp. 2011–03 (2011)
18. Tokyo Fire Department: Rescue robot (nicknamed Robochee). http://www.tfd.metro.tokyo.jp/ts/soubi/robo/05.htm
19. Nosowitz, D.: Meet Japan's Earthquake Search-and-Rescue Robots (2011). https://www.popsci.com/technology/article/2011-03/six-robots-could-shape-future-earthquake-search-and-rescue
20. Saputra, R.P., Kormushev, P.: ResQbot: a mobile rescue robot for casualty extraction. In: 2018 ACM/IEEE International Conference on Human-Robot Interaction (HRI 2018), pp. 239–240, ACM, New York (2018)
21. Engineers edge: Coefficient of Friction Equation and Table Chart. http://www.engineersedge.com
22. Engsberg, J.R., Standeven, J.W., Shurtleff, T.L., Tricamo, J.M., Landau, W.M.: Spinal cord and brain injury protection: testing concept for a protective device. J. Spinal Cord Med. **47**, 634–639 (2009)
23. EURailSafe: Head Injury Criteria Tolerance Levels. www.eurailsafe.net/subsites/operas/HTML/Section3

# Seeing the Unseen: Locating Objects from Reflections

Jing Wu$^{(\boxtimes)}$ and Ze Ji

Cardiff University, Cardiff CF24 3AA, UK
{wuj11,jiz1}@cardiff.ac.uk

**Abstract.** Inspired by the ubiquitous use of reflections in human vision system, in this paper, we present our first step exploration of using reflections to extend the FOV of cameras in computer vision applications. We make use of a stereo camera, and establish mathematical models for locating objects from their mirror reflections. We also propose a pipeline to track and locate moving objects from their reflections captured in videos. Experimental results demonstrated the efficiency and effectiveness of the proposed method, and verified the potential use of reflections in locating non-line of sight (NLOS) objects.

**Keywords:** Mirror reflection · Object tracking · Stereo vision

## 1 Introduction

Reflections are ubiquitous in our environments, and are utilized by our vision system to make us aware of our surroundings. A typical use of reflections is to extend the field of view (FOV) of our eyes to make scenes and objects, which are not directly in line of sight (NLOS), visible. For example, we use rear view mirrors of cars to tell the traffic behind, and detect oncoming vehicles at junctions by their reflections from parked cars or windows. There is little effort in the area of robotics using reflections as another means of robot perception. Inspired by such empirical use of reflections in human vision, in this paper, we present our first step exploration of using reflections to extend the FOV of cameras for not only general-purpose computer vision applications, but also specifically for applications with vision-based robot perception, such as vSLAM (Visual Simultaneous Localization and Mapping) and situation awareness.

There have been works in computer vision that try to extract useful information from reflections. Yang et al. [18] regarded a water reflection image as a special case of two-view stereo and recovered the depth of the scene using stereo matching. Depth information can also be recovered from the replica of reflections presented on transparent surfaces [19]. For a transparent surface, the reflected scenes are often mixed up with the scenes transmitted from the other side. Then it becomes a popular topic how to separate and restore the two scenes [3–5,13–15]. Reflections in eyes have also attracted research interests. Nishino et al. [9,10] estimated lighting from corneal reflections, which were then used for relighting

© Springer International Publishing AG, part of Springer Nature 2018
M. Giuliani et al. (Eds.): TAROS 2018, LNAI 10965, pp. 221–233, 2018.
https://doi.org/10.1007/978-3-319-96728-8_19

applications [10] and robust face recognition [9]. Jenkins and Kerr [7] extracted faces of bystanders from corneal reflections, and proposed its possible application in criminal investigations. There are other interesting works making use of reflections, such as Sparkle Vision [20] – a work from MIT which aims to find images hidden in reflections from random shining micro-surfaces, and the use of inconsistent reflections to expose manipulation of photos [11].

Existing works demonstrated the diverse use of reflections in computer vision applications. Reflections provide a view of the scene from a different angle, which on one hand can reveal depth information when combined with the direct view; on the other hand can extend the FOV to expose NLOS scenes and objects. Our work focuses on the latter, and differs from relevant existing works [7] in that (1) instead of restoration of static scenes, we emphasize on tracking moving NLOS objects from reflections captured in videos; and (2) we make use of a stereo camera to help locating the object.

There have been works using ultra-fast time-of-flight imaging to detect motion of NLOS objects [12] and recover their 3D shapes [17]. However this imaging relies on the use of a femtosecond laser and a streak camera which are expensive (hundreds of thousands dollars), and slow (one hour or so capturing time) [6]. Our work overcomes these limitations by using visual reflections coupled with real-time processing algorithms.

The contributions of this paper are two folds. Firstly, this paper presents the first exploration into the novel use of visual reflections in estimating movements of NLOS objects. Secondly, in a simplified lab setting, we (1) establish the mathematical model that relates the locations of the object, the reflective surface, and the observer, and (2) based on the model, propose a processing pipeline for tracking and locating the moving NLOS object.

## 2    Problem Overview

Figure 1 illustrates the idea of using reflections to reveal NLOS objects. While the target object is already out of FOV in Fig. 1 right, its reflection from the mirror is still visible to the camera. Our idea is to infer the 3D location of the object from its reflection. Although reflection is a complex phenomenon in real

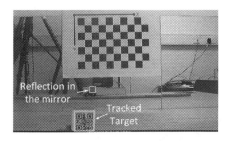
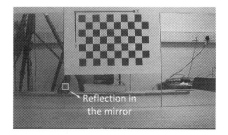

**Fig. 1.** Example frames of the moving object and its reflection, and their tracking results

world, in this initial exploration, we make a few simplifications in our laboratory set-up, which include:

- a planar mirror reflector to simplify the mathematical model and liberate the attention from image distortion and blurring;
- a binary QR code on the object to facilitate object detection and tracking.

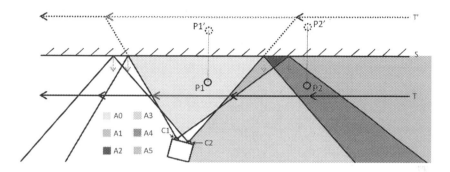

**Fig. 2.** Illustration of the simplified scenario and the reflections.

Figure 2 draws the simplified scene from top view. $S$ is the planar reflector. $C1$ and $C2$ are the two lenses of the stereo camera. The use of reflections from $S$ extends the FOV of $C1$ and $C2$. Without loss of generality, we analyse the field on the right. Look at $C1$ for example, objects in regions $A0-2$, e.g. $P1$, are directly visible to $C1$. Objects in regions $A3$ and $A4$, e.g. $P2$, are invisible to $C1$ themselves, but their reflections from $S$ are visible to $C1$. The FOV of $C1$ is thus extended to $A3$ and $A4$. Similarly, the FOV of $C2$ is extended to $A1$ and $A3$. Based on the visible contents (the object $P$ or its reflection $P'$), the field on the right can be segmented into six regions as colour coded in Fig. 2. Table 1 lists the visible contents for each region.

**Table 1.** Visibility of the object $P$ and its reflection $P'$ to camera $C1$ and $C2$.

|       | $A0$    | $A1$    | $A2$    | $A3$ | $A4$ | $A5$ |
|-------|---------|---------|---------|------|------|------|
| $C1$  | $P, P'$ | $P, P'$ | $P, P'$ | $P'$ | $P'$ |      |
| $C2$  | $P, P'$ | $P'$    |         | $P'$ |      |      |

When an object moving along a trajectory $T$, its reflection moves along the mirrored trajectory $T'$. As shown in Fig. 2, the visible section on $T'$ has extended range than that on $T$. The visible sections of $T$ and $T'$ can be recovered using stereo vision. And the extended part on $T'$ can be used to infer the locations on $T$ even they are not directly visible. The method is described in the following section.

## 3    Method

Figure 3 illustrates the pipeline of our method to recover an object's moving trajectory. The videos are captured in three sections. The calibration section captures a set of checkerboard patterns and is used to calibrate the stereo camera and estimate the location and orientation of the mirror. The movement section records the moving object, from which we detect/track the target object in 2D and reconstruct their 3D locations. The parameters estimated from the calibration section are used in the 3D reconstruction. The sequence of reconstructed 3D locations forms the recovered trajectory which is then compared with the ground-truth obtained from the evaluation section. In the following, we describe in detail the two main functional modules, i.e., target detection and tracking, and 3D reconstruction.

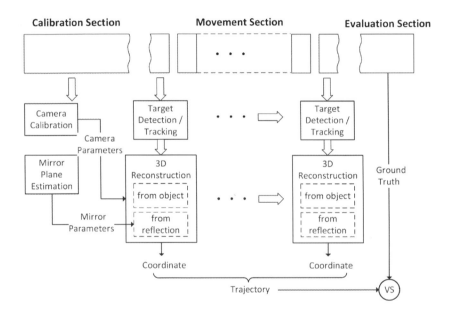

**Fig. 3.** Processing pipeline.

### 3.1    Detection and Tracking

The detection and tracking step is to find the 2D pixel locations of both the actual object and its mirror reflection in the video frames. The experiment considers only one known object. A template matching method is used for the initial detection of the object in the scene. Since the real object and its reflection are not always observable to the camera (Fig. 2), template matching will continue running with every new frame until the first detection of the target.

A registered template $t$ is first pre-determined for the search of the initial position of the object in the frames. The template matching is based on the fast normalized cross-correlation [8] that can be formulated as:

$$r(u,v) = \frac{\sum_{x,y}[f(x,y) - \bar{f}_{u,v}] \cdot [t(x-u, y-v) - \bar{t}]}{\sqrt{\sum_{x,y}[f(x,y) - \bar{f}_{u,v}]^2 \sum_{x,y}[t(x-u, y-v) - \bar{t}]^2}} \tag{1}$$

where $f(x,y)$ is the intensity value at $(x,y)$, $\bar{f}_{u,v}$ is the mean of the region shifted to position $[u,v]$ being compared with the template $t$, and $\bar{t}$ is the mean of the template.

With the first object detected, image tracking will be activated using the initial detected image patch as the tracking target. Due to various other uncontrollable factors, such as deformation caused by uneven reflective surfaces, blurred images due to poor focusing, occlusions, as well as rotations and distances from the camera, a robust image tracker is therefore needed. Correlation filter based trackers are considered highly efficient and robust in tracking through the correlation operations between the frames and the correlation filter, which is trained and updated at each subsequent time step [2].

Considering robustness and efficiency, we use the MOSSE (Minimum Output Sum of Squared Error) method [2]. Below is a summary of MOSSE. A filter $h$ is needed to map the input $x$ with a desired output $y$ by minimizing the sum of squared error between actual correlation outputs and desired correlation outputs. The correlation operations are performed in the DFT (Discrete Fourier Transform) space with high efficiency compared to the exhausted element-wise convolution computation. This can be formulated as below.

$$\min_{\hat{h}^*} \sum ||\hat{h}^* \odot \hat{x} - \hat{y}||^2 \tag{2}$$

Figure 1 shows the tracking results, where both the reflection of the object and the actual object are tracked and highlighted with bounding boxes. As can be seen, to increase the robustness of tracking, we used a binary QR code to enhance the discrimination of the target from the background.

## 3.2  3D Reconstruction

This step is to reconstruct the 3D location (i.e., the world coordinate) of the tracked object at each frame. Camera calibration and mirror plane estimation are carried out beforehand to provide the required parameters in the reconstruction.

**Camera Calibration** is to find the camera's intrinsic and extrinsic parameters, and to establish the projection from world coordinates to pixel locations. In this work, we define the origin of the world coordinate system to be at the optical centre of $C1$, and the x, y, z-axis pointing to the right, down, and away from the camera respectively. We make use of the stereo calibration app in Matlab [1] to calibrate $C1$ and $C2$, and rectify the images they captured. Figure 4 shows a pair of rectified left/right images after the stereo calibration.

**Fig. 4.** A pair of rectified images after stereo camera calibration. The lines show that the rectified images become undistorted and row-aligned.

**Stereo Vision** is a standard method to locate an object in the 3D world when the object is visible to both cameras. Suppose $(x_{p1}, y_{p1})$ and $(x_{p2}, y_{p2})$ are a pair of corresponding pixel locations of an object in the rectified left/right images. The disparity between the two pixels $d = x_{p1} - x_{p2}$ is inversely proportional to the depth of the object, and the world coordinate of the object $(X_P, Y_P, Z_P)$ can be computed using triangulation, i.e.,

$$Z_P = bf/d, \quad X_P = Z_P(x_{p1} - x_{01})/f, \quad Y_P = Z_P(y_{p1} - y_{01})/f \qquad (3)$$

where $f$, $b$, and $(x_{01}, y_{01})$ are the focal length, the baseline, and the pixel location of the camera's optical centre, and are obtained from calibration.

**Stereo Vision via Reflection** is an extension of standard stereo vision, and can locate an object when its reflected image is visible to both cameras. An example is when the object is in regions $A0$, $A1$, and $A3$ in Fig. 2. Assuming a planar reflecting surface, the reconstruction via reflection can be carried out in two steps as shown in Fig. 5. Since the virtual object $P'$ can be seen as a fixed point behind the reflector, we can first recover its world coordinate $\mathbf{X}_{P'} = (X_{P'}, Y_{P'}, Z_{P'})$ using Eq. (3). Then the coordinate of the actual object $P$: $\mathbf{X}_P = (X_P, Y_P, Z_P)$ is the mirror inversion to $\mathbf{X}_{P'}$, i.e.,

$$\mathbf{X}_P = \mathbf{X}_{P'} + 2 \cdot dist \cdot \mathbf{n}_S, \qquad (4)$$

where $\mathbf{n}_S = (n_x, n_y, n_z)$ is the unit normal vector of the planar reflective surface, $dist = |\mathbf{n}_S \cdot \mathbf{X}_{P'} + h|$ is the distance from $P'$ to the plane, and $h$ the distance from the origin of the world coordinate system to the plane.

**Locating the Mirror Plane** is important in locating an object from its mirror reflection, as the position of the virtual object depends on the position and orientation of the reflector. In this work, we simplify the mirror plane estimation by using a checkerboard pattern attached on it, as shown in Fig. 6 left. The world coordinates of the checkerboard points are recovered using stereo vision (Eq. (3)), and the position $h$ and orientation $\mathbf{n}_S$ of the mirror plane are found using the

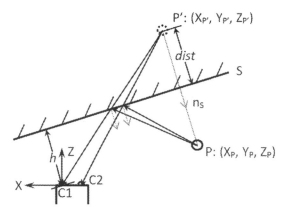

**Fig. 5.** Stereo vision via reflection. $P'$ is visible to both $C1$ and $C2$.

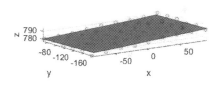

**Fig. 6.** Locating the mirror plane from checkerboard points.

M-estimator Sample Consensus (MSAC) algorithm [16] on the detected points. Figure 6 right shows a recovered mirror plane.

The orientation of the mirror plane is determined by the normal's elevation angle $\theta$ and azimuth angle $\phi$. Representing the normal using spherical coordinate $\mathbf{n}_S = (\cos\theta\cos\phi, \cos\theta\sin\phi, \sin\theta)$, from Eq. (4), the world coordinate of the real object $X_P$ can be expressed as a function

$$X_P = f(X_{P'}, \theta, \phi, h) \tag{5}$$

Analysing the partial derivatives of $f$ with respect to the mirror parameters gives important information how the estimation of the mirror affect locating the object via its reflection. In experiments, we carry out numerical analysis of this influence.

## 4    Results and Analysis

To compare the trajectories recovered from the actual object and its reflection, we move the object along tracks at different distances toward the mirror. Figure 7(a) shows the setup of the experiments. Because the object has a thickness, the images of the object and its reflection show two opposite sides of the object, and the moving trajectories for the two sides are separated. As a result, for each track, two ground-truth trajectories are used. Figure 7(b–d) visualize the recovered trajectories for each of the three tracks. Each recovered trajectory consists of a sequence of 3D locations reconstructed frame-wise from the stereo video. The sequences in black are recovered using images of the object's reflection while the green ones are recovered from images of the actual object. Both types of trajectories are compared with the according ground-truth shown as a straight line in the same colour.

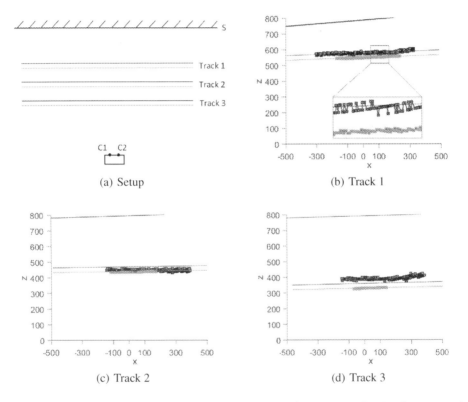

**Fig. 7.** Shown in $xz$ plane, the recovered trajectories (sequences of points) compared with ground-truth (straight lines). Black: trajectories from images of reflection; Green: trajectories from images of object. The top line in each sub-figure shows the recovered mirror plane. (Color figure online)

From Fig. 7, we observed that both the recovered trajectories are generally consistent with the ground-truth. The trajectories from reflections extend the according trajectories from objects, demonstrating the benefit of using reflections to extend the FOV of cameras. Then at a closer look, we noticed that the trajectories from reflections deviate slightly from their ground-truth, especially in Fig. 7(c) and (d). Moreover, amplifying the recovered trajectories (as shown

in the red box in Fig. 7(b)), we noticed bigger variance within the trajectory
from reflections than that within the trajectory from objects.

To quantitatively analyse the results, for each recovered trajectory, we measure its length in $x$ direction, its reconstruction error, and its variability. The
reconstruction error is calculated as the average distance from the recovered
locations to the corresponding ground-truth line. To compute the variability,
we first use SVD (singular value decomposition) to find the best fit line to the
recovered sequence of locations. The variability of the trajectory is calculated
as the standard deviation from the locations to the line. The measurements for
each recovered trajectory are shown in Table 2.

**Table 2.** Quantitative analysis of recovered trajectories

| | Track 1 | | Track 2 | | Track 3 | |
|---|---|---|---|---|---|---|
| Trajectory from | Object | Reflection | Object | Reflection | Object | Reflection |
| Length (mm) | 402.2 | 622.1 | 288.1 | 533.4 | 205.3 | 530.2 |
| Reconstruction error (mm) | 3.7 | 6.4 | 4.5 | 24.0 | 3.2 | 30.7 |
| Standard deviation (mm) | 1.3 | 4.6 | 0.8 | 5.2 | 0.5 | 7.9 |

From the table, the lengths of trajectories verified the extended FOV of
cameras using reflections. In theory, the extension becomes more significant when
object is closer to the camera. The ratio of the length from reflection to that from
object shows the trend (although not accurate, as we didn't track the reflections
for the whole visible length). We also found that when the object moves away
from the mirror toward the camera, the recovered trajectory from reflection
has increased reconstruction error and variability, but the recovered trajectory
from object maintains and even decreases the reconstruction error with decreased
variability. There are several reasons behind this observation. Firstly, it is known
that the accuracy of stereo vision in the near range far exceeds that in the far
range. From Track 1 to 3, while the object gets closer to the camera, its reflection
gets further away, which explains the trends in the accuracy changes. Secondly,
a faraway reflection increases errors in tracking, which further adversely affects
the accuracy of reconstruction. Finally, reconstruction from reflection inherently
depends on the location and orientation of the reflective surface. Deviations of
mirror estimation will cause further inaccuracies in the recovered trajectory from
reflection.

To better understand the influence from estimation of mirror parameters,
we use the recovered trajectory for Track 1 as an example and examine the
changes of the trajectory from reflection by varying each of the mirror parameters. Figure 8 shows the changes by varying (a) the distance of the origin to the
mirror $h$, (b) the elevation angle of the surface normal $\theta$, and (c) the azimuth
angle of the surface normal $\phi$. From the two views in Fig. 8(a), we can see that

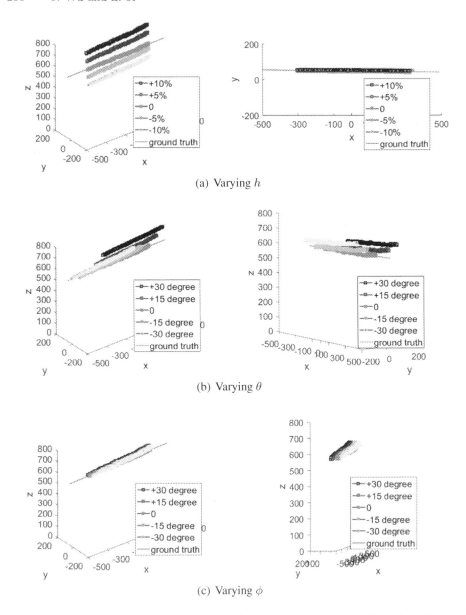

(a) Varying $h$

(b) Varying $\theta$

(c) Varying $\phi$

**Fig. 8.** Influence from estimation errors of mirror parameters $h$, $\theta$, and $\phi$. For each parameter, two views are provided to give better illustration.

estimation errors in $h$ mainly influence the depth of the trajectory, and have limited influence to $x, y$ locations. A positive deviation in $h$ results in an overestimation of the depth while a negative deviation results in an underestimation. Turning our attention to Fig. 8(b), estimation errors in $\theta$ have influence to locations in all three directions. Deviating $\theta$ from $+30°$ to $-30°$ moves the trajectory along a sheared valley shaped surface. Compared with $h$ and $\theta$, the influence from errors in $\phi$ is relatively small. We log scaled $y$-axis in the second view in Fig. 8(c) for a better visualization, and noticed a slight movement of trajectory in $y$ direction when deviating $\phi$ from $+30°$ to $-30°$. This numerical analysis gives a rough idea of the influence from estimation of mirror parameters. A more thorough analysis can be done analytically by deriving the Jacobian matrix of Eq. (5), and will be covered in our future work.

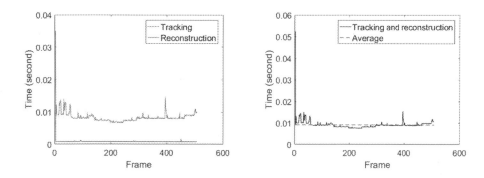

**Fig. 9.** Time efficiency of tracking and reconstruction.

Figure 9 shows the running time of the proposed method in tracking and locating the moving object on Track 1 from its reflection. The program is run on a PC with Intel Core i7-7500U CPU at 2.70 GHz and 8 GB memory. From the figure, we notice that tracking in the first frame takes the longest time of 0.035 s because of the detection in the whole image, and then drops to below 0.001 s, while the reconstruction step is relatively stable around 0.008 s. Tracking and reconstruction together takes an average of 0.009 s for each frame (110 fps), which demonstrates the real-time processing ability of the proposed method.

## 5   Conclusion and Discussion

In this paper, we proposed the idea of making use of reflections to extend the FOV of cameras, and carried out preliminary work verifying our idea in a simplified lab setting. We established the mathematical model in the simplified scene, and proposed a processing pipeline to recover an object's moving trajectory reaching out of the camera's FOV. We carried out experiments to analyse the accuracies of recovered trajectories, and how the recovery is influenced by the estimation of the reflective surface. The results verified the potential use of reflections in locating NLOS objects, and inspired more ideas for future work which will be discussed below.

As mentioned in Sect. 4, the trajectory from reflection depends on the mirror parameters. Moreover the recovery of both trajectories from reflection and object depends on the camera's intrinsic/extrinsic parameters. In order to have a thorough understanding of how the recovered trajectory is affected by all these factors, we will carry out analytical error analysis by deriving the Jacobian matrix of Eq. (5), and this will be our immediate work in the future.

A robust and accurate tracking algorithm is required to handle multiple objects and reflections, occlusions, blurry images, and deformation. We will first deploy other advanced image trackers, including the popular kernel-based KCF method [2] and its derivatives. Also, we will also implement the re-detection function to handle situations when the target is lost due to occlusions or ambiguous features. One long term challenge is automatic association of the object and its corresponding reflection, hence, allowing tracking the object by not only the registered patterns, but also fusing the reconstructed trajectories from both the reflection and object.

Ground-truth trajectories are necessary to evaluate the proposed method. However, it is difficult to extract accurate ground-truth in the current primitive lab setting with limited equipments. Currently, we obtain the ground-truth trajectories by combining detection of checkerboard points and manual measurements, which are inaccurate and affect the evaluation of reconstruction accuracy. In the future, it is desired to develop approaches to achieve more accurate ground-truth data, possibly from using more advanced equipments or using computer simulations. In the long term, creating such a benchmark dataset will benefit future research into the use of reflections as well.

An interesting direction to carry forward is to extend the mathematical model and evaluation to non-planar reflective surfaces which are more common in real world. The non-planarity is sometimes beneficial in revealing NLOS objects. An example is the convex rear view mirror on cars which gives much wider FOV than a planar mirror. Stereo vision via reflection from such non-planar surfaces is much more complex, but is more practical in real world applications, and thus will be an interesting direction to explore in our future work.

In addition to non-planar reflective surfaces, there are many other challenges in application of the proposed method to real world scenarios. For example, many surfaces are not perfectly specular, from which reflections can be dim and blurry, and makes it difficult for detection and tracking. Another fundamental question is how to differentiate images of reflections from images of objects. And the time efficiency is crucial in many applications. However, we believe the use of reflections has the potential to improve many computer vision tasks, and hope our preliminary work would inspire more interest into this challenging field.

# References

1. Matlab stereo calibration app. https://uk.mathworks.com/help/vision/ug/stereo-camera-calibrator-app.html. Accessed 13 Feb 2018
2. Chen, Z., Hong, Z., Tao, D.: An experimental survey on correlation filter-based tracking. CoRR abs/1509.05520 (2015)
3. Diamant, Y., Schechner, Y.Y.: Overcoming visual reverberations. In: Proceedings of CVPR (2008)

4. Farid, H., Adelson, E.: Separating reflections from images by use of independent component analysis. J. Opt. Soc. Am. A **16**(9), 2136–2145 (1999)
5. Guo, X., Cao, X., Ma, Y.: Robust separation of reflection from multiple images. In: Proceedings of CVPR, pp. 2195–2202 (2014)
6. Heide, F., Hullin, M.B., Gregson, J., Heidrich, W.: Low-budget transient imaging using photonic mixer devices. ACM Trans. Graph. (TOG) **32**(4), 1–10 (2013). Article No. 45
7. Jenkins, R., Kerr, C.: Identifiable images of bystanders extracted from corneal reflections. PLOS ONE **8**(12), 1–5 (2013)
8. Lewis, J.P.: Fast normalized cross-correlation (1995). http://citeseerx.ist.psu.edu/viewdoc/summary?doi=10.1.1.21.6062
9. Nishino, K., Belhumeur, P., Nayar, S.: Using eye reflections for face recognition under varying illumination. In: Proceedings of ICCV (2005)
10. Nishino, K., Nayar, S.K.: Eyes for relighting. ACM Trans. Graph. (TOG) **23**(3), 704–711 (2004). 2004 Proceedings of ACM SIGGRAPH
11. O'Brien, J.F., Farid, H.: Exposing photo manipulation with inconsistent reflections. ACM Trans. Graph. (TOG) **31**(1), 1–11 (2012). Article No. 4
12. Pandharkar, R., Velten, A., Bardagjy, A., Lawson, E.: Estimating motion and size of moving non-line-of-sight objects in cluttered environments. In: Proceedings of CVPR, pp. 265–272 (2011)
13. Sarel, B., Irani, M.: Separating transparent layers through layer information exchange. In: Pajdla, T., Matas, J. (eds.) ECCV 2004. LNCS, vol. 3024, pp. 328–341. Springer, Heidelberg (2004). https://doi.org/10.1007/978-3-540-24673-2_27
14. Schechner, Y.Y., Nayar, S.K.: Generalized mosaicing: polarization panorama. IEEE Trans. Pattern Anal. Mach. Intell. **27**(4), 631–636 (2005)
15. Szeliski, R., Avidan, S., Anandan, P.: Layer extraction from multiple images containing reflections and transparency. In: Proceedings of CVPR (2000)
16. Torr, P.H.S., Zisserman, A.: MLESAC: a new robust estimator with application to estimating image geometry. Comput. Vis. Image Underst. **78**(1), 138–156 (2000)
17. Velten, A., Willwacher, T., Gupta, O., Veeraraghavan, A., Bawendi, M.G., Raskar, R.: Recovering three-dimensional shape around a corner using ultrafast time-of-flight imaging. Nat. Commun. **3**, 745+ (2012)
18. Yang, L., Liu, J., Tang, X.: Depth from water reflection. IEEE Trans. Image Process. **24**(4), 1235–1243 (2015)
19. Yano, T., Shimizu, M., Okutomi, M.: Image restoration and disparity estimation from an uncalibrated multi-layered image. In: Proceedings of CVPR, pp. 247–254 (2010)
20. Zhang, Z., Isola, P., Adelson, E.H.: SparkleVision: seeing the world through random specular microfacets. In: Proceedings of CVPR Workshops (2015)

# The Effect of Pose on the Distribution of Edge Gradients in Omnidirectional Images

Dean Jarvis and Theocharis Kyriacou[✉]

School of Computing and Mathematics, Keele University, Staffordshire ST5 5BG, UK
{d.g.jarvis,t.kyriacou}@keele.ac.uk

**Abstract.** Images from omnidirectional cameras are used frequently in applications involving artificial intelligence and robotics as a source of rich information about the surroundings. A useful feature that can be extracted from these images is the distribution of gradients of the edges in the scene. This distribution is affected by the pose of the camera on-board a robot at any given location in the environment. This paper investigates the effect of the pose on this distribution. The gradients in the images are extracted and arranged into a histogram which is then compared to the histograms of other images using a chi-squared test. It is found that any differences in the distribution are not specific to either the position or orientation and that there is a significant difference in the distributions of two separate locations. This can aid in the localisation of robots when navigating.

## 1 Introduction

The goal of this paper is to test a bio-inspired system that can recognise and distinguish between two locations[1] using visual information, specifically information from edges within the scene. Tests will measure how changes in pose may effect this information and whether or not there is a significant difference between separate locations. Tests are made simpler by using an omni directional camera. Visual information is used as it is the primary sense that mammals use to navigate in their environments. The omnidirectional camera emulates the near omnidirectional vision of rodents and to reduce the amount the variability of images that can be taken from same position.

In the field of robotics there are many parts of a design one might want to consider. One very important ability that is required for an autonomous robot would be to navigate within its environment. Navigation can be broken down

---

[1] During the course of this paper the word "location" will refer to the immediate environment (the set of positions that share the same contextual name) of the robot for example the kitchen or the lab. Whereas "position" will be an exact measure of where the robot is (e.g. coordinates x, y). Pose defines the position (x, y) and orientation (theta) of the robot.

© Springer International Publishing AG, part of Springer Nature 2018
M. Giuliani et al. (Eds.): TAROS 2018, LNAI 10965, pp. 234–244, 2018.
https://doi.org/10.1007/978-3-319-96728-8_20

into three distinct tasks, localisation, mapping, and path finding [1]. There are in essence two ways to approach robot navigation; there are the *pure* computational methods and biologically inspired methods. Pure methods include examples such as those described in [2–4]. These methods have come a long way in producing reliable results for navigation but they often produce a lot of data and high fidelity maps that then require optimisation before they can be used efficiently (see [3]). This means that these methods have a high demand for memory and computational power. In contrast animals seem to do the same tasks without high fidelity maps, using primarily visual stimuli. Biologically inspired robotic navigation can be further broken down into two more categories; top down methods and bottom up methods. For example top down methods start by observing the behaviour of living organisms and how they react to stimuli and situations, whilst attempting to reproduce these behaviours in robots. Franz and Mallot demonstrate a review of some top down biologically inspired robot navigation methods, which take inspiration from insects and rodents [5]. In contrast bottom up methods attempt to reproduce natural navigation by looking at how individual parts of an animal may work in tandem to navigate in an environment. This could be how individual neurones fire in response to stimuli within their receptive field. Work produced by Kyriacou (see [6]) is one such example; this work focuses on producing a working computational model of head direction cells within the brain that aid in determining the orientation of the robot.

Bio-inspired computing has influenced the way in which robots localise and navigate in their environments. Sensors designed to mimic the way insects use polarised light from the sky to navigate to and from their nests as described in work by [7]. Other notable examples include teaching a system to change navigation methods based on environmental cues and the concept of Time Till Contact (TTC) which can be utilised for obstacle avoidance without feature detection by using optical flow. This can be improved by incorporating angular velocities and a Kalman filter [8–10]. Localisation using vision is essentially the ability to compare the current view to images in memory that are linked to a spatial location [11]. It has been found and discussed by Anzai [12] how the visual system in monkeys exhibits selective firing when encountered edges and textures that correspond to certain angles that exist within the visual field within the V2 region of the brain. The cells within V2 region of the visual system respond more to complex stimuli such as curves and angles. This suggests that this information is an important component of the image, the image itself being important for localisation. By developing a localisation system based on information gathered from the behaviour of the brains of animals it is hoped that the resulting system will be robust.

There have been studies that use edges and gradient information from images to compute image similarity [13, 14] and localise [15]. However there is a lack of information about how this kind of information changes with respect to the pose of the camera and whether or not it can be used as a stand-alone method to differentiate between locations in the navigable environment.

Omnidirectional images could be used to compare the views taken at different locations. Images taken using omni-directional cameras are unwrapped in such a way so as to form a continuous panorama image. During the unwrapping process there is some warping of the original image, distorting the information density, due to the nature of the omni-directional camera lens and the interpolation methods that have to be employed [16]. Omni directional images used in applications that also use image gradient distribution could potentially suffer with inaccurate comparisons due to changes in camera pose. Work in object recognition with omni-directional cameras, for example [17], could be affected by these changes in pose. There is little available research on the effect that a change in pose can have on the gradient distribution of an omnidirectional image. This study explores the effect of changing pose on the gradient distribution by comparing similarity of the histograms of gradients in images using the chi-squared test [19] as a metric of similarity.

(a) Reference position image for empirical analysis.

(b) Image after moving camera forward 80cm showing an apparent distortion on the tables.

(c) Image after rotation the reference image by 60 degrees.

**Fig. 1.** These photographs show the unwrapped omnidirectional images taken at two different positions in the same room. At first glance it seems that there is a greater apparent change in the images between the change in position compared to the change in orientation

It is hypothesised by looking at images such as those in Fig. 1, that there will be a greater difference in the gradient histograms due to position than there will be due to the orientation as the camera lens is rotationally symmetric and a change in position seems to cause a greater distortion. Also there will be a significant difference between the histograms of gradients between two different locations (between Figs. 1 and 4) that could be utilised as a determinant of location.

The aim of this study is to see how, by using the gradients of edges, a scene may be used to localise a robot within it's environment using only visual information received from it's camera. In order to test this, omni-directional images taken in the same location (room) but from different poses (in terms of position and orientation) are compared with each other by means of their edge content. Also, images taken in another location (i.e. a different room) are compared with the first set using the same method.

## 2   Method

A Sony Bloggie[2] camera with a 360 lens attachment, as shown in Fig. 2, was used to capture all the images that were used in this study. A limited perspective camera was not used due to the fact that locations would require the capture of multiple views from which to be identified. Many animals benefit from wide fields of views that allow them to be aware of more of their environment without having to move around a lot to do so. An omnidirectional camera can handle this issue better as all possible views of a position are incorporated into a single image. The room where a majority of the images were captured (GR) conveniently had a floor of tiled equilateral triangles as shown in Figs. 3a and b. This room was chosen for this reason to ensure that distances and angles between images were constant. Initially, to check if there was any inherent time dependant error due to the hardware, software, or the environment, multiple images were taken from the same pose (Fig. 3b centre point at $0°$). Images taken from this one pose were used to compute the minimum difference that could be attributed to temporal error. The Positions that images were taken from are also described in Fig. 3b, which shows the 7 positions and the various angles at which the images were

**Fig. 2.** This image shows the camera with $360°$ lens attachment mounted with velcro on the back of an RC car.

---

[2] https://www.sony.co.uk/electronics/support/webbie-hd-bloggie-cameras-mhspm-series/mhs-pm5. Last accessed: 1/05/2018.

238     D. Jarvis and T. Kyriacou

taken for a total of 24 images for the GR. The centre point has smaller angle
intervals as this is used primary to test for changes due to orientation without
changes in position. Whereas points 1–6 are used to test for changes due to
position, and changes due to changes in position and orientation.

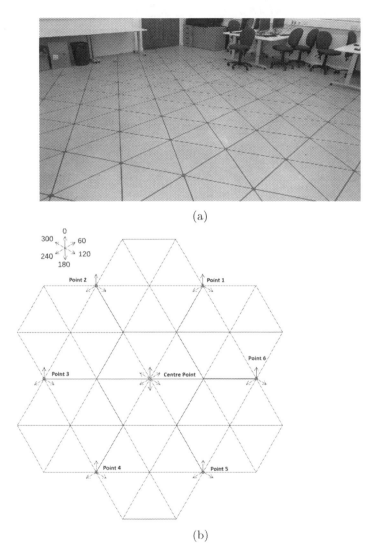

(a)

(b)

**Fig. 3.** (a) Shows the GR and its convenient tiled flooring. (b) Shows a partial layout
of the first room images were taken with all the positions and orientations marked.
Length of triangle sides are 40 cm.

For future comparison, another set of images were taken from a different room (TR), see Fig. 4 using the same angle increments as the centre point in the GR. The angular increments were kept constant with the use of a regular hexagon template. This is also another point of comparison for how changes in orientation alter the edge gradient distribution.

**Fig. 4.** This is an image of the TR from which images were used to distinguish the viability of this method as one that would be suitable to distinguish between different locations.

## 2.1   Image Processing

To process the images the OpenCV[3] library was used in conjunction with the Sony Playmemory Home software. Playmemory Home was used to unwrap the raw images into a panorama like image. OpenCV was then used to extract the gradient information from the image. To do this, Sobel operators [18] in the x and y direction were used to get two gradient images, and after this a method was used to combine these images to produce two new images. One of the resulting images being the image where each pixel value represents an angular value between 0 and 360 which is also the direction of the edge as shown in Fig. 5c. The other image being a magnitude image where each pixel value is the magnitude of the gradient as shown in Fig. 5b. The magnitude image was altered via a binary threshold where the cut off point was one fifth the maximum magnitude. This threshold was empirically chosen. The chosen threshold appeared to be a good value where prominent edges persist whilst artefacts due to low magnitude edges such as textures were removed. The resultant binary image was used as a mask to remove noisy gradients with low magnitudes that do not provide any useful information in this context. Once the gradient image had been masked the value of every non zero pixel was written to a file for comparison against other images.

## 2.2   Data Representation

The edge information from the collected images was used to produce histograms that describe the gradient distribution at each of the sampled positions in the two locations used. These histograms were then compared using openCV's *compHist* method. The *compHist* method has four different tests it can use to compare the similarity of the histograms. The one that was chosen to compare the histograms

---

[3] https://opencv.org/. Last accessed: 1/05/2018.

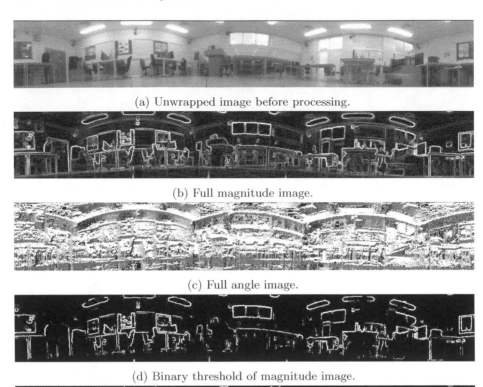

(a) Unwrapped image before processing.

(b) Full magnitude image.

(c) Full angle image.

(d) Binary threshold of magnitude image.

(e) Angle image after being masked with the binary threshold. This shows the location and direction of edges in degrees.

**Fig. 5.** This figure shows intermediate image Processing Steps. Images (b) and (c) are obtained from (a). Image (d) is obtained via a binary threshold applied to image (b). Image (d) is used to select important information from image (c). Image (e) is the final product used to produce the gradient distribution

was the chi-squared test [19] where big values of the test statistic (chi-square) mean big differences (in terms of edge distribution) in any two images being compared. Figures 6a and b illustrate how the chi-squared value represents a distance between the histograms of seemingly similar and different places.

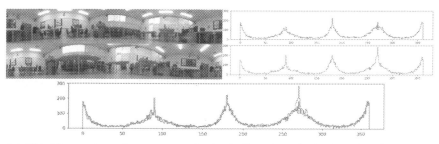

(a) This Figure shows how two seemingly similar places look when their histograms are overlaid. This would give a very small chi-squared metric as there is a small difference between the lines at any point.

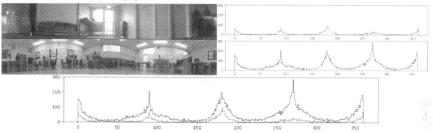

(b) This Figure shows how two seemingly different places look when their histograms are overlaid. This would give a large chi-squared metric as there is a large difference between the lines at many points.

**Fig. 6.** The x axis of the histograms are values that gradients can take in the image. The y axis is how many time a given gradient occurs.

## 3 Results

The check for temporal errors resulted in some low level differences across different frames taken from the same pose. The mean chi-squared distance from images at the same position and orientation was $860.8 \pm 98.8$, this information gives an estimate of how much error there may be within any other results due purely to external factors, e.g.: camera auto exposure calibration (no camera option to disable), light changes due to flickering lights, and sensor noise on the camera.

The main aim of this work was to check whether changes in pose are more dependant on position or orientation, therefore a comparison of the image data where only the position and only the orientation was changed was performed. To do this, for every image recoded the histogram generated from it was compared to that of the other images, resulting in a table of chi-squared results that could be used to easily visualise any relationships between the different poses from which the images were captured. The table in Fig. 7 is illustrated visually (using grey-scale to represent the chi-square value). A t-test was performed to check whether there was a significant difference between images where only position was changed and images where only orientation was changed, this was done using images from both the GR and the TR. To do this all the data points that are the result of positional changes only were averaged and data points that are the result of changes in orientation only were also averaged. These averages were used to perform the T-test. The average chi-squared distance due to changes in position was $1947 \pm 1448$ whereas the average chi-squared distance due to changes in orientation only was $1851 \pm 1005$. A rejection of the leading hypothesis is attained showing that there is no significant difference between the means ($p = 0.393 > 0.05$).

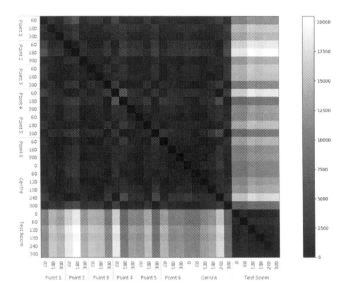

**Fig. 7.** This image shows how every image was compared to all other image. Each pixel represents a chi-squared value, resulting from a comparison of two rooms which can be found on the axis. It highlights the distinction between similar and dissimilar rooms where low values-dark correspond to comparisons of images captured at different poses in the same room (GR) and high values-light correspond to comparisons of images taken in different rooms (GR&TR). The axes of this illustration refer to the position and orientation of the corresponding image; e.g. Point 1 60 is the image taken from Point 1 at $60°$ as shown in Fig. 3b.

Using the same method of comparison (i.e. the t-test), all the data points from the Fig. 7 that corresponded to comparisons of images taken in different rooms (i.e. the light regions) were averaged and compared to the average of the data points from image comparisons of the same room (i.e. the dark regions). The mean difference between images from the same room was $1917.8 \pm 1062$ and the mean from images of different rooms was $13574.1 \pm 2920$. Due to this data the alternate hypothesis, that there will be a significant difference between the histograms of differing rooms, fails to be rejected as there is a significant difference between the means of the two sets of data ($p = 2.6 \times 10^{-95} < 0.05$).

# 4   Conclusion and Further Work

It was found that a change of position seemed to have a similar difference to a change in orientation; this was shown within the results section with the t-test showing no significant difference between the data from each. It has also been confirmed how gradient histograms as a global feature could potentially be used as a distinguishing feature between two locations. This global feature could be used as a coarse localisation feature as a fast way to limit any search space for finer localisation later. However, more research would be required to further justify this statement. This could be done by comparing images taken from multiple locations in the environment of the robot in the same way as this work has shown. How will a larger set of areas affect the robots ability differentiate between locations? The method discussed on the paper has not been designed to handle transitional locations. For example, if the robot were in a door way and could see 2 separate locations where would it say it belongs? Future work could look at developing a strategy to handle this scenario. This could possibly be accomplished by segmenting the image if there are two locations with similar chi-squared distances. Future work could also use video as opposed to still images will be used, providing multiple images per position but also the temporal link between them. This could mitigate any false positives due to a poor comparisons as the incorrect comparison would be overshadowed by the average from the other images.

# References

1. Fuentes-Pacheco, J., Ruiz-Ascencio, J., Rendón-Mancha, J.M.: Visual simultaneous localization and mapping: a survey. Artif. Intell. Rev. **43**(1), 55–81 (2015)
2. Wen, S., Zhang, Z., Ma, C., Wang, Y., Wang, H.: An extended Kalman filter-simultaneous localization and mapping method with Harris-scale-invariant feature transform feature recognition and laser mapping for humanoid robot navigation in unknown environment. Int. J. Adv. Rob. Syst. 14(6) (2017). https://doi.org/10. 1177/1729881417744747
3. Vallve, J., Sola, J., Andrade-Cetto, J.: Graph SLAM sparsification with populated topologies using factor descent optimization. IEEE Robot. Autom. Lett. **3**, 1322–1329 (2018)
4. Lowe, T., Kim, S., Cox, M.: Complementary perception for handheld slam. IEEE Robot. Autom. Lett. **3**(2), 1104–1111 (2018)
5. Franz, M.O., Mallot, H.A.: Biomimetic robot navigation. Robot. Auton. Syst. **30**(1–2), 133–153 (2000)
6. Kyriacou, T.: An implementation of a biologically inspired model of head direction cells on a robot. In: Groß, R., Alboul, L., Melhuish, C., Witkowski, M., Prescott, T.J., Penders, J. (eds.) TAROS 2011. LNCS (LNAI), vol. 6856, pp. 66–77. Springer, Heidelberg (2011). https://doi.org/10.1007/978-3-642-23232-9_7
7. Karman, S.B., Diah, S.Z.M., Gebeshuber, I.C.: Bio-inspired polarized skylight-based navigation sensors: a review. Sensors **12**(11), 14232–14261 (2012)
8. Dollé, L., Sheynikhovich, D., Girard, B., Chavarriaga, R., Guillot, A.: Path planning versus cue responding: a bio-inspired model of switching between navigation strategies. Biol. Cybern. **103**(4), 299–317 (2010)

9. Horn, B.K., Fang, Y., Masaki, I.: Time to contact relative to a planar surface. In: 2007 IEEE Intelligent Vehicles Symposium, pp. 68–74. IEEE (2007)
10. Zhang, H., Zhao, J.: Bio-inspired vision based robot control using featureless estimations of time-to-contact. Bioinspiration Biomim. **12**(2), 025001 (2017)
11. Paul, C.M., Magda, G., Abel, S.: Spatial memory: theoretical basis and comparative review on experimental methods in rodents. Behav. Brain Res. **203**(2), 151–164 (2009)
12. Anzai, A., Peng, X., Van Essen, D.C.: Neurons in monkey visual area V2 encode combinations of orientations. Nat. Neurosci. **10**(10), 1313 (2007)
13. Liu, A., Lin, W., Narwaria, M.: Image quality assessment based on gradient similarity. IEEE Trans. Image Process. **21**(4), 1500–1512 (2012)
14. Hu, R., Collomosse, J.: A performance evaluation of gradient field HOG descriptor for sketch based image retrieval. Comput. Vis. Image Underst. **117**(7), 790–806 (2013)
15. Kröse, B.J., Booij, O., Zivkovic, Z., et al.: A geometrically constrained image similarity measure for visual mapping, localization and navigation. In: EMCR (2007)
16. Jacquey, F., Comby, F., Strauss, O.: Non-additive approach for omnidirectional image gradient estimation. In: 2007 IEEE 11th International Conference on Computer Vision (ICCV 2007), pp. 1–6. IEEE (2007)
17. Cinaroglu, I., Bastanlar, Y.: A direct approach for object detection with catadioptric omnidirectional cameras. Sig. Image Video Process. **10**(2), 413–420 (2016)
18. Sobel, I.: An isotropic 3×3 image gradient operator. In: Machine Vision for Three-Dimensional Scenes, pp. 376–379 (1990)
19. Greenwood, P.E., Nikulin, M.S.: A Guide to Chi-Squared Testing, vol. 280. Wiley, Hoboken (1996)

# HRI, Assistive and Medical Robotics

# Learning to Listen to Your Ego-(motion): Metric Motion Estimation from Auditory Signals

Letizia Marchegiani[✉] and Paul Newman

Oxford Robotics Institute, University of Oxford, Oxford, UK
{letizia,pnewman}@robots.ox.ac.uk
http://ori.ox.ac.uk

**Abstract.** This paper is about robot ego-motion estimation relying solely on acoustic sensing. By equipping a robot with microphones, we investigate the possibility of employing the noise generated by the motors and actuators of the vehicle to estimate its motion. Audio-based odometry is not affected by the scene's appearance, lighting conditions, and structure. This makes sound a compelling auxiliary source of information for ego-motion modelling in environments where more traditional methods, such as those based on visual or laser odometry, are particularly challenged. By leveraging multi-task learning and deep architectures, we provide a regression framework able to estimate the linear and the angular velocity at which the robot has been travelling. Our experimental evaluation conducted on approximately two hours of data collected with an unmanned outdoor field robot demonstrated an absolute error lower than 0.07 m/s and 0.02 rad/s for the linear and angular velocity, respectively. When compared to a baseline approach, making use of single-task learning scheme, our system shows an improvement of up to 26% in the ego-motion estimation.

**Keywords:** Ego-motion estimation · Sound-based odometry
Deep learning · Multi-task learning · Acoustic sensing

## 1 Introduction

This paper explores the possibility of modelling a robot's ego-motion, relying only on acoustic sensing. Specifically, we employ the robot's ego-noise (i.e. the noise produced by the motors and actuators while generating motion) to make estimates on the vehicle's velocity. Optical sensors and lasers have commonly been employed to perform this task, as they are able to provide accurate pose estimates, by also overcoming the shortcomings of wheel odometry, such as error calculation during wheel slippage (e.g. [1,2]). The performance of Visual Odometry (VO) systems are still challenged, though, by environments characterised by moderate lighting conditions or, more generally, scarcity of textures. On the other hand, laser odometry might struggle in degenerated scenes where planar

© Springer International Publishing AG, part of Springer Nature 2018
M. Giuliani et al. (Eds.): TAROS 2018, LNAI 10965, pp. 247–259, 2018.
https://doi.org/10.1007/978-3-319-96728-8_21

areas are prevalent. Auditory perception is resilient to the scene's appearance: a property which would be particularly convenient in environments lacking structure and illumination, or in which distractions are intense. For instance, extreme scene movement could be misinterpreted as movement of the robot, and acoustic signals could be used to perform consensus checking and resolve the ambiguity. In this perspective, we envision acoustic sensing as an auxiliary source of information, on the side of more traditional odometry methods, for the development of more robust ego-motion estimation systems. Building on such premises, in this work we introduce and evaluate a framework to estimate a robot's ego-motion, using exclusively the ego-noise produced by the vehicle and recorded by the on-board microphones. Following on from recent studies that exploit deep learning for visual and laser odometry estimation [3,4], we model the vehicle's odometry using a deep neural network (DNN). In particular, we leverage regression analysis, and, similarly to the modelling strategy adopted by [5] for camera relocalisation, we apply a multi-task learning scheme. Unlike that work, however, we do not regress the robot's poses directly, but the linear and the angular velocity at which the robot has been travelling. We evaluate our system on approximately two hours of data collected at the University Parks in Oxford, UK.

To the best of our knowledge, this is the first work investigating robot ego-motion modelling employing solely the acoustic features of the ego-noise of the vehicle to estimate its velocity through a state-of-the-art regression framework.

## 2   Related Work

For long time, robot audition has mainly concerned the development of human-robot interaction frameworks (e.g. [6]). More recently, the robotics community has started investigating auditory perception in a wider perspective. A method to augment autonomous vehicles with the capability of detecting the presence of anomalous sounds (e.g. the siren of an emergency vehicle) has been introduced in [7]. Acoustic event classification in a domestic environment has been explored in [8]. In all these instances the robot's ego-noise has been examined as a limitation to the systems' performance, as introducing additional task-unrelated components to the acoustic scene, making its interpretation more challenging. Yet, robot ego-noise carries significant information which could be exploited, both for environment understanding and self-modelling. The use of ego-noise to perform terrain classification has been proposed in [9]. Sound-based self-localisation and ego-motion estimation have been approached in [10,11]. The former combines orientation estimates from inertial measurement unit (IMU) observations and audio-based distance estimation to localise a snake robot moving in a pipe. The latter proposes a classification framework to associate ego-noise to a set of predefined velocity profiles. Our work shares the aspirations of [11], while presenting a substantially different approach to velocity estimation. Rather than encoding the robot's motion into profiles known *a priori*, we propose a regression model able to provide, at any point in time, the current velocity of the vehicle. The resulting system will, consequently, be more flexible, and, as not relying on predefined behaviours, inherently more robust to changes in the environment leading to potential unexpected modifications in the robot's motion. Furthermore, we investigate the possibility of using auditory features to estimate the angular velocity of the vehicle, laying the foundations for the development of an audio-only ego-motion estimation system.

# 3 Technical Approach

Our regression analysis makes use of a deep neural network, which given as input a feature representation of the robot's motion sound, provides estimates both for the linear and angular velocity of the vehicle. A description of the features employed is presented in Sect. 3.3, while a more detailed illustration of the deep architecture utilised is delineated in Sect. 3.2.

## 3.1 Preliminaries

Our framework relies on the use of VO (cf. Sect. 1) to generate the true values of the velocities we employ to train our deep network. Visual odometry computes estimates of the robot's pose from a set of camera images by analysing the variations on those images generated by the motion of the vehicle. Different approaches and implementations have been proposed in the literature (for a review, see [12]). In this work, we utilise a stereo VO pipeline which makes use of a combination of FAST [13] corners and BRIEF descriptors [14], and applies RANSAC [15] for outlier rejection. The ego-motion is, then, computed by non-linear least squares optimisation. VO provides 6DoF pose estimates. In this case, as the motion of the robot is actually restricted to the ground plane, its pose is fully described by two translational components and one rotational component, which we use to compute the velocities.

## 3.2 Architecture

Our regression system is based on a DNN which takes as input a feature representation of the robot's ego-noise (cf. Sect. 3.3) and returns estimates for both the linear and angular velocity at which the robot is travelling. We leverage multi-task learning (MTL) to simultaneously regress both the linear and the angular velocity. Multi-task learning, indeed, allows greater generalisation, as it is able to take advantage of information in training signals of related tasks, and has been successfully used in several applications [16,17]. In this work, we opt for *hard parameter sharing*, which was firstly introduced by [18]. In the resulting architecture, the input and the first hidden layer are shared across the two tasks (i.e. linear and angular velocity estimation), while the rest of the hidden layers are not shared. This architecture was empirically chosen, as being the one yielding the best performance on our dataset. We employ for both tasks four hidden layers with a Rectified Linear (ReL) function. Our network outputs a vector $\mathbf{V} = [\hat{v}, \hat{\omega}]$, consisting of the estimates of the magnitude of the linear velocity $\hat{v}$

and the magnitude of the angular velocity $\hat{\omega}$. Similarly to [5], we define our loss function $L$ as:

$$L = \|v - \hat{v}\|_2 + \|\omega - \hat{\omega}\|_2 \qquad (1)$$

where $v$ and $\omega$ are the ground truth values we can extrapolate from our Visual Odometry system (cf. Sect. 3.1). Training is performed by minimising the Euclidean loss $L$ with $l1$ regularisation, using back-propagation.

### 3.3    Feature Representation

In audio-based classification, Mel-frequency cepstrum coefficients (MFCCs) [6] have been traditionally used as feature representations of the signals. However, recent studies proved that the performance of classification systems relying on MFCCs is greatly reduced in the presence of noise [7,19]. Our data is affected by some environmental noise, such as people talking in the proximity of the robot, construction works nearby, wind, and cars passing. Noise which is especially manifest when the vehicle is moving slowly, as the sound level (i.e. volume) of the motion tends to increase with the speed. In the attempt of being more resilient to these additional and unwanted acoustic signals, in this work we opt for a frequency representation based on Gammatone filterbanks, which have been originally introduced in [20], as an approximation to the human cochlear frequency selectivity, and later used in several contexts (e.g. [21]). Similarly to [7], we employ a time-independent representation of the sound, which is obtained by filtering the audio waveform with a bank of Gammatone band-pass filters. The impulse response of a Gammatone filter centered at frequency $f_c$ is:

$$g(t, f_c) = \begin{cases} t^{a-1} e^{-2\pi b t} \cos 2\pi f_c t & \text{if } t \geq 0 \\ 0 & \text{otherwise} \end{cases} \qquad (2)$$

where $a$ indicates the order of the filter, and $b$ is the bandwidth, which increases as the center frequency $f_c$ increases. The frequency-dependent bandwidth yield narrower filters at low frequencies and broader filters at high frequencies. Several investigations have been carried out to compute the values of the filters' parameters which best approximate the human auditory filter. In this work, following [22], we utilise fourth-order filters (i.e. $a = 4$), and approximate $b$ as:

$$b = 1.09 \left( \frac{f_c}{9.26449} + 24.7 \right) \qquad (3)$$

The center frequencies $f_c$ of the filters are distributed across the available spectrum in proportion to their bandwidth. The identification of those frequencies can be achieved by using the Equivalent Rectangular Bandwidth (ERB) scale [23]. Let $x(t)$ be the audio signal we want to analyse, the output response $y(t, f_c)$ of a filter characterised by the center frequency $f_c$ can be computed as:

$$y(t, f_c) = x(t) * g(t, f_c) \qquad (4)$$

We calculate the output response for all the filters in the bank. The energy of these output responses, expressed in dB, represents our feature representation of the audio signal in the frequency domain, which we name $GTF$. Extending the same procedure to overlapping time frames of the signal, it is possible to generate time-frequency representations which follow the frequency resolution imposed by the Gammatone filterbank, the *Gammatonegrams*. Examples of the gammatonegrams and GTF representations for frames of 1 s, recorded with the robot travelling at different linear velocities (angular velocity is negligible in those frames) are provided in Figs. 2 and 3.

Additionally, we consider also some signal statistics in the time domain, such as the short-term energy (STE) of an entire frame and the zero-crossing rate (ZCR). The zero-crossing rate indicates the number of times the signal changes its sign within a frame. Figure 1 shows a 2D normalised histogram of the ZCR and linear velocity pairs (Fig. 1a), as well as a 2D normalised histogram of the short-term energy and linear velocity pairs (Fig. 1b). We notice that the ZCR increases with the linear velocity. The same is observed for what concerns the short-term energy. Both considerations suggest that higher linear velocity are characterised by higher frequencies (due to the higher ZCR) and by a higher sound level (due to higher STE). Same behaviour is appreciable from the Gammatone filterbanks and the GTF representations (cf. Figs. 2 and 3). While no apparent pattern is observed for what concerns the angular velocity and either the ZRC or the STE, an example of how the angular velocity affects the spectrum of the ego-noise is presented in Fig. 4. The figure shows the time-independent representation of two frames, characterised by the same linear velocity ($v = 0.4\,\mathrm{m/s}$) and different angular one ($\omega \in \{0.005, 0.26\}\,\mathrm{rad/s}$). We notice that the angular velocity mainly influences the lower part of the ego-noise's frequency spectrum. In particular, a higher angular velocity is reflected into greater energy in the lower part of the frequency spectrum. The complete framework is shown in Fig. 5.

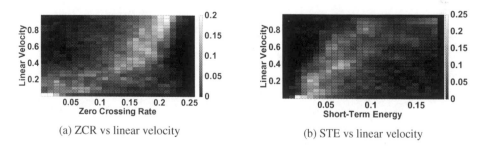

(a) ZCR vs linear velocity                  (b) STE vs linear velocity

**Fig. 1.** From left to right: 2D normalised histogram of the zero crossing rate (ZCR) and linear velocity pairs (a) and 2D normalised histogram of the short-term energy (STE) and linear velocity pairs (b). We notice that the ZCR increases with the linear velocity. The same is observed for what concerns the STE.

## 4    Experimental Evaluation

To validate our framework, we collected approximately two hours of data at the University Parks in Oxford, UK, using a Clearpath Husky A200 platform. The robot is equipped with a Bumblebee2 stereo camera, two Knowles omnidirectional boom microphones mounted in proximity of each of the two front wheels, and an ALESIS IO4 audio interface. The stereo camera is used to collect the image data that will be employed by the VO pipeline to generate ground truth values for the velocity estimates. The audio data has been recorded at a sampling frequency $f_s$ of 44100 Hz at a resolution of 16 bits. Camera images are gathered at a rate of 10 frames per second (FPS) and with $768 \times 1024$ pixel resolution. The data covers a total route of about 2 Km in length and includes portions of the park characterised by different kinds of terrain, such as grass, soil, and gravel. We made this choice to build a regression model able to generalise to different surfaces. The data was collected by manually driving the platform to obtain a wider spectrum of motion profiles and be able to encapsulate the behaviour of the robot in several circumstances. We used in total $85K$ frames of 1 s for training and $13K$ for testing. We carry out two different kinds of experiments. We first evaluate our MTL framework, varying the number of frequency channels used in the frequency representation. In particular, we consider 64 and 128 frequency channels (i.e. number of filters in the Gammatone filterbank). Secondly,

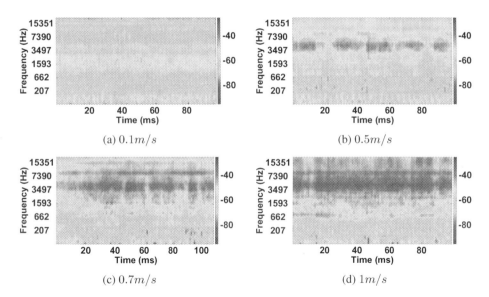

(a) $0.1m/s$

(b) $0.5m/s$

(c) $0.7m/s$

(d) $1m/s$

**Fig. 2.** Gammatonegrams of 1 s frames of ego-noise recorded with the robot travelling at different linear velocities: (a) robot is travelling at 0.1 m/s, (b) robot travelling at 0.5 m/s, (c) robot travelling at 0.7 m/s, (d) robot travelling at 1 m/s. Angular velocity is negligible in those frames. The energy of the time-frequency bins is expressed in decibel (dB) scale. The filtering is performed using 64 frequency channels (i.e. number of filters in the Gammatone filterbank) between 0 Hz and 22050 Hz.

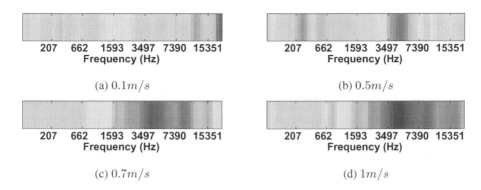

Fig. 3. GTF representations correspondent to the gammatonegrams in Fig. 2: (a) robot is travelling at 0.1 m/s, (b) robot travelling at 0.5 m/s, (c) robot travelling at 0.7 m/s, (d) robot travelling at 1 m/s. Angular velocity is negligible in those frames. The filtering is performed using 64 frequency channels (i.e. number of filters in the Gammatone filterbank) between 0 Hz and 22050 Hz.

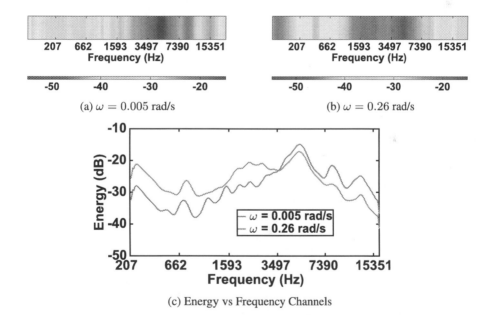

Fig. 4. The figure shows the GTF representations of two frames, characterised by the same linear velocity ($v = 0.4$ m/s) and different angular ones. Specifically, the top-left diagram (a) represents an audio frame where the vehicle is travelling at $\omega = 0.005$ rad/s, while the top-right (b) represents an audio frame where the vehicle is travelling at $\omega = 0.26$ rad/s. Energy is expressed in dB. Differences between the frequency spectra of the two frames are further highlighted in (c). We observe that a higher angular velocity is reflected into greater energy in the lower part of the frequency spectrum.

we compare the behaviour of the MTL framework with a baseline one, represented by a single-task learning scheme, where the two velocities are regressed separately by two different networks.

## 4.1   Implementation Details

We trained the networks using mini-batch gradient descent based on back propagation, employing the Adam optimisation algorithm [24]. We applied dropout [25] to each non-shared layer for both tasks' architectures with a keeping probability of 0.9. The models were implemented using the Tensorflow [26] libraries. Independently of the number of filters utilised, we confine our frequency analysis to a range between 0 Hz and $f_s/2 = 22050\,\text{Hz}$, corresponding to the maximum reliable frequency resolution available. The filtering is computed on time domain frames of 1 s with 10 ms overlap, after applying a Hamming window to avoid spectral leakage. As our VO system returns ego-motion estimates at 10 Hz, we can generate the 1 s audio frames by using a sliding window of 1 s size with 100 ms overlap. Similarly to previous works on deep learning in the auditory domain (cf. [27,28]), we randomly split our dataset into training set (85%) and test set (15%). To avoid any unwanted overlap between training and testing sets, frames in the training set and frames in the test set do not share any audio segment across the sliding windows.

## 4.2   Experiment 1: Multi-Task Learning

In this first experiment we analyse the performance of our system whilst varying the number of filters $NF$ employed. In particular, we evaluate the framework for $NF \in \{64, 128\}$. Table 1 reports the results of this experiment. In the table, $\tilde{E}_v$ and $\tilde{E}_\omega$ refer to the median absolute error in the estimation of the linear and angular velocity on the test data. No significant difference in the performance is observable when increasing the number of filters from 64 to 128, neither for what concerns the linear velocity nor in case of the angular velocity, leading to the conclusion that 64 filters have already a proper representation power for the task. The table also reports the median absolute error in the estimation of the linear and angular velocity in the MTL regression framework on the training data, indicated with $\tilde{T}_v$ and $\tilde{T}_\omega$, respectively. Figure 6 shows the normalised histograms of the absolute error in the estimation of the linear velocity (Fig. 6a) and in the estimation of the angular velocity (Fig. 6b), for $NF \in \{64, 128\}$, when following an MTL scheme.

## 4.3   Experiment 2: Single-Task Learning

In this second experiment we compare the behaviour of the MTL framework with a baseline one, represented by a single-task learning scheme. Specifically, in the STL case, we employ the same deep architecture as the one illustrated in Fig. 5, but without the shared layer, i.e. we regress the two velocities separately. Also

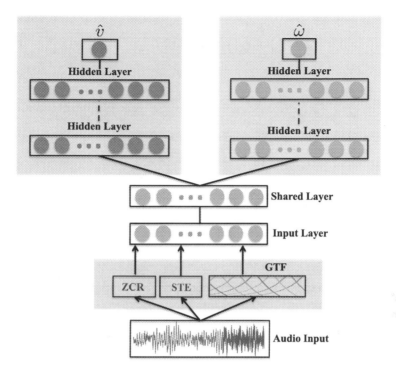

**Fig. 5.** Representation of the learning scheme used. The waveform of the original signal in the time domain is parsed and features are extracted (purple area). Specifically, ZCR indicates the zero-crossing rate of the signal, STE represents the short-term energy, and GTF is the feature representation in the frequency domain obtained after applying the Gammatone filterbank to the original signal. Features are then concatenated and fed to the DNN. The input and the first hidden layer of the networks are shared across the two task (i.e. linear and angular velocity estimation). The rest of the hidden layers (we used four in this case for both tasks) are not shared. The green structure refers to the portion of the network employed to regress exclusively the linear velocity $\hat{v}$, while the orange one refers to the portion of the network employed to regress the angular velocity $\hat{\omega}$. All hidden layers are equipped with a Rectified Linear Unit (ReLU). (Color figure online)

in this experiment, we consider two different feature representations, obtained by using either 64 or 128 frequency channels. Table 1 reports the results of this experiment. In the table, $\tilde{E}_{v_s}$ and $\tilde{E}_{\omega_s}$ refer to the median absolute error in the estimation of the linear and angular velocity on the test data, by using the STL regression framework. $\tilde{T}_{v_s}$ and $\tilde{T}_{\omega_s}$ indicate the median absolute error in the estimation of the linear and angular velocity on the training data. Figure 7 shows the normalised histograms of the absolute error in the estimation of the linear velocity (Fig. 7a) and in the estimation of the angular velocity (Fig. 7b), for $NF \in \{64, 128\}$, when following an STL scheme. We see that in this case,

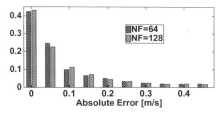

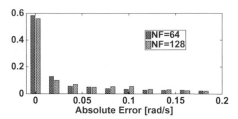

(a) Normalised Histogram of $E_v$ in the MTL case

(b) Normalised Histogram of $E_\omega$ in the MTL case

**Fig. 6.** From left to right: Normalised histogram of the absolute error in the estimation of the linear velocity $E_v$ in the MTL case (a), Normalised histogram of the absolute error in the estimation of the angular velocity $E_\omega$ in the MTL case (b). Both histograms refer to the errors on the testing data. $NF$ refers to the number of frequency channels used in the feature representation.

employing 64 frequency channels yields better performance in the linear velocity estimation, while the opposite behaviour is reported for what concerns the angular velocity.

**Table 1.** The table reports the results of the experiments. $\tilde{E}_v$ and $\tilde{E}_\omega$ indicate the median absolute error in the estimation of the linear and angular velocity in the MTL and the STL regression frameworks on the test data. $\tilde{T}_v$ and $\tilde{T}_\omega$ indicate the median absolute error in the estimation of the linear and angular velocity in the MTL and the STL regression frameworks on the training data. $NF$ refers to the number of filters used in the Gammatone filterbank.

| NF | MTL | | | | STL | | | |
|---|---|---|---|---|---|---|---|---|
| | $\tilde{E}_v$ [m/s] | $\tilde{E}_\omega$ [rad/s] | $\tilde{T}_v$ [m/s] | $\tilde{T}_\omega$ [rad/s] | $\tilde{E}_v$ [m/s] | $\tilde{E}_\omega$ [rad/s] | $\tilde{T}_v$ [m/s] | $\tilde{T}_\omega$ [rad/s] |
| 64 | **0.065** | **0.017** | 0.041 | 0.013 | 0.074 | 0.023 | 0.037 | 0.011 |
| 128 | **0.064** | **0.018** | 0.040 | 0.009 | 0.081 | 0.021 | 0.030 | 0.009 |

When comparing the behaviour of the STL system with the MTL one, we observe that the MTL scheme outperforms the STL one, independently of the number of channels used, both in the case of the linear and the angular velocity. Specifically, we obtain an improvement in the performance by 12% on $\tilde{E}_v$ and 22% on $\tilde{E}_\omega$, when $NF = 64$, and an improvement by 26% on $\tilde{E}_v$ and 14 % on $\tilde{E}_\omega$, when $NF = 128$. We also notice that the STL scheme is characterised by a lower error on the training set, in the estimation of both velocities, independently of the number of filters used. Such a behaviour is expected, as one of the advantages of MTL, especially in case of hard parameter sharing, is, indeed, to help against overfitting, increasing the generalisation capabilities of the model.

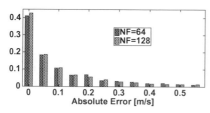
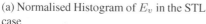

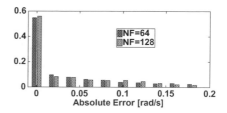

(a) Normalised Histogram of $E_v$ in the STL case

(b) Normalised Histogram of $E_\omega$ in the STL case

**Fig. 7.** From left to right: Normalised histogram of the absolute error in the estimation of the linear velocity $E_v$ in the STL case (a), Normalised histogram of the absolute error in the estimation of the angular velocity $E_\omega$ in the STL case (b). Both histograms refer to the errors on the testing data. $NF$ refers to the number of frequency channels used in the feature representation.

## 5   Conclusions

In this paper we investigated the possibility of estimating a robot's ego-motion by relying only on acoustic sensing. We performed regression analysis employing a deep neural network and followed a multi-task learning scheme to simultaneously estimate the magnitude of the linear and the angular velocity of the vehicle. Our experimental evaluation conducted on approximately two hours of data collected by an unmanned outdoor field robot proved that our framework is able to provide accurate ego-motion estimates, despite the presence of background noise and the robot travelling on different kinds of terrain. When compared to a single-task learning scheme, where the two velocities are modelled separately, our framework shows an improvement of up to 26% in the ego-motion estimation. Given those results, we envision this system being useful as an auxiliary source of odometry information on the side of more traditional odometry systems. Acoustic sensing, indeed, is not affected by lighting or scene appearance. Future work could investigate the possibility of combining the current framework with visual odometry or laser-based odometry systems in a multi-modal setting.

**Acknowledgements.** This work was supported by the UK EPSRC Programme Grant EP/M019918/1.

## References

1. Nistér, D., Naroditsky, O., Bergen, J.: Visual odometry for ground vehicle applications. J. Field Robot. **23**(1), 3–20 (2006)
2. Maimone, M., Cheng, Y., Matthies, L.: Two years of visual odometry on the mars exploration rovers. J. Field Robot. **24**(3), 169–186 (2007)
3. Nicolai, A., Skeele, R., Eriksen, C., Hollinger, G.A.: Deep learning for laser based odometry estimation. In: Robotics: Science and Systems, Workshop on Limits and Potentials of Deep Learning in Robotics (2016)

4. Konda, K.R., Memisevic, R.: Learning visual odometry with a convolutional network. In: VISAPP (1), pp. 486–490 (2015)
5. Kendall, A., Grimes, M., Cipolla, R.: PoseNET: a convolutional network for real-time 6-DOF camera relocalization. In: Proceedings of the IEEE International Conference on Computer Vision, pp. 2938–2946 (2015)
6. Marchegiani, M.L., Pirri, F., Pizzoli, M.: Multimodal speaker recognition in a conversation scenario. In: Fritz, M., Schiele, B., Piater, J.H. (eds.) ICVS 2009. LNCS, vol. 5815, pp. 11–20. Springer, Heidelberg (2009). https://doi.org/10.1007/978-3-642-04667-4_2
7. Marchegiani, L., Posner, I.: Leveraging the urban soundscape: auditory perception for smart vehicles. In: 2017 IEEE International Conference on Robotics and Automation (ICRA), pp. 6547–6554. IEEE (2017)
8. Maxime, J., Alameda-Pineda, X., Girin, L., Horaud, R.: Sound representation and classification benchmark for domestic robots. In: 2014 IEEE International Conference on Robotics and Automation (ICRA), pp. 6285–6292. IEEE (2014)
9. Valada, A., Spinello, L., Burgard, W.: Deep feature learning for acoustics-based terrain classification. In: Bicchi, A., Burgard, W. (eds.) Robotics Research: Volume 2. SPAR, vol. 3, pp. 21–37. Springer, Cham (2018). https://doi.org/10.1007/978-3-319-60916-4_2
10. Bando, Y., et al.: Sound-based online localization for an in-pipe snake robot. In: 2016 IEEE International Symposium on Safety, Security, and Rescue Robotics (SSRR), pp. 207–213. IEEE (2016)
11. Pico, A., Schillaci, G., Hafner, V.V., Lara, B.: How do i sound like? Forward models for robot ego-noise prediction. In: 2016 Joint IEEE International Conference on Development and Learning and Epigenetic Robotics (ICDL-EpiRob), pp. 246–251. IEEE (2016)
12. Scaramuzza, D., Fraundorfer, F.: Visual odometry [tutorial]. IEEE Robot. Autom. Mag. **18**(4), 80–92 (2011)
13. Rosten, E., Reitmayr, G., Drummond, T.: Real-time video annotations for augmented reality. In: Bebis, G., Boyle, R., Koracin, D., Parvin, B. (eds.) ISVC 2005. LNCS, vol. 3804, pp. 294–302. Springer, Heidelberg (2005). https://doi.org/10.1007/11595755_36
14. Calonder, M., Lepetit, V., Ozuysal, M., Trzcinski, T., Strecha, C., Fua, P.: BRIEF: computing a local binary descriptor very fast. IEEE Trans. Pattern Anal. Mach. Intell. **34**(7), 1281–1298 (2012)
15. Fischler, M.A., Bolles, R.C.: Random sample consensus: a paradigm for model fitting with applications to image analysis and automated cartography. Commun. ACM **24**(6), 381–395 (1981)
16. Collobert, R., Weston, J.: A unified architecture for natural language processing: deep neural networks with multitask learning. In: Proceedings of the 25th International Conference on Machine Learning, pp. 160–167. ACM (2008)
17. Jin, F., Sun, S.: Neural network multitask learning for traffic flow forecasting. In: 2008 IEEE International Joint Conference on Neural Networks, IJCNN 2008. (IEEE World Congress on Computational Intelligence), pp. 1897–1901. IEEE (2008)
18. Caruana, R.: Multitask learning. In: Thrun, S., Pratt, L. (eds.) Learning to Learn, pp. 95–133. Springer, Boston (1998). https://doi.org/10.1007/978-1-4615-5529-2_5
19. Chakrabarty, D., Elhilali, M.: Abnormal sound event detection using temporal trajectories mixtures. In: 2016 IEEE International Conference on Acoustics, Speech and Signal Processing (ICASSP), pp. 216–220. IEEE (2016)

20. Holdsworth, J., Nimmo-Smith, I., Patterson, R., Rice, P.: Implementing a gammatone filter bank. Annex C SVOS Final Rep.: Part A: Audit. Filterbank **1**, 1–5 (1988)
21. Marchegiani, L., Karadogan, S.G., Andersen, T., Larsen, J., Hansen, L.K.: The role of top-down attention in the cocktail party: revisiting cherry's experiment after sixty years. In: 2011 10th International Conference on Machine Learning and Applications and Workshops (ICMLA), vol. 1, pp. 183–188. IEEE (2011)
22. Toshio, I.: An optimal auditory filter. In: 1995 IEEE ASSP Workshop on Applications of Signal Processing to Audio and Acoustics, pp. 198–201. IEEE (1995)
23. Glasberg, B.R., Moore, B.C.: Derivation of auditory filter shapes from notched-noise data. Hear. Res. **47**(1), 103–138 (1990)
24. Kingma, D., Ba, J.: Adam: a method for stochastic optimization. arXiv preprint arXiv:1412.6980 (2014). Published as a Conference Paper at the 3rd International Conference for Learning Representations (ICLR) 2015
25. Hinton, G.E., Srivastava, N., Krizhevsky, A., Sutskever, I., Salakhutdinov, R.R.: Improving neural networks by preventing co-adaptation of feature detectors. arXiv preprint arXiv:1207.0580 (2012)
26. Abadi, M., et al.: TensorFlow: large-scale machine learning on heterogeneous systems (2015) Software available from tensorflow.org
27. Deng, S., Han, J., Zhang, C., Zheng, T., Zheng, G.: Robust minimum statistics project coefficients feature for acoustic environment recognition. In: 2014 IEEE International Conference on Acoustics, Speech and Signal Processing (ICASSP), pp. 8232–8236. IEEE (2014)
28. Takahashi, N., Gygli, M., Van Gool, L.: AENet: learning deep audio features for video analysis. arXiv preprint arXiv:1701.00599 (2017)

# Piloting Scenarios for Children with Autism to Learn About Visual Perspective Taking

Luke Jai Wood(✉), Ben Robins, Gabriella Lakatos, Dag Sverre Syrdal, Abolfazl Zaraki, and Kerstin Dautenhahn

Adaptive Systems Research Group, School of Computer Science, University of Hertfordshire, Hertfordshire, UK
l.wood@herts.ac.uk

**Abstract.** Visual Perspective Taking (VPT) is the ability to see the world from another person's perspective, taking into account what they see and how they see it, drawing upon both spatial and social information. Children with autism often find it difficult to understand that other people might have perspectives, viewpoints, beliefs and knowledge that are different from their own which is a fundamental aspect VPT. In this paper, we present the piloting of scenarios for our first large scale pilot-study using a humanoid robot to assist children with autism develop their VPT skills. The games were implemented with the Kaspar robot and to our knowledge this is the first attempt to improve the VPT skills of children with autism through playing and interacting with a humanoid robot.

**Keywords:** Assistive robotics · Autism · Social robotics
Human-robot-interaction

## 1 Background

The various sub domains of social robotics investigate the wide and diverse applications where social robots could be utilised, from robotic pets and educational aids [1–3] to therapeutic and assistive tools [4–7]. Research in social robotics suggests that both neurotypical children and children with special needs often appear to be enthusiastic towards interacting with social robots [8, 9]. In the late 1990s, Dautenhahn and Werry began pioneering studies investigating how robots could be used as assistive tools for children with ASC [10]. Since these first studies, there have been numerous subsequent investigations into this field, in particular with regards to the potential of robots to encourage social interaction and collaborative play amongst children with ASC [11, 12]. However, to date very little research has been conducted into the possibility of using robots to assist developing the Visual Perspective Taking (VPT) skills of children with ASC. The aim of this research presented in this paper is to present the development of scenarios that will be used in future to establish if humanoid robots such as Kaspar can assist children with ASC develop their VPT skills.

Autism Spectrum Condition (ASC) is a lifelong developmental condition that affects how people perceive the world and interact with others [13]. ASC appears in many different forms and varies in its degrees of severity ranging from severe low functioning autism, to high functioning and Asperger's syndrome. One of the most

© Springer International Publishing AG, part of Springer Nature 2018
M. Giuliani et al. (Eds.): TAROS 2018, LNAI 10965, pp. 260–270, 2018.
https://doi.org/10.1007/978-3-319-96728-8_22

**Fig. 1.** Child playing VPT game with the Kaspar robot

common manifestations of ASC is an impaired ability for social communication and interaction [14]. Individuals affected by ASC often have great difficulty with Theory of Mind (TOM) and understanding the views and desires of other people [14–20]. TOM is the ability to understand that other individuals have their own thoughts, plans and perspectives, this also extends to the attitudes, beliefs and emotions of others [15]. Because children with ASC struggle to understand that other people do not have the same thoughts as themselves it can cause them difficulty communicating and relating to other people socially.

Visual Perspective Taking (VPT) is the ability to see the world from another person's perspective, taking into account what they see and how they see it, drawing upon both spatial and social information [21]. For children with ASC it can be difficult to understand that other people might have perspectives, viewpoints, beliefs and knowledge that is different from their own. Flavell 1977 defined two levels of perspective taking: VPT1, the ability to understand that other people have a different line of sight to ourselves and VPT2, the understanding that two people viewing the same item from different points in space may see different things [21]. The research outlined in this paper details our path in creating a number of games where child with ASC can playfully explore elements that are important in developing VPT skills which are thought to be a component of Theory of Mind (TOM).

Prior to conducting the larger scale pilot-study outlined in this paper we tested the concept of using the Kaspar robot with a screen showing "what the robot sees", with three children aged between 3 and 5 that had been diagnosed with ASC in a special needs school [22]. This successful initial proof of concept led us to develop 9 games that would assist in developing children's VPT skills. The games included elements of well-known games such as "I Spy" and "Hide and Seek" that the children could play with the Kaspar robot [23]. The games involve a number of different combinations of actions, starting with moving objects into and out of the robots field of view (see Fig. 1), and then physically controlling the robot's line of sight. The key to these games is giving the children the ability to see the world from the robot's perspective and to assist them in learning about VPT. The development of these games was based on a number of factors including the literature on VPT in relation to our previous experience of developing scenarios for children with ASC [6, 24] and consultation with teachers that specialised in working with children in special needs schools to gain feedback on the games we devised. Once the games had been developed a lab trial with a single typically developing child was conducted followed by a trial with three children with ASC in a special needs school to further test and refine the games before being used in the larger scale pilot-study reported in this paper.

## 2  Method

The pilot-study outlined in this paper meant to refine our scenarios was conducted in a local special needs school with twelve children aged between 11 and 14 that had been diagnosed with ASC or similar condition. Each child took part in a three part pre-test before starting the study playing the games with the robot. Each game had a progression criterion with the children needing to successfully complete the game three times before they could move to the next game. Subsequently each child took part in a different number of sessions as the rate at which they progressed through the games varied. In total the children collectively took part in 69 sessions. Once the child had completed all of the games they took part in a post-test that was identical to the pre-test to analyse the child's progress.

In order to measure the potential impact of the games on the children, three tests were piloted with the children before and after all of their sessions interacting with the robot. These assessment tools were chosen because they have previously been used in the literature for children with ASC.

*The Smarties Test*

The smarties test is designed to establish if the child has a theory of mind by asking a series of questions about the contents of a smarties tube [25]. The tube is shown to the child then the child is asked "what do you think is inside". Very often the child would say either "chocolate", "sweets", or "smarties". When the tube is opened the child sees that there are pencils inside rather than the sweets as they had expected. The pencils are then put back into the tube and the tube is closed. Once the tube has been closed the child is then asked what their teacher (someone that has not just seen the pencils being put into the tube) would think is inside. If the child has a theory of mind they will say smarties, chocolate or something to that effect, if they do not then the child will say pencils.

*The Sally-Anne Test*

The Sally-Anne test is a well-known test, again designed to establish if the child has a theory of mind (see Fig. 2(D)) [15]. The advantage of this test is that it is more accessible to non-verbal children because the children can simply point to answer questions rather than speak. Two dolls that look different are placed on the table, one is called Sally the other is called Anne. The child has to confirm that they know which doll is called Sally at the beginning of the test. Sally has an empty basket, whilst Anne has an empty box. Sally places a ball into her basket whist she goes out to play. Anne moves the ball from the basket into her box whilst Sally is out. The child then needs to indicate where the ball is and then where Sally left it. The child is finally asked where Sally will look for her ball when she is back. If the child says the basket then they have a theory of mind, if they say the box this is an indication that they do not.

*The Charlie Test*

The Charlie test is designed to examine the child's understanding of eye gaze [26], which is important for VPT (see Fig. 2). The child answers a number of questions which revolve around the concept of eye gaze. Figure 2(A) shows an example question where the child is asked "which face is looking at you?", whilst the image is directly in front of the child. As the test becomes more complex the child is then presented with pictures of 4 different sweets and asked which one is their favourite (see Fig. 2(B)). Once the child has selected a favourite then a face referred to as Charlie is placed in the middle of the sweets looking at something different to what the child stated and an arrow is also placed on the sheet pointing at another selection that is not what the child stated or what Charlie is looking at. The child is then asked "What is Charlie looking at?". If the child states the sweet that the face is looking at then this is coded as correct, if the child stated the sweet they chose themselves, this is coded as an egocentric response. If the child states one of the other sweets this is coded as random. The Charlie test consists of 15 questions in total and similarly to the Sally-Anne test can be performed with a child that is unable to speak.

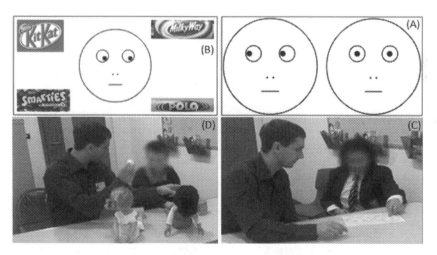

**Fig. 2.** (A, B): Example Charlie test questions, (C, D): children taking part in pre/post-test.

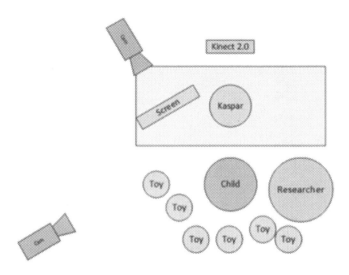

**Fig. 3.** Generic equipment layout

## 2.1   The Games

The 9 games designed for this study initially started out very simple and incrementally become more difficult. To implement these games we used the humanoid robot Kaspar and a screen next to the robot to display what the robot can see from its eyes. The games focused on the children showing the robot animal themed toys in an appropriate manner in order for the child to get the reward from the robot. The reward was the robot making the sound of the animal and perform gestures. Showing the toys to the robot in an appropriate manner meant ensuring that the toy was in the robot's field of view and as such is not too close or too far from the robot's face. The robot provided feedback to the child if the toy was not being shown in an appropriate manner. Figure 3 illustrates the basic setup for the games, however there were variations on this setup depending on the game which was being played. Two cameras and a Kinect sensor were used to gather data from the children interacting with the robot during the sessions. In addition to this the robot also recorded what the robot's field of view.

*Game 1: Show me an animal and I'll make the sound*

The first game is a VPT1 exercise as the children learn that Kaspar has a different line of sight from their own line of sight. This game involves the child freely showing Kaspar animal toys of the child's choice. In this game Kaspar looks straight ahead not moving its head or eyes, the child therefore needs to locate and move the toys into Kaspar's field of view. This game allows the child to explore what happens when they move a toy into the Kaspar's field of view, because the toy becomes visible on the screen that shows what the robot can see from its eyes. Once Kaspar can see the toy, the robot makes the sound of the animal being shown to it by the child, which serves as a reward for the child.

*Game 2: I'll ask for the animal, you find me the animal*

Building on game 1, rather than free exploration, the child now needs to find the animals that Kaspar asks for. Kaspar will ask the child to show it particular animals, and the child needs to find the corresponding animal and show it to the robot in an appropriate manner in order for Kaspar to make the animal sounds and gestures. This again classed as a VPT1 exercise as the children learn about Kaspar having a different line of sight from their own line of sight. However the child needs to collaborate with Kaspar in order to obtain the reward.

*Game 3: Make me look and I'll tell you what it is*

Similar to game 1, the children have the freedom to show Kaspar any toy without limitation and Kaspar will reward the child regardless of the toy. However, in this game the child directs where Kaspar looks rather than moving the objects into Kaspar's field of view. The objects in the room are placed so that they are viewable by the robot from where it is sitting. In this setup the child physically moves the robots head to make it look at the toys around the room. Similarly to the first two games this is classed as a VPT1 exercise, reinforcing what had been learnt in the first two games but in a different (interaction) context, it therefore requires the child to transfer what they have learnt in games 1 and 2 to a different game. An important new feature of this game is that the children learn about how someone's physical head movement and orientation affects what they can see.

*Game 4: I'll tell you what I want to see and you need to show me*

Combining aspects from both games 2 and 3, in game 4 the child controls where Kaspar looks, but must direct Kaspar's head towards the animal that the robot states that it wants to see. Again this is classed as a VPT1 exercise, reinforcing what has been learnt from the earlier games. However, in this game the children need to direct the robot's gaze according to the robot's intentions, collaborating with Kaspar and understanding the robots intention by directing the robots eye gaze towards the correct toy.

*Game 5: What you see is not the same as what I see*

As with game 2 Kaspar looks in one direction only and requests to see particular animals. However, in this task the child is given a cube with pictures of animals on the faces of the cube (see Fig. 4). When the child shows Kaspar the requested animal picture on the face of the cube, Kaspar makes the sound of that animal as a reward similar to the previous games. It is important to note that the face of the cube that is towards the child is different from the face of the cube that is facing the robot. This game is classed as a VPT2 exercise because

**Fig. 4.** Cube with animal pictures on faces

the robot and the child are looking at the same object but see different things. The child needs to understand that what he/she sees is not the same as what Kaspar sees.

*Game 6: I spy with my little eye...*

This game is based on the well-known game "I spy". The toys are placed around the room (with sufficient spacing) and the child needs to work out and pick up the toy that Kaspar is referring to and show the toy to Kaspar. Unlike all the previous games, in this game the child will not have the assistance of the screen because we are beginning to try and encourage the children to work out what Kaspar can see without referring to the screen. This is a very important step because in real life interactions with other people the child cannot see what other people can see via a screen. In these games the screen is simply used as a stepping stone to help teach the children about VPT and at this stage we want to try and get the children to complete the game without the assistance of a screen.

*Game 7: What can we see?*

This game is a VPT2 exercise in which a physical separator device is placed on the table between Kaspar and the child. As shown in Fig. 5, the separator allows three positions: in the first position, the toy can be seen by both, Kaspar and the child. In the second position the toy can be seen by Kaspar only, in the third position the toy can be seen by the child only. In this game the

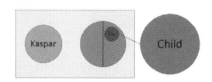

**Fig. 5.** Equipment layout diagram for game 7

child places one toy in the holder and the researcher rotates the holder into one of three positions before asking the child questions about the visibility of the object. As with game 6, the screen is not available to the child as a point of reference.

*Game 8: Who can see what?*

Similar to game 7, the child will answer questions on the visibility of toys placed in a holder, however in this game the child will place three toys into the holder and the holder has 3 different positions in terms of the toys visibility to the robot and the child (see Fig. 6). Again Kaspar asks the child questions about the visibility of the toys in the holder.

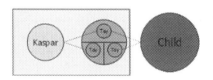

**Fig. 6.** Equipment layout diagram for game 8

*Game 9: Where will I look?*

This game is inspired by the well-established Sally-Anne test [15] that is a psychological test, used in developmental psychology to measure a person's social cognitive ability to attribute false beliefs to others. Often children with autism struggle to view a situation from another person's perspective and realise that what they want, feel, know and think is different from another person's thoughts and feelings. In this game there are two boxes, a blue box and a red box, both have lids. The child has one toy and Kaspar asks the child to put it one of the boxes then place the lid on it whist Kaspar watches. The robot says it is tired and going to have a quick nap, Kaspar will then close its eyes. Whilst Kaspar's eyes are closed and the robot is "sleeping", the researcher encourages the child to move the toy into the opposite container and place the lid on it. The researcher then asks the child to wake Kaspar up to continue playing. When the robot wakes up, the researcher asks the child to point where the robot would look for the toy. The child should point to the last place where Kaspar saw the object if they have developed TOM. Kaspar then states where it thinks the toy is i.e. where it last saw the toy. If the child does not identify this correctly the researcher explains to the child that the robot did not see the child move the toy and would have looked in the container that it last saw the toy in. This is to assist the child in learning about TOM and assess their progress.

## 3 Findings and Discussion

Because this pilot-study is the first of its kind there are a number of lessons that were learnt during the course of this study that will be taken into consideration when conducting future studies in this field, which are as follows:

**Order of Games:** Very early in this study we realised that some of the children had great difficulty in choosing which toy to show Kaspar, even though initially it was though that the children may find it easier to select a toy themselves than find the toy stated by Kaspar. As a result of this, after the first session the order of games 1 and 2 were swapped as were the order of games 3 and 4, so that the child would initially take instruction then make choices. To be consistent with this change, all of the children experienced the original order in their first session and after this were presented with the games in the new order. In our next study as part of this work we will modify the order of the games to ensure that the difficulty of the games is more reflective of how difficult the children found the games in the first pilot-study.

**Progression Criteria:** In this pilot-study initially there was a progression rule in place that the children would have to complete a game successfully on three consecutive occasions before moving onto the next game. Because this large scale pilot-study had no set inclusion criteria, the ability of the children that took part in this study varied greatly and as a result it was impossible to stick to this progression criteria as different children found different games difficult. For example, some children found physically manipulating the head of the robot to look at toys very difficult (in games 3 and 4), but found game 6 (the eye spy game) very easy. We therefore decided to be flexible with the progression criteria in the first study and use this as an exercise to re-assess and re-arrange the games for future studies and form an inclusion criteria to select the children that can benefit from the games. By using an inclusion criteria in our next study, it will be possible to have a robust progression criteria that can be adhered to.

**Level of Assistance Given:** During the sessions with the children sometimes the teaching assistant and/or the experimenter would give the child a lot of assistance in completing the games. Again, this relates to the range of abilities of the participating children being so varied, but also relates to the human nature of wanting to help the child. Giving the children assistance during the games is perfectly acceptable and a very good method of teaching the children about VPT. However, it is important that the child can complete the objective of each game on their own without assistance of the researcher or teaching assistant. In our next study it will be important to communicate this to any teaching assistants present with the children and also important for the experimenter to remember this when assessing if a child has completed a game successfully.

**Implementation of an Additional Game:** As the children progressed to the final game some of them seemed to find the concept of the robot not being able to see while its eyes were closed difficult, as a result of this we introduced an additional game that we referred to as 8.5, as it sat between game 8 and 9. This game was played with the children if they were unable to successfully complete game 9. Although game 9 was a TOM based game it was believed that going back to a very basic level in game 8.5 may assist the children in learning about VPT and ultimately TOM. The objective of game 8.5 was to assess if the children could understand the difference between what Kaspar could see with its eyes closed, eyes open, eyes obscured with a sleeping mask and eyes obscured with its hands. This game was initially completed with the children with the assistance of the screen then once the child could demonstrate they understood this, the screen was switched off to ensure that the child did not rely on the screen. This game will also be included in our next study.

**Child Specific Rewards:** During the study, one of the children requested that Kaspar would sing a song that he had heard in a film he liked. In the next session this song was added to the robots behaviours and used as a reward for the child when he completed a game and moved to the next level. This child specific reward was very effective in motivating the child to successfully complete the games and was also adopted with another child in the study. Taking this into consideration, in the next study we will establish some child specific rewards as this has such a positive impact on the children's response to the games and the robot.

**Use of the Screen:** Initially it was planned that the children would be allowed to use the screen up until game 5 but not after this. During the study it became apparent that for the children to learn about the later games and concepts it would be useful for them to be able to see the screen and learn what Kaspar can and cannot see. Therefore, we waivered this rule for this study. However, in our next study the children will have access to the screen for all of the games but will also have to complete all of the games without the screen in order to have been considered successful in completing each game.

**Charlie Pre/Post-test Questions:** It was noticed very quickly in the pre-testing that some of the children would sometimes correctly identify the side where the face was looking (left or right), but would struggle to identify if the face was looking up or down. Consequently it was ensured that the researcher conducting the test made the face look to the opposite side to which the children had chosen themselves to ensure that an accidental egocentric response was not produced. By administering the test in this way we eliminated any potential false egocentric results.

### 3.1    Conclusion

The 12 children that took part in this study all possessed different levels of ability and as a result took part in a different number of sessions. In total 69 sessions were run at the school and the games that we devised flowed well and were playable for the children. All of the children managed to complete the most basic games successfully whilst some of the more children struggled with the more complex games such as the VPT2 games but most eventually managed this successfully. One unexpected outcome from this study was that some of the children found the games we had previously considered to be easier more difficult than anticipated. In particular, the children found physically manipulating the head of the robot to look at toys placed around the room much harder than we had ever considered. In light of this in future work we will revise the order of some of these games to reflect how the children in this study performed. The final game that was a Theory of Mind exercise many of the children still struggled with, however some children did make some progress in learning about this. Generally the games worked as anticipated and the lessons learned from this first pilot-study will be taken into account when conducting our next study in the field.

## 4 Future Work

Because this research is part of the EU Horizon 2020 BabyRobot project, a project which aims to develop semi-autonomous robotic systems that can work in real world settings and assist with real world problems, a semi-autonomous implementation of the games will be implemented and tested in a school in the near future [27].

**Acknowledgments.** This work has been partially funded by the BabyRobot project supported by the EU Horizon 2020 Programme under grant 687831.

## References

1. Yoshida, S., Sakamoto, D., Sugiura, Y., Inami, M., Igarashi, T.: RoboJockey: robotic dance entertainment for all. In: SIGGRAPH Asia 2012 Emerging Technologies, p. 19. ACM (2012)
2. Tanaka, F., Ghosh, M.: The implementation of care-receiving robot at an English learning school for children. In: Proceedings of the 6th International Conference on Human-Robot Interaction, HRI 2011, Lausanne, Switzerland (2011)
3. Bartlett, B., Estivill-Castro, V., Seymon, S.: Dogs or robots—Why do children see them as robotic pets rather than canine machines? Presented at the 5th Australasian User Interface Conference (AUIC 2004), Dunedin (2004)
4. Goris, K., Saldien, J., Lefeber, D.: Probo: a testbed for human robot interaction. In: Proceedings of the 4th ACM/IEEE International Conference on Human Robot Interaction, HRI 2009, La Jolla, California, USA (2009)
5. Kozima, H., Michalowski, M., Nakagawa, C.: Keepon: a playful robot for research, therapy, and entertainment. Int. J. Soc. Robot. **1**(1), 3–18 (2009)
6. Robins, B., Dautenhahn, K., Dickerson, P.: From isolation to communication: a case study evaluation of robot assisted play for children with autism with a minimally expressive humanoid robot. In: Proceedings of the Second International Conferences on Advances in Computer-Human Interactions, ACHI 2009, Cancun, Mexico, pp. 205–211. IEEE Computer Society Press (2009)
7. Mead, R., Grollman, D.H., Lim, A., Yeung, C., Stout, A., Knox, W.B.: HRI 2018 workshop: social robots in the wild. In: Companion of the 2018 ACM/IEEE International Conference on Human-Robot Interaction, pp. 399–400. ACM (2018)

8. Michalowski, M.P., Sabanovic, S., Michel, P.: Roillo: creating a social robot for playrooms. Presented at the Robot and Human Interactive Communication, The 15th IEEE International Symposium, ROMAN (2006)

9. Martínez-Miranda, J., Pérez-Espinosa, H., Espinosa-Curiel, I., Avila-George, H., Rodríguez-Jacobo, J.: Age-based differences in preferences and affective reactions towards a robot's personality during interaction. Comput. Hum. Behav. **84**, 245–257 (2018)

10. Werry, I., Dautenhahn, K.: Applying mobile robot technology to the rehabilitation of autistic children. In: Proceedings of SIRS 1999, 7th Symposium on Intelligent Robotic Systems (1999)

11. Pennisi, P., et al.: Autism and social robotics: a systematic review. Autism Res. **9**, 165–183 (2015)

12. Sartorato, F., Przybylowski, L., Sarko, D.K.: Improving therapeutic outcomes in autism spectrum disorders: enhancing social communication and sensory processing through the use of interactive robots. J. Psychiatric Res. **90**, 1–11 (2017)

13. Wing, L.: The autistic spectrum: a guide for parents and professionals. Constable (1996)

14. Baron-Cohen, S.: Mind Blindness: An Essay on Autism and Theory of Mind (1995)

15. Baron-Cohen, S., Leslie, A.M., Frith, U.: Does the autistic child have a "theory of mind"? Cognition **21**(1), 37–46 (1985)

16. Happé, F.G.: Understanding minds and metaphors: insights from the study of figurative language in autism. Metaphor Symbol **10**(4), 275–295 (1995)

17. Baron-Cohen, S., Jolliffe, T., Mortimore, C., Robertson, M.: Another advanced test of theory of mind: evidence from very high functioning adults with autism or Asperger syndrome. J. Child Psychol. Psychiatry **38**(7), 813–822 (1997)

18. Frith, U.: Mind blindness and the brain in autism. Neuron **32**(6), 969–979 (2001)

19. Senju, A.: Spontaneous theory of mind and its absence in autism spectrum disorders. Neurosci. **18**(2), 108–113 (2012)

20. Senju, A., Southgate, V., White, S., Frith, U.: Mindblind eyes: an absence of spontaneous theory of mind in Asperger syndrome. Science **325**(5942), 883–885 (2009)

21. Flavell, J.H.: The development of knowledge about visual perception. In: Nebraska symposium on motivation. University of Nebraska Press (1977)

22. Wood, L., Dautenhahn, K., Robins, B., Zaraki, A.: Developing child-robot interaction scenarios with a humanoid robot to assist children with autism in developing visual perspective taking skills. In: Proceedings of the 26th IEEE International Symposium on Robots and Human Interactive Communication (Ro-Man), pp. 1–6 (2017)

23. Wood, L.J., Zaraki, A., Walters, M.L., Novanda, O., Robins, B., Dautenhahn, K.: The iterative development of the humanoid robot Kaspar: an assistive robot for children with autism. In: Kheddar, A., et al. (eds.) Social Robotics. LNCS, pp. 53–63. Springer, Cham (2017). https://doi.org/10.1007/978-3-319-70022-9_6

24. Robins, B., Dautenhahn, K.: Tactile interactions with a humanoid robot: novel play scenario implementations with children with autism. Int. J. Soc. Robot. **6**(3), 397–415 (2014)

25. Hogrefe, G.-J., Wimmer, H., Perner, J.: Ignorance versus false belief: a developmental lag in attribution of epistemic states. Child Dev. **57**, 567–582 (1986)

26. Baron-Cohen, S., Campbell, R., Karmiloff-Smith, A., Grant, J., Walker, J.: Are children with autism blind to the mentalistic significance of the eyes? Br. J. Dev. Psychol. **13**(4), 379–398 (1995)

27. Zaraki, A., Dautenhahn, K., Wood, L., Novanda, O., Robins, B.: Toward autonomous child-robot interaction: development of an interactive architecture for the humanoid Kaspar robot. Presented at the 3rd Workshop on Child-Robot Interaction (CRI2017) in International Conference on Human Robot Interaction (ACM/IEEE HRI 2017), Vienna, Austria, 6–9 March 2017 (2017)

# User Detection, Tracking and Recognition in Robot Assistive Care Scenarios

Ştefania Alexandra Ghiţă, Miruna-Ştafania Barbu, Alexandru Gavril(✉),
Mihai Trăscău, Alexandru Sorici, and Adina Magda Florea

Faculty of Automatic Control and Computer Science,
Politehnica University of Bucharest, Bucharest, Romania
alexandra.ghita2712@stud.acs.upb.ro,
{miruna.barbu,alexandru.gavril,mihai.trascau}@cti.pub.ro,
{alexandru.sorici,adina.florea}@cs.pub.ro

**Abstract.** The field of assistive robotics is gaining traction in both research as well as industry communities. However, capabilities of existing robotic platforms still require improvements in order to implement meaningful human-robot interactions. We report on the design and implementation of an external system that significantly augments the person detection, tracking and identification capabilities of the Pepper robot. We perform a qualitative analysis of the improvements achieved by each system module under different interaction conditions and evaluate the whole system on hand of a scenario for elderly care assistance.

**Keywords:** Assistive robotics · Person detection and tracking
Face recognition · Autonomous navigation

## 1 Introduction

Assistive and social robots that interact with and support humans in their everyday lives is a field gaining consistent interest in both research and industrial communities. Common application domains range from informing customers in commercial and exhibition venues to visitor guidance in museums, and personal assistance for elderly users.

There are already numerous vendors offering robotic solutions whose capabilities make them suitable for the above mentioned applications. However, while there is a high variety of robotic platforms, it is still currently a challenge to adapt and quickly tailor the behavior of an assistant robot from one scenario to another, according to customer requirements. Furthermore, there is often the case that the functionalities offered by the out-of-the-box robot need to be augmented by external services in order to implement meaningful interactions.

Pepper([1]) is an example of a robot that can act as an assistant for people who need information, guidance or help. It is designed by the Japanese company

---

[1] https://www.ald.softbankrobotics.com/en/robots/pepper.

© Springer International Publishing AG, part of Springer Nature 2018
M. Giuliani et al. (Eds.): TAROS 2018, LNAI 10965, pp. 271–283, 2018.
https://doi.org/10.1007/978-3-319-96728-8_23

SoftBank Robotics [1] and is the robotic platform we used for development. It is one of the first robotic machine specially designed to interact with humans with a very friendly human-like appearance. The interaction with the robot can be done by voice, gestures or touch, and it can respond back by speaking or by using visual information displayed on the tablet.

Pepper disposes of capabilities that already allow successful demo deployments in day to day environments (e.g. public offices or stores), as well as implementation of educational applications [2].

However, the specifications of application scenarios we envision (e.g. elderly user assistance) require the robot to be able to detect, track and identify people at a greater distance (e.g. more than 5 m), under more severe partial occlusion conditions and with greater accuracy than it is currently capable.

For example, in one proposed scenario, Pepper acts as an assistant for elderly people, offering the means to efficiently look for and find a particular person in order to inform about notifications regarding personal health or well-being issues (e.g. take medication, blood pressure measurements, perform physical exercises, call friends, etc.) [3,4]. The scenario considers the case of a previously unmapped enclosed space where the robot performs a random search looking for the user of interest. Upon detection of a person, the robot needs to track and move closer to the detected user in order to perform facial recognition. The robot repeats a cycle of detect - track - identify until it is able to locate and recognize the person whom it needs to inform of pending notifications.

In order to address the above challenges, this paper reports on an external processing system that improve the default capabilities of the Pepper robot with respect to the tasks of person detection and identification. The robot-detached solution was used in order to provide more computing capabilities of Pepper and the vision processing modules added to the robot are improving the capabilities of localizing, detecting and recognizing persons in various locations (distant or near). If Pepper is used as an assistive robot, it must recognize the person in order to provide personalized assistance. In Sect. 2 we provide an overview of hardware and software modules of the robot which are relevant for the given class of applications. Section 3 reviews computer vision frameworks integrated on the external implementation to augment long distance person detection and the accuracy of user identification. The architecture of the integrated system and the interplay between all modules that enable person detection, tracking and identification is presented in Sect. 4. We detail the demonstration setup and perform a qualitative analysis of the achieved improvements for different interaction settings in Sect. 5. Section 6 concludes the paper.

## 2   Pepper Description

In order to perform human-like tasks, Pepper is equipped with multiple sensors and specialized hardware for motion and perception [5].

*Vision* - Pepper has three cameras placed on its head: one of them is a 3-dimensional one that gets depth information at a resolution of $320 \times 240$ with the frame rate of 20 FPS; the other two are 2D, but are capable of receiving high resolution images of $2560 \times 1920$ at 1 FPS or images with resolution $640 \times 480$, but at a greater frequency of 30 FPS.

*Mobility* - Pepper has an advanced system for object avoidance and multiple sensors that prevent bumping into people, including lasers, sonars, accelerometer and gyroscope. In case of collision, it can maintain its stability thanks to bumpers in the base and it thus has a small chance of falling. It has an autonomy of approximately half a day, given its rechargeable battery.

*Interaction* - Pepper has 4 microphones which help it detect sound, but also localize people around it and rotate to face them. For verbal communication it uses the 2 speakers that are located in the ears. For guidance of the companion, it uses LEDs that are positioned in the eyes or around the head to signal when it is ready to speak or to mark its movements. The tactile sensors it has are useful in various situations; the same happens with the integrated tablet that displays requested information or has other applications installed on it.

At software level, the system is developed on top of the NAOqi framework [6], which is the default environment of the robot. The application we develop uses a number of built-in modules, namely the ones responsible for image acquisition, language processing and for tracking: *ALVideoDevice* (provides images from all the cameras available on the robot), *ALTracker* (tracks specific targets, like face, red ball, landmark, etc.), *ALSpeechRecognition* (recognizes sounds from the environment), *ALTextToSpeech* (converts into texts to speech) and *ALTabletService* (used for tablet interaction).

## 3    Computer Vision Framework Description

The Pepper robot has a default mode of operation called *autonomous life*[2] that lets it act alive and interact with users. This operation mode enables the robot to engage with people once they come close enough to capture the attention of the robot. However, our proposed scenario requires that the robot be able to *pro-actively* detect and move towards people that are beyond the range of its default interaction distance. Furthermore, the detection and identification of people needs to handle cases of partial occlusion of target users (e.g. sitting behind a desk), as well as different illumination levels (e.g. moving towards a well lit window, or in low-light due to the blinds being completely closed).

This prompts us to make use of external computer vision frameworks for *object detection* and *face recognition*. The increase in dataset availability and variability of training conditions (e.g. levels of illumination, occlusion or quality) have led to face recognition methods which achieve accuracies close to 100% [7] and people detection techniques with up to 80 mean average precision [8]. In this research, we used YOLO for object detection and FaceNet for face recognition.

YOLO (You Only Look Once). [8,9] is an approach for object detection in images, wrapping them in bounding boxes. The method can detect all instances

---

[2] http://doc.aldebaran.com/2-5/family/pepper_user_guide/life_pep.html#alife-pep.

of objects from a defined category list in just one pass over the image through a convolutional neural network in real-time. Therefore this methods is adequate for our aim, bringing real-time detection of objects, with excellent results at a speed of 30 frames per second, which is the maximum frame rate of the video stream offered by Pepper.

YOLO gives accurate results even if the frames it has as input are badly illuminated, have a lower quality or the target objects in them are distorted with affine transformations.

In our experiments we obtained promising results in both accuracy and detection speed, results which proved to be better than the built-in system for human tracking in Pepper, which can not detect anyone at more than 5 m (see also Sect. 5.2).

FaceNet [7] gives best results considering the face recognition task. For each face in an image, FaceNet provides an embedding of 128 elements resulted from passing the image through a deep neural network. Two vectors that are obtained from the similar faces have the property that are closer to each other. In this way, a measure of similarity can be derived and faces can be classified using Support Vector Machines or clustered with a k-means approach.

The supervised training approach used by FaceNet, which uses a large amount of labeled images, leads to better results on real-life conditions where we encounter different face positions and orientations, varied luminosity or image quality.

Using the model on Pepper, the error rate compared to a previously tested method (OpenCV face recognition system) improved by 30% (see also Sect. 5.2). FaceNet does not require any preprocessing of the image feed from Pepper and proved more robust on several edge cases. It can much better distinguish people seen from an angle, ones that are under very strong or low light, as well as people which share a dominant face characteristic (e.g. men with beard or people with same face elongation).

## 4    Architecture and Implementation

The proposed system has several components. The robotic platform is using data that comes from both internal and external processing. The internal processing refers to sensors, cameras and movement, while the external one implies image processing for obtaining the required information (i.e. detection and identification of people).

Figure 1 presents our system architecture. Image processing tasks are achieved on a remote server and the results are later passed to the robot. The need of an external processing is due to the limited computational capabilities of the robot, which do not allow using good techniques with real-time results.

Pepper is equipped with an *ASUS Xtion 3D camera*[3] offering a $320 \times 240$ resolution at 20 frames per second depth images which are aligned with the

---

[3] http://doc.aldebaran.com/2-4/family/pepper_technical/video_3D_pep.html.

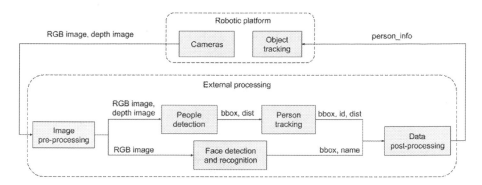

**Fig. 1.** System architecture overview.

RGB images used for people detection and face recognition. The *People Detection* module forwards bounding box (bbox) information for the detected person along with depth information to the person tracking module. This module links the current detection with the previous ones. This step is required, because the robot must track one person at a time. In a parallel processing pipeline, the RGB image is passed to the *Face Detection and Recognition module*, which is able to extract information about the position of the face and the *name* of the person it identified.

The extracted information (bounding box of detected person, id of tracking session, depth information and name) is then passed back to the robot, by a TCP connection.

On the robot side, the bounding box position and depth data is used to translate from image positions to 3D coordinates, which are required by the tracking and navigation modules. Distance information and the name of the identified person are used to trigger a specific user interaction, given by the proximity of the robot to the human actor. The object tracking, navigation and speech recognition modules we used are the ones available in the NAOqi framework, which run directly on the robot.

### 4.1    People Detection Module

One of the most important components of the proposed system is the module for people detection. The detection must be done in real-time with accurate results, such that the tracking is consistent, with no errors. As previously reported, for this task we use the YOLO network, as it fits our system well, being able to process around 40 frames per second, which covers the 30 FPS image streaming capability of Pepper in full.

The integration between the robot produced image stream and YOLO runs on a server, with high computational power. We use the *ALVideoDevice* module from NAOqi framework to access two types of already correlated image streams, RGB and depth.

We used a pre-trained YOLO network for fast detections. An example of the network's result can be seen in Fig. 2. The YOLO network result is presented in the left side of the image, while the right side shows how the detections fit the depth image. The depth image is slightly misaligned with the RGB image, as the 3D sensor is not in the same position as the 2D sensor. To be in the correct positions, the computed detections are translated in the depth image with the corresponding difference on x-y axes.

**Fig. 2.** YOLO people detection results using Pepper RGB and depth image streams.

The network result for an image is a set of bounding boxes alongside the corresponding confidence, where each bounding box represent the position of a person in image pixels. The detection is limited to top squares, which are defined by the width of the detection. This change is useful for the tracking part, so that the robot can center its head position to the upper body of the detected person.

The distance to the detected person is obtained using the bounding boxes computed by the YOLO network. For each bounding box, the distance is computed based on the median value of the pixels in that patch. The depth image is a grayscale image, where the value of each pixel represents the distance to that point, from 0.4 m to 3.68 m. The problem with the depth image is that the pixel value for the closest distance is the same as the value for the points that are further than the maximum distance. To solve this case, the system also takes into consideration the size of the detection, in order to decide if the person is close or not. When the median pixel is black, if the size of the detection is above a threshold then the distance will have the value 0.4, otherwise it will have the value 5.

### 4.2   People Tracking Module

The people tracking module is responsible with changing the pose of the robot relative to the person which is being tracked, while trying to move towards the detected person. The module receives its input from the person detection module as a rectangle with an extracted patch from the image containing the person.

The tracking module estimates the 3D position of the person. The people detection module, presented in Sect. 4.1 uses an ORB detector [10] to extract features from the patch in order to verify if the person being tracked is the same as the one in the previous step. The tracking module keeps a history of ORB features for all detected persons. This history is used in order to distinguish between individual people, as well as to continue a tracking session in case a person goes out of sight.

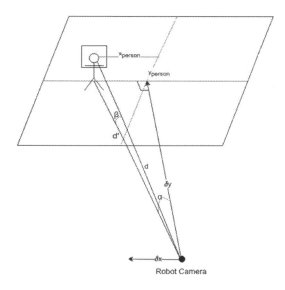

**Fig. 3.** People tracking in image representation and angular computation.

In order to estimate the relative localization of the robot with respect to the detected person we rely on computing angular approximations based on the input image and the camera parameters of the robot.

Figure 3 shows the geometry we are taking into consideration. We compute estimations of the horizontal ($\alpha$) and vertical ($\beta$) displacement angles between the robot camera and the position of the person. The value of the angles are computed as proportions from the horizontal and vertical camera fields of view, respectively. The proportion amounts are given by the pixel-wise relation between the ($x_{person}, y_{person}$) distances of the detected person patch from the center of the image and the total image width and height. Our angle approximations are thus computed by the equations: $\alpha = hfov_{camera} * (x_{person}/width_{image})$ and $\beta = vfov_{camera} * (y_{person}/height_{image})$.

To compute estimates of the actual $\delta x$ and $\delta y$ offsets with respect to the real world position of the person we must take distance information into account. We make use of *depth-to-rgb* mapping functionality to obtain the distance information for the *pixel* representing the center of the detected person patch. This procedure is however limited to the capabilities of the depth sensor, therefore

278 S. A. Ghiță et al.

we can identify three main cases depending on the distance of the robot to the person.

*Tracking within depth range.* When a new detection is registered in the tracking module, the $(x_{person}, y_{person})$ vector between the center of the image and the position registered is computed, as explained previously. Let $d$ be the distance from the robot to the tracked person. Then $d'$ in Fig. 3 is equal to $d * cos(\beta)$. Knowing the distance to the detected patch and the relative angles as previously described, the robot can estimate the distances $\delta x$ and $\delta y$ on the X and Y axes using the equations $\delta x = d * cos(\beta) * sin(\alpha)$ and $\delta y = d * cos(\beta) * cos(\alpha)$.

*Tracking outside depth range.* If the range is beyond the range of the depth sensor, yet the people recognition module registers a new target, the tracking module will use the *maximum depth sensor range* as a distance estimate to the target and will move on X and Y while maintaining the pose towards the person until the person enters the depth range.

*Tracking when under the minimum depth range.* When a person is closer to the robot than the depth range, Pepper will ask the person to turn around and face it in order to be recognized by the face recognition module.

### 4.3 Face Detection and Recognition Module

The face detection and recognition module is used to detect and identify the person with whom the robot must interact. Face recognition is needed in case Pepper is used as an assistive robot (Sect. 1), for people with special needs (elderly, illness) in an integrated smart home environment [4]. As stated in Sect. 3, the network used for facial detection and recognition is FaceNet.

The network results includes the position of the face in the image and the name of the person, with the corresponding probability. One example is presented in Fig. 4.

**Fig. 4.** FaceNet recognition results using Pepper RGB image stream.

The RGB images are taken using the NAOqi framework and then passed to the external server to the Face Detection and Recognition module, where the network obtains the detections.

The information that comes from this module is then combined with the information from the people detection module. The application only takes into the consideration the faces for which there is a person detected. This check is done based on the bounding boxes: if the bounding box of a detected face is inside the bounding box of a detected person, then the information about the face is associated with that detected person; otherwise the face is ignored, as we do not have a matching person. The second case should not happen in practice, as the YOLO network gives very good results in terms of person detection, especially if the face of that person is visible.

### 4.4  User Interaction Module

The system comprises a user interaction module. For the time being, the module is implemented for the scenario presented Sect. 1, that is giving vocal and visual notifications regarding personal health or well-being issues to the identified person and waiting for acknowledgements from that person.

When the robot reaches a person, based on the face recognition information, it knows if it reached the person it is looking for. If it cannot see the face of the person in front of it, it will alert the person by voice (e.g. "Hey, please look at me!").

After arriving near the person and drawing her attention, the robot starts reading out notifications such as: *"take your medicine"*, *"take your blood pressure"*, *"time for your exercises"*. The user can check each one using the tablet, but we also offer the possibility to go through the notifications by using voice commands.

The interaction with the user is achieved using NAOqi framework modules. The robot takes the notifications for the person from an external server and starts saying them one by one, using the module for *TextToSpeech*. It uses the *TabletService* to create a view that also displays the notifications on the tablet, such that the user can mark them as read, or can navigate forward or backward through them. The vocal commands that the robot interprets are for acknowledging a reminder or for closing the display. They are interpreted using the *SpeechRecognition* module.

The limitation of this component is determined by the *SpeechRecognition* module of the NAOqi framework. The problem with this module is that it requires good environment conditions for good results. If there is background noise, the results are not accurate, and this may cause the robot to not understand the vocal command of the person or to understand a command when there was none. This part is still to be improved by finding other mechanisms for speech recognition compatible with the capabilities of the robot.

## 5  Experiments

We performed extensive experiments for the scenario described previously, when Pepper is used as an assistive robot for people with special needs, using the architecture presented in Sect. 4.

## 5.1   Setup

The system was empirically tested in a laboratory environment with different people. The proposed scenario for testing implies that the robot begins from a random position and starts looking for a specific person to provide the notifications. The robot keeps looking around and, if it detects a person, it will move towards them; the person can be standing or sitting, it can be totally visible or partially obstructed by chairs, table, etc. If the detected person is the right one, then Pepper will read out the pending notifications, otherwise it will continue its search. The schema of the application is presented in Fig. 5.

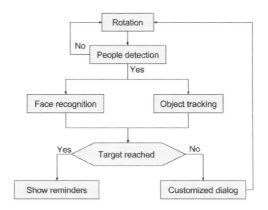

**Fig. 5.** Application flow overview.

The designed algorithm is as follows. The robot is situated in an initial position and starts a rotation, first with the head, and then with the whole body. The head performs a circular rotation, from right-top to left-top, then from left-bottom to right-bottom. We chose this kind of movement in order to inspect all the possible locations in the field of view for the current position of the robot. If there is no person detected, then it will rotate the whole body with 120°. When a person is detected both head and body rotations are stopped, and the next modules are activated, more precisely, the tracking and face recognition, which run in parallel.

The robot will track the detected person and will get closer until it reaches a predefined distance threshold. If the robot reached the target, but the face of the person is not detected, it will ask the person to look straight to it in order to identify them. If the person is recognized as the target person, Pepper will read out the pending notifications. If not, it will continue its search. Since the high level operations like detection and recognition is performed on a remote machine, the total reaction time is also influenced by the network latency. On a 100 Mbps local area network the total round-trip time is around 300 ms.

## 5.2  Qualitative Results

The application gives promising results in terms of computer vision techniques. Based on the proposed scenario and the experimental setup described in Sect. 5.1 we performed a series of qualitative assessments of the person detection and face recognition modules, comparing them to the existing robot functionality.

The experiments we made are checking the system in different conditions, as it can be seen in Tables 1 and 2. The tables present the results of the YOLO architecture and FaceNet network in comparison with the built-in modules from NAOqi. The test cases we consider are checking the behavior in two different bad lighting conditions, low-light and back-light, the detections of rotated people, the maximum distance to accurate detections and the case when there are multiple people in front of the robot. We tested YOLO in two extra cases, when a person is partially obstructed by an object and when the person is only partially in the field of view of the robot.

**Table 1.** Comparison between robot's built-in human detection module and YOLO architecture.

| Test Case | Robot's built-in human detection module | YOLO architecture for person detection |
|---|---|---|
| Obstructed person | No | Yes |
| Rotated person | Yes | Yes |
| Multiple people | 1 person error detection | accurate detection |
| Maximum distance | ~3.5m | >9.5m |
| Back-light | Yes | Yes |
| Low-light | Yes | Yes |
| Part of person out of view | No | Yes |

Table 1 presents a short comparison between *ALPeoplePerception* for person detection and those obtained using the YOLO architecture. Looking at the results, it is clear that the YOLO network gives accurate results in all the tested conditions. It detects people in all positions, even from behind, it detects people obstructed by objects or half out of the field of view. This is a major improvement compared with the built-in module, which has errors in some of the presented cases.

Table 2 presents, by comparison, the results of the NAOqi module for face detection and recognition and the results of the FaceNet architecture. FaceNet brings an improvement in recognition results, by having accurate results at a bigger distance to the camera and with a higher angle of rotation. It does not solve the case when the person is situated in contre-jour (strong back-light), but it improves the accuracy in all the other cases.

**Table 2.** Comparison between robot's built-in face detection-recognition module and FaceNet architecture.

| Test Case | Robot's built-in face detection-recognition module | FaceNet architecture |
|---|---|---|
| Rotated face recognition | Maximum 45% rotation | Maximum 80–90% rotation |
| Multiple faces detection | Yes | Yes |
| Max recognition distance | ~1.5m | ~4m |
| Back-light recognition | No | No |
| Low-light recognition | Yes | Yes |

More details about the results containing example images can be found in a separate report[4].

# 6   Conclusions and Future Work

In this work we presented a summary of findings and a proposed method regarding detecting, tracking and identifying people in an enclosed environment using the sensors from a SoftBank Pepper Robot. The sensor data, like RGB and depth images are being processed using existing people detection and people recognition frameworks on external servers in order to detect, recognize and track the person.

We proposed and validated a mechanism to usefully approximate the real world orientation and distance of a detected person relative to the robot head, based on RGB and depth image frames from the robot and the bounding box of the person within the image (computed by the YOLO network).

We further used the improved tracking capabilities to implement a map-free person finding behavior. The final application involves using the speech recognition, text to speech and tablet service modules installed on Pepper to develop an enhanced human robot interaction. Thus, the robot is able to assist a person in compliance with their personal health care and well being plans, and can be used either as a personal robot or as a robot in rehabilitation centers. Besides improving the detection and user tracking capabilities of Pepper, our solution has the advantage that it can be ported on other robotic platforms with similar sensors and voice interaction facilities.

In future work, we plan to address the motion planning issues experienced when the robot is getting really close to the user. To tackle this, a way of segmenting the human blob from the recognized patch can be used to perform better estimation of distances to the tracked person. At the same time, the work can be extended by using SLAM techniques, or by providing a previously generated

---

[4] https://goo.gl/z24ZXm.

map in which the robot can track the positions which were already visited and save the positions of the recognized persons on a global map of the environment.

**Acknowledgement.** This research was supported by AAL grant of the Romanian National Authority for Scientific Research and Innovation, CCCDI - UEFISCDI, CAMI - "The Artificially intelligent ecosystem for self-management and sustainable quality of life in AAL", project number AAL-2014-1-087 and SPARC national project grant PN-III-P2-2.1-BG-2016-0425.

# References

1. Softbank robotics - pepper robot. https://www.ald.softbankrobotics.com/en/cool-robots/pepper. Accessed 23 Jan 2018
2. Tanaka, F., Isshiki, K., Takahashi, F., Uekusa, M., Sei, R., Hayashi, K.: Pepper learns together with children: development of an educational application. In: 2015 IEEE-RAS 15th International Conference on Humanoid Robots (Humanoids), pp. 270–275, November 2015
3. Awada, I.A., Mocanu, I., Florea, A.M., Cramariuc, B.: Multimodal interface for elderly people. In: 21st International Conference on Control Systems and Computer Science - CSCS21, pp. 536–541, May 2017
4. Kunnappilly, A., Sorici, A., Awada, I.A., Mocanu, I., Seceleanu, C., Florea, A.M.: A novel integrated architecture for ambient assisted living systems. In: 2017 IEEE 41st Annual Computer Software and Applications Conference (COMPSAC), vol. 1, pp. 465–472, July 2017
5. Perera, V., Pereira, T., Connell, J., Veloso, M.M.: Setting up pepper for autonomous navigation and personalized interaction with users. CoRR abs/1704.04797 (2017)
6. Softbank robotics - naoqi framework. http://doc.aldebaran.com/2-5/ref/index.html. Accessed 23 Jan 2018
7. Schroff, F., Kalenichenko, D., Philbin, J.: Facenet: a unified embedding for face recognition and clustering. In: 2015 IEEE Conference on Computer Vision and Pattern Recognition (CVPR), pp. 815–823, June 2015
8. Redmon, J., Divvala, S., Girshick, R., Farhadi, A.: You only look once: unified, real-time object detection. In: 2016 IEEE Conference on Computer Vision and Pattern Recognition (CVPR), pp. 779–788, June 2016
9. Redmon, J., Farhadi, A.: YOLO9000: better, faster, stronger. CoRR abs/1612.08242 (2016)
10. Rublee, E., Rabaud, V., Konolige, K., Bradski, G.: ORB: an efficient alternative to SIFT or SURF. In: 2011 International Conference on Computer Vision, pp. 2564–2571, November 2011

# Hypertonic Saline Solution for Signal Transmission and Steering in MRI-Guided Intravascular Catheterisation

Alberto Caenazzo[✉] and Kaspar Althoefer

Centre for Advanced Robotics @ Queen Mary (ARQ), Queen Mary University of London, Mile End Road, London, E1 4NS, UK
{A.Caenazzo,K.Althoefer}@qmul.ac.uk

**Abstract.** Use of traditional low-impedance sensor leads is highly undesirable in intravascular catheters to be used with MRI guidance; thermal safety and quality of imaging are particularly impacted by these components. In this paper, we are showing that hypertonic saline solution, a high-impedance body-like fluid, could be a compatible and effective signal transmission medium when used in MRI-compatible catheters. We also propose a simple type of catheter design that can be steered hydraulically using the same saline solution. Integration of hydraulic steering is not required for MRI-compatibility; however efficient design can bring advantages in terms of structural simplicity and miniaturisation. Manufacturing of proof-of-concept prototypes using 3D printing is underway.

**Keywords:** Surgical robotics · MRI · Soft-robotics
Interventional electrophysiology

## 1 Introduction

Intravascular catheterization is nowadays a standard technique for many types of minimally invasive diagnostic and surgical procedures. Catheters are typically guided using fluoroscopy – however, this imaging technique uses ionizing radiation and is associated with an increase in risk of cancer and other side effects for patients and attending medical staff. Real-time Magnetic Resonance Imaging (MRI) has been recently developed as a safer, more effective alternative to fluoroscopy; however, practical implementation of MRI is not proving easy. Some intravascular procedures (e.g. interventional electrophysiology studies) require electrical signals to be transmitted outside the body – this is almost universally achieved with thin metal or otherwise low-impedance wires. Unfortunately, such components are particularly undesirable in an MRI environment as they have the potential of heating to dangerous levels; imaging artefacts may also arise, making guidance and positioning of catheters particularly difficult [1]. While methods devised to increase MRI-compatibility of "conventional" wire-based systems have been reported in literature [2, 3], these same methods are not guaranteed to solve the MRI compatibility issues completely. As a result, MRI-guided intravascular catheterisation is reported to be still largely confined to research environments [3].

## 2   Methodology

### 2.1   Conduction of Electro-Physiological Signals Through Saline Solution

Our approach takes inspiration from non-invasive examinations of the electrical signals generated by the heart, e.g. electro-cardiography. With some rough approximation, these signals are collected after passing bodily tissues; these, in turn, can be roughly approximated as normal saline solution (0.9% weight/volume), which is itself a rather poor conductor. Performance of such systems is, however, very well established. Stemming from this, we determined that hypertonic concentrations (i.e. well above normal concentration) offer good signal transmission properties when tested in narrow catheter-like lumens (1 mm internal diameter, 100+ cm in length) at similar voltages and frequencies as cardiac electrophysiological signals collected directly. Being similar in composition to human tissues and only marginally more conductive, hypertonic saline solution appears feasible as a MRI-compatible substitute of traditional low-impedance wires. The safety profile of hypertonic saline solution in case of accidental spillage into the bloodstream is also very good, with 20% and 7% considered as safe concentrations for adult and paediatric patients respectively.

DC electrical properties of saline solutions are well known. Using widely available data and equations [4], we extrapolated the following equation for resistivity vs. concentration and temperature:

$$\rho_{T^\circ C} = \frac{1}{(16.283c + 1.0074)[1 + 0.02(T - 25)]} \; [k\Omega \cdot cm] \qquad (1)$$

with $\rho$ resistivity of the solution (in k$\Omega$•cm) c weight over volume concentration (in g/100 ml), T the temperature of the solution (in degrees Celsius). Recalling Ohm's laws, the resistance of a conductor is directly dependent on its length and resistivity, while it is inversely dependent on its cross section:

$$R = \rho \frac{l}{A} [k\Omega] \qquad (2)$$

where R is the resistance (in k$\Omega$), $\rho$ resistivity of the solution (in k$\Omega$•cm), l and A respectively the length (in cm) and the cross section (in cm$^2$) of the conductor.

Assuming catheter-like dimensions of l = 150 cm and A = 0.008 cm$^2$ (approximately equivalent to a lumen of 1 mm in diameter), we used (1) and (2) to compute the resistance values for different temperatures and concentrations of NaCl (Fig. 2). Values shown in Fig. 2 are broadly in the same order of magnitude of the impedance normally encountered at interface between body and electrodes in non-invasive studies [5], albeit exclusively calculated here in terms of DC behaviour.

We conducted several experiments by sending and receiving electric signals with frequency and amplitude comparable to what encountered inside the heart (frequency = 1 Hz, amplitude = 0.1 V peak to peak) through a catheter-like lumen. The equivalent circuit schematic of the test rigs we used is shown in Fig. 3.

The experimental results proved the feasibility of the approach; a clear example is shown in the chart on top left corner of Fig. 1, replicated for clarity in Fig. 4 below. In this chart, the signal received through the catheter-like lumen follows very closely the transmitted signal (net of the 50 Hz mains noise captured by the unshielded test-rig).

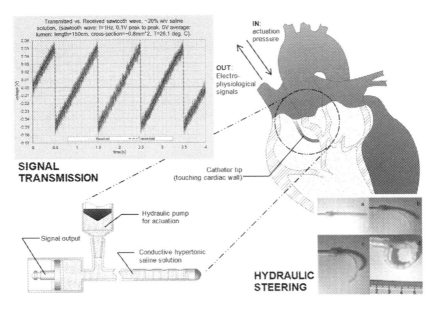

**Fig. 1.** Our vision. A catheter using the same hypertonic saline solution for signal transmission and steering is used to collect electrophysiological signals from inside the heart.

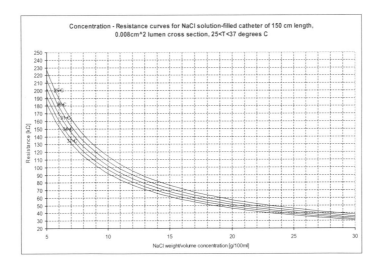

**Fig. 2.** Calculated DC concentration vs. resistance curves for saline solution in a catheter-like structure at various service temperatures.

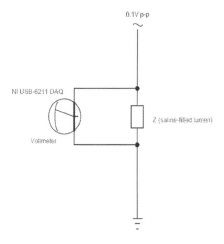

**Fig. 3.** Equivalent circuit for the experimental test-rigs.

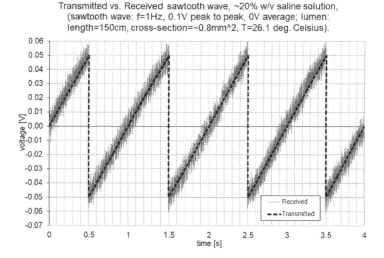

**Fig. 4.** Experimental results of signal transmission through a catheter-like geometry filled with saline solution.

## 2.2 Integration of Hydraulic Catheter Steering

We also investigated the integration of hydraulic steering using the same conductive fluid. MRI-compatible steering mechanisms can be devised without the need of an hydraulic system, e.g. using tendons or push-rods made of MRI-compatible polymers [6]. However, it can make sense to re-use/re-purpose components that are available by design in the body of the catheter – this could help in designing a smaller and/or simpler structure (reducing stress on blood vessels and being easier/cheaper to manufacture, respectively), or could even be used as part of an hybrid hydraulic-tendon system with improved mechanical characteristics [7]. Our proof-of-concept design uses a very simple 1-DOF mechanism (Fig. 5) that is steered by removing a small volume of fluid, and re-straightened by pumping in back the same volume (Fig. 6) [8, 9].

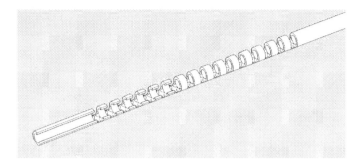

**Fig. 5.** Rendering of the simple hydraulic steerable catheter structure we are using as proof-of-concept. Note that the LHS of the structure is sectioned to show the internal lumen. In order for the catheter to work as intended, a thin silicone "skin" needs to cover the catheter structure. This is not shown in this rendering, but is visible in the real-life prototype pictures (Figs. 1, 8 and 9) and the schematic in Fig. 6.

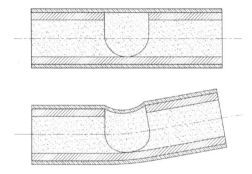

**Fig. 6.** Schematic showing the basics of the prototype hydraulic actuation. The top drawing shows a section of the catheter at rest – note the "skin" covering the entire catheter structure. The bottom configuration shows the effect of displacing some fluid from the catheter: the skin collapses over the groove, in turn causing the entire structure to bend. While not in scope for this paper or the prototypes shown here, it is noteworthy that rigorous modelling has been developed to determine the relationship between bending radius and fluid displacement. This, in turn, can allow for development of robotic control systems and trajectory-planning algorithms.

Variances in the conductive cross-section (thus in resistivity) in the catheter tip are still very limited when actuating the steering mechanism, thus not affecting the overall signal transmission properties of the whole catheter. After some initial successes with simple handcrafted samples [9], we are currently in the advanced manufacturing stages of a functional prototype, while at the same time testing designs, materials and assembly techniques that can be useful in future production. Use of 3D printing has enabled to significantly reduce the time and costs involved to test ideas, with results that are more than satisfactory considering the minuscule size of the components being printed and the consumer-grade technology employed so far (e.g. Figs. 7, 8 and 9).

**Fig. 7.** Catheter structure being printed. We used a fairly standard, consumer-grade Fused Filament Fabrication printer with a variety of materials.

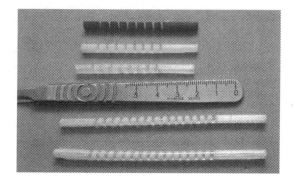

**Fig. 8.** Examples of catheter structures printed with different materials. From top to bottom: PLA (non-steerable), Nylon, Flexible TPU, PETG, PETG with silicone skin added. Note the realistic scale of the structures (3–4 mm outer diameter).

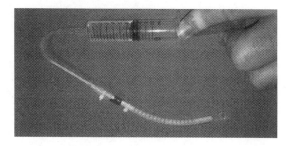

**Fig. 9.** Assembled catheter prototype being steered hydraulically. This is a PETG structure with a silicone skin of the same type as shown in Fig. 8.

# 3   Conclusions

Stemming from our positive experimental results, we can state that use of hypertonic saline solution can indeed be evaluated as a viable alternative to traditional metal/low-impedance wires for signal transmission in MRI-compatible intravascular catheters. We also examined the integration between signal transmission and hydraulic steering, as exemplified by our realistic-sized 3D-printed prototypes. More work is required to demonstrate the effectiveness of our approach in-vivo and in the actual MRI setting.

# References

1. Koning, M.K., Weiss, S., Bakker, C.J.G., Bartels, L.W., Mali, W.P.T.M.: Catheters and guidewires in interventional MRI: problems and solutions. Medica Mundi **45**(1), 31–39 (2001)
2. Bhagirath, P., et al.: Interventional cardiac magnetic resonance imaging in electrophysiology: advances toward clinical translation. Circ.: Arrhythm. Electrophysiol. **8**(1), 203–211 (2014)
3. Chubb, H., Williams, S.E., Whitaker, J., Harrison, J.L., Razavi, R., O'Neill, M.: Cardiac electrophysiology under MRI guidance: an emerging technology. Arrhythm. Electrophysiol. Rev. **6**(2), 85–93 (2017)
4. Radiometer Analytical, Conductivity, Theory and Practice, Villerurbanne, France (2004)
5. Lee, S., Kruse, J.: Biopotential Electrode Sensors in ECG/EEG/EMG Systems. Analog Devices Inc. (2008)
6. Ataollahi, A., et al.: Three-degree-of-freedom MR-compatible multisegment cardiac catheter steering mechanism. IEEE Trans. Biomed. Eng. **63**(11), 2425–2435 (2013)
7. Stilli, A., Wurdemann, H., Althoefer, K.: Shrinkable, stiffness-controllable soft manipulator based on a bio-inspired antagonistic actuation principle. In: 2014 IEEE/RSJ International Conference on Intelligent Robots and Systems (IROS 2014) (2014)
8. Haga, Y., et al.: Small diameter hydraulic active bending catheter using laser processed super elastic alloy and silicone rubber tube. In: Proceedings of the 3rd Annual International IEEE EMBS Special Topic Conference on Microtechnologies in Medicine and Biology, pp. 245–248 (2005)
9. Caenazzo, A., Liu, H., Althoefer, K.: Integrated signal transmission and hydraulic steering using hypertonic saline solution. In: MRI-Compatible Intravascular Catheters, Abstract book of the 24th Congress of EAES (2016)

# A Conceptual Exoskeleton Shoulder Design for the Assistance of Upper Limb Movement

Carlos Navarro Perez[1], Ioannis Georgilas[2], Appolinaire C. Etoundi[1],
Jj Chong[1], and Aghil Jafari[1(✉)]

[1] Faculty of Environment and Technology, University of the West of England,
Bristol, Bristol, UK
{Carlos2.Navarroperez,appolinaire.etoundi,
jj.chong,aghil.jafari}@uwe.ac.uk
[2] Faculty of Engineering and Design, University of Bath, Bath, UK
i.georgilas@bath.ac.uk

**Abstract.** There is an increased interest on wearable technologies for rehabilitation and human augmentation. Systems focusing on the upper limbs are attempting to replicate the musculoskeletal structures found in humans, reproducing existing behaviors and capabilities. The current work is expanding on existing systems with a novel design that ensures the maximum range of motion while at the same time allowing for lockable features ensuring higher manipulation payloads at minimum energy and fatigue costs. An analysis of the biomechanics of the shoulder is being done and a detailed system design for structural as well actuation elements of a parallel mechanism is given. The benefits for the use are discussed of reduced weight, maximum range of motion at minimum energy cost.

**Keywords:** Exoskeleton design · Assistive systems
Wearable technology

## 1 Introduction

There is an increase in the interest of the research community and industry for wearable technologies in recent years. The future prospects offer endless opportunities for the creation of a wide range of technological solutions for human assistance and augmentation. Orthotic and exoskeleton systems have the advantage of allowing for the enhancement of both the disabled and healthy population. As well as being able to provide medical rehabilitation, their ability to deliver repetitive movements for a longer period and at a higher intensity than manual manipulation gives them the potential to be great tools in rehabilitation training as well as in mitigating fatigue in healthy users.

The role of the shoulder complex in the human everyday interaction with its environment is necessary as it is responsible for most of the upper limb's

© Springer International Publishing AG, part of Springer Nature 2018
M. Giuliani et al. (Eds.): TAROS 2018, LNAI 10965, pp. 291–302, 2018.
https://doi.org/10.1007/978-3-319-96728-8_25

mobility. Any disruption to the function to this area of the musculoskeletal system can prove severely debilitating. As a result, a considerable amount of research has been conducted on the kinesiology and kinematics of the shoulder [1,2,4]. However, due to the kinematic complexity of the upper limb, creating a bioinspired model of the shoulder remains a challenge [5,6].

It is therefore that many existing exoskeleton designs possess the relevant structural features for shoulder articulation by emulating the kinematic requirements of the anatomical ball and socket joint that is the glenohumeral (GH) joint. Usually satisfying the centre of rotation of the shoulder's GH joint, by designing the exoskeleton around the physical shoulder, attempting to maintain the centre of rotation of the system in line with that of the GH joint [8,9]. A great number of them apply a form of the triaxial spherical linkage kinematics model of a Cardan universal joint [10–12] while some go even further and introduce some form of scapular motion in conjunction with the Cardan model [13].

On the front of actuation the structure of the shoulder's musculoskeletal system is composed of links serially connected to form a kinematically redundant system; as a result, the shoulder is a parallel mechanism. An aspect that has been explored in the form of parallel mechanism shoulder models [4,7] and new prismatic parallel actuated exoskeletons [14] for a higher control and torque.

Within this context this work is describing the bioinspired design for a novel shoulder exoskeleton for human augmentation. Although other research efforts have looked into replicating the anatomical structures found in humans, little work has been done in using bioinspired techniques to enhance the shoulder capabilities. This work is expanding on the work, of StrongArm FLx nonpowered exoskeleton [15], on the use and stabilization of the scapula and the scapulothoracic (ST) joint with a new design for the ST. The proposed approach will allow the joint to lock in place enabling the user to maintain postures that will engage the ST join for longer periods of time with minimum energy cost and physical straining.

To achieve this, the paper is organized as follows. In Sect. 2 the biomechanics of the shoulder will be described, covering the musculoskeletal operation of the different elements. In Sect. 3 the design of the exoskeleton will be analyzed and compared to the findings of the previous section. Finally Sect. 4 concludes the paper.

## 2    Biomechanics of the Shoulder

This section introduces the basic biomechanics of the shoulder. The motions are been analyzed so as to allow for easier replication by the exoskeleton design which will be presented in the following section.

In principle the shoulder girdle (SG) is comprised of three linkages; two synovial joints, between the clavicle (collarbone) and scapula (shoulder blade), and a third between the scapula and thorax.

The sternoclavicular (SC) joint is the most proximal of the joints in the shoulder and is the only anatomic joint in the shoulder complex physically attached by ligaments to the trunk at the manubrium of the sternum. It serves as a stabilizer for the movement of the scapula, with which it articulates at the acromioclavicular (AC) joint, limiting its range of motion (ROM) by keeping the scapula at a relatively constant distance, so the shoulder can swing clear of the trunk whilst transmitting part of the limb's weight to the axial skeleton [16]. The scapula needs stabilizing as it is responsible for supporting the arm at the scapulothoracic (ST) joint. It must be noted however, that the ST joint is not a true joint, but rather a functional joint, a point of contact between the anterior surface of the scapula and the posterior aspect of the thorax [1].

The outer part of the scapula, directly below the AC joint, is called the glenoid cavity. This shallow socket hosts the ball of the head of the humerus forming a synovial ball and socket joint, the GH joint. This type of joint suffers from a severe lack of stability. A group of four of the seven scapulohumeral muscles and their tendons, stabilize the shoulder by keeping the head of the humerus in place. Thus, preventing the dislocation of the GH joint. This group is known as the rotator cuff; the supraspinatus, the infraspinatus, teres minor, and the subscapularis muscle.

The Scapular motion involves the synergic movement of the shoulder girdle. This is achieved by the action of specific primary muscles responsible for scapular motion in six different directions, which are summarised in Table 1. Given that muscles can apply only pulling forces in order for the motions to be completed there is the need for synergetic action for these to achieve the movement of the scapula.

**Table 1.** Scapular motion and primary muscles

| Movement of scapula | Muscles responsible for the movement |
|---|---|
| Protraction | Serratus anterior (SA), Pectoralis minor, (Pm) assists |
| Retraction | Trapezius (middle fibres) (TM), Rhomboid minor (Rm) Rhomboid major (RM) |
| Elevation | Trapezius (superior fibres) (TS), Levator Scapulae (LS) |
| Depression | Pectoralis minor (Pm), Trapezius (inferior fibres) (TI), Latissimus dorsi (LD) |
| Lateral rotation | Trapezius (superior and inferior fibres), Serratus anterior (lower 5 digitations) |

## 3    Shoulder Exoskeleton Design

In this Section, the concept for the multidirectional actuation of the human upper limb, based on the movement of the SG is proposed. A simple bioinspired design of the exoskeleton shoulder is approached, duplicating the structure of the human skeletal girdle in which articulations and their ligaments have been substituted with homologous mechanical joints for a more predictable stability. Moreover, the muscles actuating the SG are being substituted by appropriately positioned linear actuators and the second part of the section will focus on explaining their selection and positioning. Finally, the support structure that will form the backbone of the motions will be implemented in the form of harnesses and bodily attachments and been described in the third part of the section.

### 3.1    Shoulder Skeletal Analogues

The SC joint has the mechanical equivalence of an irregular saddle joint that allows for three rotatory degrees of freedom (DoF). To substitute the SC joint a revolute joint allowed to rotate at both ends is introduced. The first rotating end, attached to the sternum, allows for elevation and depression in the frontal plane, the revolute joint (set at a 90° angle) allows for protraction and retraction in the horizontal plane and the second revolute end attaches to the clavicle analogue model allowing for posterior clavicular rotation in the sagittal plane [1].

The clavicle attaches to the acromion of the scapula via the AC joint. This gliding, or plane, joint allows for 3 DoF: two translations along the X and Y axes and a rotation around Z. However, due to the observed osteokinematics of the shoulder girdle [1] the AC joint requires of three revolute perpendicular DoF. One accounting for rotation of the scapula in the frontal plane, a second for the internal rotation of the scapula in the horizontal plane and a third one that allows for anterior and posterior tilting in the sagittal plane. Considering these characteristic, the same RRR joint derived for the SC joint is applicable for the AC joint, despite them being distinct types of synovial joints.

To avoid the necessity and therefore inclusion of the rotator cuff muscles as stabilizing agents, the GH ball and socket joint has been substituted by a gimbal system that is mechanically secured at two points without the need for any further stabilizing anchors. This design provides the stability and the DOF's necessary. The gimbal is set such that the full ROM of the system is utilized, by attaching an extreme of the gimbal's range to the humerus analogue, parallel to the sagital plain to the side of the body. This arrangement allows for the 100° of motion the gimbal is capable of in the frontal plane for glenohumeral abduction. This poses a lack of range in that orientation of 20° according to [1]. However, the actual kinematic values among persons and studies vary considerably, likely due to the different levels of flexibility of the subjects.

This leads to the scapulohumeral rhythm, where the rotation of the scapula is introduced to support the abduction of the arm with an approximate extra 60°, for a full 180° of range, or 160° in the case of the designed system. The retroversion of the humeral head, that aligns the humeral head with the scapular plane for articulation, needs to be accounted for. The gimbal joint is capable of a full 360° ROM perpendicular to the sagittal plane (with the exception of the angle range in which the body is located), since the scapular analogue will be behind the subject's shoulder and therefore positioned further behind with respect to the frontal plane than the humerus analogue and upper arm attachments.

Finally since the focus of the study is on the shoulder region the motion of the elbow is addressed only in as a passive component meant to aid and support humeral internal rotation.

## 3.2  Shoulder Muscular Analogues

The actuators are placed as to substitute the muscles of the shoulder muscu-loskeletal system suppressing stabilizing muscles unnecessary in a mechanical system and conserving those responsible for the primary force driving the actions.

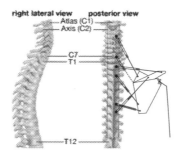

**Fig. 1.** Origin and insertion of muscle analog prismatic actuators of the posterior scapulothorathic motion.

Figure 1, represents the substitution of the muscles in Table 1. From the top following the vertebrae, the LS actuator originates from in between the C2 and C3 vertebrae, equivalent to the center of the LS biological origin. The TS originates from the external occipital protuberance and the nuchal ligament, it doesn't have an attachment to a solid surface. Although the TS aids in scapular elevation, it has its insertion at the clavicle and provides mostly neck movement function rather than scapular. Therefore, the functions of this muscle have been assumed by the LS in the design.

The Rm shown as a dotted line (Fig. 1) is attached in between the C7 and T1 vertebrae and inserts at the root of the scapular spine. Due to the quasi parallel nature of the rhomboids and LS, the functions of the Rm are suppressed and adopted by it's neighboring muscles. Next the TM originates at T2 and inserts at the medial end of the spine close to the acromium. The RM originates between T3 and T4 and inserts at the medial border of the scapula. These muscles in each of their corresponding motions act both as agonists and antagonists. Taking advantage of this aspect, the inclusion of a serratus anterior analogue can be placed at the posterior aspect of the body rather than the anterior. The analogue muscle, prismatic actuator, responsible for its motion will push instead of pulling. The antagonistic analogue inserts at the meeting point between the medial border and the inferior angle of the scapula, originating at T7. This experimental placement satisfies the rotational and the protraction trajectories. For the latter trajectory, the RM and TI muscles join in an antagonist pushing motion to provide a controlled protraction of the shoulder. The modelled TI originates at T8 and inserts at the medial third of the spine.

The LD crosses the inferior angle of the scapula. However, a study found that out of 100 cadavers dissected 57% had a less than substantial amount of muscular fibers originating from the scapula [17]. Therefore, the latissimus dorsi won't be accounted for during scapular motion.

All of the scapular motion prismatic actuators attach with a revolute joint that allows for rotation in the frontal plane, and insert with a universal joint to allow internal rotation of the scapula during protraction.

### 3.3   Glenohumeral Actuation

The design responsible for GH abduction/adduction has been approached in the same direct substitution fashion for the DA and DP muscles. The DA originates at the anterior border of the lateral third of the clavicle and the DP originates at the spine of the scapula. Both muscles and actuators insert at the deltoid tuberosity of the humerus (Fig. 2).

The deltoid middle fibers (DM) originate at the acromion and insert at the deltoid tuberosity of the humerus, whereas the SS originates at the supraspinatus fossa and inserts at the superior facet of the greater tubercle (Figs. 2 and 3). These two muscles work in synergy; the SS initiates abduction and stabilizes the GH joint as the DM completes the GH abduction.

For this substitution to be possible, the actuator for both muscles would have to be flexible to wrap over the GH joint. The proposed design for this group of two muscles is to fuse their function together at the SS position as shown in Fig. 2. Consequently, to achieve the displacement necessary for the GH abduction, a lever is introduced at the head of the humerus oriented at 110° with respect to the lateral aspect of the humerus, taking the elbow as 0°. Thus, can the actuator pull the lever behind the shoulder unobstructed, increasing the length of the lever and placing the insertion further from the fulcrum, increasing the leverage exerted on the humerus.

The LD actuator has a wide origin from the T7 to the L5 vertebrae as well as at the lower four ribs and the posterior third of the iliac crest. As a preliminary origin, the actuator will be attached at the position of the iliac crest. This actuator origin will also be off-set from the body at a distance as to preserve alignment with the rest of the exoskeleton, while allowing space for the actuator to follow the humerus without colliding with the user as the arm is flexed.

The insertion of the LD, together with the rest of the muscles responsible for rotation, poses a design problem. The posterior muscles wrap around the humerus and insert on the anterior aspect together with the muscles on the anterior aspect of the torso (Fig. 3). Making an ergonomic design for these actuators is the next challenging step in the design and development of the exoskeleton.

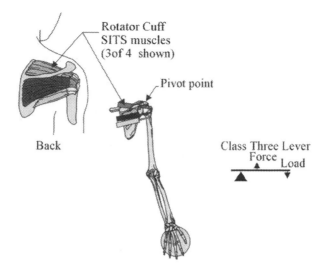

**Fig. 2.** The shoulder joint is a class three lever system (Supraspinatus: green Infraspinatus: blue Teres minor: yellow) [3]. (Color figure online)

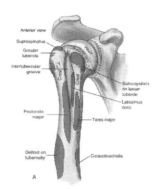

**Fig. 3.** Anterior view (A) of the right humerus [1].

### 3.4  Harness and Bodily Attachments

A suitable support system for the actuation elements need to be developed and form part of the exoskeleton design. The proposed system needs to replicate the anchoring characteristics of the biological musculoskeletal system and its operation. With this in mind a bioinspired system is being proposed that is using the same anchoring points along the spinal column.

From a posterior view of the torso, a solid spine (Fig. 4) is attached to the back via a posture brace, or corrector. The brace pulls the shoulders back and straightens the spine to prevent slouching and improve posture. The inferior aspect of the spine attaches to a lumbar pad and is secured to the waist via a safoty rock climbing sitting harness, which ensures a reduced displacement of the belt via the adjustable leg perimeter straps. This combination generates a posture feedback system. As the user extends beyond proper posture, the feedback system then provides a gentle reminder, via pressure at the shoulder straps and the spine right above where the back curves in the most, approximately between the T1 and T5 vertebrae, as well as at the lumbar pads. This pressure suggests to the user an adjustment in his or her posture to a correct position.

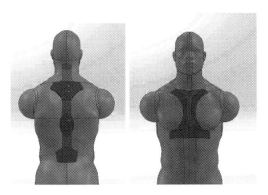

**Fig. 4.** Exoskeleton support structures. Left - A solid spine is attached to the back via a posture brace. Right - A narrow front chest support to the front. In both the anchoring points for the actuators can be seen. (Image produced in SolidWorks)

This design feature is inspired by the Strongman FLx which is designed to help remind wearers to maintain proper posture, helping to ensure proper lifting technique [15]. With this system the aim is to provide posture support and feedback. Minimising poor posture and over rotation, the adoption and inclusion of this design aims to provide a stable anchoring for the shoulder exoskeleton to the back of the user.

The superior end of the spine culminates in a tongue shape that provides the anchoring for the origin of the muscles attached at the cervical section of the spine.

From an anterior perspective, a narrow front chest support (Fig. 4.) attaches to the posture brace straps at the shoulders. Its inferior aspect, attaches to a second belt extending around the chest and connecting at the thoracic pads of the spine. The chest support houses the mechanical analogue of the sternum to which the clavicle connects to the scapula analogue. Two vertical torso adjusters lock into place from the chest belt to the waist belt preventing slippage. This arrangement completes a 5-point adjustable system. At its centre, the chest belt, a 5-point seat belt racing harness with a quick release centre buckle allows for an easy and immediate detachment.

It is proposed that the harness will follow a fitting approach similar to everyday backpacks. This aims to ensure that the harness will be close to the body, ensuring minimal discomfort and the potential of injury. The key straps are the shoulder ones that provide overall alignment while the rest ensure correct position.

The upper arm brace consists of a link that attaches at the bottom of the biceps, the distal end of the humerus, right above the elbow. This location is the point at which the circumference of the upper arm remains at its lowest when performing movements such as an arm curl, thus avoiding major discomfort while performing daily life arm movements while wearing the suit.

The distal placement of the attachment also provides the biggest leverage Include classical lever physics reference on the glenohumeral articulation and thus the shoulder complex, further justifying the placement of the attachment.

A second brace is included at the medial end of the arm under the deltoid insertion at an angle to guide the strap over the top of the biceps brachii muscle accommodating an unobstructed curl of the arm with minimal discomfort. This attachment, works as a stabilising agent tot the humeral shaft of the system by keeping the shaft parallel to the humerus. This inclusion was necessary, since the attachments allow for some displacement, as their flesh anchoring surfaces can be compressed, allowing the humerus to shift and slide under the skin. By increasing the number of attachments, the displacement is reduced.

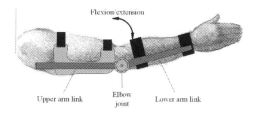

**Fig. 5.** Proposed passive elbow exoskeleton.

To ensure the compliance of the exoskeleton during internal and external rotations of the humerus in the horizontal plane's axis of rotation, a mechanical link corresponding to the forearm is introduced, leading to the inclusion of braces at the forearm and the wrist. The two links are connected by a revolute joint, coaxial with the humeroulnar (HU) elbow joint, as shown in Fig. 5. With the attachment of the foreanrm link, the extra section applies leverage on the humerus shaft upon rotation, ensuring the complient motion of the model so long as the forearm is at an angle with the humerus. This remains true even in a fully stretched arm, albeit to a smaller degree.

Finally, in Fig. 6 the complete assembly of the proposed system can be seen, with the placement of the actuators and support structures on the harnesses and attachments.

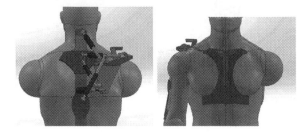

**Fig. 6.** Front and back view of the complete proposed system. (Image produced in SolidWorks)

## 4   Discussion and Future Works

To duplicate the motion of the human arm, shoulder exoskeletons are mostly designed around the three principal DOFs of the GH joint. Note that this GH model does not include translation of the glenohumeral joint caused by SC, AC, and ST motions; it's purely rotational. Upon observation, it can be seen that these designs, with or without scapular motion inclusion, rely on a single rotary actuator at its only anchoring point (to the user, rig, wall, etc.). This flaw puts all the strain of the load applied to the exoskeleton during abduction at this specific point, meaning that you will require a large motor that can bear it and still function when attempting to lift large loads.

The exoskeleton design can share the load of an action in every direction between a number of actuators, similar to the way the human body does. The key difference is that the linear actuators in the exoskeleton can perform not only pull but push and locking actions as well. This allows for a versatile use of the suit in different lifting conditions for different tasks. Moreover, due to its parallel design and it's multiple anchoring positions to the body, the design has the aim to reduce injuries due to malfunction, as the system would mechanically constraint itself, not allowing the exoskeleton to perform extreme movements at the edge of the user's arm's ROM.

To attain this ideal design however, an ergonomic solution must be explored to accommodate, in a nonobstructive way, the actuators for the rotation of the humerus at different orientations and positions. Simulations will also be necessary to determine the inclusion of the Rm actuator and the TS actuator necessary for scapular and clavicular stabilization respectively. Determining which actuators offer a stabilization purpose in the shoulder complex, unnecessary in a mechanical analogue design, will be essential. Removing unnecessary actuators from the design would reduce the total weight and bulk of the ensuing system, making it more energy efficient.

To further the security aspect of the design, the harness, should include a tension system; as the front distance decreases upon bending, the distance at the back increases. This way, the chest-rig would remain in place when bending over to any degree, avoiding asphyxiation via the chest rig, and improving the general stability of the harness.

# 5   Conclusion

This paper presented a novel conceptual robotic exoskeleton design composed of a shoulder and an arm exoskeletal structure to enable maximum range of motion while at the same time allowing for lockable features ensuring higher manipulation payloads at minimum energy and fatigue costs. This robotic exoskeleton has been designed by considering the various motions that the operator will be performing including flexion, extension, abduction, adduction and expands on current exoskeleton designs mainly focusing on existing behaviors and capabilities. Most of the reviewed devices are technically advanced, yet there is still significant need to enhance their efficiencies and reduce their cost [18]. With the design presented, dynamic force to the articulations can be provided to the upper limb by means of a set of motors in combination with a parallel mechanism. The ability to apply internal dynamic forces to the upper limb can potentially widen robotic exoskeleton applications. For instance, they could provide restoration or maintenance of motor function to different joints of the upper limb and at the same time augmenting human performances abilities. Current powered orthoses designed are nonambulatory devices [19] and therefore there is a need in the rehabilitation area of ambulatory devices capable to provide dynamic forces to the upper limb.

**Acknowledgment.** The authors acknowledge the support of the UK Engineering and Physical Sciences Research Council (EPSRC) under grant reference EP/P022588/1 and to acknowledge the support of Professor Chris Melhuish from the Bristol Robotics Laboratory, University of the West of England.

# References

1. Neumann, D., Kelly, E.: Kinesiology of the Musculoskeletal System, 2nd edn, pp. 115–165. Mosby/Elsevier, St. Louis (2010)
2. Schenkman, M., de Cartaya, V.R.: Kinesiology of the shoulder complex. J. Orthop. Sports Phys. Therapy **8**(9), 438–450 (1987)
3. Van der Helm, F.: Analysis of the kinematic and dynamic behavior of the shoulder mechanism. J. Biomech. **27**(5), 527–550 (1994)
4. Maurel, W., Thalmann, D.: A case study on human upper limb modelling for dynamic simulation. Comput. Methods Biomech. Biomed. Eng. **2**(1), 65–82 (1999)
5. Gopura, R., Kiguchi, K.: Mechanical designs of active upper-limb exoskeleton robots: state-of-the-art and design difficulties. In: 2009 IEEE International Conference on Rehabilitation Robotics (2009)
6. Tondu, B.: Estimating shoulder-complex mobility. Appl. Bion. Biomech. **4**(1), 19–29 (2007)
7. Ingram, D., Engelhardt, C., Farron, A., Terrier, A., Müllhaupt, P.: Modelling of the human shoulder as a parallel mechanism without constraints. Mech. Mach. Theory **100**, 120–137 (2016)
8. Rosen, J., Perry, J., Manning, N., Burns, S., Hannaford, B.: The human arm kinematics and dynamics during daily activities - toward a 7 DOF upper limb powered exoskeleton. In: Proceedings of 12th International Conference on Advanced Robotics, ICAR 2005 (2005)

9. Ergin, M., Patoglu, V.: ASSISTON-SE: a self-aligning shoulder-elbow exoskeleton. In: 2012 IEEE International Conference on Robotics and Automation (2012)

10. Stienen, A., Hekman, E., van der Helm, F., van der Kooij, H.: Self-aligning exoskeleton axes through decoupling of joint rotations and translations. IEEE Trans. Rob. **25**(3), 628–633 (2009)

11. Yan, H., Yang, C., Zhang, Y., Wang, Y.: Design and validation of a compatible 3-degrees of freedom shoulder exoskeleton with an adaptive center of rotation. J. Mech. Des. **136**(7), 071006 (2014)

12. Nef, T., Riener, R.: Shoulder actuation mechanisms for arm rehabilitation exoskeletons. In: 2008 2nd IEEE RAS & EMBS International Conference on Biomedical Robotics and Biomechatronics (2008)

13. Carignan, C., Liszka, M.: Design of an arm exoskeleton with scapula motion for shoulder rehabilitation. In: Proceedings of 12th International Conference on Advanced Robotics, ICAR 2005 (2005)

14. Klein, J., et al.: Biomimetic orthosis for the neurorehabilitation of the elbow and shoulder (BONES). In: 2008 2nd IEEE RAS & EMBS International Conference on Biomedical Robotics and Biomechatronics (2008)

15. StrongArm Technologies Inc.: FLX ErgoSkeleton$^{TM}$ (2018)

16. Gray, H., Standring, S., Ellis, H., Berkovitz, B.: Gray's anatomy, vol. 4, 39th edn, pp. 817–840. Elsevier Churchill Livingstone, Edinburgh (2005)

17. Di Giacomo, G., Pouliart, N., Costantini, A., de Vita, A.: Atlas of Functional Shoulder Anatomy. Springer, Milano (2008). https://doi.org/10.1007/978-88-470-0759-8

18. Maciejasz, P., Eschweiler, J., Gerlach-Hahn, K., Jansen-Troy, A., Leonhardt, S.: A survey on robotic devices for upper limb rehabilitation. J. Neuroeng. Rehabil. **11**(1), 3 (2014)

19. Johnson, G.R., Carus, D.A., Parrini, G., Marchese, S., Valeggi, R.: The design of a five-degree-of-freedom powered orthosis for the upper limb. Proc. Inst. Mech. Eng. **215**(3), 275–284 (2001)

# Swarm Robotics

# A Hormone Arbitration System for Energy Efficient Foraging in Robot Swarms

James Wilson[(✉)], Jon Timmis, and Andy Tyrrell

University of York, York YO10 5DD, UK
james.s.wilson@york.ac.uk

**Abstract.** Keeping robots optimized for an environment can be computationally expensive, time consuming, and sometimes requires information unavailable to a robot swarm before it is assigned to a task. This paper proposes a hormone-inspired system to arbitrate the states of a foraging robot swarm. The goal of this system is to increase the energy efficiency of food collection by adapting the swarm to environmental factors during the task. These adaptations modify the amount of time the robots rest in a nest site and how likely they are to return to the nest site when avoiding an obstacle. These are both factors that previous studies have identified as having a significant effect on energy efficiency. This paper proposes that, when compared to an offline optimized system, there are a variety of environments in which the hormone system achieves an increased performance. This work shows that the use of a hormone arbitration system can extrapolate environmental features from stimuli and use these to adapt.

**Keywords:** Energy efficiency · Swarm · Robotics · Foraging
Hormone arbitration

## 1 Introduction

A system's parameters can often be optimized for a given task to improve performance. This optimization will typically take into account environmental factors, thus tailoring a system such that it performs well. If a robotic system is deployed in a dynamic environment the chosen parameters must either take a suboptimal value or be re-optimized during the task, taking into account new environmental properties. The former of these options reduces the system's capability in each setting and the latter wastes time that could be spent executing the assigned task. Additionally, both of these options are difficult given that a thorough analysis of the environment would be required.

This paper shows, in a series of specific environments and tasks, that it is more energy efficient to use a hormone inspired system than an optimized timer-based system to control state transitions in a foraging swarm. Previous work on hormone-inspired systems [14] has shown that hormone systems can be used to

© Springer International Publishing AG, part of Springer Nature 2018
M. Giuliani et al. (Eds.): TAROS 2018, LNAI 10965, pp. 305–316, 2018.
https://doi.org/10.1007/978-3-319-96728-8_26

directly control the motor functions of a single robot. Similar hormone-inspired controllers have been presented in [3–5] which decide upon appropriate swarm morphology based on environmental context. These studies have shown that hormone-inspired systems can be engineered to provide an effective, computationally inexpensive method for control.

Rather than waiting for events or direct instructions, hormone systems receive information in the form of stimuli. These stimuli affect the values of virtual hormones, causing them to fluctuate over time. By having a variety of hormone values triggered by different stimuli, information about environmental aspects can be obtained by observing the relationships between each of these values.

By using a combination of hormone release, stimulated by environmental factors, and constant hormone decay, artificial hormone systems create a simple yet powerful method for controlling robots [12]. The values produced from hormone systems can be used to arbitrate the states of individuals in the swarm, meditating actions such as resting, searching or returning to the nest site.

In this paper we present a hormone-inspired system to control state transitions, rather than the discrete actuator control seen in the AHHS system [14]. Additionally, each robot in the swarm produces its own hormone without requiring a lead robot to act as an emitter, in contrast to the hormone control for the CONRO robot [12,13].

Work in this paper uses a foraging system, a well studied example in swarm robotics with a history of research on energy efficiency. Examples of this work cover improving the efficiency of search behavior [11], exploring methods of task allocation, creating periods of inactivity when workload is low [2] and increasing the efficiency of motion, reducing congestion by letting swarm members rest [7]. While these studies address the issue of energy efficiency, some even including methods of online adaptation, they do not apply a hormone arbitration system in their method of control. This paper contributes to current literature by identifying where a hormone-inspired system increases the performance of a foraging swarm or makes the swarm more robust to environmental change.

## 2    Hormone-Inspired Systems

Hormone inspired systems provide an elegant method for swarm control. Individual robots react to stimuli and can be engineered to extrapolate knowledge from environmental interactions. Through these interactions, complex swarm behaviors can be constructed in a more calculated fashion than relying upon emergent swarm behavior. These behaviors still allow for decentralized control in which no member of the swarm is solely required for task completion.

Some previous hormone-inspired implementations have been aimed at controlling the behavior of a single robot rather than a swarm, focusing more on providing a strong insight to the construction of a hormone system [14]. While others have explored swarm examples for hormone behavior arbitration, in [5] a system is evolved over several iterations to complete a task with notable improvements.

The stimuli featured in the study were in the form of virtual pheromones. The system thus required a centralized element to record pheromone values at their location, meaning that their system cannot be considered completely swarm-like by definition [10]. Additionally, the experiments carried out had no real base-line comparison to show the hormone implementation as a superior system.

Other swarm-based hormone systems have exhibited chemotatic behavior, emulating the biological diffusion of hormones in cells to organize and structure a swarm [13]. Using this system the swarm was capable of navigating and exploring an obstacle-filled environment. However, again the experiments were performed with no quantifiable base-line to compare the performance of the system against.

By examining a complex hormone system with a quantifiable measure of performance and providing a comparison optimized for each case examined, this paper will establish a precedent for future development.

## 3   Controllers

### 3.1   System 1: Hormone Arbitration

Previous work [2,7] has suggested that an energy efficient system can be produced by modifying a rest time for individual swarm members upon the completion of a task. In [7] this was done by modifying the duration of various counters to mediate the amount of time robots would spend 'sleeping' in the nest site and the length of time they would spend searching for food items. The length of these time periods were changed based on the number of collisions experienced by members of the swarm along with the successes and failures of each robot. Success and failure in this case were defined by whether the robot returned to the nest with or without a food item. This work on foraging efficiency inspired the elements that would be controlled by Eqs. 1, 2 and 3. These equations regulate the sleep period and conditions required for robots to return to the nest.

The artificial hormone system proposed in this paper is constructed from several hormone inspired equations based on those produced in [14]. By taking a base increment ($\alpha$), a decay ($\lambda$) and weighting assigned to stimuli ($\gamma$), equations can be produced which roughly mimic the behavior of hormones used for biological control.

In these equation $\alpha$ and $\lambda$ combine to make the settling point of the hormone without stimuli (calculated via $\frac{\alpha}{1-\lambda}$) when $\alpha$ is 0, the system settles at 0. $\lambda$ defines how quickly the system reacts to a lack of stimuli; the smaller the value $\lambda$ takes, the faster the system will return to the settling point without stimuli. $\gamma$ defines how quickly the hormone will deviate from the minimum settling point when stimulated. Using this simple format, multiple hormone equations can be created, each affected by different stimuli, building to arbitrate behavior states.

$$\text{Avoidance Hormone: } H_A(t) = \lambda_A H_A(t-1) + \gamma_A A \tag{1}$$

Where $A$ is a boolean value detecting whether or not the robot is avoiding another robot or surface.

$$\text{Greed Hormone: } H_G(t) = \alpha_G + \lambda_G H_G(t-1) + \gamma_G D \qquad (2)$$

Where $D$ is an boolean value representing whether or not the robot successfully returned a food item to the nest site.

$$\text{Sleep Hormone: } H_S(t) = \lambda_S H_S(t-1) + \gamma_S H_A(t-1) \qquad (3)$$

The avoidance hormone $(H_A)$ has been designed to return swarm members to the nest when an environment is too cluttered. While in the search state the robots will move randomly to explore their environment. If an obstacle is detected during this search the $H_A$ value is stimulated and increases slightly. Rather than specifying a search time, which could inhibit the discovery of food items, $H_A$ acts more dynamically; sending robots back to the nest only in the case of overcrowding. Overcrowding is detected by the relationship between $H_A$ and the greed hormone $H_G$, whenever the avoidance hormone exceeds the value of $H_G$ the robot changes state to return to the nest. To allow some small obstacle detection prior to returning to the nest and ensure that decay leads the system to settle in the search state, the $\alpha$ term in $H_G$ provides a higher settling value than in $H_A$.

The purpose of $H_G$ is to build a resistance to $H_A$, becoming less likely to return to the nest depending on the success of the robot. Upon each success this resistance will increase and then begin to decay slowly until the next success. The importance of this resistance is clear when you consider the implications of a successful robot. Either the robot has access to a large concentration of food, or the robot has minimal competition and is clearing its immediate area of food quickly.

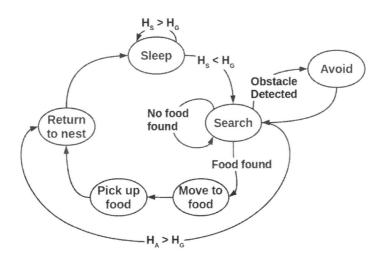

**Fig. 1.** State machine for foraging hormone system

Considering the first of these cases, a high concentration of food may attract a large number of robots, each collecting food in close quarters. Because of this, avoidance is more likely to take place. Without accounting for food density, robots with a threshold that is too low could return to the nest before discovering food items or the swarm may be allowed to aggregate too tightly in an area of low food density with a threshold that is too large. Both of these cases would waste energy and use the members of the swarm ineffectively. By allowing a certain amount of avoidance, and allowing that amount to vary based on context, better performance can be achieved.

In the second case, with food items close to the nest removed, the successful robot will then have to travel a longer distance to discover new food. If the robot has a single collision prior to traveling the greater distance, harder-to-find food items will not be discovered. This would leave a potential food source untapped. The swarm is thus more effective if successful robots are allowed to travel further and avoid more objects before returning to the nest.

In addition to controlling behavior switching, the avoidance hormone acts as a stimulant for the sleep hormone ($H_S$). The sleep hormone controls how long the robot stays in the sleep state. In this state the robot waits in a low power mode at the nest, this minimizes energy consumption when the swarm size is too large for the current work load. The amount of time spent in the low power state depends on how long $H_S$ takes to decay below the $H_G$ value. This means that time spent in the nest is dependent upon both robot success and the amount of avoidance performed while searching. The state transitions controlled by these hormone equations are illustrated in Fig. 1.

The parameters for the hormone equations (shown in Table 1) were chosen empirically to create a desirable response to environmental factors. Outside of this manual tuning no optimization was performed to increase the performance of these parameters. The parameters were also not changed across any of the experiments outlined in this paper.

Table 1. Arbitration hormone parameter values.

| $\lambda_A$ | $\gamma_A$ | $\alpha_G$ | $\lambda_G$ | $\gamma_G$ | $\lambda_S$ | $\gamma_S$ |
|---|---|---|---|---|---|---|
| 0.999 | 0.2 | 0.005 | 0.999 | 5 | 0.999 | 0.05 |

## 3.2  System 2: An Offline Optimized System

To form a comparison for the hormone arbitration controller, a simple timer-based system was produced. In this system, the functions performed by the hormones designed in the hormone inspired system were replaced with timers. In order to make this a fair comparison the timer lengths were optimized using a fitness proportionate roulette wheel genetic algorithm with elitism across 50 generations. The resultant best cases were taken as the parameters for the baseline tests. This was an attempt to simulate a system that had perfect knowledge of its environment and could choose strong parameter values prior to deployment.

The two parameters optimized where avoidance threshold $(Th_A)$ and sleep threshold $(Th_S)$. $Th_A$ represents the maximum amount of time a robot would spend avoiding obstacles prior to returning to the nest site. $Th_S$ represents the amount of time that would be spent resting in the nest upon returning. Neither of these values changed during the simulation and instead the system's performance relied upon having the best parameters for swarm size and environment type.

## 4    Experiments

The goal of the following experiments was to identify how the hormone-inspired system and the timer-based system compared. The success of the hormone-inspired system was dependent upon the rejection of the following null hypotheses:

$H_0$: The unoptimized hormone-inspired system's performance will have no significant difference from that of an optimized timer-based system in a variety of simple environments (rejected with a 95% confidence level).

$H_1$: The unoptimized hormone-inspired system's performance will have no significant difference from that of an optimized timer-based system in a dynamic environment (rejected with a 95% confidence level).

To test these hypotheses two different experiments were designed. In each of the experiments 70 repetitions were performed. The number of replicates required for consistent results was determined by performing a cumulative mean test as specified in [9]. This method of testing uses the cumulative mean of a data set, along with a calculated confidence interval to give an estimate of a range in which the true mean lies. The results produced from this indicated that 69 trials would be the minimum number of replicates required for the results of the experiments to be an accurate representation of the simulation responses.

The performance of the swarms in each of the experiments was measured by energy efficiency, calculated with Eq. 4 where $E_e$ is energy efficiency, $E_F$ is energy from total food stored, $E_C$ is total energy consumed by the swarm and $E_A$ is the total energy available in the environment from food. When food items are returned to the nest they provide the swarm with 2000 units of energy.

$$E_e = \frac{E_F - E_C}{E_A} \qquad (4)$$

To make the two proposed systems comparable the energy consumption in these experiments was based on the drive mode of the robots. Each robot consumed 8 units of energy per second while driving forwards, 4 while turning, 1 while stationary and an additional 2 while carrying a food item.

## 4.1    Simulation

All experiments were conducted in the ARGoS simulator [8] a multi robot simulator used to simulate large robot swarms. The simulated robots used in these experiments where based on the marxbot [1] a miniature wheeled robot, assumed in these tests to be capable of traveling at 10 cm/s and identifying food items within a 2 m radius.

## 4.2    Investigating the Effect of Swarm Density

**Environment.** The environment for the first set of experiments was an octagonal arena (this arena shape has previously been used in foraging research [6,7]). The arena measures 8 m × 8 m and the northern most 2 m of arena is coloured grey to represent the nest site. Outside of the nest site 100 food items have been randomly distributed (represented by the black circles as seen in Fig. 2).

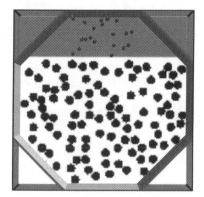

**Fig. 2.** Simulated ARGoS environment for experiment 1. The grey area represents the nest site, the black spots mark the location of food.

**Table 2.** System 2 parameters for experiment 1.

| Swarm size | System | |
|---|---|---|
| | Avoidance counter | Sleep counter |
| 5 | 1992 | 40.9 |
| 10 | 34.9 | 1960 |
| 15 | 48.9 | 3672 |
| 20 | 35.4 | 4510 |

**Experimental Setup.** In this experiment swarms of 5, 10, 15 and 20 robots were deployed in the nest area of the foraging environment. Each trial lasted 1500 s (with each time step being 0.1 s) or until each of the food items where collected and returned to the nest. The energy efficiency of the swarm was measured at the termination of the simulation and used as the measure of performance. By allowing the system to terminate early upon completion of the task, the effectiveness of the swarm was challenged in addition to the efficiency. This meant that a swarm capable of collecting food items quickly could also be rewarded, rather than completing the task and wasting energy waiting for the end of the simulation timer.

As mentioned in Sect. 3.2, the timer-based system was optimized for each swarm size before the experiments. The optimized parameter values are shown in Table 2.

**Results.** Observing the median performances in Fig. 3 it can be seen that the hormone-inspired system has an increased performance relative to the timer-based system in swarm sizes of 5, 10 and 15. Performing a Wilcoxon test on the data sets shows that this increase in performance is significant in the 5 and 10 robot case with p values (shown in Table 3) lower than 0.05, rejecting $H_0$. These results also show that, in general, efficiency decreases as the swarm size increases. This was expected as a more cluttered environment is more difficult to navigate. However, as the swarm size increased the performance of the hormone-inspired system also decreases relative to that of the timer-based system, resulting in a significantly lower performance in the 20 robot case. This suggests that the initial parameters chosen for the hormone-inspired system are more suited to swarms of a smaller size.

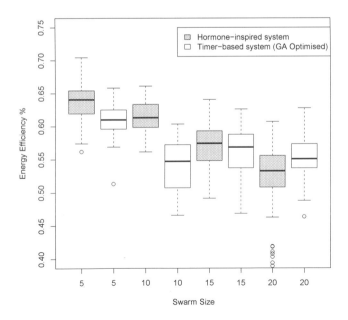

**Fig. 3.** Box plots showing energy efficiency for each swarm size and system for experiment 1

The significant increase in performance with smaller swarm sizes, compared to the timer-based system, shows that the hormone-inspired system is capable of adapting parameters to minor environmental changes. The dynamics of removing food items in this case provided a distinct enough change in environment to allow the timer-based system to adapt mid-task and thus perform better. Even the 15 robot case, in which the hormone-inspired system achieves no significant difference in performance to the timer-based system, shows the benefits of a hormone arbitration method. The hormone-inspired system is capable of achieving these results having no knowledge of the environment before performing the task.

**Table 3.** Wilcoxon rank sum tests comparing the two systems for each swarm size.

| Swarm size | P-value |
|---|---|
| 5 | $P < 0.001$ |
| 10 | $P < 0.001$ |
| 15 | 0.4034 |
| 20 | $P < 0.001$ |

In contrast to this, the significantly lower performance with a swarm size of 20 may be an issue. This swarm size became the focus of the next experiment to identify whether a larger swarm would cause a problem for the system in a more complex environment.

### 4.3   Investigating the Performance of Large Swarms in a Highly Dynamic Environment

**Environment.** The environment (shown in Fig. 4) for this experiment was very similar to that of the previous. The major differences being:

1. An extended space: the new environment kept an octagonal arena of the same dimensions as the first environment, however the arena was also extended in length to $8\,m \times 15\,m$. This was to accommodate for a second search area with different environmental properties.
2. Dynamics: $500\,s$ into the experiment the lower three walls of the octagon were removed, allowing the swarm to enter the rest of the arena.
3. Variable food density: 100 food items were scattered randomly amongst the whole environment (excluding the nest area) but an additional 50 food items are scattered in the area outside of the octagon. This substantial change in food density was an attempt to provide a challenge to the hormone-inspired system, having to quickly adjust values and the timer-based system, having to produce a robust set of parameter values to perform well with a greater environmental contrast.

**Experimental Setup.** The setup for this experiment was similar to the last. The main change was an increase to the maximum time allowed for the experiment, now 3000 s. This was done to account for the larger arena and increased travel time.

Additionally, with the changes to the arena the timer-based system's parameters were re-optimized. Using the same genetic algorithm as previously specified the value of 57.6 was chosen for $Th_A$ and 8014 for $Th_S$. This experiment was designed to test the capabilities of a large swarm size, therefore only the 20 robot swarm was examined here.

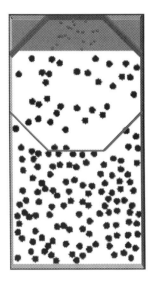

**Fig. 4.** Simulated ARGoS environment for experiment 2

**Results.** The energy efficiency of both systems in this experiment were significantly reduced, even producing some results with a negative efficiency (more energy is used than gained from foraging). The reduction in performance was expected given the increased distance the robots were required to travel to obtain food. A Wilcoxon test between the two data sets produced a P-value < 0.001 establishing a significant difference between the systems and rejecting $H_1$. Viewing the results plotted in Fig. 5 it can be seen that the hormone-inspired system outperforms the timer-based system. This shows that, while the hormone arbitration system may be less effective with a large swarm size, it is still capable of compensating for large changes in the environment to out perform the timer-based system without the need of time consuming recalibration.

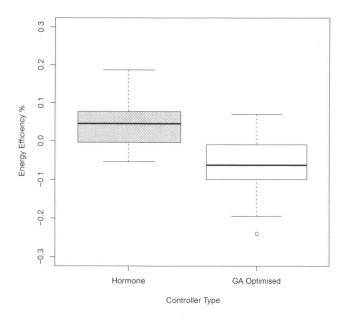

**Fig. 5.** Box plot results showing the energy efficiency for 20 robot swarm size for both systems

## 5 Conclusions and Future Work

This paper has shown that an adaptive, online hormone arbitration system can be used to increase performance (in this case energy efficiency) while foraging in environments of varying robot and food densities. In swarms of relatively small size the performance increases were significant when compared to a system with optimized but static parameter values. The performance observed in the hormone-inspired system depreciates as the size of swarm increases. However, swarms of large sizes were still capable of outperforming a simple but optimized system when introduced to an environment with more pronounced dynamic effects, rapidly changing the food density mid way through.

These results show that the system has promise but, to take this work further, the hormone system should be tested in a greater variety of dynamic environments and potentially be tested against another method of live adaptation rather than the static, optimized, system used as a comparison in this paper. It may also be beneficial to observe the relationship between the hormone equation parameters and that of the optimized parameters in the timer-based system. The optimal sleep and avoidance thresholds may offer an effective way to increase the performance of the hormone system, or potentially make the design of hormone systems for different tasks simpler in the future.

# References

1. Bonani, M., et al.: The marxbot, a miniature mobile robot opening new perspectives for the collective-robotic research. In: 2010 IEEE/RSJ International Conference on Intelligent Robots and Systems (IROS), pp. 4187–4193. IEEE (2010)
2. Charbonneau, D., Dornhaus, A.: When doing nothing is something. How task allocation strategies compromise between flexibility, efficiency, and inactive agents. J. Bioecon. **17**(3), 217–242 (2015)
3. Jin, Y., Guo, H., Meng, Y.: Robustness analysis and failure recovery of a bio-inspired self-organizing multi-robot system. In: 2009 Third IEEE International Conference on Self-Adaptive and Self-Organizing Systems. SASO 2009, pp. 154–164. IEEE (2009)
4. Kernbach, S., et al.: Symbiotic robot organisms: replicator and symbrion projects. In: Proceedings of the 8th Workshop on Performance Metrics for Intelligent Systems, pp. 62–69. ACM (2008)
5. Kuyucu, T., Tanev, I., Shimohara, K.: Hormone-inspired behaviour switching for the control of collective robotic organisms. Robotics **2**(3), 165–184 (2013)
6. Lau, H.K.: Error detection in swarm robotics: a focus on adaptivity to dynamic environments. Ph.D. thesis, University of York (2012)
7. Liu, W., Winfield, A.F.T., Sa, J., Chen, J., Dou, L.: Towards energy optimization: emergent task allocation in a swarm of foraging robots. Adaptive behavior **15**(3), 289–305 (2007)
8. Pinciroli, C., et al.: ARGoS: a modular, parallel, multi-engine simulator for multi-robot systems. Swarm Intell. **6**(4), 271–295 (2012)
9. Robinson, S.: Simulation: the practice of model development and use. Wiley, Chichester (2004)
10. Şahin, E.: Swarm robotics: from sources of inspiration to domains of application. In: Şahin, E., Spears, W.M. (eds.) SR 2004. LNCS, vol. 3342, pp. 10–20. Springer, Heidelberg (2005). https://doi.org/10.1007/978-3-540-30552-1_2
11. Schroeder, A., Ramakrishnan, S., Kumar, M., Trease, B.: Efficient spatial coverage by a robot swarm based on an ant foraging model and the lévy distribution. Swarm Intell. **11**(1), 39–69 (2017)
12. Shen, W., Lu, Y., Will, P.: Hormone-based control for self-reconfigurable robots. In: Proceedings of the Fourth International Conference on Autonomous Agents, pp. 1–8. ACM (2000)
13. Shen, W., Will, P., Galstyan, A., Chuong, C.M.: Hormone-inspired self-organization and distributed control of robotic swarms. Auton. Robots **17**(1), 93–105 (2004)
14. Stradner, J., Hamann, H., Schmickl, T., Crailsheim, K.: Analysis and implementation of an artificial homeostatic hormone system: a first case study in robotic hardware. In: 2009 IEEE/RSJ International Conference on Intelligent Robots and Systems, October 2009

# A Bio-inspired Aggregation with Robot Swarm Using Real and Simulated Mobile Robots

Sarika Ramroop, Farshad Arvin$^{(\boxtimes)}$, Simon Watson, Joaquin Carrasco-Gomez, and Barry Lennox

Robotics for Extreme Environments Lab (REEL),
School of Electrical and Electronic Engineering,
The University of Manchester, Manchester M13 9PL, UK
farshad.arvin@manchester.ac.uk

**Abstract.** This paper presents an implementation of a bio-inspired aggregation scenario using swarm robots. The aggregation scenario took inspiration from honeybee's thermotactic behaviour in finding an optimal zone in their comb. To realisation of the aggregation scenario, real and simulated robots with different population sizes were used. Mona, which is an open-source and open-hardware platform was deployed to play the honeybee's role in this scenario. A model of Mona was also generated in Stage for simulation of aggregation scenario with large number of robots. The results of aggregation with real- and simulated-robots showed reliable aggregations and a population dependent swarm performance. Moreover, the results demonstrated a direct correlation between the results observed from the real robot and simulation experiments.

**Keywords:** Aggregation · Swarm robotics · Bio-inspired
Open-source

## 1 Introduction

Swarm robotics [1] allows many simple robots to work together to carry out tasks that they would not be able to do individually. Many swarm algorithms are based on biological systems such as swarms of bees [2], flocks of birds [3], or ants colonies [4]. Using swarms can allow for greater efficiency as sub-tasks can be carried out in parallel by different groups of robots [5]. Swarms are also generally robust as the failure of a few robots in the collective has little effect of achieving the overall objective. Swarms require large numbers of robots, which means that experimentally testing algorithms can be difficult due to the cost and time required to set up and carry out the experiments. As such, before deploying algorithms on the actual robots, it is beneficial to carry out simulations to estimate an algorithm's performance.

Mona [6] is an open-hardware and open-source robot developed at the University of Manchester for swarm robotic research and teaching. In keeping with the

© Springer International Publishing AG, part of Springer Nature 2018
M. Giuliani et al. (Eds.): TAROS 2018, LNAI 10965, pp. 317–329, 2018.
https://doi.org/10.1007/978-3-319-96728-8_27

design philosophy of swarm robots, its base model is relatively simple; its only built-in sensors are infrared (IR) sensors at the front of the robot and encoders for the wheels. Additional sensors, such as vision system [7], light sensors [8], inductive charging [9], or radio frequency (RF) modules can be added as there are available input/output ports. Mona was developed in 2017 and prior to this work, there was no simulation environment for it. Any algorithms that needed to be testing required direct deployment on the hardware. Mona is also used for robot education hence a simulation environment would enable use of the robot when physical devices are not available.

The aim of this work was to select a suitable simulation environment for Mona, modelling the robot's physical and control structure, implementing aggregation algorithm for testing, and conducting comparisons of the simulated behaviour with the actual behaviour when implemented in hardware.

## 2     Background and Related Work

This section presents the background and related work for the proposed aggregation scenario and corresponding swarm robot platforms and their simulation environments.

### 2.1     The Mona Swarm Robot Platform

Mona [6] is an open-source low-cost miniature mobile robot which has been developed at the University of Manchester for swarm robotic research and teaching. It's primary advantage compared to other existing platforms is its in-built inductive charging system which allows for perpetual swarm experiments to be run [10].

Figure 1 (left) shows the overhead view of the Mona robot. It is a differential drive robot [11] with a maximum velocity of approximately 7 cm/s and makes use of an ATmega 328 chip. This can be programmed using the Arduino development environment after uploading a boot-loader to the microcontroller. There are three IR sensors which allow to robot to carry out obstacle detection [12]. After testing, the maximum range was determined to be 45 mm, with an angular range of up to 80°. The IR sensors also enable robot identification. Additionally, a light dependent resistor (LDR) shown in Fig. 1 (right) allows for light intensity measurement.

### 2.2     Aggregation Algorithm

BEECLUST (Fig. 2) is a bio-inspired swarm aggregation algorithm which was based by the tendency of young honeybees to gather in areas with temperatures between 34 °C and 38 °C [2]. Robot implementations of BEECLUST have used light intensity [2,9,13] or sound signals [14,15] instead of temperature, with the robots clustering in areas (cues) with the highest intensity of either source.

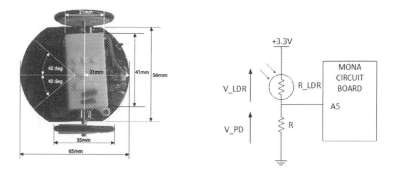

**Fig. 1.** (Left) An overhead view of the Mona robot (right) light sensing circuit

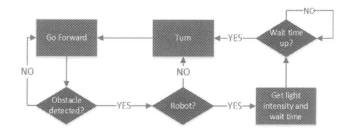

**Fig. 2.** BEECLUST algorithm state diagram for a single robot

Based on the aggregation scenario, the robot is in one of four states:

1. `forward`: robot moves forward in a straight line, while checking for obstacles
2. `obstacle`: checks if an obstacle is a robot or wall
3. `wait`: if the obstacle is another robot, the robot waits for length of time based on the measured light intensity
4. `turn`: the robot turns to avoid an obstacle/robot and then returns to `forward`.

BEECLUST has previously been implemented by platforms such as Jasmine [2] and Colias [9] which have similar characteristics as shown in Table 1.

**Table 1.** Comparison of different open-source swarm robotic platforms

| Robot | Size (diam. or $l \times w$) (mm) | Type of motion | Sensors | Sensor range |
|---|---|---|---|---|
| Mona [6] | 65 | Diff. drive | 3 IR | 45 mm, 180° |
| Jasmine [2] | 23 × 23 | Diff. drive | 6 IR, light | 60 mm, 360° |
| Colias [16] | 40 | Diff. drive | 6 IR, light | 150 mm, 360° |

## 2.3 Simulators for Swarm Robotics

The most popular simulators for swarm robotics include Gazebo, ARGoS, Player/Stage and Webots [17,18]. This section provides a review of these environments with respect to their use for simulations of BEECLUST with Mona.

Gazebo [19] is widely used for simulating robot behaviour; swarm or otherwise [18]. It provides a 3D visualisation environment and custom robots can be created in it. Gazebo is open-source and code written for robot applications can often be ported easily from Gazebo to the actual robot. Due to its popularity [17], a lot of support can be found from the active online community. However, because Gazebo renders its simulations in a 3D environment, it can be relatively computationally heavy. For swarm applications with many robots (greater than 10), the performance could be too slow.

ARGoS [20] is widely used simulator which also provides 3D simulations. It was developed as part of the Swarmanoid project [21] and is therefore used in several different swarm related research such as [22,23]. As a result, ARGoS tends to be used mainly in relation to the foot-, hand- and eye-bot robots. While ARGoS allows for fast performance with many robots, it is difficult to customise for a user-defined robot.

Webots [24] and Stage [25] are among the most recognised simulation platforms as both have existed for several years. Webots presents the same problem as Gazebo; that is, it is not suitable for large numbers of robots.

Stage [25] is described as a 2.5D simulator and can simulate robots through a range of customisable sensor modules and actuators. Environments can be simulated to include different colour cues and fixed and movable obstacles. In general, one of the disadvantages of Stage is that it only allows for differential drive robot.

Table 2 shows a comparison of the simulation environments. Due to the relative ease of simulating robots in Stage and creating the environments, and confirmation that BEECLUST can be simulated, Stage was selected to build the simulations for the Mona robots.

## 3 Experimental Procedure

### 3.1 Arena Setup

All hardware tests utilised a 72 cm × 44.8 cm arena with 3.2 cm walls (Fig. 3). LED bulbs were used to create the cue since they emit less IR radiation that halogen bulbs. This eliminates a potential source of IR interference to the robots' sensors.

The arena walls were constructed with white Lego blocks as this surface reflects IR signals well so would be easily detected by the sensors. The arena's floor was covered in black cardboard. This absorbs IR signals and prevent IR and light from being reflected and affecting sensor readings.

**Table 2.** Comparison of different open-source swarm robotic platforms

| Simulator | Visualisation | Customisation | Number of robots |
|---|---|---|---|
| Gazebo [19] | 3D | Easy | Low |
| ARGoS [20] | 3D | Hard | High |
| Webots [24] | 3D | Easy | Low |
| Stage [25] | 2.5D | Easy | Very high |

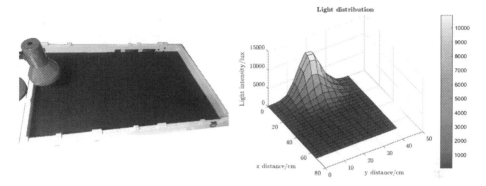

**Fig. 3.** (Left) Lego arena with one light source and (right) 3D graph showing light intensity of the arena with one light source.

The cue size was determined by Eq. 1, as adapted from [9]:

$$a_c = \beta n a_r \tag{1}$$

where $a_c$ is the area of the cue, $n$ is the number of robots, $a_r$ is the area occupied by a robot and $\beta$ is the ratio of cue to area occupied by the swarm.

Using the minimum $\beta$ value of two and the maximum number of robots of eight, a cue with radius of 16 cm was selected. This was also modelled in simulation. For a simulation only arena, a maximum of 50 robots was used. This required a cue radius of 46 cm. The arena size with selected as 100 cm × 160 cm to allow for this.

### 3.2  Experiment 1: Static Environment with Single Light Source

This experiment used a single light source at one end of the arena (Fig. 3). All the robots were turned on while the light was switched off and placed outside the general cue area. The light was then turned on. This was to allow all the robots to respond to the light at the same time.

The time taken for the robots to aggregate was recorded ($t_a$). A robot was considered to be aggregated if it was in the cue while in the waiting state or enclosed by other robots in the waiting state. Aggregation was considered to be completed when 70% of the total number of robots were aggregated [9]. This experiment was carried out with increasing the number of robots to observe the effect. For the real-robot implementation $n \in \{3, 4, 5, 6, 7, 8\}$ robots were used. This same number of robots was also used in simulation, but further tests were carried out with up to 50 robots.

**Table 3.** Experimental values or range for variables and constants

| Values | Description | Range/values |
|---|---|---|
| $n$ | Total number of robots | Real robot: $\{3, 4, 5, 6, 7, 8\}$ |
| | | Simulation: $\{10, 20, 30, 40, 50\}$ |
| $n_a$ | Number of aggregated robots | 0 to 50 |
| $s$ | Sensor value | 0 to 255 |
| $w$ | Wait time | 0 to 85 s |
| cruiseSpd | Forward speed | 4 cm/s |
| safeDist | Minimum safe distance | 1 cm |
| turnSpd | Turn speed | 1 rad/sec |
| $r_c$ | Cue radius | $\{16, 46\}$ cm |
| $t_a$ | Aggregation time | 0 to 500 s |

### 3.3  Experiment 2: Static Environment with Two Light Sources

This experiment is simular to Experiment 1, except two light sources with different light intensities were used. The light sources produced different cue sizes and were situated at opposite ends of the arena. The robots were placed outside the cue and the aggregation times were recorded. Aggregation was considered to be completed when 70% of the total number of robots were waiting in either one of the cues. This was also carried out with increasing numbers of robots.

Table 3 gives the definitions and values of any constants and variables used in the both Experiments 1 and 2. Each set of experiment was repeated 10 times and results were statistically analysed.

## 4  Simulated Robot in Stage

### 4.1  Environment Model

As shown in Fig. 3, the light source has maximum intensity at the centre. The cue was modelled in Stage using a colour gradient with shades of gray, from white (maximum intensity) to black (darkness). Each colour has an associated RGB value from which the R value was scaled to a value between 0 and 255 to represent the light sensor measurement.

The arena walls were created from a '.png' image with a black square that was scaled to the desired length, width and height values. This was set to be recognized as an obstacle.

## 4.2   Robot Model

The physical model was created using the measurement from Fig. 1. The following details how the sensors and actuators were implemented.

1. Differential drive - built into the Stage `position` model
2. IR sensors for obstacle detection - the `ranger` module is used to implement a sensor with range of 45 mm and 80°.
3. Light sensors - implemented using the `blobfinder` module, which returns colour values
4. IR sensors for robot detection - implemented using the `fiducial` model which is set to recognise objects assigned a value of "1".

Figure 4 shows the robot model in Stage, where the image on the left shows the different sensors and the image on the right shows how the fiducial model works to identify another robot.

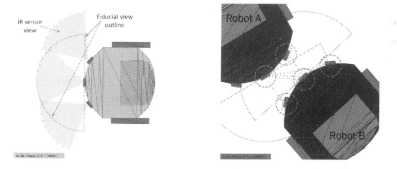

**Fig. 4.** (Left) robot sensor views and (right) The fiducial module on Robot A detects the sensors that are circled on Robot B and vice versa.

## 5   Results of Experiments

### 5.1   Experiment 1: Static Environment with Single Light Source

Figure 5 shows a randomly selected final aggregated positions of the Mona robots for real and simulated experiments where the total number of aggregated robots, $n_a$, is five.

Statistical analysis was carried out on the aggregation times obtained for both the real and simulated scenarios. The analysis of variance (ANOVA) and $F$-test method was used to disprove the null hypotheses, which states that the means for different conditions are the same. A high $F$-value (greater than 1) and a low $p$-value (less than 0.05) indicates that a factor significantly affects results. It does not indicate how it affects the result.

S. Ramroop et al.

**Fig. 5.** Aggregation of 5 real robots ($n = 7$) with: (left) real-robots and (right) simulated robots.

**Table 4.** Two-way ANOVA analysis for Experiment 1

| Source | $F$-value | $p$ value |
|---|---|---|
| Number of robots | 5.47 | 0.0005 |
| Experiment type | 0.0048 | 0.945 |
| Robots * Experiment | 0.49 | 0.785 |

Two-way ANOVA was carried out where the factors were the robot population size ($n \in \{3, 4, 5, 6, 7, 8\}$) and the type of experiment (real or simulated robots). Table 4 shows the $F$- and $p$-values that were obtained.

The $F$-value for *experiment type* is less than 1 with a high $p$-value. This suggests that the null hypothesis cannot be disproven and that data from the real and simulated experiments are very similar. However, in general, this can also indicate an error with the data.

To account for this, one-way ANOVA was carried out with the factor as the experiment type, for each value of $n$. The $F$-values were between 0.01 and 0.80 while $p$-values were between 0.3971 and 0.9387, indicating inability to disprove the null hypothesis. This validates the results of the two-way ANOVA analysis about the similarity of the real and simulated data. Hence, even though the simulation is not a perfect match, the results can be considered good enough to estimate the behaviour of the real system.

The second factor in Table 4 is the number of robots. The large $F$-value and small $p$-value indicate that population size significantly affects aggregation times. Figure 6 shows the box and whisker plot of the times for the different population sizes. The results shows clearly that increasing the population size decreases the aggregation time. This occurs because BEECLUST depends on collisions in light for aggregation to take place. Most robots in the same arena increases the likelihood of collisions. This matches the observations by Schmickl et al. [2] and Arvin et al. [9] who both noted this improved performance with more robots.

Figure 6 also shows that as the number of robots increases, the *difference* in aggregation time becomes smaller. This occurs because there is also an increased number of collisions outside of the light cue so robots need to reorient themselves continuously. The general observation was noted in [9], while Hereford [26] also observed this nonlinearity in the relationship between population size and aggregation time.

Figure 7 shows the number of robots aggregated over time for $n = 4$ and $n = 8$. Only these two cases are considered as they should provide enough contrast to see the effects of increasing population size.

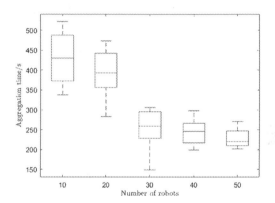

**Fig. 6.** Aggregation times for the simulated Experiment 1, using the larger arena

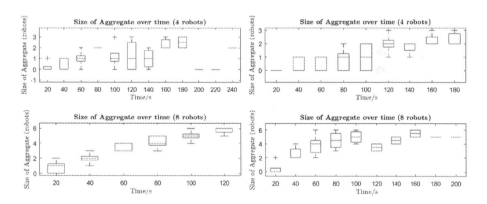

**Fig. 7.** Number of robots in the aggregate over time, for both (left) real robots and (right) simulated robots.

For case $n = 4$, there is fluctuation in the number of robots over time as the enter and leave the aggregate. This is becasue there is a lower collision rate, so robots leave the waiting state before other robots are able to collide. In contrast, for $n = 8$, there is a general increase in the aggregate size over time. This shows that a larger aggregate is more likely to increase in size since unaggregated robots have a higher probability of colliding with a robot in the wait state. Figure 7 (right) shows that when robots leave the aggregate, the overall aggregation time increases. This behaviour matches the results obtained by Arvin et al. [9]. Their aggregation graphs for dynamic environments show display similar results. Note only the initial aggregation can be compared here.

## 5.2    Experiment 2: Static Environment with Two Light Sources

The box and whisker diagram in Fig. 8 shows the collective decision of the swarm for the larger arena. The smaller population sizes were not considered here since the consensus is less obvious due to fewer collisions being required for aggregation.

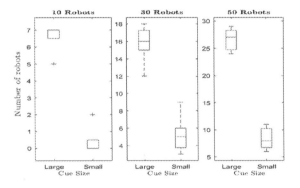

**Fig. 8.** Robots per cue, for cases $n \in \{10, 30, 50\}$

In every case, the majority of robots aggregate around the larger cue. This behaviour is observed in [2,9]. The results from Experiment 1 show enough similarity between real and simulated performances to conclude that if this was implemented in hardware, there would also be a preference to aggregate around the global optimum. Therefore, this BEECLUST property is also replicated by the Mona robots.

Table 5 shows the results of two-way ANOVA analysis where the factors were number of robots and number of cues. The data used is for $n \in \{3, 4, 5, 6, 7, 8\}$.

**Table 5.** Two-way ANOVA analysis for Experiment 2

| Source | $F$-value | $p$ value |
|---|---|---|
| Number of robots | 8.52 | $< 0.00001$ |
| Number of cues | 0.3776 | 0.5418 |
| Robots * cues | 0.1740 | 0.9710 |

The $F$- and $p$-values show that the number of robots has a significant effect on aggregation. This was also observed with Experiment 1, so is expected.

The small $F$-value and large $p$-value for number of cues means the null hypothesis cannot be discredited. This differs from the observations in [9]. They find that cue size does affect aggregation time, though to a less degree than population size. Two cues behave as a larger single cue.

It is possible that the population sizes in this analysis are too small to observe this difference and there is not a large enough difference between the population sizes. As a result, a box and whisker diagrams were also done for $n \in \{10, 30, 50\}$ with single and double cues (Fig. 9).

This more closely matches the observations in other works as the aggregation time with two cues is generally less than with a single cue.

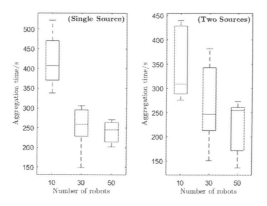

**Fig. 9.** Aggregation times for simulated Experiment 1 and simulated Experiment 2 for larger $n$ values

## 6   Conclusion

In this work, the LDR potential divider circuit was added to the Mona robots to allow them to execute the BEECLUST algorithm. Even though the short IR sensor range affects the performance, the robots were still able to achieve aggregation under a light source. The observed behaviour was comparable with other work that have been previously carried out using this algorithm. Using the ANOVA statistical method, it was determined that the Stage simulations provide behaviour close enough to the real robots' performance. For the future work, dynamic environments using single and multiple cues will be investigated.

**Acknowledgement.** This work was supported by the EPSRC (Project No. EP/P01366X/1).

# References

1. Hamann, H.: Swarm Robotics: A Formal Approach. Springer, Heidelberg (2018). https://doi.org/10.1007/978-3-319-74528-2
2. Schmickl, T., Thenius, R., Moeslinger, C., et al.: Get in touch: cooperative decision making based on robot-to-robot collisions. Auton. Agents Multi-Agent Syst. **18**(1), 133–155 (2009)
3. Turgut, A.E., Çelikkanat, H., Gökçe, F., Şahin, E.: Self-organized flocking in mobile robot swarms. Swarm Intell. **2**(2), 97–120 (2008)
4. Dorigo, M., Birattari, M., Stutzle, T.: Ant colony optimization. IEEE Comput. Intell. Mag. **1**(4), 28–39 (2006)
5. Şahin, E.: Swarm robotics: from sources of inspiration to domains of application. In: Şahin, E., Spears, W.M. (eds.) SR 2004. LNCS, vol. 3342, pp. 10–20. Springer, Heidelberg (2005). https://doi.org/10.1007/978-3-540-30552-1_2
6. Arvin, F., Espinosa, J., Bird, B., West, A., Watson, S., Lennox, B.: Mona: an affordable open-source mobile robot for education and research. J. Intell. Robot. Syst. (2018). https://doi.org/10.1007/s10846-018-0866-9
7. Hu, C., Arvin, F., Xiong, C., Yue, S.: Bio-inspired embedded vision system for autonomous micro-robots: the LGMD case. IEEE Trans. Cogn. Dev. Syst. **9**(3), 241–254 (2017)
8. Arvin, F., Krajník, T., Turgut, A.E., Yue, S.: COS$\Phi$: artificial pheromone system for robotic swarms research. In: IEEE/RSJ International Conference on Intelligent Robots and Systems (IROS), pp. 407–412 (2015)
9. Arvin, F., Turgut, A.E., Krajnk, T., Yue, S.: Investigation of cue-based aggregation in static and dynamic environments with a mobile robot swarm. Adapt. Behav. **24**(2), 102–118 (2016)
10. Arvin, F., Watson, S., Turgut, A., Espinosa, J., Krajník, T., Lennox, B.: Perpetual robot swarm: long-term autonomy of mobile robots using on-the-fly inductive charging. J. Intell. Robot. Syst. 1–18 (2017)
11. Arvin, F., Bekravi, M.: Encoderless position estimation and error correction techniques for miniature mobile robots. Turk. J. Electr. Eng. Comput. Sci. **21**(6), 1631–1645 (2013)
12. Arvin, F., Samsudin, K., Ramli, A.: Development of IR-based short-range communication techniques for swarm robot applications. Adv. Electr. Comput. Eng. **10**(4), 61–68 (2010)
13. Arvin, F., Samsudin, K., Ramli, A.R., Bekravi, M.: Imitation of honeybee aggregation with collective behavior of swarm robots. Int. J. Comput. Intell. Syst. **4**(4), 739–748 (2011)
14. Arvin, F., Turgut, A.E., Bazyari, F., Arikan, K.B., Bellotto, N., Yue, S.: Cue-based aggregation with a mobile robot swarm: a novel fuzzy-based method. Adapt. Behav. **22**(3), 189–206 (2014)
15. Arvin, F., Turgut, A.E., Bellotto, N., Yue, S.: Comparison of different cue-based swarm aggregation strategies. In: Tan, Y., Shi, Y., Coello, C.A.C. (eds.) ICSI 2014. LNCS, vol. 8794, pp. 1–8. Springer, Cham (2014). https://doi.org/10.1007/978-3-319-11857-4_1
16. Arvin, F., Murray, J., Zhang, C., Yue, S.: Colias: an autonomous micro robot for swarm robotic applications. Int. J. Adv. Rob. Syst. **11**(7), 113 (2014)
17. Ivaldi, S., Padois, V., Nori, F.: Tools for dynamics simulation of robots: a survey based on user feedback. arXiv:1402.7050 (2014)

18. Tan, Y., Zheng, Z.Y.: Research advance in swarm robotics. Def. Technol. **9**(1), 18–39 (2013)
19. Koenig, N., Howard, A.: Design and use paradigms for gazebo, an open-source multi-robot simulator. In: IEEE/RSJ International Conference on Intelligent Robots and Systems (IROS), vol. 3, pp. 2149–2154 (2004)
20. Pinciroli, C., et al.: ARGoS: a modular, parallel, multi-engine simulator for multi-robot systems. Swarm Intell. **6**, 271–295 (2012)
21. Dorigo, M., et al.: Swarmanoid: a novel concept for the study of heterogeneous robotic swarms. IEEE Robot. Autom. Mag. **20**(4), 60–71 (2013)
22. Montes de Oca, M.A., et al.: Majority-rule opinion dynamics with differential latency: a mechanism for self-organized collective decision-making. Swarm Intell. **5**(3), 305–327 (2011)
23. Ducatelle, F., Di Caro, G.A., Pinciroli, C., Gambardella, L.M.: Self-organized cooperation between robotic swarms. Swarm Intell. **5**(2), 73 (2011)
24. Michel, O.: Cyberbotics Ltd. webots: professional mobile robot simulation. Int. J. Adv. Rob. Syst. **1**(1), 5 (2004)
25. Vaughan, R.: Massively multiple robot simulations in stage. Swarm Intell. **2**(1), 189–208 (2008)
26. Hereford, J.: Analysis of BEECLUST swarm algorithm. In: IEEE Symposium on Swarm Intelligence, pp. 1–7 (2011)

# SO-MRS: A Multi-robot System Architecture Based on the SOA Paradigm and Ontology

Kamil Skarzynski[2], Marcin Stepniak[2], Waldemar Bartyna[2], and Stanislaw Ambroszkiewicz[1,2]($\boxtimes$)

[1] Institute of Computer Science, Polish Academy of Sciences,
Jana Kazimierza 5, 01-248 Warsaw, Poland
sambrosz@gmail.com
[2] Siedlce University of Natural Sciences and Humanities, Siedlce, Poland

**Abstract.** A generic architecture for a class of distributed robotic systems is presented. The architecture supports openness and heterogeneity, i.e. heterogeneous components may be joined and removed from the systems without affecting its basic functionality. The architecture is based on the paradigm of Service Oriented Architecture (SOA), and a generic representation (ontology) of the environment. A device (e.g. robot) is seen as a collection of its capabilities exposed as services. Generic protocols for publishing, discovering, arranging services are proposed for creating composite services that can accomplish complex tasks in an automatic way. Also generic protocols for execution of composite services are proposed along with simple protocols for monitoring the executions, and for recovery from failures. The proposed architecture and generic protocols were implemented as a software platform, and tested for several multi-robot systems.

## 1 Introduction

The general assumption is that multi-robot system (MRS for short) consists of an environment, and of devices that operate in the environment and may change its state. A device may be considered as an element of the environment, and the device state may be subject of change, e.g. its position. The crucial questions, for a MRS to be designed and developed, are: What is the purpose of the system? What kind of problems is it supposed to solve, or what class of tasks are to be accomplished in the system? If the system is dedicated to a fixed class of tasks, then the tasks as well as the methods for the task accomplishing may be hard-codded during the design process.

In the paper, a special kind of MRS is considered. It is supposed that the devices may be heterogeneous, and can be added to the system as well as be removed without affecting its basic functionality, i.e. the generic ability for task accomplishing. Hence, the class of the tasks is not fixed and depends on the joint capabilities of the devices currently available in the system. Since such

© Springer International Publishing AG, part of Springer Nature 2018
M. Giuliani et al. (Eds.): TAROS 2018, LNAI 10965, pp. 330–342, 2018.
https://doi.org/10.1007/978-3-319-96728-8_28

tasks can not be hard-coded in the system, there must be a language for the task specification. Intuitively, a task is an intention to change local state of the environment. That is, task consists of precondition and effect. Sometimes the precondition is not necessary. Precondition specifies initial local state of the environment, whereas the effect specifies the desired environment state after the task performance. So that, a formal representation of the environment (ontology) is needed. It is also supposed that the devices are not isolated, i.e. there is a minimum communication in the system in the form of (wireless) network. That is, each device has a network address and can receive and send messages.

Each device is autonomous and may provide some services (via its Service Manager) for a client (i.e. human user or software application). If a client has a task to be accomplished, it sends a request to the device. Then, the service may accomplish the task, if it has enough resources and capabilities. Hence, each device provides some services that correspond to some types of elementary tasks the device may accomplish. The formal specification (expressed in a language of the common ontology, e.g. OWL-S) of the type of a service consists of a precondition and an effect. The service type must be published by a device (to be joined to MRS) to a Registry. Client may discover the service, and invoke it. This constitutes the essence of the Service Oriented Architecture (SOA) paradigm in Information Technology.

Repository (the next component of MRS) is a realization of the common knowledge of the environment representation (ontology), and a storage of the current maps of the environment, i.e. instances of the ontology. Since the environment may be changed by devices, the maps must be updated.

If a client wants to realize a complex task (a sequence or partial order of the elementary tasks), then some services, that may jointly accomplish the complex task, should be discovered (in the Registry), and composed into a workflow (composite service). An additional component of MRS is needed for doing so. It is called Task Manager, and it is responsible for constructing an abstract plan in the form of partial order of service types. Then, appropriate services should be arranged. Finally, the workflow is executed and its performance is monitored. If a failure occurs (due to a broken communication or inability of a service to fulfill the arranged commitment), then failure recovery mechanisms must be applied. Simple mechanisms (in the form of protocols) consist in re-planning, and changing some parts of the workflow in order to continue the task execution.

To summarize, the software infrastructure built on MRS (for complex task accomplishing) consists of services exposed by Service Managers on devices (robots), service Registry, Task Manager, and Repository. The interactions between them are based on generic protocols for publishing, discovering, composing elementary services, arranging, execution, monitoring and recovery from failures. Note that the basis for the protocols is a formal representation of the environment (ontology) that allows to specify local states of the environment, tasks, service types, intentions, commitments, and situations resulting from failures. Roughly, this constitutes the proposed architecture called Service Oriented Multi-Robot System (SO-MRS for short).

SO-MRS architecture follows the hybrid approach based on additional infrastructure where main components of the infrastructure may be multiplied, i.e. in one MRS, there may be several independent Task Managers, Registries, and Repositories. Note that the presented approach is at higher level of abstraction than Robot Operating System (ROS) that is usually used to implement services on the devices. The main contribution consists of simple universal upper ontology, MRS architecture, and generic protocols.

## 2    Motivations and Related Work

Rapid development and ubiquitous use of intelligent devices (equipped with sensors, micro-controllers, and connected to a network) pose new possibilities and challenges in Robotics and Information Technology. One of them is creating large open distributed systems consisting of heterogeneous devices that can inter-operate in order to accomplish complex tasks. *Ambient Intelligence* (AmI), and *Ubiquitous robotics* are currently extensively explored research areas. It is supposed that in the near future humans will live in a world where all devices are fully networked, so that any desired service can be provided at any place at any time. It is worth to notice the Intelligent Physical Systems research program by NSF, and Machine-to-Machine (M2M) standards promoted by International Telecommunication Union http://www.onem2m.org/. AmI and Ubiquitous robotics require new information technologies for developing distributed systems that allow defining tasks in a declarative way by human users, and an automatic task accomplishing by the system. Openness and heterogeneity of the systems are essential because of the scalability, see Di Ciccio et al. [1], and Helal et al. [2].

Multi-robot systems and multi-robot cooperation is a vital research subject. Several architectures were proposed for a pure swarm robotics approach using large numbers of homogeneous robots (see overview by Khaldi and Cherif [3]), for behavior-based approach without explicit coordination IQ-ASyMTRe by Zhang and Parker [4], and a hybrid approaches, e.g. Distributed Robot Architecture (DIRA) Simmons et al. [5]. DIRA is closely related to SO-MRS, however, it was not fully developed.

Actually, the proposed SO-MRS architecture follows the idea of IQ-ASyMTRe by Zhang and Parker [4]. However, instead of sharing (by devices) mutually data from their sensors, SO-MRS is equipped with explicit common ontology as the basis for constructing generic protocols.

The project Service Oriented Device Architecture SODA Alliance, and its extension in the form of OASIS standard Devices Profile for Web Services (DPWS), is also of interest. Device functionality is described there in the very similar way as it is done for Web services. For an extensive overview of SOA based robotic systems (from software engineering point of view) see de Oliveira [6]. Although these approaches are also based on SOA, what makes the difference (in comparison to SO-MRS) is the lack of ontology, i.e. a *common* representation of the environment, and the language describing the representation. This very ontology is the necessary basis for constructing the generic protocols for automatic complex task execution and for recovery from failures.

It is worth to notice that the following view presented by Parker [7] is still up to date: *"A general research question in this vein is whether specialized architectures for each type of robot team and/or application domain are needed, or whether a more general architecture can be developed that can easily be tailored to fit a wider range of multirobot systems."*

It seems that there are still a lot of problems to be solved in the domain of multi-robot systems. Recent research directions are focused rather on software level. The player/stage project Gerkey et al. [8] developed software level approach whereas the more abstract software independent level is needed. An abstract (however still unsatisfactory) approach was proposed by Kramer and Magee [9] as the software engineering point of view of the problem. The idea of Jung and Zelinsky [10], and Hugues [11] of common grounded symbolic communication between heterogeneous cooperating robots is very close to the concept of common ontology, however, it was not fully developed and not continued. An interesting approach to composite services (heterogeneous robot teams) as temporal organizations with elements of recovery from failures was presented in Zhong and DeLoach [12].

Let us also cite the view on the research on MRS by Chitic et al. [13]: *"Despite many years of work in robotics, there is still a lack of established software architecture and middleware, in particular for large scale multi-robots systems. Many research teams are still writing specific hardware orientated software that is very tied to a robot. This vision makes sharing modules or extending existing code difficult. A robotic middleware should be designed to abstract the low-level hardware architecture, facilitate communication and integration of new software."*

# 3   Environment Representation

Classic representations of robotic environments (see Thrun et al. [14] for a comprehensive overview) are based on metric and topological approaches dedicated mostly to tasks related to navigation. Another approach, *Spatial Semantic Hierarchy* (SSH), Kuipers [15], is based on the concept of cognitive map and hierarchical representation of spatial environment structure. There is some object-based approaches (see Vasudevan et al. [16]) where the environment is represented as a map of places connected by passages. Places are probabilistic graphs encoding objects and relations between them. Anguelov et al. [17] proposed the environment representation composed of two object hierarchies; the first one (called spatial) related to sensor data in the form of object images or occupancy grid, and the second one (called conceptual) related to some abstract notions of the representation. The recognition of places and objects consists in matching sensor data against the abstract notions. Recent work on semantic mapping is mainly focusing on perception and recognition techniques, see Pronobis and Jensfelt [18], and an extensive survey by Kostavelis and Gasteratos [19]. Also the project KnowRob, a knowledge processing system at

RoboEarth http://wiki.ros.org/roboearth, explores this idea, see Tenorth and Beetz [20]. It seems that more abstract generic and simpler representation, in the form of upper ontology (common for humans and devices), is needed for MRS.

In the Computer Science related to Robotics, the term "ontology" is equivalent to the "general structure of the representation of a multirobot system environment". The most popular definition of ontology was given by Tom Gruber (1993) in the following way: *ontology is a specification of a conceptualization.* Conceptualization is understood here as an abstract and simplified model (representation) of the real environment. It is a formal description of concepts (objects) and relations between them. Since the model is supposed to serve the interoperability, it must be common and formally specified, i.e. the definitions of objects and relations must be unambiguous in order to be processed automatically.

Two recent standards developed by groups of the IEEE RAS and addressing robot ontologies and map representation (https://standards.ieee.org/findstds/standard/1872-2015.html and https://standards.ieee.org/findstds/standard/1873-2015.html) are closely related to upper ontology presented below. However, these ontologies are complex and include specifications even for defining processes for task execution. Our ontology is extremely simple, and is at the higher level of abstraction, i.e. it abstracts from recognition of physical objects, and is focusing only on generic attributes of the objects that can be measured, recognized or evaluated. Although the proposed ontology is simple, it is generic (abstracting from implementation details), and sufficient together with simple and universal protocols (presented roughly below) to accomplish complex tasks in open and distributed heterogeneous multi-robot systems. In its general form it is an upper ontology, and consists of the following concepts:

– attributes that define properties of object (e.g.: color, weight, volume, position, rotation, shape, texture, etc.,
– relations that express dependencies between objects,
– types of objects that specify object attributes, constraints on attribute values, and relations between sub-objects,
– object that is an instance of a type with concrete attribute values, sub-objects and relations between them.

In order to add a new type to the ontology one has to specify:

– parent type, i.e. the type that the new type inherits from,
– list of attributes of the new type,
– list of types of obligatory sub-objects, i.e. types of objects that are integral parts of the type being defined, e.g. legs in the case of the type of table,
– list of constraints specifying attribute values as ranges and/or enumerations, and obligatory relations between sub-objects.

The type inheritance provides hierarchical structure supporting management of existing types as well as creation of new types. In the presented ontology the most generic type called *Object* is inherited by two types: *PhysicalObject* and

*AbstractObject* as shown in Fig. 1. The types are for separating physical objects that are directly recognizable by robots from abstract objects that are hierarchically composed from physical objects, relations between them, and attributes.

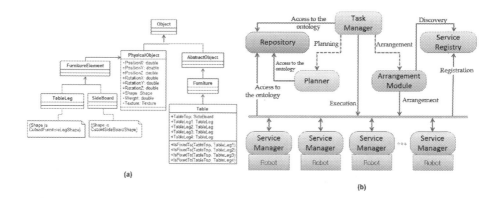

**Fig. 1.** (a) Main object types. (b) SO-MRS architecture

Descendants of *PhysicalObject* type, that are leafs in the inheritance hierarchy tree, are called *elementary types*. They are described only by *attributes* (*simple* and/or *complex attributes*) that can be recognized by robots. The type *CuboidFurnitureLeg* is an example of an *elementary type*. It is defined by the following attributes: *PositionX*, *PositionY*, *PositionZ*, *RotationX*, *RotationY*, *RotationZ*, *Shape*, *Weight*, *Texture*, and the constraint: *Shape is CuboidFurnitureLegShape*. *Shape* is a *complex attribute* consisting of its own attributes and their constraints. The constrains are important for object recognition, e.g. attribute constrains of the *FurnitureLeg* type are different than the constrains of the type corresponding to building pillars.

The *AbstractObject* branch consists of complex abstract types. Each such type is defined as a collection of types (complex and/or elementary), and relations between objects of these types. The type *CuboidRoom* is an example of an abstract type. Internal structure of an object of this abstract type is composed of elementary objects such as walls, floor, ceiling, windows, and doors, as well as the relations between these objects.

General structure of the proposed representation of the environment is defined as a hierarchy of types. Elementary type is defined as a collection of attributes with restricted ranges, whereas an abstract type is defined by some of the previously defined types (abstract and/or elementary), and relations between objects of these types. The type *Building* consists of several other abstract types like storey, passages, rooms, stairs, lifts, etc.

The attributes and relations are the basic elements for creating representation, i.e. construction of object types. A particular object (as an instance of its type) is defined by specifying concrete values of its attributes, specifying its sub-objects (if it is of abstract type) and relations between them. Instance of the

general structure (called also a map of the environment) is defined as a specification of an object of an abstract type, for example, of the type *Building*. In
order to support an automatic map creating and updating (by mobile robots),
the attributes must be recognizable and measurable by robot sensors.

## 4   Services

There are three kinds of services: physical services that may change local situations in the physical environment, cognitive services that can recognize situations
described by formulas of the language of the ontology, and software services that
process data.

A service interface consists of the following elements:

- Name of the type of service, i.e. name of an action that the service performs.
- Specification of the inputs and outputs of the service.
- The condition required for service invocation (precondition), and the effect
  of service invocation.
- Service attributes as information about the static features of a service, e.g.
  operation range, cost, and average realization time.

Precondition and effect are defined as formulas of a formal language (e.g.
OWL, or Entish [21]) describing local situations in the environment. Entish is a
simplified version (without quantifiers) of the first order logic. It has logical operators (*and, or*), names of relations (e.g., *isIn, isAdjacentTo*), names of functions
(e.g., *action, range*), and variables. A precondition formula is a description of
the initial situation, and the effect formula is a description of the final situation.

## 5   SO-MRS Architecture

Figure 1 shows the proposed architecture of multi-robot system designed according to the SOA paradigm. The system components communicate with each other
by using generic protocols. Repository stores ontology, and provides access to
object maps for the other system components. It has also a graphical user interface (GUI) for developing the ontology, and for its management.

Task Manager (TM for short) represents a client, and provides a GUI for
the client to define tasks, and to monitor their realization. The Planner provides
abstract plans for TM, that are used to construct a concrete plan (workflow)
on the basis of information on available services (provided by Service Registry).
The workflow is constructed by arranging concrete services. Arrangement is performed by TM (via the Arrangement Module) by sending requests to services
(in the form of intentions), and collecting answers as quotes (commitments). TM
controls the plan realization by communicating with the arranged services.

Service Registry stores information about services currently available in the
system. Each service, in order to be available, must be registered to Service
Registry via Service Manager (SM) that is a robot (device) interface for providing

its services for an external client. In this case, TM acts as a client. SM controls the execution of subtasks delegated by TM, and reports the success or failures to TM.

Task is defined (on the basis of the ontology stored in Repository) as a logical formula that describes the initial situation (optionally) and the required final situation in the environment. For a given task, Planner returns abstract plans that, when arranged and executed, may realize the final situation specified by the task in question. An abstract plan is represented as a directed acyclic graph where nodes are service types and edges correspond to causal relationship between the output of one service and the input of another service. The relationship determines the order of arrangement, and then also the order of execution of a concrete plan (workflow) called also a business process. A concrete plan may also include handlers responsible for compensations, and failure handling to be explained below.

# 6   Protocol for Failure Handling and Recovery

Since some ideas and methods are adopted from electronic business transactions, realization of a task is called *a transaction*. All services are invoked within a transaction that contains a dynamic set of participants. The transaction is successfully completed, if the delegated task is accomplished. Special transaction mechanism designed for handling failures has the following properties.

1. Failed services may be replaced by other services during task realization.
2. The general plan may be changed.
3. The transaction ends either after successful completion of the task, or inability to complete the task, or cancellation of the task.

The classic meaning of the term *transaction* in Information Technology goes back to the ACID properties of modifying a database. Long-running transactions avoid locks on non-local resources, use compensations to handle failures, potentially aggregate smaller ACID transactions (also referred to as atomic transactions), and use a coordinator to complete or abort the transaction. In contrast to rollback in ACID transactions, a compensation restores the original state or an equivalent one, and it is domain-specific, e.g. for a failure when transporting a cargo by one robot, a compensation may be done by arranging another robot that can continue the transport to the destination, and charging (as a penalty) the owner of the first robot for the delay.

In distributed systems, a communication protocol specifies the format of messages exchanged between two or more communicating parties, message order, and the actions taken when a message is sent or received. Based on the OASIS Web Services Transaction (WS-TX) standards, a transaction protocol, called Failure Recovery Protocol (FRP, for short), is proposed for multi-robot systems. FRP defines states of services, and types of messages exchange between Task Manager and services, see Fig. 2. The messages are sent as SOAP 1.2 envelopes, and WS-Addressing specification is used. The message format consists of the header and

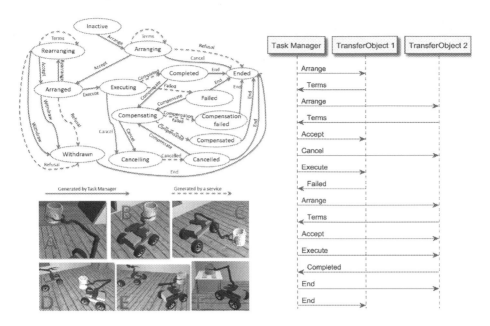

**Fig. 2.** Transaction protocol state transition diagram (top-left). "Moving a jar" scenario (bottom-left). Sequence of transaction messages in a transportation task with failure (right)

the body. The header includes information about the sender, the recipient, the message type, the message and session identifiers, and the version of the protocol. The body contains data specific to the message type, e.g. input data, output data, precondition, effect, or failure description. All necessary data required for task execution and control are transmitted in the messages of the transaction protocol. FRP allows TM to initialize particular phases of service invocation, monitor their progress, and perform additional actions, e.g. compensation. TM initializes the service execution by sending the required input data to the SM of the service. A service is invoked in accordance with the agreement made in the arrangement phase, and sends messages (via its SM and according to the protocol) to notify TM about the status of the performance of the delegated task. After successful execution, SM sends to TM the confirmation of subtask completion, e.g. changing situation in the environment to the required one. TM can also stop the service execution before its completion. This may be caused by the task cancellation by the client, a failure during execution of other services in the plan (that cannot be replaced), or by changes in the environment making the current plan infeasible. Robot may not be able to successfully complete a task. In this case, its SM notifies TM by sending a detailed description of the problem. On this basis, TM can take appropriate actions. If SM is not able to send such information, TM must invoke appropriate cognitive service (a patrolling robot, if available) to recognize the situation resulting from the failure. Compensation is performed either after a cancellation of a subtask execution by a service, or after the occurrence of a failure that interrupts the execution. It is designed to restore the original state of the environment before the execution. Since restoring that situation is sometimes impossible, the compensation may change the situation resulting from the failure to a situation from which the task realization can be continued. Note that even for simple transportation tasks (that seem to be simple) a universal failure recovery mechanism and corresponding compensations are not easy to design and implement. A concrete plan should contain predefined procedures for failure handling and compensations. For an interesting approach and an extensive recent overview on the failure handling and recovery in robotic systems, see Hanheide et al. [22].

# 7    Experiments Verifying SO-MRS

SO-MRS architecture was implemented twice. The first implementation was done within the framework of Robo-enT project (2005–2008) with mobile robots Pioneer 3 (P3-DX).

The Autero system (the RobREx project (2012–2015)) is the second implementation of revised and extended SO-MRS architecture with new version of the ontology and new protocols; see http://www.robrex.ipipan.eu/about.php?lang=en for the experiments. The system has been tested in a universal simulation environment implemented in Unity 3D. The class of tasks that can be accomplished in a real environment is always limited by the number and capabilities of available devices (robots). From the point of view of the proposed information technology (the architecture, ontology and protocols), the fact that the test environment is simulated is irrelevant. The simulation environment is generated *automatically (!)* from the contents of Repository. Service Managers are implemented as independent components that communicate with robots in the simulation environment via TCP/IP protocol. The following simple scenarios serve to illustrate the protocols.

**Scenario 1a - Moving a Jar from a Cupboard to a Platform.** The task was realized by a single *TransferObject* service on a mobile robot with a gripper. The task is defined as the precondition *Jar002 isOn ?Shelf*, and the effect *Jar002 isOn Platform001*. In the arrangement phase, precondition and effect of the task are sent in an *Arrange* message to the Service Managers that can provide the *TransferObject* service. Two services of this type are registered in the system, so that, two Service Managers (representing these services) receive the same query. Service Managers respond with *Terms* messages, each of them contains a commitment. Additional service attributes (maximum service execution time, and price) are also specified. Service 2 has a shorter execution time whereas service 1 requests much lower price. So that, service 1 is selected for the task. The SM of service 1 is notified by an *Accept* message, whereas the SM of service 2 receives a *Cancel* message. The precondition is sent within an *Execute* message initializing execution phase. After receiving this message, the Service Manager starts the task execution by moving the robot closer to the cabinet so that the object to be transported is within the range of the robot gripper. Then, the object is grabbed, the gripper is set to the transport position, and the robot approaches the platform on which the jar is put down. Then, SM sends a *Completed* message containing the description of the resulting situation. In this scenario, one service is needed for the task, so that, after the successful service execution, the task is considered as completed and transaction can be ended. The Task Manager does this by sending an *End* message to the Service Manager.

**Scenario 1b.** Failures might occur during the transportation, e.g. the robot drive was out of order. In such a situation, the robot has a control unit that can communicate with other system components. It also has an active gripper. Hence, it puts the transported object to the ground, and sends (via its SM) a *Failed* message to the Task Manager containing information about the location of the jar (i.e. the formula `Jar002.PositionX = 12.5 AND Jar002.PositionY = 1.3 AND Jar002.PositionZ = 7`). This allows the Task Manager to take an action in order to complete the task. In this scenario there is another service of the same ( *TransferObject*) type available. So that, TM arranges this service by passing, in the precondition, the situation (the new position of the jar) received from the damaged robot. The second service is executed, i.e. the operative robot goes to the position, picks up the jar, moves it to the destined position, and puts the jar on the platform. Screen shots of Fig. 2 show the following steps: A – robot 1 approaches and grips the jar. B – robot 1 transports the jar. C – a failure; the drive of robot 1 is out of order. D – robot 2 approaches the jar and grips it. E – robot 2 transports the jar. F – robot 2 puts the jar on the target platform. Figure 2 also shows the complete FRP protocol message exchange sequence while performing the task in Scenario 1b. Failed *TransferObject 1* service does not participate in the re-arrangement process. The second *Arrange* message is sent only to *TransferObject 2* service. The *End* message is sent to both services, indicating the end of the transaction. More complex tasks (with failures during execution) were also tested, see http://www.robrex.ipipan.eu/about.php?lang=en for video of the experiments.

## 8   Conclusion

The SO-MRS architecture is a proposal of a new information technology consisting of a generic environment representation (upper ontology), specification of the system components, and generic protocols for realizing the system functionality, i.e. automatic accomplishing of complex tasks, along with a protocol for failure handling and recovery. Since our approach is based on generic protocols, it should scale for large MRS. The next steps of the development of the architecture are: incorporating humans (by enriching the ontology) to inter-operate with robots, implementing new intelligent devices and new sophisticated scenarios, and applying performance metrics.

# References

1. Di Ciccio, C., Mecella, M., Caruso, M., Forte, V., Iacomussi, E., Rasch, K., Querzoni, L., Santucci, G., Tino, G.: The homes of tomorrow: service composition and advanced user interfaces. EAI Endorsed Trans. Ambient Syst. **1**(1) (2011)
2. Helal, S., Mann, W., El-Zabadani, H., King, J., Kaddoura, Y., Jansen, E.: The gator tech smart house: a programmable pervasive space. Computer **38**(3), 50–60 (2005)
3. Khaldi, B., Cherif, F.: An overview of swarm robotics: swarm intelligence applied to multi-robotics. Int. J. Comput. Appl. **126**(2) (2015)
4. Zhang, Y., Parker, L.E.: IQ-ASyMTRe: forming executable coalitions for tightly coupled multirobot tasks. IEEE Trans. Robot. **29**(2), 400–416 (2013)
5. Simmons, R., Singh, S., Hershberger, D., Ramos, J., Smith, T.: First results in the coordination of heterogeneous robots for large-scale assembly. In: Rus, D., Singh, S. (eds.) Experimental Robotics VII, vol. 271, pp. 323–332. Springer, Heidelberg (2001). https://doi.org/10.1007/3-540-45118-8_33
6. de Oliveira, L.B.R.: Architectural design of service-oriented robotic systems. Ph.D. thesis, Université de Bretagne Sud (2015)
7. Parker, L.E.: Current research in multirobot systems. Artif. Life Robot. **7**(1–2), 1–5 (2003)
8. Gerkey, B., Vaughan, R.T., Howard, A.: The player/stage project: tools for multi-robot and distributed sensor systems. In: Proceedings of the 11th International Conference on Advanced Robotics, vol. 1, pp. 317–323 (2003)
9. Kramer, J., Magee, J.: Self-managed systems: an architectural challenge. In: Future of Software Engineering, 2007. FOSE 2007, pp. 259–268. IEEE (2007)
10. Jung, D., Zelinsky, A.: Grounded symbolic communication between heterogeneous cooperating robots. Auton. Robots **8**(3), 269–292 (2000)
11. Hugues, L.: Collective grounded representations for robots. In: Parker, L.E., Bekey, G., Barhen, J. (eds.) Distributed autonomous robotic systems 4, pp. 79–88. Springer, Tokyo (2000). https://doi.org/10.1007/978-4-431-67919-6_8
12. Zhong, C., DeLoach, S.A.: Runtime models for automatic reorganization of multi-robot systems. In: Proceedings of the 6th International Symposium on Software Engineering for Adaptive and Self-Managing Systems, pp. 20–29. ACM (2011)
13. Chitic, S.-G., Ponge, J., Simonin, O.: Are middlewares ready for multi-robots systems? In: Brugali, D., Broenink, J.F., Kroeger, T., MacDonald, B.A. (eds.) SIMPAR 2014. LNCS (LNAI), vol. 8810, pp. 279–290. Springer, Cham (2014). https://doi.org/10.1007/978-3-319-11900-7_24
14. Thrun, S., et al.: Robotic mapping: a survey. Explor. Artif. Intell. New Millennium **1**, 1–35 (2002)
15. Kuipers, B.: The spatial semantic hierarchy. Artif. Intell. **119**(1), 191–233 (2000)
16. Vasudevan, S., Gächter, S., Nguyen, V., Siegwart, R.: Cognitive maps for mobile robots - an object based approach. Robot. Auton. Syst. **55**(5), 359–371 (2007)
17. Anguelov, D., Biswas, R., Koller, D., Limketkai, B., Thrun, S.: Learning hierarchical object maps of non-stationary environments with mobile robots. In: Proceedings of the Eighteenth Conference on Uncertainty in Artificial Intelligence, pp. 10–17. Morgan Kaufmann Publishers Inc. (2002)
18. Pronobis, A., Jensfelt, P.: Large-scale semantic mapping and reasoning with heterogeneous modalities. In: 2012 IEEE International Conference on Robotics and Automation (ICRA), pp. 3515–3522. IEEE (2012)

19. Kostavelis, I., Gasteratos, A.: Semantic mapping for mobile robotics tasks: a survey. Robot. Auton. Syst. **66**, 86–103 (2015)
20. Tenorth, M., Beetz, M.: KnowRob - a knowledge processing infrastructure for cognition-enabled robots. Part 1: the KnowRob system. Int. J. Robot. Res. (IJRR) **32**(5), 566–590 (2013)
21. Ambroszkiewicz, S.: Entish: a language for describing data processing in open distributed systems. Fundam. Informaticae **60**(1–4), 41–66 (2004)
22. Hanheide, M., Göbelbecker, M., Horn, G.S., Pronobis, A., Sjöö, K., Aydemir, A., Jensfelt, P., Gretton, C., Dearden, R., Janicek, M., et al.: Robot task planning and explanation in open and uncertain worlds. Artif. Intell. **247**, 119–150 (2015)

# Robotics Applications

# ROS Integration for Miniature Mobile Robots

Andrew West$^{(\boxtimes)}$, Farshad Arvin, Horatio Martin,
Simon Watson, and Barry Lennox

Robotics for Extreme Environments Lab (REEL), School of Electrical and Electronic
Engineering, The University of Manchester, Manchester M13 9PL, UK
andrew.west@manchester.ac.uk

**Abstract.** In this paper, the feasibility of using the Robot Operating
System (ROS) for controlling miniature size mobile robots was investigated. Open-source and low-cost robots employ limited processors, hence
running ROS on such systems is very challenging. Therefore, we provide
a compact, low-cost, and open-source module enabling miniature multi
and swarm robotic systems of different sizes and types to be integrated
with ROS. To investigate the feasibility of the proposed system, several
experiments using a single robot and multi-robots were implemented and
the results demonstrated the amenability of the system to be integrated
in low-cost and open-source miniature size mobile robots.

**Keywords:** Robot Operating System (ROS) · Mobile robots
Swarm robotics · Communication

## 1 Introduction

The Robot Operating System [1] (ROS) is an open-source, Linux based framework which allows for the rapid implementation of hardware and software, particularly in research settings. Hardware includes individual components such as
LiDAR units and actuators, up to complete integrated platforms, and the software available extends from joint transformations [2] and robot visualisation [3]
to Simultaneous Localisation And Mapping (SLAM) and path planning [4].

At its core, it consists of a publish/subscribe model for communication, where
'topics' made up of predefined message structures can be communicated between
multiple 'nodes' in the network. These topics, for example 'odometry', can be
accessed by any nodes in the network, allowing for easy scalability of publishers
and subscribers. Hardware and software acting as publishers and subscribers
can readily communicate with other components in the system in a well defined
manner. A more detailed description of the communications protocol can be
found in [1].

For many ROS has become the *de facto* choice when designing and operating robots, thanks in part to its extensive functionality and ubiquity through
freely available packages. For swarm robotics [5], ROS already contains software

© Springer International Publishing AG, part of Springer Nature 2018
M. Giuliani et al. (Eds.): TAROS 2018, LNAI 10965, pp. 345–356, 2018.
https://doi.org/10.1007/978-3-319-96728-8_29

packages for simulation, for example 'micros_swarm_framework' [6], as well as interfaces to other simulation and control software such as ARGoS [7], ASEBA [8] and Webots [9], however, native ROS compatible swarm hardware is incredibly limited.

Common examples of swarm robots including the E-puck [10], Khepera [11], Alice [12], Jasmine [13], Colias [14], Swarmbot [15], PSI [16], Marxbot [17], eSwarBot [18], Kilobot [19], and S-bot [20] have very limited to no native hardware ROS implementation, and any custom packages that do exist are out of date. In nearly all cases researchers are unable to readily leverage the functionality of ROS at the hardware level. As a consequence they may have to spend unnecessary time and energy recreating solutions that already exist or using extra software via a ROS bridge.

In this study, we introduce a methodology for enabling small microcontroller based robots to interact with the ROS framework wirelessly without a computer on-board, to allow development, control and monitoring in conjunction with ROS using native packages. This compatibility from hardware to software can help bridge the gap between simulation and experiment in swarm robotics.

## 2   ROS for Miniature Mobile Robots

The Robot Operating System requires a master device, typically a laptop or desktop PC, to act as a central server in the network. Other devices running ROS are capable of connecting to the master, upon which they are then able to send and receive messages on any established topics with each other, including the master.

Unfortunately, this requirement to have the ROS core node running on slave systems, as well as the master, limits its implementation in small robots to those running small form factor laptops, or single board computers such as the Intel NUC, Raspberry Pi 3, or the ODROID-XU4 which are all capable of running the ROS core node as master or slave. By the standards of very small swarm robots, these devices can be too large, heavy, and power hungry to be utilised.

One method to circumvent this is to enable less powerful microcontrollers to be able to publish and subscribe to ROS topics, without the need for a full instance of ROS. The `rosserial` family of nodes allow for small microcontroller-based platforms such as Arduino to communicate with a specialised node running on a separate fully fledged computer which handles publishing and subscribing to ROS topics with the rest of the network on its behalf. The `roserial` nodes convert data from normal structured XMLRPC protocol handled by TCP natively in ROS [1] to serialised data out to the microcontroller, this node also deserialises data from the microcontroller back into the correct message structures to be sent around the conventional ROS network.

This functionality of `rosserial` is very effective when hardware needs to be integrated into ROS that is not already ROS compatible. The microcontroller acts as a bridge to the hardware and `rosserial` then acts as another bridge from the microcontroller to ROS. Figure 1 demonstrates how nodes across the

ROS network can communicate with microcontrollers allowing for interaction of non-ROS compatible hardware. The drawback to this solution is that the micro-controller is typically connected physically to a computer system running ROS via USB and ultimately the non-ROS compatible robot hardware still requires a computer on-board [21], a solution that is not suitable for very small robots.

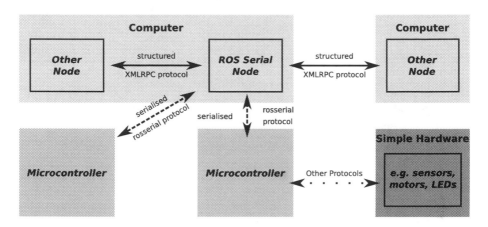

**Fig. 1.** Diagram of rosserial interaction between computer running ROS and multiple microcontrollers.

Through the use of a modified node handler hardware (as is made possible in the `rosserial` packages), making use of a WiFi connection instead of a wired USB connection, each robot can independently connect to a remote computer running the ROS core node over a network, and begin automatically publishing and subscribing to topics without a computer running ROS on-board.

This remote computer runs a `rosserial_server socket_node` node to enable multiple connections from many microcontroller devices, allowing for scalability to multiple robots. The microcontroller based robots can now communicate with each other directly whilst the remote computer handles communications. The published and subscribed messages can be directed to individual microcontrollers, resulting in robot to robot communication via the remote computer running the relevant nodes. Furthermore, it is also possible for other nodes on the remote machine or other machines in the network to publish and subscribe to these messages. This allows for robots to receive centralised commands if desired, but more importantly it can be used for debugging, data logging and integrating other software and hardware quickly by leveraging the existing functionality of ROS.

The use of the native `rosserial` packages that are supported as part of the basic ROS install means that users can easily get a functioning and up-to-date version of the package. This removes the need for the Authors, or other contributors to write their own custom packages, and more importantly keep it up to date.

## 3    Hardware Description

A ROS module has been developed to investigate the feasibility of the proposed system. The module was attached to a low-cost open-source mobile robot, *Mona*. In this section, the design of the Mona robot and the developed ROS module are presented.

### 3.1    Mona Robot

Mona (see Fig. 2) is a low-cost and open-source robotic platform [22], which has been developed at the University of Manchester for education and research purposes. Mona uses the Arduino platform for programming, hence it is easily possible to add available modules and libraries which have been developed as part of the Arduino project.

The robot deploys an AVR microcontroller (ATMEGA328) as the main processor. It uses five short-range infra-red (IR) proximity sensors ($2 \pm 0.5$ cm) for obstacle and neighbour robot detection [23]. Mona has two micro gear-head motors with encoders. The motors' rotational speeds are controlled by pulse-width modulation (PWM) approach. The pulse-width, is a one byte command (between 0 and 255) which changes the length of pulse resulting in changing rotational speed of the motors. The macroscopic model of the utilised DC motors that have been used in Mona was presented in [24].

**Fig. 2.** (Left) Mona platform; Arduino based (ATMEGA328 Mini/Pro) robot including five IR proximity sensors, 3.7 V Li-Po battery, micro gear-head motors with encoders, and USB interface. (Right) Mona robot equipped with a ROS-WiFi module to be controlled/monitored using ROS commands.

Mona uses a 3.7 V, 350 mAh Li-Po battery which provides approximately 2 h of autonomy. To increase the robot's autonomy time, an inductive charging system providing a continues power source for long term autonomy of multi robotic systems have been proposed [25]. Since Mona has been developed to support various modules, it supports three serial communication standards including: UART, I$^2$C, and SPI. In this work, ROS module communicates with Mona using Arduino's native serial UART at the baud rate of 9600 bps.

## 3.2  ROS Extension Module

The add-on Mona ROS module is a board manufactured at the University of Manchester accommodating a Teensy 3.2 microcontroller, programmed using the Arduino IDE, and an ATWINC1500 WiFi solution from Microchip. The module mounts on top of Mona via supports, with header pins making connection to the Mona battery for power, and a serial connection for inter-board communications as shown in Fig. 2. The perpetual charging option for the Mona [25] mitigates the extra power draw from the microcontroller and low power WiFi chip, however, the ROS extension module also has the capability to carry extra batteries, therefore maintaining or increasing the run time of the Mona despite the extra power consumption.

Each module has a user specified hardware identification number from 0 to 15 in this feasibility study, which is expandable up to 250 robots using physical address lines. In theory, the actual number of robots is limited by the bandwidth of the network, as robots are added more connections are made which take up capacity, however, a limit was not observed in this study using a consumer grade wireless network router.

The use of `rosserial` as a way of including microcontroller-based platforms such as Arduino into ROS can introduce unacceptable overheads in terms of computation time and memory requirements when using standard Arduino hardware, and has lead others to implement their own alternative protocols [21]. A Teensy 3.2 by comparison allows for faster clock speeds (6 times faster than an Arduino Uno) and larger memory (8 times the flash memory and 32 times the RAM), enabling the use of `rosserial` directly whilst remaining low power, low size and low mass. This use of native ROS packages ensures better long term support, but also lowers the barrier to entry for new users as they often include well written documentation and tutorials, as well as community generated support and materials. This is in stark contrast to many available non-native packages which typically do not have the same wealth of support.

In keeping with the accessible and user-friendly design of Mona, the ROS module is programmed entirely using the Arduino IDE, using standard freely available libraries for basic functionality and to include ROS functionality. This module can easily be programmed to remove or add extra ROS functionality, including publishers, subscribers and services.

The serial connection between the ROS module and the robot base allows for commands to be sent and data to be retrieved from a Mona (see Fig. 3). The ROS module initiates a subscriber to a topic with a name encoded with the hardware defined ID of the ROS module. In this study, the topic for Mona robots consists of a 'Twist' message comprised of linear velocity components for $x, y, z$ in ms$^{-1}$ and angular velocity for roll, pitch, yaw in rad.s$^{-1}$ for control of individual Mona robots motion (only x and yaw are required for Mona). The module is also capable of creating a publisher, with a topic also encoded with the ID of the module, for reporting for example the odometry and status of the Mona robot it is attached to.

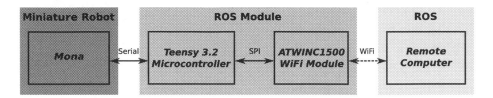

**Fig. 3.** Overview of the ROS module design and interface between the miniature robot and ROS running on remote computer.

The ROS module then sends and receives data to the computationally inferior Mona at a more manageable rate and data size. The use of a secondary module minimises computational impact of ROS integration, and preserves any embedded swarm behaviour of the Mona robot, whilst offering interaction expected of more sophisticated robots with velocity input, odometry and status output.

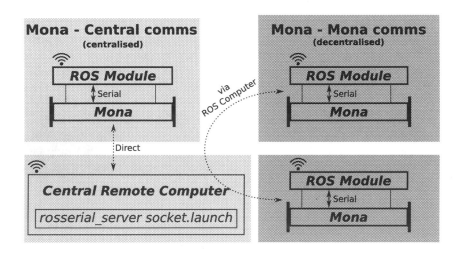

**Fig. 4.** Architecture of the developed ROS system

Figure 4 shows how Mona robot to Mona robot communications are achieved. Topics produced by the ROS modules can be directly published or subscribed to, with messages travelling via the remote computer running a so-called socket server node via `rosserial_server socket.launch`. The remote computer does not necessarily have to remain passive in this configuration, as from this machine commands can be published or subscribed to, either directly or by using a ROS node (see Fig. 4). This optional direct interaction is what enables users to include additional ROS packages and nodes, hardware, visualisation and recording into their research quickly, or use ROS merely as a conduit for inter-robot communications.

The module automatically connects to the network via WiFi, with the network details contained on the Teensy, and then automatically tries to connect to the remote machine, whose IP address is also recorded on the Teensy. The module detects drop outs in either of these connections and will automatically begin to re-establish a connection. The benefit of this behaviour is that the ROS modules have a 'plug-and-play' usability and do not suffer if the required ROS nodes have not yet been initialised or if WiFi drops out. More modules can be quickly added or removed from the network without the rest of the system running into issues. Connection time from power on to connecting to the ROS master is approximately $5 \pm 2$ s.

This methodology can be utilised not just for robots, but for any device that can communicate with the ROS module board through serial or $I^2C$, enabling sensors or other hardware to directly publish and subscribe to ROS topics, without the need for a fully fledged computer.

## 4    Experiments

Several experiments have been conducted to investigate the feasibility of the proposed ROS Module to control miniature size simple mobile robots. From the remote PC hundreds of messages were successively published to a topic subscribed to by the ROS Module with a queue size of 1. Upon receiving a message, the ROS Module then undertakes any actions required and publishes a message on a different topic. Both inbound and outbound messages were identified using a incrementing integer counter somewhere in the message structure.

If an inbound message is missed by the ROS Module, for example if it is engaged in computation, the incrementing counters of the inbound and outbound messages become mismatched. The mismatch in counters after multiple inbound messages were assessed to measure the fraction of missed messages. The message success rate $m_s = 1 - N_{\text{missed}}/N_{\text{total}}$ was used as a metric of the system performance, where $N$ is number of messages. The frequency of message publication, $f_p$, was varied to assess at what frequencies the ROS Module is safe to work at.

The standalone ROS Module was assessed, along with its performance in conjunction with a single Mona robot and performance of all systems when operating with multiple ROS Module and Mona robot pairs in more swarm like condition.

## 5   Results

This section presents the obtained results from experiments with different configurations: (i) ROS Module only, (ii) ROS Module communicating with Mona robot, and (iii) multi ROS Module Mona robot pairs in unison.

### 5.1   ROS Module Only

From the remote pc 1000 ROS Int16 messages were published at a rate between 1–250 Hz with the value of the Int16 data equal to an incremental counter (0–999), this was repeated 10 times. Upon receiving the message the ROS module published a separate ROS Int16 message with the difference between an internal incrementing counter and the value in the inbound message. If every message is handled correctly the value the ROS module publishes is constant, for every missed message there is a difference of 1 between the counters.

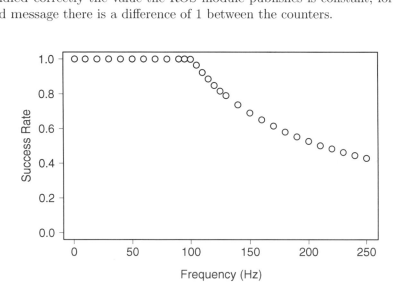

**Fig. 5.** Ratio of successfully received messages at varying frequencies.

Figure 5 shows how incoming published messages get missed by the ROS Module at $f_p > 100$ Hz. This was repeated using ROS Twist messages, which are larger than simple Int16 messages, and no differences in $m_s$ across the publishing frequencies was observed, suggesting that the size of the ROS message is not a dominant factor in limiting message success rate. This upper limit can be attributed to the various checks and overheads incurred when using rosserial. The required 'spinOnce()' command which carries out these checks in the main loop on the ROS Module microcontroller was timed, and it was observed that every 2.5 s the time required to execute this function increases from 0.2 ms to approximately 10 ms. The 10 ms timing holding up the ROS module would be an equivalent maximum message handling rate of approximately 100 Hz. This periodic extended execution time of the necessary ROS overheads may be the cause in an apparent throttling to <100 Hz.

## 5.2   Single Robot

In this set of experiments, the remote computer running a ROS core node and `rosserial_server socket_node` established connection with one ROS Module connected to a Mona robot and sent 500 Twist messages to the robot. The Mona robot then replies with one byte upon receiving data back to the ROS Module, the number of messages which do not result in a reply from the Mona robot are recorded. The experiment was repeated 10 times and the average results shown in Fig. 6. It is apparent that the maximum message frequency is decreased when the Mona robot is attached to the ROS module, with a maximum $f_p$ which can consistently maintain total message success at roughly 50 Hz.

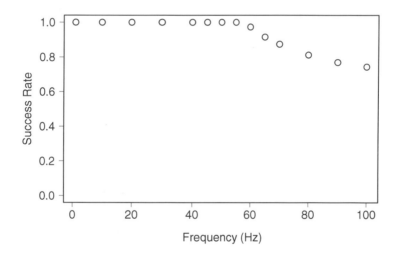

**Fig. 6.** Message success rate for varying publishing frequency when ROS Module integrated with Mona.

The reduction in maximum $f_p$ may be due to the code native to the Mona robot. The Mona uses various checks to ensure behaviours such as obstacle avoidance are executed properly, the resulting total time of all this code is around 20 ms. This equates to a maximum message handling rate of approximately 50 Hz, in concordance with the maximum frequency the Mona is capable of. Considering a baud rate of 9600 between the ROS Module and the Mona, with the Mona receiving a maximum of $2 \times 64$ bit data (for linear and angular velocity), the resultant rate would be on the order of 75 Hz, greater than what is observed. If the code of the Mona was updated to be more responsive, it may be that the bandwidth of the serial connection could then become the bottleneck.

### 5.3 Multi Robot

In this set of experiments, we tested the proposed ROS integration module using a multiple robot configuration. The method used for a single Mona robot was repeated, whilst increasing the total number of robots on the network subscribing a topic. The ROS Modules have unique IP addresses, and unique publisher topics, however, all modules subscribe to a single topic published at a set rate. Publishing to this topic would result in all active robots recieving a data and acting upon it, mimicking the most demanding network and computational requirements.

The maximum publish rate remained at approximately 50 Hz, though some robots appeared to have slightly better or worse response rate compared to the single unit tested previously, which maintained a 100% success rate to 55 Hz. The variations in the maximum publish frequency of $\pm 4$ Hz between units is due to hardware heterogeneity of Mona robots and the ROS module which were reported in [14, 26, 27]. The similar behaviour regardless of number of robots suggests that there is little to no penalty incurred for operating this many additional robots with ROS modules.

Considering a TCP packet consists of a 20 bytes overhead for the WiFi data connection between the ROS Module at the remote computer, a serialised ROS message to be sent has an additional 8 bytes of overhead, and the actual Twist message data consists of 6 * 64bit values (48 bytes), a total of 76 bytes sent per message. Typical WiFi can handle 0.75 Mbytes/sec, equivalent to 10000 Twist messages per second, meaning that hundreds of Monas with integration modules could send/receive messages at a rate of $\approx$50 Hz. Clearly, for the relatively small number of robots in this study the limit to message rate is dominated by the speed of the ROS module with the overheads associated with using `rosserial` and the Mona Arduino hardware and software. The computational power of the machine running the required ROS nodes can be disregarded as a bottleneck, as it is orders of magnitude faster than the robot mounted components. To allow for a margin of safety in future research, a frequency of $f_p \leq 50$ Hz is preferable for this current implementation of the ROS module, network, Mona robot, and with this many ROS module-Mona pairs active at one time.

The Mona robots have on-board their own fast routines for behaviours, feedback and control. For most swarm applications the ROS integration would most likely operate on a slower 10 Hz rate for monitoring and high level control, as ROS inherently does not support real-time control. In contrast, the 50 Hz achieved in this feasibility study is more than adequate for this use case.

## 6   Conclusion

In this paper, a low-cost system ($<$£30) for controlling open-source miniature robots using ROS was proposed. The system includes a Teensy 3.2 and a WiFi module which were attached to an additional board developed at The University of Manchester as an extension module for Mona. The reliability of the system was tested with two different configurations which were frequency of the communication and size of the group for multi and swarm robotic scenarios. The results showed that frequency of $f_p \leq 50$ Hz demonstrates a reliable connection between the Mona robots and the rest of the ROS network. For the future work, decentralised control of a swarm of robots using the developed ROS module will be investigated.

**Acknowledgement.** This work was supported by the EPSRC Projects (Project No. EP/P01366X/1 and Project No. EP/P018505/1).

# References

1. Quigley, M., et al.: ROS: an open-source robot operating system. In: ICRA Workshop on Open Source Software (2009)
2. Foote, T.: TF: the transform library. In: 2013 IEEE International Conference on Technologies for Practical Robot Applications (TePRA). Open-Source Software Workshop, pp. 1–6, April 2013
3. Kam, H.R., Lee, S.H., Park, T., Kim, C.H.: RViz: a toolkit for real domain data visualization. Telecommun. Syst. **60**(2), 337–345 (2015)
4. Guimarães, R.L., de Oliveira, A.S., Fabro, J.A., Becker, T., Brenner, V.A.: ROS navigation: concepts and tutorial. In: Koubaa, A. (ed.) Robot Operating System (ROS). SCI, vol. 625, pp. 121–160. Springer, Cham (2016). https://doi.org/10.1007/978-3-319-26054-9_6
5. Hamann, H.: Swarm Robotics: A Formal Approach. Springer, Heidelberg (2018). https://doi.org/10.1007/978-3-319-74528-2
6. Pinciroli, C., Beltrame, G.: Buzz: an extensible programming language for heterogeneous swarm robotics. In: 2016 IEEE/RSJ International Conference on Intelligent Robots and Systems (IROS). IEEE, October 2016
7. Pinciroli, C., et al.: ARGoS: a modular, parallel, multi-engine simulator for multi-robot systems. Swarm Intell. **6**(4), 271–295 (2012)
8. Magnenat, S., Rétornaz, P., Bonani, M., Longchamp, V., Mondada, F.: ASEBA: a modular architecture for event-based control of complex robots. IEEE/ASME Trans. Mechatron. **16**(2), 321–329 (2011)
9. Michel, O.: Cyberbotics ltd. Webots$^{TM}$: professional mobile robot simulation. Int. J. Adv. Robot. Syst. **1**(1), 5 (2004)
10. Mondada, F., et al.: The e-puck, a robot designed for education in engineering. In: Proceedings of the 9th Conference on Autonomous Robot Systems and Competition, vol. 1, pp. 59–65 (2009)
11. Mondada, F., Franzi, E., Ienne, P.: Mobile robot miniaturisation: a tool for investigation in control algorithms. In: Yoshikawa, T., Miyazaki, F. (eds.) Experimental Robotics III. LNCIS, vol. 200, pp. 501–513. Springer, Heidelberg (1994). https://doi.org/10.1007/BFb0027617
12. Caprari, G., Siegwart, R.: Mobile micro-robots ready to use: Alice. In: IEEE/RSJ International Conference on Intelligent Robots and Systems, pp. 3295–3300. IEEE (2005)
13. Kernbach, S., Thenius, R., Kernbach, O., Schmickl, T.: Re-embodiment of honeybee aggregation behavior in an artificial micro-robotic system. Adapt. Behav. **17**(3), 237–259 (2009)
14. Arvin, F., Murray, J., Zhang, C., Yue, S.: Colias: an autonomous micro robot for swarm robotic applications. Int. J. Adv. Robot. Syst. **11**(113), 1–10 (2014)

15. Mondada, F., Pettinaro, G.C., Guignard, A., Kwee, I.W., Floreano, D., Deneubourg, J.L., Nolfi, S., Gambardella, L.M., Dorigo, M.: Swarm-bot: a new distributed robotic concept. Auton. Robots **17**(2–3), 193–221 (2004)
16. Hilder, J., Horsfield, A., Millard, A.G., Timmis, J.: The psi swarm: a low-cost robotics platform and its use in an education setting. In: Alboul, L., Damian, D., Aitken, J.M.M. (eds.) TAROS 2016. LNCS (LNAI), vol. 9716, pp. 158–164. Springer, Cham (2016). https://doi.org/10.1007/978-3-319-40379-3_16
17. Bonani, M., et al.: The marxbot, a miniature mobile robot opening new perspectives for the collective-robotic research. In: IEEE/RSJ International Conference on Intelligent Robots and Systems (IROS), pp. 4187–4193. IEEE (2010)
18. Fernandes, A., Couceiro, M.S., Portugal, D., Santos, J.M., Rocha, R.P.: Ad hoc communication in teams of mobile robots using zigbee technology. Comput. Appl. Eng. Educ. **23**(5), 733–745 (2015)
19. Rubenstein, M., Ahler, C., Hoff, N., Cabrera, A., Nagpal, R.: Kilobot: a low cost robot with scalable operations designed for collective behaviors. Robot. Auton. Syst. **62**(7), 966–975 (2014)
20. McLurkin, J., Smith, J., Frankel, J., Sotkowitz, D., Blau, D., Schmidt, B.: Speaking swarmish: human-robot interface design for large swarms of autonomous mobile robots. In: AAAI Spring Symposium (2006)
21. Araújo, A., Portugal, D., Couceiro, M.S., Rocha, R.P.: Integrating arduino-based educational mobile robots in ROS. J. Intell. Robot. Syst. **77**(2), 281–298 (2014)
22. Arvin, F., Espinosa, J., Bird, B., West, A., Watson, S., Lennox, B.: Mona: an affordable open-source mobile robot for education and research. J. Intell. Robot. Syst. (2018)
23. Arvin, F., Samsudin, K., Ramli, A.R.: Development of IR-based short-range communication techniques for swarm robot applications. Adv. Electr. Comput. Eng. **10**(4), 61–68 (2010)
24. Arvin, F., Bekravi, M.: Encoderless position estimation and error correction techniques for miniature mobile robots. Turk. J. Electr. Eng. Comput. Sci. **21**, 1631–1645 (2013)
25. Arvin, F., Watson, S., Turgut, A.E., Espinosa, J., Krajník, T., Lennox, B.: Perpetual robot swarm: long-term autonomy of mobile robots using on-the-fly inductive charging. J. Intell. Robot. Syst. (2017)
26. Arvin, F., Turgut, A.E., Krajník, T., Yue, S.: Investigation of cue-based aggregation in static and dynamic environments with a mobile robot swarm. Adapt. Behav. **24**(2), 102–118 (2016)
27. Schmickl, T., et al.: Get in touch: cooperative decision making based on robot-to-robot collisions. Auton. Agents Multi-Agent Syst. **18**(1), 133–155 (2009)

# Feature and Performance Comparison of the V-REP, Gazebo and ARGoS Robot Simulators

Lenka Pitonakova$^{(\boxtimes)}$, Manuel Giuliani, Anthony Pipe, and Alan Winfield

Bristol Robotics Laboratory, University of the West of England, Bristol, Bristol, UK
contact@lenkaspace.net

**Abstract.** In this paper, the characteristics and performance of three open-source simulators for robotics, V-REP, Gazebo and ARGoS, are thoroughly analysed and compared. While they all allow for programming in C++, they also represent clear alternatives when it comes to the trade-off between complexity and performance. Attention is given to their built-in features, robot libraries, programming methods and the usability of their user interfaces. Benchmark test results are reported in order to identify how well the simulators can cope with environments of varying complexity. The richness of features of V-REP and the strong performance of Gazebo and ARGoS in complex scenes are highlighted. Various usability issues of Gazebo are also noted.

## 1 Introduction

Simulation is a useful scientific tool that can complements more traditional experimental approaches [1]. Choosing a suitable simulator is important, as different simulation environments offer different performance, model detail and built-in features, all of which may affect the success and the merit of a simulation-based study. In this paper, features and performance of three open-source simulators for robotics, V-REP [2], Gazebo [3] and ARGoS [4], are thoroughly analysed and suggestions about what types of projects they are suitable for are provided. All of the three simulators allow for programming in C++, allowing us to make reasonable comparisons between their features and performance. At the same time, the simulators represent clear alternatives when it comes to the trade-off between simulation complexity and speed.

Other simulators, such as Matlab [5,6], Webots [5,6], Player/Stage [5,7–9], Gazebo [5,7–9], USARSim [5,8,9], SARGE [8] and TeamBots [7], have previously been described and compared. While some comparisons were rather informal [6,8], others involved ranking simulators based on specific evaluation criteria. For example, in [9], programming language support, documentation, user interface and debugging techniques of simulators were evaluated. In [5], the evaluation criteria included simulator physical fidelity, functional fidelity, ease of development and cost.

To the best of our knowledge, no formal comparison between V-REP, ARGoS and Gazebo has been conducted before. Inspired by [5,7,9], it is therefore our

M. Giuliani et al. (Eds.): TAROS 2018, LNAI 10965, pp. 357–368, 2018.
https://doi.org/10.1007/978-3-319-96728-8_30

aim to provide a ranked evaluation of the simulator characteristics in Sect. 2. Moreover, similarly as in [9], the simulator performance is evaluated on a set of benchmark experiments in Sect. 3.

## 2    Simulator Characteristics

All tests were performed in the 64-bit Ubuntu Linux 16.04 environment running on a computer with 4x Intel Core i7 2.2 Gz processor, 8 GB RAM and Intel HD Graphics 6000 graphics card. The built-in capabilities, model library, programming methods and user interface of the simulators are compared in Table 1.

**Table 1.** Simulator characteristics ranked as rich (green), neutral (white) and poor (red). Ranking was performed by considering characteristics in the same row (i.e., of the same type) relatively to each other.

| V-REP | Gazebo | ARGoS |
|---|---|---|
| Available for MacOS, Linux and Windows. Binary packages are available for all platforms. | Available for MacOS, Linux and Windows. A binary package is only available for Linux Debian. Installed via the command line using third-party package managers on other systems. | Available for MacOS and Linux. Binary packages are available for Linux. On MacOS, ARGoS is installed via the command line using a third-party package manager. |
| **Built-in capabilities** | | |
| Default **physics engines** include: Bullet 2.78, Bullet 2.83, ODE, Vortex and Newton. | Only the ODE **physics engine** is available by default. It is, however, possible to build Gazebo from source with a different physics engine. | A 2D and a 3D custombuilt **physics engines** with very limited capabilities are available by default. |
| Includes a code and a scene **editor**. | Includes a code and a scene **editor**. | Includes a Lua script editor but no scene **editor**. |
| **Meshes** can be **manipulated** (e.g., cut) by robots in real time. | No **mesh manipulation** is available. | No **mesh manipulation** is available. |
| **Scene objects** can be fully **interacted** with (e.g., moved or added) by the user during simulation. The world returns to its original state when the simulation is reset. | **Scene objects** can be fully **interacted** with (e.g., moved or added) by the user during simulation. The world does not return to its original state when the simulation is reset. | **Scene objects** can be **moved** by the user during simulation. |

(continued)

**Table 1.** (*continued*)

| | | |
|---|---|---|
| **Outputs** include video, custom data plots and text files. | **Outputs** include simulation log files, video frames as pictures and text files. | **Outputs** include video frames as pictures and text files. |
| Includes particle systems. | No particle systems are available. | No particle systems are available. |
| **Robot and other models** | | |
| Provides a large variety of **robots**, including bipedal, hexapod, wheeled, flying and snake-like robots. Also provides a large number of robot actuators and sensors. | A less diverse library of default **robots**, that mostly includes wheeled and flying robots. Third-party robot models are available, but their documentation is often poor. | A fairly small library of **robots**, only including the e-puck [11], eyebot [13], Kilobot [17], marXbot [12] and Spiri [14] robots. |
| **The default models** are very detailed and therefore appropriate for high-precision simulations. It is possible to simplify the models directly in V-REP. | **The default models** are fairly simple and are therefore more appropriate for computationally complex simulations. | **The default models** are fairly simple and are therefore more appropriate for computationally complex simulations. |
| **Meshes** are **imported** as collections of subcomponents. It is therefore possible manipulate individual parts of an imported model and to change their textures, materials and other properties. | **Meshes** are **imported** as single objects. Models that contain multiple subcomponents have to be assembled in Gazebo from multiple DAE files, each corresponding to one subcomponent. | **Mesh importing** is not available. Object representations are programmed using OpenGL. |
| It is possible to **simplify, split and combine meshes**. This makes it possible to optimise the triangle count of imported models and to manipulate meshes (e.g., to cut them) with robot actuators. | Imported **meshes cannot be changed**. A model therefore has to be optimised in third-party 3D modeling software. This may be difficult during iterative development. | N/A |
| **Programming methods** | | |
| **A scene is saved** in a special V-REP format. All scene editing therefore has to be done using the V-REP interface. | **A scene is saved** as an XML file. This makes it possible to e.g. create a bash script that changes the scene and then runs a simulation. | **A scene is saved** as an XML file. This makes it possible to e.g. create a bash script that changes the scene and then runs a simulation. |

(*continued*)

**Table 1.** (*continued*)

| | | |
|---|---|---|
| There are various options for **programming** functionality, including scripts attached to robots, plug-ins, ROS nodes [10] or separate programs that connect to V-REP via the RemoteAPI. | Functionality can be **programmed** either as compiled C++ plug-ins or as ROS [10] programs. Lack of scripting makes it difficult to run quick tests with ad-hoc solutions. | Robots can be **programmed** either through Lua scripts or in C++. |
| Scripts can be included in robot models and are often used to **describe the models** and their capabilities. | It is difficult to recognise how a third-party robot **model works** or what plug-ins it uses. The plug-in list is only available in the Model Editor. | Some **documentation** of the robots is provided in ARGoS, but most of how a robot works needs to be deducted from code examples. |
| "CustomUI" API, based on QT[15], is used to create **custom interfaces**. Custom UI controllers can be attached to individual robots. For example, it is possible to display a robot's camera output when the robot is clicked on. | **Custom interfaces** can be created as plug-ins by using the default QT API [15]. However, the interfaces can only be attached to the whole scene and not to individual robots. | **Custom interfaces** can be created in C++ by sub-classing an ARGoS API class. The interfaces can be attached to the whole scene or to individual robots. |
| All scripts and **plug-ins provided with the default robot models** and example scenes worked. | Many **plug-ins provided with the default robot models** did not work. Some on-line examples were difficult to run due to a large number of dependencies and differences in ROS versions. | A few **examples are provided** on the ARGoS website, all of which worked. |
| Good API **documentation**, a large library of tutorials and code examples and a large user community are available. Regular **updates** have been provided since 2013. | A fairly comprehensive **documentation**, step-by-step tutorials and a large user community are available. Gazebo is likely to be **supported** in the future, since a development road map is available on the website. | Good **documentation**, but a small user community are available. Development has not been regular. |
| **User interface (UI)** | | |

(*continued*)

**Table 1.** (*continued*)

| | | |
|---|---|---|
| **No freezing issues** with the interface were experienced. | **The interface froze** a number of times and the program, and sometimes the computer, had to be restarted. This occurred, e.g., when editing robot models, starting or stopping the simulation, and in other instances. | **No freezing issues** with the interface were experienced. |
| **All functionality is fairly intuitive** and follows general conventions known from similar applications. | **The UI usability** is relatively low. For example, the top application tool bar sometimes disappears, it is not possible to copy and paste multiple objects, or to save a scene into the same file after making changes to it. | The UI is very limited, but all **functionality is fairly intuitive** and follows general conventions known from similar applications. |
| **The model library** is distributed with V-REP and it is thus always available regardless of Internet connectivity. | **The model library** is not distributed with Gazebo, and it is instead available on-line. On multiple occasions, the library could not be accessed because Gazebo could not connect to its server, even though the computer was connected to the Internet. | **The robot models** are distributed with ARGoS and it is thus always available regardless of Internet connectivity. |
| **The model library** is organised into folders based on model category. User can create their own folders for their own models. | **The model library** is a long list of models and particular model types (e.g., robots) can be difficult to find. | **Different robot types** are natively a part of ARGoS and can be found by querying command-line documentation. |

V-REP offers the largest repertoire of features including, most notably, a scene editor, 3D model importing, mesh manipulation, video recording and an API for remotely connecting to a simulation. Also, its model library is relatively large and well-documented. Gazebo also offers a scene editor and 3D model importing, however, no mesh editing is available and the imported models need to be optimised in third-party software. Gazebo relies on ROS [10] when it comes to remote connectivity. Notably, Gazebo crashed a number of times on our computer system and its interface was generally slow during testing (see details in Table 1). Furthermore, and again only tested on our computer system, some of its example code could not be compiled or did not run properly. Finally, ARGoS offers the smallest amount of features compared to the other two simulators. It has no scene editor and 3D models cannot be imported into it. Also, by comparison, its robot library and documentation are limited.

One advantage of Gazebo and ARGoS over V-REP is the ability to define a scene in a XML file. This is convenient, for example, when multiple experiments with varying parameter values need to be generated and run automatically. On the other hand, a V-REP experiment can only be specified in a V-REP scene file via the V-REP graphical interface. It is therefore difficult to vary experimental parameters, especially when running V-REP from the command line. While V-REP offers up to nine optional command-line arguments that can be supplied to a simulation, a more involved parameter specification would have to be handled, for example, by a plug-in that could parse parameter text files. Such a plug-in is currently not distributed with V-REP.

## 3    Simulator Performance

### 3.1    Methods

There were two types of benchmark test performed with each simulator:

- **The GUI benchmark** involved running a simulation of robots that moved in a straight line and avoided obstacles in real-time. The simulators were run along with their user interfaces. Each simulation took one minute.
- **The headless benchmark** involved running the same simulation as in the GUI benchmark, that lasted five minutes. The simulators were run from the command line without their user interfaces.

There were two types of simulation environment:

- **Small scene**, where robots were put on a large 2D plane.
- **Large scene**, where an industrial building model with approximately 41,6000 vertices was imported into the simulator (Fig. 1a). Since it was not possible to import the model into ARGoS, 5,200 boxes, corresponding to 41,6000 vertices, were randomly placed in the environment (Fig. 1b).

Robot models were selected from a library of models available in each simulator, so that a sensible similarity, in terms of robot geometry and controller capabilities, was achieved (Fig. 2). In ARGoS, a flying instead of a wheeled robot was used, since all wheeled robots in ARGoS are handled by a relatively simple 2D physics engine. In V-REP, the original e-puck model was simplified in order to decrease its vertex count. Each benchmark test was run with 1, 5, 10 and 50 robots in both environments.

At the beginning of each benchmark experiment, a simulator was restarted. The computer was not running any other applications, apart from those normally required by its operating system, and a simple CPU and memory monitoring application. V-REP was running in "threaded rendering" mode during the GUI benchmarks.

**Fig. 1.** The "Large scene" environment in (a) V-REP and Gazebo, and (b) ARGoS.

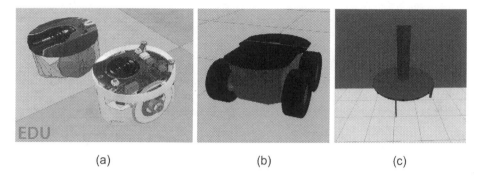

**Fig. 2.** (a) The simplified (left) and the original (right) e-puck [11] models in V-REP. (b) The Pioneer 3AT [16] model in Gazebo. (c) The eye-bot [13] model in ARGoS.

The simulation in both V-REP and ARGoS was updated 10 times per second, i.e., $dt = 100$ ms. In Gazebo, 10 times more simulation steps per second were needed ($dt = 10$ ms), otherwise some robots exhibited strange movement dynamics, such as rocking behaviour on a straight horizontal plane.

Three performance metrics were used to evaluate the simulator performance. *Real-time factor*, $R$ = simulated time/real time, the amount of *CPU usage*, $C$, and the amount of *memory usage*, $M$. When $R > 1$, a simulation could run faster than real time and vice versa. When $C > 100\%$, a simulator could utilise multiple processor cores. Two values for $C$ and $M$ were noted for Gazebo GUI experiments, corresponding to the usage of gzclient (visualisation) and gzserver (simulation), respectively.

## 3.2 Results

ARGoS achieved the highest simulation speed in the GUI experiments with up to 50 robots in the Small scene and with up to 5 robots in the Large scene, while utilising the smallest amount of resources (Table 2). Gazebo outperformed ARGoS in other experiments, especially when the Large scene was used in the Headless benchmark (Tables 2 and 3). However, Gazebo usually required the largest amount of memory when it was running in the GUI mode, and a median amount in the Headless mode. V-REP combined with ODE usually achieved the lowest simulation speed. Using Bullet 2.78 often significantly increased the performance of V-REP.

**Table 2.** Simulator performance in the GUI mode. The best (green) and the worst (red) performance are indicated.

| | V-REP + Bullet 2.78 | V-REP + ODE | Gazebo + ODE | ARGoS + Point-Mass3D |
|---|---|---|---|---|
| 1 robot + Small scene | $R \geq 1$ $C = 180\%$ $M = 235$ MB | $R \geq 1$ $C = 190\%$ $M = 225$ MB | $R \geq 1$ $C = 100 + 9\%$ $M = 225 + 58$ MB | $R \geq 1$ $C = 7\%$ $M = 85$ MB |
| 5 robots + Small scene | $R = 0.52$ $C = 395\%$ $M = 380$ MB | $R = 0.37$ $C = 395\%$ $M = 360$ MB | $R \geq 1$ $C = 100 + 19\%$ $M = 305 + 58$ MB | $R \geq 1$ $C = 10\%$ $M = 88$ MB |
| 10 robots + Small scene | $R = 0.11$ $C = 400\%$ $M = 536$ MB | $R = 0.099$ $C = 400\%$ $M = 530$ MB | $R \geq 1$ $C = 100 + 30\%$ $M = 402 + 58$ MB | $R \geq 1$ $C = 13\%$ $M = 89$ MB |
| 50 robots + Small scene | Not feasible | Not feasible | $R = 0.87$ $C = 100 + 105\%$ $M = 1410 + 358$ MB | $R = 0.9$ $C = 103\%$ $M = 93$ MB |
| 1 robot + Large scene | $R = 0.96$ $C = 205\%$ $M = 235$ MB | $R = 0.53$ $C = 200\%$ $M = 225$ MB | $R \geq 1$ $C = 100 + 10\%$ $M = 264 + 58$ MB | $R \geq 1$ $C = 32\%$ $M = 90$ MB |
| 5 robots + Large scene | $R = 0.18$ $C = 400\%$ $M = 325$ MB | $R = 0.1$ $C = 400\%$ $M = 310$ MB | $R \geq 1$ $C = 100 + 25\%$ $M = 333 + 58$ MB | $R \geq 1$ $C = 60\%$ $M = 97$ MB |
| 10 robots + Large scene | $R = 0.052$ $C = 400\%$ $M = 433$ MB | $R = 0.036$ $C = 400\%$ $M = 460$ MB | $R \geq 1$ $C = 100 + 40\%$ $M = 425 + 58$ MB | $R = 0.86$ $C = 120\%$ $M = 97$ MB |
| 50 robots + Large scene | Not feasible | Not feasible | $R = 0.57$ $C = 100 + 100\%$ $M = 1450 + 426$ MB | $R = 0.052$ $C = 107\%$ $M = 106$ MB |

In general, $R \geq 1$ could be achieved by all simulators until all available CPU power was used. The cut-off point, in terms of the number of robots, was always the lowest for V-REP, i.e. the simulation in V-REP slowed down in smaller experiments, compared to the other simulators. Furthermore, the simulation speed decrease due to insufficient CPU power was generally less severe for Gazebo than for V-REP and ARGoS.

Running Gazebo and ARGoS in the Headless mode (Table 3) increased $R$ in environments where maximum CPU power was utilised by the GUI mode. On the other hand, $R$ was often smaller in the Headless mode of V-REP, compared

**Table 3.** Simulator performance in the Headless mode. The best (green) and the worst (red) performance are indicated.

|  | V-REP + Bullet 2.78 | V-REP + ODE | Gazebo + ODE | ARGoS + Point-Mass3D |
|---|---|---|---|---|
| 1 robot + Small scene | $R = 4.1$ $C = 200\%$ $M = 165$ MB | $R = 3.12$ $C = 200\%$ $M = 160$ MB | $R = 42.85$ $C = 100\%$ $M = 107$ MB | $R = 300$ $C = 6.3\%$ $M = 18$ MB |
| 5 robots + Small scene | $R = 0.38$ $C = 400\%$ $M = 320$ MB | $R = 0.32$ $C = 400\%$ $M = 320$ MB | $R = 10$ $C = 100\%$ $M = 130$ MB | $R = 150$ $C = 100\%$ $M = 20$ MB |
| 10 robots + Small scene | $R = 0.09$ $C = 400\%$ $M = 470$ MB | $R = 0.08$ $C = 400\%$ $M = 480$ MB | $R = 5.26$ $C = 100\%$ $M = 150$ MB | $R = 21.42$ $C = 144\%$ $M = 20$ MB |
| 50 robots + Small scene | Not feasible | Not feasible | $R = 1.06$ $C = 100\%$ $M = 356$ MB | $R = 0.52$ $C = 103\%$ $M = 25$ MB |
| 1 robot + Large scene | $R = 1.91$ $C = 200\%$ $M = 165$ MB | $R = 0.58$ $C = 200\%$ $M = 160$ MB | $R = 18.75$ $C = 100\%$ $M = 174$ MB | $R = 15.78$ $C = 139\%$ $M = 31$ MB |
| 5 robots + Large scene | $R = 0.2$ $C = 400\%$ $M = 270$ MB | $R = 0.11$ $C = 400\%$ $M = 250$ MB | $R = 5.88$ $C = 100\%$ $M = 192$ MB | $R = 5.45$ $C = 157\%$ $M = 45$ MB |
| 10 robots + Large scene | Not feasible | Not feasible | $R = 3.09$ $C = 100\%$ $M = 211$ MB | $R = 1.59$ $C = 130\%$ $M = 47$ MB |
| 50 robots + Large scene | Not feasible | Not feasible | $R = 0.60$ $C = 100\%$ $M = 423$ MB | $R = 0.03$ $C = 105\%$ $M = 55$ MB |

to its GUI mode. There were two factors that contributed to this result. Firstly, $R$ of the Headless mode was calculated over a longer period of time (simulated five rather than one minute) and its average, rather than its maximum, value was reported. Secondly, $R$ of the Headless mode took into account not only the actual simulation time, but also the time needed to initialise and close the simulation. This in some cases took a significant amount of time, especially when ODE physics engine was used with V-REP.

Finally, V-REP demonstrated the most optimal CPU utilisation. It automatically spawned new threads when it was necessary and it could thus fully utilise all available CPU cores. Gazebo only utilised a single CPU core per process. In the GUI mode, Gazebo ran two processes, gzclient and gzserver, that could each utilise a maximum of 100% of CPU power. In the Headless mode, only a single core was utilised, as only the gzserver process was running. The multi-threaded core utilisation by ARGoS worked in general but problems were experienced in larger experiments. The CPU usage was notably smaller when more robots were added to the environment. Furthermore, unlike V-REP, ARGoS requires the user to specify the desired number of threads, rather than automatically spawning new threads when it is necessary.

It is notable that the 3D models used in ARGoS and Gazebo were fairly simple compared to those used in V-REP, even though effort was made to simplify the V-REP robot model (Fig. 2). Moreover, the ARGoS physics engine was much simpler than those used by V-REP and Gazebo. It is therefore expected that using third-party libraries to cope with various aspects of the simulation that are currently not covered in ARGoS, such as calculating more complex physics dynamics, or working with imported 3D meshes, would decrease the simulator's performance. Similarly, it is expected that more complex 3D models would decrease the performance of Gazebo compared to V-REP.

In order to confirm that the mesh complexity played a major role in V-REP, we ran experiments with the Kilobot robots [17], that could only move forward and did not have the sensing or controller capabilities of e-pucks, but consisted of very simple 3D meshes. In the Kilobot experiments, up to six times higher $R$ could be achieved, using only about an eighth of the computer's resources. In another experiment, the building model in the Large scene was simplified from around 41,600 to around 2,000 vertices. This increased $R$ by up to 66%. Another kind of optimisation involved decreasing the number of simulation update loops per second from ten to two (i.e., $dt = 500$ ms). This increased $R$ by up to 150%, while decreasing memory usage by up to 15%. These results suggest that it is possible to significantly increase the performance of V-REP by carefully setting simulation parameters and by optimising 3D models used in the simulation.

## 4    Conclusion

V-REP is the most complex and the most resource-hungry of the three simulators. However, it offers a number of useful features, such as multiple physics engines, a comprehensive model library, the ability of a user to interact with the world during simulation and, most importantly, mesh manipulation and optimisation. Moreover, V-REP automatically spawns new threads on multiple CPU cores and therefore utilises the full amount of CPU power when it is necessary. It is therefore suitable for high-precision modelling of robotic applications such as object transportation or area surveillance, as well as of various industrial applications, where only a few robots are required to operate at the same time.

ARGoS, on the other hand, is a suitable choice for simulations of swarm robotics tasks, such as collective foraging, flocking, or area coverage. Compared to V-REP, ARGoS trades-off robot, environment and physics complexity for superior performance. An XML-based simulation settings file is also very convenient, especially when a large variety of simulations need to be generated automatically. However, there are multiple important features missing from ARGoS, most notably the ability to import 3D meshes into the simulator. Currently, users that are not willing to spend time and effort on programming new robot models in OpenGL, have fairly limited choices.

Gazebo occupies the space between V-REP and ARGoS. While it is much closer to V-REP in terms of features, its interface and default robot models are much simpler and resemble those found in ARGoS. It is notable that Gazebo outperformed ARGoS in the larger simulation environments studied here, which suggests that it is a more suitable choice for large swarm robotics experiments. However, our experiments showed that the usability of Gazebo is relatively poor. Firstly, while it can import 3D meshes, there are no editing options, making it difficult to alter and optimise models. Another problem is the interface that has a number of issues and fails to follow established conventions. Finally, difficulties were noted when installing dependencies for Gazebo and for many of its third-party models. While not necessarily severe by themselves, these issues together could have a negative impact on a research project.

In the future, it would be interesting to conduct a user survey regarding the features and simulator usability in order to obtain a more robust comparison. It would also be interesting to evaluate the extent of the reality gap in the default simulator robot models.

**Acknowledgements.** This work was supported by EPSRC Programme Grant "Robotics for Nuclear Environments", grant ref: EP/P01366X/1. We would like to thank Farshad Arvin, Tareq Assaf, Giovanni Beltrame, Paul Bremner, Ales Leonardis, Carlo Pinciroli, Chie Takahashi, Simon Watson and Craig West for sharing their opinions and insights into various aspects of simulation work. We would also like to thank Xavier Poteau, who created the sample industrial building CAD model.

# References

1. Andrews, P.S., Stepney, S., Timmis, J.: Simulation as a scientific instrument. In: Stepney, S., Andrews, P.S., Read, M.N. (eds.) Proceedings of the 2012 Workshop on Complex Systems Modelling and Simulation, pp. 1–10. Luniver Press (2012)
2. Rohmer, E., Singh, S.P.N., Freese, M.: V-REP: a versatile and scalable robot simulation framework. In: Proceedings of the 2013 IEEE/RSJ International Conference on Intelligent Robots and Systems (IROS 2013). IEEE Press, Piscataway (2013). https://doi.org/10.1109/IROS.2013.6696520
3. Koenig, N., Howard, A.: Design and use paradigms for Gazebo, an open-source multi-robot simulator. In: Proceedings of the 2004 IEEE/RSJ International Conference on Intelligent Robots and Systems (IROS 2004), pp. 2149–2154. IEEE Press, Piscataway (2004)
4. Pinciroli, C., Trianni, V., et al.: ARGoS: a modular, parallel, multi-engine simulator for multi-robot systems. Swarm Intell. 6(4), 271–295 (2012)
5. Craighead, J., Murphy, R., Burke, J., Goldiez, B.: A survey of commercial & open source unmanned vehicle simulators. In: Proceedings of the 2007 IEEE International Conference on Robotics and Automation (ICRA 2007), pp. 852–857. IEEE, Piscataway (2007)
6. Žlajpah, L.: Simulation in robotics. Math. Comput. Simul. 79, 879–897 (2008)
7. Kramer, J., Scheutz, M.: Development environments for autonomous mobile robots: a survey. Autonom. Robot. 22(2), 101–132 (2007)
8. Harris, A., Conrad, J.M.: Survey of popular robotics simulators, frameworks, and toolkits. In: Proceedings of the 2011 IEEE Southeastcon, pp. 243–249 (2011)
9. Staranowicz, A., Mariottini, G.L.: A survey and comparison of commercial and open-source robotic simulator software. In: Proceedings of the 4th International Conference on PErvasive Technologies Related to Assistive Environments (PETRA 2011). ACM, New York (2011). https://doi.org/10.1145/2141622.2141689
10. Quigley, M., Gerkey, B., et al.: ROS: an open-source robot operating system. In: Proceedings of the ICRA 2009 Workshop on Open Source Software (2009)
11. Mondada, F., Bonani, M., et al.: The e-puck, a robot designed for education in engineering. In: Goncalves, P.J.S., Torres, P.J.D., Alves, C.M.O. (eds.) Proceedings of the 9th Conference on Autonomous Robot Systems and Competitions (ROBOT-ICA 2009), vol. 1, no. 1, pp. 59–65 (2009)
12. Bonani, M., Longchamp, V., et al.: The MarXbot, a miniature mobile robot opening new perspectives for the collective-robotic research. In: Proceedings of the 2010 IEEE/RSJ International Conference on Intelligent Robots and Systems (IROS 2010), pp. 4187–4193. IEEE Press, Piscataway (2010)
13. Ducatelle, F., Di Caro, G.A., et al.: Self-organized cooperation between robotic swarms. Swarm Intell. 5(2), 73–96 (2011)
14. Spiri Specifications. http://pleiadesrobotics.com. Accessed 18 Apr 2018
15. QT. https://www.qt.io. Accessed 18 Apr 2018
16. Pioneer 3AT Specifications. http://bit.ly/2D2VfSR. Accessed 18 Apr 2018
17. Rubenstein, M., Ahler, C., Nagpal, R.: Kilobot: a low cost scalable robot system for collective behaviors. In: Proceedings of the 2012 IEEE International Conference on Robotics and Automation (ICRA 2012), pp. 3293–3298. Computer Society Press of the IEEE, Washington, D.C. (2012)

# A Hybrid Underwater Acoustic and RF Localisation System for Enclosed Environments Using Sensor Fusion

Jose Espinosa[1]($\boxtimes$), Mihalis Tsiakkas[2], Dehao Wu[1], Simon Watson[1], Joaquin Carrasco[1], Peter R. Green[1], and Barry Lennox[1]

[1] School of Electrical and Electronic Engineering,
The University of Manchester, Manchester, UK
joseluis.espinosamendoza@postgrad.manchester.ac.uk
[2] KIOS Research and Innovation Center of Excellence,
Department of Electrical and Computer Engineering,
University of Cyprus, Nicosia, Cyprus

**Abstract.** Underwater localisation systems are traditionally based on acoustic range estimation, which lacks the accuracy to localise small underwater vehicles in enclosed structured environments for mapping and surveying purposes. The high attenuation of electromagnetic waves underwater can be exploited to obtain a more precise distance estimation over short distances. This work proposes a cooperative localisation system that combines an acoustic absolute localisation system with peer-to-peer distance estimation based on electromagnetic radio frequency (RF) attenuation between multiple robots. The proposed system is able to improve the position estimation of a group of Autonomous Underwater Vehicles (AUVs) or Remote Operated Vehicles (ROVs) for exploring enclosed environments.

## 1 Introduction

The exploration of underwater infrastructure is usually completed by either divers or remotely operated vehicles (ROVs) which are tethered. In industries such as Oil & Gas or offshore wind, the infrastructure is often in open water, which is easily accessible. The inspection of wet nuclear storage facilities is significantly more challenging. The radiation levels preclude the use of divers and the enclosed and cluttered (either structured or unstructured) environment means that traditional ROVs are difficult to operate due to snagging of the tether on objects. The University of Manchester has been developing a small-scale ($40 \, \mathrm{cm} \times 30 \, \mathrm{cm} \times 30 \, \mathrm{cm}$) tetherless underwater inspection vehicle, AVEXIS$^{\mathrm{TM}}$ [1], for the inspection of wet nuclear storage ponds of nominal size $50 \, \mathrm{m} \times 25 \, \mathrm{m} \times 5 \, \mathrm{m}$. To enable the deployment of these vehicles, a robust communications and localisation system is required. Figure 1 shows the system overview

This work was supported by CONACyT, Innovate UK (KTP10410), Forth Ltd. and The University of Manchester Dalton Cumbrian Facility.

© Springer International Publishing AG, part of Springer Nature 2018
M. Giuliani et al. (Eds.): TAROS 2018, LNAI 10965, pp. 369–380, 2018.
https://doi.org/10.1007/978-3-319-96728-8_31

of the Communications and Positioning System (CaPS) which is being developed. To enable both global localisation and the transfer of video without the use of a tether, a hybrid system is being developed which utilises both acoustic and radio frequency (RF) transmissions. The acoustic system provides global localisation with low accuracy and low data rate communication (command and control), whilst the RF system allows for relative localisation with high accuracy and high data rate communication (video). Neither system provides all of the functionality required on its own, given the size and power requirements of the AVEXIS$^{\text{TM}}$ vehicles. This paper will present the fusion algorithms developed for combining the absolute (acoustic) and relative (RF) localisation data. The remainder of this paper is organised as follows. Section 2 provides an overview of existing underwater localisation systems. Section 3 defines the mathematical problem and Sect. 4 presents numerical simulation results. Section 5 draws conclusions and discusses further work.

## 2    Underwater Localisation Systems

Common methods of mobile robot localisation, such as Global Positioning Systems (GPS) and odometry are not available for underwater robots. Visual or optical methods for simultaneous localisation and mapping (SLAM) are extremely difficult and computational heavy in environments with low visibility, high turbidity, lack of landmarks or low saliency [2]. There are other underwater systems that provide a rough estimate of the position via swarm aggregation behaviours like the "relay chain" presented in [3] but this systems lack the precision of traditional localisation systems as the position rather to be an absolute measure it is determined by the initial and end position of the "relay chain". The alternative technologies used underwater are acoustics and RF.

### 2.1    Acoustic Localisation

Acoustics are widely used for underwater localisation, however the acoustic channel is affected by a number of factors including limited bandwidth, long propagation delays and phase and amplitude fluctuations [4]. The primary issues

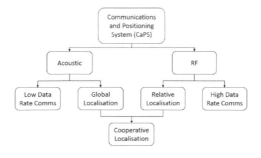

**Fig. 1.** Communications and Positioning System (CaPS) overview

in enclosed, cluttered environments are multipath and the loss of line-of-sight (LOS). Most underwater localisation systems transmit acoustic signals between a vehicle and reference beacons at known locations. Accuracies can vary between m and cm depending on the operating frequency (6 kHz to 300 kHz), however the operating distance decreases as the frequency (and accuracy) increases (>10 km to <7 m) [5,6]. The distance between the vehicle and the beacon can be estimated using methods such as Time of Arrival (ToA) or Time Difference of Arrival (TDoA) [7]. The actual position of the robot can be estimated using Multidimensional Scaling (MDS) [8], Least Squares (LS) [9] or other similar methods. Commercially available systems are too large to be deployed on the small-scale vehicles being developed for the nuclear applications, so a new system is being developed.

## 2.2 RF Localisation

RF-based underwater localisation systems are not widely used, primarily due to the high attenuation of the EM waves in sea water. An RF localisation system for enclosed environments was proposed in [10] which utilised an array of RF beacons along the edge of the environment and at fixed depths to estimate the distance to a single robot. The nuclear application environments use fresh water, rather than salt water, so the attenuation of the EM waves is reduced. By exploiting the high attenuation, distance estimates between two RF transducers can be obtained from the received signal strength information (RSSI) [11]. The measurement error can be less than 3 cm, however the range is limited by the operating frequency and is mostly <6 m [12,13] making it viable only for short range applications.

## 2.3 AVEXIS™ CaPS

To overcome the limitations of both the existing acoustic and RF underwater localisation systems, a new hybrid system is proposed, shown in Fig. 2. An acoustic positioning system (APS) will provide long-range, global position estimates of single robots. Utilising a swarm of vehicles, peer-to-peer (P2P) RF relative distance estimates can also be obtained by interchanging simple messages and measuring the RSSI of the received package. By fusing the two sets of data with an Extended Kalman Filter, a more accurate global position estimate can be obtained. A swarm of robots is used to not only improve the position estimates, but to allow multi-hop transmission of real-time video using RF. Groups of vehicles can also be used to localise robots which descend into cluttered spaces where LOS to the acoustic base-stations is lost.

## 3   Problem Formulation

Given an underwater environment with $n$ mobile robots, the localisation problem is to obtain the mean state of the robots, $\hat{X} \in \mathbb{R}^{3n}$, and its covariance matrix,

$P_{\hat{X}_k} \in \mathbb{R}^{3n}$ at each time interval, $k$, given the column vector, $Z$, which contains the measured positions of the robots

$$\tilde{p}_i = \begin{bmatrix} \tilde{x}_i & \tilde{y}_i & \tilde{z}_i \end{bmatrix}^T,$$

where $\tilde{x}_i$ and $\tilde{y}_i$ are obtained using the APS and $\tilde{z}_i$ is obtained using an on-board depth sensor (DS). The APS can also provide a $\tilde{z}_i$, but it is not as accurate as the DS. $Z$ also contains the information of the pair wise range measurement (PRM) between the $n$ robots (from the RF relative localisation), denoted by $\tilde{\delta}_{i,j}$, where $i$ and $j$ are the robot's numbers of the P2P range measurement. Therefore:

$$Z = \begin{bmatrix} \tilde{p}_i & \dots & \tilde{p}_n & \tilde{\delta}_{1,2} & \dots & \tilde{\delta}_{n-1,n} \end{bmatrix}^T.$$

The $Z$ vector measurements are considered to have an inherent measurement error which is different for each vehicle in the system, where $\sigma_g$, $\sigma_r$, and $\sigma_d$ are the standard deviations of the APS, the PRM and the DS respectively. It is considered that:

$$\sigma_g > \sigma_r > \sigma_d.$$

The APS, PRM, and DS information of all the robots in the group is known by a central computing node. The state estimation algorithm used to fuse the elements of the sensor suite, is based on the Classical Estimation Theory applied to the Conditional Mean for Linear Gaussian Measurements presented in [14]. It is assumed that the APS, PRM and DS have a linear measurement model

$$Z = HX + V, \tag{1}$$

where $X$ is the real positions of the robots

$$p_i = \begin{bmatrix} x_i & y_i & z_i \end{bmatrix}^T.$$

$X$ is a normally distributed variable with a mean $\bar{X}$ and a covariance $P_X$; $X \sim N(\bar{X}, P_X)$ and the noise, $V$, is also a normally distributed variable with zero mean and covariance $R$; $V \sim N(0, R)$. The measurement matrix $H$ that represents the relationship between the APS and PRM is assumed to be known

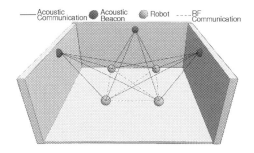

**Fig. 2.** System configuration with the number of robots $n = 4$

and deterministic. If $R > 0$, and the system's noise is decoupled, $X$ and $V$ are orthogonal, meaning that $\overline{XV^T} = 0$. Using the solution provided in [14] the error covariance can be calculated as

$$P_{\bar{X}} = (P_X^{-1} + H^T R^{-1} H)^{-1}. \tag{2}$$

The covariance matrix, $R$, is a diagonal matrix dependant on $\sigma_g$, $\sigma_r$, and $\sigma_d$. $R$ can be generated for $n$ robots using the following expression:

$$R = \text{diag}(I_n \otimes \text{diag}(\sigma_g I_2, \sigma_d), \sigma_r I_{R_c})^2, \tag{3}$$

where $\otimes$ is the Kronecker product and $I_n$ denotes the $n \times n$ identity matrix. The vector $X \in \mathbb{R}^{3n}$, whilst the sizes of $Z$, $H$, and $R$ are dependant on the number of robots ($n$) and the second binomial coefficient given by

$$R_c = \binom{n}{2} = \sum_{i=1}^{n} i = \frac{n}{2}(n+1). \tag{4}$$

Therefore $Z \in \mathbb{R}^{3n+R_c}$, $R \in \mathbb{R}^{(3n+R_c) \times (3n+R_c)}$ and $H \in \mathbb{R}^{(3n+R_c) \times 3n}$. As there is no prior information about $X$, it can be assumed that $P_X \to \infty$, therefore $P_X^{-1} \to 0$, allowing it to be removed from (2). Hence, using the solution in [14]

$$\hat{X} = \bar{X} + P_{\bar{X}} H^T R^{-1} (Z - H\bar{X}). \tag{5}$$

Since a numerical value for $\bar{X}$ is not available at initialisation, $\bar{X} = H^+ Z$, where $H^+$ denotes the left inverse of $H$. It is set to

$$\hat{X} = (H^+ + P_{\bar{X}} H^T R^{-1} (I - HH^+)) Z. \tag{6}$$

$\hat{X}$ is a column vector containing the estimated position of the robots

$$\hat{p}_n = \begin{bmatrix} \hat{x}_n & \hat{y}_n & \hat{z}_n \end{bmatrix}^T$$

in the $x$, $y$ and $z$ axis of each of the robots after the APS, PRM and the DS information is fused, e.g.

$$\hat{X} = \begin{bmatrix} \hat{p}_1 & \dots & \hat{p}_n \end{bmatrix}^T.$$

To obtain a correct estimation of the robots' positions, the measurement matrix $H$ for the system needs to be constructed. The PRM obtains a measurement of the distance between the robots, therefore in a 3D environment it is represented by the Euclidean distance given by:

$$\delta_{i,j} = ||p_i - p_j|| = \sqrt{(x_i - x_j)^2 + (y_i - y_j)^2 + (z_i - z_j)^2}$$

The euclidean distance cannot be represented in a matrix form, therefore a linearisation has to be completed around the APS and DS position estimates for each time, $k$, of each robot. The simplified linearisation expression for $\delta_{i,j}$ is

$$\text{L}(\delta_{i,j}) = \tilde{\delta}_{i,j}^{-1} (\tilde{p}_i \quad \tilde{p}_j)^T (p_i \quad p_j). \tag{7}$$

The solution in (7) can be extrapolated to any $n$ as the distances are independent from each other, therefore the measurement matrix $H$ can be constructed as shown in Algorithm 1 ($0_a$ denotes the zero vector in $\mathbb{R}^a$).

---

**Algorithm 1.** $H$ matrix generator

---

**procedure** MAKE H

    $D_c \leftarrow$ *list of all possible pair combinations in* $[i,n]$

    $H = I_{3n}$

    **for** all pairs $(i, j) \in D_c$ **do**

        $k_1 = 3(i - 1), \ k_2 = 3(j - 1), \ k_2 = 3(R_c - j)$

        $T = (0_{k_1}^T \ \tilde{\delta}_{i,j}^{-1}(\tilde{p}_i - \tilde{p}_j)^T \ 0_{k_2}^T \ -\tilde{\delta}_{i,j}^{-1}(\tilde{p}_i - \tilde{p}_j)^T \ 0_{k_3}^T)$

        $H \leftarrow \begin{pmatrix} H \\ T \end{pmatrix}$

---

If $n = 2$ the measurements matrix $H$ is

$$H = \begin{pmatrix} I_3 & 0 \\ 0 & I_3 \\ \tilde{\delta}_{1,2}^{-1}(\tilde{p}_1 - \tilde{p}_2)^T & \tilde{\delta}_{1,2}^{-1}(\tilde{p}_2 - \tilde{p}_1)^T \end{pmatrix}$$

and the covariance matrix $R$ is

$$R = \begin{pmatrix} \sigma_g^2 I_2 & & & & \\ & \sigma_d^2 & & & \\ & & \sigma_g^2 I_2 & & \\ & & & \sigma_d^2 & \\ & & & & \sigma_r^2 \end{pmatrix}.$$

$Z = \begin{bmatrix} \tilde{p}_1 & \tilde{p}_2 & \tilde{\delta}_{1,2} \end{bmatrix}^T$ and $X = \begin{bmatrix} p_1 & p_2 \end{bmatrix}^T$. The previous model is used to estimate the positions of the robots when they are static and it is possible to take many samples of their position and distances with the APS, PRM and DS. This approach is not optimal when the robots are either moving through he environment, drifting or both. For this reason a filter was designed using the same $H$ and $R$ matrices. Equations (2) and (5) were modified such that:

$$P_{\hat{X}_k} = A(P_{\hat{X}_{k-1}}^{-1} + H_k^T R^{-1} H_k)^{-1} A^T + Q, \tag{8}$$

and

$$\hat{X}_k = (A - K_k H_k)\hat{X}_{k-1} + (AK_k)Z + u_k, \tag{9}$$

where

$$K_k = P_{\hat{X}_{k-1}} H_k^T (H_k P_{\hat{X}_{k-1}} H_k^T + R)^{-1}. \tag{10}$$

Assuming that the robots will act as an integrator, $A = I_{3n}$. $Q = \alpha I_{3n}$ was found to be a good option, with a tuning constant, $\alpha$, $u_k$ the control input vector of the robots and $P_{\hat{X}_0} = 0$.

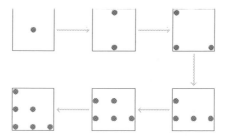

**Fig. 3.** Top view of the positions of the robots as the number of robots $n$ is increased for the simulations. The blue dots represent the robots. (Color figure online)

## 4   Numeric Simulations

This section show results for the dynamic and steady state estimation algorithms of various groups of robots done via numeric simulations in MATLAB. To analyse the performance of the steady state estimation algorithm, several simulations were performed in which the standard deviation of the APS, PRM and DS remained constant, while the number of robots and positions were modified. In the first set of simulations the number of robots increases from $n = 2$ to $n = 30$ while keeping them in static positions. The standard deviations of the APS, PRM and DS were $\sigma_g = 0.3$, $\sigma_r = 0.1$ and $\sigma_d = 0.01$. The APS standard deviation value is chosen based on the accuracy of the AVEXIS$^{\text{TM}}$ Acoustic Positioning System presented in [7], the PRM based on the RSSI distance estimation accuracy based in [10] and the DS value based on the MS5837-30BA pressure sensor datasheet. For these simulation sets, the robots were static in the environment and 1000 sets of measurements of the APS, PRM and DS for each robot were simulated and used for the localisation algorithm, before increasing $n$ all numeric simulations assume a constant depth among all the vehicles. When increasing the number of robots, the new robot was placed at a predefined position, as shown on the Fig. 3. The reason for the selection of these locations was to have a structured set of positions for each $n$, rather than randomly positioning the robots in the environment. To analyse the performance of the robots in the static scenario as the number of robots increases, the following metrics are proposed:

$$\mu_{\text{CaPS\_static}} = \frac{1}{2n} \sum_{r=1}^{n} (\sigma(\hat{x}_r) + \sigma(\hat{y}_r)) \tag{11}$$

and

$$\mu_{\text{APS\_static}} = \frac{1}{2n} \sum_{r=1}^{n} (\sigma(\tilde{x}_r) + \sigma(\tilde{y}_r)). \tag{12}$$

$\mu_{\text{CaPS\_static}}$ and $\mu_{\text{APS\_static}}$ are the mean of the $X$ and $Y$ axis standard deviations for all the robots' estimated positions in the static environment for the CaPS and the stand alone APS respectively expressed in m. The metrics were chosen as they show the accuracy of the CaPS and the APS over of a set of measurements for robots in the same position. $\sigma_{\hat{z}}$ is not taken in count as the $z$ axis positioning has the same accuracy for both cases. Figure 4 compares the result of the metrics over the first set of simulations. It can be seen that the $\mu_{\text{CaPS\_static}}$ metric reduces its value as the number of robots increases, showing that the performance of the CaPS increases with the number of robots. It is important to note that the performance of the $\mu_{\text{CaPS\_static}}$ metric improves considerably with only two robots in the environment, while at higher number of robots, the increased performance of adding another robot might not be perceptible. The CaPS's accuracy is also affected by the formation of the robots within the environment. Figure 5 shows the accuracy of the state estimation for each of the robots in different formations of $n = 4$. The red and blue ellipses around each robots shows the APS and the CaPS standard bivariate deviations respectivly on the $X$ and $Y$ axis after $10,000$ iterations of static localisation. Figure 5 shows that the accuracy varies for different formation shapes and for each of the robots within specific formations. Table 1 shows the means of $\sigma_{\hat{x}}$ and $\sigma_{\hat{y}}$ for each formations and the formation ratio $\sigma_{\frac{x}{y}} = \frac{\sigma_{\hat{x}\text{mean}}}{\sigma_{\hat{y}\text{mean}}}$. If $\sigma_{\frac{x}{y}} \sim 1$ the formation has a similar mean accuracy on both axis, $\sigma_{\frac{x}{y}} > 1$ means the formation is more accurate in the $Y$ axis, and for $\sigma_{\frac{x}{y}} < 1$ the formation is more accurate on the $X$ axis. It can be seen in Table 1, that formations in which the robots keep a horizontal or vertical shapes reduces the $Y$ and $X$ axis accuracy respectively, while diagonal formations, such as Shape d, have a even accuracy on both axis. It is also worth noticing that some formations will increase the accuracy of specific robots, such as Shapes e and f, where the central robots have a more accurate position estimation compared to the external robots. These formations properties need to be considered for high level formation control and mission planning.

For the dynamic scenario, the robots were placed at the same position as in the static scenario (Fig. 3) at time $k = 0$. For $k > 0$, a change in position was applied for each robot. To simulate the movement of the robots, an input vector, $u_k$, was applied for to each robot.

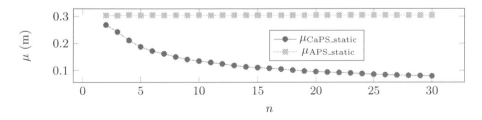

**Fig. 4.** Performance of the state estimation system with various number of robots. The robots are set in static positions within the environment. The metric value is the mean average $\mu_{\text{CaPS}}$ for 100 simulations of 1000 iterations each for every number of robots $n$.

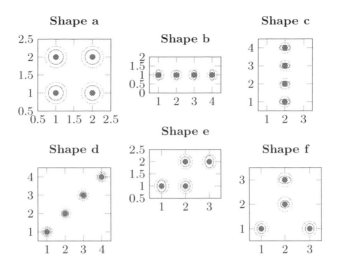

**Fig. 5.** Top view of the positions of the robots with the number of robots $n = 4$ and distance in meters. The X and Y axis are in meters. The red ellipse represent the localisation accuracy of the APS alone, the blue ellipse represents the localisation accuracy after fusing the APS with the PRM. (Color figure online)

**Table 1.** Accuracy of the CaPS depending on the robots' formation

| Shape | $\sigma_{\hat{x}_{\mathrm{mean}}}$ | $\sigma_{\hat{y}_{\mathrm{mean}}}$ | $\mu_{\mathrm{CaPS\_static}}$ | $\sigma_{\frac{x}{y}}$ |
|---|---|---|---|---|
| a | 0.2057 | 0.2047 | 0.2052 | 1.004 |
| b | 0.1549 | 0.2713 | 0.2131 | 0.5709 |
| c | 0.2707 | 0.1544 | 0.2125 | 1.7532 |
| d | 0.2122 | 0.2141 | 0.2131 | 0.9911 |
| e | 0.1949 | 0.2280 | 0.2114 | 0.8548 |
| f | 0.2005 | 0.1817 | 0.1911 | 1.1034 |

$$u_0 = \begin{bmatrix} u_{x,1} & u_{y,1} & 0 & \dots & u_{x,n} & u_{y,n} & 0 \end{bmatrix}^T,$$

where $u_{x,i}$ and $u_{y,i}$ are the control inputs for the robots to move in a triangular trajectory as seen in Fig. 6. Movement noise was also applied to simulate drift and uncertainties while moving, collisions were not simulated. (13) shows the equation that simulates the change in position for each robot.

$$p_n(k) = p_n(k-1) + 0.001V_k + u_k, \tag{13}$$

where $V_k$ is uniformly distributed random number in the interval $(0, 1)$. Figure 6 shows the results of the dynamic simulations for $n = 4$. It can be seen that the estimation of the CaPS is always within a few centimetres of the real position of the robot. To analyse the performance of the localisation system for each set of robots, a metric parameter $\mu_{\mathrm{CaPS\_dynamic}}$ was proposed, which measures the average error between the real position of each of the robots and the estimated position over the $M$ samples. $\mu_{\mathrm{CaPS\_dynamic}}$ is defined as follows

**(A) Movement of robots for dynamic state estimation**

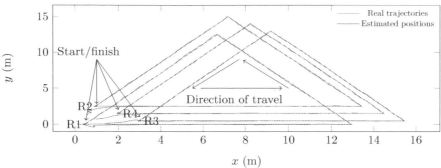

**(B) Error of the position estimation for each robot**

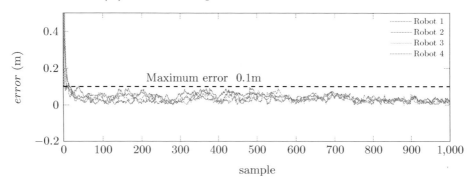

**Fig. 6.** (A) Movement of the robots within the environment for the state estimation with the number of robots $n = 4$. The robots are moving in a triangle trajectory and stopping at the end. (B) Graph of the error of the position estimation for each robot. The maximum error is $0.1$ m.

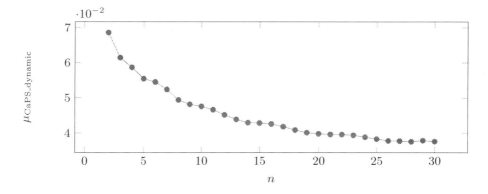

**Fig. 7.** Mean of $\mu_{\text{CaPS\_dynamic}}$ after 100 simulations of 1000 iterations of the state estimation system with increasing number of robots. The robots are moving within the environment

$$\mu_{\text{CaPS\_dynamic}} = \frac{1}{M} \sum_{k=1}^{M} e_k, \tag{14}$$

where

$$e_k = \frac{1}{n} \sum_{i=1}^{n} ||p_i(k) - \hat{p}_i(k)||. \tag{15}$$

Figure 7 shows the mean of $\mu_{\text{CaPS\_dynamic}}$ for 100 simulations of the dynamic state estimation algorithm. Similar to the static case, the performance of the system increases in a exponential decay fashion as the number of robots is incremented. The average $\mu_{\text{CaPS\_dynamic}}$ of the CaPS when $n = 2$ is 0.068 m and converges to $\sim$0.037 m as $n \to 30$.

## 5    Conclusions and Further Work

The numeric simulations showed that the hybrid CaPS, which has been proposed, can provide a better estimation of the robot's position when compared to the stand alone APS. The range of the system is also greater than an pure RF localisation system and there is the potential to localise robots who have lost LOS to the anchors. Figures 4 and 7 show that the accuracy is higher as the number of robots increases for both the static and dynamic scenarios. However, as $n$ grows, the computational requirements of the measurement matrix $H$ also increase according to (4). The shape of the robots' formation also affects the accuracy of the CaPS, as a whole and for each of the robots within the formation. Determining the optimal shape for the required task is a necessary to obtain the most accurate position estimate. In order to create a more realistic model for the numeric simulations, underwater RSSI range estimation experiments are needed to fully characterise the error distribution of both, the APS and the P2P range measurement, as this work considers them as normally distributed. The experiments to generate these models are currently ongoing. A planned extension of this work is to simulating indirect localisation where one or more robots are not able to be localised by the APS, only via P2P from other robots. This scenario will be common when exploring locations that are difficult to access or where LOS to the APS is blocked by an obstacle. There are a number of hardware constraints which also need to be considered in the final implementation of the CaPS system. Current simulations are restricted to a plane, as the antennas currently being used have a radiation pattern which is limited to a 30° elevation angle between the robots. Designing an antenna capable of radiating in a predictable manner will enable the system to have more accurate RSSI range estimations even when the robots are not in the same plane, allowing more complex formations and exploration algorithms. For practical applications the global number of robots in the environment will be determined by a number of factors such as the size of the environment, the requirements of the communications system (the number of nodes needed for the multi-hop video transmission), the desired deployment time and cost. With respect to the CaPS, there is work to be completed on understanding how the vehicles will form the formations and how many will be required (fixed formations or ad-hoc formations). This will depend on the total number of robots deployed in the ponds. Finally, the approach on this paper is assuming a centralised system for the information sharing and the position estimate computing. An extension of this work is to modify the information sharing to allow a decentralised approach for the position estimates. This type of approach will share the computing requirements among all the robots involved and will be more tolerant for loss in the line-of-sight acoustic/RF communication.

# References

1. Griffiths, A., Watson, S., Dikarev, A., Greeen, P., Lennox, B., Poteau, X.: AVEXIS aqua vehicle explorer for in-situ sensing. IEEE Robot. Autom. Lett. **1**, 282 (2016)
2. Meireles, M., Lourenco, R., Dias, A., Almeida, J., Silva, H., Martins, A.: Real time visual slam for underwater robotic inspection. Oceans (2014)
3. Schmickl, T., et al.: CoCoRo - The self-aware underwater swarm, pp. 120–126 (2011). cited By 0
4. Tan, H.-P., Diamant, R., Seah, W.K.G., Waldmeyer, M.: A survey of techniques and challenges in underwater localization. Ocean Eng. **38**(14–15), 1663–1676 (2011)
5. Garcia, J.-E., Kyamakya, K., Jobmann, K.: Positioning issues in underwater sensor networks. In: Proceedings of the 1st Workshop on Positioning, Navigation and Communication (WPNC 2004) (2004)
6. Kinsey, J.C., Smallwood, D.A., Whitcomb, L.L.: A new hydrodynamics test facility for UUV dynamics and control research. In: Oceans 2003. Celebrating the Past ... Teaming Toward the Future (IEEE Cat. No. 03CH37492), vol. 1, pp. 356–361, September 2003
7. Dikarev, A., Griffiths, A., Watson, S., Lennox, B., Green, P.: Combined multiuser acoustic communication and localisation system for μAUVs operating in confined underwater environments. In: IFAC Workshop on Navigation Guidance and Control of Underwater Vehicles (2014)
8. Tarro, P., Bernardos, A., Casar, J.: Weighted least squares techniques for improved received signal strength based localization. Sensors **11**, 8569–8592 (2011)
9. Latasoudas, G., Sidiropoulos, N.: A fast and effective multidimensional scaling approach for node localization in wireless sensor networks. IEEE Trans. Signal Process. **55**, 5121–5127 (2007)
10. Park, D., Kwak, K., Kim, J., Chung, W.K.: 3D underwater localization scheme using EM wave attenuation with a depth sensor. In: International Conference on Robotics and Automation (ICRA) (2016)
11. Park, D., Kwak, K., Chung, W.K., Kim, J.: Development of underwater short-range sensor using electromagnetic wave attenuation. J. Ocean. Eng. **41**, 318–325 (2015)
12. Kwak, K., Kim, J., Park, D., Chung, W.K.: Localization of unmanned underwater vehicles using EM wave in structured environment. In: 2012 Oceans - Yeosu, pp. 1–2, May 2012
13. Park, D., Kwak, K., Kim, J., Chung, W.K.: Underwater sensor network using received signal strength of electromagnetic waves. Intell. Robot. Syst. (IROS), 1052–1057 (2015)
14. Lewis, F., Xie, L., Popa, D.: Optimal and Robust Estimation with and Introduction to Stochastic Control Theory. CRC Press, Boca Raton (2008)

# Towards a Comprehensive Taxonomy for Characterizing Robots

Manal Linjawi(✉) and Roger K. Moore

Department of Computer Science, University of Sheffield,
211 Portobello, Sheffield S1 4DP, UK
{malinjawi1,r.k.moore}@sheffield.ac.uk

**Abstract.** Every day a new robot is developed with advanced character-istics and technical qualities. The increasingly rapid growth of robots and their characteristics demands bridging between the application require-ments and the robot specifications. This process requires a supporting conceptual structure that can capture as many robot qualities as pos-sible. Presenting robot characteristics through the proposed conceptual structure would enable designers to optimize robot capabilities against application requirements. It would also help application developers to select the most appropriate robot. Without a formal structure, an accu-rate linking between the robot domain and the application domain is not possible. This paper presents a novel theoretical representation that can capture robot features and capabilities and express them as descrip-tive dimensions to be used to develop a capability profile. The pro-file is intended to unify robot description and presentation. The pro-posed structure is reinforced with several layers, sections, categorizations and levels to allow a detailed explanation of robot characteristics. It is hoped that the proposed structure will influence the design, develop-ment, and testing of robots for specific applications. At the same time, it would help in highlighting the corresponding outlines in robot application requirements.

**Keywords:** Robot capabilities profile · Robot features
Robot characterization

## 1 Introduction

There are many types of robot. In general, each robot has its individual fea-tures, capabilities, and corresponding application requirements. Defining both which robot should be used for what application and what application is best for which robot is a complicated process. It demands mapping between the appli-cation requirements and the robot capabilities. This requires a comprehensive taxonomy of robot descriptions. Most of the existing robot taxonomies and clas-sifications (e.g., domain [19], field [17], size [4], ontology [15]) focus on several characteristics but do not include all of them. These classifications are not enough to bridge the gap between the two domains, nor are they adequate for comparing

© Springer International Publishing AG, part of Springer Nature 2018
M. Giuliani et al. (Eds.): TAROS 2018, LNAI 10965, pp. 381–392, 2018.
https://doi.org/10.1007/978-3-319-96728-8_32

one robot with another. Also, the continual development of robot characteristics, the frequent updating of application requirements, and the lack of consistency in naming conventions among the relevant fields, all hinder the mapping process. There is, therefore, a need to present robot characteristics in an abstract structure to capture the fixed as well as the dynamic characteristics. These characteristics should include all aspects of robot features, capabilities, interactions and reasons for robot performance, presented as skills and intelligence. Consequently, the proposed structure requires new dimensions in identifying and describing individual robots, an objective that is a considerable challenge in the continuously expanding field of robotics. Moreover, this structure should support the robot domain with robot capability profiles (as a set of outlined hierarchies for robot characteristics) and, at the same time, it needs to provide the application domain with a corresponding layout for straightforward comparison and analysis of robot requirements.

There is a substantial, well-structured document of over 300 pages, known as the Multi-Annual Roadmap (MAR) [19]. It accompanies the Strategic Research Agenda (SRA) to analyse robot technology and robot market details. It is updated annually by expertise formed by euRobotics aisbl, to prioritize the technology and the strategic development shaping European research development and innovation (R&D&I). The MAR contains a detailed explanation of robot characteristics; however, using the MAR to characterize robots is a complex process. In addition, the MAR does not include all robot characteristics (e.g., emotion, social capabilities, cognitive interactions). In this study, we propose a consistent conceptual structure that captures robot features, capabilities and interactions, adopting the levels used in the MAR where possible, and innovating where necessary. Hence, we propose not to replace the MAR, but to extend it by encompassing the MAR system of ability levels within a straightforward taxonomy that is supported by a layered hierarchy. The proposed model has been presented to roboticists during the development process and refined through their feedback.

## 2    The Proposed Conceptual Structure

The proposed conceptual structure defines the embedded relations between technical and operational capabilities, and features of any particular robot. To accommodate the complexity of these relations in describing a robot, the proposed structure allocates robot characteristics within three main layers [12] in a graphical presentation, as presented in Fig. 1. Each layer is further divided into sections and subsections. Some of the sections present robot capabilities and others capture more elements of the robot. Each robot capability may be characterized using the ability levels provided in MAR [19], if available. The ability levels are presented from no capability to full capability with specific intermediate levels. To designate a specific technical ability for any given robot, at least one of the concept levels for that specific capability should score more than 0. However, some capabilities are not covered by MAR, which highlights areas in need of further attention. Describing robot characteristics is an important aspect in robot classification, but due to page limitations, this paper mainly focuses on the second layer, 'robot technical capabilities'.

## The First Layer: Robot Features

This layer captures the robot components, including the hardware, the software and their specifications, as presented in Fig. 1, layer (1). The robot components and the specifications are fundamental in determining the robot capabilities and interaction types [1,11]. They are considered as key aspects in robot assessment and improvement. The hardware concepts include: external and internal sensors, external and internal actuators, internal structure (including kinematics and kinetics), external structure, embodiment, locomotion, electronics, mechanics, materials, etc. The software concepts include: operating system, software modules including different versions, memory size, sensory memory (instinct data/imitating data), network connections, system engineering, system architecture, system theories, system integration and system of systems. This layer also includes other robot specifications that depend on the hardware and software together, such as the robot interface (command line, GUI, speech, pen, etc.) or robot presentation medium (physical robot, simulated robot, hologram robot, etc.). A robot's hardware and software together determine some of the robot capabilities, interaction types [1] and consequently defines the robot limitations [11]. Therefore, the robot capabilities are presented in the structure in layers above the feature layer (1). However, in MAR [19] there are several types of capabilities that describe the robot hardware and software components, thus they are located in the first layer of the structure. These capabilities are:

- The parameter adaptability, presented in 5 levels.
- The component adaptability, presented in 5 levels.
- The mechatronics configurability, presented in 5 levels.

## The Second Layer: Technical Capabilities

Some robots are limited to one capability while others have multiple capabilities. Therefore, listing robot capabilities is an important aspect of robot identification. Technical capabilities are divided into three sections: robot capabilities, interaction capabilities and intelligence/skill capabilities. Each section depends on the outcomes from the lower section/layer underneath it, presented as a upside funnel, in Fig. 1.

1. Robot capabilities, presented in Fig. 1, layer (2), section (A), represent capabilities produced by the robot's hardware (HW) and software (SW) features in layer (1). Hence, robot technical capabilities are located above the robot features.
2. Interaction capabilities, presented in section (B), are produced by robot capabilities in section (A), and are therefore located in the section above the robot capabilities.

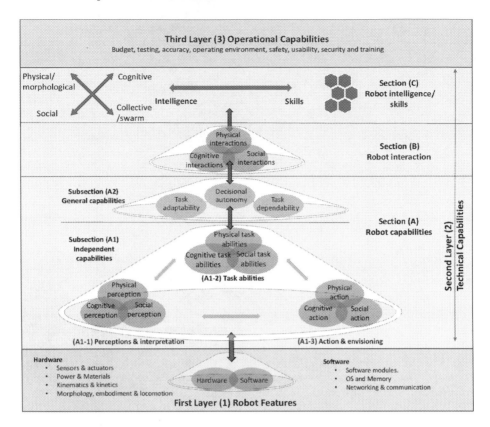

**Fig. 1.** The hierarchical conceptual structure captures robot characteristics and allocates them in different layers. Each layer/section depends on the layer/section underneath it (emphasized in the graph by the upside down funnels). Layer (1) covers the hardware and software components. Layer (2) captures the three sections (A, B and C) of the technical capabilities. Robot capabilities section (A) is divided into two subsections: Independent capabilities subsection (A1) holds any possible capability that does not depend on another for its performance. General capabilities subsection (A2) holds all capabilities that are dependent on other capabilities for its performance. Robot interaction section (B) describes the robot interaction types. Robot intelligence/skills section (C) describes skills obtained by the robot to support a specific intelligence. Each skill is presented as a cell in a honeycomb. The group of skills are presented in a honeycomb to illustrate the interdependent relationships between the skills, to present a robot with a specific intelligence. Layer (3) captures all the operational capabilities of the robot.

3. Robot intelligence, presented in section (C), depends on skills and behaviour that emerge from robot interactions in section (B). Therefore, robot intelligence is located above the interaction capabilities.

## Section (A): Robot Capabilities

Robot capabilities are divided into two types. The first type is 'independent capabilities', and includes any capability that could be installed alone in the robot and might not rely on any other capability, as presented in Fig. 1, layer (2), section (A), subsection (A1). The second type is 'general capabilities', and includes any capability that depends on any of the 'independent capabilities', as presented in Fig. 1, layer (2), section (A), subsection (A2).

**Subsection (A1): Independent Capabilities.** The independent capabilities are not contingent on any other capabilities in their performance. They are grouped according to a perception-action cycle [2], as shown in Fig. 1, layer (2), section (A), subsection (A1). The cycle captures the flow of actions that take place within the robot. Therefore, the independent capabilities are grouped into three sub-subsections: (A1-1) Perception and interpretive capabilities, (A1-2) Robot task abilities, (A1-3) Robot actions and envisioning. They are allocated in this section because each of these capabilities can be used alone without the need of the existence of other capabilities. Some robots might have only perception and other robots might perform a manipulation task repeatedly without perception. Although, some robots perform manipulation according to perception, which identifies them with a perception capability and manipulation capability.

*(A1-1) Perception and Interpretive Capabilities.* Capabilities in this sub-subsection provide the robot with the act of perceiving. Robot perception is described by the following three concepts:

1. Robot perception categories: there are three categories of perception: (1) Physical perception to capture perception of objects. (2) Cognitive perception to capture perception of information. (3) Social perception to capture perception of people. These are presented in Fig. 1, layer (2), section (A), subsection (A1), sub-subsection (A1-1).

2. Robot perception types: according to MAR [19], there are six types of perception, each type given a number of levels:
   (a) Perception abilities (9 levels).
   (b) Tracking abilities (7 levels).
   (c) Recognition abilities (13 levels).
   (d) Sensing static surrounding perception abilities (7 levels).
   (e) Self-location (8 levels).
   (f) Interpretive ability in the robot (10 levels).

3. Robot modes of perception, also known as the 'interaction modes', define the data collection methods used by the robot to perform the perceptive capabilities. There are several perception modes such as visual, auditory or physical (mechanical, magnetic, chemical, etc.) [17].

*(A1-2) Task Abilities.* The robot task abilities, as presented in Fig. 1, layer (2), section (A), subsection (A1), sub-subsection (A1-2), are divided into three categories: (1) Physical tasks: to describe the mobility and manipulation ability of the robot. (2) Cognitive tasks: to capture the ability of the robot in performing any informatics or data manipulation, such as learning, reasoning and problem-solving. (3) Social tasks: to describe the social ability of the robot, such as emotions, relationships, behaviours, and personality [3,5]. There are no defined social concepts, descriptions or levelling presented in MAR for social tasks. Therefore, identification of social indicators to describe the degree of these social tasks is suggested as a research area. Table 1 illustrates the categorization of task capabilities, sub-types and their levels.

**Table 1.** Categories of robot task abilities, types, sub-types and their levels.

| Types, subtypes and levels of robot task capabilities | |
| --- | --- |
| Physical tasks | – Robot motion capabilities, captures the system's moving ability through:<br>  • Unconstrained motion of the robot, presented in 8 levels<br>  • Constrained motion, presented in 6 levels<br>– Robot manipulation capabilities, captures the system's manipulation ability through:<br>  • Grasping capabilities, presented in 9 levels<br>  • Holding capabilities, presented in 6 levels<br>  • Handling capabilities, presented in 10 levels |
| Cognitive tasks | – Learning abilities, also known as 'acquiring knowledge', presented in 16 levels<br>– Reasoning abilities, presented in 9 levels |
| Social tasks | – Define indicators for different degree of social capabilities such as emotion, not presented in MAR, and are a proposed research area |

*(A1-3) Actions and Envisioning Capabilities.* This is the third subsection of robot capabilities, as presented in Fig. 1, layer (2), section (A), subsection (A1), sub-subsection (A1-3). A robot would not be able to perform an action unless it is listed as one of its available capabilities which has been described previously in the robot task ability. The ability of a robot to act purposefully and to assess the impact of its actions are separate abilities. These concepts are described in the following section:

– A robot's ability to act purposefully, presented by MAR in 10 levels, is categorized into: (1) Physical purposeful action, towards objects. (2) Cognitive purposeful action, towards information. (3) Social purposeful action, towards social members.
– A robot's envisioning abilities identify the impact of the action on the environment, presented by MAR in 9 levels. They are categorized as: physical envisioning, cognitive envisioning and social envisioning capabilities.

**Subsection (A2): General Capabilities.** The general capabilities are part of the robot capability section (A), within the technical capability layer (2), as presented in Fig. 1, layer (2), section (A), subsection (A2). These general capabilities depend on other capabilities to perform the most suitable and appropriate perception/action cycles [2]. To describe some of these general capabilities of the robot, the following concepts are defined by MAR:

1. Decisional autonomy (12 levels).
2. Task adaptability: system ability to carry on tasks between multiple agents (5 levels).
3. System dependability: ability to perform tasks without errors (8 levels).

## Section (B): Interaction Capabilities

A robot's interactions rely on its existing capabilities, such as perception, task abilities and actions. The sequence of performing these capabilities as robot actions towards an environment is termed the 'interaction cycle', or the 'robot-world feedback loop' [20]. The execution of the interaction cycles create tasks and/or behaviours. These tasks and/or behaviours generate a specific skill, which demonstrates a distinct intelligence, such as social, physical/morphological, cognitive or collective intelligence, presented in the next section.

The accumulated interaction cycles performed by a robot define its interaction towards object, information and/or social members to determines the interaction category. This section is divided into three categories, as presented in Fig. 1, layer (2), section (B): (1) Physical interaction, which captures the robot's connection with its environment. (2) Social interaction, which captures a robot connecting with other social members. (3) Cognitive interaction, which captures a robot connecting to any information system. Robot interaction categories, types and levels are listed in Table 2. All other robot interaction classifications are also included in this section (B), such as paradigms, roles, social models of interactions, interaction length/period, social robot interaction types, interaction media, interaction mode and interaction architecture.

## Section (C): Intelligence/Skills Capabilities

The third section of the technical capabilities layer encompasses a robot's intelligence/skills, as presented in Fig. 1, layer (2), section (C). Robot intelligence outlines the purpose of a robot's performance and describes the external perception of its actions [16]. It also clarifies what sort of intelligence the designer aims to present in the robot by expressing the ultimate cause of the robot's actions/behaviour captured through specific skills. Therefore, the intelligence in this section is defined by specific skills, behaviours and interactions [5,8]. The intelligence/skill explanation is an essential aspect for robot description, robot comparison and robot taxonomy. There are several types of intelligence that might be acquired by the robot [5,10,14]. Each intelligence is represented by specific skills, adopted from Gardener's theory of multiple intelligence [14]:

**Table 2.** Interaction categories, types and levels.

| Interaction categories, types and levels | |
| --- | --- |
| Physical | – Object interaction: presented in 8 levels |
| Cognitive | – Robot-to-robot interaction: level of interaction between robots in carrying out tasks, presented in 8 levels |
| | – System-to-system interaction: degree of information exchange, not presented in MAR, and is a proposed research area |
| Social | – Human-robot interaction: to capture users interactions, presented in 9 levels |
| | – Human-robot interaction feedback: user perception of robot state, presented in 9 levels |
| | – Human interaction levels of extent: integrating information through extended social interaction, presented in 8 levels |
| | – Cognitive social interaction complexity: presented in 5 levels |
| | – Human interaction modality: including different modalities of human interaction, presented in 6 levels |
| | – Social interaction learning: presented in 4 levels |
| | – Human-cognitive robot interaction: presented in 8 levels |

- Physical-morphological intelligence, such as bodily-kinaesthetic skills or visual-spatial skills.
- Cognitive intelligence, such as learning skills or logical-mathematical skills.
- Social intelligence, such as emotional behaviour skills or musical skills.
- Collective intelligence, which captures emerging skills in combining either heterogeneous or homogeneous robots, such as collaboration or cooperative skills.

**The Third Layer: Operational Capabilities**

The operational capabilities covers the following concepts with regard to a robot: cost, duration, safety, security, testing, training, acceptance, usability, re-usability, reliability, versatility, robustness and the operational environment (e.g., ground, aerial, or underwater [17,19]), as presented in Fig. 1, layer (3).

# 3   Illustration of the Conceptual Structure

To demonstrate the ability of the conceptual structure to capture robot characteristics in a profile, different robots are presented through out the conceptual structure.

## 3.1   Social Robots

Social robots are engaged in diverse social scenarios. The social aspect of the robot could be situated in any of the social categories throughout the conceptual structure. The following examples demonstrate the conceptual structure in presenting social robots. The first example is to illustrate the Zeno robot [7] in a capability profile. In the first layer, Zeno would be situated as having both hardware and software. In the second layer, if Zeno is programmed with social perception and social recognition abilities to identify people, it would be situated in the social perception category. If Zeno is programmed to name the identified person and greet him, it would be situated in the social task abilities category. If Zeno is programmed to act purposefully with social intent, then it would be situated in the social action category. The interaction categories are defined by Zeno's social interaction cycles. If Zeno is programmed to perform a greeting, for example, waving and shaking hands, then it would have two skills to support both the physical/morphological and the social intelligence. If Zeno is programmed to say 'hello', presenting some verbal/linguistic skills, it would support social intelligence. In the third layer, the operational capabilities of Zeno need to be defined, such as cost, duration of performance, safety issues, tests and training, as well as the acceptance and usability rate and operational environment capabilities.

Another example is to illustrate how the NAO robot [6] performance is captured via the conceptual structure. For this example, a NAO robot is programmed to perform a sequence of activities. In the first and third layer of the conceptual structure, the NAO would cover the same concepts as described above with the robot Zeno. In the second layer, the programmed activities within the NAO would describe its capabilities presented in section (A) and section (B). As an illustration for the NAO performance: the NAO's first activity is to recognize a predefined red ball on the floor among other unknown objects. Performing this activity requires the robot to have object recognition and object interpretation capabilities. The second activity is to recognize some predefined faces of people in the room and move towards them. Performing this activity requires the robot to have social perception, self-location perception, social agent location perception and physical mobility capabilities. The third activity is to have a social conversation and perform a dance. Performing this activity requires the NAO to have social interaction and motion capabilities. The NAO robot needs to have some basic levels of decisional autonomy and it is not performing any task adaptability nor any task dependability covered in subsection (A2). In section (C), the activities performed by the NAO robot present the robot with searching and social skills. These skills enhance the robot's appearance as a robot with social intelligence.

## 3.2   Simulated Robots

An important aspect should be clarified when applying this conceptual structure to simulated robots. The physical aspect of the simulated robot is presented as part of the hardware section in the first layer of the robot features. Using BabyX [9] as an example of an interactive simulated robot, BabyX would be situated as having both hardware and software. In the second layer, if BabyX is programmed to identify and track an object, it would be situated in the physical perception category. If BabyX is performing learning then it would be situated in the cognitive task ability category. BabyX's interaction cycles will define the motivation in presenting a specific skill. If BabyX's interactions present some verbal/linguistic skills then it will demonstrate social intelligence. If BabyX is programmed to perform interaction for the purpose of presenting learning skills, then it will display cognitive intelligence. For the third layer, the operational capabilities within BabyX (such as cost, safety, training, acceptance and usability) need to be defined.

### 3.3   Swarm Robots

Applying the conceptual structure to present the performance of swarm robots requires presenting the individual swarm robot capability in one profile (by using the same concepts applied for the social robot) and the whole swarm system in another profile.

### 3.4   Reconfigurable Robots

Using the conceptual structure to present the capabilities of reconfigurable robots, requires presenting each module capability in an individual profile and any combined modules in another capability profile.

## 4   Advantages of the Conceptual Structure

The conceptual structure aims to provide a clear description of robot characteristics. It outlines robot specifications in layers, categories and levels to present a comprehensive robot capabilities profile. The structure can be used in various ways. The most desired benefit of the capability profile is the link between robot capabilities and application requirements. The growth of robot capabilities in laboratories and the corresponding increase in requirements, needs an extensive bridging model. Therefore, embedding this conceptual structure within a robot-application mapping framework would improve robot deployment and application selection. The conceptual structure outlines the linking process between requirements and robot characteristics. For any robot application it will define the most appropriate robot. It will also indicate what changes are needed within the robot in order to fulfil a specific application requirement. Moreover, the conceptual structure will enable the mapping of any given robot to its most suitable application, where it can clarify the most advanced features of the robot that are essential for a particular application.

Some robotic fields are more developed than others. Demonstrating these robots in profiles using the conceptual structure highlights their advanced characteristics, which will help laboratories develop new approaches by mixing available robot characteristics. Therefore, presenting robot capability profiles helps to develop robots by using existing capabilities in the same field or from different fields [18]. On the other hand, presenting robot capability profiles will clarify the effectiveness and limitations of each robot, allowing better development and business decisions.

Furthermore, applying the conceptual structure and presenting robots in the different dimensions namely: layers, sections, categories and levels, and classifies them. It filters robots along one or more of the conceptual dimensions and matches them to others. This will lead to a taxonomy/classification for various robot types, even from different fields. From a broader perspective, the layers of the conceptual structure are broad and flexible enough to capture current robot characteristics and any future features that might be developed. Additionally, providing a flexible structure to include diverse interests from both industry and academia, helps in understanding the contrasting interests and approaches. Thus, the conceptual structure can be considered as a point of reference to resolve different views from a range of disciplines into one harmonized pattern. Finally, the conceptual structure presents a new method for outlining robot descriptions, specifications, evaluations and validations [13].

## 5   Conclusions

Bridging the gap between robot application (benefits, purpose and requirements) and technology (features and capabilities) is an important but challenging task. The aim of this paper is to describe a novel theoretical model to capture robot features and their capabilities in the robotic domain and to match them accordingly to the requirements of particular applications. Therefore, the proposed conceptual structure provides outlined features to accommodate comparably detailed profiles. It also aims to enhance the robotic field and its literature by providing a schematic model of classification to improve robot development and deployment. It is important that the conceptual structure adopts the levels used in MAR where possible, and innovates to expand MAR where necessary. This work differs from existing taxonomies in that it classifies robots through their capabilities. The theoretical aspects of the classification are presented in this paper, along with brief examples. The practical application of the classification is an outcome of this research and lies outside of the capacity of the current paper.

## References

1. Breazeal, C.: Social interactions in HRI: the robot view. IEEE Trans. Syst. Man Cybern. Part C (Appl. Rev.) **34**(2), 181–186 (2004)
2. Cutsuridis, V., Hussain, A., Taylor, J.G.: Perception-Action Cycle: Models, Architectures, and Hardware. Springer, New York (2011). https://doi.org/10.1007/978-1-4419-1452-1

3. Dautenhahn, K.: Socially intelligent robots: dimensions of human–robot interaction. Philos. Trans. R. Soc. Lond. B Biol. Sci. **362**(1480), 679–704 (2007)
4. Dobra, A.: General classification of robots. Size criteria. In: Proceedings of Robotics in Alpe-Adria-Danube Region (RAAD), pp. 1–6. IEEE (2014)
5. Fong, T., Nourbakhsh, I., Dautenhahn, K.: A survey of socially interactive robots. Robot. Auton. Syst. **42**(3), 143–166 (2003)
6. Gouaillier, D., et al.: Mechatronic design of NAO humanoid. In: 2009 IEEE International Conference on Robotics and Automation, pp. 769–774, May 2009
7. Hanson, D., et al.: Zeno: a cognitive character. AI Magazine, and Special Proceedings of AAAI National Conference, Chicago (2009)
8. Kihlstrom, J.F., Cantor, N.: Social intelligence. In: Sternberg, R.J. (ed.) Handbook of Intelligence, pp. 359–379. Cambridge University Press (2000)
9. Lawler-Dormer, D.: Baby x: digital artificial intelligence, computational neuroscience and empathetic interaction. In: Proceedings of the 19th International Symposium on Electronic Art. ISEA International (2013)
10. ManagementMania:   Thorndike's   intelligence   theory   (2016).   https://managementmania.com/en/thorndikes-intelligence-theory
11. McGrenere, J., Ho, W.: Affordances: clarifying and evolving a concept. In: Graphics Interface, pp. 179–186 (2000)
12. Moore, R.K.: The future of speech-based services: bringing in the benefit. In: COST 249 Workshop on Voice Operated Telecom Services (2000)
13. Moore, R.K.: Section 1: users guide. In: EAGLES Handbook of Standards and Resources for Spoken Language Systems, vol. 1, no. 1, pp. 1–28. Speech Research Unit, DRA Malvern, Worcestershire (1993)
14. Pal, H.R., Pal, A., Tourani, P.: Theories of intelligence. Everyman's Sci. **39**(3), 181–192 (2004)
15. Prestes, E., et al.: Towards a core ontology for robotics and automation. Robot. Auton. Syst. **61**(11), 1193–1204 (2013)
16. Schaefer, K.E., Billings, D.R., Hancock, P.A.: Robots vs. machines: identifying user perceptions and classifications. In: Proceedings of Cognitive Methods in Situation Awareness and Decision Support (CogSIMA), pp. 138–141. IEEE (2012)
17. Siciliano, B., Khatib, O.: Springer Handbook of Robotics. Springer, Heidelberg (2016). https://doi.org/10.1007/978-3-540-30301-5
18. Sita, E., Studley, M., Dailami, F., Pipe, A., Thomessen, T.: Towards multimodal interactions: robot jogging in mixed reality. In: Proceedings of the 23rd ACM Symposium on Virtual Reality Software and Technology, VRST 2017, pp. 78:1–78:2. ACM (2017)
19. SPARC Robotics, eu-Robotics AISBL, Brussels, Belgium: Robotics Multi-annual Roadmap for Robotics in Europe, Horizon 2020 (2016)
20. Winfield, A.: Robotics: A Very Short Introduction. Oxford University Press, Oxford (2012)

# Implementation and Validation of Kalman Filter Based Sensor Fusion on the Zorro Mini-robot Platform

Philipp Bolte, Joyce Martin, Reza Zandian, and Ulf Witkowski$^{(\boxtimes)}$

South Westphalia University of Applied Sciences,
Luebecker Ring 2, 59494 Soest, Germany
{bolte.philipp,witkowski.ulf}@fh-swf.de
http://www.fh-swf.de/embedded-sys

**Abstract.** This paper focuses on the implementation of a Kalman filter for a sensor fusion task and the testing and validation of the implementation by using a test platform. Implementation device for the sensors and the fusion algorithm is the mini-robot platform Zorro that is equipped with multiple sensors. In order to internally develop a consistent model of the robot's world sensor data has to be fused. The fused data is used to control the behavior of the robot that should be able to act autonomously. To test the sensor fusion and the resulting behavior a Teleworkbench test system has been developed that supports video recording and analysis of the robot's behavior complemented by wireless transmission of robot's internal sensor and state data. Both, the video data and the sensor data are matched and displayed at operator's computer of the Teleworkbench system for detailed analysis.

**Keywords:** Sensor fusion · Kalman filter · Test platform
Teleworkbench · Zorro mini-robot

## 1 Introduction

Robots being able to act autonomously need several sensors to get internal robot data as well as information about the environment. Depending on the set of tasks different types and numbers of sensors are required [1]. Typical sensors for autonomous robots are infrared and ultrasound sensors to locally sense for obstacles, laser scanner might be used to sense for obstacle more far away or to get information about location of walls and open space, an IMU can be used to estimate the robots movements, this is often complemented by incremental encoders to get speed data of motors or wheels. For object identification and advanced navigation camera sensors can be used. Usually the sensors have different modalities, different range and resolution. Therefore it's a challenge to combine the available sensor data to get a consistent and as complete as possible view of the robot status and its environment. A behavior generation unit

© Springer International Publishing AG, part of Springer Nature 2018
M. Giuliani et al. (Eds.): TAROS 2018, LNAI 10965, pp. 393–404, 2018.
https://doi.org/10.1007/978-3-319-96728-8_33

often uses all sensor data to analyze robot's situation and to decide on next steps. A powerful tool to combine sensor data is sensor and data fusion [2].

We have designed the Zorro mini-robot platform to be able to do experiments with single and multiple robots with reasonable space requirements. Several sensors including a micro-controller with floating point unit have been integrated into the robot base platform. If a camera sensor is required, a smartphone can be attached to the robot's base and connected via USB to the microcontroller. Image processing and complex behavior planning is performed on the smartphone's processing unit that today provides high processing power. Even for simple robot tasks like odometry sensor fusion is very helpful. If the robot does not have access to an external localization system the robot has to estimate its own position and heading based on odometry that usually uses data from the incremental encoders of the motors and wheels. To reduce drift of calculated position and heading other sensor data as provided by an IMU or compass can be used.

In order to fuse the data from the different sources a Kalman filter approach has been tested and integrated. Because of the complexity of the fusion algorithms and for better testing our Teleworkbench platform is used. This platform supports wireless capture of robot's sensor data and status data for off-line experiment analysis [3]. The analysis option is complemented by a video capture of the robot when performing experiments. Based on the video data the robot's position and heading is extracted and saved for the analysis of the robot's performance and the features of the implemented algorithms including sensor fusion. For the development of a new fusion algorithms usually one robot is used, in this case one robot has to be tracked only by the video system. When experiments with multiple robot's are performed a LabVIEW based tracking software is used that supports the online tracking of multiple robots in parallel including the performance analysis of the robots.

Main focus of this paper is the development of sensor fusion algorithms based real data of the robot sensors captured by the Teleworkbench. The fusion algorithm is tested and optimized using MATLAB due to provided analysis options. The video capture feature of the Teleworkbench is used to analyze the fusion algorithm including the achieved advances based on the sensor fusion, here in term of position estimation and heading of the robot.

The paper is organized as follows: In Sect. 2 the Zorro mini-robot and integrated sensors are introduced. Section 3 explains the implemented Kalman filter for advanced odometry that is based on data from the incremental encoder and a compass sensor. The Teleworkbench for experiment analysis is presented in Sect. 4. Section 5 discusses performed experiments and achieved advances based on the sensor fusion. A conclusion is given in Sect. 6.

## 2   The Mini-robot Zorro

The Zorro robot platform has been developed to enable real world robotic experiments with a relatively low barrier to be able to do necessary programming. Due to its small diameter of 11 cm it can be used for experiments on the table or in medium sized labs or it can be used for multi-robot experiments with reasonable space requirements [4]. Zorro is two-wheeled platform as depicted in Fig. 1. Core processing element is the microcontroller STM32L496, an ARM Cortex M4 from ST. This controller calculates the speed and torque control of the two motors, reads the data from all integrated sensors and provides a USB interface to optionally integrate a smartphone into the robot platform. Also basic behaviors like driving simple pattern as line, arc and turn are implemented on the microcontroller. Tasks that are significantly more complex are to be implemented on the smartphone. For the bidirectional communication between the microcontroller and the smartphone a protocol has been defined that supports transmission of all sensor data to the smartphone and vice versa. An important task of the smartphone is to provide video capture and image processing. Because of the today's high quality image sensor of smartphones and the available processing power, experiments on e.g. vision based navigation becomes possible.

**Fig. 1.** Zorro robot platform. Left: base platform with drive system, microcontroller and several integrated sensors; right: Zorro base with attached smartphone for video capturing and advanced processing

## 2.1 Integrated Sensors

Main sensors that are integrated into the base platform are eight infrared sensors (STMicroelectronics VL6180XV0NR/1), used for obstacle detection in context of navigation, an inertial unit (TDK InvenSense MPU-9250) with integrated accelerometer, gyroscope and compass, motor speed encoders and motor current sensors (TI INA219), and battery control (Linear Technology LTC2943) to check for battery status. A block diagram of the robot's base module is depicted in Fig. 2.

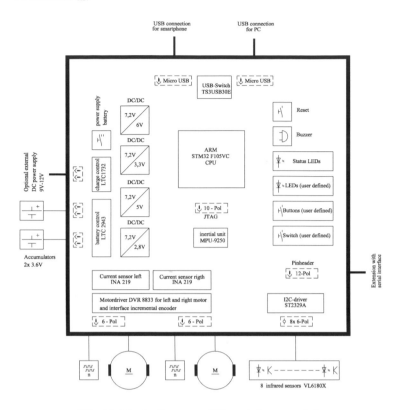

**Fig. 2.** Block diagram of Zorro's base module

If a smartphone is connected to the robot's base additional sensors become available depending on the smartphone model. Typical additional sensors are an IMU, compass, GPS, brightness, sometimes air pressure and thermometer and even heart rate senor that is usually not important in robot context. The most powerful sensor of smartphones is the camera that enables together with the smartphone's computing power object detection and recognition, scene analysis and in general vision based behavior including navigation. In mobile robotics the combination of different sensor data helps to complete the multimodal view of the robot.

In case several sensors are used in parallel it's a challenge to combine the different sensor data to a consistent view. I.e., the combination of sensor data may complete the view of the robot. Or the combination helps to have more accurate data or data with higher confidence about the robot state or situation. The underlying process is called sensor fusion. In this paper the sensor fusion is used to get more accurate information about the robot's position and heading direction when the robot is moving in its environment. In the following section the fusion of data of the incremental encoders and the compass sensor is discussed. Objective is to increase the performance of the odometry of the robot.

## 3   Kalman Filter Based Sensor Fusion

The knowledge of the robot's pose in its environment is essential when acting autonomously following a special driving strategy. An odometry system can be used to track the robot's motion state when starting at known position with known heading. Odometry is described as the integration of incremental small pose changes of a vehicle based on the velocity of its wheels [5]. The kinematic model is based on the mechanical structure of the robot and its involved motion constraints [6]. The incremental integration of it results in the actual pose of the robot with respect to its initial pose. The simplified discrete kinematic model of the Zorro platform is defined as:

$$\hat{\underline{x}}_n = \begin{bmatrix} x_{I,n} \\ y_{I,n} \\ \theta_n \end{bmatrix} = \begin{bmatrix} x_{I,n-1} \\ y_{I,n-1} \\ \theta_{n-1} \end{bmatrix} + \Delta t \begin{bmatrix} \cos\theta & -\sin\theta & 0 \\ \sin\theta & \cos\theta & 0 \\ 0 & 0 & 1 \end{bmatrix} \begin{bmatrix} \frac{R}{2} & \frac{R}{2} \\ 0 & 0 \\ \frac{R}{2L} & -\frac{R}{2L} \end{bmatrix} \begin{bmatrix} \dot{\varphi}_{R,n} \\ \dot{\varphi}_{L,n} \end{bmatrix} \quad (1)$$

with:

$\hat{\underline{x}}_n$: A-priori pose of the robot
$x_I$, $y_I$: Robot position in the environment
$\theta$: Heading direction
$R$: Radius of the wheels
$L$: Distance of the contact points to the centre
$\dot{\varphi}_R$, $\dot{\varphi}_L$: Angular velocity of the wheels

This model does not cover all aspects of the motion of the robot (e.g. deviations in the radius of the wheels and their distance to the centre of the axis, alignment errors, uneven surfaces, wheel slip [7]) to achieve a manageable complexity.

Measurement errors and deviations from the model lead to an increasing pose error over the time due to the integration of the input values and the non-existent internal dynamics of the system. Therefore the heading direction of the robot is additionally measured with a magnetometer.

$$y_n = \begin{bmatrix} 0 & 0 & 1 \end{bmatrix} \underline{x}_n = \varphi_n \quad (2)$$

The state space model of the system is shown in Fig. 3. The uncertainties of motion during one time step $(w_n)$ and the magnetometer measurements $(v_n)$ are approximated by Gaussian noise with known variance.

A Kalman filter was used to fuse the heading direction estimation of the odometry with absolute heading direction measurements from the magnetometer. The Kalman filter is a data fusion approach that uses a time discrete state space model and represents the uncertainties by white Gaussian noise. The variance of the estimation is minimized given those constraints [8]. The structure is shown in Fig. 4.

Two cumulative steps are applied for each iteration. The pose of the robot is predicted using the kinematic model of the robot given in Eq. 1.

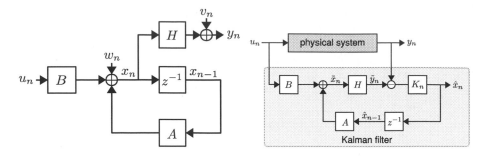

**Fig. 3.** Structure of a noisy discrete state space system

**Fig. 4.** Structure of the Kalman filter

The variance of the heading direction estimation increases during this step:

$$p_n = p_{n-1} + \sigma_{predict} \tag{3}$$

Then, the estimation of the heading direction is updated by utilizing the magnetometer measurements. The uncertainty of the estimation decreases after a measurement $(\hat{p}_n)$. The degree of correction (Kalman gain $k$) is determined by the variances of the estimation and measurement.

$$\hat{\theta}_n = \theta_n + k_n(\theta_{mag,n} - \theta_n) \tag{4}$$

$$k_n = \frac{p_n}{p_n + r} \tag{5}$$

$$\hat{p}_n = (1 - k_n)p_n \tag{6}$$

The used data fusion approach is only able to correct the estimation of the heading direction because this value is directly measured by the magnetometer. The measurement $y$ is independent from the position $x_I$, $y_I$. Nevertheless, the correction of the heading direction will also reduce the position error because the integration of the position data depends on the heading direction.

## 4   Teleworkbench for Experiment Analysis

The evaluation of the developed pose tracking algorithm was done using the Teleworkbench shown in Fig. 5. The driving manoeuvre of the robot is captured with a camera. Each camera frame is tagged with a timestamp. A patch with a geometric figure is mounted on top of the robot to enable the extraction of the robot's pose. At the same time the sensor and actuator data from the robot is continuously wirelessly transmitted to a PC using a Bluetooth connection. The experiment analysis is performed off-line. A Python program extracts the pose trajectory of the robot. The gathered data from the wheel encoders and the magnetometer is processed off-line by the described Kalman filter using MATLAB. The evaluation of the designed tracking algorithm is also performed using MATLAB. The set of matched pose trajectories recorded by the camera and estimated using the sensor data from the robot can be used multiple times for testing different algorithm configurations. This approach allows the flexible adoption of the parameters of the Kalman filter without the need of rerunning the experiment multiple times. The reuse of input data for the data fusion algorithm enables a direct performance evaluation between different configurations. The captured data for certain driving manoeuvres can be stored to avoid the need of repeating an experiment.

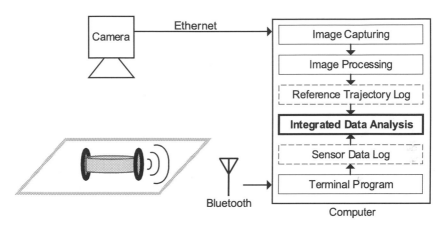

**Fig. 5.** Structure of the teleworkbench

## 4.1  Video Recording and Processing

The driving manoeuvre is captured using a camera that is mounted orthogonal in a height of 2 m above the playground. The lens of the camera causes a radial distortion and its misalignment in relation to the sensor introduce tangential distortion [9]. The raw images from the camera are processed to correct lens distortions. The information density is further increased by transferring the colour image into a binary one which represents if a pixel is consistent with the colour of the patch. The exact pose of the robot is captured by multiple convolutions of the patch in different scales and rotations with the binary image. The results of the convolutions are filtered by a threshold. The absolute pose of the robot is determined by averaging the position and the rotation of the fitting convolutions. The final results of the extracted poses over time are stored in a CSV logfile for further processing by the integrated data analysis.

## 4.2  Wireless Capture of Sensor Data

The software of the MCU acquires and processes the raw data from the wheel encoders and the magnetometer. The pre-processed data is transmitted to a

PC using a Bluetooth connection with the serial port profile (SPP). The data is transmitted together with a timestamp as an ASCII formatted comma separated string. The first column specifies the data source (e.g. wheel encoder) using an enumeration. The time of reading is stored in the second column as a timestamp and the actual sensor value in 32 bit float representation is added in the third column. A standard terminal program was used to receive the data and to store it in a logfile. Each line of the log file consists of one sensor reading. This file can be imported to the workspace of MATLAB using its integrated CSV parser. This approach provides a simple but powerful solution for recording sensor data of the robot on a computer.

### 4.3   Integrated Data Analysis

The evaluation of the tracking performance is done by implementing an integrated data analysis using MATLAB. The data samples from the camera system and the sensor values from the robot need to be matched. Therefore a synchronization method is required. The robot optically indicates the start of a driving manoeuvre by toggling an LED. At the same time the transmission of the sensor data over Bluetooth is started. The camera is recording with a constant frame rate which enables a temporal matching of both data sources. The designed Kalman filter is applied to the set of sensor data. Each wheel encoder data used for the prediction step is followed by a magnetometer reading that updates the estimation. The resulting trajectory over the time is matched with the reference path gathered from the video recording. The performance of the tracking algorithm was evaluated depending on the tested driving manoeuvre. For driving a straight line e.g. the lateral error $\Delta y$ was compared. A direct measurement of the variances of both the wheel encoder and the magnetometer data for optimizing the performance of the Kalman filter is not possible because the robot is moving and the reference data is noisy as well. The main advantage of the reference system is the absolute measurement of pose in contrast to the iterative odometry system. The ratio between process and measurement noise that determines the strength of correction can be adjusted in a way that the error of estimation decreases. The resulting Kalman filter parameters providing good performance can be used for developing an optimal on-line odometry system.

### 4.4   Robot Tracking

For the development and testing of the sensor fusion algorithms an off-line approach has been used. I.e., data from the robot and video data has been processed off-line using MATLAB to do detailed step by step analysis of the implemented algorithm. For the analysis of multi-robot experiments the same Teleworkbench setup as depicted in Fig. 5 with photograph in Fig. 6 is used, but the on-line tracking of multiple robots is performed via a LabVIEW frontend. For unique identification a special pattern is used that allows robot identification, localization and heading extraction of the robots. An example experiment setup and related screenshot of the extracted robot position is shown in Fig. 7.

**Fig. 6.** Teleworkbench environment: 2 m by 2 m playground with overhead gig-vision camera and computer on the right for experiment setup and analysis

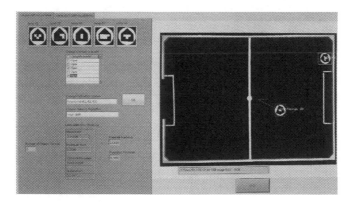

**Fig. 7.** Example multi-robot experiment with automatic tracking. GUI with selected templates and report of tracking performance and recorded scene with overlay of robot position, heading and trajectory

## 5   Experiments with the Zorro Platform

The developed integrated data analysis was tested with various driving manoeuvres (e.g. driving a straight line or an arc). The results for driving a line is a vivid example of the capabilities of the developed Kalman filter. Therefore the

robot was supposed to drive a straight line with a velocity of about 5 cm/s. The
lateral position $y$ and the heading direction $\theta$ for one sample dataset are shown
in Figs. 8 and 9.

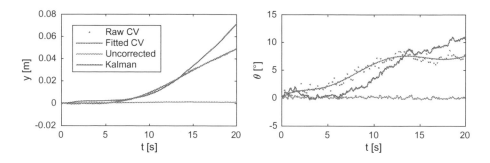

**Fig. 8.** Lateral position $y$          **Fig. 9.** Heading direction $\theta$

Due to the integrated driving controller of the Zorro robot both wheels are
rotating at the same angular velocity. The lateral position $y$ of the uncorrected
odometry system is constant over the time. The real path of the robot is not
ideal straight due to the existent process noise. The magnetometer is measuring
the drift of the heading direction which causes the Kalman filter to compensate
the lateral drift to a certain degree. The slope of the lateral position error of
the Kalman filter output rises with a significant lower slope although it is not
directly affected by the data fusion.

The experiment results for driving an arc show that the correction of the
heading direction has also a positive effect on the geometric distance error for
this manouvre. The robot has driven a circular path with a radius of 5 cm with
an average velocity of 10 cm/s. The evaluation of the geometric distance error $\Delta s$
of the uncorrected path and the Kalman filter output as well as the estimation
of the heading direction $\theta$ for one run are shown in Figs. 10 and 11.

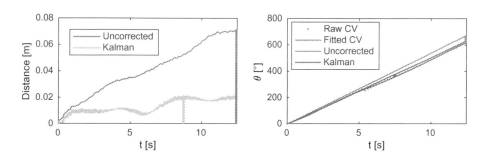

**Fig. 10.** Geometric distance error $\Delta s$          **Fig. 11.** Heading direction $\theta$

Even the circlealthough the model parameters are not affected by it. The position deviation of the robot is based on the heading direction. Therefore a drift in the heading direction caused by model parameter uncertainties increases the position error. The Kalman filter compensates those uncertainties to a certain degree as shown in Fig. 11.

The usage of the magnetometer to determine the heading direction of the robot is only suitable for environments where the homogeneous magnetic field of the earth is not distorted. Further experiments were performed to evaluate the homogeneity of the magnetic field in the environment. The total magnetic flux density was used as an indicator for field inhomogeneity. This value should be almost constant for all locations of the robot in the soccer playground. But ferromagnetic materials in the surrounding of the magnetometer concentrate the field lines of the magnetic field as it can be caused by iron screws. Figure 12 shows the measured magnetic flux density when driving nearby a screw.

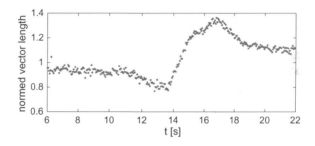

**Fig. 12.** Punctual magnetic perturbance and the resulting change in flux density when the robot is driving oven a screw that is used in the playground setup

The external magnetic field is concentrated at some positions caused by screws because a screw forms a magnetic dipole itself. The flux density slightly decreases when the robot is approaching a screw. In close proximity to the screw the magnetic flux density is increasing rapidly which magnetises the soft iron components of the robot. Therefore the magnetic flux density does not immediately reaches the initial level. Disturbances of the magnetic field lead to heading direction error. The ability to detect those abnormalities and to adapt the degree of heading direction correction would further improve the performance of the data fusion approach.

## 6   Conclusions

The Zorro mini-robot platform has been introduced as tool for development of sensor fusion algorithms. Mobile robots are usually equipped with several sensors of different modality to sense the environment. In order to get useful and confident information from all the sensor data sensor and data fusion algorithms can be used to process the captured sensor data. As application example the development of an odometry system has been discussed that is based on fused data of the incremental encoders and the compass sensor. For development detailed testing of the algorithm MATLAB has been used as a powerful off-line data processing tool. The analysis of the performance of the fusion algorithm has been done by using the Teleworkbench system that supports video based capturing of the robot movements as well as data capturing of the robot's sensor data.

It was shown that by fusing data from the incremental encoders and the magnetometer the performance of the odometry is increased. The heading direction is estimated with higher confidence. As a result the robot's driving trajectory can be calculated with less deviation. The performance of the implemented Kalman filter has been successfully confirmed by the Teleworkbench system by analyzing the robot's actual path. In future work the fusion algorithm should be extended by an additional sensor system that is based on UWB (Ultra-Wide Band) localization technique. The mean deviation of this radio based localization system is about 5 cm. But by combining the already implemented odometry system and the UWB system we expect to significantly reduce static error when performing odometry.

# References

1. Siegwart, R., Nourbakhsh, I.R., Scaramuzza, D.: Introduction to Autonomous Mobile Robots. The MIT Press, London (2011)
2. Castanedo, F.: A review of data fusion techniques. Sci. World J. 2013, Article ID 704504 (2013)
3. Tanoto, A., Rückert, U., Witkowski, U.: Teleworkbench: a teleoperated platform for experiments in multi-robotics. In: Tzafestas, S.G. (ed.) Web-Based Control and Robotics Education, vol. 38, pp. 287–316. Springer, Dordrecht (2009). https://doi.org/10.1007/978-90-481-2505-0_12
4. Sitte, J., Witkowski, U., Zandian, R.: Learning with small autonomous robots. In: Kim, J.-H., Karray, F., Jo, J., Sincak, P., Myung, H. (eds.) Robot Intelligence Technology and Applications 4. AISC, vol. 447, pp. 341–355. Springer, Cham (2017). https://doi.org/10.1007/978-3-319-31293-4_28
5. Groves, P.D.: Principles of GNSS, Inertial, and Multi-sensor Integrated Navigation Systems. Artech House, Boston (2008)
6. Siciliano, B., Khatib, O.: Springer Handbook of Robotics. Springer, Berlin, Heidelberg (2008). https://doi.org/10.1007/978-3-540-30301-5
7. Borenstein, J., Everett, H.R., Fend, L.: Where Am I: Sensors and Methods for Mobile Robot Positioning. University of Michigan, Michigan (1996)
8. Marchthaler, R., Dingler, S.: Kalman-Filter: Einfuehrung in die Zustandsschaetzung und ihre Anwendung fuer eingebettete Systeme. Springer, Wiesbaden (2017). https://doi.org/10.1007/978-3-658-16728-8
9. Weng, J., Cohen, P., Herniou, M.: Camera calibration with distortion models and accuracy evaluation. IEEE Trans. Pattern Anal. Mach. Intell. 14(10), 965–980 (1992)

# Evaluation of a Robot-Assisted Therapy for Children with Autism and Intellectual Disability

Daniela Conti[1([⊠])] [iD], Grazia Trubia[2] [iD], Serafino Buono[2] [iD], Santo Di Nuovo[3] [iD], and Alessandro Di Nuovo[1] [iD]

[1] Sheffield Robotics, Sheffield Hallam University, Sheffield, S1 1WB, UK
{d.conti,a.dinuovo}@shu.ac.uk
[2] IRCSS Oasi Maria SS, Via Conte Ruggero 73, 94018 Troina, EN, Italy
{gtrubia,fbuono}@oasi.en.it
[3] University of Catania, Via Teatro Greco 84, 95124 Catania, Italy
s.dinuovo@unict.it

**Abstract.** It is well established that robots can be suitable assistants in the care and treatment of children with Autism Spectrum Disorder (ASD). However, the majority of the research focuses on stand-alone interventions, high-functioning individuals and the success is evaluated via qualitative analysis of videos recorded during the interaction.

In this paper, we present a preliminary evaluation of our on-going research on integrating robot-assisted therapy in the treatment of children with ASD and Intellectual Disability (ID), which is the most common case. The experiment described here integrates a robot-assisted imitation training in the standard treatment of six hospitalised children with various level of ID, who were engaged by a robot on imitative tasks and their progress assessed via a quantitative psycho-diagnostic tool. Results show success in the training and encourage the use of a robotic assistant in the care of children with ASD and ID with the exception of those with profound ID, who may need a different approach.

**Keywords:** Autism spectrum disorder · Intellectual disability
Socially assistive robotics · TEACCH · VB-MAPP

## 1 Introduction

Autism Spectrum Disorder (ASD) can often comorbid with some level of Intellectual Disability (ID) [20], in fact it has been reported that 54% of children with ASD have an Intellectual Quotient (IQ) below 85 [3], which encompasses four ID levels: "mild", "moderate", "severe" and "profound", characterised by significant limitations in both intellectual function and in adaptive behaviour. These limitations result in problems with reasoning, learning or problem-solving as well as communication and social skills difficulties. Imitative deficits are very often observed in children with ASD [9, 23]. The presence of ID makes therapeutic interventions more difficult and, therefore, there is need of the technological aid [7].

© Springer International Publishing AG, part of Springer Nature 2018
M. Giuliani et al. (Eds.): TAROS 2018, LNAI 10965, pp. 405–415, 2018.
https://doi.org/10.1007/978-3-319-96728-8_34

Considered the complexity and the wide amplitude of this "spectrum", which encompasses different disabilities and severity levels, it is appropriate the use of a multi-modal intervention that can be adapted to the individual's needs in order to obtain the best benefits from the therapy. As the same medicine cannot be offered to all types of patients, similarly robot interactions need to be customized as per the state and conditions of the individual patients [18]. Therefore, the controllable autonomy of robots has been exploited to provide acceptable social partners for these children [1]. Indeed, several studies have shown that some individuals with ASD prefer robots to humans and that robots generate a high degree of motivation and engagement in individuals who are unlikely or unwilling to interact socially with human therapists (see [16] for a review). Recent studies have successfully presented robots as mediators between humans and individuals with ASD [10]. For instance, Duquette et al. [8] show improvements in affective behaviour and attention sharing with co-participating human partners during an imitation task solicited by a simple robotic doll.

Furthermore, social robots may be especially beneficial for individuals with ASD who face communication difficulties because practicing communication can be less intimidating with a robot than with another person [2, 12].

For this reasons, robotics research has shown numerous benefits of robot assistants in the treatment of children with ASD [5, 17, 22] however, most of the studies focused on ASD individuals without ID or neglected to analyse comorbidity. In fact, very little has been done in this area and it could be considered as one of the current gaps between the scientific research and the clinical application [4]. The aim to use robots in a clinical setting is to reduce the therapist's workload by allowing the robot to take over some parts of the intervention. This includes, monitoring and recording the behaviour of the child, engaging the child when they are disinterested, and adapting between levels of intervention. This enables the therapist to oversee different children and plan the required intervention for every child on an individual basis [10].

However, while a qualitative analysis is usually considered by the previous research, e.g. via analysis of video-recorded human-robot interaction, the quantitative analysis that can be made through the use of standardized psycho-diagnostic tools is often lacking [7, 11].

The work presented here is part of the ongoing EU H2020 MSCA-IF CARER-AID project, which aims to fully integrate a robot-assistant within a standard treatment of hospitalised children with ASD and ID, i.e. the TEACCH (Treatment and Education of Autistic and related Communication Handicapped Children) approach [13].

The main aim of the present study was to verify the applicability of the robot-assisted therapy to lower ID levels, which are the most difficult to treat as support for a psycho-diagnostic and training tool previously standardized and validated in the psychological field. To this end, we introduced in the therapy a robot-assisted intervention, in which the rehabilitation tasks were developed and adapted to the children level according to a psycho-diagnostic instrument: Verbal Behaviour Milestones Assessment and Placement Program (VB-MAPP) [19], which is a standardised tool designed for children with ASD. In fact, the tool was used at the beginning (Ex-Ante) to identify the tasks to implement on the robot, and at the end (Ex-Post) of the training to quantitatively assess the result of the robot-assisted therapy.

## 2   Materials and Method

### 2.1   Participants

Six children (n = 6, Males = 6, *M*-chronological age = 104.3 months, range = 66–121, *SD* = 18.6), all males, were selected among patients diagnosed with ASD and ID. Specifically two participants were diagnosed with profound ID level, two severe ID level, one moderate ID level and one with mild ID level, as shown in Table 1.

**Table 1.** Participants description (age in months)

| P | CA | Leiter IQ | AE | ID level |
|----|-----|-----------|-----|----------|
| 01 | 103 | 22 | 22 | Profound |
| 02 | 121 | 22 | 22 | Profound |
| 03 | 118 | 27 | 29 | Severe |
| 04 | 116 | 38 | 31 | Severe |
| 05 | 66 | 53 | 26 | Moderate |
| 06 | 102 | 56 | 35 | Mild |

For each child, Table 1 presents the Age Equivalent (AE) expressed in months, which is calculated as the average of the *Growth Scores* (GS) associated to the different Chronological Age (CA) groups. These are based on the performance of typically developed children in the test manual [19].

All the participants are currently receiving treatment at the IRCCS Oasi Maria SS of Troina (Italy), a specialized institution for the rehabilitation and care of intellectual disabilities. Participants' ASD and ID levels have been diagnosed before the beginning the study with the standard psycho-diagnostic instruments: Leiter-R, WISC, PEP-3, VABS, ADI-R, and CARS-2. For more details and explanation see [6]. All children had verbal language absent or limited exclusively to verbal stereotypes.

All children follow a clinical daily program of training using the TEACCH approach with psychologists and highly specialized personnel. The core of TEACCH is that structured teaching can effectively work with children with autism.

Ethical approval was obtained, all the parents signed consent forms before their children were included in the study. The robot-assisted therapy could be discontinued at any time if the therapeutic team believed it was appropriate for the child.

### 2.2   Verbal Behaviour Milestones Assessment and Placement Program (VB-MAPP)

Gross motor imitation abilities of the participants were evaluated using the Verbal Behaviour Milestones Assessment and Placement Program (VB-MAPP) [19]. The VB-MAPP is a criterion-referenced assessment tool, curriculum guide, and skill tracking system that is designed for children with developmental disabilities. VB-MAPP considers skills that are balanced and sequenced along three different levels of child development (1 = 0–18 months, 2 = 18–30 months, and 3 = 30–48 months).

We administered the VB-MAPP in the standard form to each participant to evaluate the level of the participants in order to identify the starting level and program the robot training accordingly. The VB-MAPP protocol evaluates each milestone score by giving 1 for the correct fully execution of the task, 0.5 a partial execution, 0 for error or no imitation.

## 2.3   The Robot and the Experimental Procedure

The robot used for experimenting the robot-assisted therapy was the Softbank Robotics Nao, which is a small toy-like humanoid robot, very popular for child-robot interaction studies [5, 7]. Nao is 58 cm high, weights 4.3 kg and can produce very expressive gestures with 25° of freedom (DoF) (4 joints for each arm; 2 for each hand; 5 for each leg; 2 for the head and one to control the hips). Nao can detect faces and mimic eye contact moving the head accordingly, it can also vary the colour of LEDs in eyes' contour to simulate emotions, and it can capture a lot of information about the environment using sensors and microphones. Nao is programmed with a graphical programming tool, named *Choregraphe* [15].

The robot was programmed to implement the VB-MAPP tasks of levels 1 (Fig. 1), which were then adapted and applied to match the specific level of the participants.

| Gross Motor Imitation | | |
|---|---|---|
| Stomp one foot | Left/hold 1 leg (bent at knee) | |
| Kick | Stomp both feet together | |
| Lift foot/point toes up & down | Squat | |
| Shake foot | Cross legs standing | |
| Place feet together | One foot in front of other | |
| Spread feet apart | Cross legs sitting | |
| Place foot forward | Stomp both feet (alternating) | |
| Place foot backward | Tap table with palms | |
| Hop with two feet | Turn palms up and down | |
| Hop on one foot | Elbows at waist/palms up | |
| Clap hands | Elbows at waist/palms down | |
| Arms up (over head) | Elbows at waist/palms sideways | |
| Arms out to side | Hands together over head | |
| Hands to cheeks | Make circle to side with 1 arm | |
| Hands cover mouth | Make circles to side with 2 arms | |
| Arms out in front | Grab wrists | |
| Arms out to back | Wave with hand/up & down | |
| Arms to side/move up and down | Wave with hand/side to side | |
| Hands on head | Rub hands (palms together) | |
| Hands on shoulders | Wash hands movement | |
| Hands on knees | Tongue out | |
| Hands on waist | Tongue out & side to side | |
| Touch toes | Tongue out/up and down | |

**Fig. 1.** Tasks of VB-MAPP (level 1) that were implemented with the robot. For each child, we selected 3 tasks (T1, T2, T3) that he was not able to perform and trained him with the assistance of the robot.

(a)            (b)

**Fig. 2.** (a) the *visual schedule* for the robot-assisted therapy; (b) A child returning the visual schedule after a daily session.

The robot-assisted tasks were designed after preliminary evaluation and planning with the therapeutic team, who administered the VB-MAPP for the experiment. After analyse performance in each relevant skill area the clinician selected for each child, three gross motor imitation tasks (T1, T2 and T3) that the children were not able to do or did not perform properly, i.e. that received a milestone score of 0 or 0.5.

The experimental procedure comprised a preliminary session to decrease the novelty effect. The robot was presented to all the children in a non-therapeutic setting for a total of approximately 10 min.

The actual experimentation started after 7 days following the preliminary encounter. The experimental study includes a total of 14 training encounters over one month, i.e. 3 sessions per week. The experiments were carried out in the same room in which is where children usually do their treatment sessions.

Each session was approximately of 6–8 min per child including 1-min breaks to let children rest. The gross motor imitation procedure was repeated six times for each task, and video was recorded by NAO.

In this paper, we present the results after the first 7 training encounters.

The robot-assisted therapy was included in the TEACCH program among the standard activities, which are identified via a specific visual schedule (Fig. 2a and b).

**Fig. 3.** An example of training with robot-assisted.

Visual schedules are designed to match the individual needs of a child. A visual schedule communicates the sequence of upcoming activities or events through the use of objects, photographs, icons, words, or a combination of tangible supports. A visual schedule tells a child where he/she should be and when he/she should be there.

During a training encounter, the robot was deployed on a table, in order to be approximately at the same height of the child, initially at a distance of at least 1 m. The child was allowed to move backwards or forwards to be more comfortable.

Taking into account the Proximal Development Zone [21], we decided to engage the children with activities of a slightly higher level of their current competencies, but still simple enough to be comprehended.

The training encounters comprised three sessions, one for each task. In each session, the children were encouraged to imitate the task performed by the robot. Tasks were proposed daily in a randomized modality to avoid stereotypical learning. First, the robot verbally presented the behaviour to perform in a simple and clear language, then, it solicited the child to imitate its movements while doing them (Fig. 3).

The robot addressed the child by his name to make the intervention more personalized. At the end of each session, the child was free to rest in an adjacent area in the room about for 1 min.

A professional educator, selected among those involved in the everyday treatment, was always present to represent a "secure base" for the children [4]. The educator used *prompts* in order to encourage the production of a new behaviour in presence of a defined stimulus. During sessions, the educator's *prompts* were systematically reduced so that the behaviour produced by the child became responsive to the stimulus and not to the *prompt* response. The professional educator gave a positive verbal reinforcement ("good" and/or "right") along in some cases with a physical reinforcement (a caress). Moreover, the types of reinforcement used have been previously defined with clinicians and consisted of reinforcement variation. These reinforcements were different for each child and were connected directly to responses, behavior and to the child's difficulties.

## 2.4 Measures and Evaluation

Before the start of the experiment to evaluates the impact of the robot-assisted imitation therapy, the therapeutic team administered the VB-MAPP psycho-diagnostic and training instrument. The VB-MAPP was administered Ex-Ante by a qualified clinician, without the robot.

To further analyse the child behaviours during the interaction, used the imitation criterion [6], which is the percentage of time the child was actively imitating the robot's movements when prompted.

The interactions were recorded using the NAO webcam to measure the children's tasks during the sessions. After, all video episodes of the tasks were coded separately by two researchers, with the use of a record sheet divided into seconds, who were separately compiled. Inter-coder agreement score was 0.94, producing a reliability (measured by Cohen's kappa) of 0.85. Discrepancies were resolved via discussion.

# 3    Results and Discussion

In Fig. 4, we report the comparison between the time spent by the children in imitating the robot movements in the first therapeutic session (Ex-ante) and the improvement shown after the robot-assisted training (Ex-post). In both cases, the children were interacting with the robot without educator *prompts*.

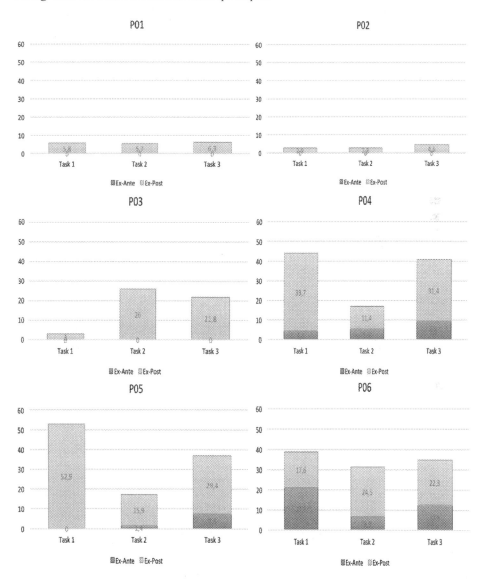

**Fig. 4.** Imitation time. The graphs show the percentage of time spent by each child (P01–06) in imitating the robot. Ex-ante is the result at the first encounter, before the robot-assisted training. Ex-post is the increase of imitation time at the end of the robot-assisted therapy.

Children P01, P02 slightly increased their imitative time, but this didn't result in learning any of the imitative tasks as shown in Fig. 5. This is because, even if they tried, the imitation was partial and incorrect. All the others significantly increased their imitation time and were able to successfully execute the imitative tasks after the training with the robot.

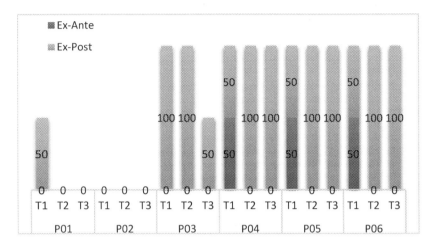

**Fig. 5.** Score of VB-MAPP for each task (T1, T2, T3) Ex-Ante and Ex-Post the robot training (Color figure online)

Figure 5 reports the scores of VB-MAPP psycho-diagnostic instrument Ex-Ante (before the robot-assisted training) and Ex-Post (after the robot training).

We can see that in the Ex-Ante condition all 6 children had a score of 0 and this is because the tasks were selected among those the children were not able to perform. Only in three children and for a single task (T1) the initial score was 0.5, i.e. a partial and incorrect execution of the task (blue line).

Children with mild, moderate, and severe ID were successful at the end of the therapy, in fact they were able to perform adequately the VB-MAPP tasks. On the other side, two children with profound ID did not benefit from the robot-assisted therapy as they were not able to perform any task. This is could be due to their mental age equivalent to less than a 2 years old child that identify also difficulties in comprehension of stimuli. However, in the psychometric assessment P01 increased T1 to 0.5, i.e. he was able to learn a partial execution, even if not fully correct.

The video analysis shows that all children increased the time spent in imitating the robot. More significant is the progress of those that learned how to perform the task, while it is negligible, around 5%, the increase of the two children that were not successful.

# 4   Conclusion

Results of our clinical experiment confirm that the robotic-assisted therapy can be successfully integrated into the standard treatment of autistic children with mild, moderate and severe intellectual disability. Indeed, the scores of the psycho-diagnostic instrument VB-MAPP show that these children significantly increased their imitative level and acquired the capability to perform three new tasks.

However, the participants with a profound intellectual disability did not learn any tasks and show a modest (5%) increase in the gross motor imitation of the robot. This is related to their mental conditions as both children have been diagnosed with profound ID and have difficulties in comprehending the stimuli. In fact, children with more intellectual disability were less engaged than other participants. In this regard, their behaviour with the robot was comparable to their behaviour with other human beings. This result is also supported by the studies of Pioggia et al. [14], where the participants who got less benefit by the robot-assisted therapy were the ones with a more severe form of autism and also with the lowest IQ.

This suggests that there is the need to find more advanced solutions and approaches for persons with profound ID. This is the case that requires more care and, thus, the robot-assisted therapy may be very welcome by the therapeutic team, who can reduce their workload by allowing parts of the treatment be taken over by a robot.

Due to the relatively low number of participants and the absence of a control group, results of this study only indicate the underlying potential of research in this field. The use of an automatic method for assessing the response of different types of patients during the interaction with robots is of ultimate importance. This will also allow the autonomous change of the robot's behaviour according to the current response of the patients, this feature is also of great interest for future work.

**Acknowledgments.** The authors gratefully thank all children, parents, and educators D. Maccarrone, G. Artimagnella and S. Nigro.

This work was supported by the European Union's H2020 research and innovation program under the Marie Skłodowska Curie Action - Individual Fellowship (CARER-AID) grant agreement no. 703489.

# References

1. Adams, A., Robinson, P.: An android head for social-emotional intervention for children with autism spectrum conditions. In: D'Mello, S., Graesser, A., Schuller, B., Martin, J.-C. (eds.) ACII 2011. LNCS, vol. 6975, pp. 183–190. Springer, Heidelberg (2011). https://doi.org/10.1007/978-3-642-24571-8_19
2. Alemi, M., Meghdari, A., Basiri, N.M., Taheri, A.: The effect of applying humanoid robots as teacher assistants to help iranian autistic pupils learn english as a foreign language. In: Tapus, A., André, E., Martin, J.C., Ferland, F., Ammi, M. (eds.) Social Robotics. LNCS (LNAI), vol. 9388, pp. 1–10. Springer, Cham (2015). https://doi.org/10.1007/978-3-319-25554-5_1

3. Baio, J.: Prevalence of autism spectrum disorders: autism and developmental disabilities monitoring network, 14 sites, United States, 2008. Morbidity and Mortality Weekly Report. Surveillance Summaries, vol. 61, no. 3. Centers for Disease Control and Prevention (2012)
4. Bowlby, J.: A Secure Base: Clinical Applications of Attachment Theory. Taylor & Francis, Abingdon (2005)
5. Conti, D., et al.: Robots in education and care of children with developmental disabilities: a study on acceptance by experienced and future professionals. Int. J. Soc. Robot. **9**, 51–62 (2017)
6. Conti, D., et al.: Use of robotics to stimulate imitation in children with autism spectrum disorder: a pilot study in a clinical setting. In: Proceedings of the 24th IEEE International Symposium on Robot and Human Interactive Communication, ROMAN, pp. 1–6 (2015)
7. Diehl, J.J., et al.: The clinical use of robots for individuals with autism spectrum disorders: a critical review. Res. Autism Spectr. Disord. **6**(1), 249–262 (2012)
8. Duquette, A., et al.: Exploring the use of a mobile robot as an imitation agent with children with low-functioning autism. Auton. Robots **24**, 147–157 (2008)
9. Edwards, L.A.: A meta-analysis of imitation abilities in individuals with autism spectrum disorders. Autism Res. **7**(3), 363–380 (2014)
10. Esteban, P.G., et al.: How to build a supervised autonomous system for robot-enhanced therapy for children with autism spectrum disorder. Paladyn J. Behav. Robot. **8**(1), 18–38 (2017)
11. Kim, E., et al.: Bridging the research gap: making HRI useful to individuals with autism. J. Hum.-Robot Interact. **1**, 26–54 (2012)
12. Kozima, H., et al.: Interactive robots for communication-care: a case-study in autism therapy. In: 2005 IEEE International Workshop on Robot and Human Interactive Communication, ROMAN 2005 (2005)
13. Mesibov, G.B., et al.: The TEACCH Approach to Autism Spectrum Disorders. Springer, Boston (2004). https://doi.org/10.1007/978-0-306-48647-0
14. Pioggia, G., et al.: Human-robot interaction in autism: FACE, an android-based social therapy. In: The 16th IEEE International Symposium on Robot and Human Interactive Communication, RO-MAN 2007, pp. 605–612. IEEE (2007)
15. Pot, E., et al.: Choregraphe: a graphical tool for humanoid robot programming. In: Proceedings - IEEE International Workshop on Robot and Human Interactive Communication, pp. 46–51 (2009)
16. Rabbitt, S.M., et al.: Integrating socially assistive robotics into mental healthcare interventions: applications and recommendations for expanded use. Clin. Psychol. Rev. **35**, 35–46 (2014)
17. Robins, B., et al.: Scenarios of robot-assisted play for children with cognitive and physical disabilities. Interact. Stud. **13**(2), 189–234 (2012)
18. Shukla, J., Cristiano, J., Amela, D., Anguera, L., Vergés-Llahí, J., Puig, D.: A case study of robot interaction among individuals with profound and multiple learning disabilities. In: Tapus, A., André, E., Martin, J.C., Ferland, F., Ammi, M. (eds.) Social Robotics. LNCS (LNAI), vol. 9388, pp. 613–622. Springer, Cham (2015). https://doi.org/10.1007/978-3-319-25554-5_61
19. Sundberg, M.L.: Verbal Behavior Milestones Assessment and Placement Program: The VB-MAPP. AVB Press, Concord (2008)
20. Underwood, L., et al.: Mental health of adults with autism spectrum disorders and intellectual disability. Curr. Opin. Psychiatry **23**(5), 421–426 (2010)
21. Vygotsky, L.: Interaction between learning and development. Read. Dev. Child. **23**(3), 34–41 (1978)

22. Wainer, J., et al.: A pilot study with a novel setup for collaborative play of the humanoid robot KASPAR with children with autism. Int. J. Soc. Robot. **6**(1), 45–65 (2013)
23. Williams, J.H.G., et al.: A systematic review of action imitation in autistic spectrum disorder. J. Autism Dev. Disord. **34**, 285–299 (2004)

# Towards an Unmanned 3D Mapping System Using UWB Positioning

Benjamin McLoughlin[✉], Jeff Cullen, Andy Shaw, and Frederic Bezombes

Liverpool John Moores University, Liverpool L3 3AF, UK
b.mcloughlin@2011.ljmu.ac.uk

**Abstract.** The work presented in this paper is part of a Horizon 2020 project known as DigiArt, with an aim to deploy an unmanned ground vehicle (UGV) mounted with a 3D scan LiDAR to generate 3D maps of an archaeological subterranean environment. The challenges faced when using 3D scan LiDAR is the ability to localize the LiDAR device and account for motion to register sequential point cloud frames. Traditionally approaches such as GPS and vision based systems are unsuitable for the intended environment due to signal restrictions and low lighting conditions respectively. Therefore, this paper seeks to assess an alternative method in the form of ultra-wideband (UWB) positioning system known as Pozyx. Experimental results show an average distance error of 4.8 cm, 10 cm, 6.5 cm and 8.3 cm for clear line of sight (CLOS) and 11 cm, 10 cm, 13.8 cm and 24 cm for non-clear line of sight (NCLOS) when the receiver is orientated at for 90°, 60°, 30° and 0° respectively.

**Keywords:** UWB · Ranging · Localisation · Positioning · LiDAR

## 1 Introduction

Generating 3D maps with scan line LiDAR systems requires the registration of con-secutively acquired point cloud frames, therefore knowledge of motion between each frame is essential. Various methods have been implemented to estimate motion such as combined Global Positioning and Inertial Navigation Systems (GPS-INS) [1], monocular or stereo visual odometry techniques [2,3] and LiDAR odometry [4], which is further optimized with the addition of a monocular based vision system [5]. However, considering the intended subterranean environment, traditional approaches such as GPS and visual based systems are unsuitable due to signal restrictions and low lighting conditions [5] and are therefore prone to errors. This work explores the possibility of an alternative approach in the form of ultra-wideband (UWB) positioning [6], the UWB system used for this initial analysis is known as Pozyx [7]. UWB is a communication technique that transmits and receives narrow pulses at a nanosecond rate. Unlike conventional radio frequency identification (RFID) based systems that operate on single bands, UWB transmits over a broad area of the of the radio spectrum, from 3.1–10.6 GHz [8], the ability to transmit over this extensive

© Springer International Publishing AG, part of Springer Nature 2018
M. Giuliani et al. (Eds.): TAROS 2018, LNAI 10965, pp. 416–422, 2018.
https://doi.org/10.1007/978-3-319-96728-8_35

bandwidth decreases the power spectral density, therefore enabling UWB based systems to avoid interface with other RF signals [6,9]. Positioning using UWB consists of static reference anchor nodes placed in an environment and a rover tag fixed on the platform that is in question. Locating a node in a wireless system involves the collection of information such as ranges from the pulsed radio signal traveling between the rover node and the anchor nodes. Different types of positioning techniques such as angle of arrival (AOA), signal strength (SS) or time orientated information can be utilised to determine rover node location [6].

## 2   Methodology

### 2.1   Ranging Error Characterisation

Ranging capabilities of the Pozyx were analysed in clear line of sight (CLOS) and non-CLOS (NLOS) conditions when the receiver tag was orientated from 0–90° at 30° increments and placed along a 20 m track, with the distance between the devices was increased by 2 m at each static position.

### 2.2   Positioning Error Characterisation

Characterising the positioning performance of the UWB system included the use of a Velodyne HDL-32E LiDAR system as a means of an indoor ground truth. Both were mounted to an UGV similar to the one shown in Fig. 1.

**Fig. 1.** Similar UGV test platform.

The experiment was carried out in a controlled indoor environment where a LiDAR odometry algorithm was designed using the north and west flat walls in the operating environment for positioning, the UWB anchors were also placed on the same walls. Figure 2 shows a 2D line scan point cloud of the environment

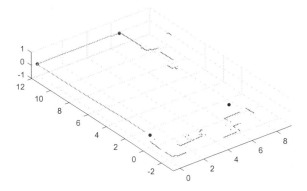

**Fig. 2.** Example point cloud map with reference identification for LiDAR positioning & UWB anchor positions

extracted from the $0°$ firing laser and also highlights the walls that are used for positioning with the LiDAR.

However, taking into account laser error, a line recognition procedure was utilised for both walls in a least squares line fitting sense, this method was chosen entirely for simplicity purposes. Point $i$ with coordinates $(x_i, y_i)$ lying on the reference wall is extracted from each point cloud scan $P_k$ acquired in the robots coordinate frame, where $i \in P_k$. The fitted line running through the points on the reference walls is parametrized with distance $r$ and angle $\alpha$, which are the distance of the UGV to the wall and its angle respectively and these variables are used to position the UGV in relation to both walls, this is demonstrated in Fig. 3 [10]. The mathematical model used was presented in [11];

$$d_i = \rho_i \cos(\theta_i - \alpha) - r \tag{1}$$

Where the total error $S_{r\alpha}$ of the points in relation to the fitted line can be written as;

$$S_{r,\alpha} = \sum_{i=1}^{N} d_i^2 = \sum_{i=1}^{N} (\rho_i \cos(\theta_i - \alpha) - r)^2 \tag{2}$$

Taking the partial derivatives to optimize $S_{r\alpha}$ and setting them to zero generates equations to solve $r$ and $\alpha$.

$$\frac{\delta S}{\delta \alpha} = 0 \qquad \frac{\delta S}{\delta r} = 0 \tag{3}$$

Solving for $r$ and $\alpha$ [11];

$$\alpha = \frac{1}{2} \alpha \tan \left( \frac{\frac{1}{N} \sum \rho_i^2 \sin 2\theta_i - \frac{2}{N^2} \sum \sum \rho_i \rho_j \cos \theta_i \sin \theta_j}{\frac{1}{N} \sum \rho_i^2 \cos 2\theta_i - \frac{1}{N^2} \sum \sum \rho_i \rho_j \cos(\theta_i + \theta_j)} \right) \tag{4}$$

$$r = \frac{\sum \rho_i \cos(\theta_i - \alpha)}{N} \tag{5}$$

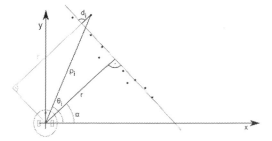

**Fig. 3.** Line fitting in a least squares sense [11]

# 3   Results

## 3.1   Ranging

Figure 4 demonstrates the results gathered concerning the range error charac-
terisation procedure. For each distance and orientation, 400 samples were taken
which equates to 20 s of activation time. The range error is seen to be considerably lower when the tag is orientated at 90° in the pitch axis as average errors
seem to stabilise around 0° with lower standard deviations. Average errors in
CLOS are not seen to rise above 10 cm, with results showing 4.8 cm, 10 cm, 6.5 cm
and 8.3 cm for 90°, 60°, 30° and 0° respectively. However, with the inclusion of
a physical barrier to simulate NCLOS situations, average errors are seen to rise
with simultaneous increases in uncertainty at each point as the tag is orientated
away from its optimal orientation of 90°, this is clearly noticeable at 30°. At
larger distances when the tag is at 0°, the two devices failed to communicate
hence why there are no data points present in the figure. Average errors in
NCLOS conditions were calculated at 11 cm, 10 cm, 13.8 cm and 24 cm for 90°,
60°, 30° and 0° respectively.

## 3.2   Positioning

Localisation capabilities of the Pozyx were tested against a Velodyne HDL-32E
scanning unit for ground truth. Figures 5 and 6 show the filtered and non-filtered
trajectories respectively of three paths that were executed using an unmanned
ground vehicle. Filtering the Pozyx signal was necessary as occasional time outs
in communications resulted in outliers. The Pozyx and Velodyne were calibrated
to operate within the equivalent co-ordinate frame. The developed Velodyne
odometry algorithm used two flat walls to position itself within the environment
and the Pozyx anchors were placed on the same walls for calibrated reference
points. The default positioning algorithm for the Pozyx was used in these initial
tests. The visual results show that the general trajectory estimation from the
Pozyx react as the UGV turns and follows a straight path. The RSME for X
and Y positions are located in Table 1 for all three paths.

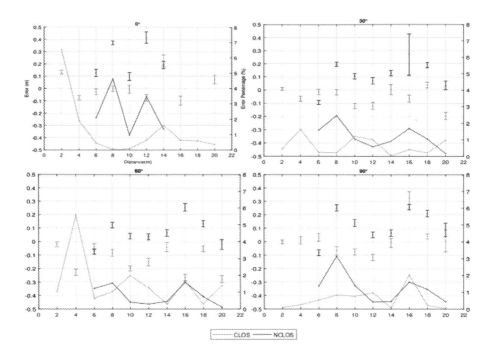

**Fig. 4.** Error statistics for CLOS & NCLOS

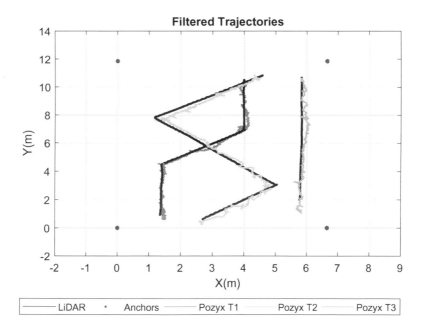

**Fig. 5.** Filtered trajectories Pozyx & LiDAR Comparison

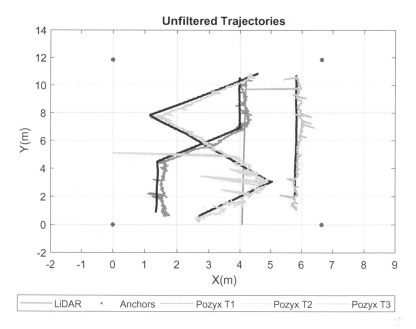

**Fig. 6.** Unfiltered trajectories Pozyx & LiDAR Comparison

**Table 1.** RMSE between Pozyx trajectories and LiDAR ground truth (m)

|  | P1 (X,Y) | P2 (X,Y) | P3 (X,Y) |
|---|---|---|---|
| RMSE(m) | 0.0949, 0.166 | 0.1693, 0.2671 | 0.1374, 0.2243 |

## 4    Conclusion

In conclusion, the results gathered prove that an UWB positioning system can be considered as an alternative method to estimate motion of a LiDAR within a subterranean environment. However, future work will include the integration of other sensors such as an inertial measurement unit (IMU) or rotary encoders that will compensate for the communications drop causing larger uncertainty in ranging measurements though state estimation algorithms such as Extended Kalman Filters (EKF) and its variants as well as the behavior of signal error in multiple operating environments.

## References

1. Christiansen, M., et al.: Designing and testing a UAV mapping system for agricultural field surveying. Sensors **17**(12), 2703 (2017)
2. Huang, A.S., et al.: Visual odometry and mapping for autonomous flight using an RGB-D camera. In: Christensen, H.I., Khatib, O. (eds.) Robotics Research. STAR, vol. 100, pp. 235–252. Springer, Cham (2017). https://doi.org/10.1007/978-3-319-29363-9_14

3. Maimone, M., Cheng, Y., Matthies, L.: Two years of visual odometry on the mars exploration rovers. J. Field Robot. **24**(3), 169–186 (2007)

4. Zhang, J., Singh, S.: LOAM: lidar odometry and mapping in real-time. In: Robotics: Science and Systems (2014)

5. Zhang, J., Singh, S.: Visual-lidar odometry and mapping: low-drift, robust, and fast. In: 2015 IEEE International Conference on Robotics and Automation (ICRA). IEEE (2015)

6. Gezici, S., et al.: Localization via ultra-wideband radios: a look at positioning aspects for future sensor networks. IEEE Sig. Process. Mag. **22**(4), 70–84 (2005)

7. Pozyx Labs. Pozyx Accurate Positioning. https://www.pozyx.io/. Accessed 10 Feb 2018

8. Aiello, G.R., Rogerson, G.D.: Ultra-wideband wireless systems. IEEE Microw. Mag. **4**(2), 36–47 (2003)

9. Liu, H., et al.: Survey of wireless indoor positioning techniques and systems. IEEE Trans. Syst. Man Cybern. Part C (Appl. Rev.) **37**(6), 1067–1080 (2007)

10. Correll, N.: Introduction to Autonomous Robots. CreateSpace Independent Publishing Platform (2014)

11. Siegwart, R., Nourbakhsh, I.R., Scaramuzza, D.: Introduction to Autonomous Mobile Robots. MIT Press, Cambridge (2011)

# The Multimodal Speech and Visual Gesture (mSVG) Control Model for a Practical Patrol, Search, and Rescue Aerobot

Ayodeji O. Abioye[1]([✉]), Stephen D. Prior[1], Glyn T. Thomas[1],
Peter Saddington[2], and Sarvapali D. Ramchurn[1]

[1] Faculty of Engineering and the Environment, University of Southampton,
Southampton, UK
aoa2g15@soton.ac.uk
[2] Tekever Ltd, Southampton, UK

**Abstract.** This paper describes a model of the multimodal speech and visual gesture (mSVG) control for aerobots operating at higher nCA autonomy levels, within the context of a patrol, search, and rescue application. The developed mSVG control architecture, its mathematical navigation model, and some high level command operation models were discussed. This was successfully tested using both MATLAB simulation and python based ROS Gazebo UAV simulations. Some limitations were identified, which formed the basis for the further works presented.

**Keywords:** mSVG (Multimodal speech and visual gesture) ·
Aerobot (Aerial robot) · HCI (Human computer interaction) ·
Visual gesture · Speech · MCPU (Multimodal control processing unit) ·
nCA (Navigational control autonomy) · Sbc (Single board computer)

## 1 Introduction

The rise in the popularity of small unmanned aerial vehicles (UAVs) in agriculture, aerial survey and inspection, transportation and logistics, surveillance and monitoring, search and rescue operation support, photography and videography, entertainment, sports, health care, law enforcement, environmental conservation, etc. has led to a significant increase in the number of operators, users, developers, researchers, beneficiaries, and other stakeholders with varying interest levels. This paper is interested in how the increasing leagues of human operators interact with small multi-rotor UAVs. According to [1], "It is clear that people use speech, gesture, gaze and non-verbal cues to communicate in the clearest possible fashion." [2,3] identified the need for smart and intuitive control interaction methods for aerobots (aerial robots) on higher nCA autonomy levels. This paper focuses on a UAV patrol, search, and rescue application scenario in the Alps. In

M. Giuliani et al. (Eds.): TAROS 2018, LNAI 10965, pp. 423–437, 2018.
https://doi.org/10.1007/978-3-319-96728-8_36

this paper, an alternative method of interacting with multirotor aerial robots, otherwise known as aerobots [2], is presented.

Consider a case in which a small multirotor UAV is being developed to (1) patrol a dangerous region of the Alps, (2) provide signposting information to climbers, (3) alert search and rescue teams in case of any incidence, and (4) support search and rescue efforts or team operations. If such a patrol UAV would be required to interact with climbers when needed, how would the UAV register the climbers requests? As climbers would not normally have the UAVs RC controller, an intangible HHI-like multimodal speech and visual gesture interaction method would seem more suitable for such scenarios.

## 1.1   A Case of the Matterhorn

An application of the mSVG interaction method on a patrol, search, and rescue robot could be the Alps in Southcentral Europe, where sporting activities such as climbing, mountaineering, hiking, cycling, paragliding, mountain biking, rafting, skiing, snowboarding, curling, and snow shoeing, are quite popular. People visiting these places for the first time could easily get lost if not very careful, climbers could fall when anchored on deceptively rigid surfaces, and people new to certain sports could get hurt, particularly when caught in stormy weathers. Therefore, patrol UAVs could be dispatched to assist local search and rescue operation efforts immediately after a storm. For example in the Matterhorn, about 1,700 rescue missions are conducted annually [4]. These high number of rescues is because the Matterhorn is home to numerous glaciers, which are laced with countless deep crevasses, many of which are hidden by snow that can give way without warning, swallowing up climbers and skiers in the process [4]. With the limited number of resources and man power, how can this operation be run more efficiently? Aerobots could be particularly useful in performing patrol, searching areas, and transporting small supplies. Patrol UAVs could fly along predefine routes, warning climbers of hidden crevasses, because signs on routes are easily covered by snow. The patrol UAVs could also be used to keep track of climbers progress during it regular flyovers. This could help find climbers in distress even before a call for help is made, which reduces the time between fall and call, potentially shortening rescue time, which in turn increases a rescued climbers survival chances - especially in situations where every second counts. In addition to this, a fallen climber may be unconscious, and therefore may be unable to call for help themselves, the UAV could make the call after failing to establish communication with the climber. Also, climber tracking information collected during patrol could be used to narrow down the search area in the event of an emergency or if a climber goes missing.

The UAV could also be used to provide verbal signposting, alerting climbers of their proximity to deep crevasses hidden by snow. Signs are probably unusable here because they could be easily covered by snow. According to [4] "people never know how close they are to the limits, every mistake they make could be their last". A typical signposting interaction could be - a UAV informs a lone climber, *"hello, deep crevasse 400 m ahead"*, and the lone climber could respond with *"ok"* as an affirmative or *"repeat"* to have the UAV repeat itself. Prior to the climb, all climbers and mountaineers would have already been briefed on appropriate UAV responses, and how to ask for help. They may also choose to opt out of being helped by the UAV during it routine fly over, if they think that this may be distracting, in which case the UAV avoids interacting with the climbers. The climber stick a *"don't disturb"* QR code patch on their backpack, which the UAV scans on approach and flies away instead, except it is an emergency. Patrol UAVs could also warn climbers of rapidly changing weather conditions and advise them on the nearest refuge points. In the event that the patrol UAV comes across a fallen lone climber, it could potentially alert climbing parties nearby to act as first responders, if they are quite close to the incident site, while also alerting the central control room of the emergency.

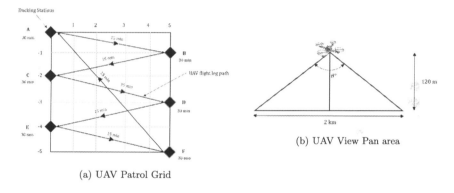

(a) UAV Patrol Grid

(b) UAV View Pan area

**Fig. 1.** $5 \times 5$ km$^2$ patrol area grid in six flight legs and with six docking stations.

An array of UAVs with front and downward facing cameras, thermal cameras, on-board navigational aid (GPS), on-board sense and avoid (proximity sensors), microphone, speaker, etc. could be used to execute this patrol operation as described in Figure 1a. Immediately after a storms, such small patrol UAVs augmented with on-board computation abilities via single board computers with microphone arrays, cameras, a speaker, and other sensors, could be dispatched to patrol and search specific hotspot areas in grids of $5 \times 5$ km$^2$. But how should such an mSVG control interface be effectively developed? This paper describes our approach in developing an mSVG control method for a small multirotor UAV. We developed a mathematical model, converted this into a program algorithm, tested this in MATLAB, and then performed a graphical simulation using a ROS Gazebo firefly UAV simulator. The idea is to run all the computation required for the mSVG on a single board computer, and couple this to the flight controller of a typical UAV, with the SBC communicating with the UAV flight controller via waypoint navigation (nCA Tier 1-III model).

## 2 Literature Review

Due to the complexity of the current HCI control interfaces, sometimes two operators may be required to control a single UAV [5]. For example, in a search and rescue mission, it may be difficult for the pilot to, simultaneously, control the UAV while effectively searching for missing persons. In order for robots to reduce human workload, risk, cost, and human fatigue-driven errors, it is crucial to make the human-robot interaction effective, efficient, and natural, through multiple modalities of contact, dialogue, and gestures [6]. The need for intuitive control interaction interfaces for aerobots beyond tier-one components of the nCA autonomy model opens up an opportunity to explore smart novel interaction techniques [3].

### 2.1 Multimodal Interface Overview

It is often assumed that "Multimodal interfaces can support flexible, efficient, and expressive means of human-computer interaction, that are more akin to the multimodal experiences human experience in their physical world" [7–9]. Hence HCI researchers are constantly trying to find ways to endow computers, machines, and robotic systems with intuitive and natural multimodal interaction abilities similar to the human-human experience. This is possible because of the advancement in non-desktop embedded computing, more powerful mobile devices, and more affordable sensors [9]. According to [10], humans tend to exhibit more implicit behaviours, utilizing a combination of short verbal and nonverbal gestures in communicating their intentions, when performing tasks under stressed conditions, with resource constraints, and under time pressure, as is often the case in the space, military, aviation, and medical domains. [11] discovered that HERMES, a humanoid robot assistant, appeared more user-friendly, intelligent, and cooperative, when endowed with the ability to interact via a multimodal combination of speech, vision, and haptics. According to [12], soldiers often use a combination of verbal and visual lexicons, to communicate manoeuvres with each other, hence incorporating robots into these existing human ISR teams often presents a human-robot interaction challenge. [13] observed that speech control is particularly effective for task requiring short control communications, but may perform poorly for longer communication tasks, or in longer continuous operations. Therefore, multimodal interfaces are explored further.

### 2.2 Multimodal Interfaces in Aerial Robotics

A multimodal speech and gesture communication with multiple UAVs in a search and rescue mission, was investigated by [14] using the Julius framework [15] and Myo device for speech and gesture respectively. The result of their simulation experiment showed that a human operator could interact effectively and reliably with a UAV via multiple modalities of speech and gesture, in autonomous, mixed-initiative, or teleoperation mode. [16] investigated the use of natural user interfaces (NUIs) in the control of small UAVs using the Aerostack software framework. Their project was aimed at studying, implementing, and validating NUIs efficiency in human UAV interaction. In their experiment, they captured whole body gestures and had visual markers (for localization and commands) via a Parrot AR Drone 2.0 camera, captured hand gestures via the Leap motion device, and speech command was captured via the ROS implementation of the CMU PocketSphinx library. These researchers demonstrated that natural user interfaces are effective enough for higher level UAV communication. [12,17] investigated the performance of a speech and gesture multimodal interface for a soldier-robot team communication during an ISR mission, even considering complex semantic navigation commands such as *"perch over there* (speech + pointing gesture), *on the tank to the right of the stone monument*(speech)" [17,18]. In a related research by [19], the researchers suggested that multimodal speech and gesture communication was a means to achieving an enhanced naturalistic communication, reducing workload, and improving the human-robot communication experience, especially when factoring in that only a minimal training is required to execute this communication method by the operator. [20] also investigated the effectiveness of speech and gesture communication in soldier-robot interaction. [21] observed participants' behaviour around UAVs and studied how the participants' interacted with the UAV, particularly how the users combined speech and two hand gestures in communicating control intentions to the UAV. [22,23] conducted elicitation study to determine intuitive gestures for controlling UAVs. [24] investigated human and UAV swarm interaction using spatial gestures.

## 3   Multimodal Speech and Visual Gesture (mSVG)

### 3.1   The mSVG Model

The mSVG technique is basically the multimodal combination of speech and visual gesture, a method that leverages familiar human-to-human type interaction in human aerobotic interaction. This combination could be simultaneous, sequential, or complementary. The underlying architecture of how this technique is designed to work is as described in Fig. 2. Let the speech and visual gesture input be $s$ and $v$ respectively, and let $f$ and $g$ be the respective processing functions, which generates the control symbols $f(s)$ and $g(v)$ as shown in Fig. 2.

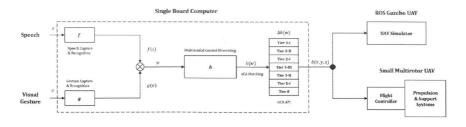

**Fig. 2.** mSVG design architecture control capture, processing, and execution.

Then the control command $w$ processed at the multimodal control processing unit (MCPU) is a function of control symbols $f(s)$ and $g(v)$ as shown below:

$$w = f(s) \otimes g(v) \tag{1}$$

$h(w)$ is the resultant control output generated after the multimodal combination of both the speech and the visual gesture input at the MCPU. This is then passed on to an nCA autonomy model API to match $h(w)$ with the coordinate increment/decrement parameters $\delta(x, y, z)$ via a delta $\Delta$ parameter, depending on the nCA autonomy level of the UAV [3]. This is described by the following equation as:

$$\delta(x, y, z) = \Delta h(w) \tag{2}$$

The delta parameter is a function generated by the nCA API to modify the MCPU output, $h(w)$, to enable compatibility with different nCA navigational control autonomy levels. For the Tier 1-III nCA model component, $\Delta = 1$. Therefore, $\delta(x, y, z) = h(w)$. The coordinate increment/decrement parameters $\delta(x, y, z)$ specifies the change in the aerobots 3-dimensional position with respect to its current position.

### 3.2   Mathematical Model

The processing operation in the multimodal control processing unit (MCPU) stage can be mathematically described through the use of relational set theories. The universal command set used consists of navigational and scenario commands, which are as presented in Tables 1 and 2. The symbol "$u$" is a numeric modifier parameter specifying amount of navigational increment/decrement as used in Table 1. Control keyword and modifiers are also highlighted in block letters. The current position of the aerobot in the world environment is represented by the $x$, $y$, and $z$ coordinate components. Where $dx$, $dy$, and $dz$ are unit conversion parameter from simulation to world environment, for example $dx = dy = dz = 1$ in the simulation test.

**Table 1.** Navigaitional commands and control expressions with example usage

| S/N | Navigational command | Control expression | Command example | |
|---|---|---|---|---|
| 1 | Forward | $x + udx$ | Go FORWARD HALF metre | $x + 0.5dx$ |
| 2 | Backward | $x - udx$ | Go BACKWARD ONE metre | $x + dx$ |
| 3 | Right | $y + udy$ | Step RIGHT | $y + 0.5dy$ |
| 4 | Left | $y - udy$ | Step LEFT TWO metres | $y - 2dy$ |
| 5 | Up | $z + udz$ | Climb UP ONE metre | $z + dz$ |
| 6 | Down | $z - udz$ | Go DOWN HALF metre | $z + 0.5dz$ |
| 7 | Hover | $z = u$ | HOVER THREE metres | $z = 3$ |
| 8 | Land | $z = 0$ | Land | $z = 0$ |

$$\mathcal{U}_{ctrl} = \mathcal{U}_{speech} \cup \mathcal{U}_{gesture}$$

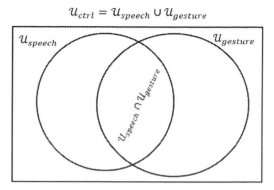

**Fig. 3.** Speech and Gesture control command set model.

Let us consider that the universal set of control commands $\mathcal{U}_{ctrl}$, listed in Tables 1 and 2, could be issued as either speech or gestures commands. Then the universal command set can be described as $\mathcal{U}_{ctrl} = \mathcal{U}_{speech} \cup \mathcal{U}_{gesture}$. Where $\mathcal{U}_{speech}$ is speech only commands, and $\mathcal{U}_{gesture}$ is gesture only commands. Figure 3 presents a set model describing this relationship. Commands that can be issued via either speech or gestures are represented as commands found at the intersection of both method $\mathcal{U}_{common} = \mathcal{U}_{speech} \cap \mathcal{U}_{gesture}$.

For the first phase of this work, all commands were implemented as speech commands, and only a few higher level scenario commands were implemented as gestures as described in Fig. 4. Lets consider an hypothetical set of speech commands,

$$\mathcal{U}_{speech} = [\{ok\}, \{weather\}, \{signpost\}, \{there\}, \{that\}, \{selfie\}, etc.] \qquad (3)$$

Which can be denoted as

$$\mathcal{U}_{speech} = [s_1, s_2, s_3, \ldots, s_n] \qquad (4)$$

Where $n$ is the total number of climber-user speech control vocabulary available. Similarly, $\mathcal{U}_{gesture}$ could be an hypothetical set of climbers' visual gesture commands,

$$\mathcal{U}_{gesture} = [\{ok \text{ - thumbs up}\}, \{leave \text{ - wave away}\}, \{what \text{ - open palm}\},$$
$$\{that \text{ - point object}\}, \{there \text{ - point place}\},$$
$$\{selfie \text{ - picture board symbol}\}, etc.] \qquad (5)$$

Which can also be denoted as

$$\mathcal{U}_{speech} = [g_1, g_2, g_3, \ldots, g_n] \qquad (6)$$

Where m is the total number of climber-user gesture control vocabulary available. Using these notations, a typical series of control commands could be a sequence of

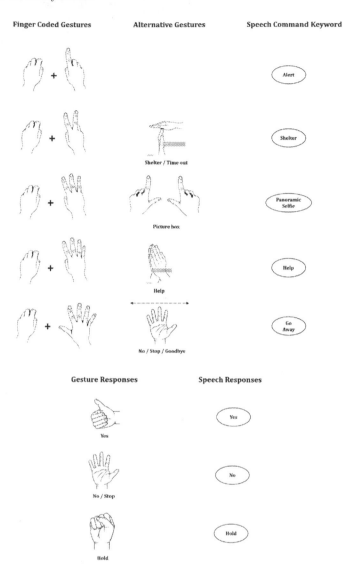

**Fig. 4.** Finger coded climber gestures and corresponding speech commands.

$$(t_1, G_1), (t_2, G_2), (t_3, S_3), (t_4, G_4 + S_4), (t_5, S_5 + G_5), (t_6, S_6), etc. \qquad (7)$$

Where $t_i$ is the sequential time component, $S_i$ is the speech command component, and $G_i$ is the gesture command component. These commands could be sequential, for example - $(t_1, S_1)$ followed by $(t_2, G_2)$ and so on; or simultaneous, as in - $(t_4, G_4 + S_4), (t_5, S_5 + G_5), etc.$ While sequential commands consist of only one gesture or speech components in each time component $t_i$, simultaneous commands consist of both speech and gesture component at the same time component $t_i$. In spatio-temporal terms, a speech and gesture command is considered simultaneous if the time between capture is no more than 0.5 s, otherwise it is considered a sequential command and one would be executed after the other. In order words

$$\text{Command Selection} = \begin{cases} \text{Simultaneous}(G + S) & \text{if } t \leq 0.5s \\ \text{Sequential}(G, S) & \text{if } t > 0.5s \end{cases} \tag{8}$$

Simultaneous command could be emphatic or complementary. A simultaneous command is emphatic if it repeats the same command using the alternative modality, whereas it is complementary when it provides additional information not given in the alternative modality. For example, *"Hold (Speech) + Fist (Gesture for hold)"* issued within 0.5 s apart only emphasis the command for the UAV to "hold" its position. Whereas a command *"Go Forward (Speech) + Two-fingers (Gesture for numeric modifier two)"* issued within 0.5 s of each other, results in the aerobot advancing two metres in the Forward direction. In this case, the gesture command complements the speech command.

### 3.3   High Level Command Operation

The last section discussed navigational control command operations. This section discusses examples of scenario command operations that could be executed by a search and rescue patrol aerobot in the wild. Navigation commands emulates low level nCA interaction while scenario commands emulates higher nCA level models. Table 2 presents some scenario commands.

**Table 2.** Scenario commands and synonyms

| S/N | Scenario command | Command synonyms |
| --- | --- | --- |
| 1 | Alert | - |
| 2 | Shelter | - |
| 3 | Panoramic selfie | Panoramic, Selfie, Panorama |
| 4 | Help | Operator |
| 5 | Go away | Away, Patrol |

**Shelter Command Computation**
The UAV knowledge base includes the UAVs world map shown in Fig. 5, as a computable lookup table, accessible during multimodal control processing. Figure 5 shows the crevice and shelter map/table implemented in the MATLAB and Python based Gazebo Simulation test.

From Fig. 5, the relative North degree direction of the crevices, shelters, and other objects of interests can be computed as follows:

$$\tan \alpha = \frac{y_{sh1} - y_{uav}}{x_{sh1} - x_{uav}} \tag{9}$$

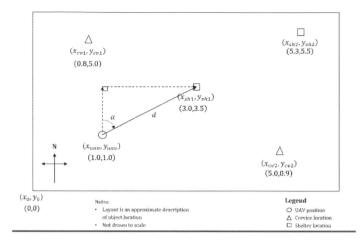

**Fig. 5.** UAV world map showing UAV position, crevices, and shelter locations.

Therefore, the bearing angle

$$\alpha = \arctan(\frac{y_{sh1} - y_{uav}}{x_{sh1} - x_{uav}}) \tag{10}$$

The distance between the UAV and the shelter shown in Fig. 5, can be computed as

$$d^2 = (x_{sh1} - x_{uav})^2 + (y_{sh1} - y_{uav})^2 \tag{11}$$

Therefore, the nearest shelter to climber can be said to be *"d km in the $\alpha°$ North direction"*, where $x$ and $y$ components are measured in km. In general, the equations for computing the distance and direction of any object located at point '$x$, $y$' on the map, from the user/climber/operator/UAV '$x_{uav}$, $y_{uav}$' are

$$\alpha = \arctan(\frac{y - y_{uav}}{x - x_{uav}}) \tag{12}$$

$$d = \sqrt{(x - x_{uav})^2 + (y - y_{uav})^2} \tag{13}$$

Interpreted as the map object of interest is *"d km in the $\alpha°$ North direction"* from the user. In addition to these, the UAV could beam a *"red arrow"* light on the ground with the arrow pointing in the direction of travel. Also, the UAV could travel the initial 50 m with the climber, before flying away.

**Panoramic Selfie Command Computation**
From Fig. 6a, capture location 1 components can be computed as

$$x_{cl1} = x_{up} - d\sin\theta_{up} \tag{14}$$

$$y_{cl1} = y_{up} - d\cos\theta_{up} \tag{15}$$

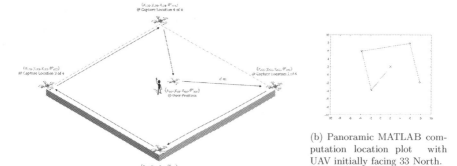

(a) Panoramic selfie capture location description.

(b) Panoramic MATLAB computation location plot with UAV initially facing 33 North.

**Fig. 6.** Panoramic selfie capture.

For capture location 2 - 4 :

$$x_b = x_a + \sqrt{d^2 + d^2} \sin(\theta_a + 90) \tag{16}$$

$$y_b = y_a + \sqrt{d^2 + d^2} \cos(\theta_a + 90) \tag{17}$$

Where subscript '$a$' denoted parameters refers to parameters from the previous location, and '$b$' subscripted parameters refers to the parameters for the current location being computed.

**Patrol Command Computation**
As was shown in Fig. 1a, the patrol operation can be broken down into the following components: (1) UAV flies at 0.5 m altitude, (2) Briefly stopping at 4 intermediate stop points between two docking stations (e.g. A and B) to pan and scan area under. The stop points between point A and point B is computed using the following expression in both the MATLAB and Python implementation

$$(x_n, y_n) = (x_p + 0.2(x_b - x_a), y_p + 0.2(y_b - y_a)) \tag{18}$$

Five points including final point B. Where $p$ is the previous state and $n$ is the next state. And the '$a$' and '$b$' subscripted coordinate '$x$' and '$y$' corresponds to the UAV's location A and B coordinate component. Figure 7 shows this python based ROS Gazebo implementation of the UAV patrol operation.

434    A. O. Abioye et al.

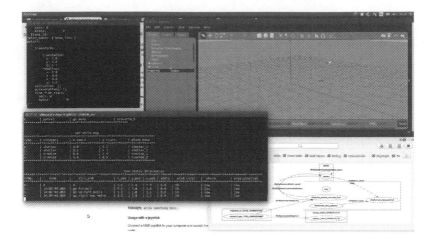

**Fig. 7.** Python implementation with rotors gazebo UAV simulator.

## 4    Result and Discussion

### 4.1    Test and Implementation

Speech is captured via a microphone, processed and recognised using the CMU Sphinx ASR with custom-defined phonetic dictionary containing only the set of command vocabulary, in order to increase recognition speed and accuracy. Figure 8a shows a screenshot of the speech recognition engine identify captured speech, and describing aerobot navigation response such as "iQuad moving forward..." Visual gesture is captured via a camera connected to the aerobot single board computer (SBC) computer. In the preliminary work, a simple finger-coded visual gesture control commands set was developed to be recognised through a combination of two OpenCV algorithms Haar cascade for hand tracking and convex hull for finger counting.

### 4.2    MATLAB and ROS Gazebo Simulation

Based on the mathematical set model, the mSVG control navigation was simulated in MATLAB, which was then implemented in python for easy integration of algorithm on a single board computer (in this case, Odroid XU4 SBC), and simulated on a rotors gazebo firefly UAV simulator in an open world environment. In each case, a series of command such as 'go forward', 'go up half metre', 'go right one metre', 'hover at three metre', 'and', 'hover', 'go forward backward two half metre', 'patrol', etc. were successfully tested. Figure 8b shows a portion of the decision tree as implemented for forward and backward navigation command operations.

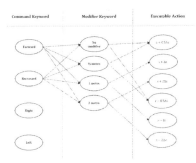

(a) CMU ASR speech recognition on Odroid XU4 single board computer (SBC) terminal screen.

(b) Relative 1-D (x-axis, forward-backward) Navigation Symbol Decision Tree.

**Fig. 8.** Speech ASR and control navigation implementation.

# 5   Conclusion - Limitations and Further Works

In this paper, the authors described the growing application of small multi-rotor UAVs otherwise called aerobots, with a particular focus on high level nCA operation such as a patrol, search, and rescue application scenario in the Matterhorn area of the Alps. An overview of multimodal interfaces was presented with further emphasis on related multimodal interface research in aerial robotics. The multimodal speech and visual gesture (mSVG) architecture model developed by the researchers was then presented along with some mathematical model description and a few high level command operation examples. A summary of the implementation and test was given as a result consequence of the developed models.

The main limitations of the proposed system is (1) its susceptibility to speech corruption during capture, due to the noise generated by the multirotor propulsion systems and other loud ambient noise such as in stormy weathers, (2) the effect of poor visibility level on visual gesture capture, as could be the case at night, or in cloudy or misty weather. The next phase of this research is already underway to determine the range of effectiveness of the mSVG method under varying noise and visibility levels. This could inform the possibility of working around this or developing techniques that may extend this range, thereby extending the usefulness of the propose mSVG technique over a much wider application area. Also, a comparison of the mSVG and RC joystick in terms of training time, same nCA Tier task completion rate, and cognitive workload requirement, is currently being conducted. Further works may also consider the application of some artificial intelligence algorithm such as deep neural network in recognising hand gestures in complicated outdoor environments.

**Acknowledgement.** This research was financially supported by the Petroleum Technology Development Fund (PTDF) of the Federal Government of Nigeria. Accessible via the following PTDF Reference Number: 16PHD052 and PTDF File Number: 862.

# References

1. Green, S., Chen, X., Billinnghurst, M., Chase, J.G.: Human robot collaboration: an augmented reality approach a literature review and analysis. Mechatronics **5**(1), 1–10 (2007)
2. Abioye, A.O., Prior, S.D., Thomas, G.T., Saddington, P.: The multimodal edge of human aerobotic interaction. In: Blashki, K., Xiao, Y. (eds.) International Conferences Interfaces and Human Computer Interaction, pp. 243–248. IADIS Press, Madeira (2016)
3. Abioye, A.O., Prior, S.D., Thomas, G.T., Saddington, P., Ramchurn, S.D.: Multimodal human aerobotic interaction. In: Isaías, P. (ed.) Smart Technology Applications in Business Environments, pp. 39–62. IGI Global (2017)
4. Root, S., Air Zermatt: The Matterhorn 101 - This is all you need to know about the Matterhorn (2016). https://www.redbull.com/int-en/the-horn-air-zermatt-matterhorn-rescue-team. Available 2016-10-17; Accessed 2017-06-07
5. Aeryon Labs Inc.: Whitepaper - intuitive control of a micro UAV (2011). https://aeryon.com/whitepaper/ituitivecontrol. First Available 2011-02-07; Accessed 2016-01-22
6. Fong, T., Nourbakhsh, I.: Interaction challenges in human-robot space exploration. In: Proceedings of the Fourth International Conference and Exposition on Robotics for Challenging Situations and Environments. Number January 2004, pp. 340–346 (2000)
7. Oviatt, S.: Multimodal interfaces. In: Jacko, J.A., Sears, A. (eds.) The Human-Computer Interaction Handbook: Fundamentals, Evolving Technologies, and Emerging Applications, 1st edn, pp. 286–304. Lawrence Erlbaum Associates, Incorporated, London (2003)
8. Preece, J., Sharp, H., Rogers, Y.: Interaction Design: Beyond Human-Computer Interaction, 4th edn. Wiley, Glasgow (2015)
9. Turk, M.: Multimodal interaction: a review. Pattern Recognit. Lett. **36**(1), 189–195 (2014)
10. Shah, J., Breazeal, C.: An empirical analysis of team coordination behaviors and action planning with application to human-robot teaming. Hum. Factors: J. Hum. Factors Ergon. Soc. **52**(2), 234–245 (2010)
11. Bischoff, R., Graefe, V.: Dependable multimodal communication and interaction with robotic assistants. In: Proceedings - IEEE International Workshop on Robot and Human Interactive Communication, pp. 300–305 (2002)
12. Harris, J., Barber, D.: Speech and gesture interfaces for squad level human robot teaming. In: Karlsen, R.E., Gage, D.W., Shoemaker, C.M., Gerhart, G.R. (eds.) Unmanned Systems Technology Xvi, vol. 9084. SPIE (2014)
13. Redden, E.S., Carstens, C.B., Pettitt, R.A.: Intuitive Speech-based Robotic Control. U.S. Army Research Laboratory (Technical Report ARL-TR-5175) (2010)
14. Cacace, J., Finzi, A., Lippiello, V.: Multimodal Interaction with Multiple Co-located Drones in Search and Rescue Missions. CoRR abs/1605.0, pp. 1–6 (2016)
15. Lee, A., Kawahara, T., Shikano, K.: Julius an open source real-time large vocabulary recognition engine. In: Eurospeech, pp. 1691–1694 (2001)
16. Fernandez, R.A.S., Sanchez-lopez, J.L., Sampedro, C., Bavle, H., Molina, M., Campoy, P.: Natural user interfaces for human-drone multi-modal interaction. In: 2016 International Conference on Unmanned Aircraft Systems (ICUAS), Arlington, VA, USA, pp. 1013–1022. IEEE (2016)

17. Barber, D.J., Howard, T.M., Walter, M.R.: A multimodal interface for real-time soldier-robot teaming. **9837**, 98370M (2016)
18. Borkowski, A., Siemiatkowska, B., Szklarski, J.: Towards semantic navigation in mobile robotics. In: Engels, G., Lewerentz, C., Schäfer, W., Schürr, A., Westfechtel, B. (eds.) Graph Transformations and Model-Driven Engineering. LNCS, vol. 5765, pp. 719–748. Springer, Heidelberg (2010). https://doi.org/10.1007/978-3-642-17322-6_30
19. Hill, S.G., Barber, D., Evans, A.W.: Achieving the vision of effective soldier-robot teaming : recent work in multimodal communication. In: Proceedings of the Tenth Annual ACM/IEEE International Conference on Human-Robot Interaction Extended Abstracts, pp. 177–178 (2015)
20. Kattoju, R.K., Barber, D.J., Abich, J., Harris, J.: Technological evaluation of gesture and speech interfaces for enabling dismounted soldier-robot dialogue. **9837**, 98370N (2016)
21. Ng, W.S., Sharlin, E.: Collocated interaction with flying robots. In: Proceedings - IEEE International Workshop on Robot and Human Interactive Communication, pp. 143–149 (2011)
22. Cauchard, J.R., Jane, L.E., Zhai, K.Y., Landay, J.A.: Drone & me: an exploration into natural human-drone interaction. In: Proceedings of the 2015 ACM International Joint Conference on Pervasive and Ubiquitous Computing, pp. 361–365 (2015)
23. Obaid, M., Kistler, F., Kasparaviciute, G., Yantaç, A.E., Fjeld, M.: HowWould you gesture navigate a drone? A user-centered approach to control a drone. In: Proceedings of the 20th International Academic Mindtrek Conference, Tampere, Finland, pp. 113–121. ACM, New York (2016)
24. Nagi, J., Giusti, A., Gambardella, L.M., Di Caro, G.A.: Human-swarm interaction using spatial gestures. In: IEEE International Conference on Intelligent Robots and Systems (Iros), pp. 3834–3841 (2014)

# Camera-Based Force and Tactile Sensor

Wanlin Li[1], Jelizaveta Konstantinova[1], Yohan Noh[3], Akram Alomainy[2],
and Kaspar Althoefer[1(✉)]

[1] Centre for Advanced Robotics @ Queen Mary (ARQ), Queen Mary University of London,
Mile End Road, London, E1 4NS, UK
{wanlin.li,j.konstantinova,k.althoefer}@qmul.ac.uk
[2] School of Electronic Engineering and Computer Science (EECS),
Queen Mary University of London, Mile End Road, London, E1 4NS, UK
a.alomainy@qmul.ac.uk
[3] Centre for Robotics Research (CoRe), King's College London, Strand, London,
WC2R 2LS, UK
yohan.noh@kcl.ac.uk

**Abstract.** Tactile information has become a topic of great interest in the design
of devices that explore the physical interaction with the external environment.
For instance, it is important for a robot hand to perform manipulation tasks, such
as grasping and active touching, using tactile sensors mounted on the finger pad
to provide feedback information. In this research we present a novel device that
obtains both force and tactile information in a single integrated elastomer. The
proposed elastomer consists of two parts, one of which is transparent and is
wrapped in another translucent one that has eight conical sensing elements underneath. Two parts are merged together via a mould. A CCD camera is mounted at
the bottom of the device to record the images of two elastomer mediums illuminated by the LED arrays set inside of the device. The method consists of evaluating the state of the contact surface based on analysis of the image of two elastomers. The external deformation of the elastomer is used to measure three force
components $F_z$, $M_x$ and $M_y$. The measurement is based on the area changes of
the conical sensing elements under different loads, while the image of the inner
transparent elastomer captures the surface pattern, which can used to obtain tactile
information.

**Keywords:** Force sensor · Tactile sensor · Optical-based

## 1 Introduction

Tactile perception became an important aspect of sensation for robot design as it could
convey useful information about the interaction of the body with the external environment (i.e. detection of mechanical stimulation and temperature) [1]. Human beings have
an extremely powerful perception system that detects various tactile stimuli. The hand
is one of the most dexterous parts and using the feedback of the contact from the fingers,
we can interact with the environment and perform dexterous manipulations. The same
principle applies for robot design, a robotic hand could perform advanced manipulations

© Springer International Publishing AG, part of Springer Nature 2018
M. Giuliani et al. (Eds.): TAROS 2018, LNAI 10965, pp. 438–450, 2018.
https://doi.org/10.1007/978-3-319-96728-8_37

if feedback from the tactile sensor was available [2]. However, tactile sensing in robots is relatively backward comparing to that of human in terms of every-day manipulations, for example, grasping a small object [11]. In spite of the sensing area, tactile sensors are single-functional with less degrees of freedom comparing with the human hand [3].

Tactile sensors have attracted a lot of attention from researchers in the past few years. Yousef [4] gives an overall review of tactile sensing for human-like manipulation in robotics. When considering the performance of tactile sensors, one important aspect of the sensor is to consider the information of the contact surface, especially when the surface is curved or irregular. This is important for grasping and in-hand manipulations, where greater contact area with the surface provides a more stable grasp, and recognizing the contact material where different materials have different physical properties (i.e. surface texture and hardness) [12].

Among all categories of recent tactile sensors, optical-based sensor shows an admirable compliance due to their soft structure employing elastomers. Compared to the conventional electromagnetic sensing methods, such as resistive or capacitive-based sensors that largely depend on the transmission of electrical signals, the optical tactile sensor has a high-resolution camera that can capture the geometry of the contact surface, as well as being able to measure the contact force. Thus, it can recognize multi-modal information of the physical properties of the contact object.

An ideal artificial optical tactile sensor has to be miniature, with high resolution, but low power consumption and a compliant mechanism [4]. With the rapid development of miniature cameras and image processing techniques, the investigations of optical tactile sensor have been quite popular in the past ten years. One of the early trials is introduced by Schneiter [5] where a reflective elastomer is applied as the physical medium along with the optical fibers for light generation. A CCD camera was used to measure the reflective light and estimate the thickness of the elastomer at every sampling point. Currently there are several typical tactile sensors [6] [10] that are optical-based and they all have the capability for acquiring tactile information. The TACTIP sensor [2] is a biologically-inspired sensing device with dome structure, composed of a silicone outer skin with inward facing nodule pins. The sensor is capable of sensing pressure force, shear force, surface strain for detecting edges, and texture. The Optical Three-axis tactile sensor [8] is a domelike robotic finger that is capable of sensing normal and shearing force. The GelSight tactile sensor [9] is a soft flat-shape sensor that has the unique characteristic of being able to capture the geometry of the contact surface and restore it in 3D configuration in computer.

We propose a design of an optical-based three-axis tactile and force sensor, to improve the capability of the current robot touch sensors to provide a larger measuring range of force and tactile information. The proposed sensor can obtain the force information by measuring three wide-range force components that are loads (Fz) and two moments (Mx and My), with the use of a combination of elastomers and force sensitive structure, and obtain the tactile information by using a camera to capture the pattern of the contact surface via a transparent silicone.

## 2   Sensor Design

We are introducing a new miniature sensor that is comparable to the size of human finger. The CAD design and schematic design of the device is shown in Fig. 1. The proposed tactile sensor consists of the following parts: Elastomer part, Force sensitive structure, LED arrays and CCD camera.

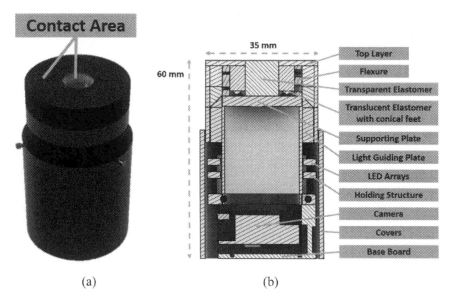

(a)                                                    (b)

**Fig. 1.** Force and tactile sensor design. (a) CAD design. (b) Schematic design.

The touch medium of the device is the elastomer part together with the flexure (a force sensitive structure). The elastomer part is composed of two elastomers coated with a hollow membrane on top. The flexure has a three degree of freedom with three cantilever structure and its rigid structure can effectively stabilize the soft elastomer part. Both the elastomer part and flexure are placed on a hard surface which is a transparent acrylic sheet. The elastomer part is illuminated with white light through the LED arrays placed in side of the device. In addition, LED arrays are used to provide an optimal condition for image capture. 3D-printed covers outside of the device are used to block the external light from coming inside and cause disruptions to the inner illumination. The camera captures deformations in both elastomers to measure the applied force based on the deformations of eight individual legs circularly allocated on the bottom side of the outside elastomer and the tactile information based on the pattern presented by the transparent inner elastomer. The tactile sensor gives a high-resolution sensing with a spatial resolution of 2 microns.

## 2.1   Elastomer Part

The elastomer part consists of three parts that are two elastomers and one membrane, as it is shown in Fig. 2. The inner elastomer composes a long transparent cylinder that traverses both the membrane and the outside elastomer. The outside elastomer is a translucent hollow cylinder with eight miniature conical legs symmetrically attached at the bottom side of the cylinder. A hollow membrane is attached to the top of the cylinder. The three components are merged together so they can be treated as an integrated part, or named as the elastomer part. Since the elastomer part is soft and compliant, it produces good deformation when external load is applied.

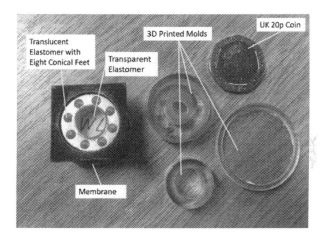

**Fig. 2.**  Elastomer part and the corresponding molds.

The properties of the elastomer play an important role in the tactile sensor and can largely affect the sensing range. An ideal elastomer material should be of low viscosity and good elasticity. Thickness and hardness are two important properties for the sensor design. A thick elastomer can carry out a larger degree of deformation.

In our sensor, the inner transparent cylinder elastomer is made of Solaris® from Smooth-On Inc. To make the inner part, Solaris® part A and part B need to be degassed in the vacuum chamber before mixing, then both parts were mixed with a ratio of 1:1. Further on, the mixture is placed into the vacuum chamber again for degassing since the stirring process might generate some bubbles, which are detrimental for the elastomer performance. Then we pour the silicone mixture into the 3D printed mold and leave the silicone into the room temperature to cure within 24 h. No additive liquid is needed during the mixing of part A and B since the softness of Solaris® has already met our needs. The hollow elastomer with eight conical legs is made from silicone (Ecoflex® 00-50 from Smooth-On Inc). The steps to make this translucent elastomer are similar but EcoflexA® 00-50 takes less time to cure (three hours). No additive liquid is required either. Moreover, we brush silver powder all over the surface of the hollow translucent elastomer, as well as the eight conical feet on the bottom side in order to increase the reflection of the elastomer itself, which leads to a better capture. The hollow membrane is made of dyed silicone (Ecoflex® 00-50 with Silc Pig® pigments). We need to pre-mix the Silc Pig® in the container before dispending and then add the colorant to Ecoflex® 00-50 part A, mix well before adding part B and wait for cure. Figure 2 shows the transparent elastomer, translucent elastomer with eight conical legs and the membrane with some 3D printed molds.

## 2.2   Force Sensitive Structure

The force sensitive cantilever structure is used to encircle the elastomer part to stabilize and enhance the robustness of measurements. This flexure structure has three degrees of freedom.

The force sensitive structure (flexure) consists of a hollow monolithic cylinder with three thin symmetrical horizontal cantilevers (with thickness of 2.3 mm) in a circular arrangement. The external and internal diameters of the flexure are 25 and 20.2 mm, respectively. Each cantilever is linked to the rest of the flexure with short supports which allows displacement to be formed either upwards or downwards between the slots (with height of 0.78 mm of each cantilever). The tolerance of the flexure is thus 0.78 mm. Forces applying on the top of the flexure give a direct impact on the horizontal cantilevers and cause the deflection of the slots, while the bottom of the flexure remains fixed. The cantilever design ensures the minimal coupling effects between axial and lateral force components. Thus, the cantilevers bend only along the vertical axis when an axial loading is applied and twist and bend along the vertical and horizontal axes when a lateral load is applied.

The combined force sensitive structure together with the elastomer part is shown in Fig. 3. During the contact, the deflection of the cantilever structure in the flexure is resulting in the deformation and horizontal displacement of eight conical legs in the elastomer part, the deformation of the cantilever structure is analyzed during finite element simulations.

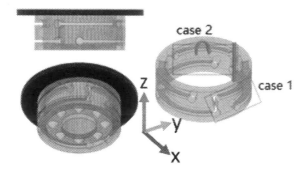

**Fig. 3.** CAD design of the force sensitive structure (two red square areas represent case 1 and case 2). In case 1, the flexure is designed to deform only along the vertical axis when an axial loading is applied (just show one of the three symmetrical cantilever structure). In case 2, the flexure is designed to twist and bend along the vertical and horizontal axes when a lateral loading is applied (just show one of the three symmetrical cantilever structure). (Color figure online)

Based on the CAD design shown in Fig. 3, we use a 3d printer Stratasy Objet30 Prime to print this MRI compatible flexure with a polymer material (VeroClear-RGD810) that has high robustness and low hysteresis. Since the device should be isolated from the external light source, we sprayed the printed transparent flexure with black dye paint. The mechanical properties of the polymer are summarized in Table 1. One feature is that the material has a heat deflection temperature (HDT) of over 45 °C which ensures that minimum deflection will occur in terms of the contact under human body temperature or room temperature.

**Table 1.** Force sensitive structure material property

| Property | RGD810 |
| --- | --- |
| Tensile strength | 50–65 MPa |
| Elongation at break | 10%–25% |
| Flexural strength | 75–110 MPa |
| Flexural modulus | 2,200–3,200 MPa |
| HDT, °C at 0.45 MPa | 45–50 °C |
| Shore hardness (D) | 83–86 D |
| Polymerized density | 1.18–1.19 g/cm^3 |
| Poisson's ratio | 0.38 |

### 2.3   Illumination and Image Capture

A key aspect of the sensor is the way the elastomer part is illuminated. A white LED array is placed on the base of the housing for sensor illumination. The light from each of the LEDs travels through the light guiding plates which have 45-degree angle on one end to guide and reflect the light to the supporting plate and thus illuminate the elastomer part. The LEDs are of size 3 mm with 30-degrees viewing angel, soldered on a 3D printed electronic housing made of VeroClear-RGD810. Transparent acrylics with 1/8-inch thickness are cut as the light guiding plates and supporting plate, using the laser cutter PLS6.150D.

A CCD camera is placed at the bottom of the sensor to capture the deformations of both the transparent elastomer and eight feelers when contacting an external surface. The camera needs to be small, as well as having the white balance and automatic light correction. The USB webcam Logitech c270 satisfies all the requirements and has a HD 720p widescreen with noise reduction.

To give a better understanding of the working principle of tactile sensor, a thumb is placed on the top of the surface. The deformations of the elastomer part which can be segmented as two sections, one is the center area and the other one is the outer area. Initially when there's no contact between the sensor and the thumb, the center area shows the natural environment scene (assuming the default environment is black), see Fig. 4(a). Then we apply a normal force with our thumb and the camera can capture an image shown in Fig. 4(b). The pattern image (the fingerprint) is shown the central area, of which the surface geometry can be clearly recorded, and the deformations of eight conical feet are recorded at the outer area, of which the shape of each conical feet and horizontal displacement (it reaches the maximum normal force and there is no horizontal displacement for the normal force in this case) can be processed to evaluate the corresponding normal force. Finally, when we apply a force with lateral moment, the camera can capture an image shown in Fig. 4(c), where there will be both the changes of conical feet's shapes and the horizontal displacements.

 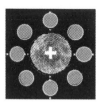 

Image pattern of sensing element     Applying normal force     Applying lateral moment

**Fig. 4.** The corresponding deformation when normal force and lateral moment is applied on the force and tactile sensor.

## 3   Prototype Sensor Performance

### 3.1   Simulation Result

FEA is a numerical method to investigate the performance of the target, make sure the target works within the expected range and optimize the design of the target before manufacturing. In our design, we apply the FEA to investigate the behavior of the force sensitive structure, using the material VeroClear-RGD810 (the material property is in Table 1). According to [7], we aim to design a flexure structure that can measure a maximum force of up to 20 N (equals to 200 gm of force). The amount of deformation under vertical and lateral loadings are shown in Fig. 5, The simulation result in Fig. 6 shows the force sensitive structure measures the maximum normal force of 20 N and the maximum lateral torque (around the x-axis and y-axis) of ± 87.5 N/mm. The parameters of the flexure are given in force sensitive structure in sensor design. Besides, the sensor also provides a force overloading protection which means if the load is too heavy for flexure to sustain, the cantilevers will bend and physically contact with the solid part of the cylinder. Thus, the flexure can sustain a maximum of around 25 N before a damage occurs.

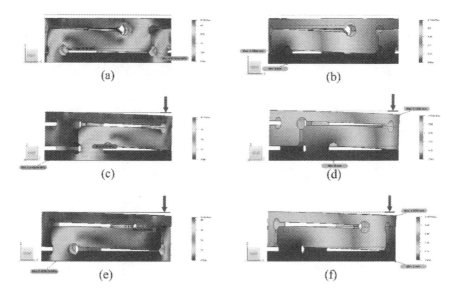

**Fig. 5.** FEA simulation performed with Fusion 360 Simulation Tool, showing the mechanical behavior under normal and lateral loadings of the force sensitive structure. (a) Stress behavior under normal force Fz = −20 N. (b) Displacement behavior under normal force Fz = −20 N. (c) Stress behavior under normal force Fz = −7 N and Mx = −87.5 N/mm. (d) Displacement behavior under normal force Fz = −7 N and Mx = −87.5 N/mm. (e) Stress behavior under normal force Fz = −7 N and My = 87.5 N/mm. (f) Displacement behavior under normal force Fz = −7 N and My = 87.5 N/mm.

Then we apply the FEA to investigate the behavior of the elastomer part. The parameters of the elastomer part are based on the parameters of the flexure structure to ensure the size and the extent of deformation of both are matched. The material used for FEA is Ecoflex® 00-50 and Solaris®. The material properties of Ecoflex® 00-50 are density of 1.07e-06 kg/mm^3, Young's modulus of 0.08 Mpa, tensile strength of 2.2 MPa. The material properties of Solaris® are density of 0.99e-06 kg/mm^3, Young's modulus of 0.1 Mpa, tensile strength of 1.2 MPa. These values are based on information shown by Ecoflex® Series - Smooth-On Inc. and Solaris® - Smooth-On Inc. Simulation result in Fig. 7 shows the elastomer part measures the maximum normal force of 1.5 N and the maximum lateral torque (around the x-axis and y-axis) of ± 3 N/mm. The amount of deformation of the elastomer part shows a linear relationship with vertical and lateral loadings, and the strain at contact area of each conical leg also demonstrates a linear relationship with vertical loadings, as is shown in Fig. 8.

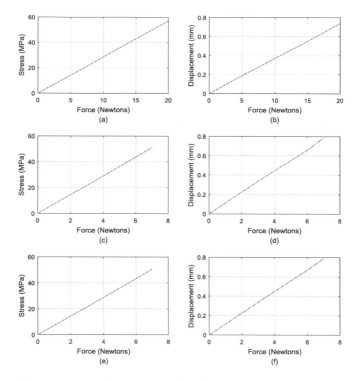

**Fig. 6.** Von Mises stress and displacement of the force sensitive structure using FEM. Stress against force components in (a) Fz, (c) Fz and Mx (d) Fz and My. Displacement against force components in (b) Fz, (d) Fz and Mx (f) Fz and My.

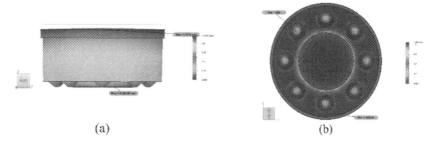

**Fig. 7.** FEA simulation performed with Fusion 360 Simulation Tool, showing the mechanical behavior under normal and lateral loadings of the elastomer. (a) Displacement behavior under normal force Fz = −1.5 N. (b) Strain behavior under normal force Fz = −1.5 N.

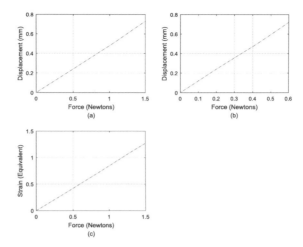

**Fig. 8.** Displacement of the elastomer part and equivalent strain at the contact area of the conical leg tip using FEM. Displacement against force components in (a) Fz, (b) Fz and My. Stress against force in (c) Fz.

Finally, we apply the FEA to investigate the behavior of the combination of both force sensitive structure and the elastomer part, based on the material used above. Simulation result in Fig. 9 shows the flexure can be nicely assembled with the elastomer part and largely expand the sensor's measuring range with the maximum normal force of

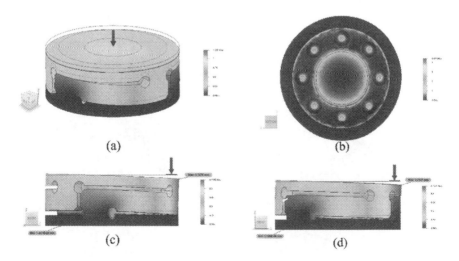

**Fig. 9.** FEA simulation performed with Fusion 360 Simulation Tool, showing the mechanical behavior under normal and lateral loadings of the combination of the force sensitive structure and the elastomer part. (a) Displacement behavior under normal force Fz = −22.5 N. (b) Strain behavior under normal force Fz = −22.5 N. (c) Displacement behavior under normal force Fz = −7.6 N and Mx = −95 N/mm. (d) Displacement behavior under normal force Fz = −7.6 N and My = 95 N/mm.

22.5 N and the maximum lateral torque (around the x-axis and y-axis) of ± 95 N/mm. The displacements of both flexure and the elastomer part are linear against force components and the strain at the tip of the elastomer's conical leg is also proportional to the applied force, thus we can establish a map between the deformations of the conical legs and the external force.

## 3.2   Experimental Result

We create a user interface for the tactile sensor in MATLAB, as is shown in Fig. 10. The top left is the live video of the webcam. There are two spaces in the bottom left part, the left one is the capture of the present image and the right one is the calibration image. In the right part of the interface, we segment the capture image into 9 parts (8 images of conical legs Pin 1 to Pin 8 and the center is for the tactile information). When no load is applied on the sensor, the camera captures an image as the calibration image. Then we do the calibration. The sensor can detect three force components Fz, Mx and My. In normal load testing, a normal force is applied by directly adding different weights (from 10 grams to 100 grams with a step of 10 grams and from 100 grams to 1000 grams with a step of 100 grams) on the center of the tactile sensor's membrane along z-axis. We capture each weight image in sequence and save them in a database. In lateral load testing, the sensor is fixed and a string is stretched along the x-axis and y-axis, respectively. One end of the string is connected to the transparent elastomer in the center and the other end is connected to the loads hanging along the corresponding axis. Lateral loads with different weights (from 10 grams to 100 grams) are connected with the string and the weights images along x-axis and y-axis are captured in sequence, respectively.

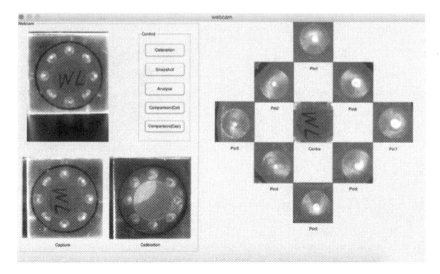

**Fig. 10.** User interface of the tactile sensor when 100 grams lateral load along x-axis is applied on the sensor.

During the test, we add different weights and could capture the images shown in Fig. 10. As can been seen, both the force information and tactile information (the initial of a signature) can be observed during the sensing and the image in the center of the camera can be quickly saved for further processing.

## 4 Conclusion

In this work, we introduce the hardware design of a novel optical-based force and tactile sensor that can sense both force information and tactile information in one single elastomer. When pressing an irregular object on the sensor, an overall force applied on the whole structure can be presented as the force information via the change of eight feet and the transparent elastomer can show the contact pattern (the future work is to demonstrate the force distribution together with the pattern in more details as the tactile information), so that we can obtain these two information based on a single elastomer. The device is based on a combination of the force sensitive structure and an elastomer part. The measurement range of the proposed sensor in simulation shows the sensor can sustain a maximum of 22.5 N loads in vertical direction through center and separately, a maximum of 95 N/mm horizontal moments Mx and My at the edge. The calibration proves a maximum of 1000 grams axial load and 200 grams lateral load in practice. A calibration matrix is obtained based on these two cases (normal force and normal force combined with two lateral moments) using the regression method. Markers will be added on the transparent elastomer surface for future work. The number of the conical legs can be reduced to three instead of eight to measure the three axis force components and this could also reduce the computation during the real-time processing.

**Acknowledgments.** This work was supported in part by the EPSRC in the framework of the NCNR (National Centre for Nuclear Robotics) project (EP/R02572X/1) and the Innovate UK funded and q-bot led project WormBot.

## References

1. Ohka, M., Mitsuya, Y., Higashioka, I., Kabeshita, H.: An experimental optical three-axis tactile sensor for micro-robots. Robotica **23**, 457–465 (2005)
2. Winstone, B., Griffiths, G., Pipe, T., Melhuish, C., Rossiter, J.: TACTIP - tactile fingertip device, texture analysis through optical tracking of skin features. In: Lepora, N.F., Mura, A., Krapp, H.G., Verschure, P.F.M.J., Prescott, T.J. (eds.) Living Machines 2013. LNCS (LNAI), vol. 8064, pp. 323–334. Springer, Heidelberg (2013). https://doi.org/10.1007/978-3-642-39802-5_28
3. Lazzarini, R., Magni, R., Dario, P.: A tactile array sensor layered in an artificial skin. In: Proceedings of the IEEE/RSJ International Conference on Intelligent Robots and Systems, Human Robot Interaction and Cooperative Robots, vol. 3, pp. 114–119 (1995)
4. Yousef, H., Boukallel, M., Althoefer, K.: Tactile sensing for dexterous in-hand manipulation in robotics—A review. Sens. Actuators Phys. **167**(2), 171–187 (2011)
5. Schneiter, J.L., Sheridan, T.B.: An optical tactile sensor for manipulators. Robot. Comput.-Integr. Manuf. **1**, 65–71 (1984)

6. Yuan, W., Li, R., Srinivasan, M.A., Adelson, E.H.: Measurement of shear and slip with a GelSight tactile sensor. In: 2015 IEEE International Conference on Robotics and Automation (ICRA), pp. 304–311 (2015)
7. Noh, Y., Sareh, S., Back, J., Althoefer, K.: A three-axial body force sensor for flexible manipulators. In: 2014 IEEE International Conference on Robotics and Automation (ICRA), pp. 6388–6393. IEEE (2014)
8. Ohka, M., Morisawa, N., Yussof, H.: Trajectory generation of robotic fingers based on tri-axial tactile data for cap screwing task. In: IEEE International Conference on Robotics and Automation, ICRA 2009, pp. 883–888. IEEE (2009)
9. Yuan, W., Srinivasan, M.A., Adelson, E.H.: Estimating object hardness with a gelsight touch sensor. In: 2016 IEEE/RSJ International Conference on Intelligent Robots and Systems (IROS), pp. 208–215. IEEE (2016)
10. Johnson, M.K., Adelson, E.H.: Retrographic sensing for the measurement of surface texture and shape. In: 2009 IEEE Conference on Computer Vision and Pattern Recognition, CVPR 2009. pp. 1070–1077. IEEE (2009)
11. Konstantinova, J., Stilli, A., Althoefer, K.: Force and proximity fingertip sensor to enhance grasping perception. In: 2015 IEEE/RSJ International Conference on Intelligent Robots and Systems (IROS), pp. 2118–2123. IEEE (2015)
12. Konstantinova, J., Stilli, A., Althoefer, K.: Fingertip Fiber Optical Tactile Array with Two-Level Spring Structure. In Sensors **17**(10), 2337 (2017)

# Short Papers

# What Comes to Mind When People Are Asked Questions About Robots?

Stanislava Naneva[1]($\boxtimes$) (iD), Thomas L. Webb[1] (iD),
and Tony J. Prescott[2] (iD)

[1] Department of Psychology, The University of Sheffield, Sheffield S1 2LT, UK
{snaneval, t.webb}@sheffield.ac.uk
[2] Department of Computer Science, The University of Sheffield, Sheffield S1 4DP, UK
t.j.prescott@sheffield.ac.uk

**Abstract.** Scientists and practitioners often seek to understand people's attitudes towards new technologies, such as robots. Attitude Representation Theory suggests that what people think and feel about a category is likely to depend on the specific representation that comes to mind when asked questions about that category. The aim of this research was therefore to explore what members of the general public think about when asked questions about robots. A short survey was conducted with 33 members of the general public in Sheffield. It was found that participants most frequently associated the word *robot* with descriptive words such as "metallic" and "artificial". Approximately half of the participants mentioned fictional robots, suggesting that people's attitudes toward robots may not be grounded in reality. Research into people's attitudes toward robots therefore needs to (i) consider what representations people are likely to base their attitudes on and (ii) find ways to help them to ground these representations in the reality of the technologies.

**Keywords:** Robots · Attitudes · Attitude Representation Theory

## 1 Introduction

Fictional representations of robots (e.g., those portrayed in films or other media) may affect people's attitudes and behaviour toward real robots [1]. This could be problematic as portrayals of robots in fiction rarely reflect the reality of current technology [1]. Attitude Representation Theory [2] could help to explain variability in attitudes toward robots [3] as it suggests that people's broader evaluations of a category (e.g., robots) is likely to be affected by their subjective representation of that category. In other words, how people think and feel about robots is likely to be shaped by the specific representation that comes to mind when the question is posed. The aim of the present research was, therefore, to investigate what members of the general public associate with the word *robot* and whether fictional or non-fictional robots are more salient representations of the robot category.

© Springer International Publishing AG, part of Springer Nature 2018
M. Giuliani et al. (Eds.): TAROS 2018, LNAI 10965, pp. 453–454, 2018.
https://doi.org/10.1007/978-3-319-96728-8

## 2   Method

A short survey with 33 members of the general public was conducted in Sheffield. Participants were approached as they were walking through a public space and asked four questions: *"What comes to mind when you hear the word robot?"*, *"Can you list the first three robots that come to mind?"*, *"Do you work in an area related to robotics?"*, and *"Have you ever visited Sheffield Robotics?"*.

## 3   Results

The data was analysed using an approach based on manifest content analysis [4]. The majority of responses (36%) reflected participants' associations between robots and words reflecting the artificial or non-organic features of robots, such as "metallic", "mechanical", and "artificial". In general, participants mentioned more fictional (50%) than non-fictional (37%) robots, although this difference was not statistically significant. Further exploration of the data revealed that participants most frequently mentioned robots from Star Wars (13% of mentions) and industrial robots (10% of mentions).

## 4   Discussion

The findings suggest that fictional representations of robots are frequently brought to mind when people are asked to think about robots. While this study cannot speak to the relationship between people's representations of robots and their attitudes, it does provide some incentive to consider the effect that fictional representations of robots may have on people's beliefs about robots. Attitude Representation Theory [2] may be a useful way to explain the variability in people's attitudes toward robots [3] and future research will attempt to measure the extent to which exposing people to different fictional and non-fictional representations of robots can influence their attitudes toward robots in general.

## References

1. Kriz, S., Ferro, T.D., Damera, P., Porter, J.R.: Fictional robots as a data source in HRI research: exploring the link between science fiction and interactional expectations. In: 19th IEEE International Symposium on Robot and Human Interactive Communication, pp. 458–463. IEEE, New York (2010)
2. Lord, C.G., Lepper, M.R.: Attitude representation theory. Adv. Exp. Soc. Psychol. **31**, 265–343 (1999)
3. Takayama, L., Ju, W., Nass, C.: Beyond dirty, dangerous and dull: what everyday people think robots should do. In: 3rd ACM/IEEE International Conference on Human Robot Interaction, pp. 25–32. ACM, New York (2008)
4. Hsieh, H.F., Shannon, S.E.: Three approaches to qualitative content analysis. Qual. Health Res. **15**(9), 1277–1288 (2005)

# Beyond "To Me, To You": Combining Implicit and Explicit Communication for Cooperative Transport in Humanoid Robotic Systems

Naomi Gildert[✉], Jon Timmis, and Andrew Pomfret

York Robotics Lab, Department of Electronic Engineering,
University of York, York YO10 5DD, UK
ng668@york.ac.uk

Effective cooperation and communication between robots is essential for the completion of many tasks in a dynamic environment. Humans are uniquely adept at cooperating and communicating and so a robotic solution could be potentially found by mimicking human behaviour.

In psychology, our ability to cooperate is known as *joint action* [5]. A fundamental facilitator to joint action is how we communicate. When cooperating, we use both explicit communication (the direct transfer of information, i.e. through speech), and implicit communication (implying information through an action). For humans, the latter often manifests itself in the form of force feedback, where an individual senses the force being exerted by the person they are cooperating with and coordinates their joint movements appropriately [4].

When humans cooperate on a task such as carrying a box between them, the individuals typically use a combination of explicit and implicit communication. For example, this could be giving a verbal instruction and then applying pressure to the object to enact that instruction. This task also requires adaptability as the most appropriate combination of the two forms of communication depends on the task and its context.

We propose the development of a system that mimics joint action in humans to produce a new form of cooperation between two humanoid robots using an adaptive combination of implicit and explicit communication.

The system will be efficient, as interpreting information through implicit cues could reduce the amount of data being transferred explicitly. It will also be fault tolerant, as the system will be able to compensate for a failure in one communication type by favouring the other.

As demonstrated in [3], no existing work has investigated the combination of using both explicit and implicit communication to fully exploit the advantages of each. The proposed system will implement this novelty, resulting in a more adaptive and efficient system.

The desired behaviour will be achieved by integrating three aspects of key robotic research areas: implicit communication in swarm robotics, internal simulation, and dynamic leadership.

Multiple explicit communication protocols in robots already exist, but a suitable form of implicit communication must be established for this system. Force

© Springer International Publishing AG, part of Springer Nature 2018
M. Giuliani et al. (Eds.): TAROS 2018, LNAI 10965, pp. 455–456, 2018.
https://doi.org/10.1007/978-3-319-96728-8

consensus will be employed as it is the mechanism that is the most similar to implicit communication used by humans when cooperating on similar tasks. Previous successful implementations in swarms demonstrate its validity [6].

A mechanism is required that will enable the robots to evaluate a given situation and adjust what combination of implicit and explicit communication to use to better solve that task. An internal model, based on the consequence engine employed in [7], and scene recall will be used to add two complexities to the system: firstly, the robots will be able to recall past experiences and simulate potential next steps to adapt to different environments and different objects they have to manipulate. Secondly, the internal model will employ constraints and restrictions related to the successful manipulation of the object that will dictate what combination of explicit and implicit communication to use.

Whilst the main novelty lies in the system adapting communication methods during task execution, further complexity will be added to enable the robots to maintain efficiency in task execution by adapting the exchange of leadership to dynamic environments. Dynamic leadership will be integrated into the framework by using a hybrid system similar to those explored in [2].

The system will be implemented on two Nao robot platforms [1], first in simulation using the V-Rep simulator, and then deployed on real robots. The efficacy of the system will be tested through a series of experiments that will evaluate the successful manipulation and manoeuvre of a range of objects by the two robots, through a variety of environments.

By integrating these areas of robotics into a single system for the first time, and exploring the novelty of the adaptive communication employed, this work will result in a new form of adaptive cooperation between humanoid robots.

# References

1. Who is nao? https://www.ald.softbankrobotics.com/en/robots/nao
2. Chaimowicz, L., Kumar, V., Campos, M.F.: A paradigm for dynamic coordination of multiple robots. Auton. Robots **17**(1), 7–21 (2004)
3. Gildert, N., Timmis, J., Pomfret, A.: The need for combining implicit and explicit communication in cooperative robotic systems. Frontiers in Robotics and AI (2018, in review)
4. Reed, K., Peshkin, M., Hartmann, M.J., Grabowecky, M., Patton, J., Vishton, P.M.: Haptically linked dyads are two motor-control systems better than one? Psychol. Sci. **17**(5), 365–366 (2006)
5. Sebanz, N., Bekkering, H., Knoblich, G.: Joint action: bodies and minds moving together. Trends Cogn. Sci. **10**(2), 70–76 (2006)
6. Wang, Z., Schwager, M.: Multi-robot manipulation without communication. In: Chong, N.-Y., Cho, Y.-J. (eds.) Distributed Autonomous Robotic Systems. STAR, vol. 112, pp. 135–149. Springer, Tokyo (2016). https://doi.org/10.1007/978-4-431-55879-8_10
7. Winfield, A.F.T., Blum, C., Liu, W.: Towards an ethical robot: internal models, consequences and ethical action selection. In: Mistry, M., Leonardis, A., Witkowski, M., Melhuish, C. (eds.) TAROS 2014. LNCS (LNAI), vol. 8717, pp. 85–96. Springer, Cham (2014). https://doi.org/10.1007/978-3-319-10401-0_8

# Towards Self-repair with Modular Robots During Continuous Motion

Robert H. Peck$^{(\boxtimes)}$, Jon Timmis, and Andy M. Tyrrell

Department of Electronic Engineering, University of York, York, UK
rp1060@york.ac.uk

By using a number of modules that are able to reconfigure for a variety of tasks, modular robots have many potential advantages over single robots designed specially for single tasks. In unstructured, or otherwise previously unknown, environments modular robots should be able to adapt by reconfiguring [4] and maintain operation. Such reconfiguration allows the use of modular robots in roles for which there would be conflicting design requirements for a single robot. It also enables self-repair, that is to say the removal of failed modules and their replacement by spare or redundant units. While there is existing work on fault tolerance for modular robots, only a limited number of studies have considered the process involved in removing a failed module from its location in the multi-robot structure [2, 3]. In both studies the group of robots remained motionless while the repair took place. Neither study allowed for the operation of collective tasks before the failure occured. We consider that there may be advantages to performing self-repair while the group maintains its motion.

To this end we propose a hypothesis: *Modular robots using a self-repair strategy which can operate while the group maintains collective motion will be able to complete their mission faster, and more effectively, than robots of the same hardware design which are using a self-repair strategy which requires the system to stop and repair before resuming motion.*

A potential advantage of our proposed approach is that in time critical situations self-repair during continuous motion can offer a speed advantage over stopping to self-repair or fault masking strategies which attempt to maintain motion despite the presence of a damaged module. This could be especially useful for robots entering, for example, a nuclear reactor where more damage will be sustained the longer the robots are in the thermally and radiologically challenging environment. A modular robot which could carry out such a dynamic self-repair should be able to complete its task within the reactor faster and so survive better and provide the opportunity for more reuse in future. Other advantages of self-repair during motion may include the ability to repair while crossing obstacles or resisting environmental forces.

We plan a series of experiments, both simulated and real, using a new hardware platform currently in the early stages of development, see Fig. 1. When a module is injected with a fault (assumed for our purposes to be a total failure of all actuators, communications and sensors) while robots docked together in a suitable configuration are moving, the group may attempt to remain in motion with the failed module in place, to stop and repair or to repair while

© Springer International Publishing AG, part of Springer Nature 2018
M. Giuliani et al. (Eds.): TAROS 2018, LNAI 10965, pp. 457–458, 2018.
https://doi.org/10.1007/978-3-319-96728-8

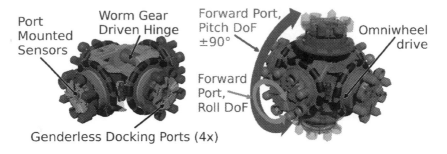

**Fig. 1.** The Omni-Pi-tent robot concept. A design which combines: an omniwheel drive, enabling a wide range of group locomotion methods; genderless docking similar to RoGenSid [1] to allow single-sided disconnection from failed modules; and SMORES like pitch-roll degrees of freedom allowing a wide range of 3D structures to form. The platform will use a Raspberry Pi Zero W and, similarly to HyMod, will feature a 3D printed body. An initial V-REP simulation of the platform has been constructed and used to demonstrate docking and actuator use, hardware is under development.

continuing their task. In the simplest scenarios this dynamic form of self-repair will act like stationary self-repair similar to [2] or [3] but with a velocity transform applied. Further work shall focus on dynamic self-repair in 3D structures where in some scenarios robots must climb across one another to perform repairs, the robot shown in Fig. 1 will allow such 3D movement. It is expected that as well as speed differences there will be other measures of performance in which fault masking, stationary self-repair and self-repair during continuous motion differ, for example energy use. In a fault masking strategy, energy will be expended dragging the failed module. Stationary self-repair would typically take increased time. Self-repair while moving will require robots to travel at a range of speeds and may consume extra energy due to those modules which must move faster than the rest of the group to get themselves into position to dock while group motion continues. Our experiments will clarify which strategy is most efficient. In some cases tasks will be completable only when some of the strategies are used. See https://www.york.ac.uk/robot-lab/dsr/ for a video of the strategies.

The general principles learned while studying self-repair during motion should be of use for the self-repair of robots in environments where the act of stopping to self-repair is impossible, for example with fixed-wing drones.

# References

1. Hossain, S.G.M., et al.: RoGenSid: a rotary plate genderless single-sided docking mechanism for modular self-reconfigurable robots. In: ASME 2013 IDETC/CIE, V06BT07A011-V06BT07A011 (2013)
2. Mathews, N., et al.: Mergeable nervous systems for robots. Nat. Commun. **8**, 439 (2017)
3. Murray, L.: Fault tolerant morphogenesis in self-reconfigurable modular robotic systems. Ph.D. thesis, University of York, York, UK (2013)
4. Rus, D., et al.: Self-reconfiguring robots. Comms. ACM **45**(3), 39–45 (2002)

# Toward a Cutter Suction Dredger Robot: Multi-agent Learning for Decision Making

Changyun Wei[✉], Fusheng Ni, and Shuang Jiang

College of Mechanical and Electrical Engineering, Hohai University,
NO. 200 Jinling Bei Road, Changzhou 213022, Jiangsu Province, China
weichangyun@hotmail.com

**Abstract.** Cutter Suction Dredgers (CSD) are widely used for removing earth from the bottom of a stream, river or lake for the purposes of deepening a navigational channel or obtaining sands for landfill. Currently, dredgers are controlled by human operators manually. During the dredging process, the operators are required to fully concentrate on various instruments. Driver fatigue of the operators often leads to operational accidents and low efficiency of production. In order to release the operators from heavy workload, we are aiming at designing an intelligent multi-agent learning framework for the development of the next generation of cutter suction dredgers. The novel feature of the framework is that reinforcement learning is employed for learning agents to obtain optimal control policy from experience.

**Keywords:** Cutter suction dredger · Multi-agent systems
Dredger robot · Reinforcement learning

## Concept and Research Objectives: Beyond the State of the Art

The key components of a cutter suction dredger usually include a cutter head, a cutter ladder, a suction pipe, a discharge pipe, several dredger pumps, a working spud pole and an auxiliary spud pole, as shown in Fig. 1. The cutter head associated with its drive and the suction pipe are mounted on the ladder that is suspended by the pontoon of the dredger. The cutter head is an efficient tool for excavating the soil that will be sucked up by pumps and then transported to the disposal place through a slurry pipeline. During the dredging process, the cutter suction dredger does not use any propulsion to drive it. Instead, it is a stationary dredger, but it moves around the working spud pole. Such a movement is called a swing, achieved by pulling and slacking on the fore sideline wires of two side anchors. Thus, the dredging trajectory is an arc round a fixed point (i.e., the working spud pole). After a swing movement, the cutter suction dredger can move forward by means of a hydraulic cylinder.

The objectives of the intelligent multi-agent system introduced in this work is to obtain the optimal control policy. Specifically, the solids level in the pipeline

© Springer International Publishing AG, part of Springer Nature 2018
M. Giuliani et al. (Eds.): TAROS 2018, LNAI 10965, pp. 459–461, 2018.
https://doi.org/10.1007/978-3-319-96728-8

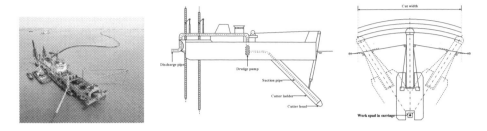

**Fig. 1.** Genearl layout of a cutter suction dredger.

cannot be too low for maintaining good production; the solids level cannot be too high either because the high density of slurry in a pipeline can potentially increase the risk of solid setting and, consequently, lead to pipeline blockage [1].

The challenge of the multi-agent system is that the environment is dynamic and uncertain as the knowledge about the characteristics of the underwater soil are not known in advance. Learning is an effective way for an agent to adapt its behaviour based on feedbacks from the environment. In order to obtain the optimal control policy, the multi-agent system seeks to tightly integrate a Soil Cutting Agent (SCA) and a Soil Transport Agent (STA). The former agent is responsible for learning the control policy of swing, spud, ladder and anchor movements for soil cutting, while the latter agent is supposed to learn the control policy of pumps for slurry transport. To obtain the final optimal control policy, we need to synthesize the objectives of two agents, because the performance of the SCA can directly influence the slurry density in the pipeline, which is the key parameter for the STA to make appropriate adjustments.

Reinforcement learning is a formal methodology that has been successfully evaluated in many agent domains, in which the agent can learn through trial-and-error iterations with its environment [2]. In order to build such a learning system, we first need to construct a Markov Decision Process model of the dredging process. Then the SCA and STA can iteratively update their respective Q-values using historical data and online feedbacks. To form the optimal control policy, we should take account of Q-values of each objective so as to balance their interests. Thus, a multi-objective reinforcement learning framework is proposed to realise such a goal. We hope that such a learning framework can set up a decision making module that supports the development of a fully intelligent dredger robot. The learning framework will be first tested in a dredging simulator in the Engineering Research Center of Dredging Technology of Ministry of Education in China, and then evaluated in a real cutter suction dredger in future.

# References

1. Tang, J.Z., Wang, Q.F., Bi, Z.Y.: Expert system for operation optimization and control of cutter suction dredger. Expert Syst. Appl. **34**(3), 2180–2192 (2008)
2. Mnih, V., Kavukcuoglu, K., Silver, D., Rusu, A.A., Veness, J., Bellemare, M.G., Graves, A., Riedmiller, M., Fidjeland, A.K., Ostrovski, G.: Human-level control through deep reinforcement learning. Nat. **518**(7540), 529 (2015)

# Intuitive Interfaces in Human-Robot Interaction

Andrew Holmes, Areeb Sherwani, Emma Kok, Fady Ghattas,
Gianmarco Pisanelli, Xin Wen, Jonathan M. Aitken[✉], Iveta Eimontaite,
Chelsea Sabo, and David Cameron

Sheffield Robotics, University of Sheffield, Sheffield, UK
{aholmes5,asherwani1,ekkok1,frezk1,gpisanelli1,xwen7,
jonathan.aitken,i.eimontaite,c.sabo,d.s.cameron}@sheffield.ac.uk

**Abstract.** This study explores the intuitiveness of four user interfaces (UI) for controlling a mobile robot (BOE Bot): Electromyography, Oculus Rift, joystick, and speech recognition. Intuitiveness was assessed through two means: participants success in navigating the robot through a maze after self-directed training, and scores on usability questionnaires.

**Keywords:** Human-robot interaction · Interfaces · Performance

## 1 Introduction

There has been few controlled empirical experiment about intuitive interfaces: for example Huttenrauch et al. [3] involved only 6 users in the design of robots and did not involve a real robot. Khan [4] investigated the preferred methods of communication to intelligent service robots (ISB) and found speech to be the most preferred method of communication (82%), followed by touch screen (63%), gesticulating (51%), and written command (45%).

Previous research observed improved attitudes and reduced negative affects after use of well-suited HRI [7]. The nature, style and attitude towards robots will be highly individualised to each operator [2], therefore the HRI used will play a significant role in user experience. This paper investigates four user-interfaces (UIs) and their effect on the user: Electromyography (EMG: electrical activity of muscle tension), Oculus Rift (virtual reality), joystick, and speech recognition.

## 2 Methodology

29 volunteers from the University of Sheffield (69%male) with average age 28.34 (10.94) took part using all four UI in this study. Participants' attitude was measured with the Negative Attitudes Toward Robots (NARS) subscale 1 and the Robot Anxiety Scale (RAS) subscale 2 [6] The intuitiveness of each interface was

D. Cameron–This work was supported by the Sheffield University Research Experience Network (SURE Network) Program.

© Springer International Publishing AG, part of Springer Nature 2018
M. Giuliani et al. (Eds.): TAROS 2018, LNAI 10965, pp. 462–464, 2018.
https://doi.org/10.1007/978-3-319-96728-8

measured with the System Useability Scale (SUS) [1] and the subscale on interface quality from the Post-Study System Usability Questionnaire (PSSUQ) [5].

Participants had to navigate robot over a maze consisting straight lines, identified point fo stopping, turning right and left, and going over a bridge. The instructions for participants indicated guidelines on how each UI was operated (go forwards/backwards, turn left/right, speed up/down, spin left/right, and stop).

## 3    Results, Discussion and Conclusions

Participants' NARS and RAS scores did not significantly reduce after the HRI ($Z < -0.69$, $p > .49$) and there was no effect of age or gender.

Several one way within participants ANOVA's showed a significant effect of controlling method on user experience of interface quality ($F(3, 26) = 35.84$, $p < .001$), system usability and learnability ($F(3, 26) = 67.33$, $p < .001$), the number of errors made ($F(3, 24) = 17.34$, $p < .001$), and time taken to complete the maze ($t$) ($F(3, 24) = 24$, $p < .001$).

Bonferroni corrected post hoc tests revealed that joystick performed significantly better than any other interfaces across all variables, followed by oculus rift. Joystick was rated as the most intuitive UI, and this might be a result of people's familiarity with the interface and the simplicity of the technology (Table 1).

**Table 1.** Mean and standard deviations of time taken to complete the maze (t) and number of errors with each interface (E) as well as average scores for Post-Study System Usability Questionnaire (PSSUQ) and System Useability Scale (SUS)

| UI | PSSUQ | SUS | Errors ($E$) | Time ($t$), s |
|---|---|---|---|---|
| EMG | $3.24 \pm 1.52$ | $48.10 \pm 17.94$ | $12.88 \pm 9.65$ | $600 \pm 363.79$ |
| Speech | $3.82 \pm 1.68$ | $46.47 \pm 21.15$ | $14.68 \pm 12.79$ | $537.82 \pm 372.93$ |
| Oculus Rift | $2.85 \pm 1.09$ | $58.45 \pm 18.09$ | $5.64 \pm 3.73$ | $275.25 \pm 193.59$ |
| Joystick | $1.61 \pm 0.52$ | $88.45 \pm 7.86$ | $2.03 \pm 1.68$ | $83.41 \pm 23.59$ |

## References

1. Brooke, J., et al.: SUS-a quick and dirty usability scale. In: Usability Evaluation in Industry, vol. 189, no. 194, pp. 4–7 (1996)
2. Cameron, D., Aitken, J.M., Collins, E.C., Boorman, L., Chua, A., Fernando, S., McAree, O., Martinez-Hernandez, U., Law, J.: Framing factors: the importance of context and the individual in understanding trust in human-robot interaction. In: IEEE/RSJ International Conference on Intelligent Robots and Systems (2015)
3. Huttenrauch, H., Green, A., Norman, M., Oestreicher, L., Eklundh, K.S.: Involving users in the design of a mobile office robot. IEEE Trans. Syst. Man Cybern. Part C (Appl. Rev.) **34**(2), 113–124 (2004)

4. Khan, Z.: Attitudes towards intelligent service robots. Technical report (1998)
5. Lewis, J.R.: Psychometric evaluation of the post-study system usability questionnaire: the PSSUQ. In: Proceedings of the Human Factors and Ergonomics Society Annual Meeting, vol. 36, pp. 1259–1260 (1992)
6. Nomura, T., Suzuki, T., Kanda, T., Kato, K.: Measurement of negative attitudes toward robots. Int. Stud. **7**(3), 437–454 (2006)
7. Stafford, R., Broadbent, E., Jayawardena, C., Unger, U., Kuo, I.H., Igic, A., Wong, R., Kerse, N., Watson, C., MacDonald, B.A.: Improved robot attitudes and emotions at a retirement home after meeting a robot. In: 2010 IEEE RO-MAN, pp. 82–87 (2010)

# Towards Computational Models of Insect Motion Detectors for Robot Vision

Qinbing Fu$^{(\boxtimes)}$, Cheng Hu, Pengcheng Liu, and Shigang Yue

Lincoln Centre for Autonomous Systems(L-CAS), University of Lincoln,
Lincoln, UK
qifu@lincoln.ac.uk

In this essay, we provide a brief survey of computational models of insect motion detectors and bio-robotic solutions to build efficient and reliable motion-sensing systems. Vision is an important sensing modality for autonomous robots, since it can extract abundant motion features from a visually cluttered and dynamic environment. However, modelling a dynamic vision system for motion detection in both a cheap and robust manner is still an open challenge. In nature, animals, that have experienced millions of years of evolutionary development, can be prominent models to study motion-detecting strategies. This essay introduces a few state-of-the-art bio-inspired motion detectors and corresponding robotic applications, in order to demonstrate the effectiveness of mimicking insect motion perception strategies for robot vision and gather cross-disciplinary attention.

Insects are well-known as experts in motion perception [1, 2]. They have a smaller number of visual neurons compared to vertebrates, but compact visual systems for sensing motion, timely and accurately. It appears that motion perception is an essential ability for insects, from avoiding predators to foraging. Biologically visual systems are mysterious, but researchers have always been attempting understanding the underlying characteristics and functionality. There are a good number of motion sensitive neurons or pathways that have been identified in insects like the locusts and flies. Here, we introduce two categories of motion detectors – the translating and the looming sensitive neural systems; these have been successfully modelled as embedded vision systems in machines like aerial vehicles (UAVs or MAVs), as well as ground mobile robots.

Firstly, the flies' motion perception strategies have motivated numerous computational models for sensing translating movements. A remarkable model of an elementary motion detector is based on a 'correlate-and-delay' type of Hassenstein-Reichardt detector. This model depicts non-linearly spatiotemporal computations between two adjacent units in the field of view to calculate local motion direction, namely optic flow. Based on this theory, there have been a lot of computational models and applications to navigation of flying robots, in order to mimic different insect behaviours like take-off, landing, tunnel crossing and terrain following and etc [1, 2]. In addition, the well-known fly optical flow-based collision avoidance strategy has been used widely in both UAVs [1, 2] and MAVs [3]. Such an approach simulates optical flow vector fields perceived by flies' compound eyes, which relies upon the physical structure of the environment.

© Springer International Publishing AG, part of Springer Nature 2018
M. Giuliani et al. (Eds.): TAROS 2018, LNAI 10965, pp. 465–467, 2018.
https://doi.org/10.1007/978-3-319-96728-8

Secondly, a few looming sensitive neuronal models have been applied as effective collision detectors; these are inspired by two lobula giant movement detectors in locusts, i.e., LGMD1 and its neighbouring neuron LGMD2. The LGMD1 has been pinpointed to play dominant roles in adult locusts for perceiving looming objects that approach. It can react to expanding edges of an approaching object well. Its functionality has been achieved and validated in an autonomous micro-robot (Fig. 1) [4]. On the other hand, the LGMD2 matures early in juvenile locusts. It applies a similar collision-detecting strategy like the LGMD1, yet it is only sensitive to dark looming objects – a sensitivity to light-to-dark luminance change. Such a specific collision selectivity has been realised by 'ON and OFF' mechanisms, and verified also by the mobile robot [5]. Moreover, a case study recently has demonstrated the usefulness of combining both looming sensitive neuronal models for collision recognition and avoidance in dynamic scenes [6].

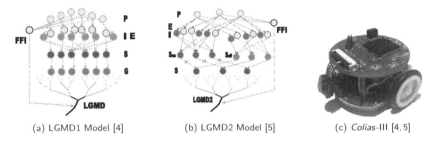

(a) LGMD1 Model [4]        (b) LGMD2 Model [5]        (c) *Colias*-III [4, 5]

**Fig. 1.** From insect motion-perception systems (a), (b) to robot vision applications (c)

In summary, we have given some examples of the computational modelling of insect motion detectors for robot vision-based tasks like collision avoidance. These bio-inspired models have not only been providing effective solutions to robotics but also easing the understanding of very complex biologically visual processing in animals. Our future work will focus on the computational modelling of insect motion detectors, visually guided behaviours and swarm intelligence for promoting the collaborative research between Neuroscience and Robotics.

# References

1. Serres, J.R., Ruffier, F.: Optic flow-based collision-free strategies: from insects to robots. Arthropod Struct. Dev. **465**, 703–717 (2017)
2. Franceschini, N.: Small brains, smart machines: from fly vision to robot vision and back again. Proc. IEEE. **102**, 751–781 (2014)
3. Green, W. E., OH, P. Y.: Optic-flow-based collision avoidance. IEEE Robot. Autom. Mag. 96–103 (2008)
4. Hu, C., Arvin, F., Xiong, C., Yue, S.: Bio-inspired embedded vision system for autonomous micro-robots: the LGMD case. IEEE Trans. Cogn. Dev. Syst. **93**, 241–254 (2017)

5. Fu, Q., Hu, C., Yue, S.: Bio-inspired collision detector with enhanced selectivity for ground robotic vision system. In: 27th British Machine Vision Conference (2016)
6. Fu, Q., Hu, C., Liu, T., Yue, S.: Collision selective LGMDs neuron models research benefits from a vision-based autonomous micro robot. In: IEEE/RSJ International Conference on Intelligent Robots and Systems (IROS), pp. 3996–4002 (2017)

# Robots Claiming Space: Gauging Public Reaction Using Computer Vision Techniques

Jacques Penders, Jing Wang, Deepayan Bhowmik, Alessandro Di Nuovo,
Alessandro Soranzo, Joe Rolph, Inna Popa, Simone Varrasi, Alexandr Lucas,
Daniela Conti, Jay Young, Lyuba Alboul, Emily Collins, Jonathan M. Aitken,
James Law, and David Cameron[✉]

Sheffield Robotics, Sheffield, UK
{j.penders,jing.wang,deepayan.bhowmik,a.dinuovo,a.soranzo,j.rolph,
inna.popa,simone.varrasi,a.lucas,d.conti,jay.young,l.alboul}@shu.ac.uk,
{e.c.collins,jonathan.aitken,j.law,d.s.cameron}@sheffield.ac.uk

## 1 Introduction

Robots are increasingly being used outside of controlled environments (*e.g.*, factory floors or research labs) and in more complex, social shared-spaces, such as exhibitions events, care-homes, or in schools. In these environments, people may need to learn robots' behaviours to accommodate them; across the long-term, people may habituate towards robots' behaviours and even presence (*e.g.*, children lose interest in a robot during long-term interaction [3]). The long-term dynamics of public's interest in, and habituation towards, robots in shared-spaces is not yet well established.

We introduce a long-term study of robots in a social shared-space and Sheffield Robotics' investigation into the dynamics of the public's interest and habituation towards the robots. This abstract describes our establishing of the interdisciplinary project combining (1) social robotics research to gauge public interest in robots in everyday shared-spaces and (2) computer vision based analysis of site security camera footage to give (unobtrusive) people count and directional flow measurement.

The study has two key aims: (1) Explore factors affecting habituation towards robots in long-term interactions, particularly people's use of the shared-space around the robot (2) Develop effective and reliable non-invasive measures of public interest towards robots.

## 2 Study Design and Environmental Description

The long-term study (lasting a full academic year) explores a population's initial interest, and then habituation, towards robots in a shared-space. We anticipate regular users of the space may regard the robots as just 'part of the furniture' or even a mild inconvenience over time. Within the long-term study, we manipulate the robots used, their behaviour/functionality, and the context of the shared-space to explore factors affecting people's use of the shared-space and habituation

© Springer International Publishing AG, part of Springer Nature 2018
M. Giuliani et al. (Eds.): TAROS 2018, LNAI 10965, pp. 468–470, 2018.
https://doi.org/10.1007/978-3-319-96728-8

towards robots. Across the study, the introduction of robots is staggered based on their complexity in behaviour and morphology: simple robots and behaviours first (*i.e.*, Guardian; Pioneer LX); more attractive and cunning robots are used later (*i.e.*, FETCH; Pepper).

The research-site comprises a newly-opened atrium at Sheffield Hallam University: built for staff, students, and visitors on campus, it also serves a pass-through for commuters. This site is ideal for a long-term study, given the public-access and regular use. Fig. 1 shows the designated robot shared-space. Crowd and individual behaviour - and their use of space - is monitored via security camera footage.

**Fig. 1.** Gauging public interests to robots in daily life using computer vision based flow analysis.

## 3 Public Behavioral Pattern Analysis Using Computer Vision

Video footage is captured using one overhead and three wall-mounted security cameras to analyse people's behavior towards robots, during working hours on weekdays. This set-up minimises intrusion into the environment (compared to staging with RGB-D cameras) to observe authentic behaviour. We have conducted primary analysis for busier times (1:00–2:00pm), using a popular aggregated channel feature (ACF) algorithm [2] to count people in the scene via upper-body detection for persons. This identifies how busy the environment is, from which, we can explore the impact of crowd density on robot interaction. Recordings are compared on a week on week basis, in hourly fashion.

Individuals' movement is calculated using optic flow analysis [1]; individual body parts' motions are aggregated to give motion for each detected individual. We divide the visual scene into quadtree-structure regions for fine-grain analysis of the robot's shared-space (Fig. 1). Finally, we average collective motions in each region for directional flow (*red* lines on white discs) to give coarse-grain cues of public attention to robots.

## 4   Summary

This abstract outlines our research interest, and study-layout in a long-term study of human robot interaction in shared-spaces. We identify suitable data-collection and analysis techniques for large volumes of crowd- and individual-level interactions with robots. Further development in this study, explores a robot's appearance and/or behaviour's influence on crowds and examines changes in interaction with robots in a shared-space.

## References

1. Barron, J.L., Fleet, D.J., Beauchemin, S.S., Burkitt, T.A.: Performance of optical flow techniques, pp. 236–242 (1992)
2. Dollár, P., Appel, R., Belongie, S., Perona, P.: Fast feature pyramids for object detection. IEEE Trans. Image Process. **36**(8), 1532–1545 (2014)
3. Kanda, T., Sato, R., Saiwaki, N., Ishiguro, H.: A two-month field trial in an elementary school for long-term human-robot interaction. IEEE Trans. Rob. **23**(5), 96–971 (2007)

# SLIDER: A Novel Bipedal Walking Robot without Knees

Ke Wang$^{(\boxtimes)}$, Aksat Shah, and Petar Kormushev

Robot Intelligence Lab, Dyson School of Design Engineering,
Imperial College London, London, UK
{ke.wang17,aksat.shah09,p.kormushev}@imperial.ac.uk

**Abstract.** This extended abstract describes our work on SLIDER: a novel bipedal robot with knee-less legs and hip sliding motion. Compared with conventional anthropomorphic leg design, SLIDER's leg design enables the robot to have very lightweight legs and is suitable to perform agile locomotion. To validate this design, we created a dynamics model and implemented a walk pattern generator capable of walking with a speed of 0.18 m/s in Gazebo. Currently, a physical prototype is under construction for real-world testing. The initial mechanical design and the control strategy for SLIDER are introduced.

**Keywords:** Bipedal Walking · Legged Robot Design
Gait Pattern Generation

## 1 Introduction

Most bipedal robots have knees with actuators mounted on the thighs, making their legs relatively heavy. This design either limits the robot's ability to perform agile behaviors (jumping, push recovery, etc.) or requires powerful motors to accomplish them. Here we propose a novel design for a bipedal robot called SLIDER that replaces the conventional legs which have knees with knee-less legs. A vertical hip sliding motion is added, to compensate for the missing degree of freedom (DOF) of the knee. To the best of our knowledge, there is no such existing bipedal robot design in the published research. The only similar robot design that we know of is in a video by Schaft [1] whose design details, however, are unknown. The purpose of building SLIDER is to explore novel designs for bipedal robots and novel actuation mechanisms.

## 2 Mechanical Design

SLIDER is 96 cm tall and has a weight of 18 kg. Each leg has 5 DOFs: hip pitch, hip roll, hip slide, ankle roll and ankle pitch. The novel aspect of SLIDER's design lies in its compact and lightweight vertical hip sliding mechanism. The top half of each leg consists of a one-axis gantry with four guide rods and a belt fixed internally, as

© Springer International Publishing AG, part of Springer Nature 2018
M. Giuliani et al. (Eds.): TAROS 2018, LNAI 10965, pp. 471–472, 2018.
https://doi.org/10.1007/978-3-319-96728-8

shown in Fig. 1. The inner shaft is attached to the pulleys moving along the belt controlling the sliding motion, while the outer shaft is responsible for the hip pitch motion as shown in Fig. 1. To further minimize the weight of the leg, a carbon rod is used for the bottom half. At the bottom of each leg a rubber ball is added to absorb the energy when the foot contacts the ground, as shown in Fig. 1. A prototype is currently under construction in our lab.

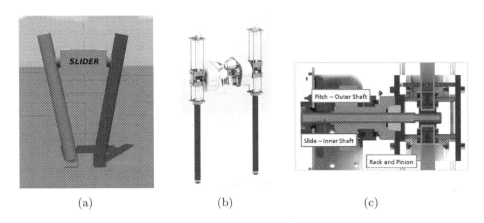

(a)                              (b)                              (c)

**Fig. 1.** (a) SLIDER model simulated in Gazebo. (b) A rendering of the initial mechanical design. (c) The inner view of the motor box.

## 3    Control Strategy and Future Work

To validate the walking capability of SLIDER, we created a model in Gazebo that has the same kinematic and dynamic properties as the physical version of SLIDER, as shown in Fig. 1. We adapted our previous two-stage gait pattern generation approach [2] to match the novel kinematics of SLIDER. In this approach an average velocity of the center of mass is given as a reference. At the first stage an inverted pendulum model is used to calculate the foot position and timing in sagittal and coronal plane. This information is then passed to the second stage and a Multi-Body Dynamic model is used to compute the trajectory of each joint. We implemented joint controllers in Gazebo to follow the reference trajectories, enabling SLIDER to walk stably with a speed of 0.18 m/s.

In the future, we will continue building and improving the design of SLIDER. Addtionally, we plan to add ZMP feedback to the controller to achieve more stable and faster walking.

## References

1. The Schaft robot video. https://www.youtube.com/watch?v=iyZE0psQsX0
2. Kryczka, P., Kormushev, P., Tsagarakis, N., Caldwell, D.G.: Online regeneration of bipedal walking gait optimizing footstep placement and timing. In: Proceedings of IEEE/RSJ International Conference on Intelligent Robots and Systems, IROS 2015, Hamburg, Germany (2015)

# Casualty Detection for Mobile Rescue Robots via Ground-Projected Point Clouds

Roni Permana Saputra[1,2]([✉]) and Petar Kormushev[1]

[1] Robot Intelligence Lab, Dyson School of Design Engineering,
Imperial College London, London, UK
{r.saputra,p.kormushev}@imperial.ac.uk
[2] Research Centre for Electrical Power and Mechatronics,
Indonesian Institutes of Sciences - LIPI, Bandung, Indonesia

**Abstract.** In order to operate autonomously, mobile rescue robots need to be able to detect human casualties in disaster situations. In this paper, we propose a novel method for autonomous detection of casualties lying down on the ground based on point-cloud data. This data can be obtained from different sensors, such as an RGB-D camera or a 3D LIDAR sensor. The method is based on a ground-projected point-cloud (GPPC) image to achieve human body shape detection. A preliminary experiment has been conducted using the RANSAC method for floor detection and, the HOG feature and the SVM classifier to detect human body shape. The results show that the proposed method succeeds to identify a casualty from point-cloud data in a wide range of viewing angles.

## 1 Introduction

Searching and detecting injured humans, i.e. casualties, in a disaster scene is one of the key challenges for autonomous mobile rescue robots in search and rescue (SAR) missions. Even though a number of successful studies have been conducted for human-presence detection methods *based on 2D images*, such as pedestrian detection [1], it remains challenging to use these methods for casualty detection by mobile robots in SAR scenarios. There are many reasons why this is difficult: (i) the fact that the casualty is lying down on the ground creates many more diverse orientations compared to a standing person with respect to the camera; (ii) the floor is right under the body which makes depth segregation more challenging; (iii) the camera viewing angle and the robot orientation in 3D keep changing depending on the terrain. Using 3D shape information such as point-cloud data could be one of the alternatives for dealing with this casualty detection challenge. Therefore, in this work, we aim to develop a novel approach utilising point-cloud data for casualty-detection applications.

## 2 Proposed Methodology

Figure 1 illustrates the flowchart of the proposed method for detecting a casualty based on point cloud data. A ground-projected point-cloud (GPPC) image is

© Springer International Publishing AG, part of Springer Nature 2018
M. Giuliani et al. (Eds.): TAROS 2018, LNAI 10965, pp. 473–475, 2018.
https://doi.org/10.1007/978-3-319-96728-8

used in this process to achieve the casualty detection process. This GPPC image is generated by projecting the point-cloud data onto the detected ground plane (i.e. floor). In order to detect the floor, the RANSAC algorithm (Random sample consensus) is used to estimate and fit a plane model to the point-cloud data [2]. Once the ground plane is detected, all the points associated to this plane, i.e. inliers, are removed. Then, the remaining points are projected orthogonally onto the plane to produce the GPPC image. Afterwards, this image is used as an input for executing the human body shape detection algorithm to detect the casualty in the image. In this preliminary work, we used a person-detection algorithm based on HOG features and SVM classifier [1].

## 3   Preliminary Experimental Results and Conclusion

Preliminary experiments have been conducted to evaluate the proposed method. In this experiment an ASUS Xtion RGB-D camera was used to obtain point-cloud data. For each conducted test, the camera was tilted at a random angle towards the ground to test the plane detection. Figure 2 demonstrates the casualty detection process and results using the proposed method. The preliminary test results prove that this method can successfully detect the casualty from point-cloud data and potential to become an essential part of autonomous mobile rescue robots. In the future work, we are planning to integrate this casualty detection module into mobile rescue robot—called ResQbot—that we have developed [3].

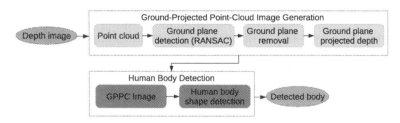

**Fig. 1.** The proposed methodology for casualty detection via ground-projected point-cloud image.

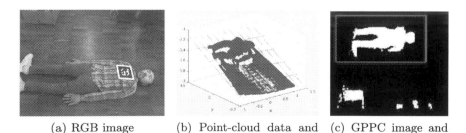

(a) RGB image       (b) Point-cloud data and       (c) GPPC image and
                        detected plane                  detected human body

**Fig. 2.** Preliminary experimental results from casualty detection using the proposed method.

# References

1. Dollar, P., Wojek, C., Schiele, B., Perona, P.: Pedestrian detection: a benchmark. In: Computer Vision and Pattern Recognition, CVPR, pp. 304–311. IEEE (2009)
2. Yang, M. Y., Förstner, W.: Plane detection in point-cloud data. In: Proceedings of the 2nd International Conference on Machine Control Guidance, vol. 1, pp. 95–104, Bonn (2010)
3. Saputra, R.P., Kormushev, P.: ResQbot: a mobile rescue robot for casualty extraction. In: 2018 ACM/IEEE International Conference on Human-Robot Interaction (HRI 2018), pp. 239–240. ACM, New York (2018)

# State Estimation of Delays in Telepresence Robot Navigation Using Bayesian Approaches

Barnali Das[(✉)], Gordon Dobie, and Stephen Gareth Pierce

Department of Electronic and Electrical Engineering,
University of Strathclyde, Glasgow, UK
{barnali.das,gordon.dobie,s.g.pierce}@strath.ac.uk

## 1 Introduction

Telepresence systems allow a human operator to control and navigate a mobile robot around the remote environment and interact with their audiences through video conferencing. Telepresence robots suffer significant challenges during navigation due to communication time delays. If the time delays are not compensated to estimate the robot pose correctly in the remote site, the robot may crash due to inaccurate pose estimation by the operator. In this work, we propose a Bayesian approach to model such delays using state estimation techniques that are useful for robust navigation.

Robot state estimation in dynamical systems is essential in real world applications, as the actual state is undetermined and sensors provide only a sequence of noisy measurements. Extended Kalman filter (EKF) generally acquires an estimate of the true state from noisy sensor measurements. However, when a filtering processor is attached to a network, there is a communication time lag. Additional time is required if there is a need to post process the raw sensor data for updating the state of the dynamical system. As a result a delay is introduced between the acquisition of measurement and its availability to the filter.

This paper proposes state estimation techniques of delayed navigation of telepresence robots. Considering a small delay in the system, an augmented state Kalman filter (ASKF) [2] is proposed. As any delayed measurement carries information about a past state, the current state cannot directly be corrected only using the measurement. The past state corresponding to a delayed measurement should be determined before using the delayed measurement in the state estimation. The current state is then corrected after correcting the appropriate past state. We also assume that the delay is not precise and hence the uncertain delay is modelled using a probability density function (PDF) [2]. To our best knowledge, the proposed approach is first of its kind in compensating delay in telepresence robot navigation.

## 2 Proposed Methodology

Two most significant systematic errors, generated by unequal wheel diameters and the uncertainty in the effective wheelbase were measured and modelled using

© Springer International Publishing AG, part of Springer Nature 2018
M. Giuliani et al. (Eds.): TAROS 2018, LNAI 10965, pp. 476–478, 2018.
https://doi.org/10.1007/978-3-319-96728-8

a well-known UMBmark [1] method. This is followed by a number of state estimation steps governed by the equations below.

In this research, the robot navigation is dependent on raw sensor data which,
we assume, is corrupted with significant random delay (*e.g.*, communication,
processing *etc.*). The sensor data arrivals to the filter is not consistent and arrives
at a different time steps. Considering $\tau$ is the number of delayed time steps, we
have defined the measurement equation as,

$$z_k = h(x_{k-\tau}, v_{k-\tau}), \tag{1}$$

By augmenting several states, the current measurement, containing information
of the past state, can be used to directly correct the augmented state vectors
using ASKF. This means, when the delay is given, we can determine the corresponding past state in the augmented vector. The past state is updated using
the delayed measurement and the current state is simultaneously corrected in
the augmented vector. The augmented state vector can be estimated recursively
via the EKF algorithm. Equations for multi step delays representing the process
model and the measurement model are given in Eqs. 2 and 3 respectively, where,
$x_k$ is the augmented state vector defined by $\begin{bmatrix} x_k^T\ x_{k-1}^T\ \cdots\ x_{k-n}^T \end{bmatrix}^T$ and $n$ is the
maximum number of delayed time steps.

$$x_{k+1} = \left[ \begin{bmatrix} f(x_k, u_k) \\ I & 0 & 0\ 0 \\ 0 & \ddots & 0\ \vdots \\ 0 & 0 & I\ 0 \end{bmatrix} x_k \right] + \begin{bmatrix} w_k \\ 0 \\ \vdots \\ 0 \end{bmatrix} \tag{2}$$

$$z_k = h\left( \begin{bmatrix} 0 \\ \vdots \\ I \\ \vdots \\ 0 \end{bmatrix}^T \begin{bmatrix} x_k \\ \vdots \\ x_{k-\tau_k} \\ \vdots \\ x_{k-n} \end{bmatrix} \right) + \begin{bmatrix} 0 \\ \vdots \\ v_{k-\tau_k} \\ \vdots \\ 0 \end{bmatrix} \tag{3}$$

We believe this time delay cannot be measure properly due to the uncertainty
and assume the delayed steps as a random variable with a corresponding PDF.

## 3   Results and Conclusions

To demonstrate and evaluate our proposed hypothesis, we have built an experimental framework on a commercially available telepresence robot, Beam+, due
to its telepresence capability controlled via WiFi. We customised an open-source
ROS driver *rosbeam*[1] and installed within BEAM+, replacing its original control
software to perform experiments in a controlled environment. We have captured

---

[1] https://github.com/xlz/rosbeam.

the robot's navigation data using a VICON motion capture system. In initial experiments, we measured systematic errors of the robot using the UMBmark method which is then used to simulate the robot's erroneous navigation. With the estimation of noisy VICON measurement we shall apply EKF to compensate navigation error. As the next step we intend to apply ASKF and PDF to further improve the navigation. Our initial experiments have shown good noise estimation of robot navigation which is the first step of this work-in-progress research.

## References

1. Borenstein, J., Feng, L.: UMBmark: a benchmark test for measuring odometry errors in mobile robots. In: SPIE Mobile Robots X, vol. 2591, pp.113–125 (1995)
2. Choi, M., Choi, J., Chung, W.: State estimation with delayed measurements incorporating time-delay uncertainty. IET Control Theory Appl. **6**(10), 2351–2361 (2012)

# Printable Soft Grippers with Integrated Bend Sensing for Handling of Crops

Khaled Elgeneidy[1,2(✉)] 🆔, Pengcheng Liu[1,2] 🆔, Simon Pearson[1] 🆔,
Niels Lohse[3] 🆔, and Gerhard Neumann[2] 🆔

[1] Lincoln Institute for Agri-Food Technology, University of Lincoln,
Lincoln LN2 4ST, UK
KElgeneidy@Lincoln.ac.uk
[2] Lincoln Centre for Autonomous Systems, University of Lincoln,
Lincoln LN2 4ST, UK
[3] Intelligent Automation Centre, Loughborough University,
Loughborough LE11 3TU, UK

Handling delicate crops without damaging or bruising is a challenge facing the automation of tasks within the agri-food sector, which encourages the utilization of soft grippers that are inherently safe and passively compliant. In this paper we present a brief overview of the development of a printable soft gripper integrated with printable bend sensors. The softness of the gripper fingers allows delicate crops to be grasped gently, while the bend sensors are calibrated to measure bending and detect contact. This way the soft gripper not only benefits from the passive compliance of its soft fingers, but also demonstrates a sensor-guided approach for improved grasp control.

Soft pneumatic actuators have been utilized as grippers as they generate a bending motion analogous to grasping when pressurized [1]. Commonly soft grippers are made from stretchable silicone rubbers that are shaped using 3D printed molds following a multi-stage lamination and curing process [2]. This process is simple and inexpensive to implement, yet it is limited in terms of its accuracy and repeatability due to its manual nature. Thus, more automated approaches are being considered for a faster, more accurate and consistent production of soft robotic components [3, 4]. Another key challenge for soft grippers, is the limited feedback and control over their grasping performance [5]. A sensor-guided soft gripper would be more reliable as it can detect contact with its targets and control the pneumatic supply accordingly, so that excessive bending that could damage delicate targets or result in unstable grasps can be avoided. In this work we present a customizable soft gripper with integrated bend sensing, which can be entirely printed using common 3D printers and commercially available material filaments (NinjaFlex and conductive PLA). The softness of the gripper fingers enables fruits and vegetables to be grasped gently, while the integrated bend sensors are calibrated to provide bending feedback and simple contact detection to avoid damage or bruising. By tuning the print settings of a fused filament fabrication process utilizing a dual extruder, flexible air-tight soft grippers and flexible resistive sensors were successfully printed (Fig. 1). Bending the sensor causes a change in the overall resistance of the sensing tracks, which can be converted to a voltage output and calibrated against the bending angle. The sensor's response exhibits some drift as it is the case with other resistive sensors, yet it provides a low-cost solution that can easily customized and

© Springer International Publishing AG, part of Springer Nature 2018
M. Giuliani et al. (Eds.): TAROS 2018, LNAI 10965, pp. 479–480, 2018.
https://doi.org/10.1007/978-3-319-96728-8

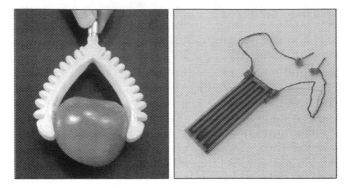

**Fig. 1.** (a) A directly printed two-fingered soft gripper gently grasping a tomato. (b) A printed flexible strain sensor sample showing the conductive tracks (black) and flexible body (yellow).

directly welded to the soft gripper fingers. This results in a printable soft gripper with integrated bend sensing that can be customized according to the application needs.

An experiment was conducted to systematically test printed soft finger equipped with the strain sensors, in order to calibrate the sensor's feedback against the measured bending angle. Results of our previous work showed that simple empirical models can be derived to accurately describe the free-bending response of individual soft actuators based on the generated sensory feedback [6]. Hence, simple contact detection can be achieved by comparing the measured bending response to the previously modelled free-bending response at the same input pressure. This is currently being extended for a soft gripper prototype to sense grasping different fruits and vegetables based on the combined sensory feedback from opposing fingers and the supplied pressure. Thus, the printable soft grippers with integrated bend sensing would benefit from the softness of its fingers to passively adapt to different delicate targets, while processing the additional sensory feedback to achieve a better controlled grasping operation.

# References

1. Ilievski, F., Mazzeo, A.D., Shepherd, R.F., Chen, X., Whitesides, G.M.: Soft robotics for chemists. Angew. Chemie Int. Ed., **50**(8), 1890–1895 (2011)
2. Marchese, A.D., Katzschmann, R.K., Rus, D.: A recipe for soft fluidic elastomer robots. Soft Robot. **2**(1), 7–25 (2015)
3. Zolfagharian, A., Kouzani, A.Z., Khoo, S.Y., Moghadam, A.A.A., Gibson, I., Kaynak, A.: Evolution of 3D printed soft actuators. Sens. Actuators Phys. **250**, 258–272 (2016)
4. Yap, H.K., Ng, H.Y., Yeow, C.-H.: High-force soft printable pneumatics for soft robotic applications. Soft Robot. **3**(3), 144–158 (2016)
5. Hughes, J., Culha, U., Giardina, F., Günther, F., Rosendo, A.: Soft manipulators and grippers: a review. Front. Robot. AI **3**, 1–12 (2016)
6. Elgeneidy, K., Neumann, G., Jackson, M., Lohse, N.: Directly printable flexible strain sensors for bending and contact feedback of soft actuators. Front. Robot. AI **5**, 1–14 (2018)

# Towards Real-Time Robotic Motion Planning for Grasping in Cluttered and Uncertain Environments

Pengcheng Liu[1,2(✉)], Khaled ElGeneidy[1,2], Simon Pearson[2],
M. Nazmul Huda[3], and Gerhard Neumann[1]

[1] Lincoln Centre for Autonomous Systems (L-CAS), University of Lincoln,
Lincoln, UK
{pliu,kelgeneidy,gneumann}@lincoln.ac.uk
[2] Lincoln Institute for Agri-Food Technology (LIAT), University of Lincoln,
Lincoln, UK
spearson@lincoln.ac.uk
[3] School of Computing, Electronics and Mathematics, Coventry University,
Coventry, UK
ab9467@coventry.ac.uk

Adaptation to unorganized, congested and uncertain environment is a desirable capability but challenging task in development of robotic motion planning algorithms for object grasping. We have to make a tradeoff between coping with the environmental complexities using computational expensive approaches, and enforcing practical manipulation and grasping in real-time. In this paper, we present a brief overview and research objectives towards real-time motion planning for grasping in cluttered and uncertain environments. We present feasible ways in approaching this goal, in which key challenges and plausible solutions are discussed.

Motion planning is an essential aspect for robotic system and control. Prevailing solutions such as sampling-based push-grasping [1, 2], optimization-based approaches [3, 4] and learning from demonstration [5] (LfD) have demonstrated their effectiveness in specific motion planning task. However, sampling-based approaches are computationally inefficient for manipulator motion planning [3, 4], optimization-based methods typically require hand-coded cost functions to achieve and formulate the desired behaviors [5]. In unorganized, congested and complex environments diffused with rigid and deformable objects, robotic motion planning for object grasping has been proven an intractable task. LfD approaches guided by human expert are plausibly the more approachable solutions towards this problem, because of their implicit behavior learning from expert demonstrations and less dependence on analytical models. Nevertheless, cluttered environment brings some challenging issues need to be solved under this method, for instance, coping with deformable obstacles. Deformable objects (e.g., flexible pipes, clothes, curtains) present different features from rigid ones because of their texture and deformability, and their infinite degrees of freedom make the configuration very intractable to recover. They may also cause uncontrolled robotic motion during grasping and/or manipulation. Towards this end, the preliminary research questions that we are approaching include how to optimally grasp and rearrange the

M. Giuliani et al. (Eds.): TAROS 2018, LNAI 10965, pp. 481–483, 2018.
https://doi.org/10.1007/978-3-319-96728-8_49

movable deformable obstacles to reach the target object? And how to find good grasp configurations that are reachable in a cluttered environment?

Based on our previous work [5], the goal of work-in-progress (as shown in Fig. 1) is to make steps forward through exploring the idea of expert guided trajectory optimization by LfDs as a strong influence on robotic motion planning for grasping. In real-world cluttered scenarios, it might be impossible for the robot to directly reach the target by following a collision-free trajectory and traversing between static and movable objects. Thus, this work has potential applications in push-grasping in various domains and scenarios diffused with rigid and deformable objects. For example, automated vegetable harvesting and fruit picking in agriculture, and autonomous garbage (e.g., protection suit, respirator, slightly flexible wires, and curtains) sorting in nuclear facilities. Admittedly, it is extremely hard to find cost functions that can be used to realize high quality paths in such scenarios as it is intractable to determine when and how these obstacles can be pushed/rearranged. This will be investigated in our ongoing works.

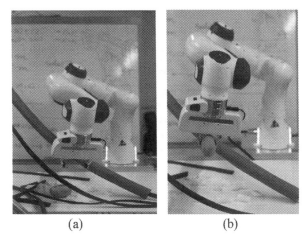

(a)                                    (b)

**Fig. 1.** (a) Motion planning and (b) grasping in cluttered environment diffused with rigid and deformable objects.

# References

1. Uddin, M., Moll, M., Kavraki, L., Rosell, J.: Randomized physics-based motion planning for grasping in cluttered and uncertain environments. IEEE Robot. Autom. Lett. **3**, 712–719 (2018)
2. Dogar, M., Hsiao, K., Ciocarlie, M., Srinivasa, S.: Physics-based grasp planning through clutter (2012)
3. Ratliff, N., Zucker, M., Bagnell, J.A., Srinivasa, S.: CHOMP: gradient optimization techniques for efficient motion planning. In: IEEE International Conference on Robotics and Automation, ICRA 2009, pp. 489–494. IEEE (2009)

4. Schulman, J., Duan, Y., Ho, J., Lee, A., Awwal, I., Bradlow, H., Pan, J., Patil, S., Goldberg, K., Abbeel, P.: Motion planning with sequential convex optimization and convex collision checking. Int. J. Robot. Res. **33**, 1251–1270 (2014)
5. Osa, T., Esfahani, A.M.G., Stolkin, R., Lioutikov, R., Peters, J., Neumann, G.: Guiding trajectory optimization by demonstrated distributions. IEEE Robot. Autom. Lett. **2**, 819–826 (2017)

# Attitudes Towards Social Robots:
# A Protocol for a Systematic Review

Marina Sarda Gou[1(✉)], Stanislava Naneva[1], Thomas L. Webb[1],
and Tony J. Prescott[2]

[1] Department of Psychology, The University of Sheffield,
Sheffield S10 2TN, UK
msardagoul@sheffield.ac.uk
[2] Sheffield Robotics, Sheffield S1 3JD, UK

**Abstract.** People's attitudes likely play a significant role in the extent to which they are willing to accept and use new technologies, including social robots. Although a number of studies have sought to assess people's attitudes toward social robots; to date, there has been no attempt to integrate these insights. We therefore propose to conduct a systematic review to summarize existing evidence on people's attitudes toward social robots and understand the factors that influence these attitudes. Research measuring people's attitudes and anxiety toward, trust in, and acceptance of social robots will be identified via a systematic search of four electronic databases. The proposed review will consider attitudes toward social robots from different domains, and whether and how the nature of the sample, intended use of the robot and so on influence outcomes.

**Keywords:** Attitudes · Social robots · Anxiety · Trust · Acceptance

## 1 Introduction

Whilst the use of robotics in fields such manufacturing is well established, people's attitudes towards the application of robotics in typically human-dominated fields (e.g., healthcare) seem to be somewhat negative [1]. It is necessary to understand people's attitudes toward social robotics and the factors likely to influence them in order to understand likely uptake and acceptance of social robotics. Unfortunately, the reviews published to date have focused primarily on healthcare and education [2, 3]. Their aim was not to analyze systematically the factors that influence people's attitudes towards robots. Therefore, a systematic review on this topic would be help to synthesize this knowledge and understand people's attitudes towards robots.

## 2 Method

The proposed review addresses two primary questions: (1) Does current evidence suggest that people have positive or negative attitudes toward social robots? (2) What factors influence people's attitudes toward, trust in, acceptance of, and anxiety associated with social robots?

© Springer International Publishing AG, part of Springer Nature 2018
M. Giuliani et al. (Eds.): TAROS 2018, LNAI 10965, pp. 484–485, 2018.
https://doi.org/10.1007/978-3-319-96728-8

The following electronic databases will be searched, using pre-specified search terms, for peer-reviewed articles and unpublished literature: PsycINFO and PsycARTICLES (Ovid), IEEE Xplore, and ProQuest. Google Scholar will be used to identify relevant grey literature and articles not found in the previously mentioned electronic databases (only the first 100 sources identified by Google Scholar will be considered for each combination of search terms) The social robots' design characteristics, capabilities, and domain of application, along with the type of exposure to the robot (e.g., direct human-robot interaction) and the primary outcomes (e.g., affective attitudes) will be extracted and synthesized. Descriptive information for all studies included in the review will be presented in a table. The findings from individual studies will be combined and summarized using a narrative approach. However, a meta-analysis will be considered if it is possible to calculate the average valence of participant's attitudes in a substantial proportion of the primary studies and to standardize this information in a manner that will permit it to be synthesized across studies The full protocol of the proposed review has been registered and can be viewed on the PROSPERO database (CRD42017057331).

## 3  Discussion

The proposed systematic review will synthesize our current understanding of people's attitudes toward social robots and the factors that influence these attitudes. By so doing, it will provide a foundation for research on the social, moral, and philosophical implications of rapid developments in new technology, as well as the basis for research that investigates ways to ensure that people's beliefs about such technology are grounded in reality, rather than representations from science fiction that likely shape many people's attitudes.

## References

1. MacDorman, K.F., Vasudevan, S.K., Ho, C.-C.: Does Japan really have robot mania? Comparing attitudes by implicit and explicit measures. AI Soc. **23**(4), 485–510 (2009)
2. Broadbent, E., Stafford, R., MacDonald, B.: Acceptance of healthcare robots for the older population: review and future directions. Int. J. Soc. Robot. **1**(4), 319–330 (2009)
3. Benitti, F.B.V.: Exploring the educational potential of robotics in schools: a systematic review. Comput. Educ. **58**(3), 978–988 (2012)

# Towards a Cognitive Architecture Incorporating Human Feedback for Interactive Collaborative Robots

Dito Eka Cahya$^{(\boxtimes)}$ (iD) and Manuel Giuliani$^{(\boxtimes)}$ (iD)

Bristol Robotics Laboratory, University of Bristol and University of the West
of England, Bristol, UK
dito.cahya@bristol.ac.uk, manuel.giuliani@brl.ac.uk

**Keywords:** Cognitive architecture · Collaborative robots · Human feedback

## 1 Introduction

The development of new collaborative robotic platforms opens the new possibility of human-robot collaborative scenarios provided that they are controlled by excellent control programs. Interactive collaborative robots need to be autonomous and possess social cognitive skills such as multimodal communication capability, recognise models of the environment and other agents, and aware of human attention and intention. On top of that, interactive collaborative robots must also able to interact fluently, learn from the interaction, and react appropriately to unprecedented situations. It is evident that the capabilities which are expected from interactive collaborative robots are too complicated to be achieved by static control programs. To successfully perform human-robot collaboration, we argue that interactive collaborative robots must be controlled by a cognitive architecture [1] that integrates multiple cognitive software modules. Inspired by the concept of Humanistic Intelligence [2], we also believe that the cognitive robot architecture must exploit the feedback from the human whom it is interacting with because humans possess superior cognitive capabilities that can be utilised by the cognitive robot architecture to enhance its cognitive skills.

## 2 CEMIRA - Cognitive Robot Architecture

To implement our idea, we present the concept of CEMIRA (Cognitive Embodied Multimodal and Interactive Robot Architecture) which is designed to interact with non-expert users by incorporating both verbal and non-verbal human feedback in the loop of its components. CEMIRA combines the strength of existing software modules with our proposed modules which is shown in Fig. 1 and described below:

- Situation Assessment Module: Translates information from the sensors into symbolic representations of the world conditions and human actions.

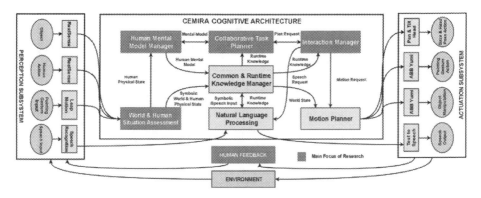

**Fig. 1.** CEMIRA Cognitive Architecture

- Knowledge Manager Module: Acts as the symbolic facts storage and connects all cognitive modules.
- Mental Model Module: Maintains the symbolic interpretation of human feedback in the form of intentions, beliefs, and preference models.
- Collaborative Task Planner Module: Synthesises shared plans containing the actions of all agents involved in a given task.
- Natural Language Processing Module: Recognises basic speech statements or commands from human and verbalises symbolic facts into sentences.
- Interaction Manager Module: Defines the cognitive behaviours of the robot by acting as a decision maker and plan execution monitor.

CEMIRA follows several principles to successfully incorporates human feedback. First, it incorporates an attention mechanism to select which feedback modalities it should focus on in a given situation. Second, input modalities are processed in parallel using the concept of Embodied Multimodal Fusion (EMF) [3]. Third, it utilises fast and predictive data processing to maximise its percieved interactivity by human.

## 3   Future Works

CEMIRA is being developed as part of the first author's PhD research. Future works involve the completion of CEMIRA modules and the integration of CEMIRA with ABB Yumi collaborative robot as the actuator and the Intel RealSense sensor that detects non-verbal human feedback (eye gaze, head pose, hand gesture). Finally, we will evaluate CEMIRA in a human-robot collaboration scenario, in which human and robot talk about and move coloured blocks, by analysing how the system will perform with and without the human feedback incorporation.

# References

1. Sun, R.: The importance of cognitive architectures: an analysis based on CLARION. J. Exp. Theor. Artif. Intell. **19**, 159–193 (2007). https://doi.org/10.1080/09528130701191560
2. Mann, S.: Wearable computing-toward humanistic intelligence. IEEE Intell. Syst. **16**(3), 10–15 (2001)
3. Giuliani, M.: Comparing Classical and Embodied Multimodal Fusion for Human-Robot Interaction (2011)

# Top-Down Bottom-Up Visual Saliency for Mobile Robots Using Deep Neural Networks and Task-Independent Feature Maps

Uziel Jaramillo-Avila[1]([✉]), Adam Hartwell[1], Kevin Gurney[2], and Sean Anderson[1]

[1] Department of Automatic Control and Systems Engineering,
University of Sheffield, Sheffield S1 3JD, UK
{ujaramilloavila1,ahartwell1,s.anderson}@sheffield.ac.uk
[2] Department of Psychology, University of Sheffield, Sheffield S10 2TN, UK
k.gurney@sheffield.ac.uk

Visual saliency is a biological mechanism for shifting visual attention to important objects in the environment, where important objects could be hazards, or items associated with a task [1]. This approach to analysing visual scenes reduces the computational burden on vision systems by only focusing on a few important stimuli rather than the whole scene. Visual saliency is therefore potentially important for robots, to enable effective and safe operation in unstructured environments [2].

Visual saliency models can contain a bottom-up and/or a top-down component [3]. The bottom-up and top-down components have particular, respective advantages. The bottom-up component is typically fast and does not require training via machine learning algorithms. Bottom-up methods should also be more robust, because they do not require object recognition to operate successfully. The top-down component is essential, however, for task-dependent actions where a robot would need to recognise important objects to complete a task.

Machine learning algorithms are typically used for top-down visual saliency, e.g. via support vector machines [4]. Recently, deep neural networks have been applied to the task of top-down bottom-up visual saliency, exploiting the accuracy of deep networks in image recognition for the top-down component [5]. However, methods that combine deep neural networks for top-down visual saliency and task-independent feature maps for bottom-up saliency have not yet been developed. This is a gap in the literature, which this work aims to address.

In this investigation, we combined a well-known approach to bottom-up visual saliency, using task-independent feature maps, based on e.g. colour contrast, intensity contrast and orientation contrast [6], with a deep convolutional neural network (CNN) based on the Tiny-YOLO architecture [7]. The resulting bottom-up and top-down saliency maps (spatially calibrated maps of salient features) were fused using a weighted sum, which combined the output of both processing streams into a single saliency map to drive visual attention [8].

To evaluate the visual saliency scheme we generated data from a small mobile robot, a Turtlebot, in an indoor environment, and implemented the visual saliency algorithm on an NVIDIA Jetson TX2, which is a processing board for

© Springer International Publishing AG, part of Springer Nature 2018
M. Giuliani et al. (Eds.): TAROS 2018, LNAI 10965, pp. 489–490, 2018.
https://doi.org/10.1007/978-3-319-96728-8

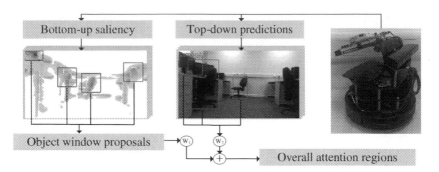

**Fig. 1.** Scheme for top-down bottom-up visual saliency. The Turtlebot with mounted Jetson TX2, on the right, generates and processes each map. In this example the top-down CNN fails to detect the chair to the right of the image, which is successfully detected by the task-independent map in the bottom-up pathway.

embedded systems with a small GPU (256 CUDA cores). The Jetson TX2 was also used to control movements of the Turtlebot, using an installation of Robot Operating System (ROS), so the control and visual processing was integrated on a single board.

We found that the bottom-up and top-down components worked as expected. However, a key early result from this pilot study was the observation that the top-down CNN would occasionally miss objects in the environment that were more robustly detected by the bottom-up task-independent feature maps (Fig. 1). Therefore, the fusion of bottom-up task-independent maps and top-down deep net maps appears promising for robust visual saliency in mobile robots.

# References

1. Itti, L., Koch, C.: Computational modelling of visual attention. Nat. Rev. Neurosci. **2**(3), 194–203 (2001)
2. Jiang, L., Koch, A., Zell, A.: Salient regions detection for indoor robots using RGB-D data. IEEE Int. Conf. Robot. Autom. 1323–1328 (2015)
3. Borji, A., Itti, L.: State-of-the-art in visual attention modeling. IEEE Trans. Pattern Anal. Mach. Intell. **35**(1), 185–207 (2013)
4. Judd, T., Ehinger, K., Durand, F., Torralba, A.: Learning to predict where humans look. IEEE Int. Conf. Comput. Vis. 2106–2113 (2009)
5. Anderson, P., He, X., Buehler, C., Teney, D., Johnson, M., Gould, S., Zhang, L.: Bottom-up and top-down attention for image captioning and VQA. arXiv Preprint, arXiv:1707.07998 (2017)
6. Itti, L., Koch, C., Niebur, E.: A model of saliency-based visual attention for rapid scene analysis. IEEE Trans. Pattern Anal. Mach. Intell. **20**, 1254–1259 (1998)
7. Redmon, J., Farhadi, A.: YOLO9000: better, faster, stronger. IEEE Int. Conf. Comput. Vis. Pattern Recogn. 6517–6525 (2017)
8. Kimura, A., Yonetani, R., Hirayama, T.: Computational models of human visual attention and their implementations: a survey. IEICE Trans. Inf. Syst. **96**(3), 562–578 (2013)

# Author Index

Printed in the United States
By Bookmasters